THE MAYA AND THEIR CENTRAL AMERICAN NEIGHBORS

The ancient Maya created one of the most studied and best-known civilizations of the Americas. Nevertheless, Maya civilization is often considered either within a vacuum, by subregion, and according to modern political borders or with reference to the most important urban civilizations of central Mexico. Seldom are the Maya and their Central American neighbors of El Salvador and Honduras considered together, despite the fact that they engaged in mutually beneficial trade, intermarried, and sometimes made war on each other. *The Maya and Their Central American Neighbors* seeks to fill this lacuna by presenting original research on the archaeology of the whole of the Maya area (from Yucatan to the Maya highlands of Guatemala), western Honduras, and El Salvador.

With a focus on settlement pattern analyses, architectural studies, hieroglyphs, and ceramic analyses, this ground-breaking book provides a broad view of this important relationship, allowing readers to understand ancient perceptions about the natural and built environment, the role of power, the construction of historical narrative, trade and exchange, multi-ethnic interaction in pluralistic frontier zones, the origins of settled agricultural life, and the nature of systemic collapse.

Geoffrey E. Braswell is a Professor of Anthropology at the University of California, San Diego.

THE MAYA AND THEIR CENTRAL AMERICAN NEIGHBORS

Settlement patterns, architecture, hieroglyphic texts, and ceramics

Edited by Geoffrey E. Braswell

Routledge
Taylor & Francis Group
LONDON AND NEW YORK

First published 2014
by Routledge
2 Park Square, Milton Park, Abingdon, Oxon OX14 4RN

and by Routledge
711 Third Avenue, New York, NY 10017

Routledge is an imprint of the Taylor & Francis Group, an informa business

© 2014 Geoffrey E. Braswell for selection and editorial matter; individual contributions, the contributors

The right of Geoffrey E. Braswell to be identified as the author of the editorial material, and of the authors for their individual chapters, has been asserted in accordance with sections 77 and 78 of the Copyright, Designs and Patents Act 1988.

All rights reserved. No part of this book may be reprinted or reproduced or utilized in any form or by any electronic, mechanical, or other means, now known or hereafter invented, including photocopying and recording, or in any information storage or retrieval system, without permission in writing from the publishers.

Trademark notice: Product or corporate names may be trademarks or registered trademarks, and are used only for identification and explanation without intent to infringe.

British Library Cataloguing in Publication Data
A catalogue record for this book is available from the British Library

Library of Congress Cataloging in Publication Data
Braswell, Geoffrey E.
The Maya and their Central American neighbors: settlement patterns, architecture, hieroglyphic texts, and ceramics / Geoffrey E. Braswell.
p. cm.
Includes bibliographical references and index.
1. Maya pottery. 2. Maya architecture. 3. Inscriptions, Mayan. 4. Mayas—Antiquities. 5. Mexico—Antiquities. 6. Central America—Antiquities. I. Title.
F1435.3.P8B73 2014
972.81—dc23
2013035980

ISBN: 978-0-415-74486-7 (hbk)
ISBN: 978-0-415-74487-4 (pbk)
ISBN: 978-1-315-79828-8 (ebk)

Typeset in Bembo
by Book Now Ltd, London

Printed and bound by CPI Group (UK) Ltd, Croydon, CR0 4YY

To E. Wyllys Andrews V, scholar, advisor, mentor, and friend

CONTENTS

List of figures   xi
List of tables   xv
List of contributors   xvii

1   The ancient Maya and their Central American neighbors   1
     Geoffrey E. Braswell

PART I
El Salvador and Honduras   23

2   Practices of spatial discourse at Quelepa   25
     Wendy Ashmore

3   Ancient Quelepa, colonial San Miguel: shifting cultural frontiers and rogue colonialism in eastern El Salvador   56
     Kathryn Sampeck

4   Shifting fortunes and affiliations on the edge of ruin: a ceramic perspective on the Classic Maya collapse and its aftermath at Copan   83
     Cassandra R. Bill

PART II
The highlands of Guatemala — 113

5 The other Preclassic Maya: interaction, growth, and depopulation in the eastern Kaqchikel highlands — 115
Geoffrey E. Braswell and Eugenia J. Robinson

6 The other Late Classic Maya: regionalization, defense, and boundaries in the central Guatemalan highlands — 150
Eugenia J. Robinson

PART III
The southern Maya lowlands — 175

7 A tangled web: ceramic adoption in the Maya lowlands and community interaction in the early Middle Preclassic as seen in the K'awil complex from Holmul, Peten, Guatemala — 177
Niña Neivens de Estrada

8 The royal port of Cancuen and the role of long-distance exchange in the apogee of Maya civilization — 201
Arthur A. Demarest

9 Real/fictive lords/vessels: a list of MARI lords on the newly discovered Andrews Coffee Mug — 223
Markus Eberl

PART IV
The eastern periphery of Belize — 243

10 The dynastic history and archaeology of Pusilha, Belize — 245
Christian M. Prager, Beniamino Volta, and Geoffrey E. Braswell

11 Follow the leader: Fine Orange pottery systems in the Maya lowlands — 308
James J. Aimers

PART V
Yucatan — 333

12 The role and realities of *popol nahs* in northern Maya archaeology — 335
George J. Bey III and Rossana May Ciau

13 Alternative narratives and missing data: refining the
    chronology of Chichen Itza   356
    Beniamino Volta and Geoffrey E. Braswell

PART VI
Before and beyond: a comparative perspective   **403**

14 Peer-polity interaction in the Norte Chico, Peru,
    3000–1800 BC   405
    Winifred Creamer, Jonathan Haas, and Allen Rutherford

Index   426

FIGURES

1.1	The Maya and their Central American neighbors	3
2.1	Map of Quelepa	28
2.2	Map of Quelepa highlighting features attributed to Uapala times	28
2.3	Map of Quelepa highlighting features attributed to Shila times	29
2.4	Map of Quelepa highlighting features of Lepa times	29
2.5	Quelepa Altar 1, the Jaguar Altar, in 1969	32
2.6	Caches at Quelepa Strs. 3 and 4 (Shila times)	35
2.7	Caches at Quelepa Str. 29 (Lepa times)	39
3.1	Navigation map of Sonsonate	72
3.2	Navigation map of "Isalcos"	74
3.3	Navigation map of San Salvador	74
3.4	Navigation map of San Miguel	75
4.1	Late Classic cream paste tradition polychromes	85
4.2	Decorated types of the Late Classic polished black/brown tradition	86
4.3	Plain types of the Late Classic polished black/brown tradition	87
4.4	Late and Terminal Coner Sesesmil Incised	88
4.5	Honduran Jicatuyo supersystem jar types	89
4.6	Chilanga Red-Painted Usulutan	90
4.7	Sevodeso Negative Incised	91
4.8	Late and Terminal Coner Sesesmil Incised	92
4.9	Ulua/Yojoa polychromes	93
4.10	Raul Red Type	95
4.11	Group 10L-2: the royal residential compound of the final ruler of Copan	97
4.12	Tohil Plumbate	98
4.13	Las Vegas polychrome	99
4.14	Map of Early Postclassic settlement in Group 11-L	100

4.15	Tamoa Red-on-Buff ladle censer	101
4.16	Hourglass-shaped censers with fillet appliqué rim	101
5.1	Middle and Middle/Late Preclassic sites of the eastern Kaqchikel highlands	122
5.2	Late and Terminal Preclassic sites of the eastern Kaqchikel highlands	132
6.1	The Guatemalan highlands	151
6.2	Map of Santa Rosa	155
6.3	Map of Rucal	156
6.4	Map of the Late Classic site types in the Antigua Valley	160
6.5	Santa Rosa	163
6.6	Comparison of Cotzumalguapan and Antigua Valley stelae	164
7.1	Map of Holmul site center	182
7.2	Katun Red Group	185
7.3	Jobal Red Group	186
7.4	Sak White Group	188
7.5	Eknab Black Group	190
7.6	Mo Mottled Group	191
7.7	Calam Burnished Ware	193
8.1	Some of the major transport and exchange routes of the Classic period	202
8.2	The Pasion–Usumacinta transport and exchange route	203
8.3	The Pasion River and Verapaz *transversal* exchange routes	205
8.4	The Cancuen region at the direct highland–lowland interface	206
8.5	Epicenter peninsula and ports of Cancuen	208
8.6	Northern port complexes, jade production area, and range structure	209
8.7	The east port complex	211
8.8	Various views of the royal palace of Cancuen	213
8.9	A subroyal palace complex	214
8.10	The western and eastern "detour" routes of late eighth-century Cancuen	216
8.11	Hypothetical reconstruction of the highland "feasting ballcourt" at Cancuen	217
9.1	Photos of the Andrews Coffee Mug	224
9.2	Two vessels of the Dynastic Vase tradition	225
9.3	Hieroglyphic text of codex-style vessel K6751	226
9.4	Rollout drawing of the hieroglyphic text of the Andrews Coffee Mug	231
9.5	Emblem on the Andrews Coffee Mug compared to the logo of MARI	232
9.6	E. Wyllys Andrews V's name and Skylifter's name	234
9.7	A court scene involving Dos Pilas king K'awiil Chan K'inich	236
9.8	MARI king list from the Andrews Coffee Mug	238

10.1	The Southern Belize Region	247
10.2	Masonry of Southern Belize	249
10.3	Partial map of Pusilha, Belize	251
10.4	The Maya bridge of Pusilha, showing modern suspension bridge	253
10.5	Major architectural groups north of the Machaca River	254
10.6	Major architectural groups north of the Machaca River, showing location of the Bulldozed Mound	254
10.7	Gateway Hill Acropolis south of the Machaca River	255
10.8	The Moho Plaza	256
10.9	Plans of the Operation 3 structure and the Operation 5 structure	260
10.10	Offering crypt Burial 6/1	261
10.11	Eccentric lithic artifacts associated with the Burial 8/4 royal tomb	263
10.12	The Operation 8 structure	264
10.13	Late Classic ceramics recovered from the Burial 8/4 royal tomb	265
10.14	Three jade diadems from the Burial 8/4 royal tomb	266
10.15	The Stela Plaza	268
10.16	The royal genealogy of Pusilha	273
10.17	Monuments showing rulers known only from iconography	276
10.18	Stelae dedicated by Ruler A	277
10.19	Stelae dedicated by Ruler B	278
10.20	Variants of the Pusilha emblem glyph	280
10.21	Proper names of stelae at Caracol and Pusilha	281
10.22	Stela H, dedicated by Ruler C	284
10.23	Stela K, dedicated by Ruler D	288
10.24	Stela M, dedicated by Ruler E	290
10.25	Stela E, dedicated by Ruler G	293
10.26	Late stelae dedicated by "Ruler" X5 and Ruler X2	295
11.1	Lamanai Silho Fine Orange Vessel	312
11.2	Comparison of Fine Orange Ware and Chichen Red Ware	314
11.3	Comparison of Fine Orange Ware and Chichen Red Ware	319
11.4	Comparison of Fine Orange Ware and Chichen Red Ware	320
11.5	Chichen Red Ware	321
11.6	Zalal Gouged-Incised from Lamanai	322
11.7	Comparison of Fine Orange Ware and Chichen Red Ware	323
11.8	Comparison of Lamanai pottery with Chichen Red Ware	323
11.9	Vessels with effigy supports and notched basal flanges	324
11.10	"Totonac motives"	325
11.11	Architectural elements	325
11.12	Descending figures	327
11.13	Vessel from Lamanai Structure N10-48	327
11.14	Diving God dish from Marco Gonzalez	328
11.15	Column bases at Chichen Itza	328
11.16	Lamanai vessel 1896/4	328
11.17	El Tajin relief carving	329

12.1	Reconstruction drawing of a *popol nah* at Kiuic	336
12.2	Map of northern Yucatan with sites mentioned in the text	337
12.3	The interior of Ek Balam GT-20, a *popol nah*	338
12.4	Exterior view of Ek Balam GT-20, showing its stair	339
12.5	Kiuic N1015E1015 and Labna Str. 7, two *popol nahs*	341
12.6	Reconstruction drawing of the Late Classic Yaxche Group at Kiuic	342
12.7	Terminal Classic "super-*nahs*"	346
13.1	The northern Maya lowlands, showing the location of Chichen Itza and other sites	357
13.2	Excavations conducted by UCSD staff in 2009	358
13.3	Chichen Itza, showing the location of Maya-style and International-style architecture	359
13.4	Ceramic chronologies for Chichen Itza	363
13.5	Platform AC3 of the Great Terrace	369
13.6	Test pit 101, south profile	370
13.7	Temple of the Three Lintels	371
13.8	Section and elevation of the Castillo-sub	371
13.9	The Castillo, an early International-style structure	372
13.10	Histogram of individual hieroglyphic dates from Chichen Itza	376
13.11	Individual calibration of radiocarbon dates from Chichen Itza and Balankanche	378
13.12	Test pit 109, south profile	379
13.13	Structure of Bayesian calibration model	380
13.14	Pooled mean of the Castillo radiocarbon dates	381
13.15	Results of Bayesian calibration compared to individual calibration	382
14.1	Map of the Norte Chico region	406
14.2	Clearing a looter's pit at Pampa San Jose	409
14.3	Examples of Norte Chico circular court and mound sites	411
14.4	Radiocarbon dates from Norte Chico sites	412
14.5	Caballete, showing "modular" construction	413
14.6	Thiessen polygon analysis of all identified Late Archaic sites in the Norte Chico	415
14.7	Sequential remodeling of a temple at Huaricanga	418
14.8	Upright figure with fangs and claws holding a staff	419
14.9	Stela at Huaricanga and the Lanzon	421

TABLES

6.1	Frequencies of types of Late Classic sites, Antigua Valley	154
6.2	A comparison of Late Classic defensive features	159
9.1	Comparison of snake kings on Dynastic Vases and on carved monuments	227
9.2	Chronology of the glyphic text on the Andrews Coffee Mug	231
10.1	Hieroglyphic dates from Pusilha	269
10.2	The ancient rulers of Pusilha and their biographies	272
10.3	The chronology of the rulers of Pusilha	274
11.1	Fine Orange systems and supersystems	315
13.1	Hieroglyphic dates associated with buildings from Chichen Itza and its hinterland	373
13.2	Radiocarbon dates from Chichen Itza and Balankanche	377
14.1	Contemporaneity of sites in the Fortaleza and Pativilca valleys based on radiocarbon dates	414

CONTRIBUTORS

James J. Aimers is Associate Professor in the Anthropology Department of the State University of New York at Geneseo and studies the ceramics of the ancient Maya. He is the editor of *Ancient Maya Pottery: Classification, Analysis, and Interpretation* (University Press of Florida, 2012).

Wendy Ashmore is Professor of Anthropology at the University of California, Riverside. She received her PhD from the University of Pennsylvania and has conducted archaeological research in Guatemala, Honduras, and Belize. Her research examines spatial organization and meaning among the ancient Maya and their neighbors. Her most recent volume is *Voices in American Archaeology* (co-edited with Dorothy T. Lippert and Barbara J. Mills, SAA Press, 2010).

George J. Bey III is the Chisholm Foundation Chair of Arts and Sciences at Millsaps College. He co-directs the Bolonchen Regional Archaeological Project, where he carries out excavations at the Maya site of Kiuic and directs the project's ceramic analysis. Bey has previously worked at Tula and the site of Ek Balam and publishes primarily in the areas of pottery economics and the evolution of complex societies.

Cassandra R. Bill is a Research Fellow of the Middle American Research Institute at Tulane University and teaches in the Department of Anthropology at Capilano University. Her specialty is the analysis of ancient pottery from Honduras and Belize.

Geoffrey E. Braswell is Professor of Anthropology at the University of California, San Diego. He is the editor of three previous volumes, including *The Ancient Maya of Mexico* (Equinox, 2012). He is the director of the Toledo Regional Archaeological

Project (Belize) and currently serves as co-editor of the journal *Latin American Antiquity*.

Winifred Creamer is Distinguished Research Professor of Anthropology at Northern Illinois University. Since 1999 her primary research focus has been on the development of early complex society on the coast of Peru in the Norte Chico region.

Arthur A. Demarest is the Ingram Professor of Anthropology at Vanderbilt University. He is the author of over 200 articles and a dozen books, including *Ancient Maya: The Rise and Fall of a Rainforest Civilization* (Cambridge Uinversity Press, 2005). He is the co-director of the ongoing Cancuen Archaeological Project and is also engaged in ethical approaches to archaeology, community development, and sacred site protection.

Markus Eberl is Assistant Professor of Anthropology at Vanderbilt University and works as an archaeologist and epigrapher in the Maya area. He directs the Tamarindito Archaeological Project in Guatemala. Among his recent publications are the monograph *Community and Difference* (Vanderbilt University Press, 2013) and an article on birth and personhood in highland Mexican codices.

Jonathan Haas first conducted archaeological fieldwork on the coast of Peru in 1976 and is presently concluding research in the Norte Chico region. He is the MacArthur Curator of the Americas at the Field Museum, Chicago.

Rossana May Ciau holds an advanced degree in archaeology from the Autonomous University of Yucatan. Her thesis examined architecture from the Mirador Group at Labna, where she carried out extensive field research. Since 2000 she has directed the excavations of the Yaxche Group at Kiuic as well as other projects in northern Yucatan and has published extensively on Kiuic and the rise of Maya society in the Puuc region.

Niña Neivens de Estrada is a PhD candidate in the Department of Anthropology at Tulane University. Her research focuses on Preclassic Maya ceramics and monumental architecture. She is writing a dissertation on the earliest ceramics found at Holmul and Tikal, Guatemala.

Christian M. Prager is Associate Lecturer at the Department of Anthropology of the Americas, University of Bonn. His recent doctoral thesis focuses on Classic Maya religion. He conducted epigraphic fieldwork at Pusilha, and his key areas of research are Maya epigraphy, religions of the Americas, and the cognitive science of religion. He serves on the board of Wayeb and also is an editor of the journal *Mexicon*.

Eugenia J. Robinson is Professor of Anthropology at Montgomery College, Maryland. She is director of the Proyecto Arqueológico del Área Kaqchikel in

Guatemala, which pursues regional archaeological research in the Kaqchikel central highlands

Allen Rutherford is a PhD candidate in anthropology at Tulane University. He is conducting his dissertation research in the Huaura Valley, Peru, focusing on sociopolitical development among late prehispanic frontier communities. He has also conducted research in southern Turkey and the southwest United States.

Kathryn Sampeck is an Assistant Professor of Anthropology at Illinois State University. Her research focuses on the archaeology and ethnohistory of Spanish colonialism, Mesoamerican literacy, the social history of commodities, and archaeological landscapes. Sampeck has been a fellow of the John Carter Brown Library and the John D. Rockefeller Library, Colonial Williamsburg.

Beniamino Volta is a PhD candidate in anthropology at the University of California, San Diego. His specialty is the quantitative study of urbanism in the Maya region. Volta has worked at Pusilha, Chichen Itza, and other sites in Yucatan, and is currently conducting research at Uxul, Campeche.

1

THE ANCIENT MAYA AND THEIR CENTRAL AMERICAN NEIGHBORS

Geoffrey E. Braswell

Central America is often left out of books on the Maya. Focusing on the Maya in isolation, without including their neighbors, is a mistake. Indeed, our knowledge is enormously enriched when we see the Maya – along with their allies, enemies, and trading partners – as embedded in a world that includes their neighbors to the south. These neighbors include Nahua peoples of Chiapas, southern Guatemala, and El Salvador, Lenkan speakers of Honduras and El Salvador, Xinka of southern Guatemala, and pockets of Oto-Manguean speakers in most of these places.

The ancient Maya are famous for their large stone pyramids, hieroglyphic writing system, complicated calendar, and beautiful stone sculpture. Yet none of these accomplishments were unique to their civilization. Instead, these cultural achievements were shared across southern Mexico and northwestern Central America, an area that scholars call Mesoamerica. Nonetheless, Maya civilization is often studied either within a vacuum, by subregion, or according to modern political borders. As a result, many textbooks and edited volumes consider the southern lowlands of Guatemala and Belize but omit the Maya highlands and northern lowlands of Yucatan. When archaeologists do seek a broader context for the ancient Maya, they usually look to the northwest and consider only the most powerful urban civilizations of central Mexico – the Olmecs, Teotihuacanos, Toltecs, and Aztecs. Seldom are the Maya and their southeastern Central American neighbors of El Salvador and Honduras considered together, despite the fact that they engaged in mutually beneficial trade, intermarried, and occasionally made war and conquered each other. Central America is often left out of books on the Maya. Focusing on the Maya in isolation, without including their neighbors, is a mistake. Indeed, our knowledge is enormously enriched when we see the Maya – along with their allies, enemies, and trading partners – embedded in a world that includes their neighbors to the south.

One purpose of *The Maya and Their Central American Neighbors* is to begin to rectify this by presenting original research spanning the whole of the Maya area, including the too often overlooked northern lowlands of Mexico (Bey 2006: 16). We also consider the linguistically mixed regions of southern Guatemala and western Honduras – where the Maya lived alongside people who spoke other languages – and non-Maya eastern El Salvador. In order to achieve more balance, each of the major regions considered in our book is given two or three chapters. Because of the enormous expansion of research in recent decades, it is no longer possible to treat within a single volume all the advances in our understanding of the ancient Maya, let alone those of the many complex and more simply organized peoples who lived to their south and southeast. Our treatment here must be limited and is admittedly biased towards our own research interests. We credit these to one man and the intellectual legacy he has given us.

This volume is the second resulting from sessions held in honor of E. Wyllys Andrews V at the seventy-fifth annual meeting of the Society for American Archaeology (SAA) in Saint Louis in 2010. The first volume (Braswell 2012a) and session focused on important recent developments in our understanding of the prehistory of the northern lowlands, that corner of the Maya world where the Andrews family has made a singularly strong mark. The second session, organized by Winifred Creamer, considered Will Andrews's important and continuing contributions to our understanding of the prehistory of Central America, especially through projects he directed in El Salvador and Honduras. Andrews's impact as a scholar and mentor has also influenced research in Guatemala and Belize, particularly in regards to our understanding of ancient pottery. This volume includes some chapters derived from our Central American session and several others that round out our coverage of Mesoamerica, from Yucatan to El Salvador.

The current work considers a wide variety of topics, methodologies, and cultures of Mesoamerica. For this reason, I have not endeavored to write a synthetic introduction of the sort that began *The Ancient Maya of Mexico: Reinterpreting the Past of the Northern Maya Lowlands* (Braswell 2012b). Nonetheless, several themes run throughout this book, ones that parallel Andrews's own interests and – in some cases – that are derived directly from his work. First, the volume is organized according to different regions of southeastern Mesoamerica. If we include early work, Andrews has conducted archaeological field research in most of these regions (Figure 1.1): Quelepa (El Salvador), Copan (Honduras), Seibal (Guatemala), and Komchen (Yucatan, Mexico). Second, many of the individual chapters focus on the origins of complex society in southeastern Mesoamerica or on its disintegration. By this, I refer to the earliest Preclassic (Formative) pottery and permanent settlement, and also to the famous "Maya Collapse" of the Terminal Classic period. Third, Andrews's and our own studies of ceramics and architecture have concentrated on interregional cultural interaction, the spread of ideas and symbolic systems, and identity. A fourth thread in both this volume and Andrews's research is the royal court, specifically the excavation of palaces in order to understand chronology, collapse, and broader issues related to political structure, economic organization, and power. Associated with this is the perception of how royal courts are understood through dynastic history. A fifth theme that runs through this work is the patterning of ancient settlement. Andrews's own impact on settlement studies was most strongly seen in his mapping and demographic research with William Ringle in northwest Yucatan (Ringle and Andrews

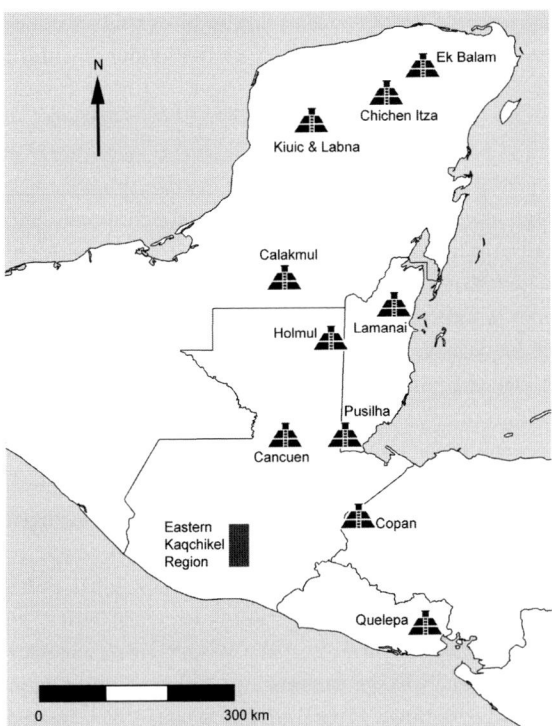

FIGURE 1.1 The Maya and their Central American neighbors: sites marked with pyramid symbols are the subjects of chapters in this volume; the mapped portion of the Eastern Kaqchikel highlands is shown in dark gray. Additional relevant sites are shown in Figures 8.3, 10.1, 12.2, 13.1, and 14.1.

1990). Two contributions to our volume build directly on Andrews's dissertation research at Quelepa, El Salvador, by analyzing architecture and settlement patterns at that site. The final and clearest strand running through and unifying our work is Will Andrews himself. Most of the contributors to this volume are his students, and all of us have benefited greatly from his thoughts, research, and guidance.

The book is structured by area, beginning with non-Maya El Salvador and multi-ethnic Honduras. These are discussed in three chapters. The second section is dedicated to highland Guatemala and its relations to non-Maya peoples living in the Pacific piedmont and on the south coast. The Maya highlands form an area that too often is ignored outside of the world of Guatemalan archaeology. The third section comprises three chapters that focus on the southern and central lowlands of Guatemala and Mexico, while the two chapters of Part IV consider the eastern periphery of Belize. The next two chapters discuss the northern lowlands, an area that, despite its importance, is not often given equal weight in discussions of the Maya outside of Mexico. The final contribution examines the Norte Chico of Peru, an area far removed from Mesoamerica, but presents an important theoretical analogy that has been used to understand Maya state formation.

Rather than follow the areal order of the sections of this book, in this introduction I emphasize the theoretical and substantive aspects of our work that tie it together into a single volume.

Preclassic origins

The origins of Preclassic village life, the adoption of agricultural economies, and the first use of pottery in southeastern Mesoamerica are pivotal topics of Maya archaeology. But it is fair to say that they have not been subject to sustained research at the level they deserve. Andrews has made particularly important contributions to these subjects through his definition of the Uapala sphere in the southeastern periphery of Mesoamerica (Chapter 2; Andrews 1976), his description of Middle Preclassic architecture and ceramics in northwest Yucatan (Andrews 1988, 1990), his reappraisal of the Swasey complex (Andrews and Hammond 1990), his general discussion of early ceramic spheres in the Maya lowlands (Chapter 7; Andrews 1990), and, most recently, his identification of very early pottery in the northern Maya lowlands (Andrews and Bey 2011; Andrews et al. 2008).

Experiments with horticultural life ways began in many regions of southeastern Mesoamerica during the late Archaic (or Preceramic) period (Chapter 5; Neff et al. 2006; Pohl et al. 1996). Nonetheless, evidence for permanent villages dating to before about 1100 BC (calibrated) is limited largely to the Pacific Coast and piedmont region of southern Chiapas and Guatemala, highland Honduras, the Salama Valley of Alta Verapaz (Sharer and Sedat 1987: 428), and perhaps Kaminaljuyu (Popenoe de Hatch 1997, 2002). Moreover, most sites where there is strong evidence for pottery dating to this early time are in regions where a close linguistic affiliation with Mayan languages seems unlikely. Put another way, we still lack unambiguous evidence that the lowland Maya lived in Early Preclassic villages and made pottery much before about 1100 BC (Lohse 2010: 343). Despite this, research at sites including Cahal Pech, Blackman Eddy, Cuello, Colha, Seibal, Altar de Sacrificios, Tikal, Komchen, and Kiuic demonstrate that settled villages where pottery was produced certainly existed during the period 1000 to 800 BC and perhaps a century earlier. There is still debate as to whether all of these early sites were inhabited by "Maya" (e.g., Ball and Taschek 2003) and whether or not the phrase "Early Preclassic" should be used to describe the time period when such pottery was first produced (see Chapter 7, note 1). Incised symbols on the earliest known pottery of the Maya lowlands are related to a complex that first appeared several centuries earlier and farther west during the Early Preclassic period. Nevertheless, their first manifestation in the Maya lowlands occurred at a time very close to the arbitrary beginning of the Middle Preclassic, at 900 bc (uncalibrated). If the Terminal Archaic and Middle Preclassic of the Maya lowlands were separated by an Early Preclassic period, current evidence suggests it did not last much more than a hundred years (Cheetham 2005: fig. 3.2; Garber and Awe 2009; cf. Lohse 2010). Thus, after nearly 2,000 years of experimentation with horticulture, the first permanent villages with pottery-using occupants developed quite rapidly in the Maya lowlands. There is no long Early Formative sequence for the Maya lowlands comparable to those of the Valley of Oaxaca, southern Veracruz, the Basin of Mexico, or the Pacific coast of Guatemala and Chiapas.

In Chapter 7, Niña Neivens de Estrada discusses an early ceramic complex from the site of Holmul, Guatemala. In a very real sense, Holmul is where archaeological studies of Maya pottery began (Merwin and Vaillant 1932), so it is fitting that some of the earliest pottery in the Maya lowlands should be found there. Pottery belonging to the K'awil complex (1000–850 BC) was recovered from architectural fill contexts at Holmul and cross-dated by comparison with similar "Pre-Mamom" pottery (i.e., lowland ceramics dating to a time before the second half of the Middle Preclassic) from sites in Belize and Guatemala. An important aspect of Neivens de Estrada's study is that, following Andrews's (1990) example, she viewed collections of early pottery from all the important southern lowland sites with Pre-Mamom ceramics. The K'awil complex shows close ties with the Cunil/Kanocha (defined first at Cahal Pech and Blackman Eddy), Eb (Tikal), and Xe/Real Xe (Altar de Sacrificios and Seibal) complexes from Peten and western Belize. In fact, it contains the full range of forms, slip colors, and incised designs represented at these early sites as well as types that were previously unreported. Among these is Jobal Red, with a distinctive red micaceous slip that sometimes contains specular hematite. The closest similarities to Jobal Red are found not in the Maya lowlands but in the Pacific coast and highlands of Guatemala, in accord with some speculations about the origins of Mayan languages. Incised white wares at Holmul also point to contacts with these areas.

Neivens de Estrada clearly disagrees with scholars who argue that the presence of pan-Mesoamerican (or "Olmec," if one is so inclined) incised motifs implies an influx of non-Maya people at the time that settled village life appeared in the Maya lowlands. In fact, she points to a growing body of evidence from Holmul and elsewhere that continuous occupation began in the eastern lowlands at least 300 years earlier, during the Terminal Archaic period. Instead of positing migration, she suggests that the earliest potters and pottery consumers at Holmul participated in a very large network over which ideas about ceramics and symbols were shared. Interaction was closest and most frequent among Holmul and its near neighbors in the central Peten and western Belize, but inter-community ties also indirectly linked Holmul to more distant sites in northern Belize, southwestern Peten, the southern Maya region, and even highland Mexico.

Chapter 5, by Eugenia Robinson and me, considers the origins of complexity in the Maya highlands of Guatemala, specifically within the departments of Sacatepequez and Chimaltenango. In the eastern half of the Kaqchikel region, we surveyed some 350 square kilometers of terrain, stretching from the southwestern slopes of Alotenango Volcano almost to the Motagua River (see Figures 1.1 and 5.1). Moreover, we conducted excavations at several sites. Tantalizing evidence of landscape modification and the introduction of cultigens can be found dating back well into the Archaic period, but – as elsewhere in Guatemala (Neff *et al.* 2006) – we still lack clear evidence of living floors, hearths, and other features dating to this early occupation. Although a gradual *in situ* development from Terminal Archaic seasonal foraging and horticulture to settled village life seems likely, sites with unambiguous evidence of this pattern are still lacking. In part, this is because of the extremely dynamic and ever changing landscape of the southern Maya highlands, where volcanic eruptions, earthquakes, and all too frequent landslides bury, disturb, or obliterate many sites. But this is also a reflection of how little archaeological research has been targeted at searching for pre-ceramic occupations.

As in the Maya lowlands, there is little evidence of a long Early Preclassic tradition. In the Kaqchikel highlands, a few sherds with Pacific and piedmont affinities suggest ties to that region. The Arevalo complex at Kaminaljuyu (Popenoe de Hatch 1997, 2002) might date to the very end of the Early Preclassic, but this is still uncertain and seeming less and less likely. Recent work at nearby Naranjo does not resolve the status of Arevalo but does demonstrate occupation as early as 900 BC (Arroyo 2010). As in the lowlands, there is abundant evidence for permanent occupation in the Middle Preclassic. The earliest Middle Preclassic sites of the eastern Kaqchikel region are quite small and lack visible mounds or monumental architecture. In contrast, evidence for incipient complexity dating to the early first millennium BC can be found at Las Charcas-phase Naranjo at roughly the same time as similar developments occurred at "pre-Mamom" sites in the southern Maya lowlands.

In great contrast to Kaminaljuyu, however, social and political complexity was slow to arrive in the eastern Kaqchikel highlands. There are many sites in this region that date to the late Middle Preclassic and early Late Preclassic, but they too seem to lack artifical platforms visible on the current ground surface. Burials do not clearly demonstrate inherited, rather than achieved, status. Over time – and especially by the Late Preclassic period – connections between the Kaqchikel region and the Valley of Guatemala seem to have dwindled. Thus, as the great chiefdom of Kaminaljuyu developed in the Valley of Guatemala, the highlands to the east appear to have maintained simpler principles of political organization and were not absorbed into that polity. During the second half of the Late Preclassic, much of the eastern Kaqchikel highlands were abandoned. This happened earlier and more completely in the north and to a lesser degree in the south. Abandonment might have been stimulated by climate change and "pull" factors attracting settlers to Kaminaljuyu. Like Teotihuacan and Monte Alban, Kaminaljuyu exerted a centripetal force attracting a larger and larger population focused on the site and its immediate environs. Nonetheless, we stress that we can find no evidence of political domination of the eastern Kaqchikel highlands during the Late Preclassic. Remaining populations seem to have had very little interaction with their neighbors to the east.

Settlement patterns and site planning

Chapter 5 also considers settlement patterns in the eastern Kaqchikel highlands and notes that there is a single level of settlement in both the Middle and Late Preclassic. Several other chapters look explicitly at settlement patterns and site planning. In Chapter 6, Robinson focuses on the Antigua Valley during the Late Classic period – a time of much greater political complexity than the Preclassic. She makes several intriguing observations. First, important sites in the settlement hierarchy often were located in defensible hills. Borhegyi (1965) noted this pattern for the Postclassic period, but

Robinson extends his observation back in time. Nonetheless, compared with areas farther west in the highlands, there is limited evidence for man-made defensive features. Instead, site location seems to have been chosen in order to take advantage of lines of site and view sheds, perhaps for communication and organizing defense of the sites in the valley below. Second, the importance of defensible locations seems to have varied within the valley. At its northern end, such locations were paramount. But in the southern and central valley, settlements were more open. Third, the Antigua Valley marks the northernmost extension of Cotzumalguapan-style sculpture containing hieroglyphs (other related but illiterate, cruder, and simpler monuments are found throughout the Late Classic Kaqchikel highlands) and participated in the same general ceramic sphere. Combining settlement, artistic, and ceramic data, Robinson proposes that the Antigua Valley was an acculturative frontier zone, where K'iche'an peoples of the Kaqchikel highlands interacted with foreign Cotzumalguapan elites from the Pacific coast and piedmont. Finally, citing paleoecological data, Robinson argues that the Late Classic collapse of the Valley of Antigua corresponded in time to the lowland Maya Collapse and might have been triggered by a drought beginning in the late eighth century.

Two chapters consider settlement and site planning at Quelepa, located far outside the Maya region in eastern El Salvador (see Figure 1.1). Will Andrews conducted his dissertation fieldwork at the site, later published as an important monograph (Andrews 1976). In the more than 40 years that have passed since this research, no similarly extensive work has been conducted at an archaeological site in eastern El Salvador. In Chapter 2, Wendy Ashmore considers the impact of human and natural landscape on site planning at Quelepa. Following Andrews, she notes clear and distinct breaks in the location of structures at the site during different periods. Like the Valley of Antigua during the Late Classic period, Quelepa can be considered as occupying an acculturative frontier zone throughout its long history. Ashmore stresses alternating westward (i.e., towards Mesoamerica) and eastward (beyond Mesoamerica) orientations in material culture. In terms of settlement, it is most striking that Late Classic Lepa construction did not seek to cover or obliterate earlier platforms dating to the Preclassic and Early Classic periods. Instead, the Lepa-phase center of the site was shifted *laterally* to the west. This had the effect of preserving the ruins, tying them to the surrounding natural landscape, and linking the newly arrived inhabitants of Quelepa (people with ties to Veracruz) to the distant but local past. Ashmore discusses the importance of this in terms of inhabitation, materiality, and social memory.

In Chapter 3, Sampeck returns to Quelepa and considers its position more broadly within Mesoamerican and Central American worlds. She sees it not as occupying a fixed boundary but instead as being within a loosely allied frontier that fostered greater agency. At times – as Ashmore also sees in site planning – Quelepa seemed to be "inward looking" towards Mesoamerica (during the early Uapala and late Lepa phases), but at other times it looked outwards towards Central America (especially during the Shila phase, when architecture and site planning were distinctly non-Maya in character). Sampeck cautions that we should not interpret the cultural affiliations of the site in these terms alone. During all periods, obsidian procurement patterns and technology indicate closer connections with southeastern Mesoamerica than with lower Central America. During the Shila phase, Quelepa pottery reflects clear continuities with earlier local materials and even ties with the Maya region and western Honduras, despite the fact that the site employed a new architectural style and site-planning norms that were distinctly non-Mesoamerican in character. Quelepa, then, exhibits its own particular and inimitable position, engaging in the kind of independent and "roguish" behavior possible only in an acculturative frontier. Its leaders picked and chose from a wide variety of traditions at will, in a way that Sampeck construes as "thumbing [their] nose[s]" at the Mesoamerican heartland. What seems to have been particularly important to Central America southeast of the Maya region was preserving political forms that were less centralized than the states that emerged in the Early Classic period. Such resistance to – or resilience in the face of – political change maintained independence and allowed for greater local expressions of agency.

Turning to later documents of the colonial period, especially the Hack Atlas, Sampeck notes that San Miguel (a colonial town not far from Quelepa) was depicted as *the* important place in El Salvador, of even greater consequence than the capital, San Salvador. During much of the early colonial period, in fact, San Miguel and eastern El Salvador had stronger ties with Honduras and pivotal events there than with the capital. The people of historical eastern El Salvador therefore continued a long-standing tradition of rogue colonialism first exhibited at Quelepa in a region far from centralized control. As a result, for millennia the inhabitants of eastern El Salvador enjoyed more freedom of action.

Winfred Creamer, Jonathan Haas, and Allen Rutherford return to settlement studies in the final chapter of the volume. This contribution, whose lead author was Will Andrews's first doctoral student at Tulane and organized our SAA session, is a wonderful example of *lagniappe*, a French Creole word meaning "a little something for nothing" and which has roots that fittingly traverse both Spanish and Quechua. The chapter examines late Archaic settlement in the Norte Chico zone of Peru, a region sometimes said to be the home of the first civilization in the world. Although the culture discussed is far from Mesoamerica, the theoretical question and methodology employed by the authors – the origins of complexity as revealed through settlement pattern studies – have clear parallels with the Maya region. Creamer and her colleagues use Colin Renfrew's (1986) model of peer-polity interaction to examine the emergence of large, multiple mound sites. It is important to remember that Renfrew, too, included the Maya (illustrated by Copan, Honduras) as an important example of his model. During the period from about 3000 to 1800 BC, at least 30 sites characterized by huge mounds and sunken circular plazas flanked by upright monoliths were occupied. Not all were contemporary, but 12 such sites flourished around 2200 BC in a relatively small and constricted region. The repetition of architectural features, the even spacing of sites on the landscape, and the placement of smaller sites midway between the largest sites all suggest competition, the maintenance of boundaries, and the existence of communication routes linking the major sites. Moreover, the remarkable similarities seen among all sites imply a shared culture. All of these are consistent with Renfrew's notion of peer polities and, although the word "state" is not at all appropriate in this case, with what he calls Early State Modules.

Creamer and her colleagues look in detail at data documenting competition for resources, competitive emulation, and symbolic entrainment – aspects of Renfrew's model that are critical in identifying peer-polity interaction. Curiously, they find that site location and form are open, and that there is no other indication of conflict. They therefore suggest that, during this early pre-state stage in Andean history, Carneiro's (1970) model for the origin of the state does not apply. It could be that many of the attributes of peer polities, such as competitive emulation, high levels of exchange, and competition for resources might also be characteristic of some social, territorial, and economic groups that existed before the emergence of chiefdoms and expansive warfare. Moreover, cooperation among intermarried and economically interacting groups might also have fostered the emergence of peer-polity structure at a simpler political level. Thus, I suggest that the phenomenon described by Creamer and her colleagues also is consistent with the tribal network model proposed by Braun and Plog (1982).

There is no comparable example for the Late Archaic or Early Preclassic Maya. Nonetheless, a network of highly interactive polities sprang up across the Pacific piedmont and the southern Maya lowlands by the early Middle Preclassic, and slightly later in the Maya highlands and northern lowlands. For many reasons, survey in such regions is much more difficult than in arid coastal Peru, but it seems that the early Maya were quite different from the people of the Norte Chico in several respects. First, the density of large, impressive sites with public architecture was much lower. Although we now have evidence of public architecture at Seibal around 1000 BC (Inomata *et al.* 2013), nothing comparable is yet known in the Maya region before about 600 BC. Second, early Maya social and political systems were not as stable as those of the Norte Chico. In Peru, this early "civilization" grew slowly over about 800 years and, after a period of stability, contracted slowly over another 700 years – both apparently with relatively little change in basic political structure. This gradual arc contrasts with the rapid appearance of the first agricultural villages (the stage most analogous to the Norte Chico, although in the Maya area the first villagers made pottery), followed quickly by individually aggrandizing chiefdoms and the emergence of states in the Maya lowlands. There, the entire process took something like 600 to 1,000 years. Thus, while both regions shared an arrangement of similar looking sites linked by culture, exchange, emulation, and competition, the results of peer-polity interaction in the Maya region were remarkably different than those in the Norte Chico.

Kingship, royal courts, and architecture during the Classic period

Four chapters in our volume examine specific aspects of rulership, palace architecture, and the royal courts of the ancient Maya in Guatemala, Mexico, and Belize. The authors of these contributions approach their topic from different scales, ranging from texts painted on ceramic vessels, to public propagandistic statements of legitimacy carved on larger monuments, to the architecture associated with rulership, to the function of cities as both dynastic seats and places of commerce.

At the smallest scale, Chapter 9, by Markus Eberl, considers Late Classic Dynastic Vases (Martin 1997), a well-known class of Codex-style painted vessels. These were produced during the eighth century AD near the modern border between Guatemala and Mexico. The Dynastic Vases contain hieroglyphic texts painted in black and red on a cream background. The texts on the vessels all share a particular form and content; they are king lists that contain accession dates in Calendar Round form. The subjects of these texts are the rulers of the Snake Head kingdom, which by AD 636 was centered at Calakmul, one of the largest and most powerful Maya cities (Grube 2004; Marcus 2012). The vessels themselves, however, date to a time when the power of the Snake Head kings was in serious decline (Braswell *et al.* 2004; Martin and Grube 2008). Such simple texts seem at first glance to be factual documents. Nonetheless, many of the rulers they describe are unknown from other sources, some kings are presented in a chronological order contradicted by the texts on carved monuments, a few important kings are omitted, and the vase texts consistently mix historical individuals with the subjects of legend or myth. Eberl argues that, rather than interpret the Dynastic Vases as factual documents, pure propaganda, or myth, we should consider them as emic statements reflecting how the Maya viewed the past. Their perspective appears to have blended all three categories for rhetorical purposes.

Using a rather delightful conceit – a coffee mug painted in honor of Will Andrews in the style of a Dynastic Vase – Eberl shows precisely how the ancient Maya texts functioned. The simple repetitive "staccato" structure of such texts provides the appearance of a chain of rulers that was unbroken from the distant past to the present, creating the impression of inevitability and order. This, rather than historical accuracy, was the intended message encoded on the pots.

In Chapter 10, Christian Prager, Beniamino Volta, and I consider ancient kingship at the Maya city of Pusilha, Belize. We first describe archaeological research conducted during the past decade and then consider the hieroglyphic texts that are known from the site. Like the Dynastic Vases discussed by Eberl, these texts date to the Late Classic period and contain information about the lives and actions of rulers. Unlike the painted texts of the Snake Head kings, these hieroglyphic inscriptions are carved on large monuments called stelae and, for the most part, describe historically current or relatively recent events. What we know about the lords of the Kingdom of the Avocado (the ancient name of Pusilha) is derived from public texts erected by rulers in order to celebrate their actions, ancestry, and legitimacy.

Six kings and one queen can be placed within a historical chronological framework. The reigns of two additional rulers cannot be precisely determined, a third can be placed in time but has a name that is thoroughly illegible, and a fourth did not employ the emblem glyph of Pusilha. Two of the kings of Pusilha used a paramount title seen only at the greatest of all Maya cities. Beyond the range of historical texts (AD 571–798), legendary individuals who lived in AD 81 and AD 159 are discussed. One of these early kings, nicknamed Decorated (or Foliated or Leaf) Ajaw, is also mentioned in the texts of several powerful Maya cities. Thus the rulers of Pusilha linked themselves to their counterparts at Tikal, Calakmul, Copan, and other polities by referring to the same legends.

Despite this allusion to a shared past, in one regard the lengthy texts of Pusilha are exceptional: they contain no clear, direct, and unambiguous reference to a powerful and archaeologically known Maya kingdom. Moreover, no such allusion to Pusilha is found in the texts of any other site, including those just a few kilometers away in southern Belize. It seems that the royalty of Pusilha tried hard to remain independent of the political and military conflicts characteristic of the southwestern Peten (Chapter 8), a region from which the settlers of the site might have come. At the same time, powerful neighbors to the south, west, and north of Pusilha seem to have cared little for an independent polity located in the underpopulated eastern frontier of the Maya world. Pusilha, then, might represent another example of the success of roguish colonialism.

Chapter 12, by George Bey and Rossana May Ciau, discusses a particular architectural form that is common in the northern lowlands and is known as the *popol nah* or "mat house." Such structures served as council houses where groups met to discuss and make decisions regarding their lineage, community, and polity. Such structures, called *nim ja* (great houses) in Kaqchikel Mayan, were identified long ago at major Postclassic sites of the Maya highlands. They also were known in a somewhat different form at Postclassic Mayapan. It was not until the late 1980s that such structures began to be identified at Classic Maya cities.

According to Bey and May Ciau, the earliest *popol nahs* were built in Yucatan – especially the Puuc region – at the dawn of the Late Classic period. They argue that the first appearance of this type of open and public platform represents a change in political structure. By about AD 550, the northern lowlands underwent a transition from simply organized communities to polities ruled by powerful lineage councils. Within the span of just two centuries, such councils were superseded by the centralized rulership of the Late Classic *ajaw* system. Thus, after AD 750, *popol nahs* became less important in the northern lowlands and were incorporated into palace compounds. In the aftermath of the collapse of the northern Maya lowlands, a new kind of structure appeared in many locales: the C-shaped building. Bey and May Ciau suggest that this represents the rebirth of open, public architecture and council-based decision-making. The *popol nah*, therefore, signifies the emergence of segmentary rule, its replacement by centralized kingship, and the reappearance of segmentary political systems after about AD 950.

Rather than consider texts or a particular type of structure, Arthur Demarest examines an entire city. In Chapter 8, he discusses the history and function of the Late Classic port of Cancuen. A relatively small Maya site built in an oxbow in the Rio Pasion, Cancuen consists of little more than a series of palaces and port complexes. It became an important place because it occupied a strategic position at the crossroads of critical transportation routes. Positioned at the head of navigation of the Pasion, Cancuen was the lowland site farthest upstream on the river, located at a point that linked the Maya highlands with a vast river system flowing northwards and opening into the Gulf of Mexico. Goods critical to the maintenance of elite power that flowed out of the highlands through Cancuen included quetzal feathers, jade, obsidian, and cloth. At the northern foot of the karstic mountains, Cancuen also could access an important east–west trade route from Chiapas to southern Belize, linking sites as distant as Palenque and Pusilha.

Demarest describes the various port facilities, palaces, lithic production sites, and ballcourts that constitute Cancuen. He notes that the site flourished as a distant ally of Calakmul but reached its apogee as an independent power in the aftermath of the collapse of the predatory Dos Pilas kingdom, located downriver. For a period of roughly 40 years at the end of the eighth century, the roguish merchant kings of Cancuen thrived and prospered at the crossroads of the lowland and highland Maya worlds. They did so by jockeying for power with their neighbors, and by employing symbolic and ritual language that could be understood by both highlanders and lowlanders alike.

Terminal Classic collapse and reorganization in the early Postclassic period

Three chapters tackle the subject of the "Classic Maya Collapse," perhaps the most enduring topic in Maya archaeology and one that unites scholars working from Chiapas to Yucatan to Honduras (e.g., Culbert 1973; Demarest *et al.* 2004). The contributions in our volume approach this subject from perspectives that are heavily influenced by Andrews's work. All three consider ceramics, and two focus on sites that have been at the center of his research and writing: Copan and Chichen Itza.

In Chapter 4, Cassandra Bill describes the Late Classic, Terminal Classic, and Early Postclassic pottery of Copan, Honduras, and demonstrates the power of detailed modal analysis as a way of creating fine-grain ceramic chronologies; at least two subphases of the four temporal blocks she describes are less than a century long.

Bill emphasizes changes in the ceramic inventory of Copan during the Classic to Postclassic transition and presents them as an example of similar processes that occurred across much of the southern Maya lowlands. Although the details of these changes are unique to Copan, Bill stresses that the basic pattern was the same at other sites where dynastic rule and populations collapsed. As the Late Classic drew to a close, there was a sharp decline in the production of elite wares, a constriction of the size of interaction spheres, and a concomitant rise in regionalization. At Copan, this process began during the lifetime of the last king (AD 750–*ca.* 820) and was particularly acute during the post-dynastic occupation of the final royal palace compound (AD 820–850/900). Those last few years were marked by a dramatic decline in local production industries linked to a loss of potters and the consumers of their wares.

The post-dynastic pottery of Copan during the ninth century is Terminal Classic in nature because it represents a continuation – albeit in a greatly attenuated form – of Late Classic traditions established during the reigns of the last five Copan rulers. But the pattern of decline described by Bill began during the Late Coner subphase (AD 750–820); thus much of that complex also can be considered Terminal Classic in character. In great contrast to the Late and Terminal Coner subphases, pottery of the Early Postclassic Ejar complex consists of "a radically different domestic inventory." The best explanation for this is that the royal center of Copan was abandoned at the end of the Classic period and was later reoccupied by a "new group with distinct pottery-making practices and different wide-reaching connections with external regions." Had Copan not been abandoned and resettled by new people, its Early Postclassic ceramic complex would have witnessed continuity in local pottery-making practices, as was the case at tenth-century Lamanai (Chapter 11) and Chichen Itza (Chapter 13). Most of us who work at Copan consider it likely that the settlers of the Postclassic Ejar phase were speakers of Lenkan, not Mayan.

In sum, the thrust of Bill's argument is that Copan is similar in many ways to lowland Maya sites that saw a rapid decline at the end of the eighth century. That decline was not just political but also demographic. The end of monument erection at about AD 790, the cessation of all known construction by about AD 810, and the decline of ceramic richness and variety during the late eighth century are consistent with population loss and a weakening of the power of the last *ajaw* of Copan. Divine kingship ended at Copan with his death during the period 810–822. Bill makes clear that ceramic evidence implies that the remaining population abandoned the city within decades of this event. These conclusions should not sound new to archaeologists who work in Guatemala or Belize, or even to those whose knowledge of Copan is limited to literature published more than 20 years ago. But they do represent a return to a traditional perspective through Bill's careful, detailed, and thorough refutation of a revisionist collapse narrative proposed in the early 1990s.

Proponents of the revisionist account argued that most of the Early Classic Copan kings were legendary rather than real, that the site was built primarily during the Late Classic period, that population levels remained close to their peak until after AD 900, that population loss was triggered by anthropogenic environmental destruction, that the local forest did not begin to recover from human degradation until after 1200, that the demographic decline was gradual, that Copan was not abandoned until 1250 or even later, and that the pottery inventory of the period 900–1250 represented an extension – with the addition of some new types and the loss of others – of the Late Classic ceramic complex (Freter 1988, 1992, 1994, 1996, 1997; Paine and Freter 1996; Paine *et al.* 1996; Webster and Freter 1990a, 1990b; Webster *et al.* 1992, 1993, 2000, 2004). This hypothetical extension was called the "late Coner" subphase and was described as a continuation of local utilitarian Late Classic ceramic traditions. This is precisely the opposite of the pattern carefully documented by Bill in Chapter 4. That a Classic Maya ceramic phase – even with two subphases – could last a full 700 years is indeed a remarkable proposal. Bill's research proves it is false.

The revisionist narrative was not based on empirical ceramic analysis. This is because its proponents worked outside of the site center in groups where pottery sherds are especially eroded. Instead, they relied on a series of more than 2,200 obsidian hydration dates determined through measurements made using an optical microscope. Such a technique is qualitative and indirect because it does not actually measure the amount of water adsorbed by an obsidian artifact. Virtually all aspects of these dates have been questioned. First – and fundamentally important – obsidian, just like ceramics, is highly subject to erosion. The technique should not be employed where there is a strong likelihood that obsidian hydration rinds are subject to significant weathering, as suggested by ceramic erosion at Copan (Braswell 2003). This is because eroded rinds yield late hydration dates. Second, the interpretation of the phenomenon observed by the qualitative optical approach has been challenged (Anovitz et al. 1999); it is almost certainly a Schlieren line representing not a hydration boundary but an inflection point where water concentration declines at a maximum rate. Third, the mathematical model of simple hydration – rather than concentration-dependent hydration – was incorrect (Braswell 1992: 132; 2003). Fourth, claims made for the precision of the method surpass those determined by the Rayleigh criterion; it is impossible to make such fine measurements with an optical microscope. Fifth, no attempts were made by the original researchers to measure at Copan itself the environmental variables that directly affect hydration (Braswell 1992; 1997: 265). Sixth, scholars ignored the central tendency in the distribution of dates and focused instead on the late tail end. This is an incorrect approach to statistical data (Cowgill and Kintigh 1997). Data sets all have outliers, and very large sets tend to have large numbers of outliers; a single date of AD 1250 out of 2,200 certainly cannot be interpreted as indicating that population continued until that time. Seventh, there was little attempt to understand error margins; even small differences in temperature can dramatically impact hydration dates (Braswell 1992: 135–9). Eighth – and most critical of all – two independent laboratories (MURR and the Diffusion Laboratory) tried to reproduce the results of obsidian hydration dating at Copan and failed (Braswell 1997: 266; 2003). They found that virtually all obsidian artifacts exhibit significant weathering, that many actually have no hydration rind at all (and hence "date" to the present), that hydration measurements do not even form a consistent sequence (i.e., that the oldest artifacts recovered from sealed contexts sometimes yield the most recent dates), and that very different measurements can be made from different sides of the same artifact. In the late 1980s and 1990s, at least three laboratories employed the Copan technique at other sites in the Maya area. These include Tak'alik Ab'aj (Dillon et al. 1988; Neff et al. 1993), Xunantunich (LeCount et al. 2002), Dos Pilas (Stiver 1994), and Kaminaljuyu (Michael Gottesman, personal communication 1998). In all these cases, the optical qualitative technique yielded unsatisfactory dates. In sum, the results of obsidian hydration dating as employed at Copan in the late 1980s and early 1990s have been utterly irreproducible.

The question of the timing of the demographic collapse at Copan was not ultimately resolved by any chronometric means, although radiocarbon dating has played a role (Fash et al. 2004; Manahan 2004; Manahan and Canuto 2009). Instead, it was solved by careful excavations in Group 10L-2 by Will Andrews (Andrews and Bill 2005; Fash et al. 2004) and in El Bosque by Kam Manahan (2003), and by the subsequent meticulous and detailed ceramic analyses of Cassandra Bill (Bill 1997). Their work, and that of environmental specialists (McNeil et al. 2010), has closed the debate concerning the collapse at Copan. The political and demographic collapse began during the eighth century and was completed in the ninth century.

Copan was abandoned early in the Terminal Classic period. Nonetheless, some ancient Maya cities did survive the Maya Collapse. One of these was Lamanai (Pendergast 1985, 1986), which served as an example for the revisionists at Copan. At Lamanai, the Terminal Classic period witnessed a contraction of settlement and population, but the site also saw a continuation through Early Postclassic times up to the present. The survival of Lamanai likely was related to its position on the New River lagoon, the largest body of freshwater in Belize. Although Lamanai is not located on the Caribbean shore, it had easy and rapid access to Postclassic coastal trade routes via the river. It therefore was connected to the Postclassic Mesoamerican World (*sensu* Smith and Berdan 2010).

Early Postclassic Buk pottery (AD 962–1200/1250) represents a continuation of long-established traditions of ceramic production and also manifests new ideas that circulated widely along the coastal trade route. Many of the motifs, forms, and surface treatments characteristic of this style may have originated in the Gulf Coast region of Veracruz and spread into the Maya lowlands on the heels of the Collapse. They became particularly important at Chichen Itza during the Sotuta phase, and some continued at Mayapan after the decline of the Itza. The first half of the Buk phase at Lamanai was contemporary with Early Postclassic Chichen Itza (Chapter 13), and the last 50 years or so overlapped with the rise of Mayapan.

In Chapter 11, James Aimers considers the Early Postclassic pottery of Lamanai, especially those vessels that he classifies as belonging to the Fine Orange supersystem. Fine Orange pottery – containing no temper – is a horizon marker for much of the Maya lowlands. It first appeared in the southern Maya lowlands at about AD 830 and ceased to be manufactured around AD 1050/1100. Although one complete Fine Orange vessel was found at Lamanai (see Figure 11.1), Aimers notes that true examples of the ware are quite uncommon at the site. Instead, the potters that supplied Buk-phase Lamanai produced a lot of vessels incorporating design motifs from Fine Orange Ware, especially from Silho Fine Orange consumed by the elites of Chichen Itza. These designs appear frequently on funerary vessels at Lamanai, so probably served a religious purpose or were used in statements of identity and affiliation.

Using Fine Orange-like pottery as a jumping-off point, Aimers asks us to re-examine two often ignored concepts in type-variety classification: ceramic systems and supersystems. Ceramic systems are based entirely on superficial aspects of pottery – what it looks like, not the characteristics of its paste. As Aimers stresses, it is the visible traits that often tell us what consumers desired in the pots they purchased. In contrast, ceramic taxa that include paste characteristics provide information on technology and place of origin. Ceramic supersystems are broader categories that incorporate multiple systems and show even more general and less specific commonalities of surface appearance.

By focusing on systems and supersystems rather than types, groups, and wares, Aimers is able to begin to answer a big question: How did Mesoamerican potters interact over vast areas? Fine Orange supersystem pottery manifests an elite style, one that served as an integrative mechanism in the expanding world religion focused on the god Quetzalcoatl/Kukulkan (Ringle et al. 1998). This cult and the inauguration rites at its center created elite ties across Mesoamerica throughout the Postclassic period. Fine Orange supersystem pottery played an important role in the cult.

The great Terminal Classic to Early Postclassic city of Chichen Itza is the subject of Chapter 13. In our contribution, Ben Volta and I discuss the chronology of the site from many perspectives: indigenous documents, pottery, hieroglyphic texts, architectural styles, and radiocarbon dates. Excavations conducted in recent years (Braswell and Peniche May 2012; Schmidt 2011) have provided a wealth of new information concerning construction stages and ceramics (Chung 2009; Pérez de Heredia Puente 2010, 2012). Combining different lines of evidence, we conduct a Bayesian analysis of temporal data in order to create a more precise chronology for the city. Along the way, we correct some errors regarding the material culture and history of Chichen Itza.

Chichen Itza was founded in the Preclassic period, but the city as we know it began to form after AD 600. The earliest structures that have survived are deeply buried and date to the Late Classic period. During the late ninth century, older platforms were destroyed or buried and buildings in the Puuc or Maya style were constructed. These are associated with Yabnal pottery, especially what is called "Say" (Pérez de Heredia Puente 2010, 2012), "Tintin" (Chung 2009), or "Early" Slate Ware (Chapter 13). There is absolutely no Sotuta pottery associated with the construction of Maya-style structures – an important correction to earlier works, including our own (e.g., Braswell and Peniche May 2012: 230; Cobos 2004; Grube and Krochock 2011: 176). A very few sherds of what appear to be medium-fired Slate Wares also have been found in the fill of Maya-style structures. These can be called "Early Dzitas" (Chung 2009) or considered to be a local variant of Muna Slate (Johnson 2012; Pérez de Heredia Puente 2010). Nonetheless, we are not yet convinced that a full Cehpech ceramic complex ever existed at Chichen Itza (cf. Pérez de Heredia Puente 2010). The period AD 870–900 not only saw the construction of numerous Maya-style structures but also witnessed the carving of many hieroglyphic texts. Because this first great florescence of Chichen Itza is contemporary with the apogee of the Classic Puuc phenomenon, it is reasonable to refer to the years AD 870–900 there as the Terminal Classic.

In contrast, comparably little is known about the period AD 900–950/980. There are no hieroglyphic texts at Chichen Itza that date to this period, and only a few major buildings – such as the Castillo-sub – were built during this time. Volta and I argue that the early tenth century, the period that saw the collapse of the Puuc region and the near to complete abandonment of many inland sites, also was a time of significant reorganization at Chichen Itza. The hieroglyphic hiatus and dramatic slowdown in construction of the early tenth century might even be symptoms of a short-term population loss.

Like Lamanai, Chichen Itza emerged from the Terminal Classic and experienced a renaissance during the period AD 950/980–1050/1100. All of the major visible structures of the Great Terrace, built in the new International style, date to this period. A few Maya hieroglyphic texts are known, as are many more examples of foreign-looking name phrases. The pottery of this second golden age belongs to the Sotuta complex, which – like the Buk complex at Lamanai – contains foreign stylistic ideas and elite imports, but otherwise is fundamentally derived from local Late and Terminal Classic antecedents. Recognizing the great continuity in utilitarian ceramics, we nonetheless see differences in material culture sufficient to warrant assigning the Sotuta phase and final period of glory at Chichen Itza to the Early Postclassic period. Thus, although the contemporary Postclassic Ejar complex of Copan represents a complete break from the past, the Early Postclassic complexes of Lamanai and Chichen Itza display continuation. All three sites participated in new, broad, and international connections with greater Mesoamerica. That greater Mesoamerica also included Quelepa (Chapter 2).

The legacy of E. Wyllys Andrews V

Will Andrews has made important contributions to our understanding of the origins of settled village life in the Maya region and lower Central America, studied ceramics from a broad comparative perspective, conducted the first extensive archaeological project in eastern El Salvador, directed settlement studies in Mexico, excavated and interpreted a royal palace occupied during and after the reign of the last Copan king, and provided important insights into the processes and events of the Maya Collapse – especially at Copan and Chichen Itza. As authors in our volume show, his research questions and methods have stimulated a wide range of scholars to conduct work in his footsteps.

Seven of the contributors to this volume were PhD advisees of Will Andrews, and he served on the committees of two more. Two authors are current Tulane graduate students, and another contributor was an undergraduate student of that institution. As of spring 2013, Andrews's direct academic legacy comprises 36 PhDs and five MAs, and there are still four more graduate students in the pipeline. We are all thankful for his inspiration and also for the vision of clear reasoning that he champions and urges us to pursue. Wendy Ashmore quips that Will has always encouraged his friends, collaborators, and students to stick "just [to] the facts, ma'am." We dedicate this book to Will with the hope that we have not strayed too far from them.

References

Andrews, E. Wyllys, V (1976) *The Archaeology of Quelepa, El Salvador*. New Orleans: Middle American Research Institute, Tulane University.

—— (1988) Ceramic Units from Komchen, Yucatan, Mexico. *Cerámica de cultura maya* 15: 51–64.

—— (1990) The Early Ceramic History of the Lowland Maya. In *Vision and Revision in Maya Studies*, ed. Flora S. Clancy and Peter D. Harrison, pp. 1–19. Albuquerque: University of New Mexico Press.

Andrews, E. Wyllys, V, and George J. Bey III (2011) The Earliest Ceramics of the Northern Maya Lowlands. Paper presented at the eighth Tulane Maya Symposium, New Orleans.

Andrews, E. Wyllys, V, and Cassandra R. Bill (2005) A Late Classic Royal Residence at Copán. In *Copán: The History of an Ancient Maya Kingdom*, ed. E. Wyllys Andrews V and William L. Fash, pp. 239–314. Albuquerque, NM: School of American Research.

Andrews, E. Wyllys, V, and Norman Hammond (1990) Redefinition of the Swasey Phase at Cuello, Belize. *American Antiquity* 55: 570–84.

Andrews, E. Wyllys, V, George J. Bey III, and Christopher Gunn (2008) Rethinking the Early Ceramic History of the Northern Maya Lowlands: New Evidence and Interpretations. Paper presented at the 73rd annual meeting of the Society for American Archaeology, Vancouver.

Anovitz, Lawrence M., J. Michael Elam, Lee R. Riciputi, and David R. Cole (1999) The Failure of Obsidian Hydration Dating: Sources, Implications, and New Directions. *Journal of Archaeological Science* 26: 735–52.

Arroyo, Bárbara (ed.) (2010) *Entre cerros, cafetales y urbanismo en el Valle de Guatemala: Proyecto de Rescate Naranjo*. Guatemala City: Academia de Geografía e Historia de Guatemala.

Ball, Joseph W., and Jennifer Taschek (2003) Reconsidering the Belize Valley Preclassic: A Case for Multiethnic Interactions in the Development of a Regional Culture Tradition. *Ancient Mesoamerica* 14: 179–217.

Bey, George J., III (2006) Changing Archaeological Perspectives on the Northern Maya Lowlands. In *Lifeways in the Northern Maya Lowlands: New Approaches to Archaeology in the Yucatán Peninsula*, ed. Jennifer P. Mathews and Bethany A. Morrison, pp. 13–37. Tucson: University of Arizona Press.

Bill, Cassandra R. (1997) *Patterns of Variation and Change in Dynastic Period Ceramics and Ceramic Production at Copan, Honduras*. PhD dissertation, Department of Anthropology, Tulane University. Ann Arbor, MI: University Microfilms.

Borhegyi, Stephan F. de (1965) Settlement Patterns of the Guatemalan Highlands. In *Handbook of Middle American Indians*, Vol. 2: *Archaeology of Southern Mesoamerica, Part I*, ed. Gordon R. Willey, pp. 59–75. Austin: University of Texas Press.

Braswell, Geoffrey E. (1992) Obsidian-Hydration Dating, The Coner Phase, and Revisionist Chronology at Copán, Honduras. *Latin American Antiquity* 3: 130–47.

—— (1997) La cronología y la estructura del colapso en Copán, Honduras. *Los investigadores de la cultura Maya* 5, pp. 262–73. Campeche, Mexico: Universidad Autónoma de Campeche.

—— (2003) Obsidian Hydration and the Demographic Collapse of Copan: Recent Methodological and Theoretical Advances. Paper presented at the 102nd annual meeting of the American Anthropological Association, Philadelphia.

—— (ed.) (2012a) *The Ancient Maya of Mexico: Reinterpreting the Past of the Northern Maya Lowlands*. Sheffield: Equinox.

—— (2012b) The Ancient Maya of Mexico: Reinterpreting the Past of the Northern Maya Lowlands. In *The Ancient Maya of Mexico: Reinterpreting the Past of the Northern Maya Lowlands*, ed. Geoffrey E. Braswell, pp. 1–40. Sheffield: Equinox.

Braswell, Geoffrey E., and Nancy Peniche May (2012) In the Shadow of the Pyramid: Excavations of the Great Platform of Chichen Itza. In *The Ancient Maya of Mexico: Reinterpreting the Past of the Northern Maya Lowlands*, ed. Geoffrey E. Braswell, pp. 227–58. Sheffield: Equinox.

Braswell, Geoffrey E., Joel D. Gunn, María del Rosario Domínguez Carrasco, William J. Folan, Laraine A. Fletcher, Abel Moralez López, and Michael D. Glascock (2004) Defining the Terminal Classic at Calakmul, Campeche. In *The Terminal Classic in the Maya*

Lowlands: Collapse, Transition, and Transformation, ed. Arthur A. Demarest, Don S. Rice, and Prudence M. Rice, pp. 162–94. Boulder: University Press of Colorado.

Braun, David P., and Stephen Plog (1982) Evolution of "Tribal" Social Networks: Theory and Prehistoric North American Evidence. *American Antiquity* 47: 504–25.

Carneiro, Robert L. (1970) A Theory of the Origin of the State. *Science* 189: 733–8.

Cheetham, David J. (2005) Cunil: A Pre-Mamom Horizon in the Southern Maya Lowlands. In *New Perspectives on Formative Mesoamerican Cultures*, ed. Terry G. Powis, pp. 27–38. Oxford: Archaeopress.

Chung, Heajoo (2009) *La cronología de Chichén Itzá*. Paju: Korea Studies Information.

Cobos, Rafael (2004) Chichén Itzá: Settlement and Hegemony during the Terminal Classic Period. In *The Terminal Classic in the Maya Lowlands: Collapse, Transition, and Transformation*, ed. Arthur A. Demarest, Prudence M. Rice, and Don S. Rice, pp. 517–44. Boulder: University Press of Colorado.

Cowgill, George L., and Keith W. Kintigh (1997) How Random Errors in Dates Increase Apparent Lengths of Intervals. Paper presented at the 62nd annual meeting of the Society for American Archaeology, Nashville.

Culbert, T. Patrick (ed.) (1973) *The Classic Maya Collapse*. Albuquerque: University of New Mexico Press.

Demarest, Arthur A., Don S. Rice, and Prudence M. Rice (eds) (2004) *The Terminal Classic in the Maya Lowlands: Collapse, Transition, and Transformation*. Boulder: University Press of Colorado.

Dillon, B. D., John. A. Graham, Janet L. Scalise, and F. Wood (1988) Preliminary Obsidian Hydration Results from Pacific Piedmont Guatemala: Abaj Takalik, Retalhuleu. In *Obsidian Dates IV: A Compendium of the Obsidian Hydration Determinations Made at the UCLA Obsidian Hydration Laboratory*, ed. Clement W. Meighan and Janet L. Scalise, pp. 128–9. Los Angeles: University of California Press.

Fash, William L., E. Wyllys Andrews V, and T. Kam Manahan (2004) Political Decentralization, Dynastic Collapse, and the Early Postclassic in the Urban Center of Copán, Honduras. In *The Terminal Classic in the Maya Lowlands: Collapse, Transition, and Transformation*, ed. Arthur A. Demarest, Don S. Rice, and Prudence M. Rice, pp. 260–87. Boulder: University Press of Colorado.

Freter, AnnCorrine (1988) *The Classic Maya Collapse at Copán, Honduras: A Regional Settlement Perspective*. PhD dissertation, Department of Anthropology, Pennsylvania State University. Ann Arbor, MI: University Microfilms.

—— (1992) Chronological Research at Copan. *Ancient Mesoamerica* 3: 117–33.

—— (1994) The Classic Maya Collapse at Copan, Honduras: An Analysis of Maya Rural Settlement. In *Archaeological Views from the Countryside: Village Communities in Early Complex Societies*, ed. Glenn M. Schwartz and Steven E. Falconer, pp. 160–76. Washington, DC, and London: Smithsonian Institution Press.

—— (1996) Rural Utilitarian Ceramic Production in the Late Classic Period Copán Maya State. In *Arqueología Mesoamericana: Homanaje a William Sanders*, Vol. 2, ed. Alba G. Mastache, Jeffrey R. Parsons, Robert S. Santley, and María Carmen Sierra Puche, pp. 209–30. Mexico City: Instituto Nacional de Antropología e Historia.

—— (1997) The Question of Time: The Impact of Chronology on Copan Prehistoric Settlement Demography. In *Integrating Archaeological Demography: Multidisciplinary Approaches to Prehistoric Population*, ed. Richard R. Paine, pp. 21–42. Carbondale: Center for Archaeological Investigations, Southern Illinois University.

Garber, James F., and Jaime J. Awe (2009) A Terminal Early Formative Symbol System in the Maya Lowlands: The Iconography of the Cunil Phase (1100–900 BC) at Cahal Pech. *Reports in Belizean Archaeology* 6: 151–9.

Grube, Nikolai (2004) El origen de la dinastía Kaan. In *Los cautivos de Dzibanché*, ed. Enrique Nalda, pp. 117–31. Mexico City: Instituto Nacional de Antropología e Historia.

Grube, Nikolai, and Ruth J. Krochock (2011) Reading between the Lines: Hieroglyphic Texts from Chichén Itzá and its Neighbors. In *Twin Tollans: Chichén Itzá, Tula, and the Epiclassic to Early Postclassic Mesoamerican World*. Rev. ed., ed. Jeff K. Kowalski and Cynthia Kristan-Graham, pp. 157–93. Washington, DC: Dumbarton Oaks.

Inomata, Takeshi, Daniela Triadan, Kazuo Aoyama, Victor Castillo, and Hitoshi Yonenobu (2013) Early Ceremonial Constructions at Ceibal, Guatemala, and the Origins of Lowland Maya Civilization. *Science* 340(6131): 467–71.

Johnson, Scott A. J. (2012) *Late and Terminal Classic Power Shifts in Yucatan: The View from Popola*. PhD dissertation, Department of Anthropology, Tulane University. Ann Arbor, MI: University Microfilms.

LeCount, Lisa, Jason Yaeger, Richard M. Leventhal, and Wendy Ashmore (2002) Dating the Rise and Fall of Xunantunich, Belize: A Late and Terminal Classic Lowland Maya Secondary Center. *Ancient Mesoamerica* 13: 41–63.

Lohse, Jon C. (2010) Archaic Origins of the Lowland Maya. *Latin American Antiquity* 21: 312–52.

Manahan, T. Kam (2003) *The Collapse of Complex Society and its Aftermath: A Case Study from the Classic Maya Site of Copán, Honduras*. PhD dissertation, Department of Anthropology, Vanderbilt University, Nashville. Ann Arbor, MI: University Microfilms.

—— (2004) The Way Things Fall Apart: Social Organization and the Classic Maya Collapse of Copán. *Ancient Mesoamerica* 15: 107–25.

Manahan, T. Kam, and Marcello A. Canuto (2009) Bracketing the Copan Dynasty: Late Preclassic and Early Postclassic Settlements at Copan, Honduras. *Latin American Antiquity* 20: 553–80.

Marcus, Joyce (2012) Maya Political Cycling and the Story of the *Kaan* Policy. In *The Ancient Maya of Mexico: Reinterpreting the Past of the Northern Maya Lowlands*, ed. Geoffrey E. Braswell, pp. 89–116. Sheffield: Equinox.

Martin, Simon (1997) The Painted King List: A Commentary on Codex-Style Dynastic Vessels. In *The Maya Vase Book: A Corpus of Rollout Photographs of Maya Vases*, Vol. 5, ed. Barbara Kerr and Justin Kerr, pp. 847–67. New York: Kerr Associates.

Martin, Simon, and Nikolai Grube (2008) *Chronicle of the Maya Kings and Queens: Deciphering the Dynasties of the Ancient Maya*. 2nd ed., London: Thames & Hudson.

McNeil, Cameron L., David A. Burney, and Lida Pigott Burney (2010) Evidence Disputing Deforestation as the Cause for the Collapse of the Ancient Maya Polity of Copan, Honduras. *Proceedings of the National Academy of Sciences* 107: 1017–22.

Merwin, Raymond E., and George C. Vaillant (1932) *The Ruins of Holmul, Guatemala*. Cambridge, MA: Peabody Museum of Archaeology and Ethnology, Harvard University.

Neff, Hector, Frederick Bove, T. Johnson, and Bárbara Arroyo (1993) Fechamiento através de hidratación de obsidiana en la Costa Sur de Guatemala. *Apuntes Arqueológicos* 3(1): 57–79.

Neff, Hector, Deborah M. Pearsall, John G. Jones, Bárbara Arroyo, Shawn K. Collins, and Dorothy E. Freidel (2006) Early Maya Adaptive Patterns: Mid–Late Holocene Paleoenvironmental Evidence from Pacific Guatemala. *Latin American Antiquity* 17: 287–315.

Paine, Richard R., and AnnCorinne Freter (1996) Environmental Degradation and the Maya Collapse at Copán (AD 600–1250). *Latin American Antiquity* 7: 37–47.

Paine, Richard R., AnnCorinne Freter, and David Webster (1996) A Mathematical Projection of Population Growth in the Copán Valley, Honduras, AD 400–800. *Latin American Antiquity* 7: 51–60.

Pendergast, David M. (1985) Lamanai, Belize: An Updated View. In *The Lowland Maya Postclassic*, ed. Arlen F. Chase and Prudence M. Rice, pp. 91–103. Austin: University of Texas Press.

—— (1986) Stability through Change: Lamanai, Belize, from the Ninth to the Seventeenth Century. In *Late Lowland Maya Civilization: Classic to Postclassic*, ed. Jeremy A. Sabloff and E. Wyllys Andrews V, pp. 223–49. Albuquerque: University of New Mexico Press.

Pérez de Heredia Puente, Eduardo J. (2010) *Ceramic Contexts and Chronology at Chichen Itza, Yucatan, Mexico*. PhD dissertation, La Trobe University, Bundoora.

—— (2012) The Yabnal-Motul Complex of the Late Classic Period at Chichen Itza. *Ancient Mesoamerica* 23: 379–402.

Pohl, Mary D., Kevin O. Pope, John G. Jones, John S. Jacob, Dolores R. Piperno, Susan D. deFrance, David L. Lentz, John A. Gifford, Marie E. Danforth, and J. Kathryn Josserand (1996) Early Agriculture in the Maya Lowlands. *Latin American Antiquity* 7: 355–72.

Popenoe de Hatch, Marion (1997) *Kaminaljuyú/San Jorge: Evidencia arqueológica de la actividad económica en el Valle de Guatemala, 300 a.C. a 300 d.C*. Guatemala City: Universidad del Valle de Guatemala.

—— (2002) New Perspectives on Kaminaljuyú, Guatemala: Regional Interaction during the Preclassic and Classic Periods. In *Incidents of Archaeology in Central America and Yucatán*, ed. Michael Love, Marion Popenoe de Hatch and Héctor L. Escobedo, pp. 277–96. Lanham, MD: University Press of America.

Renfrew, Colin (1986) Introduction: Peer Polity Interaction and Socio-Political Change. In *Peer Polity Interaction and Socio-Political Change*, ed. Colin Renfrew and John F. Cherry, pp. 1–18. Cambridge: Cambridge University Press.

Ringle, William M., and E. Wyllys Andrews V (1990) The Demography of Komchen, an Early Maya Town in Northern Yucatan. In *Precolumbian Population History in the Maya Lowlands*, ed. T. Patrick Culbert and Don S. Rice, pp. 215–43. Albuquerque: University of New Mexico Press.

Ringle, William M., Tomás Gallareta Negrón, and George J. Bey III (1998) The Return of Quetzalcoatl: Evidence for the Spread of a World Religion during the Epiclassic Period. *Ancient Mesoamerica* 9: 183–232.

Schmidt, Peter J. (2011) Birds, Ceramics, and Cacao: New Excavations at Chichén Itzá, Yucatan. In *Twin Tollans: Chichén Itzá, Tula, and the Epiclassic to Early Postclassic Mesoamerican World*. Rev. ed., ed. Jeff K. Kowalski and Cynthia Kristan-Graham, pp. 113–55. Washington, DC: Dumbarton Oaks.

Sharer, Robert J., and David W. Sedat (1987) *Archaeological Investigations in the Northern Maya Highlands, Guatemala: Interaction and the Development of Maya Civilization*. Philadelphia: University Museum, University of Pennsylvania.

Smith, Michael E., and Frances Berdan (eds) (2010) *The Postclassic Mesoamerican World*. Salt Lake City: University of Utah Press.

Stiver, Laura R. (1994) Obsidian Assemblages of the Petexbatun Region, Guatemala: Interim Report on Analysis from 1991–1993. Manuscript on file, Department of Anthropology, Vanderbilt University, Nashville.

Webster, David L., and AnnCorrine Freter (1990a) The Demography of Late Classic Copan. In *Precolumbian Population History in the Maya Lowlands*, ed. T. Patrick Culbert and Don S. Rice, pp. 37–62. Albuquerque: University of New Mexico Press.

—— (1990b) Settlement History and the Classic Collapse at Copan: A Redefined Chronological Perspective. *Latin American Antiquity* 1: 66–85.

Webster, David L., AnnCorinne Freter, and Nancy Gonlin (2000) *Copán: The Rise and Fall of an Ancient Maya Kingdom*. Fort Worth, TX: Harcourt.

Webster, David L., AnnCorinne Freter, and David Rue (1993) The Obsidian Hydration Dating Project at Copán: A Regional Approach and Why it Works. *Latin American Antiquity* 4: 303–24.

Webster, David L., AnnCorinne Freter, and Rebecca Storey (2004) Dating Copán Culture-History: Implications for the Terminal Classic and the Collapse. In T*he Terminal Classic in the Maya Lowlands: Collapse, Transition, and Transformation*, ed. Arthur A. Demarest, Don S. Rice, and Prudence M. Rice, pp. 231–59. Boulder: University Press of Colorado.

Webster, David L., William T. Sanders, and Peter van Rossum (1992) A Simulation of Copan Population History and its Implications. *Ancient Mesoamerica* 3: 185–97.

PART I
El Salvador and Honduras

2
PRACTICES OF SPATIAL DISCOURSE AT QUELEPA[1]

Wendy Ashmore

Work by E. Wyllys Andrews V at Quelepa opened wide a window on prehispanic times in what is now eastern El Salvador. Documenting dramatic changes in Quelepa material culture and external connections during the two best-known periods of ancient occupation, Andrews convincingly infers intrusive settlement by people with greatly different networks and cultural practices. Although such intrusive occupations of a single place are far from unique, the question lingers as to why the later builders created their new civic center adjacent to the one it superseded. Although the question cannot be answered definitively, theoretical inquiry about processes of abandonment and reuse, including the roles of social memory and forgetting, has approached fever pitch in recent decades. This chapter explores how evidence from Quelepa informs ongoing theoretical and cross-cultural interpretations.

E. Wyllys Andrews V is systematic and determined and refuses to settle for anything less than the best, in his own efforts or in those of his collaborators. For this chapter, I consider how evidence from Quelepa informs recent thinking about successive occupations of ancient civic centers. What have long intrigued me about Quelepa, most specifically, are both a finding and a question. The finding is the dramatic architectural disruption and lateral displacement of settlement there between the major periods of occupation. The question is why the later builders established a new civic center adjacent to the old, instead of on top or at some remove from it (Andrews 1976; Ashmore 1987; Low 2000: 121). I certainly do not challenge Andrews's sound conclusion that the latest resettlement of Quelepa involved new people whose networks and cultural practices differed greatly from those of earlier inhabitants of the site. Just as certainly, such repetitive occupations at this single place are far from unique – and that is the point. The phenomenon of most specific interest for this chapter is the *lateral displacement* of occupation as a correlate of new occupation episodes and the possible reasons behind such spatial repositioning. In the following pages, I explore how the prehispanic evidence from Quelepa informs ongoing theoretical and cross-cultural interpretations about practice and process in such situations. The thoughts herein are offered as a tribute to the enduring strengths of Andrews's research, analysis, and interpretation and how they facilitate fruitful continued consideration of these and many other questions.

Shaping practices of spatial discourse

This chapter draws primarily from literature on settlement and the reoccupation of places, with a perspective anchored in practice theory, materiality, and the importance of foregrounding social relations in archaeological inference.

Theoretical inquiries about the processes and consequences of sequential occupation and about the life histories of place exhibit exciting fervor, especially with regard to abandonment, resettlement, and the roles of ruins. In these discussions, some authors invoke the notion of the "persistent place," attributing long-standing or repeated occupation of a particular locale to its enduring or recurring social, economic, or ritual importance (Schlanger 1992; Zedeño and Bowser 2009). They and others frequently ascribe key roles for memory in persistence or return (Mills and Walker 2008a; Van Dyke and Alcock 2003), although yet others caution that inferring the influence of ancient memory and forgetting can be elusive or problematical (Blake 1999; Bradley 1987, 2003). Some departures, terminations, or returns to place are cyclical in nature while others are more episodic. In either case, they are linked most often to transformations in worldview or the structure of leadership (King *et al.* 2011; Laporte and Fialko 1995; Lekson 1999; Pauketat 2008; Rice 2004; Richards 1999).

Increasingly significant to discourse concerning site abandonment and return is the centrality of social actors and their active roles in making, changing, abandoning, and sometimes reoccupying space. In keeping with this recognition, many scholars find the notion of *inhabitation* a key acknowledgment of the direct engagement of people with the world around them and how they situated themselves in space. Inhabitation refers to the social impact of landscape, especially one where people have lived earlier. Whether they are descended from the builders of what in some cases have become ruins or are newcomers with no direct connections to past residents through memory or oral history, people must contend with the existence of buildings and ruins, choosing to reoccupy, build around, bury, or even raze antecedent remains (Ashmore 2004; Barrett 1999; Stanton and Magnoni 2008). Along with inhabited landscapes, architecture in particular – ruined or whole – "*mediates* the past and present" (Jones 2000: 145; emphasis in original).

Materiality and practice theory enable understanding of the inhabitation of particular places. Material culture is basic to archaeological work. *Materiality*, however, is an inherently social concept implying the mutual shaping of objects and social relations through their interaction in time and space (Jones 2000; Kopytoff 1986; Pauketat 2003). This interaction occurs through practices which, in turn, can materially inscribe space. The cumulative traces of practice constitute material stories of continuity and change in the social relations of people (Mills and Walker 2008b: 16–23).

In this chapter, I explore how evidence from Quelepa contributes to this dialogue. This, of course, first requires a review of findings from Andrews's research in eastern El Salvador.

Introducing Quelepa

Unquestionably, Will Andrews's research at Quelepa opened new insights into ancient societies of what is now eastern El Salvador (see Figure 1.1). Before his fieldwork in the late 1960s, the archaeological map east of the Río Lempa was largely vacant; standard descriptions alluded far more to potentials than to firm knowledge (e.g., Longyear 1944, 1966; Willey 1966). Ceramics, architecture, and sculpture alternately pointed to links north to the Maya and Mesoamerica and south to the "Intermediate Area" of lower Central America. Recurring questions focused on the cultural affiliations of the region in antiquity and relations to indigenous cultures of living peoples today. Although clearly there is still much to do in the area, Andrews's work made Quelepa a place to be reckoned with in all subsequent accounts (e.g., Amador 2009; Cobos 1994; Schortman and Urban 1991; Sheets 1984, 2000).

The assemblage of more than 40 structures at the site stretches along the north side of the Río San Esteban in a mapped expanse of some 50 hectares, about 8 kilometers west-northwest of the modern town of San Miguel (Figure 2.1; Andrews 1976: 4). The land is agriculturally quite productive, and from first settlement the place combined economic advantage with location uniting land, water, and a prominent mountain backdrop (ibid.: fig. 3). The combination thus plausibly centered Quelepa, as well, in a landscape rich in cosmological symbolism (Ashmore 2004; Brady and Ashmore 1999; Schaafsma and Taube 2006; Taube 2000a). Earlier observers noted large, stone-faced mounds, artificial terraces, and carved stone sculpture at Quelepa. Some also had bought pottery there for museums or private collections. Pedro Armillas began archaeological investigations at Quelepa in 1949, but the first sustained and published field research there was by Andrews. He applied state-of-the-art methods and research design for establishing culture history and for addressing issues of cultural identity and interaction. His mapping, excavations, and materials analyses depicted clearly a political, economic, and ritual center that underwent profound changes in size, internal composition, and external connections between at least 200 BC and around AD 1000 (Figures 2.2–2.4; Andrews 1976, 1977; Braswell *et al.* 1994).

Sculpture and pottery were the earliest clues to settlement and external connections. The "Jaguar Altar" from Quelepa (Figure 2.5) recalls sculpture at Kaminaljuyu and Izapa, suggesting that it was created in the last centuries BC and pointing firmly to engagement with societies to the west in Mesoamerica. Linking Quelepa pottery styles to those at Chalchuapa, Los Naranjos, and – again – Kaminaljuyu in Late Preclassic times, Andrews proposed that their makers participated in a ceramic sphere that he named *Uapala* for the pottery complex at Quelepa. Material practices at this site tied its occupants westward and northward to people with similar cultural

28 Wendy Ashmore

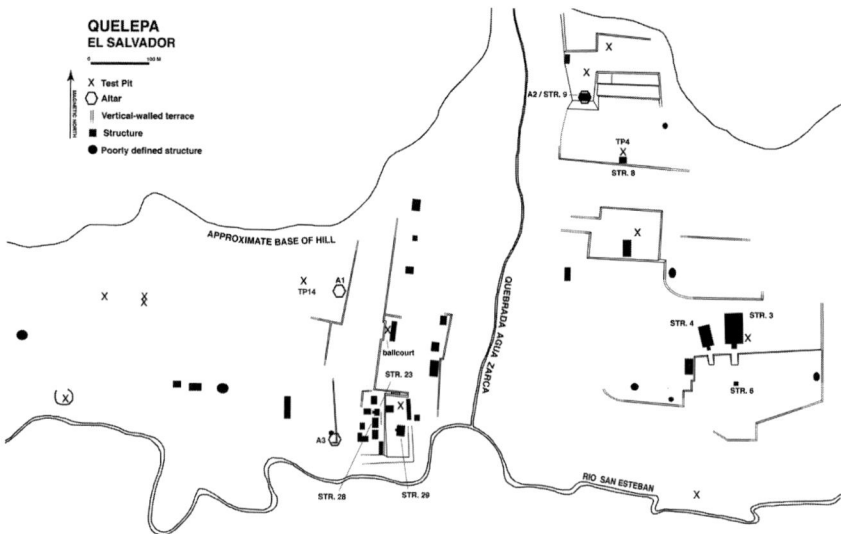

FIGURE 2.1 Map of Quelepa (adapted by Jon Spenard from Andrews 1976: fig. 2)

FIGURE 2.2 Map of Quelepa highlighting features attributed to Uapala times (adapted by Jon Spenard from Andrews 1976: fig. 2)

principles and practices. Andrews combined ethnohistoric, linguistic, and archaeological evidence to suggest that the peoples involved were proto-Lenca speakers, with roots ultimately among macro-Maya groups of southern Mesoamerica (see also Amador 2009; Sharer 1974).

Practices of spatial discourse at Quelepa   29

FIGURE 2.3   Map of Quelepa highlighting features attributed to Shila times (adapted by Jon Spenard from Andrews 1976: fig. 2)

FIGURE 2.4   Map of Quelepa highlighting features of Lepa times (adapted by Jon Spenard from Andrews 1976: fig. 2)

Evidence about architecture, settlement patterns, and the built landscape is clearer for the subsequent *Shila* and *Lepa* phases, equated respectively broadly with Terminal Preclassic to Early Classic and then Late Classic times (Figures 2.3 and 2.4). Ramps, broad monumental terraces, and prominent stepped platforms distinguish Shila construction, combining local inspiration with limited likenesses westward (Andrews 1976: 182–3; 1977: 132; Braswell *et al.* 1994: 175). The Shila center was largely abandoned before the arrival of newcomers during Lepa times (Andrews 1976: 183; Braswell *et al.* 1994: 177).

Lepa-phase construction dramatically shifts location, orientation, layout, and form. Buildings of this phase are smaller in overall size, created with smaller stones and using cruder masonry. Mesoamerican-style plaza and courtyard groups and a ballcourt are new additions (Andrews 1976: 41, 183–4; 1977: 125, 128, 133; Braswell *et al.* 1994: 175). An "acropolis" plausibly marked something akin to a royal palace, and perhaps was ultimately centered on its largest and relatively late edifice, Structure (Str.) 29 (Andrews 1976: 28).

Cultural affiliations likewise shifted in Lepa times, in which "disruption of a local tradition" and "imposition of a new and more typically Mesoamerican architectural pattern" pointed dramatically westward, as far as the Gulf Coast (Andrews 1977: 125, 128). Explanations for upheaval and subsequent resettlement include population displacement due to volcanic catastrophe and such economic goals as control of cacao production, possibly involving military invasion (e.g., Andrews 1976, 1977; Braswell *et al.* 1994; Sheets 2000: 442). Sampeck (in Chapter 3 of this volume) applies the felicitous description of both prehispanic Quelepa and nearby colonial San Miguel as occupying a "landscape of opportunity," a phrase I employ here. As discussed in my conclusions, others among Andrews's colleagues and former students, focusing on practices and change at Chichen Itza and elsewhere in Mesoamerica, indirectly make a highly plausible case for the newcomers at Quelepa combining goals of economic, military, and religious expansion (Ringle *et al.* 1998; cf. Andrews 1976: 184–5; Braswell *et al.* 1994: 176). Before treating that interpretive model, we should first focus on developments at Quelepa and how practices of spatial discourse frame the lateral displacement in Lepa times.

Lateral displacement and the discourse of space

Beyond Quelepa, multiple instances of lateral displacement are well documented in southeastern Mesoamerica, including Cerro Palenque and Los Naranjos in what is now Honduras (Joyce 1991, 2008; Baudez and Becquelin 1973) and Chalchuapa in what is now western El Salvador (Sharer 1978a). Sometimes the original focus of monumental architectural elaboration was abandoned, often a hiatus in occupation occurred, and new leaders established their own architectural bases, near but neither fully incorporating nor obscuring the earlier civic center. At Copan, lateral displacement also occurred, with partial incorporation of the older civic center rather than its abandonment (Fash 2005; Sharer 2003; Traxler 2003, 2004).

Of course, there are many potential reasons for such displacement. Sometimes establishing a new civic location marks overt rejection of earlier orders, as in the rise and fall of Akhetatan, founded hundreds of kilometers from both earlier and later Egyptian capitals (Richards 1999). Response to attempted conquest can also lead to spatial remove, as occurred during the Pueblo Revolt (Preucel 2000). In contrast, choosing to build near – but not upon or by destroying – earlier architecture can suggest *respect* for a superseded authority (Barrett 1999; Lekson 1999; Ringle *et al.* 1998). For Chalchuapa, Sharer (1978a: 211) notes continued ritual practices at El Trapiche without rebuilding following a prolonged hiatus after the devastating eruption of Ilopango in the sixth century. At Copan, Traxler (2003, 2004) compellingly infers assertive but respectful relocation of the royal court after the fifth-century intrusion by K'inich Yax K'uk' Mo' and his subsequent dynastic successors. Indeed, localization of civic authority shifted dramatically within the life histories of many Maya cities, including Copan, Tikal, Seibal, and Sayil, in each case accompanying significant local political change (Ashmore and Sabloff 2002, 2003).

Regardless of the causes of breaks in occupation or the resurgence of local authority, new nobles bolstered their expressions of authority by sometimes deferential and always proprietary architectural reference to previous monuments. That is, they acquired possession of the location of power and, in doing so, accepted the natural and architectural landscapes as unified spatial pivots of that power (Ashmore 2004; Gillespie 2008; Jones 2000; Low 2000).

Social practices and lateral displacement at Quelepa

Although lateral displacement can be empirically observed, what archaeologists seek to understand are the social dynamics that created such spatial shifts in occupation. Andrews highlights construction displacement at the onset of Lepa times as supporting other evidence of political intrusion and population replacement. That same evidence also prompts questions about the social meanings of the built environment from Uapala times forward. Of central interest to me are practices that bespeak social continuity and change between Uapala and Shila times, explosive growth in Shila times, and the radical switch in construction and deposition practices during Lepa times. My discussion centers around three sets of practices: (1) the placement of and interaction with stone *monuments*; (2) the *deposition* of objects in relation to spatial contexts; and (3) the *construction*, orientation, and destruction of architecture, as well as performance at buildings.

Monument-related practices

Three of the five monuments identified at Quelepa are monoliths. These were encountered in open, public settings, although none could be confirmed stratigraphically as being found *in situ*. For this reason, these three objects may not directly inform us about spatial organization. Their size, however, makes it most plausible that they had been created and positioned in the near vicinity, and sculpted iconography on the two larger monoliths suggests something about important spatial concepts. The remaining two of the five monuments were more surely found in place; each occupied open but more secluded locations. One of these is a multi-piece ballcourt alley-center marker. The final monument is a tight, roughly circular flat array of five stones set in a stair-side corner at Str. 23.

All three monoliths are cuboid stone basins. Altars 1 and 3 are carved on outfacing sides; the smallest, Altar 2, is uncarved. Of the three, Altar 1, the Jaguar Altar, is the largest by far – roughly 3 meters across and 85 centimeters high (Figure 2.5). The style of the carved images dates their production to the last centuries BC. Comparable imagery is known from Mesoamerica to the west, at Cara Sucia, Izapa, Kaminaljuyu, and Takalik Abaj (Andrews 1976, 1977; Miles 1965). The Quelepa basin form combines specific jaguar, serpent, and water iconography to suggest these were receptacles for water, most plausibly for ritual practices. More specifically, Altars 1 and 3 share iconographic elements with Izapa Stela 1 and with Kaminaljuyu Stelae 10 and 19, as well as with the larger compositions of which they are part. The combinations point to water ritual – perhaps rain-making – a ritual genre with long-standing relation to political authority (Coggins 1982; Lucero and Fash 2006; Smith 1984: 25; Taube 1995: 95). Such rites involved water containers of different sizes, from portable stone or clay vessels and basins to such landscape features as watery caves, ponds, rivers, lagoons, and the sea. The iconographic elements of Altar 1 plausibly signal explicitly that sacred water lay within the basin behind the sculpted exterior. Initially at least, ritual performances at these monoliths likely united leaders with the larger populace in the shared pursuit of rain, crops, and prosperity while simultaneously bearing political witness about the authority of those who conducted the events.

Augmenting implications of power and its legitimization, four-sided forms in Mesoamerica often evoke images of the cosmos and its completion and perpetual

FIGURE 2.5 Quelepa Altar 1, the Jaguar Altar, in 1969; Will Andrews kneels in the foreground (courtesy of the Middle American Research Institute, Tulane University)

re-creation (Coggins 1980; Garber *et al.* 1998; Gillespie 2008; Mathews and Garber 2004; Reilly 1996). Each side, corner, or axis of such forms had directional meaning in time and space. In southern Mesoamerica, south marked the watery underworld and, as a station in the daily transit of the sun, the night realm of danger and the dead. Perhaps water in the Quelepa basins even marked the center of a quincunx design, the five-part centering device found in many Mesoamerican spatial statements (e.g., Coggins 1980; Mathews and Garber 2004). In this regard, the basin center might have been identified as a cave portal to a watery supernatural underworld (Brady and Ashmore 1999; Schaafsma and Taube 2006). Although none of the three Quelepa stones is demonstrably in its original or other ancient position, the recorded orientation of Altar 1 suggests that those who commissioned at least its final placement possibly intended that the jaguars and serpents on its side be displayed southward, towards the distant watery underworld and the nearby Shila-era cemetery and Río San Esteban. Indeed, beyond their early association with rain-making, jaguars are night suns, fearsome forces of protection and destruction, and the avatars of kings (Saunders 1998).

Although Andrews reasonably suggests that breakage at what is now the northeast corner of the Jaguar Altar could have occurred during a move, it could also or alternatively have constituted deliberate mutilation to cancel residual threats from a powerful monument after original practitioners were out of power and had lost control of the dangerous stone (Clark 1997; Grove 1981; Pagliaro *et al.* 2003: 77). Indeed, as Clark *et al.* (2010: 5) note for Mesoamerica at large, "Stone sculptures for the Middle and Late Preclassic periods are frequently smashed, broken, defaced, and dislocated from their original locations." Destruction in any of these cases could have bespoken dramatic transformation of material form and social relations. Quelepa Altar 3, with similar carvings, points even more strongly to desecration and termination. Far more severely fragmented and worn, this basin preserves only one corner of a monument that would surely have been nearly the size of Altar 1 (Andrews 1976: 178).

The Quelepa basin monoliths, then, hint at ancient public practices, most likely performed initially by honored ritual leaders, and perhaps subsequently embodying one or more ruptures in both practices and the established social, political, and cultural order. All three basins arguably remained on display from Uapala through Lepa times. Such ruptures in settlement and cultural continuity include the intrusive occupation in Lepa times, or perhaps monument breakage occurred earlier, when leaders of Shila times asserted new authority and radically transformed the Uapala built landscape. Indeed, by Lepa times, Altars 1 and 3 could even have been rescued and revived as emblems of the deep past in this locale, perhaps despite interim desecration during the transition from Uapala to Shila times (Ambrosino *et al.* 2003: 117). Contextual evidence nonetheless implies that later practices differed dramatically from initial engagement with the monuments. Not only did excavations in the vicinity of the Jaguar Altar yield "late" sherds (Andrews 1976: 20, 37), suggesting final positioning in or after Lepa times, but the abundant pottery from Test Pit (TP) 14, northwest of Altar 1, also hints at pronounced shift in ambient practices, replacing a plausibly public arena with everyday village residence and a domestic dump. Because we cannot say where the altars were located or what their spatial associations were during individual time periods, we can only speculate as to when and where social and material breaks in monument-related practices occurred.

In contrast to the three monolithic basins, the stone mosaic stair-side "altar" at Str. 23 would always have been a setting for practices visible to only a few participants and observers near the west end of the platform summit, or from adjacent Strs. 21, 22, 27 and 28, and in the small open area they surround. What took place is unclear, but this altar could well have supported activities solidifying bonds among the relatively secluded group of occupants of the acropolis in Lepa times. Vessels smashed after abandonment of this location may attest to the targeted rejection of its earlier importance; I return to the subject of termination rituals below.

Activities at the Str. 19 ballcourt, on the other hand, would have been observed by players and potentially large groups gathered on the relatively expansive terraces north and northwest of the acropolis. These acts would have been part of a larger suite of repetitive practices of the ballgame itself and those appropriate to its observers (e.g., Fox 1996). Joyce and her colleagues (2009) write of ballgames creating and reinforcing social memory, fomenting community and even multi-community ties. The arena and adjoining open area would have permitted festive, perhaps ritual, perhaps competitive interactions among people from Quelepa and potentially much farther afield. Because the settlement of Quelepa stands out in the region for its size and the involvement of its leaders in far-flung networks, and because relatively few ballcourts are documented in eastern El Salvador, practices at this location conceivably were keys to forming and strengthening bonds within and far beyond the local community. The stone slabs that comprise this putative marker plausibly form a quincunx, analogous to the attributes I suggest for the basin monoliths (Andrews 1976: figs 70, 71). Although the Jaguar Altar might well have been situated prominently above the large, socially diverse groups present for ballgame performances in Lepa times, the inferred change in practices around that monument nonetheless make its potential relation with ballgames decidedly, if intriguingly, problematic.

Deposition practices

Practices involving Quelepa monoliths and the ballcourt seem invariably public, but other distinct practices involved the deposition of objects, variably emphasizing open view and secrecy. Open settings imply practices performed for view. Storage, pits, and caching imply secrecy and, more specifically, efforts to control knowledge about resources (Gilman 1987).

> Knowledge of the presence of caches, burials, and stores of useful or valuable commodities inside rooms or storehouses represents knowledge of a hidden dimension of social and physical space. It is mutual *knowledge that people share but not equally* – some people know more than others, or have more precise knowledge.
>
> (Hendon 2000: 49, emphasis added)

Practices of spatial discourse at Quelepa 35

All such deposits are documented at Quelepa and resemble practices of Mesoamerican materiality, and, although the people of Quelepa were *not* Maya, guarded comparisons with Maya or other Mesoamerican cases can be instructive (cf. Helms 2006; Schaafsma and Taube 2006).[2] "As a form of storage, burials and caches … are like storehouses in that they are loci where items, and sometimes people, of material and symbolic value are deposited and guarded" (Hendon 2000: 47).

As a distant comparison, Olmec La Venta Offering 4 is famous as a sealed deposit of upright stone figures, carefully arranged in a scene, whose location remained known to a select few, allowing later access without disturbance. Although deposition at Quelepa involved less directly depictive objects, patterns in content do suggest shared meaning for the community. Houk and Zaro (2011) refer to cache placement as a means of "ritual engineering," establishing the symbolic importance of key places in a civic or other social landscape (see also Bell 2007; Chase and Chase 1998; Garber *et al.* 1998).

Documented Uapala-phase caches, with the exception of Caches (Ca.) 7 and 8, had ambiguous or unknown architectural associations. These latter two were plausible dedicatory deposits, placed under the platform or terrace encountered 4 meters below the ground surface in TP 4 and near the later surface remains of Str. 8 (see Figure 2.1). Including Ca. 7 and 8, Uapala cache contents comprised locally prevalent types of pottery bowls, often in lip-to-lip pairs. In Shila times, repetitive practices of placement favored positions in the four-part layout described above, platform corners and centerlines being preferred locales in the most prominent

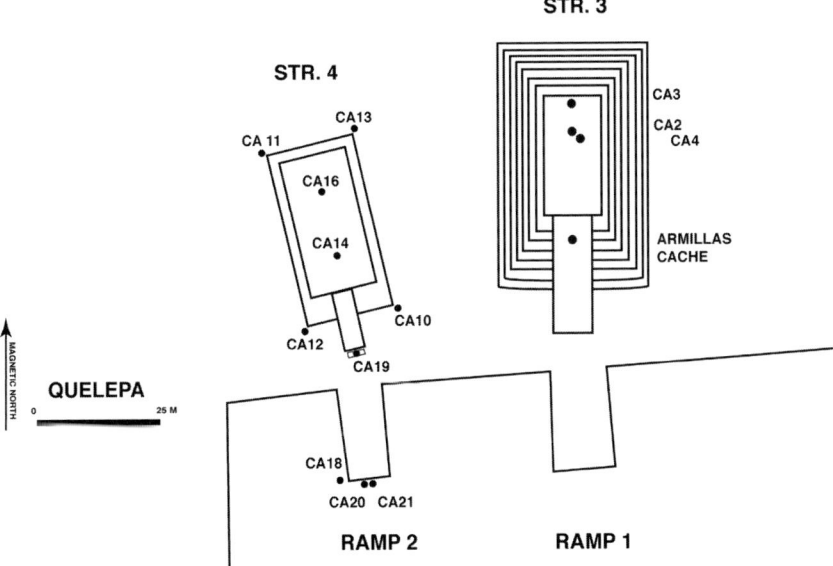

FIGURE 2.6 Caches at Quelepa Strs. 3 and 4 (Shila times) (adapted by Jon Spenard from Andrews 1976: fig. 8)

structures of the era. Lip-to-lip vessel pairs were again common in the Shila phase. Known from fewer examples, Lepa-phase deposits are quite distinct in both content and placement from preceding practices.

For Shila times, Str. 4 (Figure 2.6) illustrates how deposition practices and their preserved knowledge might have marked "paths through a sacralized architectural context" (Joyce 1992: 498; cf. Freidel and Schele 1989; Jones 2000). Despite lack of firm stratigraphic seals, Andrews suggested that the corner caches and Ca. 19 at Str. 4 could well have been dedicatory deposits. All cache vessels are local wares of the Shila ceramic complex (Amador 2009; Andrews 1976). The corner deposits comprised one or more lip-to-lip or lidded pairs of ceramic vessels.[3]

Lip-to-lip and capped vessels are common cache components in southern Mesoamerica, and their contents are frequently interpreted as incorporating sky, earth, and underworld elements of the multi-layered cosmos (Bell 2007; Chase 1988: 87; Garber et al. 1998; Houk and Zaro 2011; Joyce 1992). In the Maya area, caches and their contents constitute "creation reenactment or cosmological modeling. Such offerings were vital in the establishment and maintenance of a structure's vital connection to ancestral spirits and supernatural force" (Garber et al. 1998: 127). Although the vessel pairs in the Str. 4 corner caches all but lacked perceptible contents, the metaphor (and possibly additional perishable original contents) may nonetheless be considered.[4] Moreover, beyond the cosmological symbolism inferred for individual caches, the collective locations and contents of Str. 4 caches suggest a quincunx design.

The further distribution of caches at this imposing platform also invites comparison with a case proposed by Rosemary Joyce for Late Classic Maya Piedras Negras Str. O-13. Her narrative outlines movement from base to summit, "leading to the innermost room, where the number, diversity, and unique contents of caches suggest a peak in ritual action" (Joyce 1992: 501). Although no summit building survives at Quelepa Str. 4, a pathway with increasing seclusion – by elevation and the physical restriction of space, if not leading clearly to an enclosure – would plausibly begin at the threshold of Ramp 2, leading up to the terrace atop which the platform is built. Three caches (Ca. 18, 20, 21) lay at the base of the ramp beneath a now eroded floor; Ca. 20 was on the centerline proper. Analogous in form to the corner caches, each contained one vessel inverted on the other and was devoid of further detectable contents.

Beneath a stone slab at the threshold of the Str. 4 ramp, however, lay Ca. 19, the most elaborate cache at Str. 4. Its carefully placed contents included ten pottery vessels and a marble/onyx bowl, together with 20 jadeite beads and six shell ornaments (Andrews 1976: 13, 188). These items of material and symbolic value are noteworthy because they couple familiar local pottery with decidedly exotic mineral and shell objects – onyx, jadeite, and marine shell. The objects, therefore, bespeak the social connections of the leaders of Quelepa, those who presumably commissioned the assemblage or received its contents as gifts. Perhaps deposition beneath the cut slab, at this accessible and liminal point, allowed the cache to be exposed on select occasions, materially reinforcing memory and the meaning of the cache. At the threshold to this visually prominent construction, the cache and the stone cover called attention to the location and were perpetual testimony to the reach and authority of the leaders (Helms 1988). Memories were made and repeatedly conveyed to all in attendance at performances atop and in front of Str. 4. Moreover, in ascending this ramp, the privileged few visibly entered a place marked as restricted to those with ability to cross into other worlds, the threshold to this place defined by elevation change, physical constriction, and the information embodied in Ca. 19.

Andrews suggests that Str. 4 might have supported a perishable building on its summit (Andrews 1976: 12, 42–3). Whether or not it did, the culmination of the path would have been the two caches Ca. 14 and Ca. 16. First, privileged entrants would reach the position of Ca. 14, located beneath the floor of the platform close to the centerline. The seven ceramic vessels in that deposit resembled others at Str. 4 in pottery type – that is, they were locally made. Like Ca. 19, Ca. 14 also included exotic materials, in this case a single jadeite bead and a black stone celt. Farther north was Ca. 16, beneath the floor in what was likely the most deeply secluded place in a perishable superstructure. Its four vessels were again familiar in type and design, but Ca. 16 contained exotic objects as well. These are similar to those of Ca. 14, but the bead and celt are larger, and the celt is made of well-polished greenstone. Notably, the two objects of precious green material, the color of maize and the center place in the four-sided Mesoamerican cosmos, distinguish this most deeply hidden deposit, conceivably the most guarded knowledge, to which few had access (Reilly 1996; Taube 2000a). Most likely, only leaders and other cognoscenti were entitled to enter the inner (or upper) sanctum of this place, although ritual acts and orations performed on the spot could have told of the significance of the caches and their contents. "The pathways established by caches provided a permanent marker of impermanent human actions, until the buildings were ritually terminated" (Joyce 1992: 502). With respect to termination, Andrews (1976: 13) suggests that the putative perishable building atop Str. 4 may have burned in the mid-seventh century.

The architecture of Str. 3, which Andrews considers somewhat later than Str. 4, is more elaborate, but caching practices and the inferred path are apparently simpler (Figure 2.6). No caches were encountered at the base of either Ramp 1 or the structure ramp proper. In 1949, however, Pedro Armillas encountered an offering within the structure ramp, where it crossed the fifth and sixth terraces (Andrews 1976: 4, 16). Like caches at and above the base of Str. 4, this one featured a lip-to-lip vessel pair containing jadeite and greenstone. As at Str. 4, what is probably local pottery was joined with demonstrable exotics, attesting again to the ability of those in charge of Str. 3 to reach across distant networks for knowledge and exchange. In addition, and distinctively, the same cache incorporated layered arrangements of stone discs, pottery bowls, trios of stone balls, and, in one case, jadeite beads. Braswell et al. (1994: 175) relate the "stone balls in sets of three" to practices farther south, in lower Central America, while other features retained Mesoamerican ideas. Nonetheless, sets of three stones are also significant in Maya creation narratives and mark the hearths that center domestic life. Shila-phase discourse on political outreach thus built on familiar practices to proclaim newer and perhaps expanded political, economic, and ritual networks.

Two centerline deposits were encountered on the Str. 3 summit. Ca. 2 was located two-thirds the distance across the summit from the ramp. It consists solely of a stone disc atop a long tubular jadeite bead. In effect, it seems to be a simplified restatement of the cache Armillas found lower down in the platform ramp. Toward the north end of the summit was Ca. 3, a pair of lip-to-lip bowls, atop which sat a vaguely celt-shaped green-gray stone. Four small jars, two with lids, lay nearby (Andrews 1976: 16, fig. 29). Together, the components of Ca. 3 allude again to Mesoamerican symbols of cosmically sanctioned authority. Its four small jars recall those associated with rain-making rituals as practices farther north, thereby alluding to the watery symbolism of Altar 1 (Schaafsma and Taube 2006: 256–9).[5] Ca. 4, at the summit near Ca. 2, was quite different. Its simple polychrome bowl was likely placed intrusively during later Lepa times, discussed below. Overall, the materiality of deposition and spaces at Str. 3 reflect practices somewhat less assertively foundational than those seen at Str. 4. Nonetheless, the caches of Str. 3 seem equally concerned with extolling the effectiveness of the leaders in placing the community in far-flung networks of knowledge and exchange.

Elsewhere at Quelepa, and later in time, deposition practices differed markedly (see Figure 2.1). No corner caches are known from Strs. 23, 28, or 29, the three Lepa-era structures probed by Andrews. Ca. 23, a crushed Shila-era vessel under the north wall of Str. 23, may have been a dedicatory deposit in a new kind of location (Andrews 1976: 23). The act also could mark the cancellation of the use of the Shila-phase terrace in this spot, a view perhaps in keeping more with such depositional practice as marking *transformation* from one state to another than as solely the end or beginning (Monaghan 1998; Bell 2007; Chase and Chase 1998; Houk and Zaro 2011; Navarro Farr 2009). North of the Str. 23 wall, beneath the floor abutting it, and considered part of the same Ca. 23, Andrews encountered a Quelepa Polychrome bowl and a Lolotique Spiked censer, both from the Lepa ceramic complex and perhaps more truly forming a dedicatory deposit. To the west and in TP 14, Andrews found Ca. 25. This contained two Lepa complex jars, one each of the types Delirio Red-on-White (an intrusive type of fine-paste pottery, affiliated with Quelepa Polychrome; Andrews 1976: 147) and Obrajuelo Plain (successor to Moncagua Plain, a local Shila-phase type). These plausibly marked a dedication event, arguably in the more mundane context of an ordinary village residence (ibid.: 188). Notably, the jars combine local and foreign types in a spot near where Altar 1 joins older practices with the Lepa focus of settlement, governance, and ritual (ibid.: 146; Braswell *et al.* 1994: 176). Test pit exposure necessarily precluded stating the horizontal position of the cache relative to the plan of the Lepa-phase structure.

At the largest and possibly latest Lepa edifice, two caches hint at something like renewal practices and the assertion of authority (Figure 2.7). Cache 22 was placed in front of the bottom step of the west-facing frontal stair, near the Str. 29 centerline.

Instead of pottery vessels, its contents consisted of three Lepa ceramic discs in a stack grouped together with an obsidian knife, two obsidian flakes, a hematite chunk, and "a piece of powdery orange clay" (Andrews 1976: 28). Forty-one obsidian blades, whose deposition is considered part of the cache placement, were dispersed at and across the length of the step base. Whether or not the blades found at this liminal juncture had been used in the widespread Mesoamerican practice of bloodletting, their collective presence attests at minimum to connections westward to Mesoamerica, and specifically to obsidian sources exploited by polities in the Guatemalan highlands, western El Salvador, and Copan (Braswell *et al.* 1994: 186). Eschewing acquisition of obsidian from nearer sources in Honduras, Quelepa obsidian materiality bespeaks the selectivity and negotiating skills of its leaders. The knife, flakes, and scattered blades thus embodied the knowledge and skills of the leaders of Quelepa, and, although Andrews (1976: 188) considers the deposit possibly to be intrusive, it comprises nonetheless a statement of local access to distant resources.

Ca. 24 at the same structure was "probably contemporaneous with, or slightly later than, the final plaza floor adjacent to Str. 29" (Andrews 1976: 28). It is thus not dedicatory to the structure but constitutes a likely emblem of identity for the occupants of the building, plausibly a local ruler and perhaps the final one. Consisting of elaborate sculpted stone ballgame gear, the assemblage is eloquent testimony to the connections of the leaders of Quelepa, to important material and ritual ties

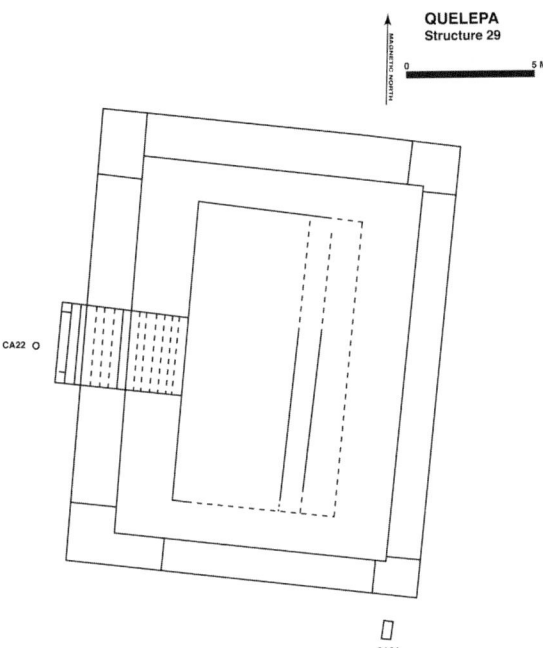

FIGURE 2.7 Caches at Quelepa Str. 29 (Lepa times) (adapted by Jon Spenard from Andrews 1976: fig. 42)

with the Gulf Coast, and perhaps to links south to the Nicoya region (Andrews 1976; Braswell *et al.* 1994; cf. Ringle *et al.* 1998). Perhaps cache deposition beneath a cut slab exterior to the structure allowed its contents to be viewed at will, as suggested for Ca. 19 of Str. 4. If so, the area for viewing Ca. 24 was far more spatially and socially restricted than that for viewing Ca. 19. Ca. 24 could also, or alternatively, indicate availability of the gear for use. In this regard, one is reminded of analogous ballgame equipment stored in the rafters of Copan Str. 9N-81, within the compound of a high-ranking noble (Webster 1989: 21–2). I discuss Quelepa Ca. 24 with respect to implications regarding construction practices in the following section.

I am proposing several instances of termination ritual at the close of Lepa times. Perhaps such rituals are also represented for the beginning of the phase, if single smashed or intact vessels, at Strs. 23 (Ca. 23, Vessel 3) and 3 (Ca. 4), can be so interpreted. Tossed piles of crushed pots and censers at Strs. 3, 23, and 29 are likely analogous to similar depositions known from sites farther west and north, where they appear as parts of either termination or renewal acts, often blurring the distinction between these categories (Amador 2009: 191; Ambrosino *et al.* 2003; Andrews 1976: 23, 24, 26–7, 111; Braswell *et al.* 1994: 177; Brown 2004; Chase 1988: 95, 98; Monaghan 1998; Tozzer 1941). Some of the smashed Lolotique Spiked censers were tossed onto the area of the Str. 23 stone-mosaic "altar," separated from it by some 20 to 40 cm of accumulated dirt (Andrews 1976: 23, 111; Braswell *et al.* 1994: 177). These acts are ascribed to the end of days at Quelepa.

Construction practices

Andrews and colleagues give thorough accounts of the shifting built environment in which monument- and cache-related practices occurred (Andrews 1976; Braswell *et al.* 1994). The key construction practices pertinent to discussion here relate to how people engaged the Quelepa landscape. These are: (1) establishing construction at each documented locale; (2) spatially shaping opportunities for participation in events; and (3) terminating individual elements and assemblages of construction and thereby prohibiting further use.

Establishing and orienting space

We may never know the number, forms, scale, or orientations for Uapala-phase structures. Nonetheless, they do not seem to have been widespread across what became Quelepa (see Figure 2.2). The scale of the monoliths attributed to the Uapala phase on stylistic grounds indicates the presence of skilled artisans and a capable labor force. Nevertheless, whether or not the creation of these huge non-portrait monuments further implies the existence of imposing architecture remains an open question (cf. Clark 1997). As I cite above, the only known Uapala structure (found in TP 4) was buried nearly 3 meters below the base of visible construction at Str. 8. The size and orientation of the structure could not be determined.

Despite the presence of this little-known Uapala settlement and continuations of some cultural principles, builders in following Shila times drastically altered the terrain at Quelepa. This was accomplished by eradicating the earlier village plan, through razing or burial as they established huge terraces, and by situating their most imposing pyramid platforms on one of the largest and southernmost of these terraces (see Figure 2.3; Andrews 1976: 182). The view for visitors arriving along the Río San Esteban must have been quite impressive, as it also would have been to local residents entering that southernmost part of the settlement. Imposing construction was framed with a watery foreground and a backdrop of hills, likely situating Quelepa in cosmic as well as topographic, political, and economic space.

Even if we grant that construction took place across the centuries of the Shila phase, the magnitude of Shila building projects would have involved sustained efforts, coerced or otherwise, by large numbers of people (Pauketat 2000: 121–2). These collective practices would surely have built community identity and solidarity. Moreover, the principal buildings were established on variably cleared and prepared ground (Andrews 1976: 9, 13). Although there is little evidence for such preparation at Str. 4, before beginning new construction at Str. 3 the *talpetate* ground surface was carefully cleared and in some places leveled. Described in the Belize Valley as a ritual "cleansing," land preparation in and beyond Mesoamerica often took place over relatively large expanses and frequently required large amounts of labor (Garber *et al.* 1998: 127; Hall and Viel 2004; Pauketat 2001: 85; Sharer 1978b: 122). The social message implicit in all these work projects is one of creating a new world and establishing a specific new place as the pivot of that world, messages that the caching practices at Strs. 3 and 4 would have enhanced. In Shila times, described as "the development and florescence of indigenous culture" (Andrews 1977: 125), new leadership seems to have taken firm hold.

With the onset of Shila-phase construction programs, and again in Lepa times, the individuals who commissioned and created the new built landscape made emphatic statements about proper arrangement of the built world. Andrews and others noted long ago that Shila terraces and construction of the East Group opened to the south, while Lepa terraces of the West Group faced east. The truly massive terrace building of Shila times transformed the landscape, obliterating the earlier Uapala settlement plan. This first potential break in social and spatial continuity allowed assertive expression of what Quelepa, its society, and – especially – its leaders were about.

The most overt statement was the creation of the extensive south-facing terraces, with most prominent buildings set towards the south or front edge of the terraces. The largest surmounting platforms similarly faced south, towards the Río San Esteban and the Shila cemetery beyond. Reference to jaguars, serpents, water and implicitly politico-ritual power on carved monoliths of Uapala times seem reiterated through south-oriented Shila construction, pointing to feline, serpent, and aquatic realms. Allusions to authority are underscored in caching practices. Although the latter were more richly developed in the program at Str. 4, builders of its later neighbor, Str. 3, chose different and more thoroughly public forms for proclaiming authority and power. That is, Str. 3 coupled a relatively abbreviated caching program of hidden knowledge with the open messages of visibly greater construction volume, higher summit elevation, more intricate vertical design, and subtle enlargement of the southern platform shape to make the edifice look even larger than it is (Andrews 1976: 14).

The arrival of the Lepa leaders, builders, and their support populace radically shifted many material practices, including how construction was set and how residents would inhabit the place they encountered. Local topography might have constrained their building choices somewhat, but they clearly valued space as providing a "landscape of opportunity." Unlike their Shila predecessors, leaders in Lepa times chose not to destroy the built landscape already in place, nor is there any evidence that Shila leaders attempted to prevent Lepa intruders from doing so. Although some burning took place, the acts do not seem to indicate conflagration or large-scale destruction. In fact, Lepa leaders did initiate dramatic shifts in building practices and orientation of construction, but they did so in ways that seem respectful, or at least tolerant, of their predecessors. The message in the new cascade of east-facing terraces may have involved adding the Quebrada Agua Zarca to the Río San Esteban as an important conceptual boundary, with the people and works of the past lying across a watercourse to the east. But east is most often a direction linked to birth and rebirth (Andrews 1976; Braswell *et al.* 1994). It seems more plausible that the Lepa occupants of the site, even though they were an intrusive group, responded to Shila constructions in ways akin to treating a revered elder or ancestor.

Nonetheless, buildings on the Lepa acropolis, and presumably their occupants, literally turned their backs on the Shila core. Of the three acropolis structures tested by excavation, two (Strs. 23 and 29) evince single western stairways giving access to their platform summit (see Figures 2.1 and 2.4). Perhaps part of the intent was to use earlier Shila monumental construction as a backdrop, as the hills to the north might have been employed by builders during the Shila phase. Although ceramic evidence attests to occupation across Quelepa in Lepa times, later leaders seemed most intent on focusing inward on the built world they had created (Barrett 1999). Indeed, Lepa ceramics were most prevalent in the West Group, and burials of the time were located there as well (Braswell *et al.* 1994: 176). Moreover, like the leaders at Los Llanitos and arguably La Laguneta (as well as distant Copan), the Lepa-phase rulers of Quelepa positioned a ballcourt directly north of the acropolis, refocusing the attention of community members and visitors on this locally newer suite of Mesoamerican ritual practices. In the Quelepa ballcourt, one of the range structures incorporates part of an earlier Shila terrace (Andrews 1976: 183), again acknowledging past construction while actively reshaping it for new practices.

Shaping space

Shila structures are situated at the edges of the aforementioned broad terraces rather than in the compact courtyard arrangements of Lepa times (Andrews 1976: 40). Unknown numbers of perishable constructions dotted the settlement from

Uapala times forward, shaping access and vistas in ways that are no longer visible. One consequence of terrace building, however, is the implied availability of what appear to have been arenas open for public gatherings.

The placement and orientation of Strs. 3 and 4 suggest that one such arena was the expanse at the base of Ramps 1 and 2. Notwithstanding the small, undated Strs. 2 and 6, the posited arena was some 2.5 hectares in area. As a comparison, this Shila arena at Quelepa was roughly half the size of the nearly coeval plaza at Chalchuapa, located in the Ney Architectural Complex of the El Trapiche/Casa Blanca portion of the larger site (Sharer 1978b: 122, fig. 38). Comparisons can also be made with arenas elsewhere in eastern El Salvador, albeit derived from likely incomplete maps of mostly unexcavated architecture possibly dating to different periods. The mapped plaza at La Laguneta is slightly smaller than that of Shila-phase Quelepa (2 hectares; Amador 2009: 35–6), and that at Los Llanitos is considerably smaller (0.2 hectares; Longyear 1944: 23). Further afield in time, space, and culture are the ceremonial plaza of Copan and the central area of Tikal (each nearly 4 hectares; Inomata 2006: 816). Of course, the social importance of scale is the capacity to accommodate gatherings. Inomata's formulas suggest that upwards of 6,000 people could have gathered easily in the Shila arena, with intense crowding allowing up to eight times that number. Clearly this was a venue where orations and other performances atop the pyramids, or even on the terrace around their bases, could attract and command the attention of many or all community members, as well as numerous and diverse visitors.

In Lepa times, gathering options were different. Perhaps people continued to assemble in the Shila arena in order to attend ritual and other performance conducted under new leadership. Undated Strs. 2 and 6 could pertain to this period. Str. 6 might have focused attention on, monitored, or even denied access to Str. 3, while Ca. 4 on the summit of Str. 3 might be a trace of respect or respectful retirement of that structure by the new lords.

On the other hand, new arenas were created during Lepa times. The cascading terraces north of the Lepa acropolis extended open areas more than 250 meters farther north. These are 60 to 100 meters wide immediately west of the ballcourt and approximately 100 meters wide between the ballcourt and Strs. 33 to 35 (see Figure 2.4). These two areas arguably had the ballcourt as their joint focus, or, reminiscent of Los Llanitos and La Laguneta, perhaps the ballcourt served as a boundary between two plazas.

When combined, the new Lepa arenas could have accommodated gatherings as large as those in Shila times, although the split terrace levels imply that access to different open spaces might not have been equal. Occupants of Strs. 33 to 35, directly east of the ballcourt, and of Str. 20, to its south-southeast, were well situated to monitor or direct activities in these plazas, and people in other acropolis locales may well have played even more central roles in managing festivities and factional or intercommunity competition.

To reiterate, ballgame gear of a distinctive Gulf Coast style was placed in Ca. 24 at Str. 29, the late and largest acropolis edifice during Lepa times. Andrews and others have remarked on this cache and how it, ceramics, and other evidence point to strong new connections with the Gulf Coast (Amador 2009; Andrews 1976, 1977; Braswell *et al.* 1994; Sheets 2000). The location of the cache outside the corner farthest from the court suggests that exotic objects might have been emblems of the foreign ties of Lepa leaders in ways analogous to the exotics in Shila caches at Strs. 3 and 4. As I have noted, cache deposition beneath a cut slab exterior to the structure might have allowed its contents to be viewed at will, as suggested for Ca. 19 at Str. 4. The number of prospective viewers at Str. 29, however, would certainly have been constrained by space more than at Str. 4. The narrative practices materialized at Str. 29 differ markedly in form from those at the Shila pyramids; nonetheless, their message of political and ritual authority seems broadly the same.

Termination or transformation

While some caching and construction practices described in this chapter might constitute termination rituals, their meanings are often difficult to interpret. Some authors have drawn intriguing distinctions between reverential and desecratory termination events, proposing material signatures for each (Ambrosino *et al.* 2003; Pagliaro *et al.* 2003). Key elements in all are burning, smashed vessels, and physical destruction, together with patterns of spatial and contextual distribution. Distinctions in material evidence frequently remain subtle, and the idea of *transformation* often seems more apt and inclusive than termination (Monaghan 1998; Sheets 2003; cf. Navarro Farr 2009).

Fire, which members of our society most frequently consider a destructive force, certainly has aspects of ritual renewal and rebirth, as in the burning of old fields to sow new ones. Fires may be utterly accidental, but in many parts of the world, including Mesoamerica, cleaning, sweeping, censing, and burning are all documented as purposeful renewal acts in ritual cycles or episodic events (Brown 2004; Rice 1999; Stevanovic 1997; Stuart 1998; Taube 2000b; Tozzer 1941). Andrews notes finding burned daub in many locations and suggests that multiple perishable structures were destroyed at different times, among them one atop Str. 4. In Shila times, burned mud-plaster floors beneath the Str. 3 summit recall the kind of structure terminations and renewals described in other places (Andrews 1976: 39; Pagliaro *et al.* 2003). The prevalence and distribution at Quelepa, however, do not necessarily imply the kind of large-scale conflagration or purposeful destruction evident in ninth-century Copan, including, as Andrews documented so convincingly, literally "bringing down" Strs. 10L-29 and 10L-33 in the royal residential compound (Andrews and Bill 2005: 302; Pagliaro *et al.* 2003: 79–80).

At the largest social scale, it can be difficult to document conquest, rebellion, and warfare unless there is overt evidence of human remains, siege architecture, or distinctive weaponry (Sheets 2003). While none of the foregoing is present at Quelepa, mortal violence might be attested as early as Uapala times. Cranial fragments were found in refuse beneath the platform near the base of Test Pit 4 (Andrews 1976: 189). Inference of military intrusion, especially at the Shila–Lepa transition, nonetheless remains plausible in that it is consistent with termination events, together with nearly wholesale replacement of old practices by new ones, sometime around AD 750 (Andrews 1976; Braswell *et al.* 1994: 175).

Social implications of lateral displacement

Let us now review highlighted sets of Quelepa practices (involving monuments, caches, construction) in relation to the observed lateral displacement of settlement and in light of wider discussions concerning social dynamics in settlement life histories.

Returning to the social implications of reorganized settlement space and foci at break points in the Quelepa time line, several practices stand out, especially related to inhabitation decisions by sequential occupants of the place. Ancient approaches to Quelepa inhabitation arguably ranged from rejection to respect. Both major transitions (Uapala to Shila and Shila to Lepa) were marked by dramatic transformations implying significant change in political leadership (Ambrosino *et al.* 2003; Gillespie 2008; Pauketat 2008). In the first transition, underlying cultural continuities were paired with assertive new political agendas. At that time, Shila leaders and builders completely eradicated visual evidence of earlier settlement and apparently rebuilt a wholly new civic center on top of the older site (Andrews 1976: 179, 182). In contrast, the phenomenon of lateral displacement was surely part of the later Shila to Lepa rupture.

Perhaps the most publicly dramatic correlate of Lepa lateral displacement was the change in settlement orientation. Mapped architecture shifted in absolute building and assemblage orientation, from south-facing terraces in the Shila East Group to east-facing terraces in the Lepa West Group. It also shifted from the monumental Shila Strs. 3 and 4 facing the Río San Esteban and visitors approaching from its banks to the Lepa Acropolis mass and affiliated structure groups opening onto the earlier settlement. Not only did new occupants in Lepa times decline to destroy the constructions visible on the settled landscape, but also they constructed a cascading line of terraces whose occupation seemed to pay homage to preceding leaders and their achievements, even as acropolis residents resolutely turned their backs on those earlier accomplishments. I suggested that the Shila platforms became the backdrop to the core of Lepa settlement, perhaps analogous in some ways to the hills framing the site to the north. Recall as well the incorporation of a Shila terrace into the Lepa ballcourt, utilizing but completely recasting the existing architecture. Indeed, this compound set of orientations – or reorientations – incorporates shifts in the range of practices discussed earlier in this chapter. That is, monument-related and depositional practices combined with construction practices to express profound transformation in social life and materiality at Quelepa.

Smaller in scale, and perhaps emblematic of the times, a very specific act bespeaks the ambiguous but at least partly respectful tone of Lepa inhabitation. Someone in the newly reconstituted community interred a Quelepa Polychrome bowl in the summit of Str. 3, close to its centerline Shila caches. This relatively high-ranking individual or party was privileged to enter into secluded and hallowed ground. Taken together with the presence of Str. 6 at the base of Ramp 1, the act could have been a termination ritual for the most prominent Shila public place. If so, it was made more in reverence than in desecration. Gillespie's comments about shifts at Olmec La Venta are thought provoking here:

> The mythic past of the earlier landscape with its monumental ancestral forms was now no longer part of the routine temporal horizon of the people who lived there, so those monuments were no longer subjected to modifications or renovations. The landscape presented its living inhabitants with a very different system of referents than before, and society was transformed in the process.
> (Gillespie 2008: 134; see also Barrett 1999)

Models for transformation and lateral displacement

As I have mentioned, Andrews (1976: 185) suggests that Lepa colonizers might have come from Veracruz. It seems likely that these newcomers had high political standing. In this way, the Lepa-phase colony was different from the ethnic enclaves discussed for portions of Teotihuacan (e.g., Spence 1992). Indeed, criteria for recognizing enclaves do not fit the Quelepa data (e.g., Braswell 2003b; Spence 1992, 2005). Comparisons with recent discussions of the impact of Teotihuacan on Maya politics, however, might be loosely instructive for Quelepa (Braswell 2003a; Stuart 2000).

Epigraphic evidence indicates that emissaries from the great Central Mexican city arrived in the Maya area in the fourth century and set about intervening in politics at select Maya capitals (cf. Braswell 2003a; Rice 2004: 102–6). Best studied among the Maya capitals are Tikal, Copan, and Kaminaljuyu. In no case did Teotihuacan assert hegemonic power, although warfare seems to have been involved in at least some cases (Cowgill 2003: 330–32; Marcus 2003: 348). Marriage of Teotihuacan-*affiliated* men with politically important local Maya women is hinted at in texts, archaeology, and bone chemistry analyses at Copan (Buikstra *et al.* 2004; Price *et al.* 2010; Sharer 2003). Nonetheless, the exact childhood origins for people interred at Tikal and Kaminaljuyu are more complicated (Wright 2005; Wright *et al.* 2010). None of the isotopic evidence demonstrates that Teotihuacan-affiliated leaders were born in Central Mexico.

A broadly similar scenario is plausible for Quelepa, although evidence there includes none of the detailed attributions possible from the epigraphic data and the human bone chemistry of the Maya cases. Rather, as Andrews (1976: 44–5) states simply: "The start of the Lepa phase is defined by the arrival of fine-paste-polychrome ceramics, cessation of major architectural activity in the East Group, and construction of a new and radically different ceremonial plazuela in the West Group." Braswell *et al.* (1994: 175, 176–7) date the onset of Lepa times to about AD 750. They also identify "the distinctively Mesoamerican termination rituals [of smashed Lolotique Spiked censers at Strs. 23 and 29 as suggesting] that the abandonment of the West Group elite ceremonial center was abrupt and total" (ibid.: 177). Otherwise the timing for the end of Lepa times is uncertain, except for Andrews's (1976: 45) assertion of "a terminal date no earlier than A.D. 950."

In the Quelepa case, Teotihuacan is of course not a candidate for the origins of the newcomers. But the foregoing discussion is relevant to the most compelling prospect for the Quelepa intruders. The Gulf Lowlands are most frequently implicated as the intruders' homeland. The evidence cited includes fine-paste ceramics, flutes or ocarinas, and wheeled figurines, all in styles strongly related to that putative homeland. Most visually dramatic links to the Gulf are the trio of yokes, plus a single *hacha* and two *palmas* of Ca. 24. The latter pair feature imposing sculpted depictions of "a feathered serpent and a depiction of Quetzalcoatl as Ehecatl, the Aztec wind god" (Braswell *et al.* 1994: 176).

Writing of ballcourts in central Veracruz, Daneels (2008: 198) notes that *palmas* "cluster in north-central Veracruz, and then, only in the Late Classic," contending in turn that the wide distribution of Veracruz elements of the ballgame, "from Durango and Sinaloa to Honduras and Salvador," marked the spread of a "Plumed Serpent cult, which took force after the decline of Teotihuacán" (ibid.: 214). Andrews and others (Andrews 1976: 185; Braswell *et al.* 1994: 176) present a similar argument; Andrews believed early on that "the only reasonable explanation is that a group strongly influenced by the latter area moved into eastern El Salvador about A.D. [750]," while acknowledging that "the nature of the new group at Quelepa is far from clear" (Andrews 1976: 184–5).

Recent analyses by some of Andrews's colleagues and former students, William Ringle, Tomás Gallareta Negrón, and George Bey, may well clarify the identity of that new group. Ringle and his colleagues (1998: 225) argue that intruders at many political, economic, and ritual centers in Mesoamerica represented a "long-lived, pan-Mesoamerican axis of politico-religious interaction focused on the cult of Quetzalcoatl … that begins to account for the appearance of 'Mexican' and 'Gulf Coast' traits in the western Peten and in Yucatan." The same authors ascribe the Epiclassic (AD 700–950) origin and expansion of the cult as coupling political reordering with doctrinal change in religion following the collapse of the Teotihuacan state (ibid.: 225–6).

More specifically, they propose that

> a quite specific mechanism was responsible for [widespread] commonalities [of materiality and practice], the spread of a regional cult focused upon Quetzalcoatl/Kukulcan in his aspects as Feathered Serpent, as Venus, as wind god, and as a patron of merchants and leaders. …
>
> The cult was based upon the establishment of a network of major shrines that transcended ethnic and political divisions. …
>
> Given that regional domestic cultures and the worship of local gods usually continued unaffected, the cult probably did not involve extensive population movements and replacements, but instead spread from several centers by means of mercenaries, pilgrimage, and local political alliances.
>
> (Ibid.: 184–5)

Moreover, "the ballgame … was transformed into a centerpiece of the Epiclassic Quetzalcoatl cult" (ibid.: 196). Those who bore intrusive cult beliefs and practices into new lands focused on place-making for new shrines and, in each, promoting the ballgame as a means of legitimating political authority (ibid.: 203; Daneels 2008). The routes they traversed to establish new shrines traced, in many cases, politico-economic and ideological networks that had been current earlier in the expansion of Teotihuacan. They see this Epiclassic cult expansion as "paralleling the medieval Christian Church or the early Islamic expansion in its ability to mobilize military might across ethnic and political boundaries" (Ringle *et al.* 1998: 225, 227).

> From an economic point of view, such centers also provide attractive venues for exchange, as the trade fairs of medieval Europe and Mecca demonstrate. In this sense, Malcolm Webb's ... dictum "the flag follows trade" might be better rephrased as *"trade follows the temple."*
>
> (Ibid.: 227, emphasis added)

The time period to which these authors point fits the Lepa intrusion (with revised dating of Lepa chronology by Braswell *et al.* 1994), and the social processes they outline plausibly account for the nature of the lateral displacement of settlement at Quelepa at that time. Mobilizing military might to extend the reach of religious beliefs, the newcomers sought to establish a new shrine in an already expansive network and to reap all the political and economic benefits such shrines bring. The selection of Quelepa as a new cult shrine may have been due to its setting in a landscape of opportunity: its local economic productivity, its external and political and economic connections, and perhaps its identity as a ritual focus since at least the carving of the Jaguar Altar. This monument might well have been moved during the Lepa phase so as to include access for non-elite residents, at the same time as they and the monument overlooked the new ballcourt and the activities taking place within it. Moreover, because Quetzalcoatl is often associated with rain-making, a cult shrine at Quelepa could draw on deep local traditions alongside intrusive new beliefs and practices (Shaafsma and Taube 2006: 250).

Several authors have suggested that the connections of Quelepa to the spreading cult involved a Pacific Coast route, with some links to Copan (Braswell *et al.* 1994: 176; Ringle *et al.* 1998: 202; cf. Parsons 1969; Zeitlin 1993: 135–8). The ballgame paraphernalia in Ca. 24 links the site ultimately to Veracruz, but, as specific evidence of expansion via a Pacific Coast route, these authors cite the Lepa-phase prominence of fine-paste ceramics (at Quelepa, Delirio Red-on-White) and the distribution of Lolotique Spiked censers, both of which are considered part of the elite pottery sub-assemblage that comprised the "hypothesized cult ceramic complex" (Ringle *et al.* 1998: 202, 221). Recall again the ceramics of Ca. 23 and 25 and the social implications of their chosen composition. The precise node(s) from which the cult carriers came to a largely abandoned Quelepa remain(s) unspecified.

In short, the respect shown by newcomers in their treatment of Shila practices and largely vacated buildings, by their choosing to inhabit this persistent location in particular and by laterally displacing the focus of their own new settlement, acknowledged simultaneously their own goals and the venerability of the local past. In so doing, they introduced to Quelepa a final prehispanic set of new practices and a new materiality of spatial discourse.

Concluding thoughts

Now we come full circle. Quelepa proves to be a "landscape of opportunity" in a new sense. That is, Andrews's research at this place continues as a rich resource for others to explore the social, political, economic, and ideological frames within which people lived across the span of local occupation. For my questions about the social dimensions of lateral displacement there, Andrews's data have been the solid ground on which new interpretive approaches can be taken. I believe the inferences drawn here attest anew to the fruitfulness of practice theory and materiality approaches and, more importantly, to how Andrews's work at Quelepa continues to inspire new thinking. Whether or not the reader agrees with my reckonings, or with Ringle and his colleagues' wonderfully provocative model, the best part of this experience has been seeing that, of course, Will has been right in his inferences all along.

Reiterating my opening contention, Will Andrews is systematic and determined and refuses to settle for anything less than the best, in his own efforts or in those with whom he collaborates. Throughout his career, he has demonstrated the best practices archaeology has to offer and has implemented those practices with sophistication and finesse. His contributions have been consistently of the highest caliber, with an immediate impact that continues to grow through time. The goal of this chapter has been to indicate some active interpretive arenas to which, in my view, the firm evidence base from Andrews's research at Quelepa contributes solid new insights. He did not explicitly set out to address these topics, and I hope he will approve my doing so with his findings. For all his research, the fullness of its reporting, and the provocative ideas his work inspires, we are all indebted to him.

Notes

1 I thank Geoff Braswell and Winifred Creamer for inviting my participation in celebration of Will Andrews's life and work. Although I have never been privileged to work in El Salvador – let alone at Quelepa specifically – the opportunity to explore evidence for ancient lives there has been an honor as well as a delight. I am deeply grateful to Tom Patterson, Fabio Amador, Christina Halperin, Brett Houk, Kyle Lovell, Katie Sampeck, Ed Schortman, and Jon Spenard for input and advice as this chapter took shape. Most of all, thanks to Will for everything he has done for the profession and for all of us.
2 Storage facilities materialize "situated and localized practice that informs constructed spaces with social meaning based on the connections people make between the act of storage and social relations" (Hendon 2000: 44). The two pits encountered at Quelepa, empty of detectable contents, were interpreted as domestic storage units. Despite their mundane context and emptiness, they nonetheless evinced special care in the preparation of durable, well-defined chambers. In one, tightly laid stone formed a flat, roughly circular base. In the other, upright stone slabs defined the base of the shaft walls. Protective care in creating these pits secured both the contents and the integrity of their remaining hidden.
3 Ca. 12, at the southwest corner, yielded the sole occurrence of both a lip-to-lip pair and a lidded vessel, and "tiny, unidentifiable fragments of bone" lay in the lidded jar.
4 The reasons for distinct additional bone-fragment contents in Ca. 12 are unclear, but Andrews (1976: 189) suggests they may be traces of "a secondary or primary infant burial." If so, Ca. 12 could conceivably have southwestern directional connotations with death and the underworld and point to the cemetery across the river. The remains

could also be from a child sacrificed as part of water ritual (Schaafsma and Taube 2006: 258–9; see also note 5 below).
5   Concerning this attribution regarding Ca. 3 of Str. 3, recall as well the water-ritual link suggested in note 4 above for Ca. 12 of Str. 4.

References

Amador, Fabio E. (2009) Atlas arqueológico de la región de oriente de El Salvador, www.famsi.org/reports/07070es/index.html (accessed 15 August 2010).

Ambrosino, James N., Traci Ardren, and Travis W. Stanton (2003) The History of Warfare at Yaxuná. In *Ancient Mesoamerican Warfare*, ed. M. Kathryn Brown and Travis W. Stanton, pp. 109–23. Walnut Creek, CA: AltaMira Press.

Andrews, E. Wyllys (1976) *The Archaeology of Quelepa, El Salvador*. New Orleans: Middle American Research Institute, Tulane University.

—— (1977) The Southeastern Periphery of Mesoamerica: A View from Eastern El Salvador. In *Social Process in Maya Prehistory: Studies in Honour of Sir Eric Thompson*, ed. Norman Hammond, pp. 113–34. London: Academic Press.

Andrews, E. Wyllys, and Cassandra R. Bill (2005) A Late Classic Royal Residence at Copan. In *Copán: The History of an Ancient Maya Kingdom*, ed. E. Wyllys Andrews and William L. Fash, pp. 239–314. Santa Fe, NM: SAR Press.

Ashmore, Wendy (1987) Architectural Expression and Social Complexity in the Southeast Mesoamerican Periphery. Paper presented at the 86th annual meeting of the American Anthropological Association, Chicago.

—— (2004) Ancient Maya Landscapes. In *Continuities and Changes in Maya Archaeology: Perspectives at the Millennium*, ed. Charles W. Golden and Gregory Borgstede, pp. 95–109. London: Routledge.

Ashmore, Wendy, and Jeremy A. Sabloff (2002) Spatial Order in Maya Civic Plans. *Latin American Antiquity* 13: 201–15.

—— (2003) Interpreting Ancient Maya Civic Plans: Reply to Smith. *Latin American Antiquity* 14: 229–36.

Barrett, John (1999) The Mythical Landscapes of the British Iron Age. In *Archaeologies of Landscape: Contemporary Perspectives*, ed. Wendy Ashmore and A. Bernard Knapp, pp. 253–65. Oxford: Blackwell.

Baudez, Claude F., and Pierre Becquelin (1973) *Archéologie de Los Naranjos, Honduras*. Paris: Mission Archéologique et Ethnologique française au Mexique.

Bell, Ellen E. (2007) *Early Classic Ritual Deposits within the Copan Acropolis: The Material Foundations of Political Power at a Classic Period Maya Center*. PhD dissertation, Department of Anthropology, University of Pennsylvania. Ann Arbor, MI: University Microfilms.

Blake, Emma (1999) Coming to Terms with Local Approaches to Sardinia's Nuraghi. In *Archaeology and Folklore*, ed. Amy Gazin-Schwartz and Cornelius Holtorf, pp. 230–39. London and New York: Routledge.

Bradley, Richard (1987) Time Regained: The Creation of Continuity. *Journal of the British Archaeological Association* 140: 1–17.

—— (2003) The Translation of Time. In *Archaeologies of Memory*, ed. Ruth M. Van Dyke and Susan E. Alcock, pp. 221–7. Malden, MA: Blackwell.

Brady, James E., and Wendy Ashmore (1999) Mountains, Caves, Water: Ideational Landscapes of the Ancient Maya. In *Archaeologies of Landscape: Contemporary Perspectives*, ed. Wendy Ashmore and A. Bernard Knapp, pp. 124–45. Oxford: Blackwell.

Braswell, Geoffrey E. (ed.) (2003a) *The Maya and Teotihuacan*. Austin: University of Texas Press.

—— (2003b) Understanding Early Classic Interaction between Kaminaljuyu and Teotihuacan. In *The Maya and Teotihuacan*, ed. Geoffrey E. Braswell, pp. 105–42. Austin: University of Texas Press.

Braswell, Geoffrey E., E. Wyllys Andrews V, and Michael D. Glascock (1994) The Obsidian Artifacts of Quelepa, El Salvador. *Ancient Mesoamerica* 5: 173–92.

Brown, Linda A. (2004) Dangerous Places and Wild Spaces: Creating Meaning with Materials and Space at Contemporary Maya Shrines on El Duende Mountain. *Journal of Archaeological Method and Theory* 11: 31–58.

Buikstra, Jane E., T. Douglas Price, Lori E. Wright, and James H. Burton (2004) Tombs from the Copan Acropolis: A Life History Approach. In *Understanding Early Classic Copan*, ed. Ellen E. Bell, Marcello A. Canuto, and Robert J. Sharer, pp. 191–212. Philadelphia: University of Pennsylvania Museum.

Chase, Diane Z. (1988) Caches and Censerwares: Meaning from Maya Pottery. In *A Pot for All Reasons: Ceramic Ecology Revisited*, ed. Charles C. Kolb and Louana M. Lackey, pp. 81–104. Philadelphia: Temple University Press [special publication of *Cerámica de Cultura Maya*, ed. Muriel Kirkpatrick].

Chase, Diane Z., and Arlen F. Chase (1998) The Architectural Context of Caches, Burials, and Other Ritual Activities for the Classic Period Maya (as Reflected at Caracol, Belize). In *Function and Meaning in Classic Maya Architecture*, ed. Stephen D. Houston, pp. 299–332. Washington, DC: Dumbarton Oaks.

Clark, John E. (1997) The Arts of Government in Early Mesoamerica. *Annual Review of Anthropology* 26: 211–34.

Clark, John E., Julia Guernsey, and Bárbara Arroyo (2010) Stone Monuments and Preclassic Civilization. In *The Place of Stone Monuments: Context, Use, and Meaning in Mesoamerica's Preclassic Transition*, ed. Julia Guernsey, John E. Clark, and Bárbara Arroyo, pp. 1–26. Washington, DC: Dumbarton Oaks.

Cobos, Rafael (1994) *Síntesis de la arqueología de El Salvador (1850–1991)*. San Salvador: Consejo Nacional para la Cultura y el Arte.

Coggins, Clemency C. (1980) The Shape of Time: Some Political Implications of a Four-Part Figure. *American Antiquity* 45: 727–39.

—— (1982) The Zenith, the Mountain, the Center, and the Sea. In *Ethnoastronomy and Archaeoastronomy in the American Tropics*, ed. Anthony F. Aveni and Gary Urton, pp. 111–23. New York: New York Academy of Sciences.

Cowgill, George L. (2003) Teotihuacan and Early Classic Interaction: A Perspective from Outside the Maya Region. In *The Maya and Teotihuacan*, ed. Geoffrey E. Braswell, pp. 315–35. Austin: University of Texas Press.

Daneels, Annick (2008) Ball Courts and Politics in the Lower Cotaxtla Valley: A Model to Understand Central Veracruz? In *Classic Period Cultural Currents in Southern and Central Veracruz*, ed. Philip J. Arnold III and Christopher A. Pool, pp. 197–223. Washington, DC: Dumbarton Oaks.

Fash, William L. (2005) Toward a Social History of the Copan Valley. In *Copán: The History of an Ancient Maya Kingdom*, ed. E. Wyllys Andrews and William L. Fash, pp. 73–101. Santa Fe, NM: SAR Press.

Fox, John G. (1996) Playing with Power: Ballcourts and Political Ritual in Southern Mesoamerica. *Current Anthropology* 37: 483–509.

Freidel, David A., and Linda Schele (1989) Dead Kings and Living Temples: Dedication and Termination Rituals among the Ancient Maya. In *Word and Image in Maya Culture: Explorations in Language, Writing, and Representation*, ed. William F. Hanks and Don S. Rice, pp. 233–43. Salt Lake City: University of Utah Press.

Garber, James F., W. David Driver, Lauren A. Sullivan, and David M. Glassman (1998) Bloody Bowls and Broken Pots. In *The Sowing and the Dawning: Termination, Dedication and Transformation in the Archaeological and Ethnographic Record of Mesoamerica*, ed. Shirley Botelier Mock, pp. 125–33. Albuquerque: University of New Mexico Press.

Gillespie, Susan D. (2008) History in Practice: Ritual Deposition at La Venta Complex A. In *Memory Work: Archaeologies of Material Practices*, ed. Barbara J. Mills and William H. Walker, pp. 109–36. Santa Fe, NM: SAR Press.

Gilman, Patricia A. (1987) Architecture as Artifact: Pit Structures and Pueblos in the American Southwest. *American Antiquity* 52: 538–64.

Grove, David C. (1981) Olmec Monuments: Mutilation as a Clue to Meaning. In *The Olmec and Their Neighbors: Essays in Memory of Matthew W. Stirling*, ed. Elizabeth P. Benson, pp. 48–68. Washington, DC: Dumbarton Oaks.

Hall, Jay, and René Viel (2004) The Early Classic Copan Landscape: A View from the Preclassic. In *Understanding Early Classic Copan*, ed. Ellen E. Bell, Marcello A. Canuto, and Robert J. Sharer, pp. 17–28. Philadelphia: University of Pennsylvania Museum.

Helms, Mary (1988) *Ulysses' Sail: An Ethnographic Odyssey of Power, Knowledge, and Geographical Distance*. Austin: University of Texas Press.

—— (2006) Glimpses of a Common Cosmos? A Brief Look South and North from Panama. In *A Pre-Columbian World*, ed. Jeffrey Quilter and Mary Miller, pp. 107–35. Washington, DC: Dumbarton Oaks.

Hendon, Julia A. (2000) Having and Holding: Storage, Memory, Knowledge, and Social Relations. *American Anthropologist* 102: 42–53.

Houk, Brett A., and Gregory Zaro (2011) Evidence for Ritual Engineering in the Late/Terminal Classic Site Plan of La Milpa, Belize. *Latin American Antiquity* 22: 178–98.

Inomata, Takeshi (2006) Plazas, Performers, and Spectators: Political Theaters of the Classic Maya. *Current Anthropology* 47: 805–42.

Jones, Lindsay (2000) *The Hermeneutics of Sacred Architecture: Experience, Interpretation, Comparison*, Vol. 1. Cambridge, MA: Harvard University Press.

Joyce, Rosemary A. (1991) *Cerro Palenque: Power and Identity on the Maya Periphery*. Austin: University of Texas Press.

—— (1992) Ideology in Action: Classic Maya Ritual Practice. In *Ancient Images, Ancient Thought: The Archaeology of Ideology*, ed. A. Sean Goldsmith, Sandra Garvie, David Selin, and Jeannette Smith, pp. 497–505. Calgary: Archaeological Association of the University of Calgary.

—— (2008) Practice in and as Deposition. In *Memory Work: Archaeologies of Material Practices*, ed. Barbara J. Mills and William Walker, pp. 25–40. Santa Fe, NM: SAR Press.

Joyce, Rosemary A., Julia A. Hendon, and Jeanne Lopiparo (2009) Being in Place: Intersections of Identity and Experience on the Honduran Landscape. In *The Archaeology of Meaningful Places*, ed. Brenda Bowser and M. Nieves Zedeño, pp. 53–72. Salt Lake City: University of Utah Press.

King, Adam, Chester P. Walker, Robert V. Sharp, F. Kent Reilly, and Duncan P. McKinnon (2011) Remote Sensing Data from Etowah's Mound A: Architecture and the Re-Creation of Mississippian Tradition. *American Antiquity* 76: 355–71.

Kopytoff, Igor (1986) The Cultural Biography of Things: Commoditization as Process. In *The Social Life of Things*, ed. Arjun Appadurai, pp. 64–91. Cambridge: Cambridge University Press.

Laporte, Juan Pedro, and Vilma Fialko (1995) Un reencuentro con mundo perdido, Tikal, Guatemala. *Ancient Mesoamerica* 6: 41–94.

Lekson, Stephen H. (1999) *Chaco Meridian: Centers of Political Power in the Ancient Southwest*. Walnut Creek, CA: AltaMira Press.

Longyear, John M., III (1944) *Archaeological Investigations in El Salvador*. Cambridge, MA: Peabody Museum of Archaeology and Ethnology.

—— (1966) Archaeological Survey of El Salvador. In *Handbook of Middle American Indians*, Vol. 4, ed. Gordon F. Ekholm and Gordon R. Willey, pp. 132–56. Austin: University of Texas Press.

Low, Setha M. (2000) *On the Plaza: The Politics of Public Space and Culture*. Austin: University of Texas Press.

Lucero, Lisa J., and Barbara W. Fash (eds) (2006) *Precolumbian Water Management: Ideology, Ritual, and Power*. Tucson: University of Arizona Press.

Marcus, Joyce (2003) The Maya and Teotihuacan. In *The Maya and Teotihuacan*, ed. Geoffrey E. Braswell, pp. 337–56. Austin: University of Texas Press.

Mathews, Jennifer, and James F. Garber (2004) Models of Cosmic Order: Physical Expression of Sacred Space among the Ancient Maya. *Ancient Mesoamerica* 15: 49–59.

Miles, Suzannah Eckholm (1965) Sculpture of the Guatemala-Chiapas Highlands and Pacific Slopes, and Associated Hieroglyphs. In *Handbook of Middle American Indians*, Vol. 2, ed. Robert C. Wauchope and Gordon R. Willey, pp. 237–75. Austin: University of Texas Press.

Mills, Barbara J., and William Walker (eds) (2008a) *Memory Work: Archaeologies of Material Practices*. Santa Fe, NM: SAR Press.

Mills, Barbara J., and William Walker (2008b) Introduction: Memory, Materiality, and Depositional Practice. In *Memory Work: Archaeologies of Material Practices*, ed. Barbara J. Mills and William H. Walker, pp. 3–23. Santa Fe, NM: SAR Press.

Monaghan, John (1998) Dedication: Ritual or Production? In *The Sowing and the Dawning: Termination, Dedication and Transformation in the Archaeological and Ethnographic Record of Mesoamerica*, ed. Shirley Botelier Mock, pp. 47–52. Albuquerque: University of New Mexico.

Navarro Farr, Olivia (2009) *Ritual, Process, and Continuity in the Late to Terminal Classic Transition: Investigations at Structure M13-1 in the Ancient Maya Site of El Perú-Waka', Petén, Guatemala*. PhD dissertation, Department of Anthropology, Southern Methodist University. Ann Arbor, MI: University Microfilms.

Pagliaro, Jonathan B., James F. Garber, and Travis W. Stanton (2003) Evaluating the Archaeological Signatures of Maya Ritual and Conflict. In *Ancient Mesoamerican Warfare*, ed. M. Kathryn Brown and Travis W. Stanton, pp. 75–89. Walnut Creek, CA: AltaMira Press.

Parsons, Lee A. (1969) *Bilbao, Guatemala: An Archaeological Study of the Pacific Coast Cotzumalhuapa Region*, Vol. 2. Milwaukee: Milwaukee Public Museum.

Pauketat, Timothy R. (2000) The Tragedy of the Commoners. In *Agency in Archaeology*, ed. Marcia-Anne Dobres and John Robb, pp. 113–29. London and New York: Routledge.

—— (2001) Practice and History in Archaeology: An Emerging Paradigm. *Anthropological Theory* 1: 73–98.

—— (2003) Materiality and the Immaterial in Historical-Processual Archaeology. In *Current Issues in Archaeological Method and Theory*, ed. T. L. Van Pool and Christine S. Van Pool, pp. 41–53. Salt Lake City: University of Utah Press.

—— (2008) Founders' Cults and the Archaeology of *Wa-kan-da*. In *Memory Work: Archaeologies of Material Practices*, ed. Barbara J. Mills and William H. Walker, pp. 61–79. Santa Fe, NM: SAR Press.

Preucel, Robert W. (2000) Making Pueblo Communities: Architectural Discourse at Kotyiti, New Mexico. In *The Archaeology of Communities: A New World Perspective*, ed. Marcello A. Canuto and Jason Yaeger, pp. 58–77. London and New York: Routledge.

Price, T. Douglas, James H. Burton, Robert Sharer, Jane E. Buikstra, Lori E. Wright, Loa P. Traxler, and Katherine A. Miller (2010) Kings and Commoners at Copan: Isotopic Evidence for Origins and Movement in the Classic Maya Period. *Journal of Anthropological Archaeology* 29: 15–32.

Reilly, F. Kent, III (1996) Art, Ritual, and Rulership in the Olmec World. In Michael D. Coe et al., *The Olmec World: Ritual and Rulership*, pp. 27–45. Princeton, NJ: Princeton University Art Museum.

Rice, Prudence M. (1999) Rethinking Classic Lowland Maya Pottery Censers. *Ancient Mesoamerica* 10: 25–50.

—— (2004) *Maya Political Science: Time, Astronomy, and the Cosmos*. Austin: University of Texas Press.

Richards, Janet E. (1999) Conceptual Landscapes in the Egyptian Nile Valley. In *Archaeologies of Landscape: Contemporary Perspectives*, ed. Wendy Ashmore and A. Bernard Knapp, pp. 83–100. Oxford: Blackwell.

Ringle, William M., Tomás Gallareta Negrón, and George J. Bey III (1998) The Return of Quetzalcoatl: Evidence for the Spread of a World Religion During the Epiclassic Period. *Ancient Mesoamerica* 9: 183–232.

Saunders, Nicholas J. (ed.) (1998) *Icons of Power: Feline Symbolism in the Americas*. London and New York: Routledge.

Schaafsma, Polly, and Karl A. Taube (2006) Bring the Rain: An Ideology of Rain Making in the Pueblo Southwest and Mesoamerica. In *A Pre-Columbian World*, ed. Jeffrey Quilter and Mary Miller, pp. 231–85. Washington, DC: Dumbarton Oaks.

Schlanger, Sarah H. (1992) Recognizing Persistent Places in Anasazi Settlement Systems. In *Space, Time, and Archaeological Landscapes*, ed. Jacqueline Rossignol and LuAnn Wandsnider, pp. 91–112. New York and London: Plenum Press.

Schortman, Edward M., and Patricia A. Urban (1991) Patterns of Late Preclassic Interaction and the Formation of Complex Society in the Southeast Maya Periphery. In *The Formation of Complex Society in Southeastern Mesoamerica*, ed. William R. Fowler, Jr., pp. 121–42. Boca Raton, FL: CRC Press.

Sharer, Robert J. (1974) The Prehistory of the Southeastern Maya Periphery. *Current Anthropology* 15: 165–87.

—— (1978a) Culture History of Chalchuapa and the Southeastern Maya Highlands. In *The Prehistory of Chalchuapa, El Salvador*, Vol. 3, ed. Robert J. Sharer, pp. 208–15. Philadelphia: University of Pennsylvania Press.

—— (1978b) Summary of Architecture and Constructional Activity. In *The Prehistory of Chalchuapa, El Salvador*, Vol. 1, ed. Robert J. Sharer, pp. 121–32. Philadelphia: University of Pennsylvania Press.

—— (2003) Founding Events and Teotihuacan Connections at Copán, Honduras. In *The Maya and Teotihuacan*, ed. Geoffrey E. Braswell, pp. 143–65. Austin: University of Texas Press.

Sheets, Payson D. (1984) The Prehistory of El Salvador: An Interpretive Summary. In *The Archaeology of Lower Central America*, ed. Frederick W. Lange and Doris Z. Stone, pp. 85–112. Albuquerque: University of New Mexico Press.

—— (2000) The Southeast Frontiers of Mesoamerica. In *The Cambridge History of the Native Peoples of the Americas*, Vol. II: *Mesoamerica*, Part 1, ed. Richard E. W. Adams and Murdo J. Macleod, pp. 407–48. Cambridge: Cambridge University Press.

—— (2003) Warfare in Ancient Mesoamerica: A Summary View. In *Ancient Mesoamerican Warfare*, ed. M. Kathryn Brown and Travis W. Stanton, pp. 287–302. Walnut Creek, CA: AltaMira Press.

Smith, Virginia G. (1984) *Izapa Relief Carving: Form, Content, Rules for Design, and Role in Mesoamerican Art History and Archeology*. Washington, DC: Dumbarton Oaks.

Spence, Michael W. (1992) Tlailotlacan, a Zapotec Enclave. In *Art, Ideology, and the City of Teotihuacan*, ed. Janet C. Berlo, pp. 59–88. Washington, DC: Dumbarton Oaks.

—— (2005) A Zapotec Diaspora Network in Classic-Period Central México. In *The Archaeology of Colonial Encounters*, ed. Gil J. Stein, pp. 173–205. Santa Fe, NM: SAR Press.

Stanton, Travis W., and Aline Magnoni (eds) (2008) *Ruins of the Past: The Use and Perception of Abandoned Structures in the Maya Lowlands*. Boulder: University Press of Colorado.

Stevanovic, Mirjana (1997) The Age of Clay: The Social Dynamics of House Destruction. *Journal of Anthropological Archaeology* 16: 334–95.

Stuart, David (1998) "The Fire Enters His House": Architecture and Ritual in Classic Maya Texts. In *Function and Meaning in Classic Maya Architecture*, ed. Stephen D. Houston, pp. 373–425. Washington, DC: Dumbarton Oaks.

—— (2000) "The Arrival of Strangers": Teotihuacan and Tollan in Classic Maya History. In *Mesoamerica's Classic Heritage: From Teotihuacan to the Aztecs*, ed. Davíd Carrasco, Lindsay Jones, and Scott Sessions, pp. 465–513. Boulder: University Press of Colorado.

Taube, Karl A. (1995) The Rainmakers: The Olmec and Their Contribution to Mesoamerican Belief and Ritual. In Michael D. Coe *et al.*, *The Olmec World: Ritual and Rulership*, pp. 83–103. Princeton, NJ: Princeton University Art Museum.

—— (2000a) Lightning Celts and Corn Fetishes: The Formative Olmec and the Development of Maize Symbolism in Mesoamerica and the American Southwest. In *Olmec Art and Archaeology in Mesoamerica*, ed. John E. Clark and Mary E. Pye, pp. 297–337. Washington, DC: National Gallery of Art.

—— (2000b) The Turquoise Hearth: Fire, Self-Sacrifice, and the Central Mexican Cult of War. In *Mesoamerica's Classic Heritage: From Teotihuacan to the Aztecs*, ed. Davíd Carrasco, Lindsay Jones, and Scott Sessions, pp. 269–340. Boulder: University Press of Colorado.

Tozzer, A. M. (1941) *Landa's Relación de las cosas de Yucatán*. Cambridge, MA: Peabody Museum of Archaeology and Ethnology.

Traxler, Loa P. (2003) At Court in Copan: Palace Groups of the Early Classic. In *Maya Palaces and Elite Residences: An Interdisciplinary Approach*, ed. Jessica Joyce Christie, pp. 46–68. Austin: University of Texas Press.

—— (2004) Redesigning Copan: Early Architecture of the Polity Center. In *Understanding Early Classic Copan*, ed. Ellen E. Bell, Marcello A. Canuto, and Robert J. Sharer, pp. 53–64. Philadelphia: University of Pennsylvania Museum.

Van Dyke, Ruth M., and Susan E. Alcock (eds) (2003) *Archaeologies of Memory*. Malden, MA: Blackwell.

Webster, David (1989) The House of the Bacabs: Its Social Context. In *The House of the Bacabs, Copan, Honduras*, ed. David Webster, pp. 5–40. Washington, DC: Dumbarton Oaks.

Willey, Gordon R. (1966) *An Introduction to American Archaeology*, Vol. 1: *North and Middle America*. Englewood Cliffs, NJ: Prentice-Hall.

Wright, Lori E. (2005) Identifying Immigrants to Tikal, Guatemala: Defining Local Variability in Strontium Isotope Ratios of Human Tooth Enamel. *Journal of Archaeological Science* 32: 555–66.

Wright, Lori E., Juan Antonio Valdés, James H. Burton, T. Douglas Price, and Henry P. Schwarz (2010) The Children of Kaminaljuyu: Isotopic Insights into Diet and Long Distance Interaction in Mesoamerica. *Journal of Anthropological Archaeology* 29: 155–78.

Zedeño, María Nieves, and Brenda Bowser (2009) The Archaeology of Meaningful Places. In *The Archaeology of Meaningful Places*, ed. Brenda Bowser and María Nieves Zedeño, pp. 1–14. Salt Lake City: University of Utah Press.

Zeitlin, Judith Frances (1993) The Politics of Classic-Period Ritual Interaction: Iconography of the Ballgame in Coastal Oaxaca. *Ancient Mesoamerica* 4: 121–40.

3

ANCIENT QUELEPA, COLONIAL SAN MIGUEL

Shifting cultural frontiers and rogue colonialism in eastern El Salvador

Kathryn Sampeck

E. Wyllys Andrews's work at the prehistoric site of Quelepa in eastern El Salvador detailed how this seemingly remote place was linked – at times in surprising ways – to both broader Mesoamerica and lower Central America. I present evidence that the curious place of eastern El Salvador persisted well into the colonial period and in fact garnered special attention from rogue colonial agents such as British pirates. Archaeological evidence of the long-distance relationships of Quelepa is placed within the context of recent scholarship to evaluate the frontier or border status of Quelepa over time. This evaluation is then extended into the colonial period on the basis of Spanish and British accounts as well as a series of maritime maps from the William Hack atlas, which dates to sometime after 1698. The historical and archaeological data of spatial, political, and economic organization indicate that colonial San Miguel was a center that eclipsed the capital city of San Salvador in several ways. The combined data suggest that the prominence of San Miguel is due in part to its long tradition of being in a boundary region, which provided the foundation for it to become a precinct for "rogue" colonialism. Rogue centers such as San Miguel, New Orleans, and Detroit contributed to colonial policies because independent agents in them tinkered with economic, political, and social practices freely at the boundaries of governmental oversight. This, in turn, provided tested methods for colonial officials to employ. In this sense, border or boundary centers such as San Miguel were not marginal but operated within the very crux of the problem of empire-building.

When E. Wyllys Andrews began his work at Quelepa in 1967, the area was a scholarly frontier. Precious little was known about the archaeology of eastern El Salvador and the region seemed to be at the very edge of Mesoamerica (see Figure 1.1). Peccorini (1913) first recorded the existence of Quelepa, and other researchers occasionally discussed the site during the following 15 years (Spinden 1915; Peccorini 1926; Lothrop 1927). Doris Stone (1959) described its orthogonal organization. Pedro Armillas conducted the first excavations at Quelepa in 1949, but no detailed report about the site or its archaeology was disseminated before Andrews's project. Andrews (1976) showed that eastern El Salvador was not a disconnected backwater but instead, at different times, had enigmatic connections that reached many regions in Central America and well into the heart of Mesoamerica. In this chapter I explore these connections and extend the analysis into the colonial period. Documentary evidence suggests that the region is a Mesoamerican example of "rogue" colonialism (Dawdy 2008). Although there is no reason to think that Quelepa was the colony of any empire until the sixteenth century, its long cultural history shows the cunning, craft, improvisation, and inventiveness that typify roguish ways. By viewing Quelepa as a renegade at the edge of Mesoamerica, we appreciate the experimentalism, creativity, and willingness that its inhabitants had to thumb their noses at the normative practices of less peripheral regions. Here I present a corollary to Dawdy's (2008: 18–19) three general points about colonialism. Europeans colonists in much of Mesoamerica often followed already established paths; in other words, they operated within a "structure of the conjuncture," a set of historical relationships that reproduced traditional cultural categories and at the same time gave them new values derived from contextual pragmatics (Sahlins 1985: 125). In this case, eastern El Salvador had the heritage of a renegade, and Atlantic World actors recognized the opportunity and elaborated upon it, manipulating the resources of the state while standing at the boundaries of state oversight and control.

Frontiers, borders, and rogue colonialism

Quelepa is usually depicted as occupying a frontier or boundary (Lange 1979; Ornat Clemente 2007; Sheets 1992). Western El Salvador and Honduras have often been viewed as the ethnic borderlands of the Maya, with the southerly reaches of Nicaragua and Costa Rica forming the edge of Mesoamerica (Baudez and Becquelin 1973; Creamer 1987; Fox 1981; Helms 1975; Lange 1976, 1979; Ornat Clemente 2007; Sharer 1974, 1984). Although Quelepa has long been considered beyond the Maya frontier, it is usually included within Mesoamerica (Sharer 1974: 165). One of the earliest formulations of this border that mentions Quelepa is Doris Stone's suggestion that the eastern frontier of Mesoamerica coincided with "the eastern limits of the Lenca territory in the Honduran highlands, going south and east of Quelepa, El Salvador" (Nicholson 1961). Fox (1981: 321) argued that the Mesoamerican boundary could be detected on the basis of declining frequency of items of "Mesoamerican high culture such as ballcourts, hieroglyphic writing, etc.," and that, in the boundary zone, "a cultural tradition arose that stood apart from traditions of both much of Mesoamerica and lower Central America and included hybrid cultural forms" (ibid.). Although the borderlands were a locale of transculturation, they seem to have been stable. Linares (1979: 26) argued for overall linguistic and cultural "stability and coherence" along the Mesoamerican frontier after 1500 BC, with changes in material culture indicating the effect of the actions of merchants rather than wholesale migration. Debates about the likelihood of the movement of people, things, and ideas permeate the study of the region. For this reason, Quelepa and the rest of southeastern Mesoamerica has been an arena for evaluating broader ideas about what material culture can tell us about the formation, maintenance, and movement of cultural, political, and economic boundaries.

The terms "frontier" and "boundary" have different nuances, but both imply territorial edges (McCarthy 2008: 203; Parker 2006: 79). Some have argued that frontiers face outward and are zones from which settlers look beyond with future colonization in mind (Green and Perlman 1985: 3–4; Kristof 1970: 127–7). Frontiers tend to have less precisely defined edges and to stand at the periphery of societies (Creamer 1987; Parker 2006). Often, the expansion of frontiers is encouraged and the regions beyond them are thought of as "pristine" or "empty," although this is rarely the case (Denevan 1992; see also Turner 1932). Elton (1996) has suggested that a frontier is a zone where different kinds of boundaries (geographic, political, demographic, economic, and cultural) intersect, affect each other, and overlap. Parker explains the dynamic of various kinds of boundaries:

> the colonization of a region (political) may result in a change in the ethnic (demographic) and linguistic (cultural) makeup of a borderland; the extraction of raw materials (economic) is conditioned by the types and quantity of resources available (geographic); population shifts (demographic) may affect the nature and distribution of material found in a borderland (cultural) and so on.
>
> (Parker 2006: 90)

The crucial point is that these shifting, interpenetrating dynamics are also contingent upon their historical context. No one constellation of factors is equally as likely as another at any given point in time because the history of interactions provides guidance and, in some cases, real constraints on the realm of possible social, economic, and political forms.

In contrast to frontiers, borders are "inner oriented" and mark the edges of sovereign units, a linear division between people and polities (McCarthy 2008: 203; see also Sharer's [1974: 174–5] employment of Wolf's [1955] idea of "open" versus "closed" societies). A border defines both social and political limits that are not to be crossed without serious consequences. To cross a border means to transgress into another realm in the social and political landscape – in other words, to move from a zone of inclusion (within the border) to a social or geographical place of exclusion (cf. Barth 1998). Efforts made by ethnically distinct populations to distinguish themselves may be even more pronounced near borders because groups struggle to maintain identity in the context of intense exchange (Barth 1969, 1994; Hodder 1982). The contrary – interchange resulting in creolization or hybridization – was conceptualized by White (1991) as a "Middle Ground," a place where populations break down and recombine practices from either side of the border (see also Kopytoff 1999; Lightfoot and Martinez 1995; Nassaney 2008; van Dommelen 1997, 1998). Was Quelepa on a frontier (looking outward) or on a border (looking inward)? Did this perspective shift over time? In particular, did early colonial encounters establish a new pattern? The Spanish conquest could have caused dramatic political, economic, and social changes such that characterizing the region as a frontier or border would be entirely inappropriate.

The question of boundaries and frontiers is especially pertinent to the understanding of rogue colonialism. Dawdy (2008: 18–19) presents three points about colonial enterprises that underscore how actors at the periphery capitalize on limited state oversight and about the ways that empires benefit from unplanned experimentation. Her three points, briefly, are that (1) colonialism is experimental and poorly controlled; (2) colonies are laboratories for modern statecraft rather than places where innovations generated in the metropole are imposed; and (3) colonial policies and practices are as much a creation of rogues and independent agents as of imperial direction (see also Cooper and Stoler 1997). Some local contingencies encouraged "circuits of seditious power and contraband flow" not because of isolation, but because the place was ideally situated in some ways for land or sea travel, a potential intersection of local smuggling and transatlantic trade (Dawdy 2008: 4, 75, 101–2). How did the foundation of native social, political, and economic practice aid or inhibit Spanish colonialism?

To address this question, I highlight a few examples of three key realms of material culture from Quelepa and eastern El Salvador: architecture, ceramics, and spatial organization. Spatial organization serves to link analyses of pre-contact and post-contact phenomena. Our understanding of the colonial period in the region depends on documentary sources because there has yet been no archaeology project focused on colonial San Miguel.

Architecture of Quelepa

Andrews (1976: 3) first broached the subject of the architecture of Quelepa, noting: "because of the scarcity of highly visible archaeological ruins and native populations, much of northern Central America has not attracted anthropologists or tourists." He then tells us in great detail about what seemed so unpromising from the surface. The architectural styles and spatial organization of Quelepa demonstrate characteristic features which, over time, situate the place either squarely within or plainly outside of Mesoamerican phenomena. The lack of clear affiliation is paralleled in other regions of the southeastern Mesoamerican boundary, such as the Comayagua Valley at the Late Preclassic settlement of Yarumela. Even though Yarumela was the apex of a primate settlement system, it lacked well-defined patio arrangements of public and elite architecture, residence rules that Dixon (1989: 261) suggests resulted from Lenca immigrants to the region, perhaps from the Quelepa area. The interaction between the Comayagua Valley and eastern El Salvador appears to have waned by about 250 BC, and Yarumela was abandoned (Dixon 1989). Interestingly enough, Quelepa architecture never shows strong resemblances to more southerly architectural forms even though artifacts clearly exhibit connections to the Intermediate Area (Ornat Clemente 2007). Thus, although these borderlands may display unclear or shifting alliances, interaction *within* the frontier occurred and probably created its own dynamic.

Uapala phase

Andrews (1976: 20, 176–8) did not find much architectural evidence of the Middle to Late Preclassic Uapala phase (see Figure 2.2), but he did uncover a Middle Preclassic jaguar altar (see Figure 2.5). This monumental sculpture shows iconographic ties to what has often been called the "Olmecoid style" and resembles most closely sculptures at Tak'alik Ab'aj, as well as at Cara Sucia, Izapa, and Kaminaljuyu (Andrews 1976: 176–8; Killion and Urcid 2001; Lowe 1989). The effort involved in creating monumental sculpture with clear iconographic and stylistic referents shows a mainstream connection to an important Mesoamerican phenomenon (Grove 1989). The shared vision expressed by the depiction of jaguar iconography on massive basalt sculpture suggests that Quelepa was one of many regions in Mesoamerica participating in a shared Preclassic ideological complex. What is more, such sculptures have not been found farther south and east. In the realm of ritual practice and perhaps elite life, Preclassic Quelepa appears to have been a border settlement that looked inward towards Mesoamerica.

Shila phase

For the Early Classic Shila phase, Andrews (1976: 38) uncovered what he calls a "local style of construction." Quelepa was one of the few places in Mesoamerica to employ ramps (see Figure 2.6). Ramps have been found, however, in Guarabuqui in the Cajon region of central Honduras (Messenger 1984). At Salitron Viejo, the largest and most politically powerful settlement in that area, three large and wide ramps led up to the site from the Río Yunque floodplain (Hirth *et al.* 1981: 9). Cobble construction for ramps is characteristic of sites in the Cajon area (Messenger 1984: 542). Andrews (1976: 38–40) excavated not just one but several ramps. Structure (Str.) 3 was the largest edifice at Quelepa and had an impressive ramp (ibid.: 13-20). Andrews noted that other examples of ramps are found at Los Naranjos (Baudez and Becquelin 1973) and Bilbao (Parsons 1969). Messenger (1984) also reported that this architectural feature suggests a distinctively local emphasis on an architectural form with ties within southern Mesoamerica.

Underscoring this distinctive pattern is Andrews's (1976: 39–40) observation that "Shila structures of any size seem to have been placed near the edges of terraces, rather than in compact, ordered groups around plazas," a pattern that he suggested was not typically Mesoamerican (see Figure 2.3). Subsequent work in Guatemalan piedmont sites has demonstrated this spatial organization. The site of Tehuacan, just west of the Lempa in El Salvador, also has similarly arranged structures. At the same time, this spatial organization is not an absolutely consistent pattern in lower Central America. The residents of Quelepa look as though they were experimenting with a novel or emergent landscape in contrast to dominant designs farther north. If the Shila-phase residents were looking towards Mesoamerica, they were thumbing their noses at the same time.

Lepa phase

By the Late to Terminal Classic Lepa phase, the construction of new architecture shifted to the southeastern corner of the West Group (Andrews 1976: 40). There, numerous platforms were compactly arranged around small terraces and plazas (see Figure 2.4). Thus, the built environment of this late phase of occupation shows a dramatic break from established patterns (see Chapter 2). At the same time, the Lepa-phase residents did not break with the past by erasing what had been built before; Shila-phase structures generally were neither dismantled nor otherwise obscured. Instead, only small, masonry-walled Lepa-phase platforms were constructed in the Shila-phase zone, and a Shila-phase terrace was covered by Str. 28, creating a new courtyard over Shila-phase terraces (Andrews 1976: 24, 40).

Str. 28 of the West Group was one of the larger mounds and exhibited typical Lepa-phase construction of crudely shaped blocks laid in mud mortar and covered with mud plaster (Andrews 1976: 24). This change in masonry architectural style shows little memory of the preceding Shila phase – gone are the ramps and the grander proportions of structures in a more dispersed pattern. Lepa architects may have largely preserved Shila-phase structures, but they did not model the built environment according to these earlier elements, their spatial distribution, or their construction. Instead, earlier structures acted as a constraint to later spatial organization. Despite these tensions or conflicts, Quelepa architecture persisted in emphasizing the typical Mesoamerican concern for single-family structures as opposed to the presence of large circular residences found at Intermediate Area sites (Messenger 1984: 542).

The dynamics of borderland interactions are also indicated in the orientation and arrangement of key structures. During the Late Classic and in the Naco Valley, site cores generally ran east–west, unlike the typical Maya north–south orientation. There, elite residences apparently surrounded temples rather than lying south of them, as in the case of many Maya sites. Moreover, in the Naco Valley, ballcourts are found on the southeast margin of site cores and – in contrast to those found in the Maya area – did not act as conduits between the sacred heavens to the north and the surface of the earth or underworld to the south (Ashmore 1987, 1991; Schortman *et al.* 2001: 323). The spatial organization of Quelepa likewise emphasized east–west orientations, and the ballcourt was not placed to be a mediating force between north and south.

Because this kind of architectural organization did not expand to the southeast (see McCafferty 2008; McCafferty and González 2009), Lepa-phase Quelepa seems to shift once again to border status, focusing inward towards Mesoamerica. Two key elements of the Lepa-phase construction give strong clues as to the direction of connections. The I-shaped ballcourt to the north of Lepa-phase architecture is one of the most southerly ballcourts in all of Mesoamerica (Andrews 1976: 174). Ballcourts are uniquely Mesoamerican and provide a space for the practice of shared ideas, whether of sport, elite power, or mythic re-enactment (Whittington 2001). Fox (1996: 489) stresses that the number and distribution of ballcourts can indicate the degree of political hierarchy, with highly centralized polities having fewer ballcourts located only in larger centers. This "tool of social negotiation" was the setting for multi-staged ritual practices and sponsored feasting that re-created social and political order.

The social realm of the ballcourt at Quelepa was further reinforced by the artifacts of Cache 24 in Str. 29, which contained a *hacha*, large and small *palmas*, and three plain yokes, all of a style strongly resembling ballgame sculpture from Veracruz (Andrews 1976: 169–75). The distribution of such Veracruz-style sculpture makes a curious leapfrog from the Gulf Coast to El Salvador. Similar items are found commonly in the highlands and Pacific coast of Guatemala but are rare through Chiapas, Tabasco, and Campeche. This spotty distribution implies either opportunistic appropriation or a discontinuous Guatemalan/Salvadoran/Gulf Coast interaction sphere rather than the widespread ideological sharing found in the Uapala phase. During the Lepa phase, Quelepa stood in contrast to its nearest neighbors and marked the frontier of this facet of Mesoamerican social enterprise.

Shifts in architectural affiliations

The history of the built environment at Quelepa shows notable shifts in its degree of connectedness to Mesoamerican trends. The earliest evidence is for labor-intensive and publicly outstanding works centered on ritual practice. The Early Classic marked a distinct shift to an intra-border style in contrast to patterns farther north in Mesoamerica. One important reason for this exclusion of the west was the devastating effects of the volcanic eruption of Ilopango around AD 535 (Dull *et al.* 2001; Earnest 1999). While eastern El Salvador was unscathed owing to the direction of the blast, the west was devastated (Sheets 1983). Other smaller eruptions occurred in western El Salvador around AD 650 – Loma Caldera, which covered in ash an area of 50 to 100 square kilometers, including Joya de Ceren, and El Boqueron, which erupted sometime between AD 785 and 995 and impacted an area under 300 square kilometers (McKee 2007). During the Early Classic, Quelepa was essentially cut off from central and western El Salvador, but not from central and western Honduras or lower Central America. Nevertheless, residents could have chosen to elaborate or modify Olmecoid organizational schemes, clinging more tightly to tradition in the wake of natural disaster. Instead, they developed a distinctive way of organizing social space that was not beholden to schemes from either farther north or south. During the Lepa phase, this shifted to a new kind of regionalism: the emulation of Gulf Coast ritual places and a distinctly non-Maya spatial arrangement. This emphasis may correlate to increased elite oversight of the symbolic and social worlds. Quelepa had, at every stage, a consistently distinct spatial realm.

Ceramics of Quelepa

The pottery of Quelepa shows equally intriguing patterns. During the Late Preclassic Uapala phase, Quelepa had distinctive vessel forms and surface treatments that are also found in much of Honduras but not in western El Salvador. Ceramic assemblages from Laguneta, Salto Coyote, and El Cacao indicate strong stylistic similarities between eastern El Salvador and northern Honduras (Amador 2007; Gómez 2010). Thus, during this early period, the importance of borderland interaction is clearer in the case of ceramics than in spatial arrangements.

Preferences in the built environment of Quelepa during the Preclassic are echoed in the presence of particular ceramics. What seems to be a connection to the west is Usulutan resist decoration (Demarest 1986). Izalco Usulutan, identified by multiple, fine wavy resist lines, is "the key type of the Caynac period and the variant of Usulutan with the widest distribution across the southern periphery (e.g., Quelepa, Archaic Copan, Yarumela, Los Naranjos) in the Late and Terminal Preclassic (100 B.C. to A.D. 250)" (Demarest and Sharer 1982: 819). Andrews notes that this was the dominant kind of pottery during the Uapala phase, composing over half the assemblage and indicating "strong relationships with western and central El Salvador and highland Guatemala" (Andrews 1976: 180).

Usulutan decorated pottery appears first in the Middle Preclassic in western El Salvador and highland Guatemala. It is found somewhat later in the Middle Preclassic in eastern El Salvador and Honduras and does not have stylistic antecedents, as was the case in the west. Andrews (1976) argues that the pottery style spread east and north sometime after 300 BC as a result of the movement of Mayan speakers radiating outward from a heartland in western El Salvador and the Guatemalan highlands to the rest of the Uapala ceramic sphere region. He supports his model with evidence of phonological correspondences between Lenka and K'iche', the modern distribution of Lenka place names, and the distribution of Izalco Usulutan. Demarest and Sharer (1982: 820) argue that "the design modes (perhaps in some cases the actual technique) spread rapidly by trade, imitation, and stimulus diffusion … because of its distinctive character, Usulutan decoration is precisely the kind of mode which one would expect to spread rapidly by trade or other nondisruptive processes." Goralski suggests a more precise model for the use and effect of the pottery, concluding that

> Usulután pottery was likely used as a daily serving vessel for elites to reinforce status differences, as a special service ware used in ritualized feasts with other elites to force or renegotiate status differences, and as gifts given by elites to forge alliances and incur debt … economic interaction between regions of the sphere was robust, and … imported pottery may have been distributed as gifts or traded from those who could afford to sponsor or participate in long distance exchange to those who could not.
>
> (Goralski 2008: 284–5)

The relative abundance of Izalco Usulutan at Quelepa and a rapid fall-off in frequency at sites to the northeast indicate not only that Quelepa was a producer of this type, but also that trade in it helped form a distinct boundary.

Because Izalco Usulutan has been found primarily in elite contexts, researchers have suggested that it was an import controlled by elites for their own political and economic goals (Schortman and Urban 1991: 126; Urban 1993; Wonderley 1991: 164–5). Goralski (2008: 72) highlights that a problem in this interpretation is that relatively less research has been directed at commoner contexts, so class associations of Usulutan are incompletely known.

Demarest (1986) argues that two other pottery types – jars with appliqué fillets or incisions (such as Pacheco Dichrome, Placitas Red, Ulua Bichrome) and a plain buff ceramic that occurs mostly in jars and *tecomate* form – should also be included in the Uapala ceramic sphere, and that this sphere should take in the Naco Valley, Ulua Valley, and Santa Barbara regions of Honduras (Schortman *et al.* 1986: 267; see Robinson 1988 for arguments to expand the reach of the sphere).

In terms of ceramic production, paste composition analysis showed that, "at the most, trace amounts of Usulután pottery produced in El Salvador made its way northward into the rest of the Uapala Ceramic sphere and that, at least in terms of ceramic exchange, the Uapala Ceramic sphere can be divided into El Salvadoran and Honduran sub-spheres" (Goralski 2008: 255). Goralski's instrumental neutron activation analyses of Izalco Usulutan and Bolo Orange pastes indicate that most Usulutan pottery in the Uapala sphere was made at local sites, although smaller amounts of imports are found across the region. Thus, stylistic unity was likely achieved without the movement of populations *or* of high volume trade.

The widespread adoption of canons can be linked to political processes. For example, "highly influential, efficient, and organized governmental strategies were needed to achieve the degree of uniformity and standardization visible across the broad range of Late Preclassic public and private material practices" (Bachand 2006: 539). This uniformity permeated the landscape. "By repetitive action, mythologizing, and marking, places become the land of X, the realm of Y, or the place of Z – they survive as such through the work of politics" (ibid.: 628). The ceramic assemblage of Quelepa, however, displays some modes – such as nubbin supports – that occur widely on resist-decorated wares, but it does not replicate the entire corpus of western vessel forms. The pottery of Quelepa retains a distinctly eastern aesthetic even though western techniques make an appearance, perhaps contributing to the effort to construct the social and political realm of Quelepa within southern Mesoamerica.

The distinction between east and west is not straightforward. In fact, Uapala-phase pottery from Quelepa is much more similar to materials from Copan than to those from western El Salvador, lending credence to the definition of a Uapala sphere (Goralski 2008). Linares (1979: 25) cautioned that ceramic similarities "may mean different things, not just a common ethnic origin or a common language." Bachand suggested that the legacy of Olmecoid social and political interaction set a precedent in a broadly conceived southern highland zone that predisposed the region to increased conflict:

> Some highland societies, such as Miraflores, Uapala, and Solano, attained surprising degrees of cultural integration, sharing ceramic, architectural, sculptural, and domestic traditions. Ultimately, however, they were less

successful at uniting themselves within a single ideological canon. In Gramscian terms, highland hegemonic groups were less effective at incorporating the interests of others into their own. Surely they possessed the intellectual and moral leadership to do so. But unlike the Lowland Maya, highland societies were comprised of many more linguistic and ethnic factions and lived with the legacy of their chiefdom-based Olmec political heritage. Coercion, violence, and political instability were probably more common realities in highland communities.

(Bachand (2006: 578)

The key element in this case may be the issue of constructing a specific group identity through the medium of the symbolic display of a distinctive aesthetic within the competition and potential for flux of a borderland. In fact, Goralski argues that the form and decoration of Izalco Usulutan suggested that it was an "*objet d'art* as much as it [was] a vessel for food presentation" (2008: 225). Taken together, Uapala-phase sculpture and ceramics indicate that Quelepa was perhaps on a frontier or the last bulwark on a border. While some elements were truer to the canon, such as in sculpture, other facets of material culture were more playful or experimental in creating a local expression of a widely used technique.

Shila-phase ceramics seem to underscore that correspondences between Quelepa, western El Salvador, and highland Guatemala persisted but were much less striking, and the web of connections seemed to place a greater emphasis on Central America. "Ceramic ties with Copan were far stronger than with western El Salvador ... many ceramic traditions established in the Late Preclassic continue into the Early Classic" (Andrews 1976: 146) – similarities that extend to central and southwestern Honduras, the La Boquita phase of central El Salvador, and other areas of eastern El Salvador. The trajectory of exchange, however, was more east and north than west (Andrews 1977; Cobos 1994: 62; Fowler and Earnest 1985: 24). Furthermore, the recovery of small carved jadeite beads, carved leg *metates*, and pecked stone balls found in sets of three in Shila-phase deposits suggest southern, possibly Cost Rican, connections (Andrews 1976: 183).

Sheets (1992) notes that some advantages, such as cultural stability, lie in avoiding statehood of the sort seen at Classic Copan. Indeed, Andrews (1976: 183) argued for strong cultural stability in the Shila phase in part because of the close similarity of Uapala and Shila ceramics. Frontier studies have suggested we should not assume that culture change is an inevitable part of living on a frontier. In fact, some areas demonstrate "structural inertia" or resistance to change as part of a strategy of frontier life (Staski 1998). The architectural and ceramic evidence of the Shila phase presents the picture of a resolute frontier, intransigence in the face of Maya state formation.

By the Lepa phase, Quelepa ceramics are linked to the Mexican Gulf Coast, particularly southern Veracruz, and thus replicate the patterning seen in architecture and sculpture. Unlike the distinctive *palmas* and *hachas* of the ballcourt context, fine paste ceramics appear in a variety of sites in the Maya area. During the Terminal

Classic, Fine Orange vessels were used in the Río Pasion area, most notably at Seibal, in the northern lowlands (in the form of a wide array of fine wares), in small amounts at Copan and Chalchuapa, and in substantial quantities in the Ulua Valley and Quelepa (Joyce 1986). Joyce (1986) identified the distinctive white-slipped and red-painted Fine Orange ware of Delirio Red-on-White at Copan, Seibal, and Cerro Palenque. Delirio Red-on-White armadillo effigies and Altar Fine Orange Modeled-Carved vessels were recovered from a few contexts in the East Court of the Acropolis at Copan and in Bayal-phase (AD 830–930) deposits at Seibal. At Cerro Palenque, Delirio Red-on-White appears in the form of low-walled tripod bowls. Joyce (1986: 319) argues that, "if Quelepa itself was not the source of the Copan and Seibal vessels, a site within the same ceramic tradition must have been."

Quelepa, interaction spheres, and exchange networks

On the basis of the distribution of the white-slipped fine wares as well as unslipped fine wares akin to Altar Fine Orange, Joyce (1986: 313) proposes the existence of two interaction spheres, one in the southern highlands and the other along the Gulf and Caribbean coasts. Quelepa was a key node or anchor in the Terminal Classic exchange network (Joyce 1986: fig. 7b). Terminal Classic trade routes split at Quelepa; one path led north to central Honduras and the other path led northwest to Copan, the lowlands of the Pasion drainage, and Seibal. This route stood in contrast to the southern highland sphere, where evidence of Fine Orange is limited to Pabellon Modeled-Carved. This parallels the east to west distribution of Lepa-phase ceramics from Quelepa to Seibal (including intervening spots of Copan, Chalchuapa, and San Agustin Acasaguastlan; Joyce 1986: 324). White-slipped Fine Orange wares have also been found as a minor component at the site of Ciudad Vieja in central El Salvador, about midway between Quelepa and Chalchuapa (Card 2007: 582).

At the same time, central Honduras ceased interactions with the Ulua Valley but the Comayagua Valley produced Tenampua Polychrome. Both the white slip of Tenampua and its occurrence at Quelepa indicate that the southeastern highland sphere truly had an eastern focus (Joyce 1986: 325). Complementing this pattern is the observation that Ulua Polychrome is found in substantial amounts in eastern El Salvador but Tohil Plumbate is rare. The presence of Tenampua Polychrome in Lepa-phase contexts at Quelepa suggests the establishment of new exchange networks to the north and west and the reappearance of centralized control, "perhaps due to a perceived threat to regional sovereignty from outside the valley" (Dixon 1989: 266, 269). This political and economic model is presented by Joyce (1986: 326), who submits that the primate settlement distribution of Cerro Palenque, the relative poverty of that site, and its wholesale adoption of a foreign pattern of elite life are symptomatic of participation in a dendritic economy. Dendritic economies have foreign managers or local leaders who identify with a dominant foreign culture. These managers intensively exploit, often through agriculture, a region for a foreign market (Smith 1976).

This dendritic economy provided the interlinking nodes that bolstered rulership and connected different elements of the political hierarchy through symbolic markers of identity. Local rulers and the ruled had social identities distinct from "paramounts … covering vast territorial expanses" (Schortman *et al.* 2001: 312) within the network. The network results from a desire to link actors through "commitment to a common value system expressed and created through manipulation of distinctive material symbols" (ibid.: 313), such that ruling power appears part of the natural order of the world. At Naco, crab and bird imagery created a distinctive local ware, while Fine-Line pottery linked elites in the Naco Valley to the Ulua Valley and as far west as Copan and most of El Salvador (Schortman *et al.* 2001). "A symbol's material prominence … cannot be equated with its political efficacy" (ibid.: 314); nonetheless, it speaks to the effort to legitimize even if its use does not lead to inevitable and predictable results.

Much of central and eastern Honduras was characterized by small-scale yet centralized polities and social factions built upon the maneuvering of economic capital by aspiring leaders who wished to enter the exchange networks of elites (Joyce 1996; Joyce and Hendon 2000; Schortman and Urban 1994). Lange noted that the ceramic assemblages of the Greater Nicoya area are of "striking contrast" to those of Quelepa even though they lie a relatively short distance from each other, which he took to be "evidence of a significant pre-Columbian frontier based primarily on the presence/absence of shared traits, rather than on an understanding of cultural process and development" (Lange 1976: 180). He described this as a "fluid zone more properly conceived of as a buffer rather than as any defined frontier" (ibid.) which shifted through time. He also argued that, despite this fluidity, "local Central American peoples maintained strong indigenous tradition despite, and within the framework of, these repeated external pressures" (ibid.:180).

Carmack and Salgado González (2006) argue that Bagaces-period artifacts from Pacific Nicaragua demonstrate that elites controlled a long-distance exchange network of ceramics and obsidian centered on the Comayagua Valley of Honduras and Quelepa, and not on Copan and western El Salvador (see also Braswell *et al.* 1994: 176,188; Braswell *et al.* 2002). Reciprocal exchange is shown by the presence of artifacts from lower Central American regions at Quelepa. They interpret this patterning in terms of world-system political economy:

> Quelepa probably was a colonial enclave established for economic purposes by newly arrived peoples from the Gulf Coast of Mexico … that likely dominated a regional sector of an intersocietal network (world-system) that connected the Mesoamerican and Lower Central American regions … By this token, Quelepa was part of a periphery, but not a true frontier, as its inhabitants were always to some degree participants in Mesoamerican exchange systems and not an independent system.
> (Carmack and Salgado González 2006: 226)

Identities based on gender, age, kinship, and earlier political forms tend to persevere as long as they guide and organize daily activities and interactions (Schortman *et al.* 2001: 325). Lepa-phase material culture indicates that these older identities had lost their relevance. Quelepa was an innovator during the Terminal Classic period. Its material culture evinces strong connections with the Gulf Coast while at the same time reproducing other mainstream Mesoamerican features. This bespeaks the negotiation of a social and perhaps political and economic place that was inside Mesoamerica yet at the same time distinct from its neighbors. Gone was the structural inertia of the Shila phase, replaced by idiosyncratic participation in particular Mesoamerican phenomena.

It is clear that Quelepa was never peripheral in the sense of being a cultural isolate. Continuing work in eastern El Salvador (Amador 2007) has developed a broader picture that reinforces what Andrews established. Likewise, other analyses, such as Braswell's (2003) work on the evolution of lithic procurement and production strategies at the site, show that, despite the location of the Quelepa on the far southeastern periphery of Mesoamerica, its inhabitants participated in a Mesoamerican rather than a Central American exchange network. Quelepa was within the "Southeast Maya obsidian exchange sphere," and only trace amounts of material from sources within that sphere were traded to central Honduras. Braswell (2003; Braswell *et al.* 1994) indicates that the Salvadoran region as a whole participated in the Southeast Maya obsidian exchange sphere during the Terminal Classic, but by the Early Postclassic a buffer zone existed on the west of a "Lowland Maya" exchange sphere, which he claims represents an expansion of trade in obsidian from the Ixtepeque source. Most obsidian sources were located far from major settlements and often in the peripheries of the exchange spheres in which they circulated, resulting in a directed rather than a radial pattern of distribution. Braswell argues that, "the peripheral or interstitial locations of obsidian sources, the directional pattern of distribution, and the lack of clear controlling central places all suggest that obsidian extraction and circulation were governed more by demand than central planning" (2003: 155). Quelepa therefore had strong local foundations and its own, roguish take on Mesoamerican networks.

Eastern El Salvador was settled by the Pipil during the Postclassic period (Fowler 1989), but there are few archaeological remains at Quelepa dating to that time. McFarlane argues that the prestige economy of the Terminal Classic "disintegrated along with the authority of political agents that drew on this interregional latticework as a source of power" and gave way to an "incipient market system, wherein the functional or utilitarian value of imported commodities surpassed their prestige value" (McFarlane 2005: 8). Moreover, this new economy fundamentally changed political organization to "one based on corporate political strategies rather than those that singled out charismatic elites" (ibid.). It is clear that Quelepa was not a significant player in this new Postclassic economy, in contrast to areas such as Santa Barbara that witnessed population growth (Schortman *et al.* 1986). Did this marginalization during the Postclassic relegate this part of the east to a backwater during the genesis of the early modern world? The next challenge is to see how boundary relations played out during the colonial period.

Colonial San Miguel

Before 1530, eastern El Salvador was a contested zone, claimed by the governors of Nicaragua and the united province of Honduras and Higueras (Chamberlain 1947: 623, 626). No Spanish town existed east of the Lempa until 1530. The *villa* of San Miguel de la Frontera was founded by Luís Moscoso on the orders of Pedro de Alvarado, who wished to stake his claim to the southeastern edge of his dominion (Andagoya 1865: 38). This initial settlement was abandoned and the lands described as unprofitable, particularly when compared to the spectacular wealth reaped from Peru during this time. Nonetheless, eastern El Salvador seems to have been well populated, with over 200 settlements within 15 leagues of San Miguel (Chamberlain 1947: fn. 5, from *Probanza* of merits and services of Gonzalo de Armenta, Santiago de Guatemala, 1565, in AGG, Papers from the *Archivo Colonial*).

In 1534 Jorge de Alvarado sent Cristóbal de la Cueva and a sizeable army to Higueras to conquer the province and establish a port on the North Pacific to serve Guatemala, but Cueva found Andrés de Cerezeda already there. After a short period of cooperation, the relationship soured and Cueva moved on to repopulate and rebuild San Miguel and quell the brewing rebellion of indigenous residents (Chamberlain 1947: 625–6). San Miguel was reoccupied by 1535, when wrangling over the borderlands revived (ibid.: 624, 626). The border dispute lingered even after the Viceroyalty of New Spain was founded in Mexico City and the Audiencia in Panama in 1535; both claimed jurisdiction over lands around the Gulf of Fonseca. In fact, this region was a hotbed of illegal activity for those claiming control. Gómez recounts that:

> Despite royal bans to protect the indigenous villages in the region, both Pedrarias and Pedro de Alvarado not only tolerated the enslavement of indigenous peoples, but also actively participated in the illicit activity. Before the approval of the royal *cédula* of 1534 – which permitted the enslavement of "hostile" native peoples – both governors were directly involved in the traffic of enslaved native peoples between the Gulf of Fonseca and Panama. An excellent example of this can be found in Pedrarias' second letter to the Crown in 1529, when Captain Martín Estete was sent to eastern El Salvador to regulate the injustices exercised by Alvarado and his men in eastern El Salvador … What is not revealed, until much later, is that Estete was given a branding iron by Pedrarias, which was only to be used for criminals and rebels.
>
> (Gómez 2010: 45)

San Miguel was both socially and geographically more distant from San Salvador than Honduras and Higueras "because of the interest which the governors of Honduras and Higueras displayed in San Miguel and the proximity of that province to Higueras, together with the distance which separated San Miguel from Santiago de Guatemala, events in Higueras and San Miguel were henceforth to become closely intertwined" (Chamberlain 1947: 627). This close relationship also included indigenous populations. The Lempira Revolt, which began late in 1537 and involved much of the Indian population of Higueras, had parallel timing in San Miguel; the Spanish population there was reduced to half its former size as a result of the bloody uprising (ibid.: 631). Both colonial administrators and indigenous populations maintained a central Honduras–San Miguel axis.

The conflict over political control was resolved in Alvarado's favor in 1544 with the establishment of the Audiencia de los Confines, first installed at Gracias a Dios in 1544 and then transferred in 1549 to Santiago de Guatemala (Chamberlain 1947: 633, 643). The definitive union of eastern El Salvador with Guatemala was achieved by installing a key tool of royal absolute government. Chamberlain (ibid.: 639) estimated that the mid-sixteenth century population of San Miguel was about 25,000. Between a survey in 1551 of *tasaciones* and that in 1590 by Francisco de Valverde to evaluate the potential for developing an inter-oceanic route between Puerto Caballos on the Honduran coast and the Gulf of Fonseca, the population dropped by at least half (Gómez 2010: 63). Uprisings continued for the next few years, and *encomenderos* on their way to participate in the siege of the Peñol of Chilanga found placer deposits in a river. This inception of gold and silver mining in the San Miguel region "had its importance … in preventing the town [of San Miguel] from being depopulated" (Chamberlain 1947: 638).

San Miguel is a short distance from Quelepa, located along the Río Grande de San Miguel, of which the Río San Esteban is a tributary. The town was founded to mark the border of Alvarado's domain against rival claims of Gil González Dávila and Francisco Hernández de Córdoba. It was during this time that the location of the capital city of San Salvador shifted from a hilltop near present-day Suchitoto to the populous valley of present-day San Salvador. The early experiment is well preserved at the archaeological site and first capital of Ciudad Vieja, which demonstrates the tensions between the imposition of a pristine Spanish *villa* with gridded streets and a slightly askew indigenous settlement at its margins. Moreover, the pottery of Ciudad Vieja includes hybrid wares imitating or inspired by Italianate majolica forms that were produced using local pottery-making techniques and decorated in traditional styles (Card 2007; Hamilton 2009). In both spatial patterns and ceramics, the Ciudad Vieja contained all of the contradictions and strains of the colonial effort.

The ascendancy of San Miguel is indicated by its selection, along with San Salvador, as one of the two key places for Franciscan convents in the 1570s as well as its official designation of *ciudad* in 1599 (Juarros 1857: 165; Van Oss 1986). As an early colonial enterprise, San Miguel seemed to receive official rewards, particularly because the region was especially suited for the cultivation of indigo, a commodity that gained importance in the late sixteenth century and rose to the fore by the seventeenth century (Fowler 1987). The colonial city lies about 50 kilometers from the south coast and 30 kilometers from the bay of La Union. The closest bay to San Miguel is the Bay of Jiquilisco, which is much smaller than La Union. Nevertheless, San Miguel was usually described as being located on a bay favorable for docking large ships, fostering bustling maritime commerce. Early in its history, San

Miguel exhibited characteristics that encouraged the colonial experiment, yet it was a contested zone and a place to draw sharp boundaries.

The limited engagement that characterized the first few years of colonization changed by 1586 to emphasize cattle ranching and indigo processing. Fray Alonso de Ponce (Ciudad Real 1873: 235–46) recounted that the region had numerous *sitios de estancias* for cattle ranching and indigo production (see also Browning 1971: 70). This commercial expansion directly affected indigenous communities, and even settlements that were expressly protected from encroachment were subsumed into haciendas by the eighteenth century (Gómez 2010: 71). One of the recorded indigo haciendas was Quelepa (ibid.: fig. 4.2). Eastern El Salvador was centrally involved in the colonial economy.

A myth of the "pristine" or unpopulated countryside (Denevan 1992; Wylie 1993) devoid of "authentic" native populations developed over the course of the sixteenth and seventeenth centuries as a strategy to acquire and usurp land for cattle ranching and indigo production:

> The theses of abandonment and assimilation became a self-fulfilling narrative of a singular racial collective in El Salvador. The mestizo narrative they serve guarantee their own continual legitimation by quite literally limiting knowledge of the records (written, material, and cultural) of contingency and historical process that could have been used to dispel the "myth of emptiness."
>
> (Gómez 2010: 10)

Thus, areas interpreted as empty were to be filled by the expansion of the production of primary agricultural commodities.

The Hack atlas

Colonial El Salvador is well illustrated by a series of maps that let us see this region through the eyes of a rogue. The maps were drawn sometime after 1698 by William Hack, a London map- and chart-maker (see the online John Carter Brown Library catalog for information summarized here). The maps are based on a collection of Spanish charts captured by the English privateer Captain Bartholomew Sharpe when his ship, *Trinity*, seized the Spanish ship *Rosario* off the coast of Ecuador in 1681. Perhaps the greatest treasure aboard the *Rosario* was a *derrotero*, or a volume of manuscript charts of the coast with detailed sailing directions. Sharpe captured the *derrotero* just as it was about to be thrown overboard. Hack copied this work for the British crown and called it the *South Sea Wagoner*. The information in the atlas was deemed so sensitive and valuable that Hack never published it. He did, however, make a few copies.

During the colonial period, most ships sailed from the south to the north. Officially sanctioned trading ships filled with goods from the Orient crossed the Pacific and arrived at the port of Callao, near Lima, Peru. From Callao ships sailed northward to make their way to the port of Acapulco. Both official and unofficial ships, including British, Dutch, and French roguish "entrepreneurs" (pirates and privateers), stopped at other ports along the way, and inter-colony trade retained vitality despite Spanish efforts to control contraband and illegal exchange. Ports along the coast of modern El Salvador played a key part in this illicit inter-colony trade, becoming hubs of exchange of Asian merchandise, Peruvian silver, cacao, indigo, and balsam (Sampeck 2007).

If we begin in western El Salvador, in the region of Sonsonate, which lies within the Izalcos polity of the Nahua-speaking Pipil, the Hack atlas allows us to imagine a bucolic scene of several named haciendas and "works" or *obrajes* (Figure 3.1). Several of the Izalcos towns are named: Santo Domingo de Guzman and Salcoatitan (in the west) and Caluco (in the east). The Spanish city of La Santisima Trinad de Sonsonate (noted as S. Trinity) is hardly larger than the Indian pueblos. Most prominent on this map is the royal road to Guatemala, the port of Acajutla (Acahultura), and the wine cellars near the coast. The emphasis on the wine cellars is because, throughout the colonial period, wine was one of the most critical commodities traded for local goods. A lack of wine in the seventeenth and eighteenth centuries makes clear that this was not a luxury item but an essential component for the functioning of colonial society (Escalante 1992: 2/53–72). Like wine, oriental merchandise was also traded for local goods. Consistent pleadings for and denials of contraband trade in Asian merchandise suggest a fascination that was not bound by trade sanctions.

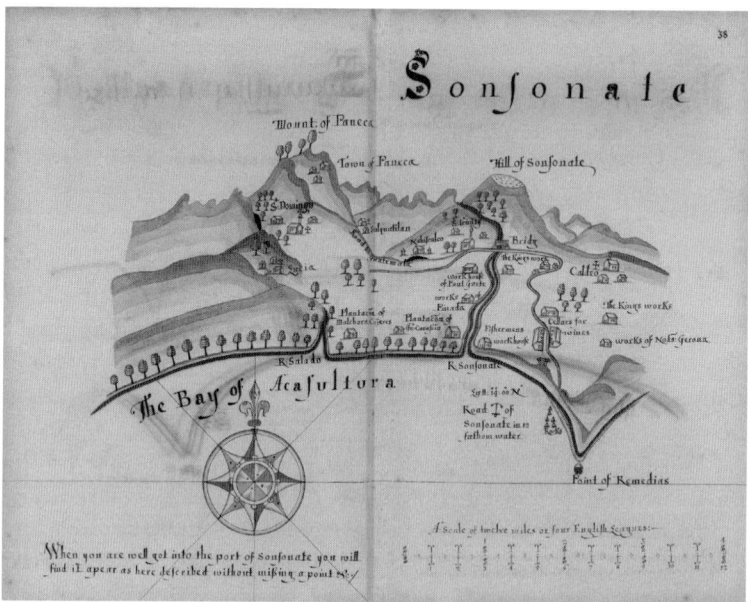

FIGURE 3.1 Navigation map of Sonsonate from the William Hack atlas (after 1698): several colonial towns are recorded, as well as private estates and indigo *obrajes*, and the road leading from the port to Sonsonate is prominently featured (original in the collection of the John Carter Brown Library, Brown University, Providence)

The Audiencia of Guatemala underwent a severe shortage of wine because of prohibitions on the imports from Peru. Spanish wine was supposed to be the only wine consumed, but shipments were few and far between for about 75 years. By the time the Hack map was made, residents complained that normal life could hardly be lived because of the severe shortage of wine. By the 1680s, Peruvian wine was prime contraband, and a few archeological sites in the region noted on the map have an unusual abundance of *botija*, or ceramic wine containers (Sampeck 2007). Thus the landscape was one of private enterprises, minimal official Spanish presence, and prominent indigenous towns. The Spanish seat of legal and official economic authority, Sonsonate, is not emphasized on the map as a rich or prime location; rather, the visual focus is the route west.

The riches of the Sonsonate–Izalcos region peaked in the sixteenth century with the ascendance of cacao in colonial trade. Cacao, the tree seed that yields chocolate, was produced on the basis of indigenous knowledge and practices (Fowler 1987; Sampeck 2007). When commodities whose production relied upon Spanish knowledge and direct control of production, such as indigo and sugar, became the focus of seventeenth-century and later colonial economies, the Izalcos region languished. Economic production never emphatically shifted to these products. San Salvador, San Miguel, and other regions of the province rose to economic prominence. The golden age of the Izalcos passed with the preference for blue dye, and it is notable that key features on this map are the *obrajes* – indigo-processing factories.

Moving southeast along the coast, the next map (Figure 3.2) shows the Balsam Coast and the mouth of the Río Lempa. No haciendas or other settlements are noted, just the distinctive shapes of the volcanoes as an aid to navigation. The following map (Figure 3.3) depicts the mouth of the Lempa in greater detail and a volcanic peak where San Salvador is located. The city itself, however, is not explicitly noted in any way. This – the seeming lack of existence of San Salvador – is the most striking feature of this series of maps, although other documents demonstrate that central El Salvador was a focus of political, social, and economic power. Why would such a place be omitted from maritime maps? One reason may be that San Salvador was a terrestrial power and not a center of maritime activity. Other inland settlements, such as Potosi, did merit notation in the Hack atlas, but such references are rare. Potosi is perhaps a special case because it loomed so large in both Atlantic and Pacific trade.

The next map (Figure 3.4) is of San Miguel and presents a scene of dense settlement. A series of towns along the royal road give an overall impression that this is a center of commerce and social life. The ample port is depicted in great detail. The overall impression is that it was *the* central place in El Salvador. Indeed, San Miguel compares handsomely in the atlas to other key cities of the time, such as Lima, Peru. The spatial extent of Lima, however, does not match that of San Miguel. An even greater contrast is with Acapulco, which barely seems to exist compared to the port and towns of the region of San Miguel. Whether or not the latter was looking outward or inward at the time, the place certainly caught the imagination of seventeenth-century Spanish mariners as well as British privateers and map-makers.

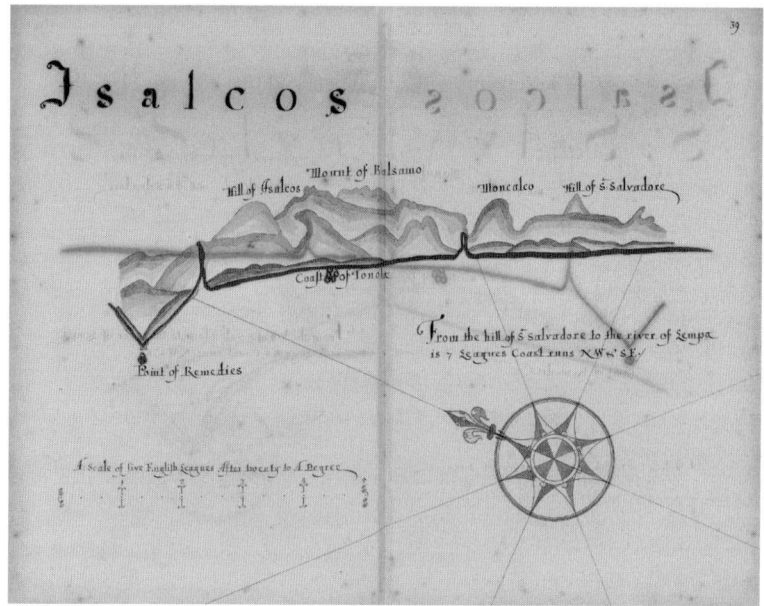

FIGURE 3.2 Navigation map of "Isalcos" from the William Hack atlas (after 1698): this region has no settlement of roads recorded on the image; the mountains are named after their primary export product – balsam – while the coast retains its Precolumbian name of Tonala.

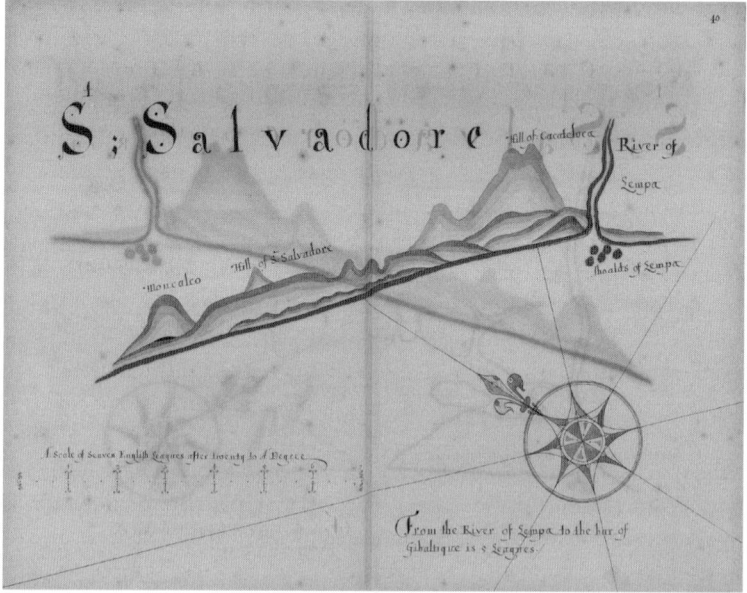

FIGURE 3.3 Navigation map of San Salvador from the William Hack atlas (after 1698): the region is bereft of settlement and roads, and the hill that marks the location of the capital city is one of the most prominent features.

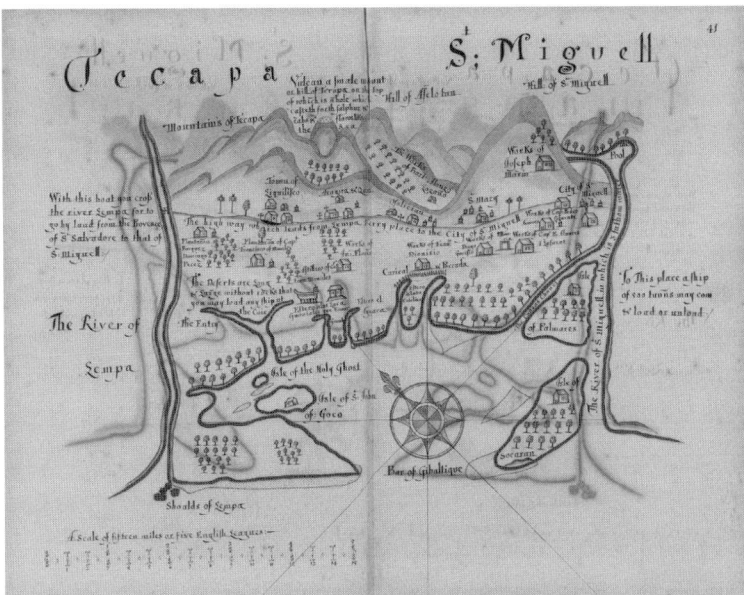

FIGURE 3.4 Navigation map of San Miguel from the William Hack atlas (after 1698): the region is filled with "works" or indigo *obrajes*, and the *camino real* is prominently drawn; the city of San Miguel is not substantially larger than other settlements.

The exaggerated importance of San Miguel suggested by sixteenth-century titles and clerical activities is borne out graphically in the seventeenth-century maps. San Miguel is accentuated even though it was not a capital city, or, more accurately, precisely because it was not. Commerce and power flowed relatively unimpeded because state oversight was minimal. San Miguel stood at the periphery of Guatemala, yet it was a center of commerce and had a long heritage of independence and of leadership within local exchange networks that are documented in precolumbian periods at the nearby site of Quelepa. The geographic location of this center and its roguish cultural heritage seem to have lent it political and economic importance to both the European and the indigenous inhabitants.

A further point is that, on the map, the position of San Miguel is rectified to be superior to (north of) the port of Jiquilisco. In other words, San Miguel lies well west of the large bay of La Union, and the more modest port in the vicinity of Jiquilisco is what is depicted. This emphasis on Jiquilisco is surprising, because La Union on the Gulf of Fonseca should be the expected eastern port of preference because of its large size and deep waters. Furthermore, the Bay of Jiquilisco is slightly farther away than that of La Union. This geographic evidence points towards a preference for an out-of-the-way place favorable to navigation.

By the eighteenth century, San Miguel witnessed dense peasant settlement and schemes of state expansion, becoming one of the 13 provinces subject to the Spanish *capitán general* of Guatemala, in the same category as Nicaragua, Costa

Rica, Honduras, and Guatemala (Bancroft 1886; Lauria-Santiago 1999: 19). This designation seems disproportionate. Why did tiny San Miguel merit such recognition? Between 1750 and 1850, Quelepa remained as a place name listed as part of the Partido de la Ciudad de Gracias a Dios, while San Miguel was part of its own partido that included 20 other places. The partido of San Salvador, in contrast, had 45 places (AGCA Sig. A3, Leg. 2885, Exp. 42102, in Sellers-García 2007: 354–5).

By the time eastern El Salvador, and particularly San Miguel, became part of a colonial enterprise, it was anything but peripheral. Navigation routes of this period in much of the jurisdiction of Guatemala had, in comparison, seen little improvement, and "travel along them was still difficult and their effective navigation still depended largely on Indians" (Sellers-García 2007: 81). By 1753, San Miguel, along with Tegucigalpa and Granada, was approved to receive monthly mail deliveries and was at the intersection of the latter two routes (ibid.: 141, fig. 4.1). The amount of mail going to San Miguel in 1768 was comparable to that for Esquipulas and Oaxaca, but only half as much as that for Sonsonate and just one-quarter that of San Salvador (ibid.: fig. 4.3). The map of routes traveled by the Archbishop Cortés y Larraz in 1770 through the diocese of Guatemala corresponds surprisingly well to the paths of interaction for the Terminal Classic. One path through central El Salvador eventually led to Los Esclavos and the capital city, and the other led nearly due north to central Honduras (ibid.: fig. 3.1). At the same time, Cortés y Larraz (1958 [1770]) reported that many of the indigenous communities throughout eastern El Salvador had disappeared completely – that is, these routes traversed "depopulated" lands.

By the mid- to late nineteenth century, the fair in San Miguel attracted more trade than the rest of the entire region (including western El Salvador; Lauria-Santiago 1999: 121,124). San Miguel and its port at La Union were depicted as "less unwholesome" than the Atlantic side (Chambers and Chambers 1896: 126). This evaluation lent a moral prerogative to legitimate British engagement in the region. The two priorities for railroad construction were first from Acajutla to Santa Ana, Ateos, and Santa Tecla and second from San Miguel to San Salvador (ibid.). By 1824, the newly independent governmental administration prioritized mail delivery to "important cities" that lay to the southeast rather than to the north of Guatemala City (Sellers-García 2007: 214). Thus, the nineteenth-century sequence for flow of commerce echoes the depictions of the Hack maps – San Salvador was disconnected from maritime trade, and a high priority was the resolution of this problem. That communication to the capital had to happen through western and eastern conduits created the opportunity for creative uses of state resources.

By the mid-nineteenth century, Ephraim G. Squier (1858: 319) noted that, in eastern El Salvador, "the native languages [had] fallen into disuse." Indigo production zones and other haciendas in the San Miguel region were noted for being "larger" and "more extensive" than those near San Salvador (Browning 1971: 84). By the 1820s, the concept of space and distance shifted to "new Central American states as bounded spaces. With the determination of boundaries came an understanding of demarcated space beyond that occupied by important roads and towns" (Sellers-García 2007: 320). The tools of colonialism – roguish experimentation beyond direct oversight – achieved their ends by symbolically and effectively wiping the slate clean of native citizens and forging an economic network that supported commodity expansion.

I suggest here that the flourishing of San Miguel in the colonial period was precisely because of its roguish heritage. It presented a landscape of opportunity and was not the result of careful state planning. The pattern of eastern El Salvador being foremost in some ways – in hosting markets and building railroads – yet at the edges of political control continued well into the nineteenth century and, one could argue, even until the present day.

This case study of frontiers and boundaries highlights that they are not merely places to pass through on the way to something better (Linares 1979: 21). If "spatial history is integral to the history of knowledge production" (Sellers-García 2007: 314), then the shift from border to frontier recounts the changing priorities in knowledge. By "living remotely either by design or by habit, Guatemalans managed to avoid both secular and ecclesiastical authorities … In Cortes y Larraz's text, 'distante' is used to describe a particular kind of remoteness: dangerous distance" (ibid.: 317). This dangerous place presented the possibility of moral and cultural corruption as well as the potential for fundamentally altering state policies. Such potential was cherished; "perhaps the center held its peripheries more closely when they remained somewhat distant, somewhat unknown" (ibid.: 337). Frontiers and boundary regions have a dynamic of their own yet are very much connected to the metropole. They are essential places for the genesis of actions and processes – such as rogue colonialism – that both precolumbian civilizations and colonial states could not do without (Gitlin 1992).

References

Amador, Fabio E. (2007) *Atlas arqueológico de la región de oriente de El Salvador.* Report to the Foundation for the Advancement of Mesoamerican Studies. Available at www.famsi.org/reports/07070es/index.html.

Andagoya, Pascual de (1865) *Narrative of the Proceedings of Pedrarias Davila in the Provinces of Tierra Firme or Castilla del Oro and of the Discovery of the South Sea and the Coasts of Peru and Nicaragua*, trans. Clements R. Markham. London: Hakluyt Society.

Andrews, E. Wyllys V (1976) *The Archaeology of Quelepa, El Salvador.* New Orleans: Middle American Research Institute, Tulane University.

—— (1977) The Southeast Periphery of Mesoamerica: A View from El Salvador. In *Social Process in Maya Prehistory: Studies in Honour of Sir Eric Thompson*, ed. Norman Hammond, pp. 113–34. New York: Academic Press.

Ashmore, Wendy (1987) Cobble Crossroads: Gualjoquito Architecture and External Elite Ties. In *Interaction on the Southeast Mesoamerican Frontier*, ed. Eugenia Robinson, pp. 28–48. Oxford: British Archaeological Reports.

—— (1991) Site Planning Principles and Concepts of Directionality among the Ancient Maya. *Latin American Antiquity* 2: 199–226.

Bachand, Bruce Robert (2006) *Preclassic Excavations at Punta de Chimino, Petén, Guatemala: Investigating Social Emplacement on an Early Maya Landscape*. PhD dissertation, Department of Anthropology, University of Arizona. Ann Arbor, MI: University Microfilms.

Bancroft, Hubert Howe (1886) *The Works of Hubert Howe Bancroft*, Vol. XII: *History of Mexico*, Vol. IV, *1804–1824*. San Francisco: The History Company.

Barth, Fredrick (1969) *Ethnic Groups and Boundaries: The Social Organization of Culture Difference*. Oslo: Universitetsforlaget.

—— (1994) Enduring and Emerging Issues in the Analysis of Ethnicity. In *The Anthropology of Ethnicity: Beyond "Ethnic Groups and Boundaries"*, ed. Hans Vermeulen and Cora Grovers, pp. 11–32. Amsterdam: Het Spinhuis.

—— (1998) *Ethnic Groups and Boundaries: The Social Organization of Culture Difference*. Long Grove, IL: Waveland Press.

Baudez, Claude F., and Pierre Becquelin (1973) *Archéologie de Los Naranjos, Honduras*. Paris: Mission Archéologique et Ethnologique française au Mexique.

Braswell, Geoffrey E. (2003) Obsidian Exchange Spheres. In *The Postclassic Mesoamerican World*, ed. Michael E. Smith and Francis F. Berdan, pp. 131–58. Salt Lake City: University of Utah Press.

Braswell, Geoffrey E., E. Wyllys Andrews V, and Michael D. Glascock (1994) The Obsidian Artifacts of Quelepa, El Salvador. *Ancient Mesoamerica* 5: 173–92.

Braswell, Geoffrey E., Silvia Salgado, Laraine A. Fletcher, and Michael D. Glascock (2002) La antigua Nicaragua: la periferia sudeste de Mesomérica y la región maya: interacción interregional (1–1522 d.C.). *Mayab* 15: 19–40.

Browning, D. (1971) *El Salvador: Landscape and Society*. Oxford: Clarendon Press.

Card, Jeb J. (2007) *The Ceramics of Colonial Ciudad Vieja, El Salvador: Culture Contact and Social Change in Mesoamerica*. PhD dissertation, Department of Anthropology, Tulane University. Ann Arbor, MI: University Microfilms.

Carmack, Robert M., and Silvia Salgado González (2006) A World-Systems Perspective on the Archaeology and Ethnohistory of the Mesoamerican/Lower Central American Border. *Ancient Mesoamerica* 17: 219–29.

Chamberlain, Robert S. (1947) The Early Years of San Miguel de la Frontera. *Hispanic American Historical Review* 27: 623–46.

Chambers, William, and Robert Chambers (1896) *Chambers's Encyclopedia: A Dictionary of Universal Knowledge*, new ed., Vol. 9. London: Chambers.

Ciudad Real, Antonio de (1873) *Relación breve y verdadera de algunas cosas de las muchas que sucedieron al Padre Fray Alonso Ponce en las provincias de la Nueva España, siendo comisario general de aquellas partes* …, 2 vols. Madrid: Imprenta de la Viuda de Calero.

Cobos, Rafael (1994) *Síntesis de la arqueología de El Salvador (1850–1991)*. San Salvador: Consejo Nacional para la Cultura y el Arte.

Cooper, Frederick, and Ann Laura Stoler (1997) Between Metropole and Colony: Rethinking a Research Agenda. In *Tensions of Empire: Colonial Cultures in a Bourgeois World*, ed. Frederick Cooper and Ann Laura Stoler, pp. 1–56. Berkeley: University of California Press.

Cortés y Larraz, Pedro (1958 [1770]) *Descripción geográfico-moral de la dioceses de Goathemala*, 2 vols. Guatemala: Sociedad de Geografía e Historia de Guatemala.

Creamer, Winifred (1987) Mesoamerica as a Concept: An Archaeological View from Central America. *Latin American Research Review* 22: 35–62.

Dawdy, Shannon Lee (2008) *Building the Devil's Empire: French Colonial New Orleans*. Chicago: University of Chicago Press.

Demarest, Arthur A. (1986) *The Archaeology of Santa Leticia and the Rise of Maya Civilization*. New Orleans: Middle American Research Institute, Tulane University.

Demarest, Arthur A., and Robert J. Sharer (1982) The Origins and Evolution of Ususlutan Ceramics. *American Antiquity* 47: 810–22.
Denevan, William M. (1992) The Pristine Myth: The Landscapes of the Americas in 1492. *Annals of the Association of American Geographers* 82: 369–85.
Dixon, Boyd (1989) A Preliminary Settlement Pattern Study of a Prehistoric Cultural Corridor: The Comayagua Valley, Honduras. *Journal of Field Archaeology* 16: 257–71.
Dull, Robert A., John R. Southon, and Payson D. Sheets (2001) Volcanism, Ecology and Culture: A Reassessment of the Volcan Ilopango Tbj Eruption in the Southern Maya Realm. *Latin American Antiquity* 12: 25–44.
Earnest, Howard H. (1999) *A Reappraisal of the Ilopango Volcanic Eruption in Central El Salvador*. PhD dissertation, Department of Anthropology, Harvard University. Ann Arbor: University Microfilms.
Elton, Hugh (1996) *Frontiers of the Roman Empire*. Bloomington: Indiana University Press.
Escalante Arce, Pedro Antonio (1992) *Códice Sonsonate: Crónicas hispánicas*, 2 vols. San Salvador: Consejo Nacional para la Cultura y el Arte.
Fowler, William R., Jr. (1987) Cacao, Indigo, and Coffee: Cash Crops in the History of El Salvador. In *Research in Economic Anthropology* 8: 139–67.
—— (1989) *The Cultural Evolution of Ancient Nahua Civilizations: The Pipil-Nicarao of Central America*. Norman: University of Oklahoma Press.
Fowler, William R., Jr., and Howard H. Earnest, Jr. (1985) Settlement Patterns and Prehistory of the Paraiso Basin of El Salvador. *Journal of Field Archaeology* 12: 19–32.
Fox, John (1981) The Late Postclassic Eastern Frontier of Mesoamerica: Cultural Innovation along the Periphery. *Current Anthropology* 22: 321–46.
—— (1996) Playing with Power: Ballcourts and Political Ritual in Southern Mesoamerica. *Current Anthropology* 37: 483–509.
Gitlin, Jay (1992) On the Boundaries of Empire: Connecting the West to Its Imperial Past. In *Under an Open Sky: Rethinking America's Western Past*, ed. William Cronon and George A. Miles, pp. 71–89. New York: W. W. Norton.
Gómez, Esteban M. (2010) *Archaeology of the Colonial Period Gulf of Fonseca, Eastern El Salvador*. PhD dissertation, Department of Anthropology, University of California, Berkeley. Ann Arbor, MI: University Microfilms.
Goralski, Craig (2008) *An Examination of the Uapala-Usulután Ceramic Sphere Using Instrumental Neutron Activation Analysis*. PhD dissertation, Department of Anthropology, Pennsylvania State University. Ann Arbor, MI: University Microfilms.
Green, S. W., and S. M. Perlman (eds) (1985) *The Archaeology of Frontiers and Boundaries*. Orlando, FL: Academic Press.
Grove, David (1989) Olmec: What's in a Name? In *Regional Perspectives on the Olmec*, ed. Robert J. Sharer and David C. Grove, pp. 8–16. Cambridge: Cambridge University Press.
Hack, William (n.d.) An Accurate Description of All the Harbours Rivers Ports Islands Sands Rocks and Dangers between the Mouth of California and the Straits of Lemaire in the South Sea of America .... Original in the collection of the John Carter Brown Library, Brown University, Providence, RI.
Hamilton, Conard C. (2009) *Intrasite Variation among Household Assemblages at Ciudad Vieja, El Salvador*. PhD dissertation, Department of Anthropology, Tulane University. Ann Arbor, MI: University Microfilms.
Helms, Mary (1975) *Middle America: A Culture History of Heartlands and Frontiers*. Englewood Cliffs, NJ: Prentice-Hall.
Hirth, Kenneth G., Gloria Lara Pinto, and George Hasemann (1981) *Segundo Informe Trimestral, Abril–Junio de 1981: Proyecto Arqueologico El Cajon*. Tegucigalpa: Instituto Hondureno de Antropologia e Historia/Empresa Nacional de Energia Electrica.

Hodder, Ian (1982) *Symbols in Action: Ethnoarchaeological Studies of Material Culture*. Cambridge: Cambridge University Press.

Joyce, Rosemary A. (1986) Terminal Classic Interaction on the Southeastern Maya Periphery. *American Antiquity* 51: 313–29.

—— (1996) Social Dynamics of Exchange: Changing Patterns in the Honduran Archaeological Record. In *Caciques, Intercambio y poder: Interacción regional en el area intermedia de las Américas*, ed. C. H. Langebaek and F. Cárdenes-Arroyo, pp. 31– 45. Bogota: Universidad de los Andes.

Joyce, Rosemary A., and Julia A. Hendon (2000) Heterarchy, History, and Material Reality: "Communities" in Late Classic Honduras. In *The Archaeology of Communities: A New World Perspective*, ed. Marcello-Andrea Canuto and Jason Yaeger, pp. 143–59. London: Routledge.

Juarros, Domingo (1857) *Compendio de la historia de la ciudad de Guatemala*, Vol. 1. Guatemala: Imprenta de Luna.

Killion, Thomas W., and Javier Urcid (2001) The Olmec Legacy: Cultural Continuity and Change in Mexico's Southern Gulf Coast Lowlands. *Journal of Field Archaeology* 28: 3–25.

Kopytoff, Igor (1999) The Internal African Frontier: Cultural Conservatism and Ethnic Innovation. In *Frontiers and Borderlands: Anthropological Perspectives*, ed. M. Rosler and T. Wendl, pp. 31–44. Frankfurt: Peter Lang.

Kristof, L. K. D. (1970) The Nature of Frontiers and Boundaries. In *The Structure of Political Geography*, ed. R. E. Kasperson and J. V. Minghi, pp. 126–31. London: University of London Press.

Lange, Frederick W. (1976) The Northern Central American Buffer: A Current Perspective. *Latin American Research Review* 11: 177–83.

—— (1979) Theoretical and Descriptive Aspects of Frontier Studies. *Latin American Research Review* 14: 221–7.

Lauria-Santiago, Aldo A. (1999) *An Agrarian Republic: Commercial Agriculture and the Politics of Peasant Communities in El Salvador, 1823–1914*. Pittsburgh: University of Pittsburgh Press.

Lightfoot, Kent G., and Antoinette Martinez (1995) Frontiers and Boundaries in Archaeological Perspective. *Annual Review of Anthropology* 24: 471–92.

Linares, Olga (1979) What is Lower Central American Archaeology? *Annual Review of Anthropology* 8: 21–43.

Lothrop, Samuel K. (1927) The Museum Central American Expedition, 1925–1926. *Indian Notes* [Museum of the American Indian, Heye Foundation, New York] 4: 12–33.

Lowe, Gareth W. (1989) The Heartland Olmec: Evolution of Material Culture. In *Regional Perspectives on the Olmec*, ed. Robert J. Sharer and David C. Grove, pp. 33–67. Cambridge: Cambridge University Press.

McCafferty, Geoffrey (2008) Domestic Practice in Postclassic Santa Isabel, Nicaragua. *Latin American Antiquity* 19: 64–82.

McCafferty, Geoffrey, and Silvia Salgado González (2009) Cuando llegaron los mexicanos? La transición entre los períodos Bagaces y Sapoa en Granada, Nicaragua. Paper presented at the Third Congress of Central American Archaeology, San Salvador.

McCarthy, Mike (2008) Boundaries and the Archaeology of Frontier Zones. In *Handbook of Landscape Archaeology*, ed. Bruno David and Julian Thomas, pp. 202–09. Walnut Creek, CA: Left Coast Press.

McFarlane, William John (2005) *Power Strategies in a Changing World: Archaeological Investigations of Early Postclassic Remains at El Coyote, Santa Barbara, Honduras*. PhD dissertation, Department of Anthropology, State University of New York, Buffalo. Ann Arbor, MI: University Microfilms.

McKee, Brian R. (2007) *Volcanism, Household Archaeology, and Formation Processes in the Zapotitan Valley, El Salvador*. PhD dissertation, Department of Anthropology, University of Colorado. Ann Arbor: University Microfilms.

Messenger, Lewis C. (1984) *Excavations at Guarabuqui, El Cajon, Honduras: Frontiers, Culture Areas, and the Southern Mesoamerican Periphery*. PhD dissertation, Department of Anthropology, University of Minnesota. Ann Arbor, MI: University Microfilms.

Nassaney, Michael S. (2008) Identity Formation at a French Colonial Outpost in the North American Interior. *International Journal of Historical Archaeology* 12: 297–318.

Nicholson, H. B. (1961) Review of *Amerikaische Miszellen: Festband Franz Termer in Freundschaft und Verehrung gewidmet von Freunden, Kollagen und Schulern zur Vollendung des 65. Lebensjahres*, by Wilhelm Bierhenke, Wolfgang Haberland, Ulla Johansen, and Gunter Zimmermann. *American Anthropologist* 63: 1109–12.

Ornat Clemente, Raquel (2007) La evolución cultural del poblamiento (eje ciudad Colón-Tabarcia) del Valle Central de Costa Rica. PhD dissertation, Department of Sciences of Antiquity, University of Zaragoza.

Parker, Bradley J. (2006) Toward an Understanding of Borderland Processes. *American Antiquity* 71: 77–100.

Parsons, Lee A. (1969) *Bilbao, Guatemala*, Vol. 2. Milwaukee: Milwaukee Public Museum.

Peccorini, Atilio (1913) Algunos datos sobre arqueologia de la Republica del Salvador. *Journal de 1a Societé des Americanistes de Paris* 10: 173–80.

—— (1926) Ruinas de Quelepa. *Revista de Etnología, Arqueología y Lingüistica* [San Salvador] 1: 249–50.

Robinson, Eugenia (1988) Ceramic Spheres of the Southwest Mesoamerican Frontier. *Cerámica de la cultura maya* 13: 10–24.

Sahlins, Marshall (1985) *Islands of History*. Chicago: University of Chicago Press.

Sampeck, Kathryn (2007) *Late Postclassic to Colonial Landscapes and Political Economy of the Izalcos Region, El Salvador*. PhD dissertation, Department of Anthropology, Tulane University. Ann Arbor: University Microfilms.

Schortman, Edward M., and Patricia A. Urban (1991) Patterns of Late Preclassic Interaction and the Foundation of Complex Society in the Southeast Maya Periphery. In *The Formation of Complex Society in Southeastern Mesoamerica*, ed. William Fowler, pp. 121–40. Boca Raton, FL: CRC Press.

—— (1994) Living on the Edge. *Current Anthropology* 35: 401–31.

Schortman, Edward, Patricia Urban, Wendy Ashmore, and Julie Benyo (1986) Interregional Interaction in the SE Maya Periphery: The Santa Barbara Archaeological Project 1983–1984 Seasons. *Journal of Field Archaeology* 13: 259–72.

Schortman, Edward, Patricia Urban, and Marne Ausec (2001) Politics with Style: Identity Formation in Prehispanic Southeastern Mesoamerica. *American Anthropologist* 103: 312–30.

Sellers-García, Sylvia Marina (2007) *Distant Guatemala: Reading Documents from the Periphery*. PhD dissertation, Department of History, University of California, Berkeley. Ann Arbor, MI: University Microfilms.

Sharer, Robert J. (1974) The Prehistory of the Southeastern Maya Periphery. *Current Anthropology* 15: 165–87.

—— (1984) Lower Central America as Seen from Mesoamerica. In *The Archaeology of Lower Central America*, ed. Frederick W. Lange and Doris Z. Stone, pp. 63–84. Albuquerque: University of New Mexico Press.

Sheets, Payson (ed.) (1983) *Archeology and Volcanism in Central America: The Zapotitán Valley of El Salvador*. Austin: University of Texas Press.

—— (1992) *The Ceren Site: A Prehistoric Village Buried by Volcanic Ash in Central America*. Fort Worth, TX: Harcourt, Brace, Jovanovich.

Smith, Carol A. (1976) Exchange Systems and the Spatial Distribution of Elites: The Organization of Stratification in Agrarian Societies. In *Regional Analysis*, Vol. II: *Social Systems*, ed. Carol A. Smith, pp. 309–74. New York: Academic Press.

Spinden, Herbert J. (1915) Notes on the Archaeology of Salvador. *American Anthropologist* 17: 446–87.

Squier, Ephraim G. (1858) The states of Central America; their geography, topography, climate, population, resources, productions, commerce, political organization, aborigines, etc., comprising chapters on Honduras, San Salvador, Nicaragua, Costa Rica, Guatemala, Belize, the Bay Islands, the Mosquito Shore, and the Honduras inter-oceanic railway. New York, Harper & Brothers.

Staski, Edward (1998) Change and Inertia on the Frontier: Archaeology at the Paraje de San Diego, Camino Real, in Southern New Mexico. *International Journal of Historical Archaeology* 2: 21–44.

Stone, Doris Z. (1959) The Eastern Frontier of Mesoamerica. *Mitteilungen* [Museum für Volkerkunde, Hamburg] no. 15, pp. 118–21.

Turner, Frederick Jackson (1932) *The Significance of Sections in American History*. New York: Henry Holt.

Urban, Patricia (1993) Naco Valley. In *Pottery of Prehistoric Honduras: Regional Classification and Analysis*, ed. John Henderson and Marilyn Beaudry-Corbett, pp. 30–63. Los Angeles: Institute of Archaeology, University of California.

van Dommelen, Peter (1997) Colonial Constructs: Colonialism and Archaeology in the Mediterranean. *World Archaeology* 28: 305–23.

—— (1998) *On Colonial Grounds: A Comparative Study of Colonialism and Rural Settlement in First Millennium B.C. West Central Sardinia*. Leiden: Faculty of Archaeology, University of Leiden.

Van Oss, Adrian C. (1986) *Catholic Colonialism: A Parish History of Guatemala, 1524–1821*. Cambridge: Cambridge University Press.

White, Richard (1991) *The Middle Ground: Indians, Empires and Republics in the Great Lakes Region, 1650–1815*. Cambridge: Cambridge University Press.

Whittington, Michael (2001) *The Sport of Life and Death: The Mesoamerican Ballgame*. London: Thames & Hudson.

Wolf, Eric (1955) Types of Latin American Peasantry: A Preliminary Discussion. *American Anthropologist* 57: 452–72.

Wonderley, Anthony (1991) The Late Preclassic Sula Plain, Honduras: Regional Antecedents to Social Complexity and Interregional Convergence in Ceramic Style. In *The Formation of Complex Society in Southeastern Mesoamerica*, ed. William Fowler, pp. 141–70. Boca Raton, FL: CRC Press.

Wylie, Alison (1993) Invented Lands/Discovered Pasts: The Westward Expansion of Myth and History. *Historical Archaeology* 27(4):1–19.

4

SHIFTING FORTUNES AND AFFILIATIONS ON THE EDGE OF RUIN

A ceramic perspective on the Classic Maya collapse and its aftermath at Copan

Cassandra R. Bill

The significance of the physical and cultural position of Copan on the southeast frontier of the Maya area has long been recognized and is reflected in the pottery of the site, which represents an eclectic mix of different regional styles and local conventions. Subtle and salient shifts within this ceramic mosaic provide a window through which to view developments in the history of Copan, including the nature of relationships between the site and other regions. Finally, the pottery of Copan reveals much about the timing and nature of the "collapse" in the early ninth century, the subsequent abandonment of the site, and repopulation during the Early Postclassic period.

What is commonly referred to as the "collapse" of Maya civilization remains a subject of much interest and some controversy among Maya scholars. We know that, sometime between AD 750 and 900, most centers throughout the southern and central lowlands of Guatemala, Belize, and southeastern Mexico (see Figure 1.1) stopped erecting monuments with hieroglyphic inscriptions, major construction programs at many sites ceased, population numbers declined, and, within a relatively short period of time, many major centers of Classic-period civilization were effectively abandoned. Despite the superficial homogeneity of this overarching theme, local details – including the timing and severity of disruptions – associated with the collapse period in the Maya lowlands varied considerably, raising issues concerning what precisely the collapse entailed, who was affected by it, and why a few centers were able to weather this storm and continue virtually uninterrupted into the succeeding Early Postclassic period.

Questions regarding the Classic Maya collapse at Copan, which are not without their own controversy (e.g., Braswell 1992; Braswell *et al.* 1996; Braswell and Manahan 2001; Fash *et al.* 2005; Webster and Freter 1990a, 1990b; Webster *et al.* 1993, 2005), can be and have been viewed from a number of different perspectives (sociopolitical, demographic, and environmental) and have been approached using a variety of data sets (archaeological, chronometric, and epigraphic). Adopting yet one more perspective and approach, I review the ceramic data pertaining to the collapse of Copan and consider what notable shifts in certain aspects of the ceramic inventory (and thus industry) suggest about changes in economic conditions and external affiliations during the period surrounding the collapse of the Classic sociopolitical order. I also examine what ceramics tell us about post-collapse occupation at Copan.

Late and Terminal Classic ceramics of Copan

Early Coner subphase (AD 650–750)

To provide a comparative backdrop for developments occurring at the end of the dynastic period – that is, in the period leading up to and including the collapse – it is informative to look at the nature of the ceramic assemblage associated with earlier, healthier times, beginning with the early Late Classic period. By all accounts, this was a dynamic period in the history of Copan: a time of both consolidation and territorial expansion, associated primarily with the reigns of the twelfth and thirteenth rulers ("Smoke-Imix-God K," or "Smoke Jaguar," who reigned from 628 to 695, and Uaxaklajun Ub'aj K'awiil, or "18 Rabbit," who subsequently ruled Copan until 738, when he was captured and killed by the king of Quirigua), and a period that corresponds roughly to the Early Coner ceramic subphase (AD 650–750).

The vibrancy of the Copan polity during the Early Coner subphase is mirrored in the vitality of the pottery-making industry at this time, which marks the peak of ceramic diversity at Copan. The most vigorous developments during this period occurred within the fine-ware industry.[1] Among innovations was the introduction of numerous new decorative treatments and forms within two ongoing fine-ware traditions: the cream paste tradition (Figure 4.1) and the polished black/brown tradition (Figure 4.2). The first of these demonstrates close links between Copan and western El Salvador, while the second evinces ties with the Maya highlands and lowlands.

The development of a widely varied inventory of fine-ware products during Early Coner times may be seen as a response within the ceramic industry to rapidly expanding demand for such goods. There is evidence for the increasing differentiation of a subroyal elite at Copan (Fash 1991: 112, 114) during the reigns of the twelfth and thirteenth rulers. The construction during the Late Classic period of more and larger elite residential compounds outside of the Main Group, including a number in outlying areas of the Copan Valley (Fash 1986: 84), further indicates a rural elite population growing in wealth and status.

Chemical compositional analyses of fine-ware pastes indicate the use of different clays and tempers in the manufacture of different varieties of decorated vessels (Bishop and Beaudry 1994). This suggests not only that a greater assortment of fine wares were produced during this period but also that an increasing number of production units or potters were involved in this enterprise. The most elaborately

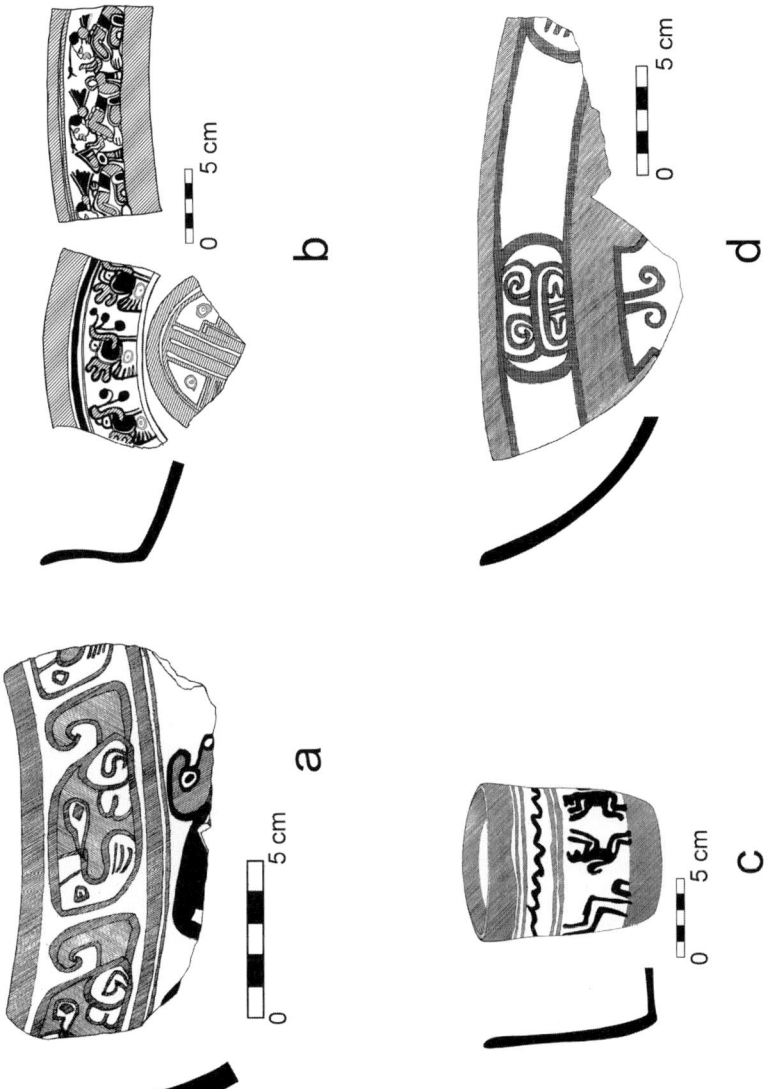

FIGURE 4.1 Late Classic cream paste tradition polychromes: (a–b) Copador Polychrome; (c–d) Gualpopa Polychrome

FIGURE 4.2 Decorated types of the Late Classic polished black/brown tradition Surlo Group: (a) Ardilla Incised-and-Excised; (b) Madrugada Modeled/Carved; (c) Madrugada Modeled/Carved vessel with stucco coating; (d) Besal Incised: Leonardo Variety

decorated vessels of the Early Coner subphase belong to the polished black/brown tradition and are unique specimens with intricately carved or incised Maya hieroglyphs and figures (Figure 4.2b–d; see Viel 1993: figs 101–2 and 104–6, and Schele and Miller 1986: plate 44, for more illustrative examples of complete vessels) that represent the finest achievements in ceramic art and technology at Copan. Contextually analogous to the finely executed figural polychromes of the lowlands, such vessels must have been produced by highly skilled artisans, who may have been commissioned by or attached to the royal court or other elite households.

Late Coner subphase (AD 750–820)

In comparison to the ascent of the polity during the Early Coner subphase, the Late Coner ceramic subphase dates to the period surrounding the decline and collapse of Copan during the reign of the final king, Yax Pasaj Chan Yopaat (who ruled from 763 to no later than 820). Two of the most notable developments within the ceramic inventory of this period are marked decreases in both the frequency and the diversity of fine wares, suggesting that fine-ware production in general fell off during the late dynastic period.

The decrease in fine wares during this time is primarily a function of the marked reduction in the production of polychrome vessels (which comprised 40 percent of the Early Coner assemblage but just 10 percent of that of the Late Coner subphase). At the same time, although certain technological modes (including pastes and polished surfaces) characteristic of the Maya polished black/brown tradition continued, decorative treatments associated with Late Coner variants are much less elaborate, and vessels with plain surfaces (Figure 4.3) or much simpler incising (Figure 4.4) replaced the more intricately carved and incised wares decorated with hieroglyphs or human figures that were produced at the beginning of the Late Classic period. All this suggests a decline in the support of highly skilled ceramic artisans.

Similar trends involving a decline in and simplification of fine wares characterize the ceramic assemblages of many other Maya sites at the end of the Late Classic period, as do an increasing regionalization of ceramic complexes and shifting ceramic sphere affiliations (Rice and Forsyth 2005; Rice 1986; Ball 1993). These patterns were also in evidence at Copan during the Late Coner subphase.

FIGURE 4.3 Plain types of the Late Classic polished black/brown tradition Surlo Group: (a) Surlo Orange-Brown: Simple Variety; (b) Surlo Orange-Brown: Blanco Variety

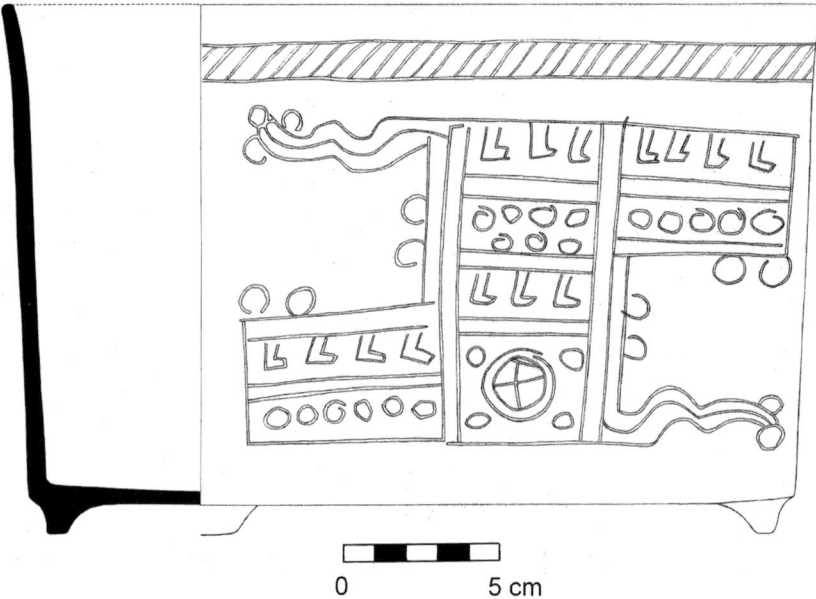

FIGURE 4.4 Late and Terminal Coner Sesesmil Incised: Sesesmil Variety of the polished black/brown tradition Surlo Group

Throughout much of the Classic period, various aspects of the material culture of Copan reflected economic, cultural, and sociopolitical interactions with external regions. Some of these regions were inhabited by Maya, others by non-Maya people, among them western El Salvador and other areas in the southeast periphery, as well as both the Maya highlands and lowlands. At the end of the Late Classic period, such far-reaching connections became sharply attenuated.

Late Classic ceramic affiliations

Given its location in the southeast periphery of the Maya area, Copan always maintained distinctive and varied extra-regional affiliations. Beginning in the Preclassic and throughout the Classic period, various elements of the utilitarian assemblage at Copan exhibited clear links to utilitarian types found at non-Maya sites in Honduras. These elements include the use of certain decorative practices (such as incising and painting jar necks and bodies) and the creation of distinctive vessel forms (Figure 4.5). Other elements of the Copan domestic assemblage that are similarly part of local Honduran traditions are certain forms of *metates* (see Willey et al. 1994: 222–3, figs 164–7) and small ceramic objects referred to as "*candeleros*" (ibid.: 207, figs 152–61). These *candeleros*, which should not be confused with similarly named but different artifacts found at Teotihuacan, are present not only at Copan but also at sites in eastern Honduras. Relationships in the local styles of domestic goods that

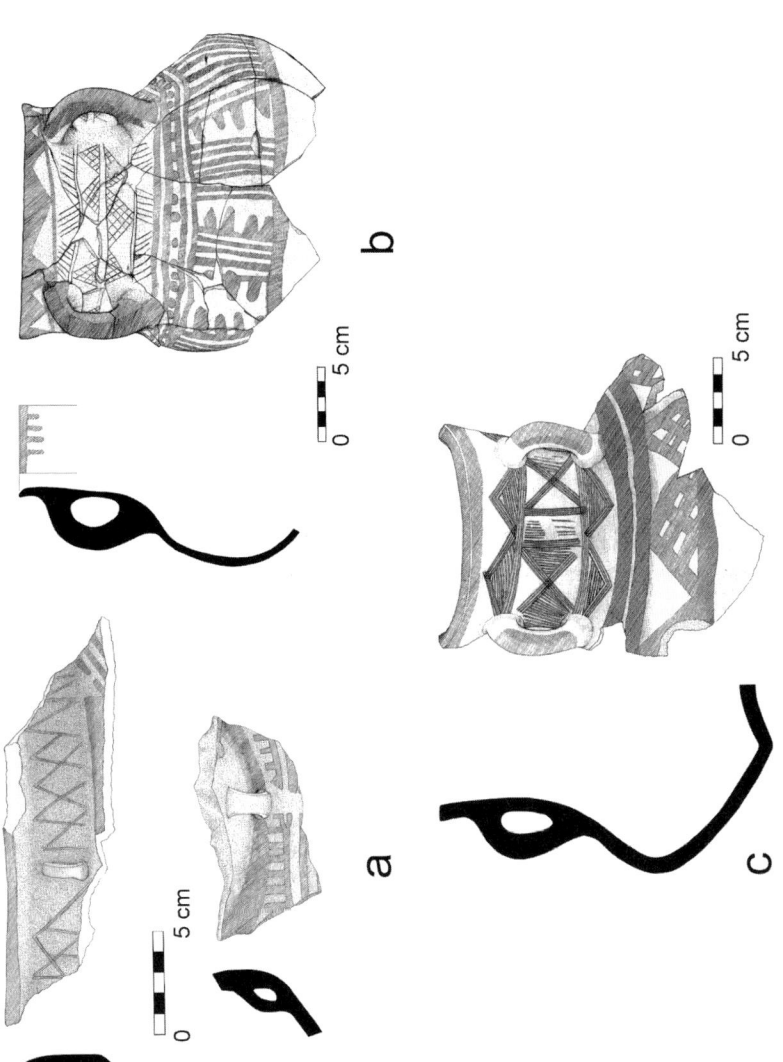

FIGURE 4.5 Honduran Jicatuyo supersystem jar types: (a) Acbi-phase Sopi Incised: Cocorico Variety; (b) Early Coner Juanita Incised; (c) Late and Terminal Coner Reina Incised

are held in common by Copan and other sites in Honduras represent utilitarian traditions shared with regions outside of the Classic Maya area. They also reflect a common cultural heritage and continuing community interaction that persisted despite the establishment of Maya rulers at Copan and the creation of elite connections between the Copan polity and the Maya region during the Classic period.

In contrast to these similarities in utilitarian goods, there appears to be little or no relationship between the fine wares manufactured at Copan after the beginning of the Late Classic period and those found at other sites in Honduras. Although there are regional similarities in some of the Early Classic fine wares (including local versions of red-painted Usulutan; Figure 4.6), Late Classic variants of the two major fine-ware traditions at Copan – the cream paste tradition (see Figure 4.1) and the polished black/brown tradition (see Figure 4.2) – were respectively and strictly shared with western El Salvador and the Maya area. Such vessels are not found, except as rare imports, in other regions of Honduras.[2]

In light of later developments, it is also noteworthy that, although fine wares imported from other parts of the southeastern periphery began to become more common in domestic assemblages at the beginning of the Coner phase, no such vessels are known to have been included in burial or other ritual assemblages during that time. In contrast, imported polychrome vessels from the Maya area have been found in at least one tomb dating to this period – the so-called Quetzal Vase (Longyear 1952: 41–2, figs 108a–b) from Tomb 2 in Group 10L-2 (see Figure 4.10), which came from the site of Altun Ha in Belize (Reents-Budet 1994: 201, 338–9, fig. 5.41).

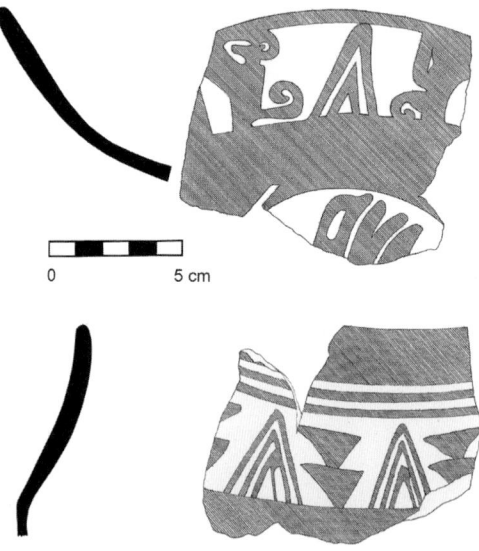

FIGURE 4.6 Chilanga Red-Painted Usulutan: Osicala Variety

FIGURE 4.7 Sevodeso Negative Incised

This pattern changed dramatically towards the end of the dynastic period. During the Late Coner subphase, production of cream paste polychrome pottery (see Figure 4.1) that had been shared with or traded to western El Salvador declined drastically (from comprising roughly 75 percent of the fine wares at the beginning of the Coner phase to approximately 25 percent at its end). The execution of Maya-style motifs and iconography on polished black/brown vessels also became less common, and new decorative treatments were introduced that involve motifs and other conventions – such as the application of a red slip (Figure 4.7) – that are seen on incised vessels from other parts of Honduras (e.g., Urban and Schortmann 1987: 376, fig. 20; Urban 1993b: 162)

During this period, the presence of vessels from the Maya lowlands also decreased substantially, while polychrome vessels produced in other parts of Honduras became much more common at Copan than at any previous time (Figure 4.8). Indeed, by the end of the dynastic period, virtually all of the imported fine wares at Copan can be classified as belonging to southeastern traditions, particularly the Ulua/Yojoa Polychrome System (Joyce 1993a, 1993b). This trend continued into the post-dynastic Terminal Coner subphase,

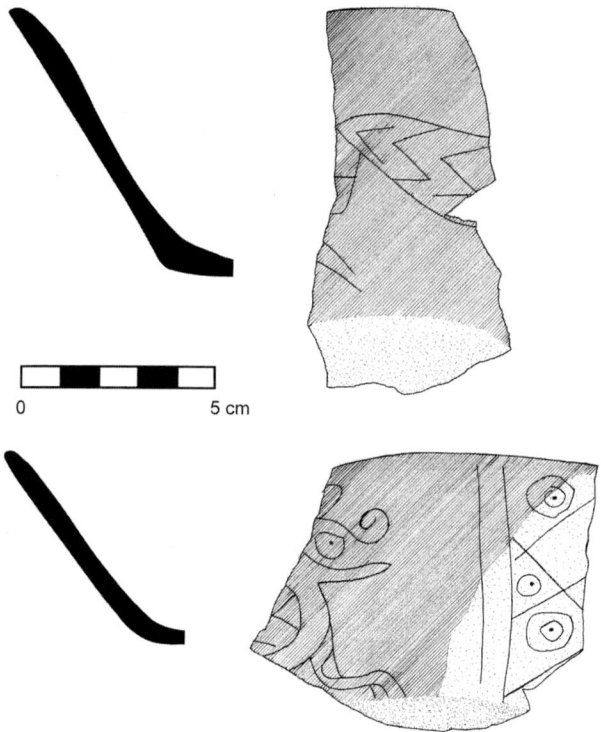

FIGURE 4.8 Late and Terminal Coner Sesesmil Incised: Facusse Variety of the polished black/brown tradition Surlo Group

at which time white-slipped dichrome and polychrome types of the southeast periphery also were introduced.

An important development during the Late Coner phase was the addition of southeastern fine wares (of the Ulua/Yojoa Polychrome System) as common and important parts of the ritual assemblage. Five of the six burials in Group 10L-2 that were associated with the final phase of construction of the royal residential compound of the last ruler contained such imported fine wares. This pattern forms a striking parallel, and equally striking contrast, to that associated with the period of the first Maya rulers of Copan during the Early Acbi subphase (AD 400–500). At that time, imported polychromes and other vessels from the Maya highlands and central lowlands were commonly placed in the richest tombs. During the Late Classic period, polychrome vessels from the Maya lowlands continued to be extremely restricted in their distribution and are rare to absent outside of the site core. In contrast, imported vessels belonging to the Honduran Ulua/Yojoa polychrome tradition are widely distributed across the Main Group and outlying residential compounds.

Certain components of the utilitarian assemblage similarly suggest a tightening of ties with western Honduras during this time.[3] As already noted, there are clear

FIGURE 4.9 Ulua/Yojoa polychromes

Classic-period similarities in form modes and decorative conventions that are shared between a number of utilitarian types at Copan and those of nearby non-Maya sites. The Late Coner variants of this regional tradition, however, exhibit particularly close parallels with other Honduran types in terms of style and the execution of decorative treatments (see, e.g., Figure 4.5c). Moreover, the same decorative techniques and motifs were incorporated into an existing, previously plain, red-slipped type belonging to another long-standing local utilitarian tradition at Copan (Figure 4.9a–b; see Bill 1997: 167–85, 188–95). One such incised jar was recovered with a polychrome jar belonging to the southeastern Ulua/Yojoa Polychrome tradition in a Late Coner burial in the royal residential complex (Figures 4.9c and 4.8c).

Thus, during the reign of the final ruler, ceramic ties between Copan and more distant Maya regions became attenuated while those with the immediate, non-Maya area became more pronounced. At the very least, the increased presence of imported Honduran polychromes at this time suggests the development or strengthening of trade relationships – and likely other forms of contact – with nearby regions that seem to have been largely excluded from the elite interaction sphere of Copan during the earlier part of the Late Classic period. The virtual replacement of previous fine-ware traditions (those shared with western El Salvador and the Maya lowlands), in both domestic *and* elite contexts, suggests an even more significant restructuring of the affiliations of Copan during the final decades of the dynastic period.

Later non-local fine wares introduced during the subsequent Terminal Coner subphase are strikingly similar to white-slipped dichromes and polychromes from the site of Quelepa in eastern El Salvador and, like the perhaps somewhat later "armadillo" vessels of the Delirio Red-on-White type (Andrews 1976: 114–16, figs 133–6; Longyear 1952: fig. 117d), may in fact have been derived from that site (Joyce 1986: 319). Thus, the Classic period occupation of Copan appears to have ended as its Preclassic roots began. The closest ceramic affiliations were with the same regions of western Honduras and eastern El Salvador that centuries earlier formed the Uapala sphere (defined by Andrews 1976: 180–81).

What happened after about AD 820 is a matter of some contention at Copan. The major focus of debate is whether there was a continuity of occupation and material culture into the Postclassic period (e.g., Webster *et al.* 2005), or whether the site and its environs were abandoned shortly after the sociopolitical collapse of the dynasty and reoccupied some time later by a different population (e.g., Fash *et al.* 2005).

Terminal Coner subphase (AD 820–850/900)

There are some indications that, following the collapse of the Copan dynasty in the early ninth century – indeed, following or attendant upon the destruction of parts of the royal residential compound (designated Group 10L-2; Figure 4.10) – there was a brief occupation or use of certain areas in that group as well as in other parts of the Copan Valley (Andrews and Bill 2005; Maca 2002). Among the contexts associated with this occupation in Group 10L-2 is trash deposited on the steps of

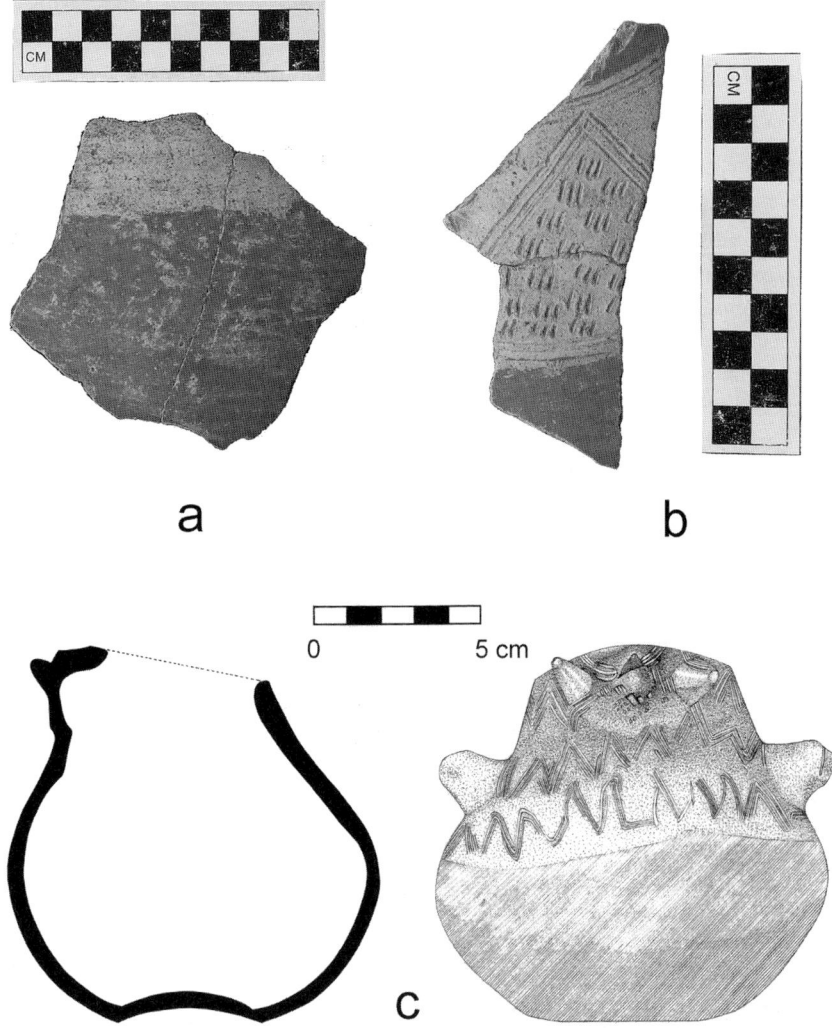

FIGURE 4.10 Raul Red Type: (a) Early Coner Sencillo Variety; (b) Late and Terminal Coner Masica (Incised) Variety; (c) Masica (Incised) Variety effigy vessel

the terrace leading into Courtyard A and on top of an altar that had been toppled from the summit of Structure (Str.) 30. Trash also accumulated on the patio and room floor of a small structure (Str. 33-S) adjacent to Yax Pasaj's residence (Str. 32).

The ceramic assemblage associated with this period of occupation, designated the Terminal Coner subphase (AD 820–850/900),[4] represents an inventory that was greatly reduced compared to that of the Late Classic. In particular, there was an even greater decline in fine wares than that seen during the Late Coner subphase. Ulua/Yojoa polychromes and southeastern white-slipped dichromes and polychromes are present, as is a very small amount of local cream paste polychrome pottery (just 3 percent of the total assemblage). The majority of fine wares associated with the Terminal Coner subphase, however, consist of simple polished brown vessels with plain or white-washed surfaces (see Figure 4.3).

The local utilitarian industry appears to have been less affected by the changing fortunes and affiliations of the ruling class at the end of the dynastic period (Bill 1997, 1998), but there were also marked differences associated with earlier and later facets of the Coner phase that represent ongoing changes within long-standing local technological traditions. In brief, the utilitarian assemblage of the Terminal Coner subphase is characterized by an overall decline in technological diversity. This includes a reduction in the number of form variants of different vessel classes, such as jars and bowls, as well as a more noticeable decline in paste variety and other technological features. This is associated with the virtual loss of one of the major utilitarian traditions at Copan.

Throughout the Classic period, the utilitarian pottery of Copan was dominated by vessels belonging to two long-standing technological traditions characterized primarily by distinctive pastes but also associated with specific kinds of surface treatments (see Bill 1997 for a more detailed description). Over time, particular form classes, such as jars, became largely restricted to each of these different traditions, a pattern suggesting the development of product specialization (Rice 1991; see also Arnold 1993: 93). That is, individual workshops or groups of potters specialized in the manufacture of a narrow range of utilitarian goods, a production strategy that increased efficiency and output.[5]

One of the most notable features of the Terminal Coner inventory is the virtual disappearance of one of these technological traditions that, by the Late Coner subphase, was employed almost exclusively in the production of *comales*, braziers, and censers. During the Terminal Coner subphase, vessels of these same classes continued to be produced but with the paste and surface treatment characteristics of the second and surviving tradition. Previously, this second tradition was used exclusively in the production of jars and large open bowls. This kind of decreasing technological diversity within product classes can be associated with one of two conditions. The first involves increasing specialization by individual production units within a ceramic industry, and is associated with a large demand market that is stable or growing. The second kind of situation in which a decrease in technological diversity within a ceramic inventory can occur is when there is a decline in the number of production units – or people producing pottery – in a region. Such a situation can logically result from an overall decline in population, resulting in both a dwindling market and fewer potters. I interpret the decrease in technological diversity evident in the Terminal Coner pottery of Copan as a reflection of this second situation. The limited technological diversity – as well as the greatly limited spatial distribution – of Terminal Coner ceramics in the Copan Valley indicates a greatly reduced occupation, suggesting a significant decline in population since the Late Coner phase. Thus, the end of the Late Coner subphase at about AD 820 witnessed not only the political fall of the Copan dynasty but also a major demographic collapse.

It is important to note, however, that, despite marked differences in the inventories of the Terminal Coner and earlier subphases (including the presence of a number of new types and varieties), 95 percent of the Terminal Coner ceramics represent a continuation of developmental trends within the same ongoing technological traditions and pre-existing (if shrinking) ceramic industries. For this reason, the Terminal Coner subphase is rightly considered to be Terminal Classic in nature, parallel to Tepeu 3 and other contemporary phases in the southern and

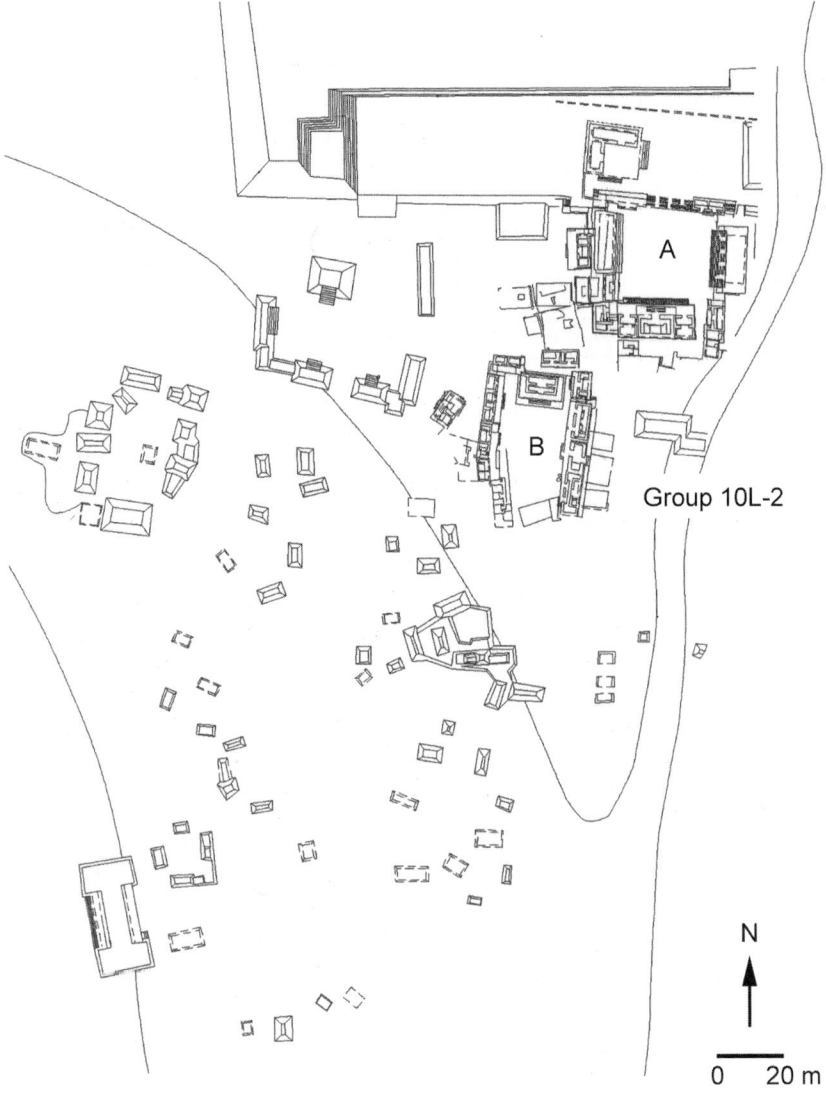

FIGURE 4.11 Group 10L-2: the royal residential compound of the final ruler of Copan, Yax Pasaj Chan Yopaat

98 Cassandra R. Bill

central Maya lowlands. Put another way, the Terminal Coner subphase implies that a small remnant population remained for some time – just how long is now the subject of discussion and is reflected in my uncertain date for the end of the subphase – in parts of the Copan Valley following the collapse of the dynasty and great demographic decline. This is in marked contrast to the subsequent Postclassic Ejar-phase ceramic inventory, which suggests a complete disjunction with earlier occupation.

Postclassic ceramics of Copan

Until recently, ceramic evidence for Postclassic activity at Copan consisted primarily of a few Plumbate vessels (Figure 4.11) and contemporary Early Postclassic types, including possible Las Vegas Polychromes (Figure 4.12). These were found in burials near the Acropolis. Because these Early Postclassic fine wares are rare and were known largely from ceremonial contexts, some have argued that the domestic types in use at Copan during the Early Postclassic period must have remained essentially those of the Late Classic Coner phase (e.g., Webster *et al.* 2005). Put another way, scholars who state that Copan did not collapse in the early ninth century imply that the Coner phase was many centuries long (*ca.* AD 650–1200+), albeit with certain fine wares added to (and others removed from) the ceramic inventory during the tenth and ensuing centuries.

Recent excavations by Kam Manahan (2000, 2002, 2003) of a small Early Postclassic group of houses located a few hundred meters south of the Acropolis

FIGURE 4.12 Tohil Plumbate

FIGURE 4.13 Las Vegas polychrome

(Figure 4.13) have now resulted in a full and well-defined ceramic assemblage for the Early Postclassic period, designated the Ejar phase (Viel 1993). Ejar-phase pottery – both utilitarian and fine wares – is dramatically different from that of the Late to Terminal Classic Coner phase (for a complete description of the Ejar-phase ceramic complex, see Bill *et al.* forthcoming; Manahan 2003: 140–209).

The Early Postclassic Ejar complex contains non-local fine wares (e.g., Plumbate) previously assigned to that phase and long recognized as marking activity at the site during this period (Longyear 1952; Viel 1993), as well as a number of other types clearly related to Postclassic pottery in other regions. These include Tamoa Red-on-Buff ladle censers (Figure 4.14) and hourglass censers with appliquéd fillets (Figure 4.15). In Manahan's excavations, these types were found directly associated – in burials and middens – with domestic wares (Figure 4.16) that are technologically and stylistically unrelated to earlier Coner-phase types. That is, there is little to nothing about Ejar-phase domestic wares that suggests the kinds of gradual developments in pre-existing ceramic industries and long-standing technological traditions that can be seen throughout the three Coner subphases or, indeed, spanning the closely related pottery

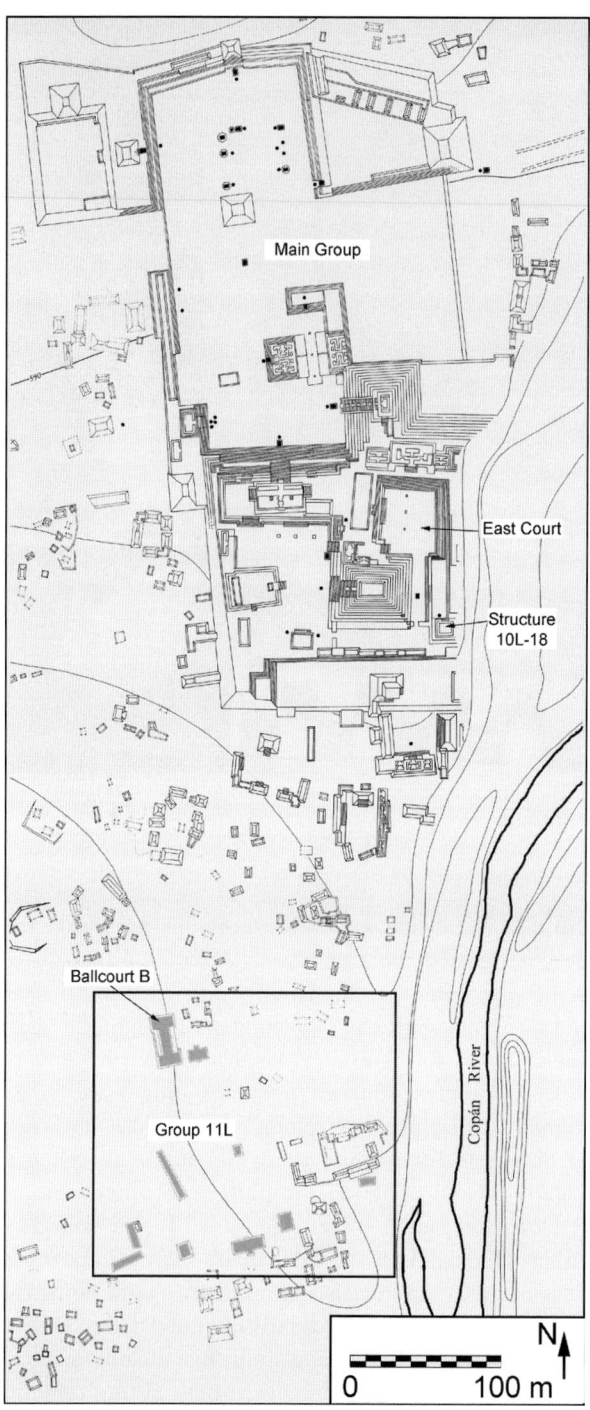

FIGURE 4.14 Map of Early Postclassic settlement in Group 11-L; shade indicates excavated structures

Ceramics and the Classic Maya collapse at Copan 101

FIGURE 4.15 Tamoa Red-on-Buff ladle censer

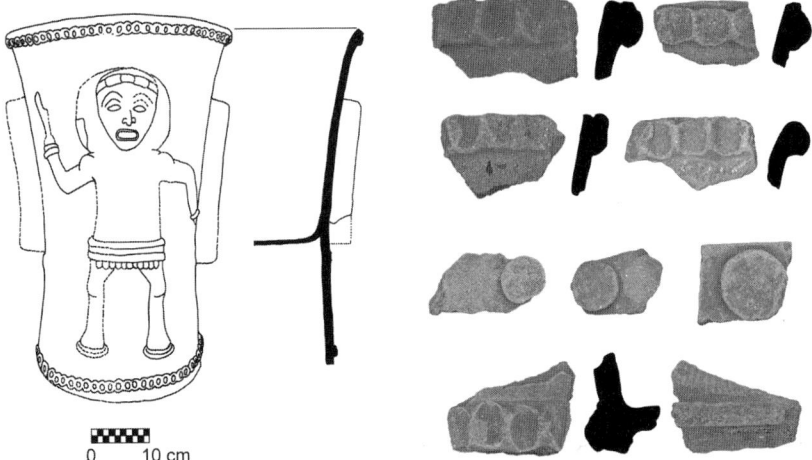

FIGURE 4.16 Hourglass-shaped censers with fillet appliqué rim (Sí Papa fillet rim type)

types of the Early Classic Acbi and Late Classic Coner phases at Copan, some of which derive from local or regional traditions that can be traced back to the Preclassic period.

Among many other differences with Coner-phase utilitarian pottery, the Ejar-phase domestic wares are much cruder and less technologically standardized than the earlier, well-made pottery of the Late Classic period. The pastes are typically extremely coarse, with large inclusions often protruding through the surface of vessel walls, and the finishing and even forming of vessels appears to have been relatively rudimentary. The features of Ejar-phase utilitarian vessels are often highly irregular, and wall thickness, rim form, and apparent rim diameter can vary considerably on a single vessel. The finishing of vessel surfaces was also typically cursory or incomplete, leaving evidence, in some cases, of the techniques used in construction. The unfinished exterior surfaces of *comales*, for example, suggest at least three different modes of manufacture, two of which involved the use of concentric coils or "shingled" slabs, the joins between which were barely blended, if at all. Other *comales* appear to have been made by pressing wet clay onto a surface covered with leaves, the impressions of which are still visible on the undersides of the vessels.

It is significant to note that Manahan (2003: 331–2) found these different techniques of *comal* construction, as well as different types of jars, to be associated with particular groups of structures. This patterned distribution in methods of manufacture and vessel form, along with the overall lack of standardization in the Ejar-phase domestic inventory, suggests a household-level mode of production (Peacock 1982: 8; Santley *et al.* 1989: 108; Santley and Kneebone 1993: 39). That is, small groups or families manufactured vessels for their own use, a striking contrast to the specialized production and valley-wide distribution systems that were associated with the pottery-making industry at Copan during the Classic period (see Bill 1997: 520–55).

Postclassic ceramic affiliations

Viewed as an entire assemblage, the Ejar-phase ceramic complex at Copan presents a picture of marked disparity between extremely crude local domestic wares and well-made imported fine wares. Specific comparisons of the Ejar-phase domestic wares with types established elsewhere are made difficult by the general lack of standardization in form and surface treatment that characterizes much of the utilitarian pottery at Copan during the Early Postclassic period. From a technological perspective, however, locally produced Ejar pottery represents an abrupt break with earlier Copan ceramic traditions in a manner analogous to that described for the Postclassic New Town complex of the Belize Valley (Sharer and Chase 1976: 288–9) and similar Postclassic complexes at other sites, such as Pusilha (Bill 2003), Cancuen (Bill *et al.* 2003), and sites in the Petexbatun region (Foias 1996), among others (Rice and Forsyth 2005).

As further discussed by Manahan (2003: 305–8, 344), the closest similarities to various features of the Ejar-phase settlement at Copan (including site layout, architectural forms, construction methods, and lithic technology) are found at sites in other regions of western and central Honduras and the eastern highlands of El Salvador. Close links between Copan and these regions during the Early Postclassic period are also indicated by certain aspects of the Ejar ceramic assemblage, such as distinctive forms of utilitarian jars that are also found in the central Santa Barbara region of Honduras (Urban 1993b: 164–5), together with the presence of imported Las Vegas Polychromes as well as seemingly related types that have a widespread distribution in Honduras during this time. Also part of the Ejar-phase inventory are decorated ladle censers that are virtually identical to those of the Tamoa Red-on-Buff type at Cihuatan, El Salvador (Fowler 1981: 206–13) and likely originated at that site (Manahan 2003: 181).

In addition to these strong connections with neighboring regions of the southeastern periphery, other external affiliations represented in the Ejar-phase artifact assemblage, among them imported vessels and obsidian from distant Mexican sources (see Manahan 2003: 328), indicate the inclusion of Copan in extensive trade and interaction networks during the Early Postclassic period.

Ladle censers, for example, have a widespread distribution during the Terminal Classic and Postclassic periods, occurring at sites in the highlands (Arnauld 1986: 426, fig. 188; Becquelin 2001: 139, 168, figs 56:2, 91:3; Ichon 1992: 196, fig. 112a–e; Wauchope 1948: 150, fig. 68a–k; Wauchope 1975: 198, 225, figs 138a–d, 168a–d) and lowlands (Adams 1971: 56–7, fig. 101d; Becquelin and Baudez 1979: fig. 203a,b; Sabloff 1975: 178–9, figs 337–40, 435e; Smith 1955: 102, figs 19c 5, 66b 2, 3; Smith and Gifford 1965: figs 12j, 14f; Smith 1971: fig. 62g–i) of the Maya area, as well as at sites in the southeast periphery (Baudez and Becquelin 1973: fig. 130i; Fowler 1981: 206–13). Among these are distinctive Mixtec-style censers, examples of which have also been recovered from other Postclassic contexts at Copan (Longyear 1952: fig. 102k; Viel 1993: fig. 107d).

Hourglass-shaped censers, similar to those with appliquéd fillet rims recovered by Manahan (2003: 172–5) from Ejar-phase contexts at Copan, also occur across a widespread area of southern Mesoamerica and have been found in Terminal Classic or Early Postclassic contexts at sites in the Maya lowlands (e.g., Chase 1985: 199; Becquelin and Baudez 1979: fig. 194c) and highlands (Wauchope 1948: 147, fig. 65; Wauchope 1975: 197, fig. 137e; Ichon 1992: 130, 198, figs 80, 113, 114), as well as in central El Salvador (Longyear 1966: 142, fig. I) and Los Naranjos, Honduras (Baudez and Becquelin 1973: figs 128l-o; 129 1-3, 5) in the southeast periphery.[6]

The most distinctive component of the Ejar-phase ceramic assemblage is Tohil Plumbate pottery (Neff 2003; Shepard 1948). Produced on the Pacific coast of southern Mesoamerica near the border of Mexico and Guatemala, Tohil Plumbate vessels are found throughout a large part of Mesoamerica, from the northern lowlands of the Yucatan peninsula (Smith and Gifford 1965: 527, fig. 12g–i) and the western Gulf Coast of Mexico (Ball 1985: 236) to the lowland Peten (Chase 1985: 194) and highland regions (Rands and Smith 1965: 135, 137, 139, fig. 18c–h; Brown 1985: 275) of Guatemala. Tohil Plumbate is also and famously known from Tula, Hidalgo, once erroneously suspected to be a source. It is striking that Las Vegas Polychromes are also known at Tula, suggesting overlapping trade networks. The circulation of Tohil Plumbate pottery extended well into lower Central America as well, occurring at sites in the Lake Yojoa region (Baudez and Becquelin 1973: 319), the central Santa Barbara region (Urban 1993b: 166), the southern Pacific region (Healy 1984: 152), and the Comayagua Valley (Baudez 1976: 141) of Honduras, as well as the Greater Nicoya region of Nicaragua (Lange 1984: 182).

Although extremely rare at Copan and other sites in Honduras, the Ejar-phase inventory also includes a small amount of Fine Orange pottery (see Chapter 11; Manahan 2003: 149–52; see also Viel 1993: 132, fig. 107a, b, e; Longyear 1952: fig. 102j), which is a distinctive marker of the end of the Terminal Classic period in the

Maya area and is particularly common in the western lowlands around the sites of Seibal and Altar de Sacrificios (Adams 1971; Rice and Forsyth 2005; Sabloff 1975).

The presence of widely shared censer types and decorative modes, as well as imported vessels from a variety of regions, in the Ejar-phase ceramic inventory is a significant contrast to the more insular or isolated nature of external affiliations represented by the ceramics dating to the end of the Classic-period Coner phase at Copan. Although the closest affiliations, and likely the most direct connections, were again with the local region of west-central Honduras and El Salvador (Manahan 2003: 344), the site of Copan – whatever the origins and linguistic identity of its Ejar-phase occupants may have been – was once more, for a brief time, part of a broader sphere of influence and interaction, and seemingly an active participant in the extensive commercial networks that characterized the Postclassic Mesoamerican world.

Summary and conclusions

Despite the fact that the *details* concerning changes in the ceramics at the end of the dynastic period may differ at Copan – as a function of the geographically remote location of the site on the southeast periphery – the *patterns* represented by these changes are the same as those seen in Terminal Classic inventories throughout the southern and central Maya lowlands (e.g., Rice and Forsyth 2005; Rice 1986). As at lowland sites, these patterns include a sharp decline in the production of fine wares – particularly of polychrome-painted pottery – as well as an increasingly regionalized ceramic complex reflecting a constriction of interaction spheres and more localized affiliations. Thus, although the collapse at Copan may have been earlier than at some other Maya sites, the impact of the demise of the Classic period sociopolitical order and demographic decline appears to have had similar effects on the local ceramic industry and inventory.

Terminal Coner pottery, contextually associated with what appears to have been a short, post-collapse occupation of the former royal residential complex (Andrews and Bill 2005) and a very few other groups in the valley (Maca 2002), is markedly different in many ways from earlier Late Classic assemblages, even those associated with the end of Yax Pasaj's reign. The Terminal Coner inventory suggests a decline in local production industries, and perhaps a constriction of local distribution spheres for goods, presumably related to a dwindling population. At the same time, however, there are clear continuities between the material culture associated with this brief post-dynastic occupation and that of the preceding dynastic period subphases. The Terminal Coner subphase is therefore Terminal Classic in character.

Conversely, the Early Postclassic Ejar assemblage represents no such kind of continuity in material culture and implies a discontinuity in pottery-making populations associated with later occupation of parts of the site and the Copan Valley. In stark contrast to Copan, those sites in the Maya lowlands that saw continuous occupation from the Terminal Classic into the Postclassic period witnessed the addition of new types and – critically – continuity in local pottery-making practices (e.g., Pendergast 1985, 1986; Rice and Forsyth 2005). The transitional nature of the assemblages from such continually occupied centers suggests a situation very different from that represented at Copan, as well as many other Maya sites where major breaks in local technological traditions occurred between the Terminal Classic and Postclassic periods. At Copan, the nature of the disjunction between the Terminal Coner and Ejar complexes, including a radically different domestic inventory consisting of crude, non-standardized vessels, implies a replacement of previous specialized production systems with what appear to have been much simpler, more "expedient" industries. This, in turn, and at the very least, indicates a major reorganization or breakdown of pre-existing economic systems. It is more likely, however, that such patterns were caused by the abandonment of Copan by its Classic-period population and a later reoccupation by a new group with distinct pottery-making practices and different wide-reaching connections with external regions. Such explanations are proposed for many sites in the southern and central lowlands where, following the Maya Collapse, major discontinuities in material culture have been noted (e.g., Foias 1996; Rice and Forsyth 2005).

The newly defined and understood Ejar-phase ceramic complex provides a means to evaluate the nature and extent of post-dynastic occupation in the surrounding region, even in those areas where the absence of obvious Postclassic markers such as Tohil Plumbate might otherwise suggest that there was no such presence. Similarly crude Ejar-phase utilitarian wares have also been found in the Río Amarillo subregion of the Copan Valley (Canuto 2002), indicating that Early Postclassic peoples settled beyond the Main Group and Copan Pocket. Continuing investigations in other portions of the Copan Valley may yet turn up more evidence of an Early Postclassic presence, and thereby enhance our understanding of this previously elusive, yet intriguing period in the history of a major center of Classic Maya civilization.

Notes

1. Throughout this chapter, the term "utilitarian wares" refers to vessels used for cooking, storage, and other domestic activities. Temper in these vessels is often coarse. Utilitarian forms include jars, *ollas*, large heavy bowls, and *comales*. The term "fine wares" refers to smaller vessels typically with finely ground temper – bowls, dishes, and cylinders that are usually carved, incised, or painted.
2. A number of finely incised polished black/brown vessels at Copan, such as the one in Figure 4.2d and a cylinder illustrated by Viel (1993: figs 101 and 102; see Schele and Miller 1996: plate 44, for a color photo of the same vessel), are partially or completely cream-slipped on the exterior. Similar kinds of incised cream-slipped vessels are common in the northern highlands of Guatemala (Smith 1952; Butler 1940) but are rare to non-existent throughout most of the lowlands (see Bill *et al.* 2002 and Castellanos *et al.* 2003 for exceptions from the Upper Pasion site of Cancuen, located at the foot of the Alta Verapaz). The same pattern pertains to so-called Classic resist (Smith 1955: 59) vessels that are also present at Copan and Quirigua. Although both types of vessels appear to have been locally produced at those two places, their resemblances to cream-slipped incised and negative-painted pottery from Alta Verapaz suggest that these two southeastern Maya centers had certain links to the highlands distinct from those of most sites in the southern and central Maya lowlands.

3   Terminal Coner deposits, as well as the latest middens of the Late Coner subphase, also incorporate utilitarian bowls and jars made with highly micaceous pastes. Such vessels appear to be imports. Micaceous-paste pottery is part of similarly late ceramic complexes from other regions, including the Naco Valley (Urban 1993a: 52) and the La Entrada region (Sato 1993: 23–4) of western Honduras and the Motagua Valley of eastern Guatemala (Schortman 1984: 464–73). It is likely that such vessels found in Late Coner contexts at Copan came from one or more of these regions.
4   The latest radiocarbon dates from Group 10L-2 – AD 810 (870) 930 and AD 810 (910) 970 (calibrated, one-sigma range) – come from two middens buried by collapsed structures in Courtyard A. These dates "are consistent with an occupation that lasted toward the end of the ninth century, but they do not rule out an earlier or later abandonment" (Andrews and Bill 2005: 302). The latest radiocarbon date associated with the Terminal Coner occupation of Group 9J-5 is AD 785 (894, 925, 935) 977 (calibrated, one-sigma range; Maca 2002: table 7.4).
5   By limiting production to a small number of specific vessel types, such as *comales* or water jars, the output levels of these few types can be increased by allowing a greater degree of routinization in specific production tasks. This kind of specialization is found among pottery-producing communities in highland Guatemala (Arnold 1978; Reina and Hill 1978) and Chiapas (Smith 1976), where, for example, one village may make water jars, another may specialize in cooking vessels, and another may go in for the production of *comales* (Rice 1991: 262–3). In fact, within such communities, specialization may be restricted not only to "a single product, but to a highly standardized version of it" (Smith 1976: 342, n. 30).
6   Impressed appliquéd fillets, in general, appear to be a relatively common decorative mode in the Postclassic period and also occur on other forms of vessels, including shallow subhemispherical bowls from Pusilha (Bill 2003: fig. 37) and collared tripod bowls and pedestal-based censers from Lamanai (Pendergast 1985: fig. 4d, f–h) and Mayapan (Smith 1971: fig. 31a–c) in the lowlands, as well as bowls and jars from Lepa-phase (AD 625 to possibly 1000) contexts at Quelepa (Andrews 1976: 102, fig. 124w-aa) and Early Postclassic contexts at Cihuatan (Fowler 1981: 144, fig. 32a–i) in El Salvador.

References

Adams, Richard E. W. (1971) *The Ceramics of Altar de Sacrificios, Peten, Guatemala.* Cambridge, MA: Peabody Museum of Archaeology and Ethnology.

Andrews, E. Wyllys, V (1976) *The Archaeology of Quelepa, El Salvador.* New Orleans: Middle American Research Institute, Tulane University.

Andrews, E. Wyllys, V, and Cassandra R. Bill (2005) A Late Classic Royal Residence at Copan. In *Copán: The History of An Ancient Maya Kingdom*, ed. E. Wyllys Andrews V and William L. Fash, pp. 239–314. Santa Fe, NM: School of American Research.

Arnauld, Marie C. (1986) *Archéologie de l'habitat en Alta Verapaz (Guatemala).* Mexico City: Centre d'Etudes mexicaines et centramericaines.

Arnold, Dean E. (1978) Ethnography of Pottery Making in the Valley of Guatemala. In *The Ceramics of Kaminaljuyú, Guatemala*, ed. Ronald K. Wetherington, pp. 327–400. University Park: Pennsylvania State University Press.

—— (1993) *Ecology and Ceramic Production in an Andean Community.* Cambridge: Cambridge University Press.

Ball, Joseph W. (1985) The Postclassic Archaeology of the Western Gulf Coast: Some Initial Observations. In *The Lowland Maya Postclassic*, ed. Arlen F. Chase and Prudence M. Rice, pp. 235–44. Austin: University of Texas Press.

—— (1993) Pottery, Potters, Palaces, and Polities: Some Socioeconomic and Political Implications of Late Classic Maya Ceramic Industries. In *Lowland Maya Civilization in the*

Eighth Century AD, ed. Jeremy A. Sabloff and John S. Henderson, pp. 243–72. Washington, DC: Dumbarton Oaks.

Baudez, Claude F. (1976) Arqueología de la frontera sur mesoamerica. *14th Mesa Redonda, Sociedad Mexicana de Antropología* 1: 133–46.

Baudez, Claude F., and Pierre Becquelin (1973) *Archéologie de Los Naranjos, Honduras*. Paris: Mission Archéologique et Ethnologique française au Mexique.

Becquelin, Pierre (2001 [1969]) *Arqueología de la región de Nebaj, Guatemala*. Mexico City and Guatemala: Centro Francés de Estudios Mexicanos y Centroamericanos and Universidad de San Carlos de Guatemala, Escuela de Historia.

Becquelin, Pierre, and Claude F. Baudez (1979) *Tonina, une cité Maya du Chiapas (Mexique)*, vol. 1. Mexico City: Mission Archeologique et Ethnologie française au Mexique.

Bill, Cassandra R. (1997) *Patterns of Variation and Change in Dynastic Period Ceramics and Ceramic Production at Copan, Honduras*. PhD dissertation, Department of Anthropology, Tulane University. Ann Arbor, MI: University Microfilms.

—— (1998) Politics, Population, and Economy: The Effects of Late Classic Sociopolitical and Demographic Change on the Ceramic Production Industry at Copan. Paper presented at the conference "Maya Culture at the Millenium" (Part I), Buffalo.

—— (2003) Preliminary Analysis of Ceramic Materials from Pusilha, Belize. In Geoffrey E. Braswell, Cassandra R. Bill, Sonja Schwake, and Christian Prager, Pusilha Archaeological Project: 2002 Annual Report, pp. 96–145. MS on file with the Institute of Archaeology, Belmopan.

Bill, Cassandra R., Michael G. Callaghan, Ronald L. Bishop, and Arthur A. Demarest (2002) Interpretaciones iniciales de la cerámica de Cancuén y el Alto Pasión. In *XV Simposio de investigaciones arqueológicas en Guatemala, 2001*, ed. Juan Pedro Laporte, Héctor Escobedo, and Bárbara Arroyo, pp. 623–34. Guatemala: Museo Nacional de Arqueología y Etnología.

Bill, Cassandra R., Michael G. Callaghan, and Jeanette Castellanos (2003) La ceramicá de Cancuén y el región del Alto Pasión. In *Proyecto Arqueológico Cancuén: informe temporada 2002*, ed. Arthur A. Demarest and Tomás Barrientos. Guatemala: Instituto de Antropología e Historia; and Nashville: Department of Anthropology, Vanderbilt University.

Bill, Cassandra R., T. Kam Manahan, and Rene Viel (forthcoming) Copán Valley. In *Pottery of Prehistoric Honduras: Regional Classification and Analysis*. 2nd ed., ed. Marilyn Beaudry-Corbett, Rosemary Joyce, and John Henderson. Los Angeles: University of California, Institute of Archaeology.

Bishop, Ronald L., and Marilyn P. Beaudry (1994) Appendix B: Chemical Compositional Analysis of Southeastern Maya Ceramics. In *Ceramics and Artifacts from Excavations in the Copán Residential Zone*, ed. Gordon R. Willey, Richard M. Leventhal, Arthur A. Demarest, and William L. Fash Jr., pp. 407–43. Cambridge, MA: Peabody Museum of Archaeology and Ethnology.

Braswell, Geoffrey E. (1992) Obsidian-Hydration Dating, the Coner Phase, and Revisionist Chronology at Copán, Honduras. *Latin American Antiquity* 3: 130–47.

Braswell, Geoffrey E., and T. Kam Manahan (2001) After the Collapse: Obsidian Production Exchange at Terminal Classic and Early Postclassic Copán. Paper presented at the 66th annual meeting of the Society for American Archaeology, April 21, New Orleans.

Braswell, Geoffrey E., Michael D. Glascock, and Hector Neff (1996) The Obsidian Artifacts of Group 10L-2, Copán: Production, Exchange, and Chronology. Paper presented at the 61st annual meeting of the Society for American Archaeology, New Orleans.

Brown, Kenneth L. (1985) Postclassic Relationships between the Highland and Lowland Maya. In *The Lowland Maya Postclassic*, ed. Arlen F. Chase and Prudence M. Rice, pp. 270–81. Austin: University of Texas Press.

Butler, Mary (1940) A Pottery Sequence from the Alta Verapaz, Guatemala. In *The Maya and Their Neighbors: Essays on Middle American Anthropology and Archaeology*, ed. Clarence L. Hay, Ralph L. Linton, Samuel K. Lothrop, and Harry L. Shapiro, pp. 250–67. New York: Dover.

Canuto, Marcello A. (2002) *A Tale of Two Communities: Social and Political Transformation in the Hinterlands of the Maya Polity of Copan*. PhD dissertation, Department of Anthropology, University of Pennsylvania, Philadelphia. Ann Arbor, MI: University Microfilms.

Castellanos, Jeanette, Cassandra R. Bill, Michael G. Callaghan, and Ronald L. Bishop (2003) Cancuén, enclave de intercambio entre las tierras bajas e altas de Guatemala: la evidencia ceramica. In *XVI Simposio de investigaciones arqueológicas en Guatemala, 2002*, ed. Juan Pedro Laporte, Bárbara Arroyo, Héctor L. Escobedo, and Héctor E. Mejía, pp. 635–48. Guatemala: Museo Nacional de Arqueología y Etnología.

Chase, Arlen F. (1985) Postclassic Peten Interaction Spheres: The View From Tayasal. In *The Lowland Maya Postclassic*, ed. Arlen F. Chase and Prudence M. Rice, pp. 184–205. Austin: University of Texas Press.

Fash, William L. (1986) Settlement History in the Copan Valley and Some Comparisons with Quirigua. In *The Southeast Maya Periphery: Problems and Prospects*, ed. Patricia A. Urban and Edward M. Schortman, pp. 72–93. Austin: University of Texas Press.

—— (1991) *Scribes, Warriors and Kings: The City of Copan and the Ancient Maya*. London: Thames & Hudson.

Fash, William L., E. Wyllys Andrews V, and T. Kam Manahan (2005) Political Decentralization, Dynastic Collapse, and the Early Postclassic in the Urban Center of Copán, Honduras. In *The Terminal Classic in the Maya Lowlands: Collapse, Transition, and Transformation*, ed. Arthur A. Demarest, Don S. Rice, and Prudence M. Rice, pp. 260–87. Boulder: University Press of Colorado.

Foias, Antonia E. (1996) *Changing Ceramic Production and Exchange and the Classic Maya Collapse in the Petexbatun Region*. PhD dissertation, Department of Anthropology, Vanderbilt University. Ann Arbor, MI: University Microfilms.

Fowler, William R., Jr. (1981) The Pipil-Nicarao of Central America. PhD dissertation, Department of Archaeology, University of Calgary.

Healy, Paul F. (1984) The Archaeology of Honduras. In *The Archaeology of Lower Central America*, ed. Frederick Lange and Doris Z. Stone, pp. 113–61. Albuquerque: University of New Mexico Press.

Ichon, Alain (1992) *Los Cerritos-Chijoj: la transición epiclásica en las tierras altas de Guatemala*. Guatemala City: Centro de Estudios Mexicanos y Centroamericanos.

Joyce, Rosemary A. (1986) Terminal Classic Interaction on the Southeastern Maya Periphery. *American Antiquity* 51: 313–29.

—— (1993a) Appendix B: A Key to Ulúa Polychromes. In *Prehistoric Pottery of Honduras: Regional Classification and Analysis*, ed. John S. Henderson and Marilyn Beaudry-Corbett, pp. 257–79. Los Angeles: University of California, Institute of Archaeology.

—— (1993b) The Construction of the Mesoamerican Frontier and the Mayoid Image of Honduran Polychromes. In *Reinterpreting Prehistory of Central America*, ed. Mark Miller Graham, pp. 51–101. Niwot: University Press of Colorado.

Lange, Frederick W. (1984) The Greater Nicoya Archaeological Subarea. In *The Archaeology of Lower Central America*, ed. Frederick W. Lange and Doris Stone, pp. 165–94. Albuquerque: University of New Mexico Press.

Longyear, John M., III (1952) *Copan Ceramics: A Study of Southeastern Maya Pottery*. Washington, DC: Carnegie Institution.

—— (1966) Archaeological Survey of El Salvador. In *Archaeological Frontiers and External Connections*, ed. Gordon F. Ekholm and Gordon R. Willey, pp. 132–56. Austin: University of Texas Press.

Maca, Alan (2002) *Spatio-Temporal Boundaries in Classic Maya Settlement Systems: Copan's Urban Foothills and the Excavations at Group 9J-5 (Honduras)*. PhD dissertation, Department of Anthropology, Harvard University. Ann Arbor, MI: University Microfilms.

Manahan, T. Kam (2000) Reexaminando los días finales de Copán: nuevos datos de la fase Ejar. In *XIII Simposio de investigaciones arqueológicas en Guatemala, 1999*, ed. Juan Pedro Laporte, Héctor Escobedo, Ana Claudia de Suasnávar, and Bárbara Arroyo, vol. 2, pp. 1149–55. Guatemala City: Museo Nacional de Arqueología y Etnología.

—— (2002) Reevaluating the Classic Maya Collapse at Copán: New Data and New Socioeconomic Implications. In *La organización social entre los mayas prehispánicos, coloniales y modernos: memoria de la Tercera Mesa Redonda de Palenque I*, ed. Vera Tiesler Blos, Rafael Cobos and Merle Greene Robertson, pp. 329–37. Mexico City: Instituto Nacional de Antropología e Historia; and Merida: Universidad Autónoma de Yucatán.

—— (2003) *The Collapse of Complex Society and its Aftermath: A Case Study from the Classic Maya Site of Copán, Honduras*. PhD dissertation, Department of Anthropology, Vanderbilt University. Ann Arbor, MI: University Microfilms.

Neff, Hector (2003) Analysis of Mesoamerican Plumbate Pottery Surfaces by Laser Ablation-Inductively Coupled Plasma-Mass Spectrometry (LA-ICP-SM). *Journal of Archaeological Science* 30: 21–35.

Peacock, D. P. S. (1982) *Pottery in the Roman World: An Ethnoarchaeological Approach*. London: Longman.

Pendergast, David M. (1985) Lamanai, Belize: An Updated View. In *The Lowland Maya Postclassic*, ed. Arlen F. Chase and Prudence M. Rice, pp. 91–103. Austin: University of Texas Press.

—— (1986) Stability through Change: Lamanai, Belize, from the Ninth to the Seventeenth Century. In *Late Lowland Maya Civilization: Classic to Postclassic*, ed. Jeremy A. Sabloff and E. Wyllys Andrews V, pp. 223–49. Albuquerque: University of New Mexico Press.

Rands, Robert L., and Robert E. Smith (1965) Pottery of the Guatemalan Highlands. In *Archaeology of Southern Mesoamerica, Part 1*, ed. Gordon R. Willey, pp. 95–145. Austin: University of Texas Press.

Reents-Budet, Dorie J. (1994) *Painting the Maya Universe: Royal Ceramics of the Classic Period*. Durham, NC: Duke University Press.

Reina, Rubén E., and Robert M. Hill II (1978) *The Traditional Pottery of Guatemala*. Austin: University of Texas Press.

Rice, Prudence M. (1986) The Peten Postclassic: Perspectives from the Central Peten Lakes. In *Late Lowland Maya Civilization: Classic to Postclassic*, ed. Jeremy A. Sabloff and E. Wyllys Andrews V, pp. 251–99. Albuquerque: University of New Mexico Press.

—— (1991) Specialization, Standardization, and Diversity: A Retrospective. In *The Ceramic Legacy of Anna O. Shepard*, ed. Ronald L. Bishop and Frederick W. Lange, pp. 257–79. Niwot: University Press of Colorado.

Rice, Prudence M., and Donald Forsyth (2005) Terminal Classic-Period Lowland Ceramics. In *The Terminal Classic in the Maya Lowlands: Collapse, Transition, and Transformation*, ed. Arthur A. Demarest, Don S. Rice, and Prudence M. Rice, pp. 28–59. Boulder: University Press of Colorado.

Sabloff, Jeremy A. (1975) Ceramics. In *Excavations at Seibal, Department of Peten, Guatemala*. Cambridge, MA: Peabody Museum of Archaeology and Ethnology.

Santley, Robert S., and Ronald R. Kneebone (1993) Craft Specialization, Refuse Disposal, and the Creation of Spatial Archaeological Records in Prehispanic Mesoamerica. In *Prehispanic Domestic Units in Western Mesoamerica: Studies of the Household, Compound, and Residence*, ed. Robert S. Santley and Kenneth G. Hirth, pp. 37–63. Boca Raton, FL: CRC.

Santley, Robert S., Philip J. Arnold III, and Christopher A. Pool (1989) The Ceramics Production System at Matacapan, Veracruz, Mexico. *Journal of Field Archaeology* 16: 107–32.

Sato, Etsuo (1993) La Entrada Region. In *Prehistoric Pottery of Honduras: Regional Classification and Analysis*, ed. John S. Henderson, Marilyn Beaudry-Corbett, John S. Henderson, and Marilyn Beaudry-Corbett, pp. 20–29. Los Angeles: University of California, Institute of Archaeology.

Schele, Linda, and Mary Ellen Miller (1986) *The Blood of Kings: Dynasty and Ritual in Maya Art*. New York: George Braziller.

Schortman, Edward (1984) *Archaeological Investigation in the Lower Motagua Valley, Department of Izabal, Guatemala*. PhD dissertation, Department of Anthropology, University of Pennsylvania. Ann Arbor, MI: University Microfilms.

Sharer, Robert J., and Arlen F. Chase (1976) New Town Ceramic Complex. In *Prehistoric Pottery Analysis and the Ceramics of Barton Ramie in the Belize Valley*, ed. James C. Gifford, pp. 532–52. Cambridge, MA: Peabody Museum of Archaeology and Ethnology.

Shepard, Anna O. (1948) *Plumbate: A Mesoamerican Trade Ware*. Washington, DC: Carnegie Institution.

Smith, Carol A. (1976) Exchange Systems and the Spatial Distribution of Elites: The Organization of Stratification in Agrarian Societies. In *Regional Analysis*, Vol. II: *Social Systems*, ed. Carol A. Smith, pp. 309–74. New York: Academic Press.

Smith, Robert E. (1952) *Pottery from Chipoc, Alta Verapaz, Guatemala*. Washington, DC: Carnegie Institution.

—— (1955) *Ceramic Sequence at Uaxactún, Guatemala*. New Orleans: Middle American Research Institute, Tulane University.

—— (1971) *The Pottery of Mayapan, including Studies of Ceramic Material from Uxmal, Kabah, and Chichén Itzá*. Cambridge, MA: Peabody Museum of Archaeology and Ethnology.

Smith, Robert E., and James C. Gifford (1965) Pottery of the Maya Lowlands. In *Archaeology of Southern Mesoamerica, Part 1*, ed. Gordon R. Willey, pp. 498–534. Austin: University of Texas Press.

Urban, Patricia A. (1993a) Naco Valley. In *Prehistoric Pottery of Honduras: Regional Classification and Analysis*, ed. John S. Henderson and Marilyn Beaudry-Corbett, pp. 30–63. Los Angeles: University of California, Institute of Archaeology.

—— (1993b) Central Santa Barbara Region. In *Prehistoric Pottery of Honduras: Regional Classification and Analysis*, ed. John S. Henderson and Marilyn Beaudry-Corbett, pp. 134–70. Los Angeles: University of California, Institute of Archaeology.

Urban, Patricia A., and Edward M. Schortman (1987) Copan and its Neighbors: Patterns of Interaction Reflected in Classic Western Honduran Pottery. In *Maya Ceramics: Papers from the 1985 Maya Ceramic Conference*, vol. 2, ed. Prudence M. Rice and Robert J. Sharer, pp. 341–95. Oxford: British Archaeological Reports.

Viel, Rene (1993) *Evolución de la ceramica de Copán, Honduras*. Tegucigalpa: Instituto Hondureño de Antropología e Historia.

Wauchope, Robert (1948) *Excavations at Zacualpa, Guatemala*. New Orleans: Middle American Research Institute, Tulane University.

—— (1975) *Zacualpa, El Quiche, Guatemala: An Ancient Provincial Center of the Highland Maya*. New Orleans: Middle American Research Institute, Tulane University.

Webster, David L., and AnnCorinne Freter (1990a) Settlement History and the Classic Collapse at Copán: A Redefined Chronological Perspective. *Latin American Antiquity* 1: 66–85.

—— (1990b) The Demography of Late Classic Copán. In *Precolumbian Population History in the Maya Lowlands*, ed. T. Patrick Culbert and Don S. Rice, pp. 37–61. Albuquerque: University of New Mexico Press.

Webster, David L., AnnCorinne Freter, and David Rue (1993) The Obsidian Hydration Dating Project: A Regional Approach and Why it Works. *Latin American Antiquity* 4: 303–24.

Webster, David L., AnnCorinne Freter, and Rebecca Storey (2005) Dating Copan Culture History: Implications for the Terminal Classic and the Collapse. In *The Terminal Classic in the Maya Lowlands: Collapse, Transition, and Transformation*, ed. Arthur A. Demarest, Don S. Rice, and Prudence M. Rice, pp. 231–59. Boulder: University Press of Colorado.

Willey, Gordon R., Richard M. Leventhal, Arthur A. Demarest, and William L. Fash Jr. (1994) *Ceramics and Artifacts from Excavations in the Copán Residential Zone*. Cambridge, MA: Peabody Museum of Archaeology and Ethnology.

PART II
The highlands of Guatemala

5

THE OTHER PRECLASSIC MAYA

Interaction, growth, and depopulation in the eastern Kaqchikel[1] highlands

Geoffrey E. Braswell and Eugenia J. Robinson

The large and powerful Preclassic centers of the Guatemalan highlands and Pacific piedmont – sites such as Kaminaljuyu and Tak'alik Ab'aj – are the focus of important and ongoing research. Although most scholars view these sites as the centers of complex chiefdoms, some have claimed that they were true cities and even the capitals of archaic states. An extraordinary claim is that Kaminaljuyu was the capital city of a territorially expansionist state encompassing the area described as the "Miraflores Ceramic Sphere" (Kaplan 2011a, 2011b). If this is the case, evidence for Kaminaljuyu domination should be found outside of the Valley of Guatemala. Our chapter discusses the results of more than 20 years of research in the Departments of Sacatepequez and Chimaltenango, just west of the Valley of Guatemala. Our principal goal is to describe evidence documenting the earliest occupation of the region during the Archaic, Early Preclassic, and Middle Preclassic periods, growth and expansion during the first part of the Late Preclassic period, and large-scale – but not universal – demographic collapse during the second half of the Late Preclassic period. Most importantly, throughout our region and over the entire span of the Preclassic period, we have no evidence of social inequality or political complexity, despite the fact that both emerged at nearby Kaminaljuyu during the Preclassic. Instead of domination by Kaminaljuyu, we see over time less and less evidence for interaction between the eastern Kaqchikel region and the great center. It is clear that the territory directly controlled by Kaminaljuyu during its Late Preclassic apogee did not extend westward out of the Valley of Guatemala and into the eastern Kaqchikel highlands, and that the notion that it was the capital of a large state corresponding to the Miraflores Ceramic Sphere is false.

How did ancient states expand? One model, proposed by Guillermo Algaze (1989, 1993), suggests that pristine civilizations grew in territory by establishing outposts, colonies, or enclaves in their peripheries. Such outposts guaranteed that growing centers would have consistent access to necessary peripheral resources. For ancient Mesoamerica, imported obsidian, exotic ceramics, and other foreign goods and preciosities are often viewed as such key resources (e.g., Smith and Berdan 2003).

Adopting an agency-based perspective, Algaze further suggests that local elites in the periphery might have cooperated with their counterparts from expanding states to further their own goals. Elite emulation and the acquisition of status-endowing goods from the core state have been proposed by some as the reason why Maya elites forged close ties with Teotihuacan (Braswell 2003b). Finally, Algaze argues that such core outposts were the most efficient means of gathering strategic resources in less hierarchically organized regions and of mitigating exchange between cores and peripheries. In Mesoamerica, Middle Formative Chalcatzingo has been interpreted as such a gateway community (Hirth 1978), and "Middle Classic" Kaminaljuyu has been viewed as a port-of-trade (Brown 1977). Important archaeological correlates of Algaze's model, therefore, include: (1) the presence of resources important to the core near proposed peripheral outposts; (2) the existence of a rural elite to be swayed by alliance, bribery, or coercion by the core state; and (3) the presence of items of trade both from the periphery in the core and from the core in and around the peripheral outposts. Furthermore, (4) the distance between the core and the peripheral zone must be sufficient to make the establishment of outposts the most viable strategy for enabling access to the relevant resources.

Jonathan Kaplan (2002a) and Juan Antonio Valdés et al. (2004) have recently applied a core–periphery approach to understanding the development of Chocola, a large Preclassic center in the piedmont zone of southwestern Guatemala. Monument 1 of Chocola, similar to Kaminaljuyu Monuments 10 and 11, suggests that a close cultural affiliation existed between the two sites (Kaplan 2008: fig. 4a–b). Moreover, *some* similarities in the ceramics and monuments of Tak'alik Ab'aj and Kaminaljuyu also demonstrate interaction between those two sites during the Late Preclassic period.[2] But how did Kaminaljuyu interact with communities *between* the Valley of Guatemala and the western piedmont of Guatemala – that is, with people who lived closer to the great highland center?

Kaplan (2011a, 2011b) has recently proposed that Kaminaljuyu was the capital of a large, expansionist state spreading from the central highlands of Guatemala to western El Salvador – that is, corresponding with what has been called the "Miraflores Ceramic Sphere" (Demarest and Sharer 1986; for an important reinterpretation of the concept, see Demarest 2011). For Kaplan, then, the highlands immediately west of Kaminaljuyu are included within the boundaries of a territorially expansive state. Given his argument, it is important to evaluate the goodness of fit of Algaze's model of state expansion to this region. A narrow task of this chapter is to consider whether archaeological evidence supports the establishment by Kaminaljuyu of outposts in the Kaqchikel region during the Late Preclassic, a period during which most researchers consider Kaminaljuyu to have been organized as a complex chiefdom. Much more broadly, the goal of our chapter is to discuss Preclassic settlement and interaction, with a focus on relations between the Valley of Guatemala and the eastern Kaqchikel highlands.

The eastern Kaqchikel highlands and the Preclassic ceramic chronology of a non-state society

The eastern Kaqchikel highlands of Guatemala are located 25 to 50 kilometers west of Kaminaljuyu and the Valley of Guatemala (see Figure 1.1). The phrase "eastern Kaqchikel" in our description of the mountains and valleys of the Departments of Sacatepequez and eastern Chimaltenango is derived from the identity and language affiliation of many of the modern inhabitants of the region. We do not mean to imply that the K'iche'an ancestors of the Kaqchikel lived in this portion of the highlands during the Preclassic, although we do believe that they had settled in the region by the beginning of the Early Classic period (e.g., Braswell 1996a; Braswell and Amador Berdugo 1999; Fahsen 2002; Popenoe de Hatch 1997, 1998, 2002).

In particular, we discuss early occupation in four areas of the eastern Kaqchikel highlands: the Antigua Valley and its major entrances and exits, and the *municipios* of Alotenango (southwest of Antigua), Sumpango (north of Antigua), and San Martin Jilotepeque (northeast of Chimaltenango). From 1988 until the present, we have conducted extensive survey and excavations in these regions. In total, more than 350 square kilometers have been surveyed and more than 450 sites have been systematically and opportunistically sampled.

The ceramics of the highlands west of the Valley of Guatemala have long been recognized as similar – but not identical – to those of Kaminaljuyu. No unambiguous, single-component Early Preclassic-period occupation has been defined in the region of our study, although we have found sherds dating to this period at Urías, Rucal, and a few other sites. A Middle Preclassic is known and defined by ceramics that are somewhat similar not only to Las Charcas materials from the Valley of Guatemala but also to pottery from the Pacific coast. Diagnostic Majadas-phase ceramics from Kaminaljuyu are unknown in the eastern Kaqchikel highlands, and, indeed, the status of Majadas as a phase, facet, or special deposit at Kaminaljuyu may still be open to some discussion (Popenoe de Hatch 1997).

The later half of the Middle Preclassic in the eastern Kaqchikel highlands historically has been known as the Sacatepequez phase, thought to be contemporaneous with the Providencia (sometimes referred to as the Providencia-Sacatepequez) phase of Kaminaljuyu (Popenoe de Hatch 1997: 9; Shook 1952: 4). At that site, the Providencia phase traditionally has been dated to 700/650–400 BC. Recently, Takeshi Inomata (2013) has proposed a revision to the Preclassic chronology of Kaminaljuyu and much of the Southern Maya Region. Fundamentally, he argues that, while Las Charcas (which he proposes has both early and late facets) dates to the Middle Preclassic period, Providencia dates to the first half of the Late Preclassic period (400–100 BC). This shift forward of three centuries is supported by a large suite of "Bayesianized" radiocarbon dates (see Chapter 13) and by ceramic comparison and cross-dating with Chicanel pottery (Inomata 2013). We accept Inomata's argument but also note the existence of formal similarities between Providencia-Sacatepequez and Mamom pottery of the Maya lowlands. Thus, we prefer to see some overlap with that phase and the end of the Middle Preclassic. Moreover, we feel that the transition from Providencia to Verbena is not particularly well dated for Kaminaljuyu, and – most critical for our region – we suspect that the Sacatepequez phase of the eastern Kaqchikel zone may end somewhat earlier than Providencia at Kaminaljuyu itself. This is because our collections with Sacatepequez-phase ceramics lack many of the diagnostics of a potential late facet Providencia. Thus – and perhaps only for the time being – we propose a date range of 500/400–250/150 BC for the Sacatepequez phase of the eastern Kaqchikel highlands and a date range of 250/150 BC – AD 150/250 for the second half of the Late Preclassic and the Terminal Classic periods.

In sum, the presence of meager amounts of Early Preclassic ceramics at a few sites suggests an early occupation dating to before about 1000 BC. Five sites have yielded pottery similar to Middle Preclassic Las Charcas materials from Naranjo and Kaminaljuyu. We date this to about 900/800–500/400 BC. The following terminal Middle Preclassic to early Late Preclassic Sacatepequez phase saw a dramatic increase in settlement during the period 500/400–250/150 BC.

The second half of the Late Preclassic is one of the more enigmatic periods of occupation in the eastern Kaqchikel highlands, and the precise date of its inception is uncertain. It is worth noting that we still have relatively few Late Preclassic dates for the central Maya highlands and only one for a site in our region of survey. This radiocarbon date, from the Golondrinas rock shelter, was determined from carbon associated with ceramics pertaining to a later period (Robinson *et al.* 2002, 2003, 2007). In the area of our surveys we found surprisingly few late Late Preclassic sherds. Braswell (1996a, 1998, 2002) argues that the San Martin Jilotepeque region was abandoned by permanent settlers during this time. Given the dearth of later Late Preclassic materials in that area and the reduced assemblage from the southern half of our survey zone, as well as the apparent isolation of the eastern Kaqchikel highlands from Kaminaljuyu throughout the period,[3] it is particularly difficult to date the inception of the later Late Preclassic. We hesitantly suggest that it began about 250/150 BC, somewhat later than suggested by the conventional Kaminaljuyu chronology (Popenoe de Hatch 2002) but also somewhat earlier than argued by Inomata (2013). The conclusion of the Preclassic in the central Maya highlands is more certain and is marked by a widespread cultural collapse and demographic decline during the late second century AD. These events were followed by the arrival of a flood of Early Classic settlers and the new Solano ceramic tradition from the northwest at about AD 200/250 (Popenoe de Hatch 1997, 1998).

Settlement and material culture during the Preclassic period

The political and economic questions related to chiefdom and state expansion are addressed here from three perspectives: settlement patterns and hierarchy in the eastern Kaqchikel region, comparative ceramic analysis, and obsidian exchange data. Excavation has been an important aspect of all our projects, but most of our excavation data come from Classic or Postclassic sites (Braswell 1996a; Robinson

1993, 1994, 1998, 2003). Limited and mixed Preclassic components were uncovered at Pachay 2 (San Martin Jilotepeque; Braswell 1996a), San Lorenzo (Parramos), and Rucal (Ciudad Vieja; Robinson and Pye 1996). The only excavated site with a clear Preclassic occupation that was not mixed with later Classic material is Urías (San Miguel Dueñas; Robinson *et al.* 2002), discussed in more detail below.

The intent of our chapter is to discuss initial settlement of the eastern Kaqchikel highlands and to assess the nature of political and economic relations between that region and the Valley of Guatemala during the Middle and Late Preclassic. From the outset, we wish to stress that we consider the eastern Kaqchikel region to be distinct from other areas. Thus, although we have always included Kaminaljuyu for comparative purposes, we have consistently interpreted relations between the eastern Kaqchikel highlands and the Valley of Guatemala in terms of the ebb and flow of exchange between partners and not as examples of domination or hegemony. Moreover, we are quite skeptical of claims that Kaminaljuyu was organized as a state – aggressively expansionist or otherwise – during the Preclassic period. Indeed, we are wary of the application of the term "state" to Classic-period Kaminaljuyu, and even somewhat cautious about using it to describe the comparatively well-organized and most certainly aggressive Postclassic kingdoms of this region (Braswell 2003a). It may be more accurate, in fact, to describe these Postclassic polities as statelets, *cacicazgos*, or *señorios*.

History of the eastern Kaqchikel research projects

This study focuses on survey and excavation data drawn from three archaeological projects that we have directed or in which we participated. References also are made to Edwin Shook's (1952) opportunistic reconnaissance of the same region and to Stephan F. de Borhegyi's (1950) survey at the base of the volcano Agua. E. Vinicio García's (1992) *tésis de licenciatura* is a synthesis of settlement in the central and western portions of the Department of Chimaltenango, an area where we have not conducted extensive survey.

In 1988, William R. Swezey of the Centro de Investigaciones Regionales de Mesoamérica, based in Antigua, initiated the Encuesta Arqueológica del Área Kaqchikel. The goals of the project were to carry out regional archaeological surveys in the Kaqchikel-speaking zone, to identify sites, and to create summary prehistories of the municipalities of the area. The project began in two areas near Antigua: the *municipio* of Alotenango, an area that spans an important corridor between the Kaqchikel highlands and the Pacific coast, and the *municipio* of Sumpango, where at least one Late Classic site had already been identified by Shook (1952; see also Robinson 1990). Sumpango was a particularly promising area for research because Castulo Puc Raxon, a resident of that *municipio*, was a member of the survey team. As a former mayor of the town, he provided secure access to the entire municipality and already knew of many sites.

After work in these two *municipios* concluded, and upon the death of both Swezey and Puc, Robinson reorganized and redefined our research as the Projecto

Arqueológico del Área Kaqchikel (PAAK). Because there had been no intensive effort to study the settlement patterns of the Antigua Region, reconnaissance next turned to the strategic north and south access points to the valley. An excavation phase of the project focused on three important sites dating to different time periods: Chitak Tzak, the protohistoric (ca. AD 1400) location of Sumpango (Robinson 1994, 1998), Santa Rosa, a Late Classic (AD 600–900) hilltop site in the northwest corridor of the Antigua Valley (Robinson 1993; see Chapter 6), and San Lorenzo, located on an eastern extension of the Chimaltenango *altiplano* and outside of the Antigua Valley, which was known from Shook's (1952) reconnaissance. Research at San Lorenzo provided important data on the Middle and early Late Preclassic, but all the excavated contexts contained temporally mixed material. As our interest in the Preclassic origins of settlement in the Kaqchikel region increased, Robinson and Mary Pye shifted excavations to Rucal. Later, Robinson led a team of investigators at Urías, which has a similar Preclassic ceramic chronology. Both of these sites are located in the southwest corner of the Antigua Valley. Excavations at Urías revealed the clearest stratigraphy and thus have become most important for understanding early settlement in the eastern Kaqchikel region (Robinson et al. 2002).

A second direct outgrowth of Swezey's Encuesta Arqueológica del Área Kaqchikel was Braswell's 1990–93 dissertation research in the *municipio* of San Martin Jilotepeque, Department of Chimaltenango. The purpose of this project, titled Ri Rusamäj Jilotepeke, was to study the relationship among obsidian outcrops, settlement, economic development, and political elaboration (Braswell 1993, 1996a, 1996b, 1996c, 1998, 2002; Braswell and Braswell 1993; Braswell and Garnica 1994; Braswell and Glascock 1998; Glascock et al. 1998). Systematic survey of an area of 138 square kilometers surrounding the San Martin Jilotepeque obsidian outcrops discovered 147 sites, including residential locations, quarry workshops, secondary workshops, and specialized workshop disposal areas. A three-tiered settlement hierarchy was developed for the region based on site area; the presence, quantity, and arrangement of visible mounds; the presence of carved or plain monuments; and the recovery of imported materials. The purpose of this hybrid hierarchy was to avoid the simple equation of population (related to site area) or the presence of elites (determined by the other criteria) with hierarchical rank (see de Montmollin 1988 for a discussion of the qualitatively different site hierarchies that may emerge when different criteria are used for their definition). In San Martin Jilotepeque, however, the four distinct criteria co-vary to a remarkable degree. In fact, consideration of the presence and quantity of mounds (Type I = artifact scatter; Type II = isolated visible mound or single group; Type III = multiple mound groups visible on the surface) yields almost precisely the same site hierarchy as that determined using all four criteria.

Both systematic and opportunistic surface collections were made in San Martin Jilotepeque. Excavations were conducted at four distinct sites: Choatalum, El Perén, Pachay, and Chuisac. The first of these is a large Postclassic quarry-workshop built atop (or, more accurately, by digging away) an Early Classic settlement of unknown size. El Perén is a Type III mound settlement dating to the Early Classic period

(Braswell 2002: fig. 10.6a). Pachay is a Type II mound site with several sculptures. The site also served as a quarry-workshop. The mounds and sculpture date to the Classic period, but a significant Type I late Middle to early Late Preclassic component was observed at Pachay 2 (locality C356328). Pachay 2 is approximately 1 hectare in area and is the second-largest Preclassic site known in San Martin Jilotepeque, but it contains no mounds. Two uncarved stelae, possibly dating to the Classic period (but see Bove 2011), also were found at Pachay 2. Finally, Chuisac is a very large Type III site dating to the Postclassic period (Braswell 2002: fig. 10.6b). It has been identified as O'ch'al Kab'owil Siwan ("Ripening-Maize Heaven Ravine"), an ethnohistorically known site associated with the Chajoma and Xpantzay (Carmack 1979; Fox 1977).

To make settlement data from each of our projects consistent, a three-tiered architectural hierarchy is adopted here. All of the Preclassic sites we identified, sampled, or excavated are assigned to the Type I category. That is, the Preclassic site hierarchy of our survey zones contains only one level. Our sites, therefore, are all individual households, hamlets, or the smallest of villages. Although greenstone beads are sometimes found, there is no clear differentiation of wealth or privileged access to special materials or labor. We have, however, some evidence of specialized ritual practice. Reports of stone pedestal sculptures (related to the Pot Belly sculptures of the Middle to Late Preclassic) and mushroom stones from Antigua and other highland regions suggest religious practices linking the Kaqchikel region to Kaminaljuyu, but these objects are scarce and their provenances need verification. In short, we picture the Preclassic eastern Kaqchikel highlands as containing small, scattered agrarian settlements organized according to egalitarian social principles. If there were settlements containing elites, either local or from Kaminaljuyu, we have been unable to find them.

The eastern Kaqchikel region during the Early, Middle, and early Late Preclassic periods

Archaic and Early Preclassic settlement

In the late 1990s, PAAK investigated the archaeology of the earliest agricultural settlers known in the eastern Kaqchikel highlands. We discovered evidence of very early occupation at the southern end of the Antigua Valley near the Guacalate River and Lake Quilisimate. John G. Jones recovered domesticated corn pollen dating to 4000 BC from cores taken from the bottom of the lake and also identified a subsequent period of early deforestation (Freidel *et al.* 2001, 2007). These data suggest that agricultural activity began during the Archaic period.

Deep strata at the Urías site, also located in the southwestern portion of the Antigua Valley (Figure 5.1), have yielded carbon dating to 1800–1280 BC (Robinson 2001). Corroborating this radiocarbon date are isolated Early Preclassic pottery sherds stylistically dated to before 1000 BC. We have recovered these sherds in excavations at both Urías and Rucal and on the surface of five other sites in the area.

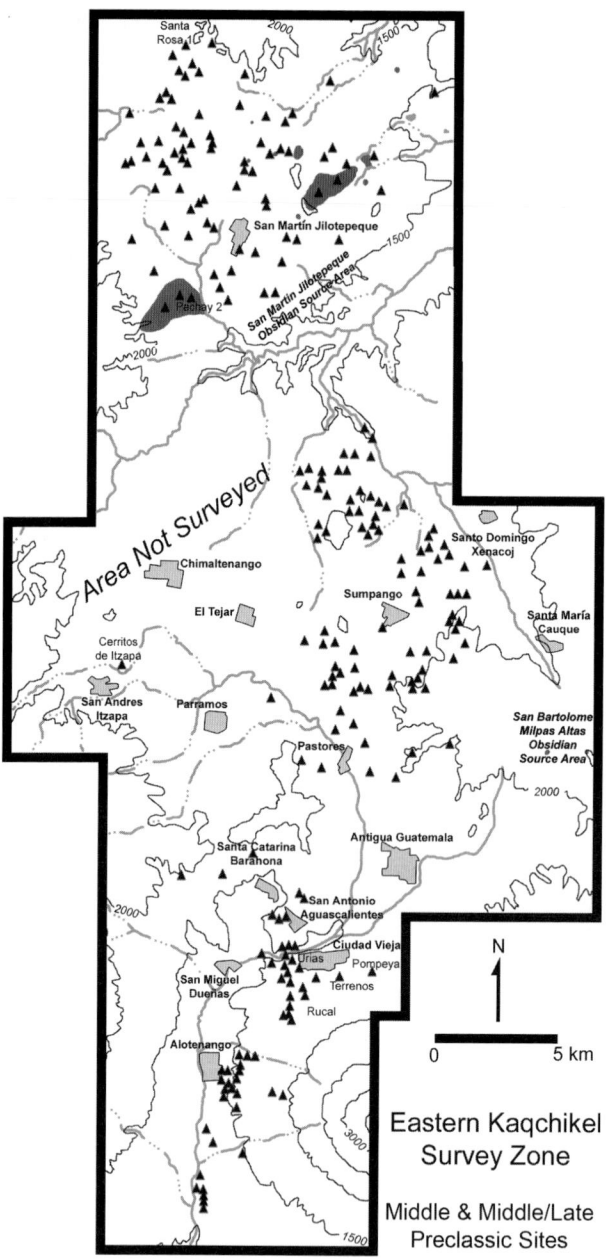

FIGURE 5.1 Middle and Middle/Late Preclassic (900/800–250/150 BC) sites of the eastern Kaqchikel highlands: note that all Agua-phase sites were also occupied during the following Sacatepequez phase. Triangles are Type I sites (sherd and lithic scatters lacking visible mound architecture); medium gray indicates natural obsidian outcrops; light gray indicates modern *cabeceras* (named in bold roman type); archaeological sites mentioned in the text are named in regular roman type; contour interval is 500 meters.

We suspect that early populations were drawn to this environmentally rich portion of the Kaqchikel highlands because of its proximity to the Pacific piedmont – the region from which early agriculture and settlers most likely spread – and because of the local abundance of water, game, and fertile soils. The region also may have held ritual significance for its first permanent settlers. Near Urías is La Casa de las Golondrinas, a rock shelter with pictographs that have yielded an AMS date of 1450–1000 BC (Robinson 2008). Thus, along with the subsistence potential of the area, the sacred nature of this location containing springs and mountains may have attracted Early Preclassic peoples (Robinson *et al.* 2007).

Middle Preclassic settlement

Survey of the Antigua Valley, Chimaltenango, and Sumpango

One important focus of Middle to early Late Preclassic settlement was the southern end of the Antigua Valley around what is now Ciudad Vieja (see Figure 5.1). Among numerous sites in this region are Urías, Rucal, Terrenos, and Pompeya (Borhegyi 1950). Together, the Middle to early Late Preclassic sites in this small area constitute 7 percent of all the sites known in the much larger Antigua Valley.

Another important zone of occupation probably existed in the Chimaltenango *altiplano*, a roughly circular, flat area surrounding the modern town of Chimaltenango. García's (1992) survey identified 16 Middle to early Late Preclassic sites in this 15-kilometer wide zone. One of these is San Lorenzo El Tejar (see Figure 5.1). Excavations and surface collections yielded ceramics, but no architectural features could be unambiguously dated to this period. García argues that several mound sites in Chimaltenango, such as Cerritos de Izapa, date to this period.[4] Nonetheless, we stress that virtually all of the surveyed or excavated Middle to early Late Preclassic sites also have Classic-period pottery. Within the survey areas, we have not yet located any Type II mound site that we can confidently date to the Preclassic period. Thus, although it is possible that some Type II sites dating to the Middle to early Late Preclassic may be found in the Chimaltenango area, the settlement hierarchy of Alotenango, Sumpango, and the Antigua Valley apparently consisted only of Type I sites. Until more excavations are conducted, the chronology of the mounds themselves is open to question.

Early Preclassic sherds were recovered from just seven sites in the Antigua Valley, but Middle to early Late Preclassic material was found at 36 sites (35 percent of the 104 sites known in the valley). In Sumpango, very few Early Preclassic sherds have been found, but 73 percent (or 82/113) of the sites known in the *municipio* have Middle to early Late Preclassic ceramics. The increase in the number of sites implies substantial population growth during the fifth through third centuries BC. Population growth, the burials of ritual specialists (see below), and the defensible location of sites all suggest the emergence of incipient complexity in the Antigua Valley and its environs during the Middle to early Late Preclassic period.

Excavations at San Lorenzo

The site of San Lorenzo El Tejar is situated on a peninsula of land surrounded by two deep ravines forming a defensible locale. It is approximately 7 kilometers northeast of Cerritos de Izapa, which may contain a Middle to early Late Preclassic mound and hence conceivably belonged to a polity centered at that site. Test excavations at San Lorenzo revealed a Preclassic burial 3.4 meters deep cut into *talpetate*, the local bedrock. Burial furniture included quartz crystals and pieces of obsidian and chert found in the chest cavity of the buried individual. We suggest that these items were once contained in a pouch tied around the neck and constitute the kit of a ritual specialist or diviner. The principal figure was accompanied by a second individual who apparently was not interred with grave goods.

Do differences in burial furniture at Middle to early Late Preclassic San Lorenzo demonstrate contrasts in individual wealth? The data from throughout the Kaqchikel highlands are somewhat ambiguous. In the western Kaqchikel region, tomb burials of this period at Semetebaj suggest that leaders had considerable status (Shook and Popenoe Hatch 1978). At Zacat, on the eastern boundary of Sumpango, Shook salvaged an exposed Preclassic burial of an individual laid out in a crypt made of uncut stone. Grave goods included red-and-black incised bowls and jars (Shook and Popenoe de Hatch 1999). This, too, was seemingly the burial of a special-status individual. Whether such status was achieved or ascribed is unknown.

Excavations at Rucal

Excavations have also provided insights concerning the construction of early villages in the Antigua area. Deep, sterile strata at Rucal consist of tumbled boulders and rocks deposited by landslides. Above these is a layer of volcanic cinder 20 centimeters thick. By 1000 BC, approximately 10 centimeters of soil had developed, covering the ash and rock and making the site suitable for occupation by agriculturalists. Sometime after this, settlers of Rucal built an earthen platform 60 centimeters high (Robinson and Pye 1996). Associated with the platform – which probably supported a perishable residential structure – were grinding stones, a miniature cache pot, and animal bones.

Excavations at Urías

At this second site in the Antigua region, our excavations revealed another platform that is 60 centimeters high and 4 meters long. Ceramic materials suggest it is roughly contemporary with the platform at Rucal. A boulder 60 centimeters wide was positioned on top of the Urías platform. The interior of the earthen mound was reinforced by stones, and at the center of its base was found a modest cache containing animal bones and a worked sherd from a red-on-buff vessel with an appliquéd face. The platform and its simple stone marker may have been an early ritual space that defined the territory of a social group (Robinson *et al.* 2001).

Stratigraphically above the low, stone-topped platform dating to about 1000 BC lay a plain stela 50 centimeters long that probably served as a territorial marker during the Middle Preclassic period. It was found lying horizontally on a floor above a cache of early Middle Preclassic ceramics. These include a red-on-black shallow bowl with a horizontal everted rim and a black incurved-wall bowl with postslip incision on its exterior (Robinson *et al.* 2002). Similar pottery has been identified at Las Charcas-phase Kaminaljuyu and Naranjo, suggesting that the stela cache was deposited early in the first millennium BC. In contrast, three problematic radiocarbon assays for this context have intercept dates in the fifth century BC, during the late Middle Preclassic. For well-known geophysical reasons, radiocarbon dates from the Middle Preclassic period are notoriously unreliable and often span the entire period.

However this dating quandary is resolved, it appears that, during the first half of the first millennium BC, customs changed from the construction of low platforms supporting stone markers to the erection of stelae with ceramic caches. The Urías stela might be contemporary with the stelae and altars from Naranjo dating to the Las Charcas phase (Arroyo 2006, 2010), appears to be roughly coeval with the earliest carved stelae in the Maya lowlands, and is significantly older than the Providencia-phase carved monuments from Kaminaljuyu and Piedra Parada. It also may be considered a precursor to the plain, large stelae that were erected during the Middle and Late Preclassic in plaza contexts throughout the highlands and Pacific coast (see Bove 2011).

Survey of San Martín Jilotepeque

Permanent occupation of San Martin Jilotepeque began near the end of the Middle Preclassic period. A total of 77 sites (52 percent of all known sites in San Martin Jilotepeque) dating to this period were discovered, but occupation is best described as broadly distributed and low in density (see Figure 5.1). We found no sculpture dating to the Preclassic, but the blank stelae at Pachay 2 could be this old. Most sites probably contained only one or two house lots, but the largest two communities, probable small villages, measured 1 hectare (Pachay 2) and 3.3 hectares in size. Santa Rosa 1, the largest of the Preclassic sites, has a single earthen mound of uncertain but probably Early Classic date. Thus at present it seems best to classify all Preclassic sites in San Martin Jilotepeque as Type I sherd scatters.

The two largest late Middle to early Late Preclassic sites are located in environmentally strategic positions. Santa Rosa 1 is situated on an open plain ideal for agriculture. Pachay 2 is adjacent to the Pachay obsidian quarries, suggesting that obsidian extraction was a motive for settlement. Nearest neighbor analysis indicates that late Middle to early Late Preclassic sites are spaced randomly with regard to each other, but we note a slight tendency for habitation sites to be located near exploited obsidian quarries (Braswell 1998).

Unlike Urías, Rucal, and a few other eastern Kaqchikel sites where both Middle Preclassic Las Charcas ceramics and even some Early Preclassic sherds related to Pacific coast types were recovered, the earliest pottery of San Martin Jilotepeque can be classified as Sacatepequez ceramics. Despite many shared similarities with (early?) Providencia-phase material from Kaminaljuyu, the late Middle to early Late Preclassic pottery of San Martin Jilotepeque is less diverse and notably impoverished.

The Valley of Guatemala

Compared with sites in the eastern Kaqchikel region, Preclassic Kaminaljuyu was a large and hierarchically organized center. Numerous monumental constructions in the Valley of Guatemala, including the colossal La Culebra mounds, date to the Providencia phase (Ericastilla Godoy and Shibata 1991; Navarrete and Luján Muñoz 1986). Pedestal sculptures (Parsons 1986), mushroom stones (Ohi and Torres 1994), figurines, and elaborate figural censers all suggest complex religious practices and craft specialization.

Three kilometers northeast of Kaminaljuyu, located near a stream and natural hill – key Mesoamerican sacred landscape features – is Naranjo, a Middle Preclassic ceremonial and residential site. Unlike Urías and Rucal, Naranjo has no Early Preclassic pottery with modes similar to Pacific coast examples. It is notable for having a mound 7 meters high, numerous ceremonial deposits, and 27 known monuments of unworked stone (Arroyo 2006, 2010). Many of the stone monuments were found placed in three lines oriented 20 degrees east of north, suggesting their ritual importance. The central structure, called Mound 1, and the southern platform were constructed during the Middle Preclassic Las Charcas phase. Mound 1 was enlarged several times during the later Providencia phase and may have become a purely ceremonial platform at that time (Arroyo 2006). Naranjo also has low earthen platforms in residential areas surrounding the ceremonial mounds. The great dimensions of these platforms indicate that they supported much larger structures than the platforms discovered at Urías and Rucal (Pereira and Arroyo 2008). In sum, Naranjo is a much larger and more complex Middle Preclassic site than anything yet known in the eastern Kaqchikel region. In addition, it is older than any site known in the northern half of our survey zone.

Las Charcas-phase ceramics have also been found in the southeastern portion of the Valley of Guatemala and are lightly scattered to the west, covering an area roughly 10 kilometers wide. Excavations at Piedra Parada (de León and Valdés 2002), 10 kilometers southeast of Kaminaljuyu, have revealed low earthen structures, approximately 50 centimeters high, like those at Urías and Rucal. This suggests that, in peripheral areas of the Valley of Guatemala, village life may have been comparable in simplicity to that of the eastern Kaqchikel highlands. Nevertheless, the abundant figurines and figural censer prongs discovered at Piedra Parada demonstrate that the site was integrated more closely ideologically with Kaminaljuyu than was the eastern Kaqchikel region.

Middle Preclassic ceramics

The Middle Preclassic Agua complex (900/800–500/400 BC)

The simple architectural and ritual remains recovered from deep stratigraphic levels at Urías and Rucal belie the complexity of material culture that existed during the early first millennium BC. Pottery from both these sites represents the earliest ceramic complex, called Agua, from the Antigua Valley, and is similar to the first well-represented pottery complex in the Valley of Guatemala, called Las Charcas. A striking feature of early ceramics from throughout the highlands is that they are neither products of primitive attempts to make pottery nor simple copies of coastal or piedmont modal combinations. Comparisons with ceramics described by Shook (1952), the latter's first-hand help with identification in 1993, a review of his many excellent yet unpublished notes and drawings, and comparisons with materials stored at the Instituto de Antropología e Historia reveal many similarities between the Agua and Las Charcas complexes. Like Las Charcas pottery known from Kaminaljuyu and Naranjo, Middle Preclassic Agua collections contain Streaky Gray Brown or black-brown bowls with arch motifs created by postslip incision. They also have wide-line impressions. Other decorated types, mostly bowl forms, have white, cream, red, or orange slips. Painted ceramics have varied surface treatments and can be described as orange-on-cream, orange-on-buff, zoned and incised red-on-buff or red-on-orange, and red-on-black/brown. Similar pottery, including Pallid Red jars and red-on-buff ceramics, has been found at other piedmont and Pacific coast sites.

Other plain Agua-complex pottery from Urías and Rucal includes a distinctive ware with a surface treatment identical to that of pottery from the piedmont and Pacific coast. This is El Balsamo Brown Ware estimated to date to 900–600 BC. The Gashed Incised type consists of jars with deep, diagonal slash incisions on the exterior of the neck or upper shoulder (Shook and Popenoe Hatch 1978). Fred Bove and Bárbara Arroyo refer to this type as Cuchillo, and Arroyo places it at 600 BC (Bárbara Arroyo, personal communication 2013). The zoned-punctate correlate, called Costeño, is part of the original El Balsamo Brown Ware and is known on the Pacific coast and at the piedmont site of Los Cerritos-Sur (Arroyo 1994). Other Agua bowls from Urías and Rucal that have zoned-punctate decoration are similar to Monte Alto Brown Ware, known from the coastal Preclassic center of the same name.

Neutron-activation analyses of Agua-complex ceramics reveal that the interaction network of the Preclassic people who inhabited Urías was at least 50 kilometers in radius. Sherds from Rucal and Urías are chemically similar to examples from the Pacific coast, piedmont, and highlands. Noteworthy ceramics with coastal pastes that were found at Urías and Rucal are two incised black examples, three others with a buff paste, and one with a cream slip. The distribution of El Balsamo Brown Gashed Incised pottery – manufactured in the piedmont – at sites in the highlands (including Rucal and Urías) and Pacific coast demonstrates that people moved goods among these three areas.

In sum, ties with Las Charcas-phase Kaminaljuyu and Naranjo are evident in the Middle Preclassic ceramics of the eastern Kaqchikel region. Naranjo ceramics are generally similar to those of the eastern Kaqchikel zone. Exceptions at Naranjo are sherds with "Olmec" or "Maya" symbols (Arroyo 2006). A few "Olmec" motifs do occur on Urías pottery, but are rare. Thus it seems likely that Kaminaljuyu did not dominate the open interaction network in which simple agricultural settlements such as Urías and Rucal participated.

The Middle/Late Preclassic Sacatepequez complex (500/400–250/150 BC)

The diagnostic pottery of the late Middle Preclassic to early Late Preclassic periods is Sacatepequez White-Paste White Ware, later renamed Xuc Ware (Shook 1952; Shook and Popenoe Hatch 1978; Shook and Popenoe de Hatch 1999; Shook et al. 1979). This pottery is highly distinctive for its bright white color derived from the paste rather than from a slip. Xuc Ware has a broad distribution, from Lake Atitlan to Kaminaljuyu and the Pacific coast. Its origin is probably the Sacatepequez highlands. Neutron-activation analyses of Xuc pottery recovered from Kaminaljuyu, sites along the Pacific coast, and settlements in the eastern Kaqchikel highlands have found the best fit with a clay sample from San Martin Jilotepeque. Shook found an unfired vessel in an exposed burial at Zacat, indicating that a production center must have been nearby (Neff *et al.* 1994). The broad distribution of Xuc Ware and its frequency in the eastern Kaqchikel region suggest that it may have been made by many potters practicing a household-industry level of production.

Other pottery types diagnostic of this time period at Kaminaljuyu were widely distributed and demonstrate that exchange in pottery – or ideas about it – occurred broadly in the highlands during the late Middle Preclassic to early Late Preclassic period. Popenoe de Hatch (1997) notes that Terra (a red-paste pottery that appears predominantly as *comales* and as a vessel form with three conical supports) and Sumpango (a cream-slip pottery with red paint that appears in jar and bowl forms) have been found principally at Kaminaljuyu but also appear at sites in the Departments of Chimaltenango and Sacatepequez. Nonetheless, these types were encountered only rarely in our survey and excavation collections – and not at all in collections from San Martin Jilotepeque; therefore they did not serve as meaningful diagnostics for dating the sites. As the Providencia phase progressed and that complex became more elaborate at Kaminaljuyu, there were fewer and fewer ceramic ties with the Sacatepequez complex of the Kaqchikel region.

Middle and Middle/Late Preclassic obsidian

Braswell has analyzed 38,436 obsidian artifacts from our various projects, as well as 2,756 artifacts from middens in the Miraflores II sector of Kaminaljuyu. Although a significant portion of the artifacts from the eastern Kaqchikel region date to the Middle and early Late Preclassic periods, as judged by their association with Agua and Sacatepequez ceramic types, most come from mixed or very meager single-component surface collections. By far the best evidence yet gathered for this early period comes from Urías, where 2,202 obsidian artifacts, many of which lay beneath a Middle Preclassic floor, were recovered during the course of excavations. Preliminary results of the analysis of 1,338 of these artifacts have been reported (Robinson *et al.* 2002) and are repeated here.

Some 277 analyzed obsidian artifacts came from the lower levels of excavations. These were accompanied by ceramics that date primarily to the Middle Preclassic Agua phase. An additional 512 artifacts came from higher stratigraphic positions and date to Sacatepequez times. All artifacts were assigned to specific types in a behavioral typology that distinguishes among four distinct lithic industries: prismatic blade production, the retouch (or uniface/biface) industry, bipolar percussion, and casual percussion. Some artifacts, notably non-diagnostic shatter and small fragmentary flakes, were assigned to an undifferentiated percussion category.

Fully 91.7 percent (N = 254) of the Middle Preclassic Agua-phase obsidian artifacts pertain to the bipolar, casual, or undifferentiated percussion industries. Only 4.0 percent (N = 11; all prismatic blade fragments) of the obsidian artifacts dating to this phase are assigned to the prismatic blade industry. During the late Middle and early Late Preclassic, the proportion represented by percussion industries dropped slightly, to 84.4 percent (N = 432), while the relative frequency of blade-related artifacts more than tripled, growing to 13.3 percent (N = 68). Given that the stratigraphically lower Agua-phase contexts contain small quantities of later Sacatepequez ceramics (i.e., there is a limited amount of mixing), it is likely that some or all of the 11 prismatic blade fragments from these levels actually date to this later period. Scholars have argued that prismatic blade technology was introduced to Chiapas, the Pacific coast of Guatemala, and western Belize at the inception of the Middle Preclassic period (Awe and Healy 1994; Clark 1988; Jackson and Love 1991). Excavations at Urías support this hypothesis and further suggest that prismatic blade production was not well established in the eastern Kaqchikel region until the end of the Middle Preclassic period.

Three geological sources are represented in our Preclassic obsidian collections. These are San Martin Jilotepeque, San Bartolome Milpas Altas, and El Chayal. The first two are located within the eastern Kaqchikel highlands (see Figures 4.1 and 4.2) and the third is some 30 kilometers northeast of Kaminaljuyu. All three are within a two-day walk from Urías. At that site, we could find no statistical difference between obsidian procurement patterns of the Middle Preclassic and later Middle to Late Preclassic periods. A total of 526 (66.7 percent) of the Preclassic obsidian artifacts from Urías come from the San Martin Jilotepeque source, 256 (32.4 percent) from El Chayal, and seven (0.9 percent) from San Bartolome Milpas Altas. El Chayal is 53 kilometers from Urías and San Martin Jilotepeque only 27 kilometers from the site. Thus, the relative quantities of obsidian from these two sources are directly related to distance. San Bartolome Milpas Altas, however, is the closest source to Urías and is located only 14 kilometers away. Material from this source fractures in an uneven and unpredictable manner. It is poorly suited for making tools and hence was never heavily exploited.

Although we have little quantitative data for other regions, the distance-decay pattern observed at Urías seems to hold for Sumpango, San Martin Jilotepeque, Alotenango, and other surveyed areas. El Chayal obsidian is found throughout the eastern Kaqchikel region, but it appears less commonly in San Martin Jilotepeque (the most distant *municipio*) than in our other survey zones. A Classic-period site at Cerro Alux, a mountain that serves as a landmark between the Kaqchikel highlands and the Valley of Guatemala, has a fairly even mixture of obsidian from the two sources.

This same pattern of distance-decay is also observed at Middle Preclassic Kaminaljuyu. Braswell has analyzed 2,756 obsidian artifacts recovered by the recent Proyecto Kaminaljuyú - Miraflores II, directed by Marion Popenoe de Hatch and Juan Antonio Valdés. Although this sample represents but a minute fraction (less than 1 percent) of the entire collection, it is drawn from the clearest single-component and transitional-phase middens excavated by that project. Among these artifacts are 51 pieces provisionally dated to the Arevalo/Las Charcas phases, six pieces from a transitional Las Charcas/Providencia context, and 106 obsidian artifacts from Providencia-phase middens. During Middle Preclassic Arevalo/Las Charcas times, obsidian was brought to Kaminaljuyu from both the El Chayal (88 percent; N = 45) and San Martin Jilotepeque sources (12 percent; N = 6). In transitional Las Charcas/Providencia and pure Providencia-phase contexts, fully 99.1 percent (N = 111) of the obsidian artifacts come from El Chayal, and only 0.9 percent (N = 1) are from the San Martin Jilotepeque source. Thus, although San Martin Jilotepeque obsidian was used at Kaminaljuyu throughout the Middle and early Late Preclassic, trade with the eastern Kaqchikel region declined significantly during the first millennium BC.

The eastern Kaqchikel region during the Late and Terminal Preclassic Periods

Late Preclassic settlement after 250/150 BC

During the Late Preclassic Verbena and Arenal phases, Kaminaljuyu emerged as the vibrant core of one of the most important polities of the southern Maya area. It is doubtful that it ever regained this level of regional importance at any later period, except perhaps during the Late Classic, when it was once again the center of a major highland polity. Although we question whether Late Preclassic Kaminaljuyu can be called a "state" – analogies with Formative Teotihuacan and with major Mississippian centers such as Moundville and Cahokia seem more appropriate – there is no question that important and influential artistic, writing, and political conventions coalesced at Kaminaljuyu during the last two centuries of the first millennium BC (e.g., Kaplan 2000; Parsons 1986). It also is probable that the predecessor of what eventually became the tradition of divine kingship existed at Kaminaljuyu at this time.[5]

In contrast to the splendor of Kaminaljuyu, the eastern Kaqchikel highlands did not grow and prosper during the second half of the Late Preclassic. Instead, the region became a depopulated buffer zone between (Ch'olan?) Mayan speakers of the Valley of Guatemala and Proto-K'iche'an people from the northwestern highlands. What is clear is that the eastern Kaqchikel region was not subject to expansionary settlement from Kaminaljuyu but instead saw a significant decline in population that in some places amounted to abandonment.

Late Preclassic settlement in Sumpango, the Valley of Antigua, and Alotenango

During the second half of the Late Preclassic (i.e., after about 250/150 BC), the number of sites decreased throughout the eastern Kaqchikel highlands (Figure 5.2). Although 73 percent of the sites surveyed in Sumpango had Middle/Late Preclassic Sacatepequez ceramics, later Late Preclassic pottery was recovered from only 12 percent (14 of 113) of the total number of sites in that *municipio*. A less profound change occurred in the Antigua region. There, 24 sites (of a total of 104) date to the Late Preclassic and Terminal Preclassic periods, representing a loss of one-third of the number of sites inhabited during the late Middle to early Late Preclassic. In contrast, the difference in the number of Middle/early Late Preclassic and later Late Preclassic sites known from Alotenango is probably meaningless, dropping from 26 to 24.[6] As in earlier Sacatepequez-phase times, all later Late Preclassic sites are designated as Type I artifact scatters.

Late Preclassic settlement in San Martin Jilotepeque

Only 24 sites (or 16 percent of all those known) dating to the second half of the Late Preclassic period were identified in San Martin Jilotepeque (Figure 5.2). Most important, sherds diagnostic of the period 250/150 BC to AD 200/250 account for just 0.8 percent of the diagnostic ceramics recovered from these sites. Thus it seems likely that this very limited occupation represents lingering Middle to early Late Preclassic settlement or precocious Early Classic reoccupation. Given that the Early Classic saw the introduction of an entirely new ceramic tradition in the region, the first possibility is most likely. San Martin Jilotepeque was abandoned by about 250/150 BC, and it did not see significant repopulation for four or five hundred years.

As in the Middle/Late Preclassic, the settlement hierarchy of the later Late Preclassic consisted of only one level, and habitation sites were positioned randomly with regard to each other. No imported ceramics were found, and the few identified sherds belong not to the Miraflores sphere of Kaminaljuyu but to the local Sacatepequez tradition.

Late Preclassic population loss and abandonment

The precise reasons why San Martin Jilotepeque was abandoned and other areas of the eastern Kaqchikel highlands suffered population loss are somewhat uncertain

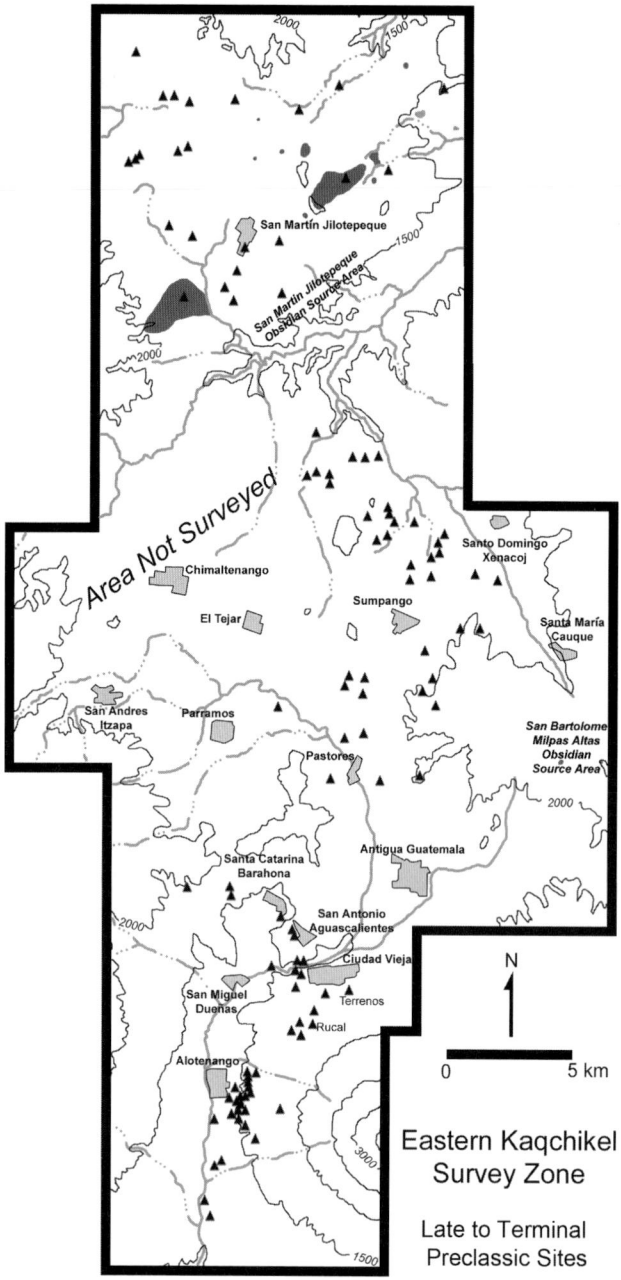

FIGURE 5.2 Late and Terminal Preclassic (250/150 BC–AD 150/250) sites of the eastern Kaqchikel highlands: triangles are Type I sites (sherd and lithic scatters lacking visible mound architecture); medium gray indicates natural obsidian outcrops; light gray indicates modern *cabeceras* (named in bold roman type); archaeological sites mentioned in the text are named in regular roman type; contour interval is 500 meters.

but may be partially understood in terms of both "push" factors, caused by the early movement of Proto-K'iche'an people – who during the Late and Terminal Preclassic periods began to make Solano tradition ceramics (Popenoe de Hatch 1997, 1998, 2002) – into the region to the northwest of our survey area, and "pull" factors attracting immigrants to vibrant and cosmopolitan Kaminaljuyu. We do not argue that these Proto-K'iche'an peoples actually moved into the eastern Kaqchikel region during the Late Preclassic. This clearly did not occur until the Early Classic period. Instead, we suggest that much of the eastern Kaqchikel region became an unoccupied buffer zone *between* these people and Kaminaljuyu. Supporting the notion of Late Preclassic pressure from the northwest is the fact that the two northern *municipios* in our survey zone (San Martin Jilotepeque and Sumpango) were dramatically depopulated, while the southern sector (the Antigua Valley and particularly Alotenango) did not suffer as drastic a loss of population after 250/150 BC.

Was population decrease during the Late Preclassic caused by local or regional environmental problems? That is, might some of the "push" factors have been environmental in nature? There is a growing body of data showing that much of the Maya region suffered significant decline during the second half of the Late Preclassic period and that this decline occurred at a time of environmental uncertainty, climatic instability, and drought felt throughout Central America (Braswell and Miller-Sisson 2013; Braswell *et al.* 2004; Freidel *et al.* 2001, 2007; Haug *et al.* 2003; Hodell *et al.* 2001; Kennett *et al.* 2012; Neff *et al.* 2006; Velez *et al.* 2011; Webster *et al.* 2007). In Peten, important cities of the Mirador Basin were depopulated and abandoned at the end of the period. In the Pacific coast and piedmont regions of southern Guatemala and Chiapas, complex chiefdoms that produced elaborate sculpture – including some examples with hieroglyphic inscriptions and a few with Initial Series Dates – ceased to erect stone monuments during the second century AD. Finally, the great florescence of Kaminaljuyu came to a close at the end of the Arenal phase at about AD 150. The roughly simultaneous decline of both the Chicanel (Maya lowlands) and "Miraflores" (central and eastern Maya highlands) exchange spheres could be linked events. When demographic decline and political fragmentation are seen to occur in so many diverse regions during the same period, it is reasonable to search for a shared environmental cause. More narrowly, although demographic decline began earlier in the Kaqchikel region than at Kaminaljuyu, the two events may have been causally linked to the same environmental changes.

One possible clue related to environmental stress is found at Kaminaljuyu itself. There, the Miraflores Canal, which drained water from the southeast end of Lake Miraflores, was constructed by the end of Providencia times (Barrientos Quezada 1997a, 1997b). A larger and more complex canal was later excavated as Lake Miraflores began to dry up – it disappeared completely by AD 250 – possibly signaling a regional drought. Popenoe de Hatch (2002: 284), however, carefully notes that there are other explanations. If the disappearance of this one lake is attributed to a regional drought (and other causes, such as overuse or tectonic activity, are possible), it may be that the Late Preclassic was a period of declining environmental conditions. Environmental data from nearby Lake Amatitlan suggest a demographic decline during the Late Preclassic. Velez *et al.* (2011) have reconstructed the late Holocene environment from multiple lines of evidence derived from a sediment core taken from the lake. They note that the Middle Preclassic, Early Classic, and Late Postclassic saw periods of population growth. This is based on evidence for deforestation and soil erosion. In contrast, the Late Preclassic, Late Classic, and Early Postclassic periods were typified by reforestation and stable soils. Most relevant, their study of diatoms indicates that the water level in Lake Amatitlan was low during the Late Preclassic, and that its trophic status – especially as measured by available oxygen – was higher during the period 250 BC to AD 125. Thus, during the second half of the Late Preclassic period, farming at Lake Amatitlan decreased dramatically, people moved away – presumably to Kaminaljuyu – and the forest recovered. What is important about this evidence is that this decline was contemporary with that of the eastern Kaqchikel region and with the remarkable surge in growth seen at Kaminaljuyu. A "push" factor could have been locally deteriorating climatic conditions, while a "pull" factor might have been greater environmental stability at Kaminaljuyu itself, created in part by hydraulic engineering projects at the site.

Corroborating data derive from Lake Quilisimate in the Antigua Valley. Cores from the lakebed show a drying episode with sharp declines in arboreal, herbal, and aquatic species. All pollen counts approached zero at 280 BC – that is, towards the end of the Sacatepequez phase. Active volcanism demonstrated by deep ash falls also correlates with population declines in the Antigua Valley during the Late Preclassic (Freidel *et al.* 2007). Perhaps, then, people left the eastern Kaqchikel region in favor of the Valley of Guatemala because environmental degradation was mitigated somewhat by water management at Kaminaljuyu and its distance from the active Pacaya volcano.

One possible cause of a Late Preclassic drought is global cooling. Two significant cooling events have been noted during the periods 200–100 BC and AD 200–350 (Braswell *et al.* 2004: fig. 8). Possible collaborating evidence of a drought caused by global cooling can be seen in the pattern of Late Preclassic abandonment. The *municipios* in our survey region that experienced the greatest Late Preclassic population loss were San Martin Jilotepeque and Sumpango. These areas are at higher elevations and are considerably cooler than the Antigua Valley, and today suffer from occasional frosts. During a period of global cooling, frosts would have been even more common, making winter agriculture even riskier. In contrast, Late Preclassic population loss was less severe in the Antigua region and minimal in low, hot, and moist Alotenango. Demographic patterns, therefore, demonstrate a shift from higher to lower elevations during the Late Preclassic. This distribution is consistent with a period of global cooling and hence may also suggest a drought.

Environmental evidence suggesting climatic instability is not limited to the Maya highlands. Hector Neff and his colleagues (2006) have collected data directly relevant to the Southern Maya Region. Pollen and charcoal indicators from sediment cores taken from the Manchon swamp in Pacific Guatemala correspond to archaeological data showing generally high levels of occupation between roughly 750 BC and AD 800. According to core MAN015, the Pacific plains and piedmont experienced stable climatic conditions with copious rainfall until about AD 50. A slight drop in metals and an increase in the Rubidium to Aluminum ratio of the soils suggest that conditions in Pacific Guatemala dried up in the first century AD. Most climatic shifts in the sediment core record from the Manchon swamp correspond to similar paleoclimate proxies derived from cores in the Cariaco Basin, Venezuela (Haug *et al.* 2003). Nonetheless, a dry period around AD 50 is not evident in the Cariaco record. There, severe dry periods took place during the first century BC and the third century AD.

To the north, Hodell and his colleagues (2001) discuss paleoclimate data determined from multiple sediment cores from Lake Chichancanab, located in southern Yucatan. They note periods of alternating dry and wet periods with a heavy deposit of gypsum – indicating reduced rainfall – from AD 90 to 230.

Even more climate data have been derived from speleothems. Stalagmites grow in caves as water drips on to the floor carrying calcium carbonate. Speleothems incorporate trace elements related to environmental conditions into their structure, and so can record long-term, high-resolution climate data. Lachniet and his colleagues (2004) discuss climate data for the period 180 BC to AD 1310 derived from a speleothem collected in the Chilibrillo Cave in the Panama Canal zone. Within that period, they note nine episodes of high $\delta^{18}O$ values that correspond to pronounced rainfall reductions. The first two of these occurred within the interval of AD 200–320, completely consistent with the Carioca Basin data but dating shortly after the decline of the Preclassic Maya. Together, these data suggest that a drought began later in southern Central America and northern South America than in the Maya region itself. Lachniet *et al.* (2004) tie these periods of drought to increased El Niño activity that greatly reduced seasonal tropical monsoons.

Closer to home, there are several analyses of speleothems from caves in Belize. The first, by Webster *et al.* (2007), comes from a sample taken from the Macal Chasm, Belize. It has low temporal resolution but implies a spike in dry conditions at the beginning of the current era. A speleothem from the Yok Balum Cave in southern Belize has yielded paleoclimate data for 40 BC until the present with 20-year temporal resolution. Kennett and his colleagues (2012) report periods of drought lasting from about AD 50 to AD 300, with particularly prolonged periods beginning about AD 150. This corresponds quite well with the collapse of Kaminaljuyu but is significantly later than decline in the eastern Kaqchikel region.

Other conceivable environmental catastrophes are local or regional in scope. These include soil exhaustion and volcanic eruption in the eastern Kaqchikel highlands. Soil exhaustion and a concomitant decrease in agricultural production, however, probably were not causal factors leading to population loss in the Antigua zone during the Late Preclassic. Patricia Farrell and her team have studied soils from this area and note that they retain extreme fertility over time because of frequent renewal by ash fall (Robinson *et al.* 2002). Moreover, the cinder content of soils and their resultant sandy texture tends to impede erosion even on steep slopes.

A more viable possibility is that a volcanic eruption may have ended settlement in some areas. In the Antigua Valley, we have uncovered evidence from two contexts of an eruption before 260 BC and probably around 400 BC (Freidel *et al.* 2001, 2007) – that is, roughly at the end of the Agua phase. Nevertheless, settlement distributions for the valley and within the eastern Kaqchikel region as a whole do not show that an eruption particularly affected populations living near Fuego volcano. In fact, the greatest loss of population during the Late Preclassic seems to have been at a later time in Sumpango and San Martin Jilotepeque, those areas farthest from active volcanoes.

Late Preclassic ceramics

One of the important utilitarian diagnostics for the post-Providencia, Late Preclassic at Kaminaljuyu is a ceramic similar to Xuc Ware called Izote Ware (Popenoe de Hatch 1997). Izote is a purple-painted white ware that differs from preceding Xuc pottery in that its decorative incision is finer. Izote forms include deep basins and jars with small handles. In Sumpango, the Antigua Valley, and Alotenango, Izote Ware is the most frequent temporal diagnostic of the second half of the Late Preclassic (Robinson 1990).

Navarro Ware is an Arenal-phase ceramic from Kaminaljuyu (dated to 200 BC to AD 100 in the traditional chronology, but to AD 50–150 by Inomata 2013). It is similar to Izote except that it has a darker paste and is white slipped. In the Department of Sacatepequez, it is called Chuya Ware. Chuya Red-on-White vessels have a characteristic red paste and a thick white slip, and often are decorated with red paint or are incised. Although the paste is quite different, Chuya Red-on-White is considered a successor to Izote Ware because of decoration and form. Robinson (1993: 35–7) describes three varieties, two of which are assigned a Late Preclassic date. The third variety may have been produced during the Early Classic period. In San Martin Jilotepeque, Chuya Red-on-White is the most common or, more accurately, least rare later Late Preclassic ceramic.

Other domestic ceramics typical of the later Late Preclassic at Kaminaljuyu have analogs in the Sacatepequez region. These are Sumpango, a red-painted red ware, and Rofino, which appears in the form of red-painted bowls with incurved rims. Important wares characteristic of the southeastern highlands, especially Usulutan resist-decorated ceramics with nubbin supports, are very rare to nonexistent in our survey collections. To us, it appears that the westernmost highland extension of this decorative mode is Kaminaljuyu. Occasional sherds of fine incised black and brown pottery, as well as incised Verbena White, show relations with Kaminaljuyu but are missing from our later Late Preclassic collections from San Martin Jilotepeque. In sum, the decorative motifs and techniques of the Miraflores Ceramic Sphere do not extend into the eastern Kaqchikel region (and, of course, the existence of the ceramic sphere has even been called into question by Demarest 2011). Furthermore, the Late Preclassic complex of the region has very little variety compared to that of contemporary Kaminaljuyu.

If there were colonial enclaves from Kaminaljuyu in the eastern Kaqchikel region, we would expect closer ceramic ties with the Valley of Guatemala than our impoverished collections demonstrate. Previously, following Popenoe de Hatch (1997), we interpreted this as indicating the development of barriers to trade. We now *also* see the attenuation of ceramic ties during the later Late Preclassic as part of a process of depopulation and site abandonment. In short, as population levels dropped in the eastern Kaqchikel highlands during the Late Preclassic, ceramic drift from Kaminaljuyu increased. Pottery does not support the conjecture of a "Miraflores state" (Kaplan 2011a, 2011b) extending west into the Kaqchikel highlands.

Late Preclassic obsidian

There can be little doubt that obsidian artifacts manufactured and used during the second half of the Late Preclassic period were recovered during the extensive surface surveys and excavations in the eastern Kaqchikel region. Nonetheless, since we have not identified single-component later Late Preclassic sites or stratigraphic levels, we have been unable to discriminate such Late Preclassic obsidian from artifacts of other periods. The dearth of such clear contexts underscores the probability of abandonment of much of the eastern Kaqchikel region.

Fortunately, the degree of interaction between the eastern Kaqchikel region and Kaminaljuyu during the second half of the Late Preclassic period can be assessed through the examination of obsidian artifacts recovered from Verbena-phase (400–200 BC in the conventional chronology, but 100 BC to AD 50 according to Inomata 2013) and Arenal-phase (200 BC to AD 100 or AD 50–150) middens excavated by the Miraflores II project. The particularly large and rich Santa Clara-phase (AD 150–200/250 in our estimation) collection, of which only a very small fraction has been analyzed, provides information on exchange between the two regions during the Terminal Preclassic period.

Some 55 obsidian artifacts were recovered from a Providencia-Verbena midden dating to the Late Preclassic period. All come from the El Chayal source, reinforcing the supposition that exchange with the eastern Kaqchikel region decreased after the Middle Preclassic. The Verbena-phase sample, however, contains both El Chayal (N = 120; 97.6 percent) and San Martin Jilotepeque (N = 3; 2.4 percent) obsidian. Recall that this is at a time when San Martin Jilotepeque itself appears to have been abandoned. During the following Arenal phase, nearly all the obsidian used at Miraflores II continued to come from El Chayal (N = 251; 99.2 percent). Trace amounts of material were imported not only from San Martin Jilotepeque (N = 1; 0.4 percent) but also from Ixtepeque (N = 1; 0.4 percent). Obsidian from the Ixtepeque source, located in Jutiapa Department, formed by far the greatest proportion of the volcanic glass used in El Salvador and Copan during all periods of prehistory. The introduction of Ixtepeque obsidian at Kaminaljuyu – even in trace amounts – is consistent with the existence of exchange linking the eastern highlands of Guatemala with western El Salvador and Honduras during the Late Preclassic period. But this trace quantity is not consistent with the especially close economic ties one would expect to see if the region was integrated by a single state, as proposed by Kaplan (2011a, 2011b).

A sample of 173 obsidian artifacts was recovered from transitional Arenal/Santa Clara-phase middens dating to the beginning of the collapse at Kaminaljuyu. All but one piece comes from the El Chayal source (N = 172; 99.4 percent); the last is from San Martin Jilotepeque (N = 1; 0.6 percent). A random sample of 294 obsidian artifacts from the numerous large Santa Clara middens excavated by the Miraflores II project was analyzed. These include material from El Chayal (N = 290; 98.6 percent), San Martin Jilotepeque (N = 2; 0.7 percent), and Ixtepeque (N = 2; 0.7 percent).

Thus, evidence from Kaminaljuyu suggests that very little obsidian from the eastern Kaqchikel region was brought to the Valley of Guatemala during the Late Preclassic, continuing a pattern of reduced interaction that began at the end of the Middle Preclassic period. It is worth noting, as well, that, although Ixtepeque obsidian was traded to Kaminaljuyu in the Late and Terminal Preclassic periods, the only material from this source recovered by our projects in the eastern Kaqchikel region comes from unambiguous Postclassic contexts. This is further evidence that trade linking western El Salvador to Kaminaljuyu did not extend west of the Valley of Guatemala into the eastern Kaqchikel region. Just as the eastern Kaqchikel highlands lack Miraflores ceramic modes, so too do they lack obsidian from a source at the eastern end of the Miraflores trade network. If there were communities of colonists from Kaminaljuyu in this region during the later half of the Late Preclassic, they were cut off from their home city and the trade network in which it participated.

Discussion: population dynamics, external relations, and the environment

There are tantalizing clues, in the form of maize pollen dating to 4000 BC, that initial human activity in the eastern Kaqchikel region began during the Archaic period. Other radiocarbon assays suggest that occupation of the region between Agua and Fuego volcanoes began no later than the second millennium BC. Nevertheless, we have found only a few pottery sherds that date to the Early Preclassic. Our earliest architecture and archaeological contexts at Urías and Rucal could date to as early as 1000 BC, but radiocarbon dates and ceramics support a date closer to 900/800 BC for the first permanent occupation.

Ceramics dating to the Middle Preclassic show similarities to materials from Las Charcas-phase Kaminaljuyu as well as to collections from sites in the piedmont and on the Pacific coast. Neutron activation analysis has shown that some ceramics with coastal modes came from the Pacific coastal area, indicating movement to the highlands of pottery – and probably people – from that zone.

Population levels in the eastern Kaqchikel highlands grew dramatically during the Middle/Late Preclassic transition (500/400–250/150 BC), mirroring similar events in the Valley of Guatemala. Nevertheless, unlike in that area, we have been unable to document through surface survey a single mound structure that unambiguously dates to this period. Instead, all our Preclassic sites are small artifact scatters lacking coeval architectural features that are visible on the modern surface. Thus, our survey of an area greater than 350 square kilometers has not revealed anything but the simplest, single-level site hierarchy for the Preclassic period. Excavations at both Rucal and Urías uncovered evidence of very low rock-and-earth platforms, but their diminutive size cannot be construed as evidence for social hierarchy or the organization of labor above the household level.

It has also proven difficult to identify clear markers of elevated status through either survey or excavation. The sole example is a late Middle to early Late Preclassic burial from San Lorenzo that we interpret as containing the remains of a diviner or other ritual specialist. The elevated status of this individual, however, might have been earned rather than ascribed, and, in any event, the burial goods were hardly overwhelming in quantity, quality, or exoticness. In sum, years of research have not revealed the existence of a chiefdom centered in our area of study, and, indeed, we have not identified a Preclassic elite of either local or foreign origin.

Economic relations during the late Middle to early Late Preclassic suggest a wide variety of ties with regions adjacent to the eastern Kaqchikel highlands. These include not only the Valley of Guatemala but also the Pacific coast and piedmont. The distribution of Xuc Ware clearly shows that pottery or ideas about ceramics were exchanged over a wide area. Overall, however, the ceramic variety of the eastern Kaqchikel region is not as rich as that of Kaminaljuyu, particularly as the early Late Preclassic progressed. The relative poverty of Sacatepequez pottery compared with the (late facet?) Providencia complex might even suggest that decline began in the eastern Kaqchikel region *before* the end of the Providencia phase at Kaminaljuyu. San Martin Jilotepeque obsidian reached its widest distribution in Mesoamerica during the Middle Preclassic (a time for which we have perhaps only 100 years of evidence of permanent occupation near the quarries), appearing as significant percentages (but in low overall quantities) of the obsidian assemblages from sites as far away as northern Peten, Yucatan, Oaxaca, and apparently even La Venta in the Olmec region. Nevertheless, it seems best to characterize the economy of our region as very limited in scale. No artifacts from these faraway regions have been found, suggesting that San Martin Jilotepeque obsidian was traded in an open, down-the-line network linking the eastern Kaqchikel region most closely with its immediate neighbors.

Throughout the Middle and early Late Preclassic periods, obsidian from the El Chayal source, which some scholars believe was controlled by Kaminaljuyu, entered the eastern Kaqchikel highlands. But the quantity of San Martin Jilotepeque obsidian used at Kaminaljuyu declined during this period. This is consistent not with the emergence of social and economic complexity in our region but rather with the development of a more closed, redistributive economy in the Valley of Guatemala. Thus, while Kaminaljuyu emerged as a complex chiefdom during the first half of the Late Preclassic period, the eastern Kaqchikel zone appears to have maintained a more egalitarian political structure and open network economy.

No colonies or enclaves of Kaminaljuyu elite were established in the region during the late first millennium. In fact, like the Middle Preclassic, the Late Preclassic was a period lacking social stratification. Most important, the northern 250 square kilometers or so of the eastern Kaqchikel region was abandoned in the second or third century BC, and population loss, albeit not as drastic, also occurred in the southern sector. In the Antigua Valley, depopulation, as measured by the surrogate variable of the number of sites, continued throughout the Terminal Preclassic period.

We are uncertain as to why depopulation occurred and do not favor environmental stress as the sole or unique causal factor. Nonetheless, increased frosts and El Niño disruptions of the seasonal monsoon led to climatic instability and drought during the Late Preclassic period. Disruptive and active volcanism also clearly merits further study. In addition, the inhabitants of the eastern Kaqchikel region could have migrated to other areas because of the movement of Proto-K'iche'an peoples to the northwest and because of the allure of more cosmopolitan centers such as Kaminaljuyu. Of course, environmental and social factors may have worked in tandem. Proto-K'iche'an peoples may have begun their migrations in the high mountains of western Guatemala because drought made conditions there difficult for agriculture. In turn, the inhabitants of the northern portion of the eastern Kaqchikel region could have left because of the same natural factors, and also to create a buffer between them and their neighbors to the northwest. We assume that most of the émigrés who left the eastern Kaqchikel region settled in the Valley of Guatemala, but it is conceivable that some were drawn to other areas, such as the western Kaqchikel region, the piedmont, and the Pacific coast.

Settlement patterns of the Classic and Postclassic periods suggest that later inhabitants of the eastern Kaqchikel region preferred to build their communities in defensible locations, often on high fingers of land surrounded by deep ravines (see Chapter 6). But many earlier settlements, including Middle/early Late Preclassic San Lorenzo, are found in the same sort of defensible locales. Nimajuyu in Sumpango and Santa Rosa are two predominantly Classic sites in our survey area that also had significant quantities of Late to Terminal Preclassic ceramics. Both sites are situated in high, defensible locations. It may be, therefore, that periodic raiding and incursions occurred not only in later times but also during the Late Preclassic period. The most likely candidates for such raiders are Proto-K'iche'an people from the northwest. We speculate, therefore, that, during the later Late Preclassic and Terminal Preclassic periods, the eastern Kaqchikel region was largely depopulated and became a buffer zone between the Valley of Guatemala and the Preclassic highland home of the ancestors of the K'iche', Tz'utujil, Chajoma, and Kaqchikel. A similar buffer zone between the Etla and other arms of the Valley of Oaxaca has been described for the period just before the emergence of Monte Alban as a regional capital (Marcus and Flannery 1996).

Conclusions

We turn now to the narrow goal of our chapter and propose an alternative analogy for population and political dynamics in the eastern Kaqchikel highlands that is more consistent with our Preclassic data. In several key respects, Algaze's model of state expansion seems inapplicable to the chiefdoms and egalitarian societies of the Preclassic Maya highlands. First, although obsidian, a resource important to Kaminaljuyu, is found at two distinct source areas in the eastern Kaqchikel region, use of material from these two sources declined at Kaminaljuyu during the Late Preclassic. Clay used to make white paste ceramics at Kaminaljuyu may have been imported from San Martin Jilotepeque or elsewhere in the Kaqchikel highlands, but again, as the Preclassic period progressed, the ceramic assemblages of Kaminaljuyu and the eastern Kaqchikel region diverged. Specifically, the rich variety of Late Preclassic ceramics at Kaminaljuyu suggests a focus on the exchange of ideas with the east rather than with the west. Second, we have been unable to identify the existence of an elite class – either local or imported from Kaminaljuyu – within the eastern Kaqchikel highlands. Indeed, during the period of greatest relevance – the second half of the Late Preclassic – much of the region was abandoned. Finally, we doubt that the short distance between the Valley of Guatemala and the eastern Kaqchikel region would have made the establishment of colonial outposts necessary. Indeed, the 95 kilometers that separate Kaminaljuyu and Chocola seem too trivial to warrant the establishment of an outpost at the latter site. The distances between cores and outposts discussed by Algaze (1993) for expansionist archaic states are an order of magnitude greater.

Although the aggressive expansions of the Sumerian, Predynastic Egyptian, and Mature Harappan civilizations into distant peripheries are inappropriate models for understanding political processes in the Preclassic Maya highlands, Teotihuacan – Algaze's fourth example – provides what may be a fitting analogy for demographic dynamics in the eastern Kaqchikel region. But it seems to us that, rather than comparing *Late Preclassic* Kaminaljuyu with *Classic* Teotihuacan (the period when the great city may have established distant outposts), an analogy with *Late Formative* Teotihuacan is much more appropriate.

At the beginning of the Late Formative period, at approximately the same time that Kaminaljuyu emerged as a paramount chiefdom, the population of the Basin of Mexico was concentrated in its southern regions. Cuicuilco, the largest of these southern sites, may have had a population of 20,000 by 100 BC. Shortly thereafter, Teotihuacan became a major central place in the northeastern portion of the Valley of Mexico, and by AD 1 it grew to some 20,000 to 40,000 inhabitants (Cowgill 1979: 55; 1997: 133). During the ensuing Tzacualli phase, the pace of growth increased, and Teotihuacan swelled to an estimated 60,000 to 80,000 inhabitants. As Teotihuacan grew, particularly during the first century AD, the rest of the Basin of Mexico became depopulated. Although it is unclear precisely when Teotihuacan became a state, it seems likely to have been shortly before or during this period of explosive growth.

During the Late Preclassic period, the eastern Kaqchikel region was depopulated and Kaminaljuyu grew to its greatest extent, much as most of the Basin of Mexico was depopulated by the Late Formative expansion of the Teotihuacan proto-state. The Late Preclassic, as Kaplan (2000, 2002b, 2011a, 2011b) and many before him have argued, was also the period of greatest political complexity and artistic achievement at Kaminaljuyu. Thus, it is reasonable to suggest that, at the close of the Late Preclassic, Kaminaljuyu was a maximal or flamboyant chiefdom on the brink of emerging as an archaic state.[7] But Kaminaljuyu never became a territorially expansionist state like Teotihuacan – perhaps in part because population levels in the Maya highlands were too low to make such a state viable and perhaps because deteriorating climatic conditions put a stop to this process. As a result, the polity instead suffered a dramatic decline during the Terminal Preclassic. Even during its peak in the Late Preclassic period, there is little evidence suggesting that Kaminaljuyu exerted direct political, military, or economic control much beyond the Valley of Guatemala. This observation holds true even for the obsidian quarries of El Chayal, an area that was remarkably open and sparsely populated during both the Preclassic and Classic periods (Suyuc Ley 2011). Although Kaminaljuyu experienced a subsequent period of Late Classic growth, it seems quite unlikely to us that it ever was organized as an archaic state.

We view the political landscape of the Late Preclassic Maya highlands and Pacific slopes not in terms of tightly packed Thiessen polygons but rather as a dispersed archipelago of large sites – including Chalchuapa, Kaminaljuyu, Chocola, Tak'alik Ab'aj, El Ujuxte, and Izapa – that each controlled relatively small territories. In between these islands of complex chiefdoms were vast areas that were more simply organized and, in many cases, lacked social stratification. One such interstitial region was the eastern Kaqchikel highlands.

Notes

1   We thank Licda Marlen Garnica, archaeologist at the Universidad San Carlos and Robinson's co-director of the PAAK, for her informed and enthusiastic help in our efforts to survey, excavate, and analyze sites in the Kaqchikel zone. Garnica's analysis of the ceramics of San Martín Jilotepeque was an indispensible contribution to Ri Rusamäj Jilotepeke. The survey of the Alotenango and Sumpango municipalities was funded by CIRMA and the Plumsock Mesoamerican Studies (1988–90) and the Organization of American States Regular Training Grant Program (Award F13581, 1989–91). Later support for survey in the Antigua zone and excavations of important sites in the valley and beyond came from a Regular Grant-in-Aid award from the Wenner–Gren Foundation for Anthropological Research (Grant 5205) and a Fulbright Research Grant (88-48337). Support for research at Chitak Tzak and Santa Rosa came from a second Fulbright Research Grant (92-66591) and funds from the owner of the Finca Santa Rosa (1991). The National Geographic Society (Grants 7218-02 and 7527-03) supported the analysis of materials and the dating of carbon samples from La Casa de las Golondrinas. Excavations and analysis at Preclassic Rucal and Urías have been supported by several institutions, including the National Geographic Society (Grants 7032-01, 6505-99, 6195-98, 5955-97, 5705-96, and 4713-92), the H. John Heinz III Charitable Fund (H0098), and Dr John Clark of the New World Archaeological Foundation (2003). Dr Patricia Farrell of the University of Minnesota, Duluth, also contributed research funds for the electrical resistivity study of Urías and soil analysis of the site and region. Special thanks are extended for the institutional support of Tulane University during the earlier phases of the work, and to Montgomery College of Rockville, Maryland, for work efforts from fall 2000 forward.

We also thank the institutions and people who facilitated our comparative analysis of highland Preclassic ceramics. The Instituto Nacional de Antropología e Historia de Guatemala permitted Robinson and Garníca to study Preclassic Kaminaljuyu ceramics in their ceramic laboratory in 2003. Dr Marion Popenoe de Hatch facilitated the review of Edwin Shook's archived notes and drawings housed in the Archaeology Section of the Universidad del Valle de Guatemala in 2002. Braswell extends a special acknowledgment to Dr Popenoe de Hatch and Dr Juan Antonio Valdés for their invitation to participate in the Kaminaljuyu-Miraflores II project and for the friendship and assistance that was extended to him while he taught at the Universidad del Valle de Guatemala.

Ri Rusamäj Jilotepeke was generously supported by the National Science Foundation (Dissertation Improvement Grant BNS-9301152), the Wenner–Gren Foundation for Anthropological Research (Grant 5650), Fulbright-IIE, a Mellon Fellowship, and the Middle American Research Institute of Tulane University. In addition to people already mentioned, we thank Edgar Vinicio García García, Paul Hughbanks, and Jennifer B. Braswell for their help in the field and laboratory. We also thank Joyce Marcus and her helpful ideas and skillful editing of our chapter.

The chronology employed in this chapter differs from that we have used in previous publications. This is due largely to new and important work by Takeshi Inomata and his colleagues that is currently in press. We are particularly thankful to Takeshi for two late-night and early-morning conversations in Brussels during which he carefully explained the basis for his new chronology and for later sharing his unpublished work with us. We also thank Valorie Aquino for sharing her knowledge of paleoclimate.

A final note of thanks is due to our longtime friend Michael Love and to Darrin Pratt of the University Press of Colorado. An earlier version of this chapter was included without our explicit permission in a volume published by that press. Pratt graciously acknowledges this error and recognizes our right to publish our data and conclusions in a place of our choosing. We welcome the chance to update our earlier paper, especially sections concerning chronology and ancient climate. We request that scholars who wish to cite our research make reference to this publication rather than the chapter in the earlier volume.

2   Popenoe de Hatch *et al.* (2011), most importantly, also note important differences in the Preclassic pottery of Kamalinajuyu, Ab'aj Tak'alik, and Chocola. They stress, in fact, that the ceramics should be assigned to three distinct traditions. We strongly concur.

3   This isolation is exhibited by ceramic divergence and distinct obsidian procurement patterns.

4   We have visited several sites in the Chimaltenango *altiplano*, including Cerritos Itzapa and Durazno (Shook 1952: 37–8), and are unable to date the mounds securely to any period. An examination of surface ceramics at both these sites revealed significant quantities of late Middle/early Late Preclassic and Classic sherds, but no later Late Preclassic sherds were recovered from Durazno. Thus, it is probable that the trends we describe for our survey region are also applicable to this zone. García's (1992) survey of the Chimaltenango region concludes that many of the mounds are probably Middle Preclassic (i.e., Sacatepequez phase) and Classic, but not Late Preclassic in date.

5   Kaminaljuyu Monument 65 depicts captives bound for sacrifice flanking what may be three consecutive (and named) rulers belonging to the same dynastic line. Nonetheless, we do not believe that the existence of divine rulership – *ajaw*ness, to make an uneasy neologism – necessarily implies the existence of a state in the political sense. Kings or, more precisely, individuals who look and act a bit like them (particularly in their use of artistic imagery) are not limited to state-level societies.

6   We have identified distinct Late and Terminal Preclassic components in these regions. In Sumpango, the number of occupied sites doubled from a Late Preclassic low of 14 (12 percent of all known sites) to 28 (25 percent) during the Terminal Preclassic period. In Antigua, however, the number of settlements continued to drop, from 36 dating to the Middle/early Late Preclassic, to 24 during the later Late Preclassic, to 11 during the

Terminal Preclassic. In Alotenango, in contrast, the number of sites with Middle/Late, Late, and Terminal Preclassic occupations is about the same. No Terminal Preclassic component has been identified in San Martin Jilotepeque because virtually no ceramics diagnostic of that period were recovered.

7   It should be obvious that, in the case of chiefdoms, we use adjectives such as "maximal," "flamboyant," and "complex" as synonymous modifiers indicating the largest, most populated, most politically elaborate, and – often – artistically "advanced" chiefdoms.

References

Algaze, Guillermo (1989) The Uruk Expansion. *Current Anthropology* 30: 571–91.
—— (1993) Expansionary Dynamics of Some Early Pristine States. *American Anthropologist* 95: 304–33.
Arroyo, Bárbara (1994) *The Early Formative in Southern Mesoamerica: An Explanation for the Origins of Sedentary Villages*. PhD dissertation, Department of Anthropology, Vanderbilt University. Ann Arbor, MI: University Microfilms.
Arroyo, Bárbara (ed.) (2006) Proyecto Arqueológico de Rescate Naranjo. Report presented to the Dirección General de Patrimonio Cultural y Natural, Guatemala.
—— (2010) *Entre cerros, cafetales y urbanismo en el valle de Guatemala: Proyecto de Rescate Naranjo*. Guatemala: Academia de Geografía e Historia de Guatemala.
Awe, Jaime, and Paul F. Healy (1994) Flakes to Blades? Middle Formative Development of Obsidian Artifacts in the Upper Belize River Valley. *Latin American Antiquity* 5: 193–205.
Barrientos Quezada, Tomás (1997a) Evolución tecnológica del sistema de canales hidráulicos en Kaminaljuyú y sus implicaciones sociopolíticas. In *XI Simposio de investigaciones arqueológicas en Guatemala, 1996*, ed. Juan Pedro Laporte and Héctor L. Escobedo, pp. 61–70. Guatemala City: Museo Nacional de Arqueología y Etnología.
—— (1997b) Desarrollo evolutivo del sistema de canales hidráulicos en Kaminaljuyú. Tesis de licenciatura, Área de Arqueología, Universidad del Valle de Guatemala.
Borhegyi, Stephan Francis de (1950) Estudio arqueológico en la falda norte del Volcán de Agua. *Antropología e Historia de Guatemala* 2(1): 3–22.
Bove, Frederick J. (2011) People with No Name: Some Observations about the Plain Stelae of Pacific Guatemala, El Salvador, and Chiapas with Respect to Issues of Ethnicity and Rulership. In *The Southern Maya in the Late Preclassic: The Rise and Fall of an Early Mesoamerican Civilization*, ed. Michael Love and Jonathan Kaplan, pp. 77–114. Boulder: University Press of Colorado.
Braswell, Geoffrey E. (1993) Ri Rusamäj Jilotepeke: investigaciones en una antigua zona productora de obsidiana: kanojkïl pa jun ojer xoral rub'anon richin chay. In *VI Simposio de investigaciones arqueológicas en Guatemala, 1992*, ed. Juan Pedro Laporte, Héctor L. Escobedo, and Sandra Villagrán de Brady, pp. 479–98. Guatemala City: Museo Nacional de Arqueología y Etnología.
—— (1996a) *A Maya Obsidian Source: The Geoarchaeology, Settlement History, and Ancient Economy of San Martín Jilotepeque, Guatemala*. PhD dissertation, Department of Anthropology, Tulane University. Ann Arbor, MI: University Microfilms.
—— (1996b) El patrón de asentamiento y producción en la fuente de obsidiana de San Martín Jilotepeque. In *IX Simposio de investigaciones arqueológicas en Guatemala, 1995*, ed. Juan Pedro Laporte and Héctor L. Escobedo, pp. 499–512. Guatemala City: Museo Nacional de Arqueología y Etnología.
—— (1996c) The Sculpture of San Martín Jilotepeque: Cotzumalguapan Influence in the Highlands or Highland Influence on the Pacific Coast? In *Eighth Palenque Roundtable, 1993*, ed. Martha Macri and Jan McHargue, pp. 441–51. San Francisco: Pre-Columbian Art Research Institute.

—— (1998) La arqueología de San Martín Jilotepeque, Guatemala. *Mesoamérica* 35: 117–54.

—— (2002) Praise the Gods and Pass the Obsidian? The Organization of Ancient Economy in San Martín Jilotepeque, Guatemala. In *Ancient Maya Political Economies*, ed. Marilyn Masson and David Freidel, pp. 285–306. Walnut Creek, CA: Altamira Press.

—— (2003a) Highland Maya Polities. In *The Postclassic Mesoamerican World*, ed. Michael E. Smith and Frances Berdan, pp. 45–9. Salt Lake City: University of Utah Press.

—— (2003b) Introduction: Reinterpreting Early Classic Interaction. In *The Maya and Teotihuacan: Reinterpreting Early Classic Interaction*, ed. Geoffrey E. Braswell, pp. 1–43. Austin: University of Texas Press.

Braswell, Geoffrey E., and Fabio E. Amador Berdugo (1999) Intercambio y producción durante el Preclásico: la obsidiana de Kaminaljuyú-Miraflores II y Urías, Sacatepéquez. In *XII Simposio de investigaciones arqueológicas en Guatemala, 1998*, ed. Juan Pedro Laporte, Héctor L. Escobedo, and Ana Claudia Monzón de Suasnávar, pp. 905–10. Guatemala City: Museo Nacional de Arqueología y Etnología.

Braswell, Geoffrey E., and Jennifer B. Braswell (1993) La obsidiana de los mayas de las tierras altas: afloramientos, canteras y talleres. In *VI Simposio de investigaciones arqueológicas en Guatemala, 1992*, ed. Juan Pedro Laporte, Héctor L. Escobedo, and Sandra Villagrán de Brady, pp. 463–78. Guatemala City: Museo Nacional de Arqueología y Etnología.

Braswell, Geoffrey E., and Marlen Garníca (1994) La escultura de San Martín Jilotepeque: influencia de Cotzumalguapa en las tierras altas o del altiplano en la costa del Pacífico? In *VII Simposio de investigaciones arqueológicas en Guatemala, 1993*, ed. Juan Pedro Laporte and Héctor L. Escobedo, pp. 185–203. Guatemala City: Museo Nacional de Arqueología y Etnología.

Braswell, Geoffrey E., and Michael D. Glascock (1998) Interpreting Intrasource Variation in the Composition of Obsidian: The Geoarchaeology of San Martín Jilotepeque, Guatemala. *Latin American Antiquity* 9: 353–69.

Braswell, Geoffrey E., and Misha Miller-Sisson (2013) The Other Maya and the Other Collapse: The Southern Maya Region during the Terminal Preclassic, *ca.* AD 100–250. Paper presented at the 18th European Maya Conference, Brussels.

Braswell, Geoffrey E., Joel D. Gunn, María del Rosario Domínguez Carrasco, William J. Folan, Laraine Fletcher, Abel Morales, and Michael D. Glascock (2004) Defining the Terminal Classic at Calakmul, Campeche. In *The Terminal Classic in the Maya Lowlands: Collapse, Transition, and Transformation*, ed. Arthur A. Demarest, Don S. Rice, and Prudence M. Rice, pp. 162–94. Boulder: University Press of Colorado.

Brown, Kenneth (1977) The Valley of Guatemala: A Highland Port of Trade. In *Teotihuacan and Kaminaljuyu*, ed. William T. Sanders and Joseph W. Michels, pp. 205–410. College Park: Pennsylvania State University Press.

Carmack, Robert M. (1979) La verdadera identificación de Mixco Viejo. In *Historia social de los Quiches*, by Robert M. Carmack, pp. 131–62. Guatemala: José de Pineda Ibarra, Ministerio de Educación.

Clark, John E. (1988) *The Lithic Artifacts of La Libertad, Chiapas, Mexico*. Provo, UT: New World Archaeological Foundation, Brigham Young University.

Cowgill, George L. (1979) Teotihuacan, Internal Militaristic Compctition, and the Fall of the Classic Maya. *In Maya Archaeology and Ethnohistory*, ed. Norman Hammond and Gordon R. Willey, pp. 51–62. Austin: University of Texas Press.

—— (1997) State and Society at Teotihuacan, Mexico. *Annual Review of Anthropology* 26: 129–61.

de León, Francisco, and Juan Antonio Valdés (2002) Excavaciones en Piedra Parada: más información sobre el Preclásico Medio del Altiplano Central de Guatemala. In *Incidents of Archaeology in Central America and Yucatán: Essays in Honor of Edwin M. Shook*, ed.

Michael Love, Marion Popenoe de Hatch, and Héctor L. Escobedo, pp 375–95. Lanham, MD: University Press of America.

de Montmollin, Olivier (1988) Scales of Settlement Study for Complex Societies: Analytical Issues from the Classic Maya Area. *Journal of Field Archaeology* 15: 151–68.

Demarest, Arthur A. (2011) The Political, Economic, and Cultural Correlates of Late Preclassic Southern Highland Material Culture: Evidence, Analyses, and Interpretations. In *The Southern Maya in the Late Preclassic: The Rise and Fall of an Early Mesoamerican Civilization*, ed. Michael Love and Jonathan Kaplan, pp. 345–86. Boulder: University Press of Colorado.

Demarest, Arthur A., and Robert J. Sharer (1986) Interregional Patterns in the Late Preclassic of Southeastern Mesoamerica: A Definition of Ceramic Spheres. In *The Southeast Maya Periphery*, ed. Patricia A. Urban and Edward M. Schortman, pp. 194–223. Austin: University of Texas Press.

Ericastilla Godoy, Sergio, and Shione Shibata (1991) Historia de las investigaciones arqueológicas en los sitios de Kaminaljuyú y el montículo de la Culebra. In *Informe*, Vol. 1: *Primer informe de exploraciones arqueológicas*, ed. Kuniaki Ohi, pp. 33–47. Tokyo: Museum of Tobacco and Salt.

Fahsen, Federico O. (2002) Who Are the Prisoners in Kaminaljuyú Monuments? In *Incidents of Archaeology in Central America and Yucatán: Essays in Honor of Edwin M. Shook*, ed. Michael Love, Marion Popenoe de Hatch, and Héctor L. Escobedo, pp. 359–74. Lanham, MD: University Press of America,.

Fox, John W. (1977) Quiche Expansion Processes: Differential Ecological Growth Bases within an Archaic State. In *Archaeology and Ethnohistory of the Central Quiche*, ed. Dwight T. Wallace and Robert M. Carmack, pp. 82–97. Albany: State University of New York Press.

Freidel, Dorothy E., John G. Jones, and Eugenia J. Robinson (2001) Paleoenvironment of the Urías Preclassic Site in the Antigua Valley, Guatemala. Paper presented at the 66th annual aeeting of the Society for American Archaeology, New Orleans.

—— (2007) Human Adaptation at Urías, Valley of Antigua, Guatemala. Paper presented at the 72nd annual meeting of the Society for American Archaeology, Austin.

García García, Edgar Vinicio (1992) Reconocimiento arqueológico de las tierras altas centrales de Chimaltenango. Tesis de licenciatura, Escuela de Historia, Universidad de San Carlos Guatemala.

Glascock, Michael D., Geoffrey E. Braswell, and Robert H. Cobean (1998) A Systematic Approach to Obsidian Source Characterization. In *Method and Theory in Archaeological Volcanic Glass Studies*, ed. Michael S. Shackley, pp. 15–65. New York: Plenum Press.

Haug, G. H., D. Günther, L. C. Peterson, D. M. Sigman, K. A. Hughen, and B. Aeschlimann (2003) Climate and the Collapse of Maya Civilization. *Science* 299: 1731–5.

Hirth, Kenneth G. (1978) Interregional Trade and the Formation of Prehistoric Gateway Communities. *American Antiquity* 43: 35–45.

Hodell, D. A., M. Brenner, J. H. Curtis, and T. Guilderson (2001) Solar Forcing and Drought Frequency in the Maya Lowlands. *Science* 292: 1367–70.

Inomata, Takeshi (2013) Middle Preclassic Maya Collapse in the Southern Maya Area. Paper presented at the 18th European Maya Conference, Brussels.

Jackson, Thomas L., and Michael W. Love (1991) Blade Running: Middle Preclassic Obsidian Exchange and the Introduction of Prismatic Blades at La Blanca, Guatemala. *Ancient Mesoamerica* 2: 47–59.

Kaplan, Jonathan (2000) Monument 65: A Great Emblematic Depiction of Throned Rule and Royal Sacrifice at Late Preclassic Kaminaljuyu. *Ancient Mesoamerica* 11: 185–98.

—— (2002a) Ethnicity and Rulership at Late Preclassic Kaminaljuyu. Paper Presented at the 101st annual meeting of the American Anthropological Association, New Orleans.

—— (2002b) From Under the Volcanoes: Some Aspects of the Ideology of Rulership at Late Preclassic Kaminaljuyú. In *Incidents of Archaeology in Central America and Yucatán: Essays in Honor of Edwin M. Shook*, ed. Michael Love, Marion Popenoe de Hatch, and Héctor L. Escobedo, pp. 311–57. Lanham, MD: University Press of America.

—— (2008) Hydraulics, Cacao, and Complex Developments at Preclassic Chocolá, Guatemala: Evidence and Implications. *Latin American Antiquity* 19: 399–413.

—— (2011a) Miraflores Kaminaljuyu: Corpse and Corpus Delicti. In *The Southern Maya in the Late Preclassic: The Rise and Fall of an Early Mesoamerican Civilization*, ed. Michael Love and Jonathan Kaplan, pp. 237–86. Boulder: University Press of Colorado.

—— (2011b) Conclusion: The Southern Maya Region and the Problem of Unities. In *The Southern Maya in the Late Preclassic: The Rise and Fall of an Early Mesoamerican Civilization*, ed. Michael Love and Jonathan Kaplan, pp. 387–411. Boulder: University Press of Colorado.

Kennett, Douglas J., Sebastian F. M. Breitenbach, Valorie V. Aquino, Yemane Asmerom, Jaime Awe, James U. L. Baldini, Patrick Bartlein, Brendan J. Culleton, Claire Ebert, Christopher Jazwa, Martha J. Macri, Norbert Marwan, Victor Polyak, Keith M. Prufer, Harriet E. Ridley, Harald Sodemann, Bruce Winterhalder, and Gerald H. Haug (2012) Development and Disintegration of Maya Political Systems in Response to Climate Change. *Science* 338: 788–91.

Lachniet, Matthew S., Stephen J. Burns, Dolores R. Piperno, Yemane Asmerom, Victor J. Polyak, Christopher M. Moy, and Keith Christenson (2004) A 1500-Year El Niño/Southern Oscillation and Rainfall History for the Isthmus of Panama from Speleothem Calcite. *Journal of Geophysical Research: Atmospheres* 109(D20).

Marcus, Joyce, and Kent V. Flannery (1996) *Zapotec Civilization*. New York: Thames & Hudson.

Navarrete, Carlos, and Luis Luján Muñoz (1986) *El gran montículo de la Culebra en el Valle de Guatemala*. Mexico: Universidad Nacional Autónoma de México y Academia de Geografía e Historia de Guatemala.

Neff, Hector, Federick J. Bove, Eugenia J. Robinson, and Bárbara Arroyo L. (1994) A Ceramic Compositional Perspective on the Formative to Classic Transition in Southern Mesoamerica. *Latin American Antiquity* 5: 333–58.

Neff, Hector, Deborah M. Pearsall, John G. Jones, Bárbara Arroyo de Pieters, and Dorothy E. Freidel (2006) Climate Change and Population History in the Pacific Lowlands of Southern Mesoamerica. *Quaternary Research* 65: 390–400.

Ohi, Kuniaki, and Miguel F. Torres (eds) (1994) *Piedras-Hongo*. Tokyo: Museo de Tabaco y Sal.

Parsons, Lee A. (1986) *The Origins of Maya Art: Monumental Stone Sculpture of Kaminaljuyu, Guatemala, and the Southern Pacific Coast*. Washington, DC: Dumbarton Oaks.

Pereira, Karen, and Bárbara Arroyo (2008) ¿Y dónde están las casas? Patron de asentamiento en la periferia de Naranjo, Guatemala. In *XXI simposio de investigaciones arqueológicas en Guatemala, 2007*, ed. Juan Pedro Laporte, Bárbara Arroyo, and Héctor E. Mejía, pp. 57–64. Guatemala City: Museo Nacional de Arqueología y Etnología.

Popenoe de Hatch, Marion (1997) *Kaminaljuyú/San Jorge: evidencia arqueológica de la actividad económica en el Valle de Guatemala, 300 a.C. a 300 d.C.* Guatemala: Universidad del Valle de Guatemala.

—— (1998) Los k'iche's-kaqchikeles en el altiplano central de Guatemala: evidencia arqueológico del período clásico. *Mesoamérica* 35: 93–115.

—— (2002) New Perspectives on Kaminaljuyú, Guatemala: Regional Interaction during the Preclassic and Classic periods. In *Incidents of Archaeology in Central America and Yucatán: Essays in Honor of Edwin M. Shook*, ed. Michael Love, Marion Popenoe de Hatch, and Héctor L. Escobedo, pp. 277–96. Lanham, MD: University Press of America.

Popenoe de Hatch, Marion, Christa Schreiber de Lavarreda, and Miguel Orrego Corzo (2011) Late Preclassic Developments at Takalik Abaj. In *The Southern Maya in the Late Preclassic: The Rise and Fall of an Early Mesoamerican Civilization*, ed. Michael Love and Jonathan Kaplan, pp. 203–36. Boulder: University Press of Colorado.

Robinson, Eugenia J. (1990) *Reconocimiento de los Municipios de Alotenango y Sumpango, Sacatepéquez*. La Antigua, Guatemala: Centro de Investigaciones Regionales de Mesoamérica.

—— (1993) Santa Rosa: un sitio defensivo en las tierras altas centrales de Guatemala. Report submitted to the Instituto de Antropología e Historia de Guatemala, Guatemala.

—— (1994) Chitak Tzak: un centro regional Postclásico Tardío de los Mayas Kaqchikel. In *VII Simposio de investigaciones arqueológicas en Guatemala, 1993*, ed. Juan Pedro Laporte and Héctor Escobedo, pp. 175–84. Guatemala City: Museo Nacional de Arqueología y Etnología.

—— (1998) Organización del estado kaqchikel: el centro regional de Chitak Tzak. *Mesoamérica* 35: 49–71.

—— (2001) Delving into the Preclassic: The Archaeology and Environment of Urías. Paper presented at the 66th annual meeting of the Society for American Archaeology, New Orleans.

—— (2003) A Sacred Maya Place: Rock Art, Rituals, and Hunting at La Casa de las Golondrinas, Guatemala. Paper presented at the Fifth World Archaeology Conference, Washington, DC.

—— (2008) Memoried Sacredness and International Elite Identities: The Late Postclassic at La Casa de las Golondrinas, Guatemala. In *Archaeologies of Art: Time, Place and Identity*, ed. Inés Domingo Sanz, Dánae Fiore, and Sally K. May, pp. 131–50. Walnut Creek, CA: Left Coast Press.

Robinson, Eugenia J, and Mary Pye (1996) Investigaciones en Rucal, Sacatepéquez: hallazgos de una ocupación del Formativo Medio en el altiplano de Guatemala. In *IX Simposio de investigaciones arqueológicas en Guatemala, 1995*, ed. Juan Pedro Laporte and Héctor L. Escobedo, pp. 487–98. Guatemala City: Museo Nacional de Arqueología y Etnología.

Robinson, Eugenia J., Marlen Garníca, Dorothy Freidel, John G. Jones, and Patricia M. Farrell (2001) El preclásico en Urías, un sitio en las tierras altas de Guatemala. In *XIV Simposio de investigaciones arqueológicas en Guatemala*, ed. Juan Pedro Laporte, Ana Claudia Monzón de Suasnavar, and Bárbara Arroyo, pp. 29–38. Guatemala City: Museo Nacional de Arqueología y Etnología.

Robinson, Eugenia J., Patricia M. Farrell, Kitty F. Emery, Dorothy E. Freidel, and Geoffrey E. Braswell (2002) Preclassic Settlements and Geomorphology in the Highlands of Guatemala: Excavations at Urías, Valley of Antigua. In *Incidents of Archaeology in Central America and Yucatán: Essays in Honor of Edwin M. Shook*, ed. Michael Love, Marion Popenoe de Hatch, and Héctor L. Escobedo, pp. 251–76. Lanham, MD: University Press of America.

Robinson, Eugenia J., Marlen Garníca, Dorothy Freidel, Geoffrey E. Braswell, and Sorayya Carr (2003) Nuevos hallazgos en La Casa de las Golondrinas, un sitio con arte rupestre en las tierras altas centrales de Guatemala. In *XVII simposio de investigaciones arqueológicas en Guatemala*, ed. Juan Pedro Laporte, Bárbara Arroyo, Hector L. Escobedo, and Hector Mejía, pp. 179–87. Guatemala City: Museo Nacional de Arqueología y Etnología.

Robinson, Eugenia J., Marlen Garníca, Ruth Ann Armitage, and Marvin W. Rowe (2007) Los fechamientos del arte rupestre y la arqueología en la Casa de las Golondrinas, San Miguel Dueñas, Sacatepéquez. In *XX Simposio de investigaciones arqueológicas en Guatemala*, ed. Juan Pedro Laporte, Bárbara Arroyo, and Héctor Mejía, pp. 959–72. Guatemala City: Museo Nacional de Arqueología y Etnología.

Shook, Edwin M. (1952) Lugares arqueológicos del altiplano meridional central de Guatemala. *Antropología e Historia de Guatemala* 4(2): 3–40.

Shook, Edwin M., and Marion Popenoe de Hatch (1978) The Ruins of El Bálsamo. *Journal of New World Archaeology* 3: 1–38.

—— (1999) Las tierras altas centrales: períodos Preclásico y Clásico. In *Historia General de Guatemala*, Vol. 1, ed. Marion Popenoe de Hatch and Jorge Luján, pp. 289–318. Guatemala: Fondo para la Cultura y el Desarrollo.

Shook, Edwin M., Marion Popenoe de Hatch, and Jamie Donaldson (1979) *Ruins of Semetabaj, Dept. of Solola, Guatemala*. Berkeley: University of California, Archaeological Research Facility.

Smith, Michael E., and Frances F. Berdan (eds) (2003) *The Postclassic Mesoamerican World*. Salt Lake City: University of Utah Press.

Suyuc Ley, Edgar (2011) The Extraction of Obsidian at El Chayal, Guatemala. In *The Technology of Maya Civilization: Political Economy and Beyond in Lithic Studies*, ed. Zachary X. Hruby, Geoffrey E. Braswell, and Oswaldo Chinchilla Mazariegos, pp. 130–51. London: Equinox.

Valdés, Juan Antonio, Jonathan Kaplan, Oscar Gutiérrez, Juan Pablo Herrera, and Federico Paredes Umaña (2004) Chocolá: un centro intermedio entre la boca costa y el altiplano de Guatemala durante el Preclásico Tardío. In *XVII Simposio de investigaciones arqueológicas en Guatemala, 2003*, ed. Juan Pedro Laporte, Bárbara Arroyo, Héctor L. Escobedo, and Héctor E. Mejía, pp. 449–60. Guatemala City: Museo Nacional de Arqueología y Etnología.

Velez, Maria I., Jason H. Curtis, Mark Brenner, Jaime Escobar, Barbara W. Leyden, and Marion Popenoe de Hatch (2011) Environmental and Cultural Changes in Highland Guatemala Inferred from Lake Amatitlán Sediments. *Geoarchaeology* 26(3): 1–19.

Webster, James W., George A. Brook, L. Bruce Railsback, Hai Cheng, R. Lawrence Edwards, Clark Alexander, and Philip P. Reeder (2007) Stalagmite Evidence from Belize Indicating Significant Droughts at the Time of Preclassic Abandonment, the Maya Hiatus, and the Classic Maya Collapse. *Palaeogeography, Palaeoclimatology, Palaeoecology* 250: 1–17.

6

THE OTHER LATE CLASSIC MAYA

Regionalization, defense, and boundaries in the central Guatemalan highlands[1]

Eugenia J. Robinson

Recent intensive investigations in the Antigua Valley of the central highlands of Guatemala reveal Late Classic regional cultural variation. Defensive features and settlement patterns indicate that the control of territory, if not actually its defense, was important during the period. Ceramic comparisons and sculptural analyses demonstrate external contacts with other parts of the highlands and the Pacific piedmont. Climatic change may explain the decline in population at the end of the period in the Antigua Valley. This chapter highlights the regionalization of highland cultures and suggests that a cultural boundary existed in the Antigua Valley, contributing to the ongoing discussion of the Late Classic Maya.

This is one of many celebratory chapters marking the retirement of Will Andrews from the Middle American Research Institute and Tulane. Following in the footsteps of Will's pioneering work at Quelepa, several of his students have carried out research outside of the Maya lowlands. This chapter – like Chapter 5 – focuses on the archaeology of the central Maya highlands west of Guatemala City and east of Lake Atitlan.

The Maya highlands form a mountainous area of Guatemala that spans approximately 35,000 square kilometers (see Figure 1.1 and Figure 6.1). Here, Mesoamerican archaeologists can investigate cultures situated in elevated terrain, as well as the challenging volcanic, topographic, and climatic circumstances created by such environments. Archaeological data from the Huista-Acatec region of the western highlands, where today people speak Jakaltek Mayan, indicate that during the Late Classic period (AD 600–900) territoriality was expressed through the building of defensive features and interregional cultural variation was shown by ceramic affiliations with the Cuchumatan mountains, the nearby Grijalva depression, the Chiapas highlands, and further afield with Kaminaljuyu, the Chixoy river basin, and the northern Maya highlands (Borgstede and Mathieu 2007).

In this chapter, I examine the proposition that other mountainous areas, such as the Antigua Valley of the central highlands, had different interregional connections

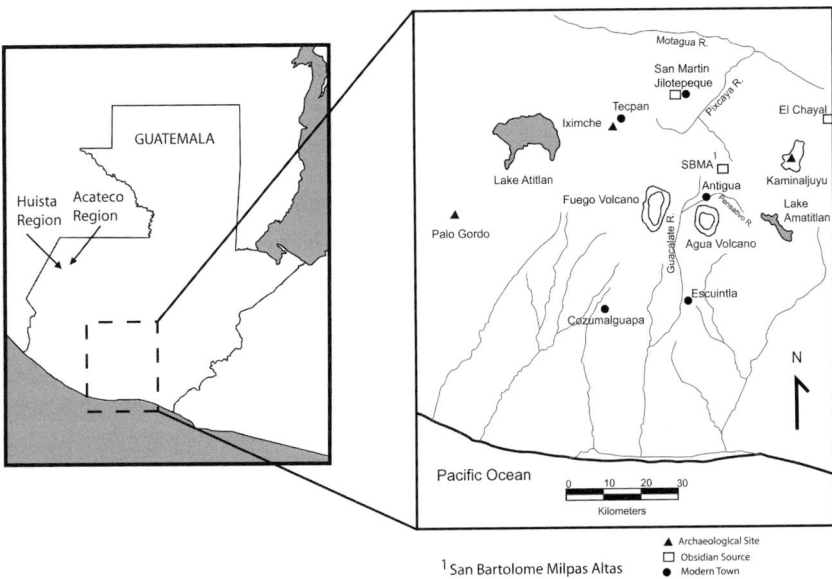

FIGURE 6.1 The Guatemalan highlands, showing the Huista-Acatec area and the Antigua Valley, archaeological sites, and towns

and settlement characteristics. Specifically, unlike the far western Huista-Acatec zone, the Late Classic Antigua Valley is interpreted to be a K'iche'an-speaking area during the Late Classic period and had sculpture in the Cotzumalguapan style, an art tradition with highland Mexican cultural affiliations centered on the cacao-rich Pacific coast piedmont of Guatemala. Both Teotihuacanos (Parsons 1969) and the Pipil (Thompson 1948) have been argued to be the originators of the style, but refined chronological divisions show that neither group was present in the southern Maya area during the Late and Terminal Classic, the periods during which Cotzumalguapan-style sculpture was made (Chinchilla Mazariegos 1996). The ethnicity and language of the Cotzumalguapan people have yet to be determined, but Oswaldo Chinchilla Mazariegos (1996, 1998) notes that after the Spanish conquest the coastal piedmont had both Pipil and Kaqchikel Maya towns, suggesting that the area was bilingual in colonial times. Classic-period settlement data from the Antigua Valley show that regional centers were often placed in defensive positions, but in contrast to the Huista-Acatec zone the quantity of protective features was much less and the architecture was simpler.

I propose that the northern end of the Antigua Valley was a boundary between archaeological cultures that expressed a mix of foreign and autochthonous architecture, sculpture, and artifacts. The data derive from survey of the valley and excavations, especially at the archaeological sites Santa Rosa, Rucal, and Pompeya. I also consider evidence for population decline at the end of the Late Classic period. In addition, this chapter provides a base for the comparison of highland cultures and contributes to the ongoing discussion of the Late Classic Maya.

The Antigua Valley

The Antigua Valley is located approximately 1,500 meters above sea level. Its location north of a corridor to the Pacific made it a node in a network of passes through steep mountains, including several volcanoes. From the valley of 16 square kilometers, passages lead southwest to the core of the Cotzumalguapan region, northwest to Lake Atitlan and the obsidian source of San Martin Jilotepeque, and east to Kaminaljuyu in the Valley of Guatemala. The deep ravines formed by the north–south trending Guacalate River and the east–west flowing Pensativo River today define routes of access in and out of the valley. Swamps and lakes in low-lying areas provided other water sources.

Dorothy Freidel *et al.* (2007) summarize the natural environment of the Antigua Valley. Because of its high elevation and latitude of 14° north, the climate is subtropical. Average temperatures in the valley vary little from season to season and range between 15 and 18° C. Peak temperatures usually occur at the end of the dry season in April. What is locally called "summer" (November to April) is generally dry, and most precipitation falls during the "winter" (May to October). Surrounded by mountains and volcanoes, the Antigua Valley actually receives less precipitation than the neighboring areas and is described as a rain-shadow valley. There are occasional droughts associated with El Niño and bouts of intense precipitation that create floods. The latter occur in association with tropical storms and hurricanes. Alluvial soils dominate the valley floor and clay loams are located near lakes and swamps. The soils of the slopes have formed from volcanic tephras and are weakly developed. Our project has recovered limited paleobotanical remains, but there is evidence that palms were grown in the southern end of the valley during the Late Classic period (Robinson *et al.* 2000). In spite of the seemingly idyllic conditions, like other parts of the Guatemalan highlands, the Antigua Valley has experienced significant volcanic eruptions from Fuego, one of the most active volcanoes in the world. There also are occasional strong earthquakes. As in other mountainous regions, seasonal rains create landslides and mudflows.

Chronology

The ceramic chronology of the Antigua Valley has been outlined and named by several authors (Borhegyi 1950; Rands and Smith 1965; Robinson *et al.* 2002). At present, temporal phases are called the Late Postclassic Medina (AD 1200–1500), the Early Postclassic Primavera (AD 800–1200), the Late Classic Pompeya (AD 550–800), the Early Classic Terrenos (AD 150/250–550), the Late Preclassic Xaraxong (250/150 BC–AD 150/250), the late Middle Preclassic Sacatepequez (500/400–250/150 BC), and the early Middle Preclassic Agua (900/800–500/400 BC). The dates for the Preclassic phases have shifted somewhat from those presented in earlier publications (see Chapter 5).

The Late Classic of the Antigua Valley, the Cotzumalguapan zone, and Kaminaljuyu are roughly contemporaneous in date. The Pompeya phase of the Antigua Valley has been dated to AD 550–800/900, according to Rands and Smith (1965). Their estimate of the absolute chronology of the Late Classic rests on comparisons with the Amatle phase (AD 600–800) and the Pamplona phase (AD 800–900) of Kaminaljuyu (Shook and Hatch 1999). Amatle Ware is common to both complexes. Our radiocarbon dates from Rucal place the end of the Late Classic in the Antigua Valley at about AD 800 (Robinson and Pye 1996).

The Late Classic ceramics from Santa Rosa (Robinson *et al.* 1993) are the best described and analyzed collection from the Antigua Valley. Descriptions of Classic pottery from Pompeya provide additional information (Garrido López 2011). Although San Juan Plumbate appears in some collections from the Antigua Valley, it occurs at very low frequencies. Analysis of surface materials from Tapexco, a Late Classic residential site near Santa Rosa, found that San Juan Plumbate formed 2 percent of the collection (Pye 1995). The sample was so small from Pompeya – just seven sherds – that its occurrence is considerably less than 1 percent in a sample of both Early and Late Classic ceramics (Garrido López 2011). Chronologies developed for sites outside the Antigua Valley date the appearance of San Juan Plumbate ceramics. At Kaminaljuyu, San Juan Plumbate is a temporal marker of the Pamplona phase, dated to AD 800–900 (Shook and Hatch 1999). In the Cotzumalguapan zone of Escuintla, San Juan Plumbate appears in the Pantaleon phase, dated to AD 700–1100 (Chinchilla Mazariegos *et al.* 2009). The very small quantity of San Juan Plumbate found in the Antigua Valley shows some temporal overlap with these other sequences in the highlands and piedmont but does not imply a strong occupation after about AD 800.

Antigua Valley research

Several archaeologists have located and mapped sites in the Antigua Valley, most of which are found in agricultural fields or coffee plantations. Edwin Shook (1952b) visited and reported a number of these. His unpublished notes (Shook 1948–50) and archives (Shook 1942, 1950, 1952a, 1964, 1969, 1972), housed at the Universidad del Valle de Guatemala, are important sources of information. His excursions to the field in the Antigua Valley area were numerous but were not conducted as part of a formal project. Shook defined the highland *palangana* ballcourt, a form with four sides of even height, which is limited to the Late Classic period (Shook 1952b; Smith 1965). Stephen Borhegyi (1950) excavated and reported Los Terrenos and Finca Pompeya, sites at the southern end of the Antigua Valley. Recent excavations of Pompeya (the name published by Shook in 1952 and in common use today) investigated the architecture, chronology, and limits of the site (Cardona Caravantes and Díaz 2010; Garrido López 2011). Sébastien Perrot-Minnot (2005) and Paulino Morales (1998) surveyed the west side of the valley. Perrot-Minnot hypothesized that the site located in the El Portal farm, named in publications "El Portal" (Perrot-Minnot 2005) or "Portal" (Shook 1952b: 34), was the most important in the valley because of its central location and the large number of sculptures (Eisen 1888; Seler 1900). Perrot-Minnot spearheaded explorations at El Portal; he mapped the site and undertook reconnaissance of the surrounding terrain. Morales (1998) led a survey of sites in the path of a new north–south road, Route 14, along the western edge of the valley near El Portal.

In 1990, Robinson undertook a complete survey of the southwest and northwest entrances and exits of the valley, a passage defined by the Guacalate River. This project, the Proyecto Arqueológico del Área Kaqchikel (PAAK), used the same methodology as the former Encuesta Arqueológica del Área Kaqchikel directed by William Swezey (Robinson 1998). During survey, we first contacted local mayors for their support and knowledge about archaeology and local people who could serve as guides in the field. Although our original intention was to survey all terrain, we learned that there are areas that do not currently have evidence of prehistoric settlement. One of these is the central portion of the valley. It has been disturbed by a redirection of the course of the Pensativo River carried out in colonial times, by the constant meanderings and flooding of the Guacalate River, by erosion and the redeposition of upslope materials on the valley floor, and by the recent expansion of residential areas.

The PAAK survey turned out to be partially opportunistic in character. In some cases, lack of access to properties in the proposed survey area prohibited our entry. Most owners of large farms, however, were gracious and willing to share information about the archaeological remains on their properties. A few times guerrilla activity in the periphery of the valley caused us to cease field activities. The political activities of the times are well described in the book *Tecpan* (Fischer and Hendrickson 2003). We also learned that it was unproductive to survey steep, wooded slopes, so we avoided such areas. José Benítez and Teresita Chinchilla of the Universidad San Carlos de Guatemala carried out survey under the auspices of the project and used some data for their theses (Chinchilla 1991; Benítez 1991). Paulino Puc Rucal often conducted field operations and contributed to the collection of data for the valley.

Settlement data

Before discussing the defensive position of some sites and comparing them to the Huista-Acatec area, I consider the Late Classic site types defined for the Antigua Valley. There are five types, based on the size of structures, the quantity and arrangement of buildings, and the presence of surface artifacts. It is possible that these types are more complicated than they now appear, because associated structures or platforms have been destroyed or buried in the agricultural areas where the sites are found. Two additional types are represented by sculpture and a burial. Table 6.1 summarizes the frequencies of these different types of sites.

TABLE 6.1 Frequencies of types of Late Classic sites, Antigua Valley

	Type 1	Type 2	Type 3	Type 4	Type 5	Burial	Sculpture	Total
Number	4	5	3	9	86	1	4	112

Type 1a

The Type 1a site is the largest in the hierarchy and has the tallest platform mounds. One example of this type of site is Santa Rosa (Figure 6.2). Edwin Shook first named the site "Ramos" for the owner of the farm where it was discovered (Shook archive 1972), but the name in use today is Santa Rosa, the current name of the farm where it is located. It has a plaza 35 meters wide and surrounding mounds attached to an enclosed *palangana* ballcourt. The mounds surrounding the plaza are 5 meters high and an attached higher "temple" on the north side (Str. 5A-1a) is 10 meters high. Our excavations located an

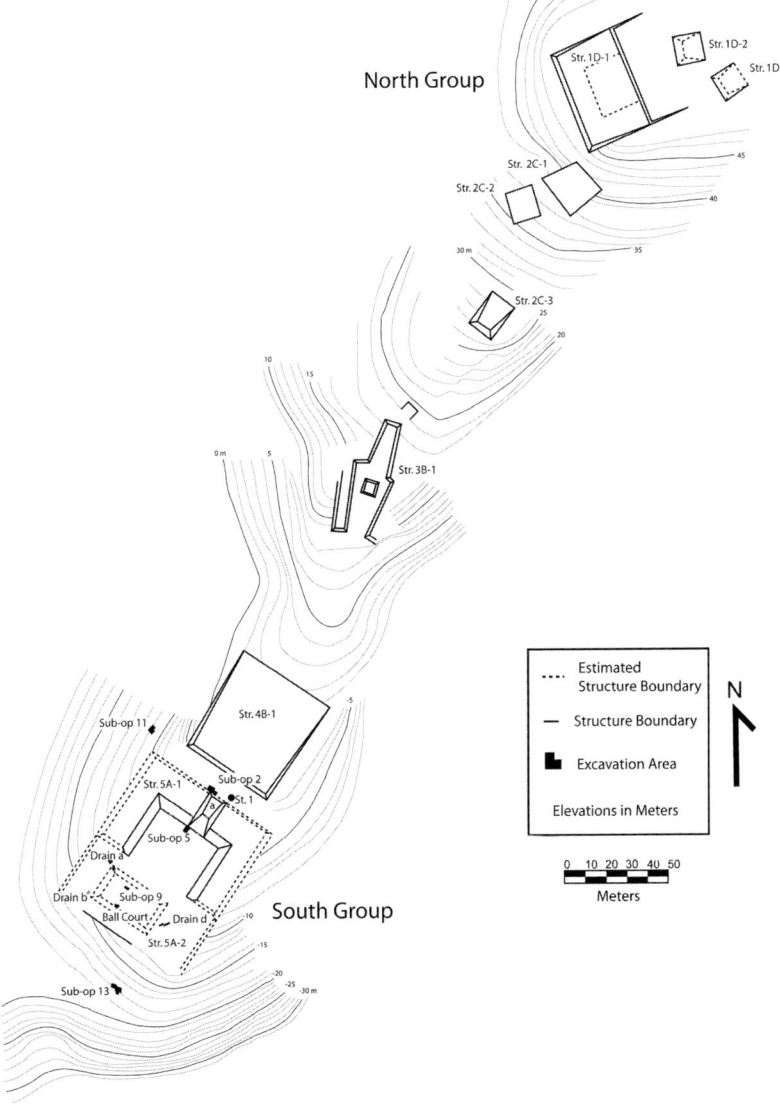

FIGURE 6.2 Map of Santa Rosa, Pastores, Sacatepequez

earthen plaza floor 3 meters below the current surface, implying that the mounds once stood 8 meters and 13 meters above the plaza. The functions of the other eight structures distributed on the higher contours of the site are unclear, but Str. 2C-3 is different because it has a large ramp 2 meters high made of *talpetate* (consolidated ash) blocks. Constructed areas of the site have a footprint of about 12,650 square meters.

Type 1b

The single site in this category is comparable in size to the Type 1a sites but has a different form. Perrot-Minnot (2005) described El Portal as an "acropolis" site; it is situated on a hill 40 meters high. It has four mound groups and a stairway made of sculpted blocks. Constructed portions of the site, not taking into account the height of the platforms, have a footprint of about 7,300 square meters.

Type 1c

Another site type is exemplified by Pompeya and Los Terrenos (published by Shook in 1952 as Terreno rather than Los Terrenos, a name used by subsequent authors) on the southern side of the valley and on the lower elevations of the Agua Volcano. According to the sketch maps made by Shook and published by Borheghi (1950: maps 2 and 3), each of these sites had a central mound group with peripheral structures oriented in

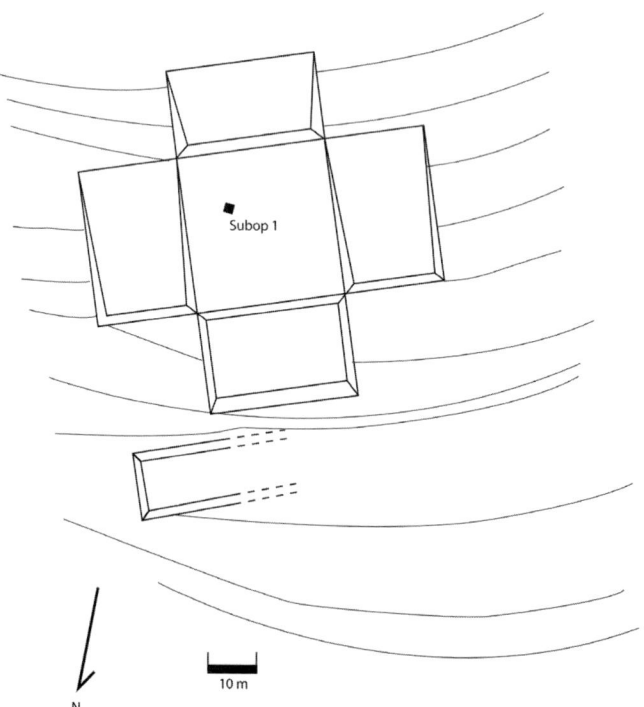

FIGURE 6.3 Map of Rucal, Ciudad Vieja, Sacatepequez

the same direction as the main plaza. Shook identified possible ballcourts, but recent observations at Pompeya make their existence uncertain (Garrido López 2011). The height of the stairway at Los Terrenos is estimated from a photograph published by Borhegyi (1950) to be 5 meters. In 2010, I determined that the tallest mound at Pompeya is 7 meters high, with a possible additional "temple" above making the structure 8.5 meters in height. Taking into account soil overlying floors, the structures could easily be taller by a meter or more. The overall construction footprint of Pompeya is approximately 5,200 square meters. This estimate includes the mounds mapped by Shook and which I observed in 2010, together with five more small structures found below ground surface at the southern end of the site (Garrido López 2011).

Type 2

Type 2 sites are smaller and less complicated than the Type 1 sites. They contain a plaza group that can measure as much as 50 meters across, but usually are smaller. Type 2 sites do not appear to have ballcourts. Rucal (Figure 6.3) is an example of a Type 2 site. It has a plaza 30 meters wide and encircling mounds 2 meters high. Because the plaza floor is located 1.5 meters below the current ground surface, the mounds were once at least 3.5 meters high. The constructed area of Rucal is approximately 3,000 square meters.

Type 3

Type 3 sites contain a single, isolated mound. Three sites, all near water sources, are defined as single structure sites: San Luis, Pastores, and San Juan del Obispo. Edwin Shook located San Luis, described it, and mapped it as a single earthen mound (Shook 195b; archive 1942). In 2010, I recorded its dimensions as about 15 by 15 meters at the base and 3 meters high. In the 1990s the site was in an open field, but now San Luis is in a forest maintained to protect a mountain spring that provides water for the towns nearby. The mound has suffered a great deal of illicit digging with cross-cutting trenches. Shook also identified Pastores, which he saw from a distance and did not visit, as a lookout site, a single mound on a promontory with a wide view-shed that overlooks the Antigua Valley (Shook 1952b; archive 1942). The mound at San Juan del Obispo, measuring 27 meters on a side, has rock piling, suggesting it once had a stone façade. Larger than the San Luis mound, it is also located near a water source. Sculpture has been found in the Pastores Finca and near the structure of San Juan del Obispo.

Type 4

Type 4 sites are low mounds or terraces. Usually they appear as undulations on the ground surface and their arrangement, orientation, and size are unclear because of plowing and cultivation. For this reason, surveyors have mentioned their presence but, because of the uncertainty of their form, have not mapped them. Many of the terrace sites lie near the base of hillsides or on them, suggesting that the slopes of the valley were used for habitation. Most Late Classic Type 4 sites have been recognized in the northern valley area. Recent excavations of earthen terraces on the hillside at the southern entrance of the Antigua Valley in the area of the site La Chacra have yielded Late Classic ceramics that date the terraces to this period (Cáceres and Herrera 2010). There are probably many more Type 4 sites than currently recognized because of disturbance or burial by eroded soils on the slopes and at the base of slopes.

Type 5

Type 5 sites are surface scatters of artifacts and usually present no evidence of structures. According to the PAAK records, they can range from 600 to 210,000 square meters in area. They probably represent the remains of both small and large residences.

Sculpture

This site type consists of isolated finds of stone sculpture. There is evidence that, in the past, such sites also had mounds. For example, Shook noted that Pavon, a site with five known sculptures, had prehistoric structures, but a local workman reported to him that the mounds had all been destroyed (Shook archive 1950). La Chacra is another example of a site with monumental sculptures but lacks mounds nearby (Shook archive 1969). Many Type 1–4 sites, and even a Type 5 surface scatter, also have sculpture.

Burial

This site type consists of burials that have been discovered but are not obviously associated with mounds or structures. A local landowner reported finding a burial on his property in the steep slopes of the town of Pueblo Nuevo. The body was accompanied by numerous ceramic vessels. There are other reports of complex burials in this same area but closer to the Guacalate River (Robinson et al. 1993).

Late Classic conflict in the highlands

Stephen Borhegyi (1965a) discussed the settlement patterns of the Guatemalan highlands in an article for the *Handbook of Middle American Indians* that drew on an earlier synthesis by Shook and Proskouriakoff (1956). Using examples from the western and central highlands, he recognized that Postclassic (AD 1000–1524) sites were elevated and fortified during this period characterized by internecine warfare (Hill 1996). In contrast, Borhegyi (1965a) noted that the Preclassic (600 BC–AD 300) and Classic (AD 300–1000) periods were times of comparative tranquility. During both of these earlier periods, many of the sites he discussed were located in open valleys. When comparing the Classic to the Preclassic period, he stated that culture became more "secularized" over time. Moreover, he suggested that sites were built on hillsides because of population growth and expansion beyond the valley floor.

Edwin Shook, Borhegyi's contemporary, once mentioned to me that the location of Santa Rosa on a high peninsula of land overlooking the Antigua Valley deviates from the Late Classic model (personal communication 1990). Moreover, other statements by Borhegyi (1965a) indicate that his model of change was more complicated than a simple progression from the open, low, and potentially peaceful settlements of the Preclassic and Classic periods to fortified, high, and defensive settlements of the Postclassic period. For example, in contradiction to his own model, he discussed Late Classic and Preclassic sites that were located on hilltops or defensive locations. Furthermore, he presented evidence that there was occupational continuity at some hilltop sites, such as Mixco Viejo in Chimaltenango and Chinautla near Guatemala City, which had Late Classic and Late Postclassic occupations (ibid.: 70–71). He also showed that Cambote in Huehuetenango, a Late Preclassic site, was situated on a defensive feature, a "tongue of land" surrounded by rivers (ibid.: fig. 2).

Borgstede and Mathieu (2007), working in the Huista-Acatec zone of the Cuchumatan Mountains of western Guatemala, have demonstrated that substantial defensive architectural and natural features were used during both the Classic and Postclassic periods. Their data demonstrate endemic conflict at these times, and their typology of defensive characteristics allows comparison with similar features in the Antigua Valley data. Table 6.2 shows that, during the Late Classic period, the Antigua Valley had only four of the Classic defensive features identified by Borgstede and Mathieu; only four of the 112 sites in the Antigua Valley incorporate these features. Four sites are on natural promontories or peninsulas in the northern end of the valley, and some of these could have functioned as lookouts. One site, El Portal, on the west side has an elevated, probably natural acropolis. Pompeya, situated on a low promontory, has terraces; these were more likely for sculpting a sloped landscape than for defensive walls.

TABLE 6.2 A comparison of Late Classic defensive features: Late Classic Huista-Acatec (and other locations in the highlands), Late Classic Antigua Valley, and Postclassic Huista-Acatec (and other locations in the highlands)

Defensive feature type	Details about defensive features	Late Classic Huista-Acatec	Late Classic Antigua Valley	Postclassic Huista-Acatec
Barriers	Protective walls and terrace walls	X	X (terrace walls)	X
Barriers	Cliffs and ravines	X		X
	Mountain top	X		X
	Promontory	X	X	X
	Mountain slope	X		X
Barriers	Ditches and moats	(possible)		
	Bodies of water	X		X
	Causeways	X		X
Barriers	Intra-site planning			X
Visibility	Relay stations and lookouts	X	X	X
Elevation	Platforms, temple pyramids, and acropoli	X	X	X
Elevation	Caves and hidden structures	X		X

Sources: Borgstede and Mathieu 2007; Borhegyi 1950; Garrido López 2011; Morales 1998; Perrot-Minnot 2005; Robinson et al. 1993; Shook 1952b.

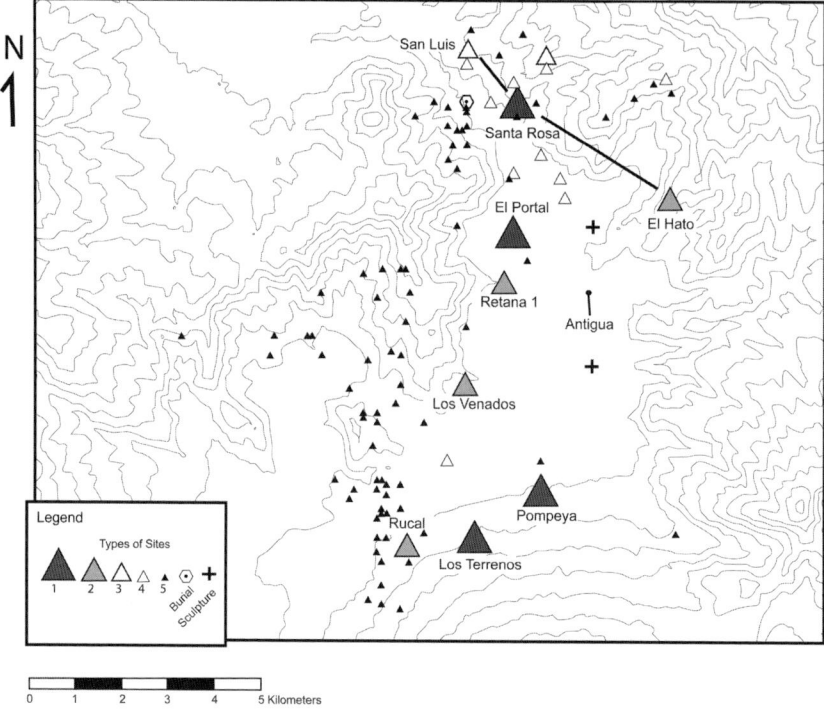

FIGURE 6.4 Map of the Late Classic site types in the Antigua Valley showing a line of sight between San Luis, Santa Rosa and El Hato

Overall, the Antigua Valley settlements of the Late Classic period reveal a less conflict-wrought cultural landscape than the Huista-Acatec region.

Settlements in the north, west, and southern portions of the Antigua Valley share some similarities (Figure 6.4). In all three regions, major centers and their satellites are found in a region about 5 km across. The spacing between Type 1 and Type 2 sites is quite regular: they are approximately 1.50 to 1.75 km apart. In the northern, central, and southern sections, defensive features are incorporated into site locations and layouts. The southern end of the valley has a seemingly less defensive open organization, but the position of Pompeya on a promontory above the base of the Agua Volcano may have provided a defensive advantage.

The southern end of the Antigua Valley (Almolonga)

Los Terrenos is located in the center of the southern base of the Agua Volcano. It once consisted of terraces, a plaza group, and a stone stairway on the north side of the group. Shook suggested that Los Terrenos might have had a ballcourt formed by two structures east of the main plaza (Shook archive 1950). A recent visit by Perrot-Minnot (personal communication 2009) found that the mounds have been entirely obliterated by agriculture. All nearby mound sites east, west, and north of Los Terrenos are classified as Types 1–3. To the south and west of Los Terrenos are Los Cerritos and Rucal, both Type 2 sites.

When Shook visited Pompeya, on a farm at that time called La Felicidad, he found that the natural slope of the volcano had seven terraces (see Borhegyi 1950: 23, map 3). Garrido López (2011) found that they were created with stone. Structures made of earth, *talpetate*, and stone were arranged around a rectangular patio on the central terrace of the site. I recently estimated that the tallest structure was 8.5 meters high and that the main plaza, perhaps filled with eroded soils that obscure its original form, was only 9 meters wide (north–south) by 100 meters long (east–west). There are two very low structures at the ends of this plaza. Shook suggested that two mounds located uphill from the plaza formed a ballcourt, although it was not of the *palangana* type and was not enclosed at the ends. Garrido López (2011) determined that these mounds could not have formed a ballcourt because they are situated on terraces of different heights.

Less than 1 km southeast of Pompeya is San Juan del Obispo, a Type 3 site consisting of one mound. A single sculpted monument was found at the site, which is located about 50 meters above the only nearby water source. During my recent visit there, trees obscured the view, but it could be that San Juan del Obispo was a satellite of Pompeya important both because of its elevation and because of its access to and potential control of water. Pompeya, Terrenos, and Rucal are each positioned about 1.50 to 1.75 km apart. This spacing suggests that these sites were the cores of territories of approximately 2.25 square kilometers in area. Today, the view from one site to another is obscured by trees and terrain cut by intermittent streams, but a view-shed analysis by Pezzarossi shows that the western site of El Portal and the northern site of Santa Rosa were both visible from Pompeya (Robinson and Pezzarossi 2011).

The southern entrance to the valley has surface sites defined by artifact scatters. Most are within reach of water sources, especially the Guacalate River. Their distribution on the landscape might have been determined by proximity to springs that reportedly existed in the past but have been sealed off by earthquakes.

The western side of the Antigua Valley

Another group of settlements exists on the west side of the valley. El Portal is the largest site in the western area. Other smaller Type 2 sites exist within a 3.5 km distance of El Portal. Los Venados is a plaza group with interior dimensions of 25 meters to a side which might have been a satellite settlement of El Portal (Morales 1998). Between El Portal and Los Venados is another site with mound sizes appropriate for a Type 2 site, although their organization is unclear (Perrot-Minnot *et al.* 2003).

The northern end of the Antigua Valley (Panchoy)

San Luis, Santa Rosa, and El Hato are three sites in the northern end of the valley that could have formed a line of sight for a territory about 5 km across. The northern valley sites are situated on promontories at high elevations. The largest is Santa Rosa, which is a plaza group with *talpetate* and earthen structures with an attached enclosed ballcourt of the *palangana* type. It is located on a promontory of land with a remarkable view of the Antigua Valley to the south and the single-mound site San Luis to the west. San Luis was described by Shook (archive 1942) as having clear views to the south. Less well known is a site called El Hato. It is now destroyed, but was situated on a promontory of land and was a simple mound group or ballcourt. Santa Rosa was visible from one of the mounds at El Hato. Such sites could have served to guard the northern end of the valley and to provide communication all the way to its center because of the clear line of sight between Santa Rosa and El Portal.

San Luis was also part of this line of sight. It may be that the placement of this site near a water source not only signaled the presence of the spring but also served as a lookout for the protection of the vital resource. Another example reinforces this pattern. Pastores, as reported by Shook (archive 1942), is also a single-mound site. It is situated north and above Santa Rosa at the location of another reported spring.

Tapexco is spatially associated with Santa Rosa, located 500 meters to the north of the Type 1 site and on an adjoining promontory. Tapexco is a large residential Type 4 and 5 site measuring 120,000 square meters in area. Still visible are some poorly defined constructions, probably the remains of low platforms and a large surface scatter. It is contemporary with Santa Rosa and is interpreted to be the residential community associated with the site.

Excavations at Santa Rosa

Our excavations in the main plaza of Santa Rosa revealed interesting features and provide a greater understanding of the archaeology of one of the largest Late Classic sites in the region (Robinson et al. 1993). In Suboperation 5, we found a hard-packed earth floor 2.4 meters below the surface. It was probably buried by eroded soils from the earthen mounds. Above the floor was about 10 cm of gray volcanic sand not found elsewhere, and hence probably not deposited by a volcanic eruption. Local informants told me that Stela 1 (see Figure 6b) was once set to the north of a temple 8.5 meters high called Str. 5A-1a. In Suboperation 2, just to the west of the original location of Stela 1, we found an andesite slab flooring and a ramp. Stone drains, uncovered by workmen at the farm, lay to the east and west sides of the ballcourt (Figure 6.5a). Smith (1965) reports drains for other closed *palangana* ballcourts. On the west side of the site, in Suboperation 11, excavations uncovered an offering of orange-slipped cylinders (Santa Rosa Anaranjado: Santa Rosa Variety) and an Amatle Hard Ware jar-neck among burned soil and a possible uncarved stela (Figure 6.6b). On the interior wall of the south side of the ballcourt (Suboperation 9) was another offering of two jars. One has red paste and a wide strap handle (Pastores Simple: Rejón Variety), while the other is red slipped and has holes around the collar (Portal Rojo: Portal Variety). This last vessel was possibly used for fermented beverages. Burials were located to the south in Suboperation 13. One was an extended burial of a 30-year-old adult dating to the Terminal Preclassic period. Secondary burials of three adults interred with an Amatle Hard Ware bowl, a fragment of a handled incense burner, and a greenstone axe were also found.

Ceramics of Late Classic Santa Rosa and Tapexco

Late Classic ceramic types found in the Antigua Valley have been described by various authors (Borhegyi 1965b; Robinson et al. 1993; Rubio 1986). Rubio's

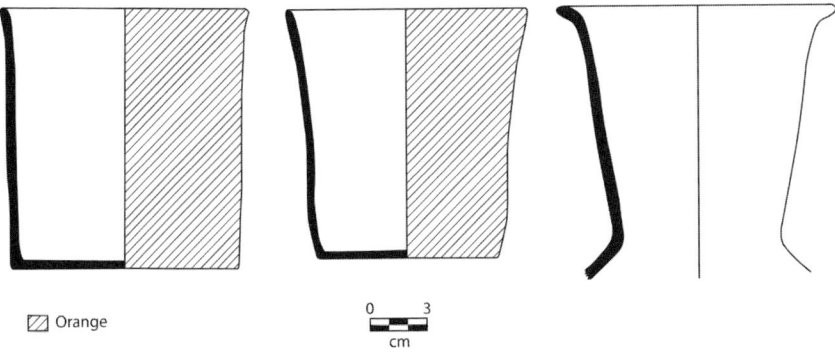

FIGURE 6.5 Santa Rosa: (a) Drain D, located on the east side of the ballcourt; (b) two cylinder vessels of the Santa Rosa Anaranjado: Santa Rosa Variety and a jar neck of Amatle Hard Ware

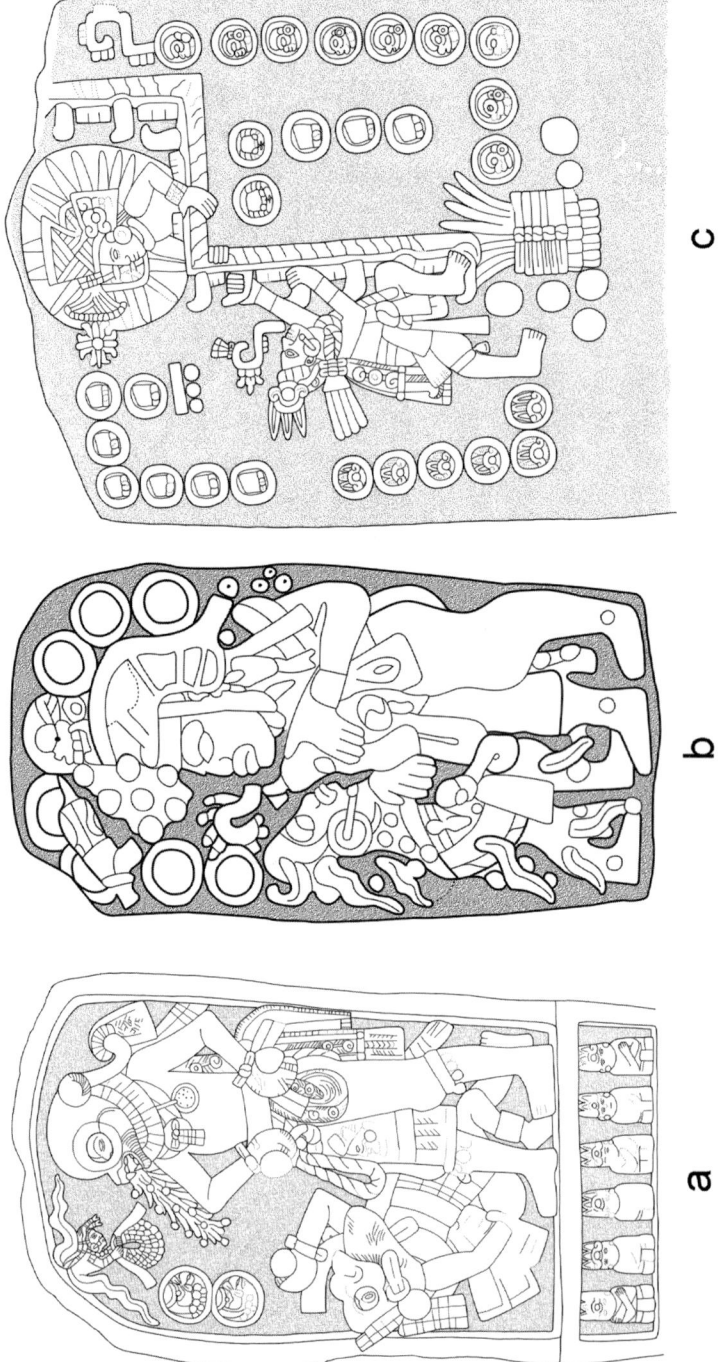

FIGURE 6.6 Comparison of Cotzumalguapan and Antigua Valley stelae: (a) El Baul Monument 27; (b) Santa Rosa Stela 1; (c) El Castillo Monument 1 (Cotzumalguapan sculpture published with permission of Oswaldo Chinchilla Mazariegos 2011)

(1986) comprehensive discussion of Amatle Hard Ware from El Baul describes it as a well-fired, plain, reddish-brown to gray pottery. Vessels are well smoothed, and sherds make a metallic sound when tapped due to a high firing temperature. Some examples have incised wavy lines or rows of appliqué buttons. The principal forms are jars, bowls, and plates. Tiquisate is a cream-colored ware that appears in bowl, vase, and tripod forms. San Juan Plumbate is a gray lustrous pottery that is found in vase, jar, and bowl forms. Pastores Simple is a red-paste type pottery (Robinson et al. 1993). Its paste has a medium texture, with a low density of quartz and black mineral inclusions. Pastores Simple is usually well smoothed. Forms include (1) jars with wide strap handles with finger impressions on the handles; (2) censers with handles; (3) bowls (one variety is mold made); (4) vases; and (5) plates or *comales*.

The analysis of a sample of 40 percent of surface-collected lots from Tapexco revealed somewhat different percentages of ceramics than at Santa Rosa (Pye 1995). Of the identifiable sherds (which constitute 45 percent of the sample), the most common kinds of pottery at Tapexco are Amatle Hard Ware (23 percent) and Pastores Simple (14 percent). Another kind of ceramic pertaining to the Late Classic period is San Juan Plumbate (2 percent). At Tapexco, the most frequently occurring form is the jar (N=128): it occurs in similar proportions in each ware; in the Amatle Hard Ware there are 87 examples and in the Pastores Simple there are 41 examples. Bowls of Amatle Hard Ware and Pastores Simple were extremely rare at Tapexco; there are only six examples in the analyzed sample. At the site center of Santa Rosa the inverse relationship is true. In the Late Classic sample, there were more bowls (N=213) than jars (N=33). One interpretation of this pattern is that food-serving and feasting activities that required ceramic bowls occurred at Santa Rosa, while food preparation and storage in ceramic jars were common activities at Tapexco. Alternative interpretations are (1) that there is a disproportionate number of bowls at Santa Rosa because they are thinner than jars and break more easily, thus their count is higher; and (2) that Tapexco actually had bowls but they were made of perishable gourds that were cut into bowl forms.

Comparing the Late Classic ceramics of the northern and southern end of the valley: Santa Rosa and Pompeya

Pottery collections from Santa Rosa and Pompeya, located at opposite ends of the Antigua Valley, are not identical. Both sites share large quantities of Amatle Hard Ware and small amounts of San Juan Plumbate, but there are differences in the red-paste ceramics. At Santa Rosa the red-paste pottery is called Pastores Simple. At Pompeya, a comparable kind of pottery is not described. Instead, the site report specifies a different red ware dated to the Late Classic by Ivic de Monterroso (1998: 632), but its attributes suggest that it actually dates to the late Early Classic period. This pottery has a brilliant paste like Early Classic Prisma ware, with crystals, pumice, and a red to rosy orange tone. Some sherds have a micaceous orange slip, or linear painted decoration and a red smoothed surface with a purple or white micaceous slip (ibid.). From the description, this pottery is unlike Late Classic Pastores Simple in paste, surface treatment, and decoration.

Borhegyi (1950) noted that some pottery from Pompeya is similar to types described for the Pacific piedmont. In particular, ceramics from Pompeya and Santa Rosa have analogues in the Santa Lucia ceramic complex of El Bilbao (Parsons 1967). The shared ceramics include Amatle Hard Ware (quite common in the highlands and called the Diamantes ceramic group at Bilbao), San Juan Plumbate, and the San Andres (polychrome) Group (Tiquisate Ware). The last is found at both Bilbao (ibid.: pl. 18d) and Pompeya but is absent at Santa Rosa.

These wares are widely distributed throughout the highlands and piedmont and thus indicate no special relationship between the Antigua Valley and the Cotzulmalguapan core site Bilbao. Utilitarian wares may be better indicators of such relationships or the lack of them. The unslipped wares from Santa Rosa are more varied in form than those of Bilbao, which are characterized by enormous urns and incurved-rim bowls or dishes. The utilitarian pottery wares of Santa Rosa and Bilbao, therefore, have little in common.

Lithic artifacts of Santa Rosa

The analysis of Late Classic chipped-stone artifacts from Santa Rosa conducted by Geoffrey Braswell revealed that the majority of the obsidian appears in the form of prismatic blade fragments (N=246; 54.3 percent). The second most frequent category is the percussion flake (N=145; 32.0 percent). Chunks, percussion blades, and a fragment of an exhausted polyhedral core reveal that lithic production took place on site. The most common obsidian source represented in the collection is San Martin Jilotepeque (N=193; 42.7 percent). Smaller quantities come from El Chayal (N=151; 33.3 percent), a high-quality source east of Kaminaljuyu, and from San Bartolome Milpas Altas (N=108; 23.8 percent), a local source of very low-quality obsidian. A small projectile point fragment was made of high-quality obsidian from the Ixtepeque source (N=1; 0.2 percent) in eastern Guatemala. Garrido López (2011) reports somewhat different obsidian procurement patterns for Pompeya. There, San Martin Jilotepeque (52 percent) is the most common source, followed by El Chayal (35 percent) and Ixtepeque (12 percent).[2]

Rucal

Our excavations in the central plaza of Rucal (see Figure 6.3) revealed two occupational components of the site (see Chapter 5 for a discussion of the Preclassic). The upper 2 meters date to the Late Classic period. We encountered a black clay floor beneath 1.5 meters of overburden and black soil and sand. This floor lay upon a prepared layer of dark brown burned gravel 20 cm thick mixed with sand and ash. This subfloor level contained a Late Classic offering of a Pastores Simple: Rejon Variety red-paste jar with a wide strap handle and an everted rim. Assay of carbon from this level yielded a date of 1230 + 60 BP (Beta 81336), equivalent to a one-sigma calibrated date of between AD 705 and 885. Perhaps the cache marks the base layer of plaza construction, implying that the site was built and occupied principally in the eighth century.

The decline of the Late Classic population of the Antigua Valley

Dorothy Freidel *et al.* (2007) present paleoclimatic data for the Antigua Valley resulting from pollen cores and phytolith studies. There were several episodes of desiccation during the Classic period, and one of them is dated to AD 785 (calibrated). Perhaps the Antigua Valley was affected quite severely by drought at the time of the beginning of the lowland Maya collapse (McNeil *et al.* 2010), and Late Classic occupation in the valley ended around AD 800.

The Antigua Valley and sculpture

The similarity of the Cotzumalguapan and Antigua Valley sculptures has long been recognized (Ford and Parsons 1969; Perrot-Minnot 2002) and demonstrates a connection between the two zones in the Late Classic. This time period must have been during an overlap of the Pantaleon phase of Cotzumalguapa and the Pompeya phase of the Antigua Valley, approximately AD 700 to 800. Possible relationships between the highlands and piedmont may have started in the Early Classic between the third and sixth centuries. Some sculptures in San Martin Jilotepeque have been found in Early Classic contexts that predate the appearance of Classic-period sculpture in the Cotzumalguapan region yet share some characteristics with that later style (Braswell 1998; Chinchilla Mazariegos 1996).

The Cotzumalguapan region is a broad expanse of piedmont terrain stretching along the south side of the volcanic highlands from Suchitepequez Department, Guatemala, to El Salvador. Within this region are numerous sites with sculpture carved in the Cotzumalguapan style or containing Cotzumalguapan iconography. Typically, however, artistic execution is crude outside of the three major Cotzumalguapan centers at the core of the zone. Located in the middle Coyolate River drainage, these centers are El Baul, Bilbao, and El Castillo. These monumental sites are separated by 1.5 km, but Chinchilla Mazariegos (1996) thinks that they functioned together as a single city because of the continuous distribution of surface artifacts between them. According to him, these sites formed the core of the polity, but there also were clusters of satellite sites. These are smaller in size and typically have one or two sculptures containing images of persons, complex iconography, and even writing. Two of these clusters exist to the east and west of the core, centered respectively at Los Cerritos Norte (25 km away on the Achiguate drainage) and Palo Gordo (35 km to the northwest on the Nahualate River). Chinchilla Mazariegos identifies a third cluster in the Antigua Valley about 40 km northeast of the core sites.

Three classes of sculptures – dressed stone monuments, sculpture in the round, and tenoned heads – found in the Antigua Valley are carved in a similar style and sport themes common to Cotzumalguapan art. Their presence demonstrates interaction between the two regions (Chinchilla Mazariegos 1996; Parsons 1969). Typical of the Cotzumalguapan style are figures with angular faces, flat feet shown from above, and anklebones depicted as small raised discs. Other characteristic elements are large circular glyphs, speech scrolls, and groups of dots. The sculptural themes of the dressed stone monuments are most commonly complex narratives depicting nobles in political and religious scenes concerning the ballgame, death, and sacrifice. Supernatural beings are often shown interacting with nobles.

Two examples of dressed stone monuments highlight features found in both the Cotzumalguapan core zone and the Antigua Valley. Although not identical, El Baul Monument 27 and Santa Rosa Stela 1 appear similar (see Figure 6.6). On both monuments, principal figures are placed on the right side of the monument and face left. On El Baul Monument 27, the principal figure dominates over a fallen ballplayer or boxer. On Santa Rosa Stela 1, the principal figure stands over a richly bejeweled but diminutive individual (see Figure 6.6b; Giraud 1972; Benítez *et al.* 1993). This latter figure has protruding ribs and is bound, which may indicate he is about to be sacrificed. Both of the main figures wear bulging protective gear on their knees, and the main figure on the El Baul monument holds balls or stone in both hands. The seven circular glyphs at Santa Rosa are associated with a death's head – the ensemble may be the name of the principal figure. A further similarity is that elements depicting speech or sounds emanate from the mouths of both individuals. The rayed headdress of the principal figure at Santa Rosa is also similar to that worn by the elevated individual on El Castillo Monument 1.

Except for tenoned heads, which probably were architectural decorations, sculptures from the Cotzumalguapa and the Antigua zone are generally not identical but instead show some creative differences. Details of Santa Rosa Stela 1 demonstrate some unique features. For example, the smaller figure, probably a sacrificial victim, is shown with curved elements and dots around his body. The curved elements might be fire; clues to their meaning exist on an unprovenienced sculpture, perhaps from the Antigua Valley, that depicts flames above a vessel in the same way (Parsons 1969: 271, pl. 63i). The dots surrounding the figure probably represent blood or water. The dots above the head of the victim on Stela 1 are associated with a possible spear thrower and perhaps indicate his name.

One of the most common themes in Cotzumalguapan art – also seen on Santa Rosa Stela 1 – is the Mesoamerican ballgame. Parsons (1991) summarizes the importance of the mythical and religious beliefs tied to this non-secular sport. He sees it representing various cosmic cycles, one of the most basic being life and death. In particular, human sacrifice after the ballgame ensured the rebirth of the sun in the east after its demise in the west. He notes also that the ballgame, although extant in the Preclassic period, served during the Late Classic period as a vehicle for the political and perhaps ideological unification of people.

In the Antigua Valley – concurrent with the florescence of sculpture in the Late Classic – there was a cessation of ritual activities at La Casa de las Golondrinas, a large rock-art site. An outcrop with at least three overhangs that create shelters, the site had ritual activities in the Preclassic, Early Classic, and Postclassic periods (Robinson *et al.* 2007). These data indicate that devotion, popular in the Early

Classic at natural shrines such as La Casa de las Golondrinas and at Pacaño, a cave site near Patzicia (Robinson *et al.* 2008), terminated during the Late Classic. This happened in conjunction with the formalization of ideological and political aspects of culture shared with the Cotzumalguapan polity and elites.

To the north of the Antigua Valley are other Late Classic sculptures from diverse and widespread locations (Benítez 2004; Braswell 1998; García García 1992; Giraud 1972, 1975; Mata 2005; Villacorta de Calderón and Villacorta 1927). The practice of using tenoned heads, stelae, and carved altars was quite common in the department of Chimaltenango, north and west of Sacatepequez, during the Late Classic period. But monuments in Chimaltenango lack carved glyphs – Chinchilla Mazariego's chief criterion for the Cotzumalguapan style. The sculptures of Chimaltenango vary, but humans, deities based on anthropomorphic forms, serpents, and jaguars occur as isolates or in combination. In this periphery, the influence of Cotzumalguapa seems less strong than it does close to the core in the Antigua Valley. The comparatively low density of sculptures may correlate with more rural and dispersed populations, but extensive excavations have yet to be carried out at numerous Late Classic sites in this area where sculptures can be deeply buried (Benítez 2004).

Conclusions: interaction in an Antigua Valley satellite cluster

Few scholars have sought to explain the cultural processes that generated the piedmont-wide Cotzumalguapan phenomenon and the incorporation of the Antigua Valley into its religious and political sphere. Ford and Parsons (1969) offered a very brief suggestion, based largely on sculptural evidence, of conquest and domination by the Cotzumalguapans. Chinchilla Mazariegos (1996) avoids assigning any social, political, or economic processes to the formation or function of satellite clusters – he merely states that they have a dendritic pattern without necessarily any economic focus.

The analysis of the defensive features of the locations of sites provides new data for the interpretation of the Late Classic sociopolitical organization. Sites such as El Portal (on a high hill) and Santa Rosa (on a projection of land) support an interpretation that elevated locations and the lines of sight between them could have facilitated communication and possibly defense for populations below the slopes. In contrast, at the southern end of the valley, Types 1, 2, and 3 sites are on contours at the base of the Agua Volcano but not on hilltops or high projections of land. The position of sites on the west and north sides of the valley might define northern and perhaps western boundaries for Cotzumalguapan sculpture and ideology. This examination of settlement patterns has provided a detailed overview of the sites and their potential for communication and defense in the Antigua Valley.

Santa Rosa, with its Cotzumalguapan-style stela, functioned as an important site within the valley. The theme of dominance displayed by an over-lording individual in Cotzumalguapan ballgame gear on Stela 1 indicates that persons with power and authority existed at this site. It was in an excellent location to protect, via surveillance, the well-populated valley to the south and to serve as part of a valley-wide communication network. It also could have served as a defensive post creating a boundary to a less acculturated populace to the north. Santa Rosa, however, was not of equal rank to other secondary sites in the Cotzumalguapan zone. It is in a peripheral location at the north edge of the Antigua Valley and occupies a high elevation. Moreover, its small size relative to other Cotzumalguapan centers and its architectural simplicity make it likely that it was a node on a network of interacting centers rather than a central place. It is unlikely that Santa Rosa served as a grand political center.

What was the culture of the Antigua Valley like in the Late Classic period? This valley, like other contact zones, could have been a dynamic area where populations with highland affiliations, possible antecedent communities, and new populations from the piedmont received and processed cultural information. Rodseth and Parker, drawing on Eric Wolf's definition of culture as a series of processes, see a frontier as a "shifting zone of innovation and recombination, through which cultural materials from many sources have been unpredictably channeled and transformed" (Rodseth and Parker 2005: 4). The cultural variety in site form and ceramic distributions in the Antigua Valley suggest some of these dynamic cultural processes were alive during the Late Classic. Acculturation is the concept that describes change that occurs when different cultures are in immediate and continuous contact. Such contact may create a decline in ethnic differences as groups and individuals take on the behavior or values of the other groups with which they have contact. Conversely, such differences may be reinforced as competition sets groups apart and accentuates cultural distinctions.

Given the data I discuss in this chapter, we can hypothesize that the Antigua Valley was an acculturative zone with some potential for defense. The archaeological culture of Santa Rosa manifests both regional highland and foreign features. The architecture has distinctive highland aspects, especially the construction of earthen platforms and the use of a *palangana*-type ballcourt. In contrast, ramps, pavements, and drains of stone such as exist at Santa Rosa – similar to other paved surfaces now known at Pompeya and Kaminaljuyu – are more likely architectural details shared by the coastal and highland groups rather than embellishments inspired by the piedmont Cotzumalguapans (Robinson *et al.* 1993; Garrido López 2011; Arroyo *et al.* 2012). The ceramics from Santa Rosa include some highland types and other types or analogues that are interregional in their distribution. These span the highlands and the Pacific piedmont and manifest the sharing of ceramic information between the two zones. Cultural processes such as elite peer interaction between local K'iche'an and foreign piedmont lords, and the emulation of Cotzumalguapan practices by local elites aspiring elevated social and political status, might explain the combination of the highland *palangana* ballcourt form with piedmont-inspired sculptures.

Santa Rosa Stela 1, the only sculpture in the Antigua Valley with circular Cotzumalguapan glyphs, throws doubt on models of peaceful interaction, emulation, and acculturation. Perhaps conflict between distinct highland and piedmont groups did exist, and people with Cotzumalguapan affiliations may have gained an upper hand at the northern end of the valley. Although it is small compared with, for example, the Valley of Guatemala, diversity in settlement patterns can be seen in the northern, western, and southern ends of the valley. Thus single cause explanations for the diverse cultural phenomena outlined here may not cover the possible variety of responses to interregional trade, ethnic diversity, or religious influences received and processed by the elites of the Late Classic Antigua Valley.

Notes

1 I extend my sincere thanks to several agencies. The Instituto de Antropología e Historia de Guatemala and Vanderbilt University provided institutional support for our survey and excavations in the Antigua Valley and its environs. The Wenner-Gren Foundation (#5202) and a Grant of Regular Training Program of the Organization of American States (1989–1991, F13581) supported the survey of the Antigua Valley. Finca Santa Rosa (1991) graciously funded excavations of the site of the same name. Work at Rucal was funded by the H. John Heinz III Charitable Foundation (#533037), and Mary Pye was a collaborator and inspiration concerning the Preclassic at that site. Throughout all phases of research, the Middle American Research Institute (MARI) of Tulane University lent logistical and institutional support. Like the other contributors to this volume, I offer special thanks to Will Andrews, the director of MARI. His support of our work in the highlands began in 1989 and has continued to the present. Thanks are also extended to Marlen Garnica, the codirector of PAAK; Paulino Puc Rucal, who became a technical director at Rucal; Lauren Okie Clark for assistance in the inking the ceramic illustrations; Guido Pezzarossi for the base map for Figure 6.4; Justin Lowry for the electronic renditions of Figures 6.1, 6.2, 6.3, 6.5b, and 6.6b; and Mike Stoianovic for help with the preparation of Figure 6.5a.
2 Geoffrey Braswell (personal communication 2012) considers it highly unlikely that the proportion of Ixtepeque obsidian at Pompeya is this high. He notes that, in the central highlands of Guatemala, Ixtepeque obsidian is exceedingly rare in contexts that predate the Late Postclassic. It seems more likely to him that this material comes from San Bartolome Milpas Altas, a little-known source of very similar-appearing lustrous, translucent, and brown obsidian. Outcrops are located just 9 km northeast of Antigua. Because of its exceptionally poor fracturing qualities, obsidian from this source did not circulate widely and is found only rarely in significant quantities beyond the Antigua Valley.

References

Arroyo, Bárbara, Lorena Paiz, Adriana Linares, and Margarita Cossich (2012) Recent Results for the Preclassic: the Naranjo and Kaminaljuyu Projects. Paper presented at the 77th annual meeting of the Society for American Archaeology, Memphis.

Benítez, José E. (1991) *Las formaciones económico-sociales preclasistas en los alrededores del Valle de Antigua Guatemala*. Licenciatura thesis, Escuela de Historía, Area de Arqueologia, Universidad de San Carlos Borromeo de Guatemala.

—— (2004) El Altar 1 de Cakhay. In *XVII Simposio de investigaciones arqueológicas en Guatemala, 2003*, ed. Juan Pedro Laporte, Bárbara Arroyo, Héctor Escobedo, and Héctor Mejía, Vol. 1, pp. 158–64. Guatemala City: Museo Nacional de Arqueología y Etnología.

Benítez, José, Teresita Chinchilla, and Eugenia Robinson (1993) La Estela 1 de Santa Rosa, departamento de Sacatepéquez. In *III Simposio de investigaciones arqueológicas en Guatemala, 1989*, ed. Juan Pedro Laporte, Héctor L. Escobedo, and Sandra Villagrán de Brady, pp. 245–53. Guatemala City: Museo Nacional de Arqueología y Etnología.

Borgstede, Greg, and James R. Mathieu (2007) Defensibility and Settlement Patterns in the Guatemalan Maya Highlands. *Latin American Antiquity* 18: 191–211.

Borhegyi, Stephan F. de (1950) Estudio arqueologico en la falda norte del volcan de Agua. *Anales de antropología e historia de Guatemala* 2: 3–22.

—— (1965a) Settlement Patterns of the Guatemalan Highlands. In *Handbook of Middle American Indians*, Vol. 2: *Archaeology of Southern Mesoamerica, Part I*, ed. Gordon R. Willey, pp. 59–75. Austin: University of Texas Press.

—— (1965b) Archaeological Synthesis of the Guatemalan Highlands. In *Handbook of Middle American Indians*, Vol. 2: *Archaeology of Southern Mesoamerica, Part I*, ed. Gordon R. Willey, pp. 3–58. Austin: University of Texas Press.

Braswell, Geoffrey E. (1998) La arqueología de San Martín Jilotepeque, Guatemala. *Mesoamérica* 35: 117–54.

Cáceres, T. Jorge Enrique, and Juan Pablo Herrera (2010) Informe de investigación arqueológica en el Predio Quinta Orotara. Km 40.8 Santa Inés del Monte Pulciano, La Antigua Guatemala, Guatemala. Unpublished MS.

Cardona Caravantes, Karla J., and Andrea María Díaz (2010) Proyecto de rescate arqueológico "Cuarta Calle Oriente, Zona 6," Ciudad Vieja, Sacatepéquez, Guatemala. Unpublished MS, submitted to the Departamento de Monumentos Prehispanicos y Coloniales, Instituto de Antropología e Historia, Guatemala.

Chinchilla, Miranda María Teresita (1991) Análisis del impacto de la conquista en las comunidades del valle de Quilisimate, Sacatepéquez, durante la primera mitad del siglo XVI. Licenciatura thesis, Escuela de Historía, Area de Arqueologia, Universidad de San Carlos Borromeo de Guatemala.

Chinchilla Mazariegos, Oswaldo Fernando (1996) *Settlement Patterns and Monumental Art at a Major Pre-Columbian Polity: Cotzumalguapa, Guatemala*. PhD dissertation, Department of Anthropology, Vanderbilt University. Ann Arbor, MI: University Microfilms.

—— (1998) Pipiles y cakchiqueles en Cotzumalguapa: la evidencia etnohistórica y arqueológica. *Anales de la Academica de Geografía e Historia de Guatemala* 73: 143–84.

Chinchilla Mazariegos, Oswaldo, Frederick J. Bove, and José Vicente Genovez (2009) La cronología del período clásico en la costa sur de Guatemala y el fechamiento del estilo escultórico de Cotzumalguapa. In *Cronología y periodización en mesoamérica y el norte de México: V Coloquio Pedro Bosch Gimpera*, ed. Annick Daneels, pp. 435–72. Mexico City: Universidad Nacional Autónoma de México.

—— (2011) *Cotzumalguapa: la ciudad arqueológica El Baúl – Bilbao – El Castillo*. Guatemala: F & G Editores.

Eisen, Gustav (1888) On some ancient sculptures from the Pacific slope of Guatemala. In *Memoirs, California Academy of Sciences* 2(2): 9–20.

Fischer, Edward F., and Carol Hendrickson (2003) *Tecpan, Guatemala*. Boulder, CO: Westview Press.

Ford, James B., and Lee A. Parsons (1969) Appendix. In Lee Parsons, *Bilboa, Guatemala: An Archaeological Study of the Pacific Coast Cotzumalguapa Region*, Vol. 2. Milwaukee: Milwaukee Public Museum.

Freidel, Dorothy, John Jones, and Eugenia Robinson (2007) Human Adaptation at Urias, Valley of Antigua, Guatemala. Paper presented at the 72nd annual meeting of the Society for American Archaeology, Austin.

García García, Edgar Vinicio (1992) Reconocimiento arqueológico de las tierras altas centrales de Chimaltenango. Licenciatura thesis, Escuela de Historía, Area de Arqueologia, Universidad de San Carlos Borromeo de Guatemala.

Garrido López, Jose Luis (2011) Proyecto arqueológico de Rescate Pompeya PARP. Unpublished MS, presented to the Dirección General de Patrimonio Cultural y Natural de Guatemala, Guatemala City.

Giraud, Rafael (1972) Nuevas esculturas líticas en el área maya. In *Atti del XL congresso internazionale degli Americanisti*, pp. 195–202. Geneva: Tilgher.

—— (1975) Esculturas monumentales olmecoides en los altos de Guatemala. In *Proceedings of the 41st International Congress of Americanists* [Mexico, 1974], Vol. 1, pp. 436–41.

Hill, Robert M., II (1996) Eastern Chajoma Political Geography: Ethnohistorical and Archaeological Contributions to the Study of a Late Postclassic Maya Polity. *Ancient Mesoamerica* 7: 63–87.

Ivic, Matilde (1998) Observaciones sobre los complejos ceramicos de Chirijuyu, Chimaltenango. In *XI Simposio de investigaciones arqueológicas en Guatemala*, ed. Juan Pedro Laporte and Héctor L. Escobedo, Vol. 2, pp. 629–33. Guatemala City: Museo Nacional de Arqueología y Etnología.

Mata Armado, Guillermo (2005) Monumento prehispánico frente al edificio de rectoria de la Universidad de San Carlos. In *XVIII Simposio de investigaciones arqueológicas en Guatemala, 2004*, ed. Juan Pedro Laporte, Bárbara Arroyo, and Héctor E. Mejía, Vol. 2, pp. 525–30. Guatemala City: Museo Nacional de Arqueología y Etnología.

McNeil, Cameron L., David A. Burney, and Lida Pigott Burney (2010) Evidence Disputing Deforestation as the Cause for the Collapse of the Ancient Maya Polity of Copan, Honduras. *Proceedings of the National Academy of Science of the USA* 107: 1017–22.

Morales, Paulino I. (1998) Sitios prehispanicos y monumentos históricos asociados a la Ruta Nacional 14 (cuenca alta del Río Guacalate). In *XII Simposio de investigaciones arqueológicas en Guatemala*, ed. Juan Pedro Laporte, Héctor L. Escobedo, and Ana Claudia Monzón de Suasnávar, Vol. 2, pp. 553–62. Guatemala City: Museo Nacional de Arqueología y Etnología.

Parsons, Lee A. (1967) *Bilbao, Guatemala: An Archaeological Study of the Pacific Coast Cotzumalhuapa Region*, Vol 1. Milwaukee: Milwaukee Public Museum.

—— (1969) *Bilbao, Guatemala: An Archaeological Study of the Pacific Coast Cotzumalhuapa Region*, Vol. 2, pp. 190–207. Milwaukee: Milwaukee Public Museum.

—— (1991) The Ballgame in the Southern Pacific Coast Cotzumalhuapa Region and its Impact on Kaminaljuyu during the Middle Classic. In *The Mesoamerican Ballgame*, ed. Vernon Scarborough and David Wilcox, pp. 195–211. Tucson: University of Arizona Press.

Perrot-Minnot, Sébastien (2002) Las esculturas prehispánicas de la región de Antigua Guatemala. In *XV Simposio de investigaciones arqueológicas en Guatemala, 2001*, ed. Juan Pedro Laporte, Héctor Escobedo, and Bárbara Arroyo, Vol. 2, pp. 709–21. Guatemala City: Museo Nacional de Arqueología y Etnología.

—— (2005) Investigaciones arqueológicas en el sitio de El Portal, Antigua, Guatemala. *Mexicon*, 27: 40–44.

Perrot-Minnot, Sébastien, Marlen Garnica, and Edgar Carpio (2003) Reconocimiento arqueológico al oeste de la cuenca de Antigua Guatemala, Sacatepéquez. Unpublished MS, submitted to the Instituto de Antropología e Historia/Consejo Nacional Para la Protección de La Antigua Guatemala, Guatemala.

Pye, Suzanne (1995) Scratching the Surface: An Analysis of a Ceramic Surface Collection at Santa Rosa, Guatemala. BA thesis, Department of Anthropology, Rutgers University.

Rands, Robert L., and Robert E. Smith (1965) Pottery of the Guatemalan Highlands. *Handbook of Middle American Indians*, Vol. 2: *Archaeology of Southern Mesoamerica, Part I*, ed. Gordon R. Willey, pp. 95–145. Austin: University of Texas Press.

Robinson, Eugenia J. (1998) William R. Swezey, 26 de febrero, 1933–9 de junio, 1989. *Mesoamérica* 19: 1–5.

Robinson, Eugenia J. and Guido Pezzarossi (2011) Los mayas del clasico tardío en la región del Valle de Antigua: defensa y agricultura en las tierras altas de Guatemala. Paper presented at the XXV Simposio de Investigaciones Arqueológicas en Guatemala, Guatemala City.

Robinson, Eugenia J., and Mary Pye (1996) Investigaciones en Rucal: hallazgos de una ocupación del formativo medio en el Altiplano de Guatemala. In *IX Simposio de investigaciones arqueológicas en Guatemala, 1995*, ed. Juan Pedro Laporte and Héctor Escobedo, Vol. 2, pp. 487–98. Guatemala City: Museo Nacional de Arqueología y Etnología.

Robinson, Eugenia J., with Geoffrey E. Braswell and Stephen Whittington (1993) Santa Rosa: un sitio defensivo en las tierras altas centrales de Guatemala. Unpublished MS, submitted to the Departamento de Monumentos Prehispanicos y Coloniales, Instituto de Antropología e Historia, Guatemala.

Robinson, Eugenia J., Marlen Garnica, Patricia Farrell, Dorothy Freidel, Kitty Emery, Marilyn Beaudry-Corbett, and David Lentz (2000) El preclásico en Urías: una adaptación ambiental y cultural en el Valle de Antigua, Guatemala. In *XIII Simposio de investigaciones arqueológicas en Guatemala, 1999*, ed. Juan Pedro Laporte, Héctor Escobedo, Ana Claudia de Suasnavar, and Bárbara Arroyo, Vol. 2, pp. 841–8. Guatemala City: Museo Nacional de Arqueología y Etnología.

Robinson, Eugenia J., Patricia Farrell, Kitty Emery, and Geoffrey E. Braswell (2002) Preclassic Settlements and Geomorphology in the Highlands of Guatemala: Excavations at Urias, Valley of Antigua. In *Incidents of Archaeology in Central America and Yucatan*, ed. Michael Love, Marion Hatch, and Héctor Escobedo, pp. 251–77. Lanham, MD: University Press of America.

Robinson, Eugenia J., Marlen Garnica, Ruth Ann Armitage, and Marvin W. Rowe (2007) Los fechamientos del arte rupestre y la arqueología en la Casa de las Golondrinas, San Miguel Duenas, Sacatepéquez. In *XX Simposio de investigaciones arqueológicas en Guatemala, 2006*, ed. Juan Pedro Laporte, Bárbara Arroyo, and Héctor Mejía, Vol. 2, pp. 959–72. Guatemala City: Museo Nacional de Arqueología y Etnología.

Robinson, Eugenia J., Marlen Garnica, and Juan Pablo Herrera (2008) Pacaño, un sitio ritual en las tierras altas de Guatemala. In *XXI Simposio de investigaciones arqueológicas en Guatemala, 2007*, ed. Juan Pedro Laporte, Bárbara Arroyo, and Héctor E. Mejía, pp. 25–33. Guatemala City: Museo Nacional de Arqueología y Etnología.

Rodseth, Lars, and Bradley J. Parker (2005) Theoretical Considerations in the Study of Frontiers. In *Untaming the Frontier in Anthropology, Archaeology, and History*, ed. Bradley J. Parker and Lars Rodseth, pp. 3–21. Tucson: University of Arizona Press.

Rubio, Rolando (1986) Estructura J-107, sitio arqueológico El Baúl, Santa Lucía Cotzumalguapa, Escuinta, Guatemala. Licenciatura thesis, Facultad de Ciencias Sociales, Universidad del Valle de Guatemala.

Seler, Cecilia (1900) *Auf alten Wegen in Mexiko und Guatemala*. Berlin: Dietrich Reimer.

Shook, Edwin M. (1942, 1950, 1952a, 1964, 1969, 1972) Archivo de sitios. Departamento de Arqueología, Universidad del Valle de Guatemala.

—— (1948–50) Notas de campo de Edwin M. Shook, Vol. 20. Departamento de Arqueología, Universidad del Valle de Guatemala.

—— (1952b) Lugares arqueológicos del altiplano meridional central de Guatemala. *Antropología e História de Guatemala* 5(2): 3–40.

Shook, Edwin M., and Marion Popenoe de Hatch (1999) Las tierras altas centrales: períodos preclásico y clásico. In *Historia general de Guatemala*, ed. Jorge Luján Muñoz, Vol. 1, pp. 289–318. Guatemala City: Asociación de Amigos del País, Fundación para la Cultura y el Desarrollo.

Shook, Edwin M., and Tatiana Proskouriakoff (1956) Settlement Patterns in Meso-America and the Sequence in the Guatemalan Highlands. In *Prehistoric Settlement Patterns in the New World*, ed. Gordon R. Willey, pp. 93–100. New York: Wenner-Gren Foundation for Anthropological Research.

Smith, A. Ledyard (1965) Architecture of the Guatemalan Highlands. In *Handbook of Middle American Indians*, Vol. 2: *Archaeology of Southern Mesoamerica, Part I*, ed. Gordon R. Willey, pp. 76–94. Austin: University of Texas Press.

Thompson, J. Eric S. (1948) *An Archaeological Reconnaissance in the Cotzumalguapan Region, Escuintla, Guatemala*. Washington, DC: Carnegie Institution.

Villacorta de Calderón, José Antonio, and Carlos A. Villacorta (1927) *Arqueología Guatemalteca*. Guatemala City: Anales de la Sociedad de Geografia e Historia de Guatemala.

PART III
The southern Maya lowlands

7

A TANGLED WEB

Ceramic adoption in the Maya lowlands and community interaction in the early Middle Preclassic as seen in the K'awil complex from Holmul, Peten, Guatemala[1]

Niña Neivens de Estrada

Recent research has greatly increased data on the earliest lowland Maya ceramics dating to the early Middle Preclassic or Pre-Mamom period. Excavations at Holmul, Peten, Guatemala, have provided a large sample of ceramics from these times. Through examination of various contemporary ceramics, I place this complex in the context of pan-Mesoamerican cultural development. This chapter is inspired by a 1990 study by Will Andrews and has benefited from his guidance throughout. My principal goal is to present examples of K'awil-phase pottery from Holmul and compare them to those from other complexes from various sites within the lowlands and highlands in order to understand the processes by which ceramic ideas were adopted by the ancient Maya.

This project was born in a dusty room on the fourth floor of Dinwiddie Hall adjacent to the displays of magnificent artifacts found in the Middle American Research Institute. The room was the location where so many budding Maya archaeologists at Tulane waited to hear their fate after completing their oral examinations. Will Andrews liked to let the student wonder for a moment or two before extending his hand to the newly minted PhD candidate. It is also the location of Will's great seminars on Mesoamerican archaeology. It was here that I first learned of the confusing state of early Middle Preclassic[2] occupation in the Maya lowlands, the problem with the term "Olmec," and the importance of comparison in ceramic analysis. These are some of the lessons taught to me by Will Andrews which eventually led me to the present study, an examination of the early Middle Preclassic ceramics from Holmul, Guatemala (see Figure 1.1).

In this chapter I offer a preliminary typological analysis of the early Middle Preclassic K'awil ceramic phase at Holmul (*c*. 1000–850 BC) and try to place it within the context of contemporaneous pottery traditions. The complex contains pottery similar to that from Cahal Pech in Belize (Cunil); Tikal (Early Eb), Altar de Sacrificios (Xe), and Seibal (Real Xe) in Guatemala; and Komchen (Ek) and Kiuic (Early Bah) in Yucatan, Mexico. These collections all share some stylistic attributes with pottery collections from other parts of Mesoamerica, such as southern Guatemala and the highlands and lowlands of Mexico. This shared style consists of an iconographic complex, usually incised on ceramics and also found on other objects, which in the past has been called "Olmec," "Olmec style," and "olmecoid" (Grove 1989; Clark and Pye 2000). I avoid this term so as not to conflate the issue of a shared iconographic complex with the influence or intrusion of a particular archaeological culture from the Gulf Coast of Mexico. Furthermore, the inclusion of a particular set of motifs on these sherds is just one component of each overall ceramic complex and not necessarily the defining characteristic of any of them.

Among Andrews's many accomplishments and contributions to the field is his pioneering work on the ceramics at Komchen, Yucatan (Andrews 1984, 1988; Andrews and Andrews 1980). His rigorous analysis of the material from that site brought him to examine many contemporaneous Preclassic collections at other sites. The result of these comparative studies is Andrews's chapter "Early Ceramic History of the Lowland Maya" (1990). When it was written, very few lowland Maya sites had been found with occupations dating to the early part of the Middle Preclassic. Among known early sites were Seibal (Sabloff 1975), Altar de Sacrificios (Adams 1971), and Cuello (Hammond 1979; Hammond et al. 1991). Andrews suggests that Maya ceramicists have much to learn from restudying previously excavated collections. He also concludes that the Xe-phase materials from Seibal and Altar de Sacrificios form a particular tradition – especially in their matte, glittery, and micaceous reds and whites – that sets them apart from other lowland Maya traditions and allies them with collections from Chiapas (Andrews 1990). Since 1990, excavations at a number of other sites in the Maya lowlands have yielded early ceramics similar to those of the Xe complex (Awe et al. 2008; Brown 2007; Cheetham 2005; Clark and Cheetham 2002; Garber et al. 2004).

Recently, the newly defined Pre-Mamom complexes at sites such as Cahal Pech (Sullivan et al. 2009; Healy et al. 2004) and Tikal (Hermes 1993a, 1993b) have led Andrews to re-examine his own conclusions regarding material from Komchen. In 2008 he described a Pre-Mamom complex for Komchen and Kiuic in northern Yucatan, which includes characteristic incised motifs found across the Maya lowlands as well as much of Mesoamerica in the Middle Preclassic period (Andrews et al. 2008). Andrews and his colleagues have now concluded that the earliest lowland Maya ceramics were probably adopted by people already inhabiting these areas, specifically as a means of displaying these incised designs (Andrews and Bey 2011; Andrews et al. 2008).

It was a fortuitous accident that I began my own studies under Will Andrews during his re-evaluation. I entered Tulane intending to study an entirely different time period, but Will soon had me fascinated by the Preclassic. My own 2005 discovery of an early Middle Preclassic phase at Holmul, Peten, Guatemala, further convinced me that this is what I wanted to study. As Will's student I have heeded his advice to examine as many excavated collections of contemporaneous material as I can (see Chapter 11) and to consider my own ceramics from Holmul within the context of the lowland Maya and the greater Mesoamerican world.

I begin this chapter with a discussion of early pottery in the Maya lowlands. I then consider excavations at Group II, Holmul, and my analysis of the pottery found there. I compare this material to that found at other sites in the Maya region. During the course of my research, I examined collections of contemporaneous material from Cahal Pech, Belize, and from Seibal, Guatemala, housed at the Peabody Museum of Archaeology and Ethnology at Harvard University. Finally, at the ceramic laboratory of the Instituto de Antropología e Historia in Guatemala City, I was able to compare sherds from various sites and regions, including Altar de Sacrificios, Rio Azul, Uaxactun, Holmul, Alta Verapaz, La Victoria, and Chiquiuitan. Viewing these sherds in person was extremely important for making interregional comparisons.

The problem of early Middle Preclassic Maya ceramics

The earliest occupation of the Maya lowlands has long been the subject of scholarly debate. Until about 1960, the Mamom ceramic complex (Smith 1955), dating to the late Middle Preclassic (600–250 BC), was considered to represent the earliest settled agricultural occupation of the Maya lowlands. In the 1960s, Altar de Sacrificios and Seibal yielded earlier "Pre-Mamom" ceramics,[3] but these were found at sites considered to be somewhat peripheral to the Peten heartland and characterized by a limited early occupation consisting of perishable structures. Somewhat later, Cuello was discovered, and great antiquity was claimed for its earliest pottery, temporarily making the Swasey complex the oldest ceramics in Mesoamerica (Hammond 1979; Kosakowsky 1987a). Andrews was instrumental in re-examining the radiocarbon dates from Cuello and, along with Hammond, argued that the Swasey phase probably dates to about 1200–900 BC (Andrews and Hammond 1990).[4] Another Belizean site, Cahal Pech, began to reveal Pre-Mamom ceramics and occupation levels in 1992, but the excavators remained cautious about claiming antiquity in part because of the controversy surrounding the Cuello dates (Awe 1992; Awe *et al.* 2008; Sullivan and Awe 2009). More recently, several sites in Belize, Guatemala, and Mexico have revealed Pre-Mamom ceramic phases, demonstrating that this early occupation is no longer an anomaly restricted to a few sites (Andrews and Bey 2011; Andrews *et al.* 2008; Cheetham 2005; Clark and Cheetham 2002). A recent article proposes that Pre-Mamom Maya pottery forms a widespread and homogeneous complex that, because of the similarity in decorated serving vessels, should be called a horizon style. David Cheetham (2005) calls this the Cunil horizon after the complex and phase named at Cahal Pech. Others prefer to see three distinct ceramic spheres in the central Maya lowlands – Swasey-Bladen (northern Belize), Eb/Cunil/Kanocha (western Belize and eastern Peten), and Xe/Real Xe (southwestern Peten; see Ball and Taschek 2003). Despite disagreements concerning how much lumping or splitting should be applied to this earliest pottery, ceramicists generally concur that at no later time are the ceramics of the Maya lowlands so similar.

Scholars considering the earliest lowland Maya ceramics were once limited to the scant data from Altar de Sacrificios, Seibal, Cuello, and – more recently – Cahal Pech. My study re-examines these earliest ceramic complexes in light of abundantly available new data. Some scholars posited that the Maya lowlands had not been populated by sedentary agriculturalists before Pre-Mamom times, and that these ceramics represented migrations from the adjacent areas of Chiapas (Andrews 1990; Clark and Pye 2000). Now that both ceramics and settlements are known across the Peten, in western and northern Belize, and – somewhat later – in northwest Yucatan, such a hypothesis is becoming increasingly untenable. Pointing to the lack of stratified deposits pre-dating Mamom at many sites, some have claimed that Pre-Mamom ceramics form a sub-complex of early Mamom (Ball and Taschek 2003). But now that new excavations at Tikal and Cahal Pech have identified numerous stratified primary deposits of Pre-Mamom pottery, this perspective also seems untenable. The relationship between Pre-Mamom and Mamom has also been questioned, some suggesting that Mamom replaced Pre-Mamom rather than developing from it (Adams 1971; Andrews 1990). Still others consider Pre-Mamom pottery to be ancestral to later Middle Preclassic pottery (Culbert n.d.; Sabloff 1975; Willey et al. 1967). The ethnicity of early villagers in the Maya lowlands also has been subject to debate, with some scholars claiming that they were Mije-Sokean speakers and others claiming an indigenous Maya identity (Ball and Taschek 2003; Garber et al. 2001; cf. Awe 1992; Cheetham 2005; Iceland 2005). Those who see Pre-Mamom peoples as having a non-Maya identity assume that the motifs found on decorated serving vessels arrived with colonizers who had ties to the Olmec region. In contrast, scholars who favor a Maya identity argue that foreign symbols were adopted by a pre-existing Maya population. The conflation of style, language, and ethnicity – a concept that may not even exist in pre-state societies – adds to this confusion.

My study uses a framework of community identity to interpret regional and local stylistic patterns in ceramics. By looking at the concept of community, I hope to move beyond some limitations of the site-specific ceramic studies of the past and undertake an examination of the majority of sites bearing evidence for this period (Yaeger and Canuto 2000). This approach also allows me to consider stylistic variation as a reflection of community without assuming that group identity is determined principally by language or ethnicity (Bartlett and McAnany 2000). I consider the natural community as the group of potters who interacted on a frequent basis in daily life and the imagined community as an identity actively chosen by villagers who participate in a broader ideological system (Isbell 2000). The imagined community is a more frequently changing category and one that individuals may choose to present at specific moments in their lives. The natural community, in contrast, is manifested in isochrestic style, a style of learning or practicing a craft activity that is interpreted as reflecting local potting groups (Sackett 1977, 1982, 1990). Isochrestic style is seen in the specific vessel forms and in form and slip color combinations at a given site or sub-site area. In contrast, iconological style refers to the symbolic content of an artifact or artwork, reflecting deliberate choices by potters to imbue their products with a particular meaning. This category is more likely to indicate imagined communities because it is an iconographic or ideological program actively chosen by potters and the consumers of the vessels, and because such iconographic content often links communities that may not have routine contact with one another.

Holmul, Guatemala

The ancient Maya site of Holmul was first excavated by Raymond Merwin between 1909 and 1911. Merwin's excavations unearthed a number of stratified burials with complete ceramic vessels that allowed the creation of the first ceramic sequence for a Maya site. Sadly, Merwin's untimely death left his important scholarship unpublished until it was taken up by George Vaillant (Merwin and Vaillant 1932). Modern excavations began in 2000 with the Holmul Archaeological Project, involving an international team of scientists under the direction of Francisco Estrada-Belli. This project looks at Holmul through a regional perspective, including mapping, land-use analysis, environmental change, human impact on the environment, and archaeological excavation within and around the six major sites in the area, starting from the initial moment of human occupation around 1300 BC (Wahl et al. 2013). The earliest pottery is found at several sites in the region and dates to around 1000 BC. During the Middle and Late Preclassic, a single major center at Cival dominated the region, and E-groups (architectural complexes commemorating the solstices and equinoxes) were constructed at many smaller sites (Estrada-Belli 2006). With the collapse of the Preclassic center at Cival around AD 250, several other sites in the area, Holmul among them, increased in population and political importance. During the Early Classic, an area of Holmul known as La Sufricaya was the setting for a new palace and ceremonial area; there are inscriptions that suggest political interaction with the central Mexican site of Teotihuacan regulated through the nearby Maya city of Tikal (Estrada-Belli et al. 2009). Several sites in the region are major ceremonial centers with palaces, ballcourts, and temple-plaza complexes that date to the Late Classic period (Tomasic 2009). The area was largely abandoned after the Terminal Classic period.

The excavations for this project have focused on Group II within the site center of Holmul (Figure 7.1). Here Merwin encountered a largely intact Early Classic temple containing a series of 23 human burials. Interpretations of Building B have concerned its role as a mortuary temple or necropolis possibly dedicated to a lincage (McAnany 1998; Taube 1998, 2004). The first burials date to the Late Preclassic period, and bodies were interred in cysts cut into the fill of an earlier phase of the temple. Later interments were in tombs within the fill, and in the interior rooms as they were successively filled during the Terminal Preclassic and Early Classic periods (Callaghan 2008).

Current research has defined a number of earlier construction phases in this building and those alongside it. The Holmul Archaeological Project found a huge deposit of Pre-Mamom ceramics in the earliest phase of Building B. These ceramics were so

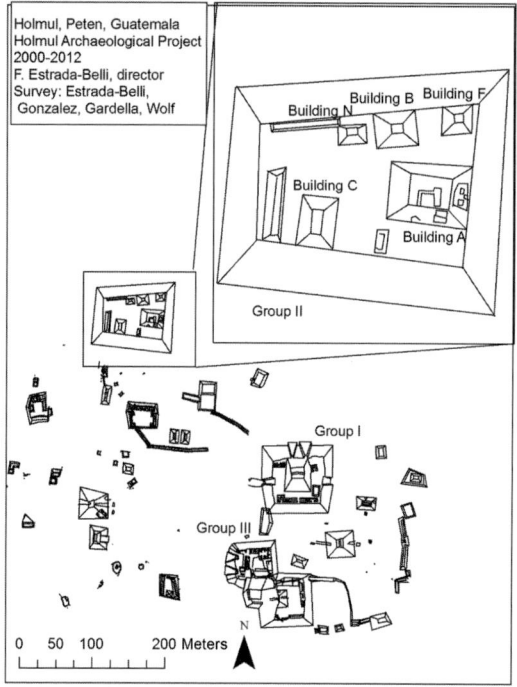

FIGURE 7.1 Map of Holmul site center (courtesy Francisco Estrada-Belli)

consistently representative of the Pre-Mamom style that we initially believed it to be a pure deposit dating to that time. Nonetheless, radiocarbon samples from charcoal imbedded in the stucco mask on the Phase 1 façade of the building date to around 400 BC, the transition from the Middle to the Late Preclassic period (Wahl et al. 2013). The platform must have been raised at about this time. The Pre-Mamom pottery we excavated, therefore, comes from a redeposited context. Further excavations focused on areas where we hoped to encounter sealed deposits from the Pre-Mamom period.

In 2007 I placed a trench in the flat open plaza next to Building B, where I expected to find a series of superimposed plaza floors. To our great surprise this area was not a vacant open plaza but had been the location of a large ceremonial structure (Building N) in the Late Preclassic period that was later completely covered and removed from view (Neivens in Estrada-Belli 2008). Building N also yielded a large sample of Pre-Mamom ceramics in the fill of each of its five construction phases, all of which date to the transition to the Late Preclassic period (c. 400–350 BC). Many of these construction fill contexts contain large quantities of Pre-Mamom ceramics, with little or no Mamom material, and a few sherds dating to the Late Preclassic period. In 2009 further investigations into Buildings B, N, and F on the north side of the Group II platform revealed the full construction sequence, which begins early in the Late Preclassic and continues until the beginning of the Early Classic period. It appears that some area nearby contained a large quantity of Pre-Mamom archaeological pottery, and that this material was collected as construction fill and deposited in Group II at the onset of the Late Preclassic period. To date, all of our Holmul Pre-Mamom ceramics come from these large Late Preclassic platforms.

Excavations at Cival, located within the regional study area of the Holmul Archaeological Project, have also encountered Pre-Mamom ceramics. At Cival these ceramics are found primarily in the ceremonial core of the ancient city, with a few discovered in the surrounding residential mounds.

Despite their later secondary contexts, the ceramic collections discussed in this chapter are believed to date to Pre-Mamom times. This is because they share vessel forms and attributes of surface decoration with established Pre-Mamom collections from other lowland Maya sites. The closest ties so far have been found with Pre-Mamom ceramics at Cahal Pech, Tikal, and Seibal, where some types are identical to those we have established at Holmul. The slip colors, pastes, and incised decoration of the early Holmul pottery differ dramatically from those of the following Mamom and Chicanel complexes, indicating clearly that this collection constitutes a coherent complex, easily distinguishable from the following Middle and Late Preclassic complexes at Holmul and elsewhere.

K'awil complex pottery from Holmul

The Holmul Pre-Mamom K'awil complex shows the closest similarities to the Cunil complex at Cahal Pech (Sullivan *et al.* 2009), Early Eb at Tikal (Culbert n.d., Cheetham n.d.), Xe from Altar de Sacrificios (Adams 1971), and Real Xe from Seibal (Sabloff 1975). The K'awil complex contains the full range of slip colors and vessel forms encountered in other Pre-Mamom complexes, and each monochrome also occurs as an incised type. The incised types usually display fine lines cut through the slip before firing. In some cases I have used the type names established at Cahal Pech and Tikal because the Holmul examples are indistinguishable from them. Other types are newly defined in the Holmul collection because they show significant differences to previously described types. The Holmul sample contains three wares: K'an Slipped Ware, Rio Holmul Slipped Ware, and Calam Burnished Ware. K'an Slipped Ware (comprising the types Katun Red, Sak White, Lak'in Red-on-White, Eknab Black, Mo Mottled, Baatz Tan, and Ochkin Orange) is the most common and is distinguished by its paste, which is yellow to pinkish yellow, with large quantities of ash and few inclusions of biotite mica, ferruginous particles, and sparitic calcite, and has a medium- to fine-grain texture. Rio Holmul Ware (containing the types Jobal Red, Xaman Red-on-White, Xpokol Incised, and Chicin'a Black) is also distinguished by its paste and is found in small quantities at both Holmul and Tikal. The paste of Rio Holmul Ware is coarse but very compact and black in color (dark brown to dark grey) and contains calcite but no ash, and vessels are often thin-walled. Calam Burnished Ware has a similar paste to K'an Slipped Ware but is not slipped. Instead the unslipped surface is burnished to create a highly polished surface (Calam Buff), sometimes with the addition of red slip in bands (Aac Red-on-Buff). Utilitarian wares are not described in this chapter, in part because of the mixed nature of the Holmul deposits and in part because unslipped wares often exhibit less visible change over time. For now, I restrict my analysis to the formal wares that can be securely identified.

Katun Red and Jobal Red Groups

Katun Red has a monochrome dull orange-red surface with well-adhered slip (Figure 7.2). This is the most common type in the collection (133 rims) and occurs in various forms: vases with direct rims, dishes with out-curving sides and exterior thickened and pointed rims, dishes with everted rims, bowls with incurving sides, jars with vertical necks, and *tecomates* with direct rounded rims. Many examples in this group have particles of mica visible to the naked eye, while in other cases this mica can be seen only with a microscope. Mica is also found in small quantities in the paste. Culbert (n.d.) defined a Pre-Mamom Joventud Red in the Early Eb phase of Tikal. This has a red-orange slip, similar to that of Katun Red at Holmul. The Uck Red of the Cunil phase at Cahal Pech is also similar to Katun Red in slip color. It has the same red-orange slip as Joventud Red in the Mamom phase but can be readily identified by its ash paste and stratigraphic position (Lauren Sullivan, personal communication 2009).

Jobal Red has a monochrome dull purple-red surface with micaceous particles in the slip (Figure 7.3). This slip occurs on a variety of vessel forms (56 rims), including bowls with slightly incurving sides and direct rims, jars with out-curving necks, dishes with out-curving sides and direct rims or exterior folded and pointed rims, *tecomates* with interior thickened rims, and vases with flared sides. The distinct red-purple color with sparkling micaceous particles of Jobal Red is so different from contemporaneous monochrome reds of nearby lowland Maya sites that it stands out clearly in the Holmul collection. Sometimes Jobal Red occurs with particles of specular hematite in the slip, and this yields a darker red-purple hue. I also identified this type in small quantities in the Tikal collection.

Jobal Red is similar to Abelino Red and Huetche White at Seibal, which also have visible mica or hematite in their slip. Katun Red, with its orange-red color, shows closer ties to the Uck Red group (Baki Red) from Cahal Pech. Lowland Maya Pre-Mamom reds from all sites other than Holmul tend to be an orange-red that is similar to the Joventud Red of the Mamom sphere. I was surprised to find that, of all the ceramic samples I have looked at, the slip color in Jobal Red resembles most closely reds from the Alta Verapaz and Pacific coast of Guatemala, both of which have a purple-hued red slip with hematite or mica particles.

Katun Red: Incised variety (57 rims) and Jobal Red: Incised variety (17 rims) are identical to the monochrome Katun Red and Jobal Red in slip color and form and have incised decoration. This decoration includes complex motifs such as cleft heads (nine examples), double merlons (two), music brackets (ten), and shark's tooth (six). Decoration also occurs in various geometric forms, such as a U shape

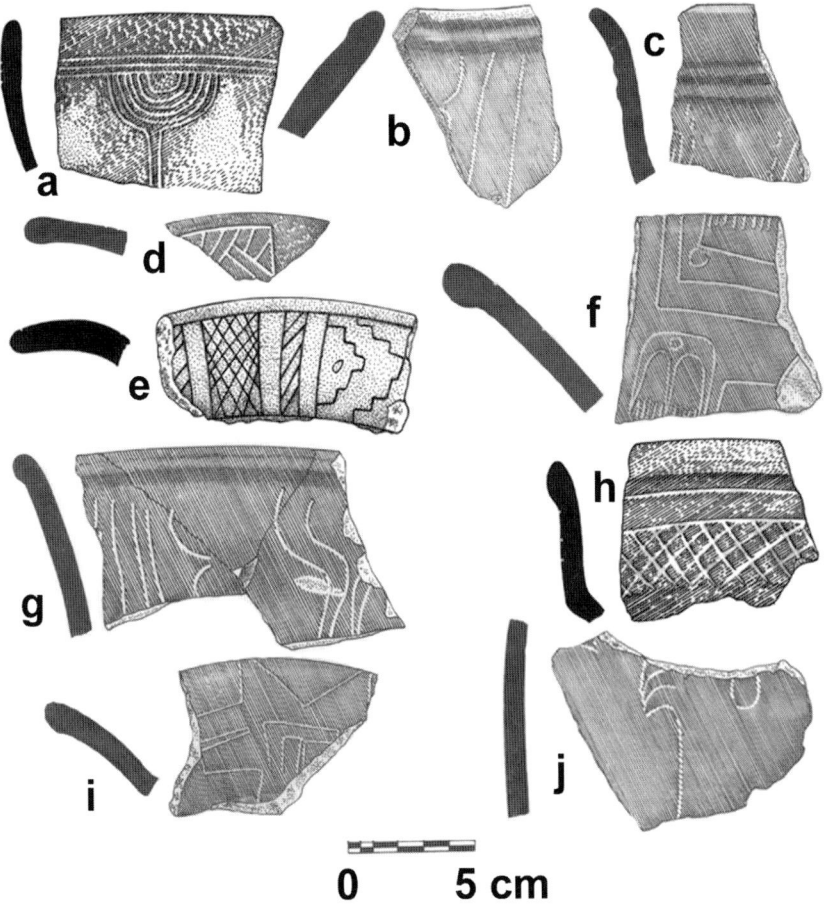

FIGURE 7.2 Katun Red Group: (a–j) Katun Red: Incised variety

(seven examples), an L shape (six), a triangle (four), circles (ten), semi-circles (six), a tassel shape (three), and a stepped fret (one). The most common incised designs are simple encircling lines (17 examples), double encircling lines (18), triple encircling lines (five), and vertical lines (four; note that these are often components of the music bracket motif). The incised designs on Katun Red: Incised variety tend to be present on the interior upper rim of wide everted-rim dishes, while on Jobal Red: Incised variety they tend to be found on the exterior of bowls with slightly out-curving sides. Incised decorations on both types also occur on the exterior rim of *tecomates* and bowls and on the interior bases of plates and bowls. *Tecomates* tend to be incised with the music bracket motif.

The incised reds from Holmul show broad similarities to ceramics from nearby sites. At Cahal Pech the incised version of the monochrome Uck Red is Baki Incised (Sullivan *et al.* 2009), which is very similar to Katun Red: Incised variety.

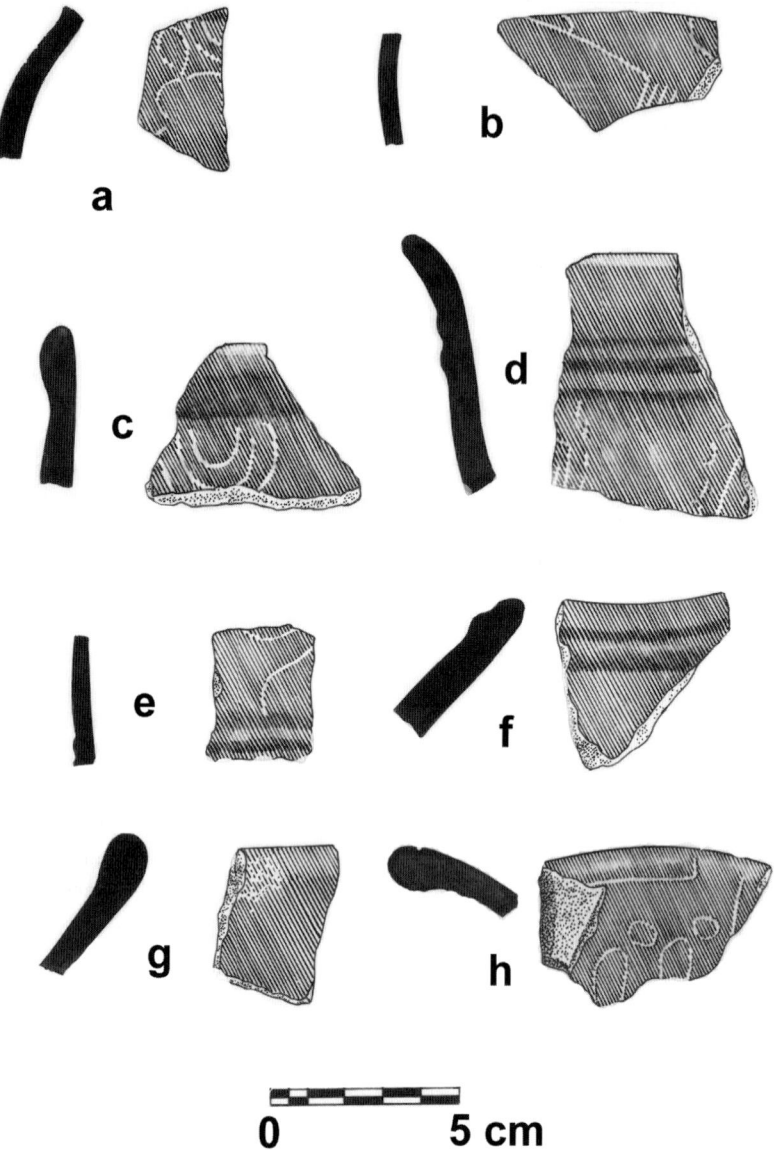

FIGURE 7.3 Jobal Red Group: (a–f) Jobal Red: Incised variety; (g) Jobal Red: Jobal variety; (h) Jobal Red: Incised variety

At Seibal it is Pico de Oro Incised (Sabloff 1975). In northwest Yucatan, it is Kin Orange-Red Incised at Komchen and currently known as Unnamed Type A at Kiuic (Andrews et al. 2008). These types all display similarities in the technology of decoration – fine-line incision usually applied after the slip but prior to firing. At Seibal there are more examples of broad-line pre-slip incising, sometimes in conjunction with fine-line post-slip incision. These broad lines often create a bordered panel along the wide-everted rim that defines the space used for the fine-line incision. The use of broad-line incision is characteristic of the following Mamom sphere and probably became more common towards the transition from the various Pre-Mamom phases to Mamom proper. This technique is seen in the Holmul K'awil collection on only a few sherds. Collections from all these sites also share similarities in the designs themselves, often displaying geometric forms with repeating sets of lines or cross-hatching, as well as the repetition of specific pan-Mesoamerican motifs such as cleft-heads, double-merlons, shark's tooth, U shape, and music brackets.

Monochrome reds with incised designs are common throughout Mesoamerica in the early Middle Preclassic period. The red at Holmul is similar to San Jose Specular Red from Oaxaca (Flannery et al. 1994), the Sachaj Group from the Salama Valley (Sharer and Sedat 1987), and Anona Specular Red from the Alta Verapaz, because all use specular hematite or mica in their slips. The most similar slip color is found at various sites on the Pacific coast of Guatemala, each with its own site-specific type name (Victoria Red, Melendrez Red, Huiscoyol Incised). These reds are similar to Jobal Red in that they have a purple hue and include particles of hematite or mica embedded in the slip. In the case of the Pacific coast collections, these micaceous particles also occur in the paste itself. This similarity in slip appearance is surprising given the distance between the two areas. I do not mean to imply a specific relationship between Holmul and any particular community on the Pacific coast, merely that the two areas used similar mineralogical products to create these slips. The minerals are found naturally in various parts of Mesoamerica and were valued for their distinct color and shininess. For whatever reason, this slip quality was preferred by, or more available to, the Holmul potters at a time when other potting communities in the Maya lowlands preferred an orange-red slip (Uck Red at Cahal Pech, Joventud Red or Chak Red at Tikal, Abelino Red at Seibal, Consejo Red at Cuello, and Kin Orange-Red at Komchen).

Sak White Group

Sak White is common at Holmul (119 rims) and occurs consistently as small plates or dishes with out-flaring sides and direct or exterior thickened rims, but also in other forms (Figure 7.4). Among these other forms are dishes with everted rims, vases with flared sides and exterior folded or direct rims, bowls with slightly incurving sides, *tecomates* with direct rounded rims, and jars with out-curving necks. Sak White is nearly identical to Cocoyal White defined at Cahal Pech, which is characterized by a creamy white to light gray slip and a high percentage of ash in the paste (Sullivan et al. 2009). While it is similar to Huetche White at Seibal in terms of slip appearance, it does not include micaceous particles and has a distinctive paste. Huetche White from Altar de Sacrificios tends to be more of a cream color than at Seibal and is therefore distinct from Sak White at Holmul. At Tikal,

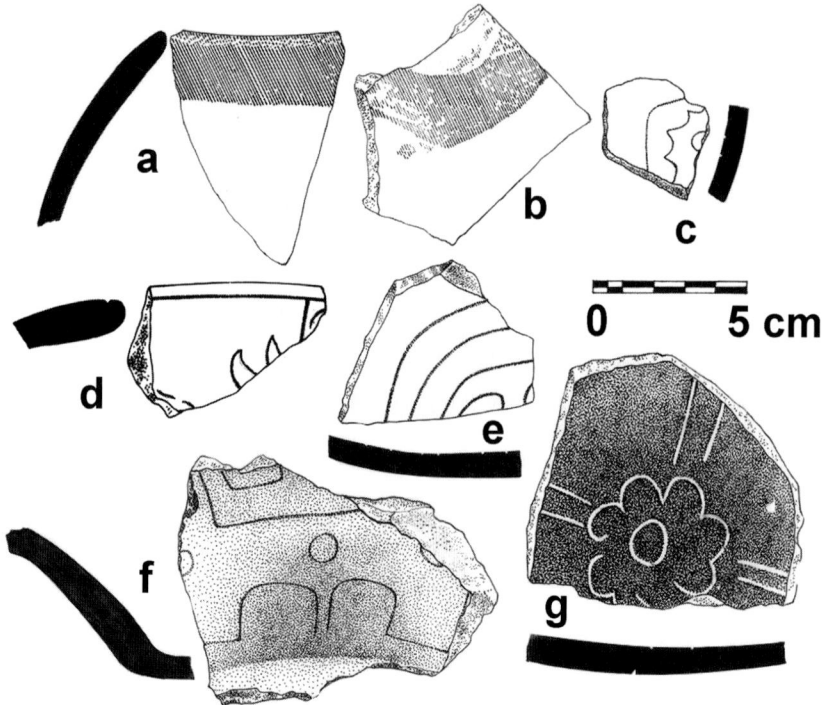

FIGURE 7.4 Sak White Group: (a–b) Lak'in Red-on-White: Lak'in variety; (c–g) Sak White: Incised variety

Bil White is nearly identical to Sak White from Holmul and Cocoyal White from Cahal Pech (personal observations 2009 and 2011).

Sak White: Incised variety is present at Holmul (22 rims) and Tikal (personal observations, 2011), although it has not yet been found at Cahal Pech (Sullivan et al. 2009). This type tends to occur on wide-everted rim plates with a white-slipped interior and is found with a variety of complex iconographic motifs. Complex motifs include cleft heads (two examples), shark's tooth (four), double merlons (one), and various geometric forms (eight). The majority of the sample exhibits simple encircling lines (six examples) or double lines (four), sometimes in combination with other motifs. Some examples have a pre-slip double broad-line incision around the rim of the everted rim plate, sometimes in conjunction with post-slip fine-line incision. This combination of pre-slip and post-slip incision is more common on white slip than other colors in the Pre-Mamom sample. This is nearly identical to Comistun Incised from Seibal and somewhat similar to Almeja Burnished Gray Incised from Komchen (Andrews et al. 2008), but Sak White: Incised variety sometimes has a darker gray surface.

Incised white types are not common at lowland Maya sites in the early Middle Preclassic and have not been recorded at Cahal Pech, Cuello, or Kiuic. Nonetheless, incised white pottery is common in other parts of early Mesoamerica – for example,

Amatzinac White at Chalcatzingo (Grove 1987) and Atoyac Yellow-White in Oaxaca (Flannery *et al.* 1994). It occurs in the Palenque area during the Chiuaan phase in a monochrome and an incised variety (Rands 1987), as well as in the Turbala group from the Salama Valley (Sharer and Sedat 1987). On the Pacific coast of Guatemala, white-slipped ceramics include Melendrez White and Ramirez Fine-White. White-slipped pottery is also known from early Middle Preclassic pottery in the Valley of Guatemala, and Xuc Ware (Sacatepequez White Paste White Ware) is ubiquitous in that area and in the eastern Kaqchikel region during the later Middle Preclassic period (see Chapter 5).

Another new type, Lak'in Red-on-White (30 rims), is characterized by the same red slip as Katun Red over the white slip of Sak White. Often the interiors of vessels are red and the exteriors white, with a band of red on the exterior rim. Also present are red slips in straight vertical lines or circles over white slip, which may occur in conjunction with a red rim. Among Lak'in Red-on-White forms are bowls with slightly incurving sides, dishes with outcurving or round sides, and plates with flared sides. A somewhat similar type found at Cahal Pech – Red-on-Buff: Variety Unspecified (A) – is rare (Sullivan *et al.* 2009) and may be more similar to Aac Red-on-Buff from Holmul. It is also similar to Tower Hill Red-on-Cream from the Bladen phase at Cuello (Kosakowsky 1987b) and Toribio Red-on-Cream from Altar de Sacrificios (Adams 1971). Sabloff (1975) classified eight sherds from Seibal as Unnamed Red-and-White Dichrome, two of which include incising; these may be similar to sherds from Holmul. Lak'in Red-on-White also occurs in an incised variety, but only a few examples have been identified so far (three rims). This type seems to have some of the same complex motifs as other Pre-Mamom incised types at Holmul, but more often has simple line incisions.

The Rio Holmul Slipped Ware includes Xaman Red-on-White (five rims), which occurs in very small quantities but with a distinct paste and slip color. The primary color of the slip is white, with the addition of a Jobal red slip on the interior or as vertical lines on the exterior. In some cases this red slip has clearly visible particles of hematite. It usually occurs on vases with vertical sides but also is found on bowls with incurving sides and on dishes with out-curving sides.

A red-on-white type is not found at Tikal or most other lowland Maya sites occupied in the Pre-Mamom period, although it is common in other parts of Mesoamerica at this time. In Pacific Coastal Guatemala, the type is named Melendrez Red-on-White (or Huiscoyol Red-on-White from Chiquiuitan, and Red-on-Cream from Tecojate, Esquintla). During the later Middle Preclassic, red-on-white varieties of Xuc Ware are common at Kaminaljuyu and in the eastern Kaqchikel region (see Chapter 5). In the Salama Valley of Guatemala, Sharer and Sedat (1987) named a similar type Xola Red-on-White. Further afield, in highland Mexico, Chalcatzingo has Manantial Orange-on-White (Grove 1987), and the Valley of Oaxaca has San Jose Red-on-White (Flannery *et al.* 1994). These types often consist of a monochrome white with the addition of bands of red paint around the exterior rims of plates and in vertical lines.

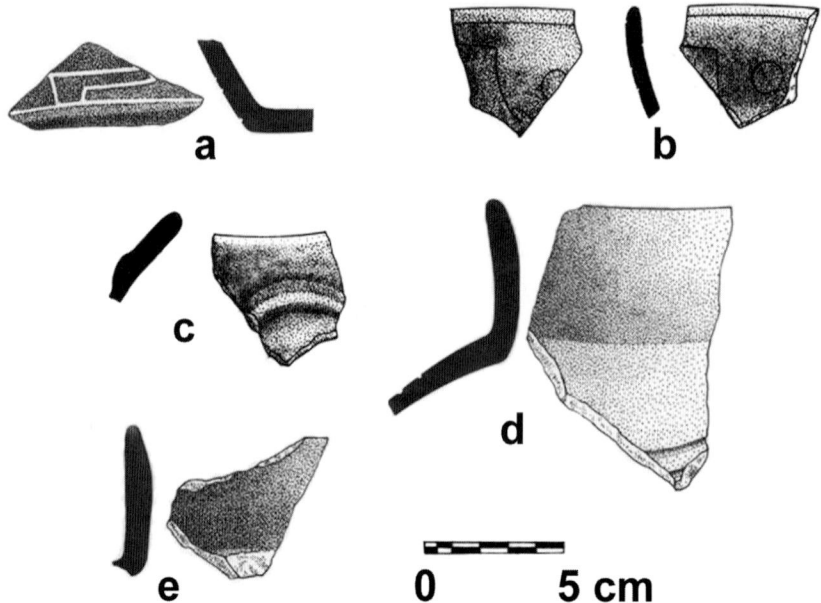

FIGURE 7.5 Eknab Black Group: (a–b) Eknab Black: Incised variety; (c) Eknab Black with appliqué; (d) Eknab Black: Incised variety; (e) Eknab Black: Eknab variety jar

Eknab Black Group

The K'awil complex at Holmul contains Eknab Black (42 rims), which is very similar to Crisanto Black, first defined at Altar de Sacrificios (Adams 1971) and later identified at Seibal (Sabloff 1975). It has a lusterless, gray-black slip, a dull surface, and an ashy gray-colored paste (Figure 7.5). Later black types tend towards a darker black or brown-black slip with a shiny surface. Eknab Black from Holmul occurs in several forms, including dishes with wide everted rims, and hemispherical bowls, but most commonly as jars with short straight-sided necks, the upper rim of which often bears an orange band. This type sometimes has a larger mottled area of orange around the rim that closely resembles examples of Ainil Orange from Tikal (Bernard Hermes, personal communication 2011).

Eknab Black: Incised variety (five rims) bears close resemblance to Chompipe Incised, defined at Altar de Sacrificios (Adams 1971), which is identical in slip, paste, and forms. Incised designs tend to occur in geometric patterns, with combinations of horizontal lines and circles. Only a few examples of this type occur in the K'awil phase, all with fine-line post-slip incision. In contrast, the Xe-phase Chompipe Incised includes examples of broad-line pre-slip incision. Black is not a common slip color at any site in the Maya lowlands during the early Middle Preclassic, occurring only in small quantities at Altar de Sacrificios, Seibal, and Holmul. It is found in greater quantities in other parts of Mesoamerica.

Ceramic adoption in the Maya lowlands **191**

Mottled (Uck) Group

Mo Mottled is a type defined by Sullivan at Cahal Pech and characterized by a variegated slip ranging from white to olive green, red, and brown (Figure 7.6; Sullivan *et al.* 2009). The paste is identical to others in K'an Slipped Ware, sometimes including a greater amount of ash giving it a gray color. Mo Mottled: Peten variety (44 rims) occurs in a variety of forms, including dishes with out-curving sides and direct or exterior thickened rims, wide-everted rim dishes, small round-sided bowls, and mushroom stands. The most common form is an open bowl with a slightly out-flaring rim and three or four flutes on the exterior, which has been

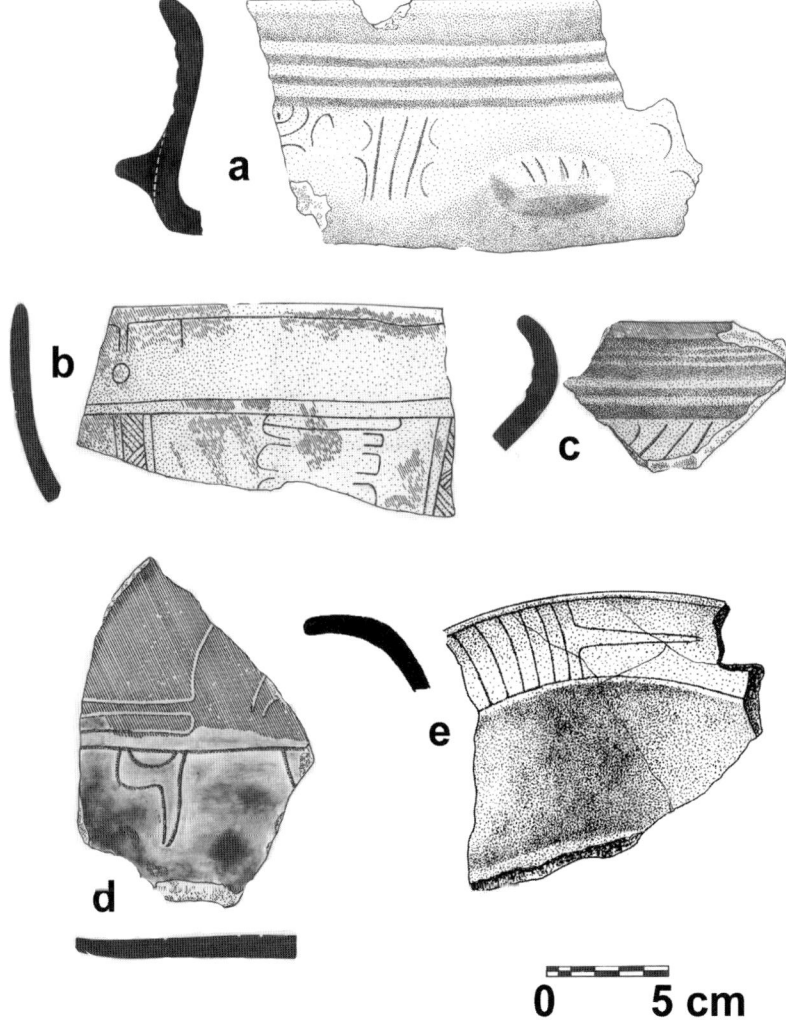

FIGURE 7.6 Mo Mottled Group: (a–e) Kitam Incised: Kitam variety

named Mo Mottled: Holmul Fluted variety (13 rims). This type is abundant at Holmul and Cahal Pech, but rare at Tikal and absent at other lowland Maya sites with Pre-Mamom occupation. A similar mottled slip is not found at any other contemporaneous site in Mesoamerica, nor does it appear as a specific type in the later Mamom sphere.

Kitam Incised: Kitam variety (61 rims) was first defined at Cahal Pech and is characterized by the same slip as Mo Mottled, with incised decoration (Sullivan *et al.* 2009). This slip color was preferred for incised design, as evidenced in the Holmul sample, which contains more examples of the incised variety than the monochrome (44). It bears the same designs and has forms similar to those of Katun Red: Incised variety. Pan-Mesoamerican motifs include the cleft head (nine examples), harpy eagle crest (two), U shape (four), and shark's tooth (one). The sample also numbers several unique motifs, among them a rounded flower with k'an cross around it. Kitam Incised: Kitam variety at Holmul also tends to combine various iconographic motifs in complex patterns. Incised decoration tends to occur on wide-everted rim plates with incised decoration on the rim encircling the interior of the vessel. Other forms are dishes with out-curving sides and exterior-thickened rims, bowls with slightly incurving sides, and vases with flared sides. A large percentage of the incised decoration at Cahal Pech occurs on this type, and at Holmul it is also the dominant incised type.

Calam Buff Group

The Holmul K'awil complex takes in Calam Buff (45 rims), which was first identified at Tikal and is characterized by its paste and burnished unslipped surface (Culbert n.d.). The paste is yellow to buff, with medium texture and calcite inclusions, similar to that of types in K'an Slipped Ware. The surface is the same color as the paste, and the smoothing surface treatment creates a rich buff to orange appearance (Figure 7.7). At Tikal the form is consistently a flaring-sided dish or vase with bolstered rim (Culbert n.d.). At Holmul this form is present, but Calam Buff dishes are much smaller than those from Tikal and are also found in equal frequencies in a variety of other forms, including plates with round sides, small rounded bowls, dishes with flared sides, incurving bowls, and jars with out-curving necks. At Holmul, the incised type is additionally present as Aute Incised: Aute variety (25 rims), which occurs on similar vessel forms and with incised designs similar to those of other incised K'awil types.

Aac Red-on-Buff was also defined at Tikal and is identical in paste to Calam Buff, with an unslipped exterior and red-slipped interior (Culbert n.d.). At Holmul, Aac Red-on-Buff (five rims) includes a red slip with micaceous inclusions similar to Katun Red slip, which is different from that at Tikal and several body sherds that are incised. These incisions usually demarcate lines of red slip. Red-on-buff is uncommon throughout Mesoamerica at this time. Nonetheless, a similar type, Cuca Red-on-Buff, occurs on the Pacific coast of Guatemala and displays similar vessel forms and decoration.

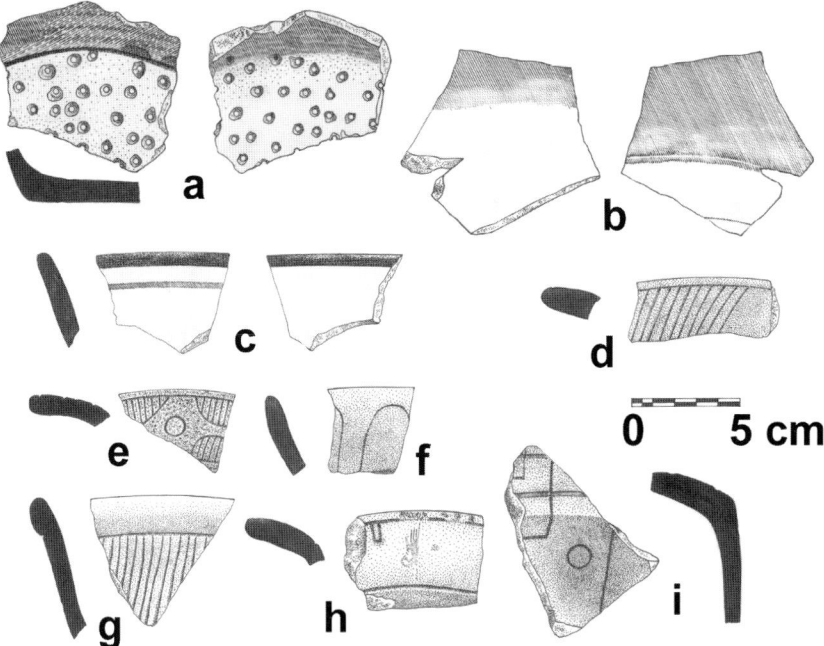

FIGURE 7.7 Calam Burnished Ware: (a) Aak Red-on-Buff colander; (b–c) Aak Red-on Buff with incision; (d–i) Calam Buff: Incised variety

Holmul in the early Middle Preclassic

We can see a number of patterns in the Pre-Mamom ceramics of Holmul. The monochrome red types are unique to the site, although Katun Red is very similar to the dull Abelino Red of Seibal and Altar de Sacrificios. Other types found at Holmul are identical to those found at nearby sites. These include Mo Mottled and Kitam Incised (which are identical at Holmul and at Cahal Pech) and Calam Buff and Aac Red-on-Buff (which are identical at Holmul and Tikal). Sak White is found only at Holmul but is very similar to Bil White from Tikal and Cocoyal White from Cahal Pech. A new type and group were created because the incised variety is so far unique to Holmul. A similar though not identical white – Huetche White – is found at Seibal. Decorated ceramics from all sites dating to this period tend to have post-slip, pre-fire incised designs. These designs occur on every slip color found at Holmul. The designs may be found on any vessel form or on any part of the vessel, but they are most frequently on the wide everted rims of plates and on the exterior rim and body of *tecomates*. The northern Yucatan sites of Komchen and Kiuic lack plates with wide everted rims, which sets them apart from the complexes of southern lowland Maya sites. In the north, incised decoration tends to occur on the exterior of vertical walled plates and dishes, a pattern present in but not dominating the Holmul collection.

The similarities between the Holmul collection and those from well-documented stratified and radiocarbon dated contexts at Tikal, Cahal Pech, and Seibal indicate the K'awil Pre-Mamom phase dates to the early Middle Preclassic, or about 1000 to 850 BC. The incised designs and forms found in the Maya lowlands at this time connect these communities with an iconographic system found throughout Mesoamerica. These Pre-Mamom ceramics show similarity to complexes from as far north as the Basin of Mexico and as far south as Honduras (Joyce and Henderson 2001).

It is now abundantly clear that the Maya lowlands were occupied by pottery-producing people in the early Middle Preclassic period, and that their connections to other communities across the landscape brought them into an ideological and iconographic system that united Mesoamerica before the end of the Early Formative/Preclassic period. Despite this, we cannot explain this phenomenon as representing immigration to a previously unoccupied wilderness. Instead, recent evidence suggests that pre-ceramic populations had occupied this area continuously from at least 2500 BC (Iceland 2005; Lohse et al. 2006; Wahl et al. 2006, 2013; see bu.edu/holmul/reports/). Their impact on the environment is seen in sediment cores from northern Belize and the central and northern Peten. It seems likely that the people impacting the environment at about 2500 BC were the ancestors of those living there at about 1000 BC.

The Holmul region was occupied continuously beginning no later than 1300 BC (Wahl et al. 2013). These people chose to adopt ceramic technology slightly later than other Mesoamerican communities, around 1100 to 1000 BC. The lack of contemporaneous architecture may indicate that these communities were not fully sedentary or that they lived in perishable structures, or it may still be a result of the small sample of known sites. The movement of people across the landscape likely brought them into contact with each other and with villagers residing in areas adjacent to the Maya lowlands, and this contact may have instigated the initial adoption of ceramic technology. The strongest ceramic similarities are found with collections from nearby lowland Maya communities, indicating that the highest degree of interaction was among neighboring sites. Secondary similarities are seen in broad patterns of incised design, slip color preference, and vessel form to those of communities in other parts of Mesoamerica. I interpret the Pre-Mamom ceramics of Holmul as indicating close connections between that site and Cahal Pech and Tikal, and that inter-community ties among the lowland Maya tied them into an interregional network of iconography and ideology that is fundamentally pan-Mesoamerican.

The Pre-Mamom K'awil complex from Holmul (c. 1000–850 BC) provides insight into the nature of ceramic adoption in the Maya lowlands. First, there is a growing body of evidence that this area was populated for at least several hundred years before the adoption of ceramics (see Chapter 5 for a parallel case), and it seems likely that the local pre-ceramic population took over ceramic technology invented elsewhere. Their interaction with people or objects from other areas of Mesoamerica is clear in the iconological style of pottery – that is, the elaborate incised designs shared with ceramics from other areas of Mesoamerica: Oaxaca, the Basin of Mexico, the Gulf Coast, Pacific and highland Guatemala, and the Maya lowlands.

The K'awil complex includes two monochrome reds, a variegated red, monochrome white, red-on-white, monochrome black, burnished buff, and red-on-buff, as well as incised versions of all these types. Similar types are found at other sites in Mesoamerica at this time, but no other contemporary lowland Maya site is currently known that had all of them. Similarities in color, incised decoration, and forms are seen across the region. Nonetheless, the closest similarities are found between Holmul and its nearest neighbors, Tikal and Cahal Pech. I interpret these similarities as isochrestic style, indicating shared similarities in the way of making this pottery. These communities of potters may have had direct contact. Alternatively, similarities may be the result of greater contact among the consumers of pottery who created a preference for certain styles.

The K'awil collection shows variation in color, form, and decoration that is greater than that seen in later complexes at Holmul. This greater variation suggests that potters were experimenting with their newly adopted craft and later simplified their production to a smaller group of preferred colors and decorations. The pottery therefore appears to be more complex at first and simpler as time passed, a phenomenon also noted after the adoption of ceramics on the Pacific coast (Blake and Clark 1999; Clark 1991). The communities around Holmul may have adopted ceramic technology in part as a way to present iconological style in a permanent medium. This iconological style was important specifically because it expressed ideology shared with various communities across Mesoamerica.

Concluding reflections on comparative analysis

This project has led me to see and handle thousands of pottery sherds from the early Middle Preclassic period. The experience has trained my eye to the similarities and differences in these collections. Paradoxically, I have tended towards "splitting" or "lumping" in different circumstances. Above all, I absolutely agree with Will Andrews that this exercise is extremely beneficial for the archaeologist. In Guatemala, the ceramic laboratory at the Instituto de Arqueología e Historia (IDAEH) provides an indispensable opportunity to view ceramics from nearly every excavated archaeological site in the country. It was especially useful to be able to hold sherds from two different sites and compare them side by side. It is essential that archaeological projects continue to provide a representative sample of ceramics and that these collections be maintained in the storage facility in a way that facilitates comparison. The utility of the IDAEH laboratory would be improved through standardization of the written identification accompanying the collections, especially by organizing them according to horizon styles or recognized ceramic spheres.

A major problem I encountered in this study was that, for many regions, each site had its own names for the ceramic types, even though these were often similar across sites. An abundance of type names can hinder efforts at interregional comparison. Some of the published ceramics were not available for study in the type collections, while some of those I was able to see had not been published. For these reasons, it was sometimes difficult to get a clear impression of the types and their distinguishing characteristics. I learned that some types with distinct names were essentially identical in appearance, differing only as to the site from which they were reported. In my effort to alleviate this problem for the Holmul collection, I have used type names established at other sites whenever possible and have created new groups only when the ceramics are truly unique to the Holmul region.

The issue of the abundance of names is but one problem with the type-variety system of ceramic analysis (Gifford 1960). This system also stipulates that a monochrome is one type while the same monochrome with incision is another type. Most vessels are not entirely covered with incised decoration, so sherds from the same pot may be classified into two different types. From the perspective of the potter, an incised version of a pot is probably little more than a decorated variety of the monochrome, not a totally different type. For the ceramic analyst undertaking cross-regional comparison, this confusion means he or she must learn two type names for every vessel color, plus two type names for every dichrome. Add to this the individual names found at each site in a particular region, and the data can quickly become unmanageable. Inter-site and interregional comparison of the sort championed by Andrews should be a goal of every ceramic study, and an effort to rectify the limitations inherent to the type-variety system is needed.

Notes

1 This project was made possible by the National Science Foundation, the National Geographic Society, the New World Archaeological Foundation, the Reinhart Foundation, the Middle American Research Institute, and private donors. I especially would like to thank those who aided in my comparative analysis: Susan Haskell and Anne Seiferly at the Peabody Museum, Harvard University; Jaime Awe and Lauren Sullivan at Cahal Pech, Belize; the staff of the ceramic laboratory at IDEAH, Guatemala City; and Bernard Hermes at Tikal, Guatemala. I also would like to thank the many scholars who have visited the Holmul laboratory and given their opinions on the Pre-Mamom material, especially Michael G. Callaghan, Diana Mendez Lee, Bernard Hermes, David Cheetham, Jaime Awe, and Lauren Sullivan. The importance of this pottery was first brought to my attention during a visit by John Clark, Don Forsyth, Richard Hansen, and Bruce Bachand, to whom I am forever indebted. The excavations and analyses presented in this chapter were supported in every way by Francisco Estrada-Belli. I would also like to thank Will Andrews for inspiring me to undertake this project and for his guidance over the past several years.

2 It is most accurate to state that the motifs on the Pre-Mamom pottery I discuss are Early Formative in style but date to calendar years that span the transition between the Early and Middle Preclassic periods. The absolute dates of these periods are still a source of confusion, in great part because traditional chronology is based on uncalibrated radiocarbon dates rather than sidereal time. Throughout this chapter, I use the phrase "early Middle Preclassic" to refer to the period 1100 to 600 BC in the Christian calendar. This is roughly equivalent to 960 to 500 bc in uncalibrated radiocarbon years. The first 60 radiocarbon years of this period (i.e., before 900 bc) fall into the traditional chronological definition of the Early Preclassic period. Nonetheless, because most of the specific time frame – 1100 to 850 BC (960–760 bc) – in which the Holmul ceramics I discuss were made falls within the early Middle Preclassic, I opt in this chapter to use this phrase.

3   In this chapter, I use the term "Pre-Mamom" in a purely chronological sense, meaning before the later Middle Preclassic period. Thus, Pre-Mamom refers to complexes viewed as ancestral to later Mamom pottery as well as to those that may not be.
4   Despite Andrews and Hammond's (1990) realignment of the Swasey phase, this range now seems too early. The Swasey complex appears to be fully Middle Preclassic in style and date, even if it is earlier than the Mamom complex (Lohse 2010). An initial date of roughly 1000 to 900 BC now seems most likely for the Swasey phase.

References

Adams, Richard E. W. (1971) *The Ceramics of Altar de Sacrificios*. Cambridge, MA: Peabody Museum of Archaeology and Ethnology.

Andrews, E. Wyllys, IV, and E. Wyllys Andrews V (1980) *Excavations at Dzibilchaltun, Yucatan, Mexico*. New Orleans: Middle American Research Institute, Tulane University.

Andrews, E. Wyllys, V (1984) Komchen: An Early Maya Community in Northwest Yucatan. *Investigaciones recientes en el area Maya: XVII Mesa Redonda*, vol. 1. San Cristobal de las Casas: Universidad Nacional e Autonoma de Mexico.

—— (1988) Ceramic Units from Komchen, Yucatan, Mexico. *Ceramica de la Cultura Maya* 15: 51–64.

—— (1990) Early Ceramic History of the Lowland Maya. In *Vision and Revision in Maya Studies*, ed. Flora Clancy and Peter Harrison, pp. 1–19. Albuquerque: University of New Mexico Press.

Andrews, E. Wyllys, V, and George J. Bey III (2011) The Earliest Ceramics of the Northern Maya Lowlands. Paper presented at the VIIIth Tulane Maya Symposium, New Orleans.

Andrews, E. Wyllys, V, and Norman Hammond (1990) Redefinition of the Swasey Phase at Cuello, Belize. *American Antiquity* 55: 570–84.

Andrews, E. Wyllys, V, George Bey III, and Christopher Gunn (2008) Rethinking the Early Ceramic History of the Northern Maya Lowlands: New Evidence and Interpretations. Paper presented at the 73rd annual meeting of the Society for American Archaeology, Vancouver.

Awe, Jaime J. (1992) Dawn in the Land between the Rivers: Formative Occupation at Cahal Pech, Belize and its Implications for Preclassic Development in the Maya Lowlands. PhD dissertation, Institute of Archaeology, University of London.

Awe, Jaime J., James Garber, and Paul Healy (2008) Contextualizing Early Maya Prehistory in Belize. Paper presented at the 73rd annual meeting of the Society for American Archaeology, Vancouver.

Ball, Joseph W., and Jennifer T. Taschek (2003) Reconsidering the Belize Valley Preclassic: A Case for Multiethnic Interactions in the Development of a Regional Tradition. *Ancient Mesoamerica* 14: 179–217.

Bartlett, Mary, and Patricia A. McAnany (2000) "Crafting" Communities: The Materialization of Formative Maya Identities. In *The Archaeology of Communities: A New World Perspective*, ed. Jason Yaeger and Marcelo A. Canuto, pp. 102–22. London: Routledge.

Blake, Michael, and John E. Clark (1999) Emergence of Hereditary Inequality: The Case of Pacific Coastal Chiapas, Mexico. In *Pacific Latin America in Prehistory: the Evolution of Archaic and Formative Cultures*, ed. Michael Blake, pp. 55–73. Pullman: Washington State University Press.

Brown, M. Kathryn (2007) *Ritual Ceramic Use in the Early and Middle Preclassic at the sites of Blackman Eddy and Cahal Pech, Belize*. Los Angeles: Foundation for the Advancement of Mesoamerican Studies.

Callaghan, Michael (2008) *Technologies of Power: Ritual Economy and Ceramic Production in the Terminal Preclassic Period, Holmul Region, Guatemala*. PhD dissertation, Department of Anthropology, Vanderbilt University. Ann Arbor, MI: University Microfilms.

Cheetham, David (2005) Cunil: A Pre-Mamom Horizon in the Southern Maya Lowlands. In *New Perspectives on Formative Mesoamerican Cultures*, ed. Terry G. Powis, pp. 27–38. Oxford: British Archaeological Reports.

—— (n.d.) The Eb Ceramic Complex and Early Interregional Interaction at Tikal, Guatemala. MS thesis, Brigham Young University.

Clark, John E. (1991) Beginnings of Mesoamerica: Apologia for the Soconusco Early Formative. In *The Formation of Complex Society in Southeastern Mesoamerica*, ed. William Fowler, pp. 13–26. Boca Raton, FL: CRC Press.

Clark, John E., and David Cheetham (2002) Mesoamerica's Tribal Foundations. In *The Archaeology of Tribal Societies*, ed. W. A. Parkinson, pp. 278–339. Ann Arbor: University of Michigan Press.

Clark, John E., and Mary E. Pye (2000) The Pacific Coast and the Olmec Question. In *Olmec Art and Archaeology in Mesoamerica*, ed. John Clark and Mary Pye. Princeton, NJ: Princeton University Press.

Culbert, T. Patrick (n.d.) Descriptions of the Preclassic Ceramics, Tikal, Guatemala (Eb Ceramic Complex; Eb Complex Collections). MA thesis, Department of Anthropology, University of Arizona.

Estrada-Belli, Francisco (2006) Lightning, Sky, Rain, and the Maize God: The Ideology of Preclassic Maya Rulers at Cival, Peten, Guatemala. *Ancient Mesoamerica* 17(1): 57–78.

—— (2008) *Investigaciones arqueológicas en la región de Holmul, Petén. Informe preliminar de la temporada 2008.* Department of Archaeology, Boston University. Available at www.bu.edu/holmul/reports/.

Estrada-Belli, Francisco, Alexandre Tokovinine, Jennifer Foley, Heather Hurst, Gene Ware, David Stuart, and Nikolai Grube (2009) A Maya Palace at Holmul, Peten, Guatemala, and the Teotihuacan "Entrada": Evidence from Murals 7 and 9. *Latin American Antiquity* 20: 228–59.

Flannery, Kent V. and Joyce Marcus, with technical ceramic analysis by William O. Payne (1994) *Early Formative Pottery of the Valley of Oaxaca*. Ann Arbor: University of Michigan, Museum of Anthropology.

Garber, James F., M. Kathryn Brown and Christopher J. Hartman (2001) *The Early/Middle Formative Kanocha Phase (1200–850 BC) at Blackman Eddy, Belize.* Los Angeles: Foundation for the Advancement of Mesoamerican Studies.

Garber, James F., M. Kathryn Brown, Jaime J. Awe, and C. Hartman (2004) Middle Formative Prehistory of the Central Belize Valley: An Examination of Architecture, Material Culture, and Sociopolitical Change at Blackman Eddy. In *The Ancient Maya of the Belize Valley: Half a Century of Archaeological Research*, ed. James F. Garber, pp. 25–47. Gainesville: University of Florida Press.

Gifford, James C. (1960) The Type-Variety Method of Ceramic Classification as an Indicator of Cultural Phenomena. *American Antiquity* 25: 341–7.

Grove, David C. (1987) *Ancient Chalcatzingo*. Austin: University of Texas Press.

—— (1989) Olmec: What's in a Name? In *Regional Perspectives on the Olmec*, ed. Robert J. Sharer, pp. 8–14. Cambridge: Cambridge University Press.

Hammond, Norman (1979) The Earliest Lowland Maya: Definition of the Swasey Phase. *American Antiquity*, 44(1): 92–110.

Hammond, Norman, Juliette C. Gerhart, Sara Donaghey, Laura J. Kosakowsky, and Duncan Pring (1991) Stratigraphy and Chronology in the Reconstruction of Preclassic Development at Cuello. In *Cuello: An Early Maya Community in Belize*, ed. Norman Hammond, pp. 23–69. Cambridge: Cambridge University Press.

Healy, Paul F., David Cheetham, Terry G. Powis, and Jaime J. Awe (2004) Cahal Pech: The Middle Formative Period. In *The Ancient Maya of the Belize Valley: Half a Century of Archaeological Research*, ed. James F. Garber. Gainesville: University of Florida Press.

Hermes, Bernard (1993a) Adiciones tipológicas a los complejos Eb, Tzec, y Manik de Tikal, Guatemala. *Revista Española de Antropología Americana* 23: 9–27.
—— (1993b) Dos reportes del laboratorio cerámico: vasijas miniatura y adiciones tipológicas para la Epoca Preclásica. In *Tikal y Uaxactún en el Preclasico*, by Juan Pedro Laporte and Juan Antonio Valdés, pp. 47–52. Mexico: Universidad Nacional Autónoma de México.
Iceland, Harry B. (2005) The Preceramic to Early Middle Formative Transition in Northern Belize: Evidence for the Ethnic Identity of Preceramic Inhabitants. In *New Perspectives on Formative Mesoamerican Cultures*, ed. Terry G. Powis, pp. 15–26. Oxford: British Archaeological Reports.
Isbell, William H. (2000) What We Should Be Studying: The "Imagined Community" and the "Natural Community." In *The Archaeology of Communities: A New World Perspective*, ed. Jason Yaeger and Marcello A. Canuto, pp. 243–66. London: Routledge.
Joyce, Rosemary A., and Julia S. Henderson (2001) The Beginnings of Village Life in Eastern Mesoamerica. *Latin American Antiquity* 12(1): 5–24.
Kosakowsky, Laura J. (1987a) *Preclassic Maya pottery at Cuello, Belize*. Tucson: University of Arizona Press.
—— (1987b) The Formative Ceramic Sequence of Cuello, Belize. In *Maya Ceramics: Papers from the 1985 Maya Ceramic Conference*, ed. Prudence M. Rice and Robert J. Sharer, pp. 15–36. Oxford: British Archaeological Reports.
Lohse, John C., Jaime Awe, Cameron Griffith, Robert M. Rosenswig, and Fred Valdez, Jr. (2006) Preceramic Occupations in Belize: Updating the Paleoindian and Archaic Record. *Latin American Antiquity* 17: 209–26.
Lohse, Jon (2010) Archaic Origins of the Lowland Maya. *Latin American Antiquity* 21: 312–52.
McAnany, Patricia A. (1998) Ancestors and the Classic Maya Built Environment. In *Function and Meaning in Classic Maya Architecture*, ed. Stephen D. Houston. Washington, DC: Dumbarton Oaks.
Merwin, Raymond E., and George C. Vaillant (1932) *The Ruins of Holmul, Guatemala*. Cambridge, MA: Peabody Museum of Archaeology and Ethnology.
Rands, Robert (1987) Ceramic Patterns and Traditions in the Palenque Area. In *Maya Ceramics: Papers from the 1985 Maya Ceramic Conference*, ed. Prudence M. Rice and Robert J. Sharer, pp. 203–40. Oxford: British Archaeological Reports.
Sabloff, Jerry A. (1975) *Excavations at Seibal: Ceramics*, pp. 46–60. Cambridge, MA: Peabody Museum of Archaeology and Ethnology.
Sackett, James R. (1977) The Meaning of Style in Archaeology: a General Model. *American Antiquity* 42: 369–80.
—— (1982) Approaches to Style in Lithic Archaeology. *Journal of Anthropological Archaeology* 1: 59–112.
—— (1990) Style and Ethnicity in Archaeology: The Case for Isochrestism. In *The Uses of Style in Archaeology*, ed. Margaret Conkey and Christine Hastorf. Cambridge: Cambridge University Press.
Sharer, Robert J., and David Sedat (1987) Preclassic Ceramics from the Salama Valley, Baja Verpaz, Guatemala. In *Maya Ceramics: Papers from the 1985 Maya Ceramic Conference*, ed. Prudence M. Rice and Robert J. Sharer. Oxford: British Archaeological Reports.
Smith, Robert E. (1955) *Ceramic Squence at Uaxactun, Guatemala*. 2 vols. New Orleans: Middle American Research Institute, Tulane University.
Sullivan, Lauren, M. Kathryn Brown, and Jaime J. Awe (2009) Refining the Cunil Ceramic Complex at Cahal Pech, Belize. *Research Reports in Belizean Archaeology* 6: 161–168.
Taube, Karl (1998) The Jade Hearth: Centrality, Rulership, and the Classic Maya Temple. In *Function and Meaning in Classic Maya Architecture*, ed. Stephen D. Houston. Washington, DC: Dumbarton Oaks.

—— (2004) Structure 10L-16 and its Early Classic Antecedents: Fire and the Evocation and Resurrection of K'inich Yax K'uk; Mo'. In *Understanding Early Classic Copan*, ed. Ellen Bell, Marcello A. Canuto, and Robert J. Sharer. Philadelphia: University of Pennsylvania Museum of Archaeology and Anthropology.

Tomasic, John J. (2009) Investigating Terminal Preclassic and Classic Period Power and Wealth at K'o, Guatemala. PhD dissertation, Department of Anthropology, Vanderbilt University. Ann Arbor, MI: University Microfilms.

Wahl, David, Roger Byrne, Thomas Schreiner, and Richard Hansen (2006) Holocene Vegetation Change in the Northern Peten and its Implications for Maya Prehistory. *Quarternary Research* 65: 380–89.

Wahl, David, Francisco Estrada-Belli, and Lysanna Anderson (2013) A 3400 Year Paleolimnological Record of Prehispanic Human–Environment Interactions in the Holmul Region of the Southern Maya Lowlands. *Palaeogeography, Palaeoclimatology, Palaeoecology* 397–80: 17–31.

Willey, Gordon R., T. Patrick Culbert, and Richard E. W. Adams (1967) Maya Lowland Ceramics: A Report from the 1965 Guatemala City Conference. *American Antiquity* 32: 289–315.

Yaeger, Jason and Marcello A. Canuto (2000) Introducing an Archaeology of Communities. In *The Archaeology of Communities: A New World Perspective*, ed. Jason Yaeger and Marcello A. Canuto, pp. 1–15. London: Routledge.

8

THE ROYAL PORT OF CANCUEN AND THE ROLE OF LONG-DISTANCE EXCHANGE IN THE APOGEE OF MAYA CIVILIZATION

Arthur A. Demarest

Maya ports and sea trade have long been subjects of archaeological investigation; however, riverine ports have seen less research. The important Classic Maya site of Cancuen, Peten, Guatemala, is an example of such a port. Standing at the crossroads of trade routes connecting the Maya highlands to the lowlands and the east–west transversal route, Cancuen was situated in a unique position and was able to capitalize on changing fortunes at the heart of the Maya world. This chapter examines the location of Cancuen along these trade routes, political ties to sites to the north, and relations with both highland and lowland peoples during the Late Classic period.

Investigations of port centers in the ancient Maya world have focused on the great and small ports on the coasts of the Gulf of Mexico and the Caribbean Sea (e.g., Andrews 1990; McKillop 1989, 1996). Inland ports not far from the coast have also been examined for their role in direct regional coastal–inland exchange circuits (e.g., Barrett and Guderjan 2006). Some port sites have been described on the lake systems of Peten Itza in the Central Peten, such as Trinidad de Nosotros and, later, Yaxha and Topoxote. These sites and others have also been part of a continuous debate in Maya archaeology concerning the importance of long-distance exchange in the rise, apogee, and decline of Classic lowland Maya civilization.

What may have been the largest and most important port of the Classic period is neither a sea nor a lake port, but a riverine site far from gulfs or seas. Nonetheless, it was a linchpin in ancient Maya exchange systems and interregional dynamics. The royal port city of Cancuen therefore adds to our understanding of the critical role of long distance exchange (see Figure 1.1).

Some history of western Peten routes of exchange and transport

Long-distance exchange routes and patterns of control over them have long been a topic of interest in Maya archaeology (Figure 8.1). Western Peten routes were important to the debate over the initial settling of the region, as well as to discussions of foreign intrusions in its collapse (e.g., Willey 1973, 1990). For the six centuries of the historically documented Classic period, the patterns are especially clear (Demarest, Woodfill et al. 2007). Epigraphy, iconography, shifts in ceramic styles and lithics, settlement patterns, and site locations all indicate clear involvement of major centers and global trends in western interregional exchange routes. All of this can be supported now by new and more precise forms of evidence,

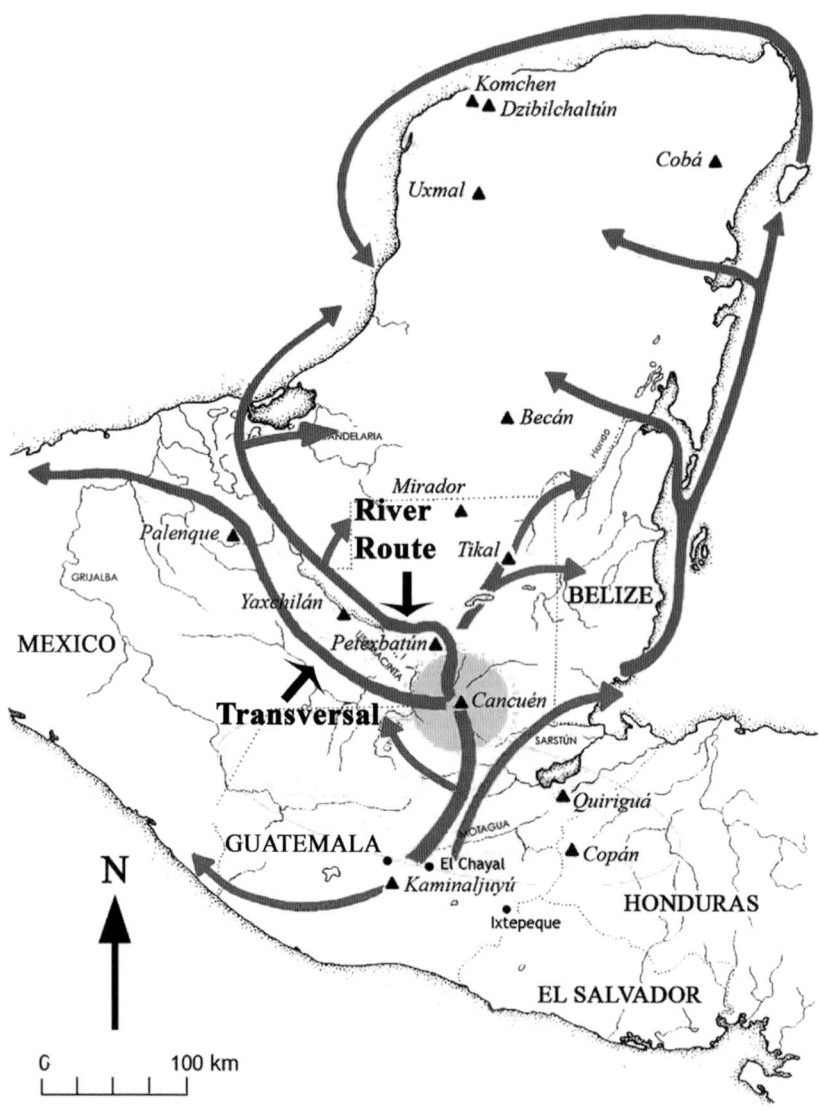

FIGURE 8.1 Some of the major transport and exchange routes of the Classic period

including the many deciphered inscriptions and the compositional tracing of ceramics (Forné *et al.* 2009, 2010; Martin and Grube 1994). In the western Peten in particular, the inscriptions are rich in political content and provide great insights into the sources and directions of influences.

Such patterns are especially clear on the Usumacinta–Pasion river artery. There a linear and sharply defined trade route on the long, wide, and highly navigable Pasion River connected the Maya world with the Usumacinta and Gulf of Mexico to the north and with the highlands and Motagua River to the south (Figures 8.1 and 8.2). It is at junctions and portages on this route that major Classic period sites were located, as well as along major tributaries. Changes in artifact and even architectural styles can be observed as global political trends varied over time (Demarest 2006a).

There were continuous attempts to maintain access to this route by the major powers of the central lowlands. These may even extend back into the Late Preclassic but can be defined more securely from Classic-period evidence. One of the most

FIGURE 8.2 The Pasion–Usumacinta transport and exchange route

evident was the central Peten influence or intrusion all along the southwestern highland–lowland river and land corridor. Central Peten ceramic styles and monuments appear along the river valley at Tres Islas, Punta de Chimino, and other sites (Bachand 2006; Demarest, Woodfill et al. 2007). Meanwhile, along the Verapaz valley route, Tzakol ceramics become prevalent in cave shrines, and a Peten-style fine monument has even been recovered from caves (Woodfill 2010; Woodfill and Andrieu 2012).

Next begins the epoch of interregional conflict between the great powers of the alliance of Tikal states and the Calakmul hegemony. These wars involved many of the centers in the west, including Dos Pilas, Machaquila, and El Peru/Waka (Demarest 2006a; Martin and Grube 1994, 2008). This pattern of central Peten influence ended abruptly in the Middle Classic period, and the Verapaz valley highland land routes and cultures became very localized. On the Pasion and the connecting land route to Calakmul there was a late seventh-century shift to the Calakmul sphere, as seen in the historical texts on monuments at Dos Pilas, El Peru/Waka, La Corona, Cancuen, and other centers (e.g., Demarest 2006a; Martin and Grube 1994). It also was in this period that the capital of the Upper Pasion kingdom was moved to Cancuen. Calakmul actually placed the first two of the rulers of Cancuen on their thrones (Martin and Grube 2008; Fahsen et al. 2003; Fahsen and Jackson 2001). This is because Calakmul had founded Cancuen as part of its expansion of Peten influences. In the eighth century the decline of Calakmul led to its influence being less direct, despite continued references to that diminished superpower in the inscriptions of many sites.

In a more direct sense it was the expansion of the Petexbatun kingdom of Dos Pilas that led to the new era of unification of the Pasion route (Demarest 2006a). It was during that period that a marriage alliance between Dos Pilas and Cancuen unified the river route once again. The marriage was much celebrated at Dos Pilas, where the queen of Cancuen had her own elaborate palace and throne. A fine sculpted panel celebrates the relationship (Wooley and Wright 1990). It appears that relations between the Petexbatun kingdom and Cancuen were always amicable (Fahsen et al. 2003). Influences can be observed at Cancuen in some buildings in the Petexbatun architectural style. Similarly, Cancuen influence at Dos Pilas may be the reason for the fine masonry palace and the Cancuen-style panel at that site.

After the defeat of El Peru/Waka in AD 743 by Tikal, there seems to have been a destabilization of the river route, with the violent destruction of Dos Pilas being the culmination of that process in AD 761 (Demarest et al. 1997). During the period of Dos Pilas alliance Cancuen had grown and thrived, but it was after the fall of Dos Pilas that its true florescence began.

All of these historical events and shifts in the style of artifacts can be attributed to the need of ruling elites to maintain the route of movement of precious goods from the highlands. The need to control the flow of jade, pyrite, quetzal and other plumage, and Pacific shell was an obvious motive for securing the Pasion and the access to the Verapaz land route to which it connected (Figure 8.3).

These goods were critical to the ritual and pageantry of the *k'uhul ajawob* but were also equally important to their patronage networks. The exchange of exotics does not mean, however, that more basic goods were not also following these same transport

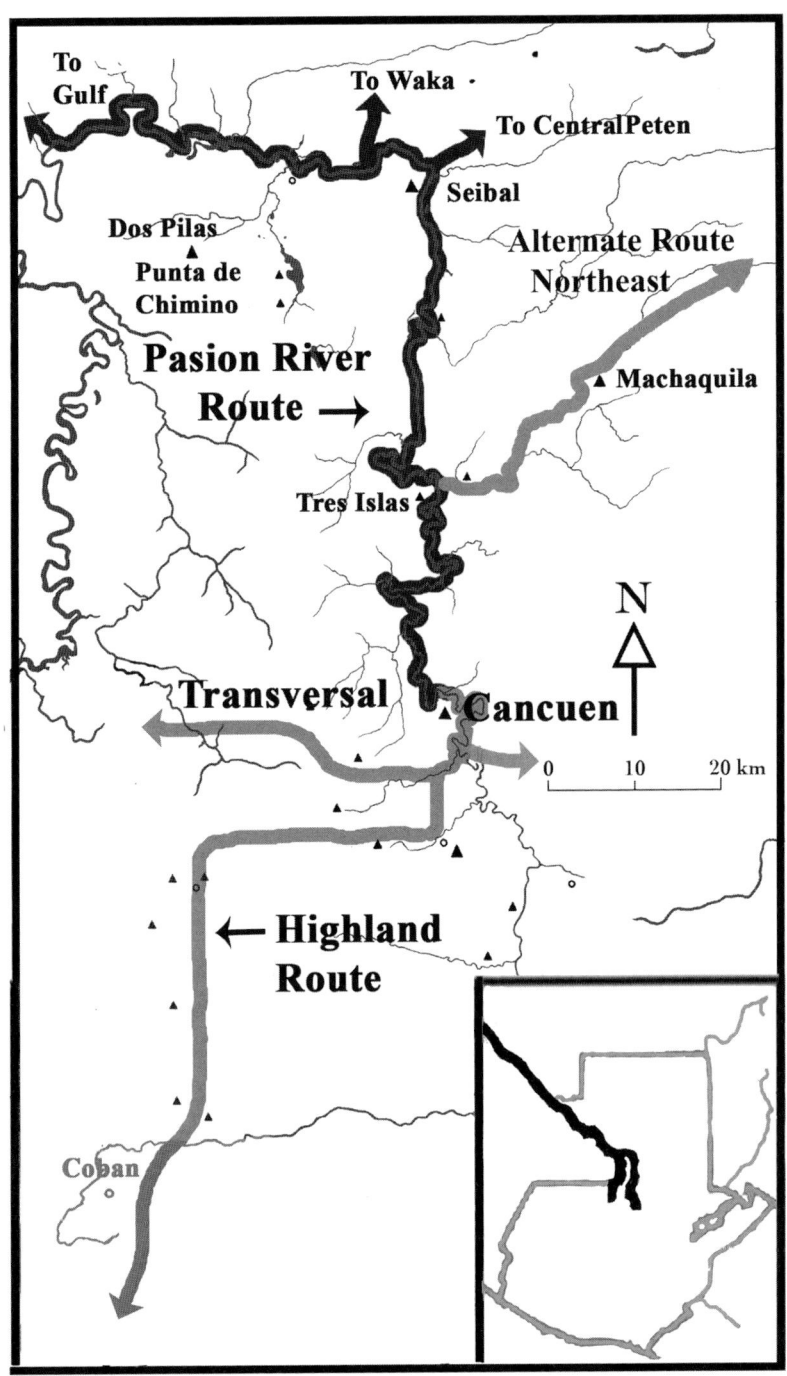

FIGURE 8.3 The Pasion River and Verapaz *transversal* and highland valley exchange routes of the western Peten

highways. Obsidian came down this route from El Chayal in every period, and it is likely that salt from Salinas de Nueve Cerros was channeled via land to the Pasion River corridor (Dillon 1977; Sears et al. 2005; Woodfill et al. 2011). Other more local exchange patterns, even in subsistence goods, may have followed segments of these pathways. The Pasion provided a channel for easy movement, making possible the exchange of perishable goods within the region if not beyond. Thus, sections of the system most probably were linked through a variety of levels and mechanisms of exchange.

Clearly the western route, and especially the Pasion River highway and its access to the Alta Verapaz valley, was of consistent importance to strategies of western and Central Peten polities. This was particularly true for the exotics that were so critical to the provisioning of royal courts and all of the myriad economic consequences of such access (McAnany 2012).

The port center of Cancuen

The port city of Cancuen was located at the intersection between the highland and lowland Maya worlds: the Peten and the southern highland and piedmont zone

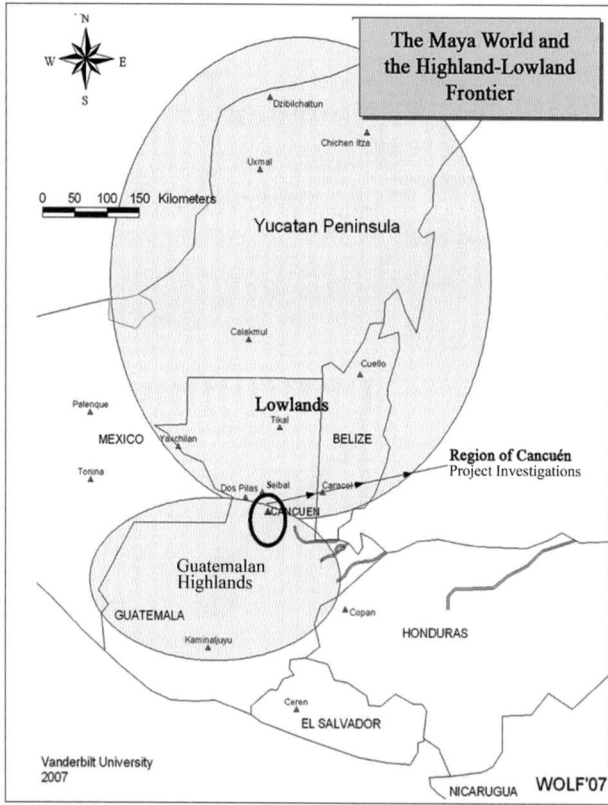

FIGURE 8.4 The Cancuen region at the direct highland–lowland interface

(Figure 8.4). These contrasting ecological realms also had strikingly different material culture even in the direct interface of the Alta Verapaz region. Cancuen and neighboring highland sites differed in ceramic styles, stone versus earthen architecture, site size, settlement patterns, monuments, and ritual assemblages. While it was first identified by Tourtellot *et al.* (1978) as the head of navigation, later decipherments of inscriptions point to the critical role Cancuen played in the political strategy of this riverine world (Fahsen and Jackson 2001; Martin and Grube 1994).

The location of Cancuen was closely related to the major trade routes and the political shifts described above. This also was the reason for its well-defined nature as a port city. The entire western trade route (Figure 8.3) from the Peten follows the single channel of the Pasion south into the highlands and the Pacific coast, passing through two narrow valleys of the Verapaz region and climbing gradually to the peak of the highlands. Moreover, the direct interface just 15 kilometers south of Cancuen, where the Sierra de Chinaja shoots up in sharp profile from the lowland floor, is very dramatic. There the streams and springs of the highlands pour out in cascades to form the Sebol River, which in turn becomes the Pasion after slowing to a navigable speed. Thus, Cancuen, at the head of navigation, defines the initiation of the Pasion–Usumacinta river route to the entire western and central lowlands (Figure 8.2).

Cancuen also sits on the east–west land route (Figure 8.3), the *transversal*, which runs along the foot of the northern side of the highlands from Chiapas in the west all the way past Salinas de Nueve Cerros and to Cancuen. In modern Mexico, the *transversal* also curves northwest following the Chiapas hills to the Gulf coast and the sites of Tabasco and Veracruz. Moreover, from Cancuen at the intersection of the southern route into the highlands and the *transversal*, the Pasion–Usumacinta river system heads north into the Peten. Along it or its tributaries were placed most of the great cities of the southwestern Peten, including El Raudal, Tres Islas, Machaquila, Seibal, Dos Pilas, Aguateca, Tamarindito, Altar de Sacrificios, Piedras Negras, Yaxchilan, and many smaller sites (Barrios *et al.* 2008; Demarest, Woodfill *et al.* 2007) It also connects to intersecting land routes that lead to other great centers, such as Calakmul, El Peru/Waka, El Mirador, Tikal, and – via the *transversal* – even to Palanque (Figure 8.3). Cancuen was thus set at a critical position as an interregional crossroads of southeastern Mesoamerica.

The head-of-navigation port and complexes of Cancuen

Over a decade of investigations at Cancuen have revealed evidence on ports, exchange, and interregional and local economic systems. The results of these investigations are detailed elsewhere (Barrientos *et al.* 2002; Barrientos, Demarest, Luín *et al.* 2006; Demarest and Barrientos 1999, 2000, 2001; Demarest *et al.* 2003, 2004, 2011; Demarest, Martínez, and Luín 2007; Demarest, Barrientos *et al.* 2008; Demarest and Martínez 2010, 2013). The history and position of the site of Cancuen and its adjacent zones provide evidence on port economy as well as insights into Maya changes in power, economics, and politics in the eighth century.

The salient feature of Cancuen was, of course, its ports (Figure 8.5). The most important of these was the true head of navigation of the Pasion at the northwestern

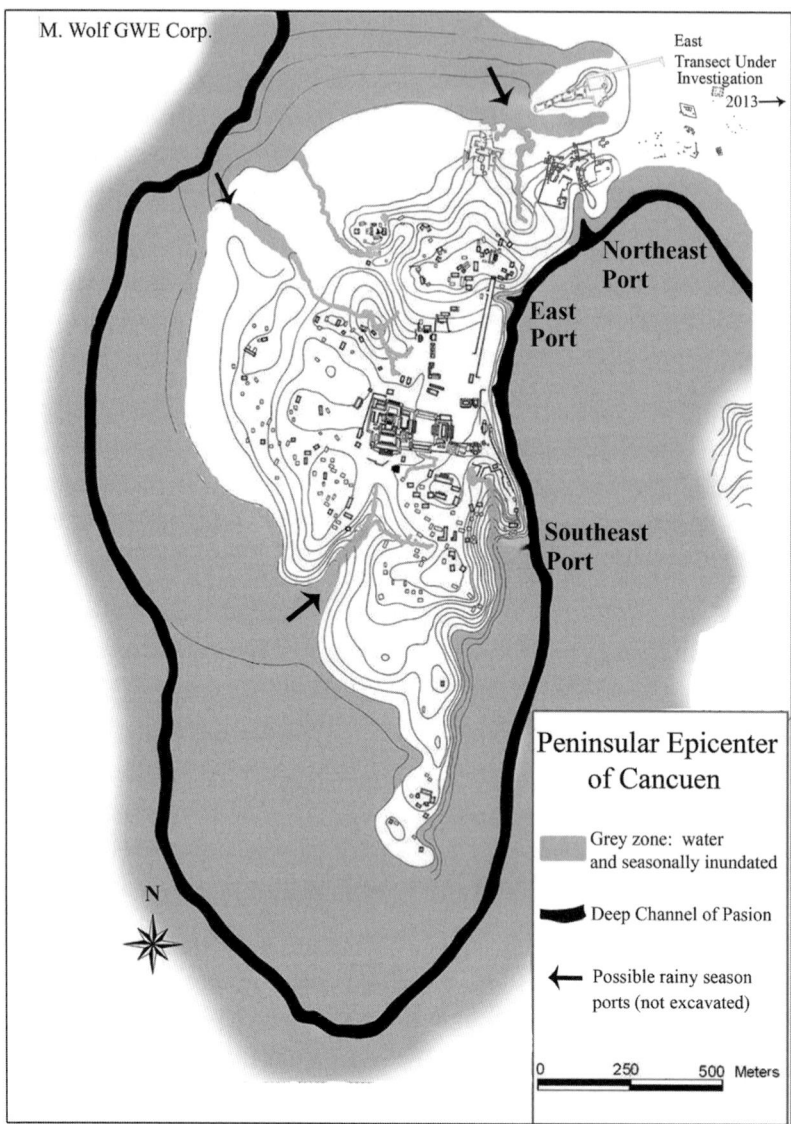

FIGURE 8.5 Epicenter peninsula and ports of Cancuen

and northeastern portages of the site. This location was where most goods from the highlands were loaded into canoes for the river route and where any lowland products for local or regional trade were unloaded from the boats for the land routes to the south into the highlands or west to Chiapas, Tabasco, and Veracruz.

The northeast port was separated only by a narrow strip of high ground from the wider northwestern port on the downriver side of the Cancuen peninsula (Figure 8.6). The port has above it a range structure with associated terraces, forming a small complex but with fine masonry and a good quantity of Peten-style

Tepeu ceramics, which are distributed only irregularly in the site (Forné *et al.* 2008, 2009). From the actual waterline to the south, artificial and reinforced natural terraces line the slope, with a gradual path running west to the higher ground above the bay. Along the slopes and atop the escarpment on all sides around the northeast and northwest portages are the complexes that serviced the head of navigation. Residential and administrative architecture of more than 50 structures covered this northern sector of the site. These were constructed in a wide range of different styles of masonry, cobble, and clay, reflecting the apparent complex mix of activities and interregional influences in this zone (Demarest, Woodfill *et al.* 2007; Demarest, Barrientos *et al.* 2008; Demarest and Martínez 2010; Demarest *et al.* 2011).

Structures were built with masonry of one type or another around one, two, or three sides depending on the slope of this irregular terrain. They include some vast platforms over 200 square meters in area, others of just 16 square meters, and every size in between. Some construction was in the style of the Verapaz piedmont and highlands, with unworked stone, good masonry, or even simply pounded clay retaining walls.

It is important to emphasize that high, elite range structure complexes delimited the northern port zone both immediately to the north and just several hundred meters to

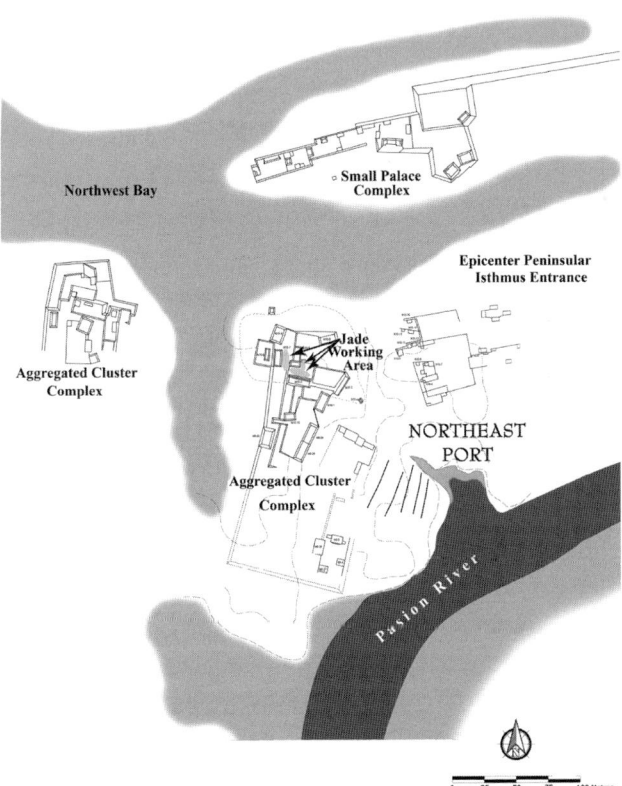

FIGURE 8.6 Northern port complexes, jade production area, and range structure

the south, with "intermediate" ranges of architecture in between. It would appear that the elites of the site, if not the state, held tight control of the head of navigation, the economic engine of Cancuen. There the variety of architecture and the mix of regional styles presumably reflect the functions of the personnel of the port, as supervisors, boatmen, rowers, porters, and merchants – the last quite possibly the nobles of the site.

In the midst of this bustling area and its dense architecture are four low mounds where artisans produced jade preforms from boulders. It was a production area almost exclusively for preforms of beads and flat pieces for earspools, but the actual finished artifacts were not produced there (Andrieu and Forné 2010; Andrieu, Jaime-Riverón, et al. 2011; Andrieu et al. forthcoming). Given the scale of production and absence of later stages of finishing, it seems most likely that the boulders of jade coming down via the highland land route were worked at the head of navigation. The zone also appears to be tightly controlled by elites with access to the area only by the isthmus or the port, both with a dominant elite complex. One massive platform area of 270 square meters directly overlooks the low, jade-working mounds. The elite enclosed location of the workshop is significant because, given the lack of later stages of crafting beyond preform production, the area of jade working was probably for export. The preform working areas directly abut the portage zone of the northern ports, convenient for movement of the heavy boulders and the export of preform products.

Multiregional influences

The head-of-navigation and other ports also had an international mixture of regional styles in artifacts fitting with the activities there. I have noted the mix of highland and lowland architecture styles, but there was also in the period from 760 to 800 a more eclectic ceramic assemblage than anywhere else in the site. These include ceramics in Tepeu lowland style, Verapaz piedmont ceramics, and, of most interest, a large quantity of pottery imported from distant Tabasco and Veracruz (Forné et al. 2008, 2009, 2010, 2013; Forné and Torres 2010).

Among the imports from Chiapas, Tabasco, and Veracruz were fine paste wares that not only lock down the date to between 760 and 800 but also illustrate the international reach of this port crossroad city. One set of types is Telchac Composite and Chicxilub Incised of the Chablekal Fine Grey ceramic ware. These have been analyzed by Ronald Bishop and his team from the Smithsonian and have been identified as a high chromium variety of this paste traceable to the Gulf coast plains of Chiapas and Tabasco (Bishop et al. 2005). Meanwhile, another fine paste ware, less common but also concentrated at port areas, was Campamento Fine Orange – a Classic-period ceramic from the Tabasco/Veracruz border zone (Forné et al. 2010). These indications of western influence reflect long-distance exchange with those zones, most probably via the route that became most important in the late eighth century – the *transversal* that ran by land from the Cancuen area to the west along the base of the highlands of Guatemala and Chiapas to the Gulf coast plain (Demarest et al. 2009).

The international associations of the head-of-navigation ports are also revealed by the presence in the northern port zone of a significant percentage of obsidian from Central Mexican sources, which provided much of the obsidian consumed along the Gulf coast of Veracruz. Although small, the levels are twice those of other Classic-period Maya sites and at the level of Terminal Classic sites over a century later (Andrieu and Quiñonez 2010; Andrieu, Quinoñes and Rodas 2011). The role of the northern ports as the true international center of the site is made clear by all of these western materials at the points of loading and unloading materials for land and river transport. Their date and distant connections together show that the political and economic agenda of Cancuen had turned in its final half century to the western *transversal*, which helped fuel the eighth-century apogee.

Other port complexes

Several other ports lie on the east and west side of the peninsula with their access primarily focused on the epicenter (Figure 8.5). Two of most thoroughly excavated of these are also among the best understood after investigations from 2003 to 2005 (Alvarado 2004; Alvarado et al. 2006; Demarest, Martínez et al. 2008; Demarest et al. 2011; Demarest and Martínez 2010). Like the head-of-navigation northern ports, both of these portages consist of protected natural bays and both had a

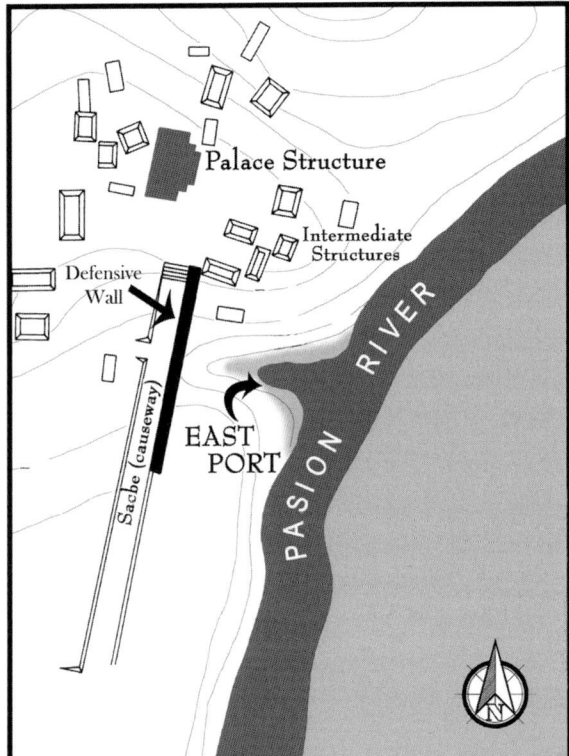

FIGURE 8.7 The east port complex

masonry range structure complex placed directly on the port on its northern side in a position allowing the supervision of activities. Like the head-of-navigation northeast port, these more southern epicenter ports are still used today as local portages for transport to and from the Cancuen peninsula.

One portage on the due eastern side of the peninsula (Figure 8.7) was associated with a *sacbe* that ran directly into the epicenter core zone from the port bay. A possible docking terrace with ramps has been thoroughly investigated (Alvarado 2004; Alvarado et al. 2006). A cobble terrace just above water level could have served as a wharf for the portage of goods to and from the site epicenter. Above and, again, just north of the port sat a small palace complex, apparently placed so as be in a supervisory position. The range structure associated with this palace had its own bench and a corbelled vaulted audience chamber, clearly the complex of subroyal elite of great importance (Jackson 2002, 2003).

It is telling that this port complex, so linked to the site core, had defensive constructions added to it in the final years of the site, if not in its final months. A low stone wall crosses over the *sacbe*, indicating its addition at the final brief moments of military danger and an attack on the site at about AD 800. On the *sacbe* itself were recovered two unburied young adult male skeletons (Berryman and Novotny 2003). We speculate that these were victims of the final assault that destroyed Cancuen. It is also telling that in the final stage of the endangered site the emphasis was on the defense of this epicenter port access. Other probable port areas led in from the western loop of the river to the epicenter.

Yet another epicenter port complex was excavated because it is currently used as the entrance to the site and camp and was intensively studied prior to camp construction. A fine masonry structure, largely dismembered by looting and stone-borrowing activity, stood on the northern side of the bay. There were rich burials beneath its base, and it was associated with a variety of other structures of various types. This bay turns north, leading into the site epicenter near the royal ballcourt of Taj Chan Ahk, described below. This port provided access to the ceremonial courtyards of the site but not necessarily to those of the highest elite nature, like the ports on the west. Another southwest port is a bay that could have led directly to the procession way into the westernmost elite entrance to the royal palace (Figure 8.5). Such portages probably served only to carry products and illustrious visitors to the site center for ceremonial visits and local provisioning. The particular well-placed southwestern bay has yet to be investigated.

In sum, these southern ports were direct entrances that brought goods into the epicenter and perhaps also marked the beginnings of ritual and political visits. The northern ports probably served more as the basic transfer points for the head of navigation.

The eighth-century florescence of Cancuen and its manifestations

The ports of Cancuen, the strategic position of the site, its alliances, and the decline of competing centers led together to a great florescence in the eighth century, particularly the period of great internationalism from 750 to 800 (Barrientos and Demarest 2007; Demarest, Barrientos *et al.* 2008). This was the culmination of a century and a half of historical changes at Cancuen as a port center, an apogee which saw the polity as an independent power exerting a variety of strategies of alliances, ballgames, and ritual visits to create new opportunities for trade and exchange. Avoidance of the contemporary chaos downriver by use of the *transversal* also helped to open up access to the west, leading to the florescence of the site.

This wealth was most manifest in the royal palace, which covered an area almost equal to the central acropolis of Tikal, even though Cancuen was by comparison a small site (Barrientos 2012; Barrientos and Demarest 2012; Demarest 2006b). The palace covered an area of over 40,000 square meters and had 11 courtyards (Figure 8.8). Some rooms towered to over 8 meters in height, and most were covered with elaborate

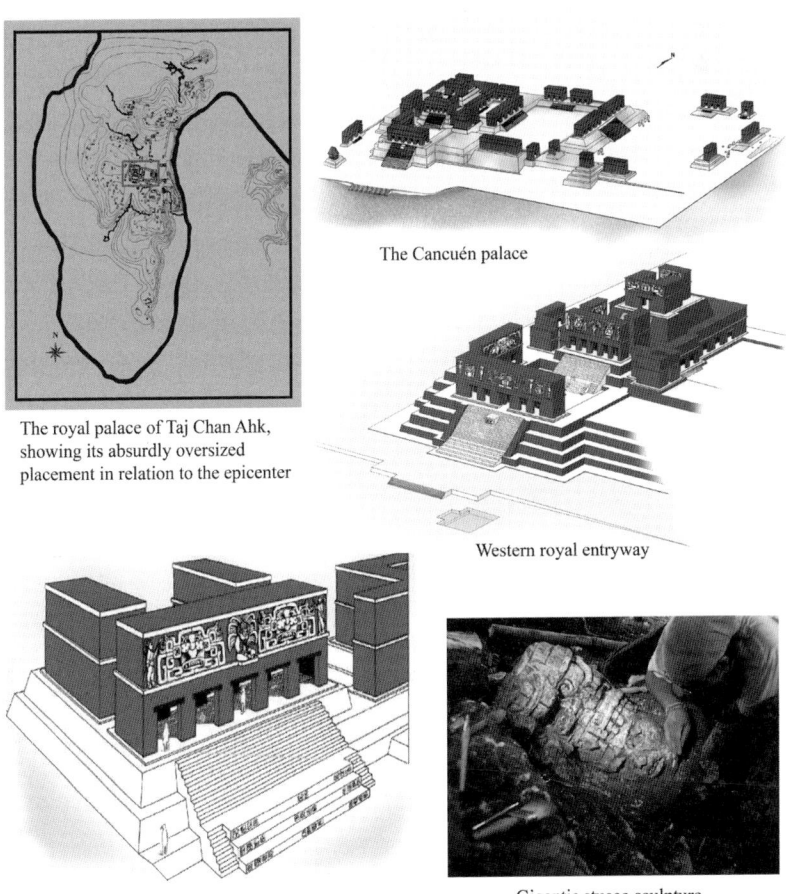

The Cancuén palace

The royal palace of Taj Chan Ahk, showing its absurdly oversized placement in relation to the epicenter

Western royal entryway

One of the many high ostentatious structures in the palace with hieroglyphic stairway

Gigantic stucco sculpture

FIGURE 8.8 Various views of the royal palace of Cancuen

three-dimensional stucco portraits of seated and standing kings, deities, and sentinels 2 to 3 meters high. The palace was carefully designed to awe visitors, particularly peer or vassal high lords arriving from the southern and east portages. One procession way led past the sacred cistern at the entrance to the royal palace, a large stucco-lined red-painted pool of nearly 80 square meters and over 2 meters deep, made of fine stone masonry. Beyond that rose a great stairway leading to the entrance structure, with its tall audience chambers and massive stucco portraits. Two passageways led through into an inner courtyard. There, in addition to more crafted stucco portraits, was the hieroglyphic staircase. It celebrates festivals and rites between the last ruler of Dos Pilas, K'awiil Chan K'inich, and the young king Taj Chan Ahk of Cancuen, whose reign oversaw the apogee of the site after AD 760 and marked the period of Cancuen's florescence (Fahsen *et al*. 2003). Further courtyards had smaller, more exclusive areas, fine sculptured panels covered with descriptions of dynastic history, and stuccoed stairways leading up to the beautifully constructed royal throne room (Barrientos, Demarest, Alvarado *et al*. 2006). It was a skilled architectonic power-generating machine, with ever more exclusive patios and ever more actual glyphic historical texts, designed to impress noblemen, lords, and even the visiting k'uhul ajawob (Barrientos 2014).

But the central palace was only one manifestation of wealth during this apogee. The Cancuen peninsula had many noble palaces and oratories, some of these quite impressive (Figure 8.9). Notably, a number were placed at strategic locations, with one identified above each of the three excavated ports. Others nearer to the site center had spectacular stucco portraits like those of the royal palace. The proliferation of architecture on the narrow peninsula – of the palace, elites, their retainers, kitchens, port complexes, and ballcourts – led to the covering of any land for possible field or garden zones. The population of the center not only was made up of

FIGURE 8.9 A subroyal palace complex, M7-28//M7-8

elites but also consisted of a wide variety of retainers and people in service occupations, probably many involved in port activities.

As the wealth of Cancuen grew, it was reflected in other architecture and landscaping. The built environment also included a ritual water system that moved through the site in narrow stone channels of less than a meter wide, running between stone cisterns, natural springs, and the ballcourt (Alvarado 2011; Alvarado and Mencos 2007; Barrientos, Demarest, Alvarado *et al.* 2006). In addition to the palace cistern mentioned above, a second cistern further north was 51 square meters in area and over 3 meters deep, and was made of fine masonry covered in red plaster. The water system filled part of the area between the ceremonial architecture, and one end of it connected to a ballcourt – an entrance to the underworld. The ballcourt of ruler Taj Chan Ahk was covered with stucco water symbols and also contained the finely carved Panel 3 (Fahsen and Barrientos 2006; Fernandez Aguilar 2010), which ties the lords to the sacred water system and the river as masters of the Pasion. The symbolism in the very aquatic name of the ruler, Fiery Great Tortoise (Taj Chan Ahk), asserts the role of the *k'uhul ajaw* and of his capital as a center of power over the Pasion and its waters.

The ballcourts and exchange strategy

One of the other impressive constructions of the epicenter was the ballcourt of the king Taj Chan Ahk (Figure 8.10, lower right), who reigned during most of the period of florescence. It displayed the great water lord in two of its altars, each portraying a royal ballgame. The fine sculptured Panel 3 identifies the ballcourt as that of Taj Chan Ahk. The altars of the ballcourt (Fahsen and Barrientos 2006) also display how its port control and its ritual devices served together to form alliances with other lords to carryout proxy wars against other centers to secure the new and old trade routes. Altar 2 (Figure 8.10, lower left) portrays a royal ballgame between Taj Chan Ahk and a lord who conquered a site named "White Mountain" (*Sac Witz*; Fahsen and Barrientos 2006). This action was possibly taken in the name of Taj Chan Ahk, who is portrayed as the superior lord in the imagery. White Mountain may be a reference to the *transversal* site of Raxruja Viejo, which is about 15 kilometers southwest of Cancuen. One of its white karst towers was turned into a pyramid temple by the construction of platforms and stelae in front of it during the Late Classic period (Demarest and Martinez 2013). It sits at a critical juncture of the *transversal*, heading west by land along the base of the Sierra de Chinaja karst, which marks the beginnings of the highlands. Thus, the ballgame, control of the ports, and the architectural and ritual displays of the center helped together to assert Cancuen access, if not control, of the land route west to Chiapas and Tabasco, the alternative route to the troubled, militarized middle Pasion River of the late eighth century (Demarest *et al.* 2009).

Altar 2 also records that the companion of the ruler of Cancuen captured a lord of Machaquila (Fahsen and Barrientos 2006). Such a proxy war might have maintained or reasserted Cancuen's control of the other end of its late eighth-century trade route: the river and land route east via Machaquila to the central and eastern Peten, an alternative

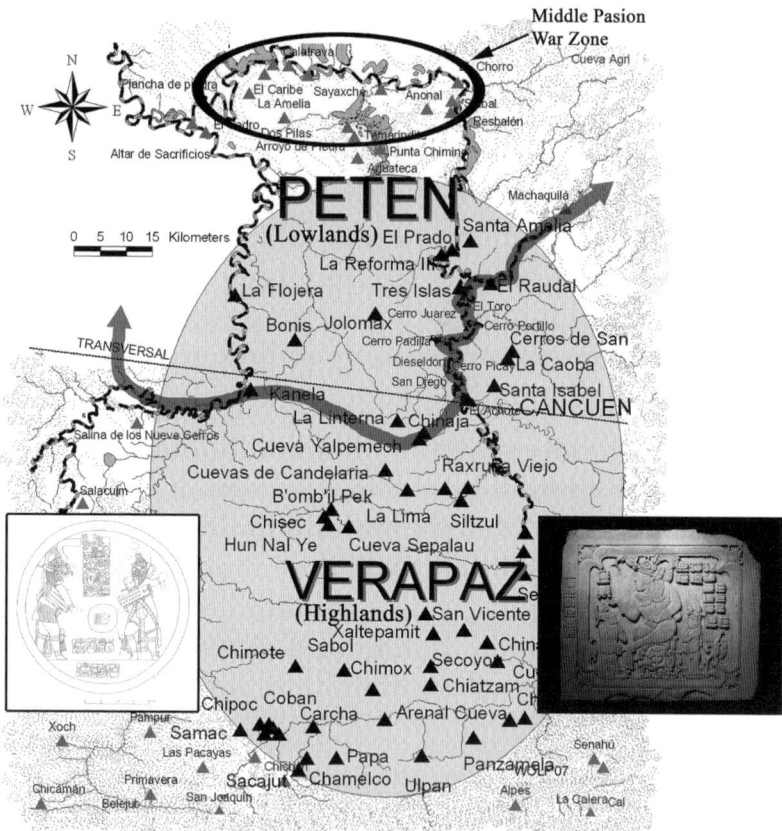

FIGURE 8.10 The western and eastern "detour" routes of late eighth-century Cancuen: (lower left) Altar 2; (lower right) Panel 3

route to the east (Figure 8.10). Trade along this route probably was controlled by Cancuen for 40 years, a period of hiatus in the monuments of Machaquila. Control of eastward trade also gave Cancuen a pathway around the chaos of the middle Pasion.

There are two other ballcourts at Cancuen. One is a standard but finely built ballcourt that can be seen from the royal palace. The final example (Figure 8.11) is a sprawling highland-style "feasting ballcourt" (cf. Fox 1996) in the center of the peninsula (Torres 2011). It was surrounded by middens of broken serving and cooking vessels, reflecting again the alliance-formation mechanisms of Cancuen. The events hosted at Cancuen for visiting highland neighbors probably were intended to help secure peacefully their own region and the southern route into the highlands themselves. The ceramics here, as elsewhere in the site, reflect its interregional ties. Simpler local and Verapaz piedmont ceramics are predominant (Torres 2011; Forné et al. 2008, 2009).

FIGURE 8.11   Hypothetical reconstruction of the highland "feasting ballcourt" at Cancuen

Conclusions: Cancuen and the role of long-distance exchange

Taken together, the constructions, monuments, ballcourts, and ritual settings of Cancuen show how its ports led to its wealth and power in the eighth century. In turn, all of those features also served to reinforce that power and elite control over ports, jade, obsidian, and probably shell and other commodities as they passed through the center at the head of navigation.

The role of ports in ancient Maya society has been much explored. Cancuen, however, as a riverine port so far inland from both the Gulf and Caribbean coasts, provides a somewhat different perspective. Its nature and history demonstrate its importance to elites, and especially the ruling dynasties of the Peten who controlled routes of exchange in exotics and perhaps other commodities.

The relative degree of importance of long-distance trade has been much discussed in Maya archaeology. Skepticism of its importance has correctly emphasized the self-sufficiency of the Peten subregions in most basic subsistence goods and material needs. Nonetheless, as with other riverine Classic centers – but even more so – the position, wealth, and history of Cancuen emphasize that long-distance exchange routes were central to the interests of ruling elites. Such routes determined wars and alliances, the flow of tribute and commodities, the positioning of sites, and other features of society as a whole. Those influences and impacts only increased as the elites, number of centers, and demand for status goods grew during the eighth century.

Cancuen therefore stands as testimony to the major role of ports, site strategy, and long-distance exchange in the Classic period. Its sudden demise remains a mystery, but that event must reflect changes in these same critical patterns of long-distance exchange. The Postclassic ushered in a new period during which such dynamics of exchange continued to be of great import via the Gulf and Caribbean routes, leaving out such riverine port centers as Cancuen. Furthermore, the central role of trade shifted away from elite exotics and more to commodities. Nonetheless, the critical role of ports and long-distance exchange would only grow greater in the new manifestations of Terminal Classic and Postclassic Maya civilization.

References

Alvarado, Carlos (2004) Excavaciones en el puerto principal de Cancuen: temporada 2003. In *Proyecto Arqueológico Cancuen: informe temporada 2003*, ed. Arthur A. Demarest, Tomás Barrientos, Brigitte Kovacevich, Michael Callaghan, Brent Woodfill, and Luís F. Luín, pp. 345–64. Guatemala City: Instituto de Antropología e Historia de Guatemala.

Alvarado, Carlos, Carrie Anne Berryman, Ana Novotny, and Kristen Demarest (2006) Investigaciones en el puerto principal de Cancuen. In *Proyecto Arqueológico Cancuen: informe de temporada 2004–2005*, ed. Tomás Barrientos, Arthur A. Demarest, Claudia Quintanilla, and Luís F. Luín, pp. 435–53. Guatemala City: Instituto de Antropología e Historia de Guatemala.

Alvarado, Silvia (2011) *Análisis funcional de las reservas de agua en Cancuen*. Licenciatura thesis, Universidad de San Carlos, Guatemala City.

Alvarado, Silvia, and Elisa Mencos (2007) CAN 48: Excavaciones en la cisterna o reserva de agua norte. In *Proyecto Arqueológico Cancuén: informe no. 8, temporada 2007*, ed. Horacio Martínez, Arthur A. Demarest, Mélanie Forné, and Luís F. Luín, pp. 79–113. Guatemala City: Ministerio de Cultura y Deportes de Guatemala.

Andrews, Anthony P. (1990) The Role of Trading Ports in Maya Civilization. In *Vision and Revision in Maya Studies*, ed. Flora S. Clancy and Peter D. Harrison, pp. 159–67. Albuquerque: University of New Mexico Press.

Andrieu, Chloé, and Mélanie Forné (2010) Producción y distribución del jade en el mundo maya: talleres, fuentes, y rutas del intercambio en su contexto interregional: vista desde Cancuen. In *XXIII Simposio de investigaciones arqueológicas en Guatemala, 2009*, ed. Bárbara Arroyo, Lorena Paiz Aragón, Adriana Linares Palma, and Ana Lucia Arroyave, pp. 947–56. Guatemala City: Museo Nacional de Arqueología y Etnología.

Andrieu, Chloé and Douglas Quiñonez (2010) Análisis lítico. In *Proyecto Arqueológico Cancuen: informe final no. 10, temporada 2010*, ed. Arthur Demarest and Horacio Martínez, pp. 164–84. Guatemala City: Ministerio de Cultura y Deportes de Guatemala.

Andrieu, Chloé, Olaf Jaime-Riverón, Maria Dolores Tenorio, Thomas Calligaro, Juan Carlos Cruz Ocampo, Melania Jimenez, and Mikhail Ostrooumov (2011) Últimos datos sobre la producción de artefactos de jade en Cancuen. In *XXIV Simposio internacional de arqueología*, ed. B. Arroyo, A. Linares Palma and L. Paiz Aragón, pp. 1017–26. Guatemala City: Museo Nacional de Arqueología y Etnología.

Andrieu, Chloé, Douglas Quiñonez, and Edna Rodas (2011) La lítica de Cancuen. In *Proyecto Cancuen: informe final no. 11, temporada 2011*, ed. Arthur A. Demarest, Horacio Martínez, Claudia Quintanilla, and Paola Torres, pp. 262–73. Guatemala City: Ministerio de Cultura y Deportes de Guatemala.

Andrieu, Chloé, Melanie Forné, and Arthur Demarest (forthcoming) El valor del jade: producción y distribución del jade en el sitio de Cancuen. In *El jade y otras piedras verdes: perspectivas interdisciplinarias e interculturales*, ed. Walburga Wiesheu and Gabriela Guzzy. Mexico City: Instituto Nacional de Arqueología e Historia.

Bachand, Bruce R. (2006) *Preclassic Excavations at Punta de Chimino, Peten, Guatemala: Investigating Social Emplacement on an Early Maya Landscape*. PhD dissertation, Department of Anthropology, University of Arizona. Ann Arbor, MI: University Microfilms.

Barrett, Jason W., and Thomas H. Guderjan (2006) An Ancient Maya Dock and Dam at Blue Creek, Rio Hondo, Belize. *Latin American Antiquity* 17: 227–39.

Barrientos, Tomás (2014) *The Royal Palace of Cancuen: The Structure of Lowland Maya Architecture and Politics at the end of the Late Classic Period*. PhD dissertation, Department of Anthropology, Vanderbilt University. Ann Arbor, MI: University Microfilms.

Barrientos, Tomás, and Arthur A. Demarest (2007) Cancuen: puerta al mundo maya. In *XX Simposio de investigaciones arqueológicas en Guatemala, 2006*, ed. Juan Pedro Laporte, Bárbara Arroyo, and Héctor Mejía, pp. 611–28. Guatemala City: Museo Nacional de Arqueología y Etnología.

—— (2012) Geografía sagrada y poder político en las ciudades Mayas del Río La Pasión: Dos Pilas, Aguateca y Cancuén. In *Ciudades Mesoamericanas*, ed. Horacio Cabezas Carcache. Guatemala City: Universidad Mesoamericana.

Barrientos Tomás, Arthur A. Demarest, Brigitte Kovacevich, Michael Callaghan, and Luís F. Luín (eds) (2002) *Proyecto Arqueológico Cancuen: informe de temporada 2002*. Guatemala City: Instituto de Arqueología e Historia de Guatemala.

Barrientos, Tomás, Arthur A. Demarest, Silvia Alvarado, Horacio Martínez, Marc Wolf, and Luís Fernando Luín (2006) Hidráulica, ecología, ideología y poder: nueva evidencia y teorías en el Sur de Petén. In *XIX Simposio de investigaciones arqueológicas en Guatemala, 2005*, ed. Juan Pedro Laporte, Bárbara Arroyo, and Héctor Mejía, pp. 291–302. Guatemala City: Museo Nacional de Arqueología y Etnología.

Barrientos Tomás, Arthur A. Demarest, Luís F. Luín, Claudia Quintanilla, and Elisa Mencos (eds) (2006) *Proyecto Arqueológico Cancuen: Informe de Temporada 2004–2005*. Guatemala City: Ministerio de Cultura y Deportes de Guatemala.

Barrios, Edy, Claudia Quintanilla, Bethany Myers, Diana Belches, Antonieta Cajas, Carlos Espigares, Orlando Moreno, Fredis Ruano, and Marc Wolf (2008) Excavaciones en El Raudal, Rio Santa Amelia, Sayaxche, El Peten. In *Proyecto Arqueológico Cancuén informe no. 9, temporada 2008*, ed. Arthur Demarest, Horacio Martínez, Mélanie Forné, Claudia Quintanilla, and Luis F. Luín, pp. 257–329. Guatemala City: Ministerio de Cultura y Deportes de Guatemala.

Berryman, Carrie Anne, and Ana Novotny (2003) Analisis osteológico. In *Proyecto Arqueologico Cancuen: temporada 2003*, ed. Arthur A. Demarest, Tomás Barrientos, Brigette Kovacevich, Michael Callaghan, Brent Woodfill, and Luís F. Luín, pp. 515–28. Guatemala City: Instituto de Antropología e Historia.

Bishop, Ronald, L., Erin L. Sears, and M. James Blackman (2005) A través del Río del Cambio. *Estudios de Cultura Maya* 26: 17–40.

Demarest, Arthur A. (2006a) *The Petexbatun Regional Archaeological Project: A Multidisciplinary Study of the Maya Collapse*. Nashville: Vanderbilt University Press.

—— (2006b) Sacred and Profane Mountains of the Pasion: Contrasting Architectual Paths to Power. In *Palaces and Power in the Americas*, ed. Jessica J. Christie and Patricia J. Sarro, pp. 117–40. Austin: University of Texas Press.

Demarest, Arthur A., and Tomás Barrientos (eds) (1999) *Proyecto Arqueológico Cancuén: informe no. 1, temporada 1999*. Guatemala City: Instituto de Antropología e Historia de Guatemala.

—— (2000) *Proyecto Arqueológico Cancuén: informe no. 2, temporada 2000*. Guatemala City: Instituto de Antropología e Historia de Guatemala.

—— (2001) *Proyecto Arqueológico Cancuén: informe no. 3, temporada 2001*. Guatemala City: Instituto de Antropología e Historia de Guatemala.

Demarest, Arthur A., and Horacio Martínez (eds) (2010) *Proyecto Arqueológico Cancuen: informe final no. 10, temporada 2010*. Guatemala City: Ministerio de Cultura y Deportes de Guatemala.

—— (2013) *Proyecto Arqueológico Cancuen, informe final temporada 2013*. Guatemala City: Ministerio de Cultura y Deportes de Guatemala.

Demarest, Arthur A., Matt O'Mansky, Claudia Wooley, Dirk Van Tuerenhout, Takeshi Inomata, Joel Palka, and Héctor Escobedo (1997) Classic Maya Defensive Systems and Warfare in the Petexbatun Region. *Ancient Mesoamerica* 8: 229-523.

Demarest, Arthur A., Tomás Barrientos, Brigitte Kovacevich, Michael Callaghan and Luís F. Luín (eds) (2003) *Proyecto Arqueológico Cancuén: informe no. 4, temporada 2002*. Guatemala City: Instituto de Antropología e Historia de Guatemala.

Demarest, Arthur A., Tomás Barrentos, Brigette Kovacevich, Michael Callaghan, Brent Woodfill, and Luís F. Luín (eds) (2004) *Proyecto Arqueológico Cancuen: informe no. 4, temporada 2003*. Guatemala City: Instituto de Antropología e Historia de Guatemala.

Demarest, Arthur A., Horacio Martínez, and Luís F. Luín (eds) (2007) *Proyecto Arqueológico Cancuén: informe no. 7, temporada 2006*. Guatemala City: Dirección General del Patrimonio Cultural y Natural.

Demarest, Arthur A., Brent Woodfill, Tomás Barrientos, Federico Fahsen, and Mirza Monterroso (2007) La ruta altiplano-tierras bajas del occidente, y el surgimiento y caída de la civilización Clásica Maya. In *XX Simposio de investigaciones arqueológicas en Guatemala, 2006*, ed. Juan Pedro Laporte, Bárbara Arroyo, and Héctor Mejía, pp. 27–44. Guatemala City: Museo Nacional de Arqueología y Etnología.

Demarest, Arthur A., Tomás Barrientos, Melanié Forné, Marc Wolf, and Ronald Bishop (2008) La nueva historia de la puerta a las Tierras Bajas: descubrimientos recientes sobre la interacción, arqueología y epigrafía de Cancuén. In *XXI Simposio de investigaciones arqueológicas en Guatemala, 2007*, ed. Juan Pedro Laporte, Bárbara Arroyo, and Héctor Mejía, pp. 515–31. Guatemala City: Museo Nacional de Arqueología y Etnología.

Demarest, Arthur A., Horacio Martínez, Méanie Forné, Claudia Quintanilla, and Luís F. Luín (eds) (2008) *Proyecto Arqueológico Cancuen: informe no. 9, temporada 2008*. Guatemala City: Ministerio de Cultura y Deportes de Guatemala.

Demarest, Arthur A., Horacio Martínez, Marc Wolf, Paola Torres, Waleska Belches, Chloé Andrieu, Luís F. Luín, Matt O'Mansky, and Claudia Quintanilla (2009) Economía interna relaciones internacionales de Cancuen y de sitios de su reinado. In *XXII Simposio de investigaciones de arqueología en Guatemala, 2008*, ed. Juan Pedro Laporte, Bárbara Arroyo, and Héctor E. Mejía, pp. 655–74. Guatemala City: Museo Nacional de Arqueología y Etnología.

Demarest, Arthur A., Horacio Martínez, Paola Torres, and Claudia Quantanilla (eds) (2011) *Proyecto Arqueológico Cancuen: informe final no. 11, temporada 2011*. Guatemala City: Ministerio de Cultura y Deportes de Guatemala.

Dillon, Brian (1977) *Salinas de los Nueve Cerros, Guatemala*. Socorro, NM: Ballena Press.

Fahsen, Federico, and Tomás Barrientos (2006) Los monumentos de Taj Chan Ahk and Kan Maax. In *Proyecto Arqueológico Cancuen: informe de temporada 2004–2005*, ed. Tomás Barrientos, Arthur Demarest, Luís F. Luín, Claudia Quintanilla, and Elisa Mencos, pp. 35–56. Guatemala City: Ministerio de Cultura y Deportes de Guatemala.

Fahsen, Federico, and Sarah E. Jackson (2001) El panel de Cancuen: nuevos datos e interpretaciones sobre la dinastía de Cancuen en el periodo Clásico. In *Proyecto Arqueológico Cancuen: informe temporada 2001*, ed. Arthur Demarest and Tomas Barrientos, pp. 21–32. Guatemala City: Ministero de Culturo y Deportes de Guatemala.

Fahsen, Federico, Arthur A. Demarest, and Luís F. Luín (2003) Sesenta años de historia en la escalinata jeroglífica de Cancuen. In *XVI Simposio de investigaciones arqueologicas en Guatemala 2002*, ed. Juan Pedro Laporte, Ana Claudia Suasnavar, and Bárbara Arroyo, pp. 703–13. Guatemala City: Museo Nacional de Arqueología y Etnología de Guatemala.

Fernandez Aguilar, Carlos Enrique (2010) Símbolos de poder: análisis simbólico-cognitivo de los estucos de la estructura M7-1 de Cancuen. Licenciatura thesis, Universidad del Valle, Guatemala City.

Forné, Mélanie, and Paola Torres (2010) Análisis cerámico. In *Proyecto Arqueológico Cancuén informe final no. 10, temporada 2010*, ed. Arthur Demarest and Horacio Martínez, pp. 113–63. Guatemala City: Ministerio de Cultura y Deportes de Guatemala.

Forné, Mélanie, Silvia Alvarado, Paola Torres, and Diana Belches (2008) Análisis cerámico de Cancuén y su región: perspectivas cronológicas y culturales. In *Proyecto Arqueológico Cancuen: informe final no. 9, temporada 2008*, ed. Arthur A. Demarest, Horacio Martínez, Melanie Forné, Claudia Quintanilla, and Luís F. Luín, pp. 139–85. Guatemala City: Ministerio de Cultura y Deportes de Guatemala.

Forné, Mélanie, Arthur A. Demarest, Horacio Martínez, Paola Torres, Silvia Alvarado, and Claudia Arriaza (2009) Intercambio y afiliación cultural en Cancuén: la complejidad cultural en las vísperas del colapso. In *XXII Simposio de investigaciones arqueológicas en Guatemala, 2008*, ed. Juan Pedro Laporte, Bárbara Arroyo, and Héctor E. Mejía, pp. 1017–36. Guatemala City: Museo Nacional de Arqueología y Etnología.

Forné, Mélanie, Ronald L. Bishop, Arthur A. Demarest, M. James Blackman, and Erin L. Sears (2010) Gris Fino, Naranja Fino: presencia temprana y fuentes de producción, el caso de Cancuen. In *XXIII Simposio de investigaciones arqueológicas en Guatemala, 2009*, ed. Bárbara Arroyo, Lorena Paiz Aragón, Adriana Linares Palma, and Ana Lucia Arroyave, pp. 1163–82. Guatemala City: Museo Nacional de Arqueología y Etnología.

Forné, Mélanie, Chloé Andrieu, Arthur A. Demarest, Paola Torres, Claudia Quintanilla, Ronald L. Bishop, and Olaf Jaime-Riverón (2013) Crisis y cambios en el Clásico Tardío: los retos económicos de una ciudad entre las Tierras Altas y las Tierras Bajas mayas. In *Millenary Maya Societies: Past Crises and Resilience*, ed. Charlotte Arnauld, pp. 49–61: www.mesoweb.com/publications/MMS/3_Forne_etal.pdf.

Fox, John W. (1996) Playing with Power: Ballcourts and Political Ritual in Southern Mesoamerica. *Current Anthropology* 37: 483–509.

Jackson, Sarah (2002) Operación 25A: investigaciones en la zona este del Grupo M9. In *Proyecto Arqueológico Cancuen: informe no. 3, temporada 2001*, ed. Arthur A. Demarest and Tomás Barrientos, pp. 129–52. Guatemala City: Instituto de Antropología e Historia de Guatemala.

—— (2003) Operaciones 25A y 25E: excavaciones en M9-1 y sus patios aledaños. In *Proyecto Arqueológico Cancuén: informe temporada 2002*, ed. Arthur A. Demarest, Tomás Barrientos, Brigette Kovacevich, Michael Callaghan, and Luís F. Luín, pp. 165–200. Guatemala City: Instituto de Antropología e Historia de Guatemala.

Martin, Simon, and Nikolai Grube (1994) Evidence for Macro-Political Organization amongst Classic Maya Lowland States. Available at www.mesoweb.com/articles/martin/macro-politics.pdf.

—— (2008) *The Chronicle of the Maya Kings and Queens: Deciphering the Dynasties of the Ancient Maya*. 2nd ed., London: Thames & Hudson.

McAnany, Patricia C. (2012) Artisans, Ikatz, and Starcraft: Provisioning Classic Maya Royal Courts. In *Merchants, Markets, and Exchange in the Pre-Columbian World*, ed. Kenneth G. Hirth and Joanne Pillsbury. Washington, DC: Dumbarton Oaks.

McKillop, Heather I. (1989) Development of Coastal Maya Trade: Data, Models, and Issues. In *Coastal Maya Trade*, ed. Heather I. McKillop and Paul Healy, pp. 1–18. Peterborough, Ontario: Trent University Press.

—— (1996) Ancient Maya Trading Ports and the Integration of Long Distance and Regional Economies: Wild Cane Cay in South Coastal Belize. *Ancient Mesoamerica* 7: 49–62.

Sears, E. L., Ron L. Bishop, and M. J. Blackman (2005) Las figurillas de Cancuen: el surgimiento de una perspectiva regional. In *XVIII Simposio de investigaciones arqueológicas en Guatemala*, ed. Juan Pedro Laporte, Bárbara Arroyo, and Héctor E. Mejía, pp. 771–80. Guatemala City: Museo Nacional de Arqueología y Etnografía.

Torres, Paola (2011) Los juegos de pelota como evidencia de un sitio fronterizo: el caso de Cancuen. Licenciatura thesis, Universidad de San Carlos de Guatemala, Guatemala City.

Tourtellot, Gair, III, Jeremy A. Sabloff, and Robert Sharick (1978) *Excavations at Seibal: A Reconnaissance of Cancuen.* Cambridge, MA: Peabody Museum of Archaeology and Ethnology.

Willey, Gordon R. (1973) *The Altar de Sacrificios Excavations: General Summary and Conclusions.* Cambridge, MA: Peabody Museum of Archaeology and Ethnography.

—— (1990) General Summary and Conclusions. In *Excavations at Seibal, Department of Peten, Guatemala,* ed. Gordon R. Willey. Cambridge, MA: Peabody Museum of Archaeology and Ethnography.

Woodfill, Brent (2010) *Ritual and Trade in the Pasión-Verapaz Region, Guatemala.* Nashville: Vanderbilt University Press.

Woodfill, Brent, and Chloé Andrieu (2012) Tikal's Early Classic Domination of the Great Western Trade Route: Ceramic, Lithic, and Iconographic Evidence. *Ancient Mesoamerica* 23: 189–209.

Woodfill, Brent, Mirza Monterroso, Erin Sears, Donaldo Castillo, and José Luis Garrido (2011) Proyecto Salinas de Nueve Cerros: Resultados de la Primera Temporada de Campo. In *XXIV Simposio de investigaciones arqueológicas en Guatemala 2010,* ed. Bárbara Arroyo, Lorena Paiz Aragón, Adriana Linares Palma, and Ana Lucia Arroyave, pp. 135–48. Guatemala City: Museo Nacional de Arqueología y Etnología.

Wooley, Claudia, and Lori Wright (1990) Operación DP7: investigaciones en el Grupo L4-4. In *Proyecto Arqueológico Regional Petexbatun: informe preliminar no. 2, segunda temporada,* ed. Arthur A. Demarest and Stephen Houston. Guatemala City: Instituto de Antropología e Historia.

9
REAL/FICTIVE LORDS/VESSELS
A list of MARI lords on the newly discovered Andrews Coffee Mug

Markus Eberl

Among E. Wyllys Andrews V's private collection of "Mesoamerican" artifacts is a Maya ceramic vessel with a hieroglyphic inscription. Although its recent provenance is well known – it was presented to him during his retirement party in 2009 – its archaeological context remains obscure. Here I discuss the vessel and its glyphic text. The ceramic vessel is consistent with the Dynastic Vase tradition and celebrates the history of the Middle American Research Institute (MARI) lords. Comparable king lists on other Dynastic Vases are of ambiguous historical value because they link attested late rulers with obscure early rulers who rarely appear in other sources. In the case of the Andrews Coffee Mug, I discuss why William Gates is missing and what this implies for MARI's origins. By situating the Dynastic Vases in their social and cultural context, I argue that text structure and content create a discourse in which unverifiable propositions attain the quality of unquestionable truth.

> It was as if God had decided to put to the test every capacity for surprise and was keeping the inhabitants of Macondo in a permanent alteration between excitement and disappointment, doubt and revelation, to such an extreme that no one knew for certain where the limits of reality lay.
> (Gabriel García Márquez, *One Hundred Years of Solitude*, 1967)

A ceramic cylindrical vessel with a long hieroglyphic inscription has recently been donated to E. Wyllys Andrews V's private collection in New Orleans (Figure 9.1). Nicknamed the "Andrews Coffee Mug," the vessel and its glyphic text are complete and very well preserved. While its archaeological provenance is unknown, the style of the mug and its textual content provide, as the following detailed analysis shows, sufficient information to place it in the Dynastic Vase tradition.[1] Its text elucidates the history of Middle American Research Institute (MARI) lords. By omitting William Gates, it offers a peculiar perspective into the origins of the MARI.

224 Markus Eberl

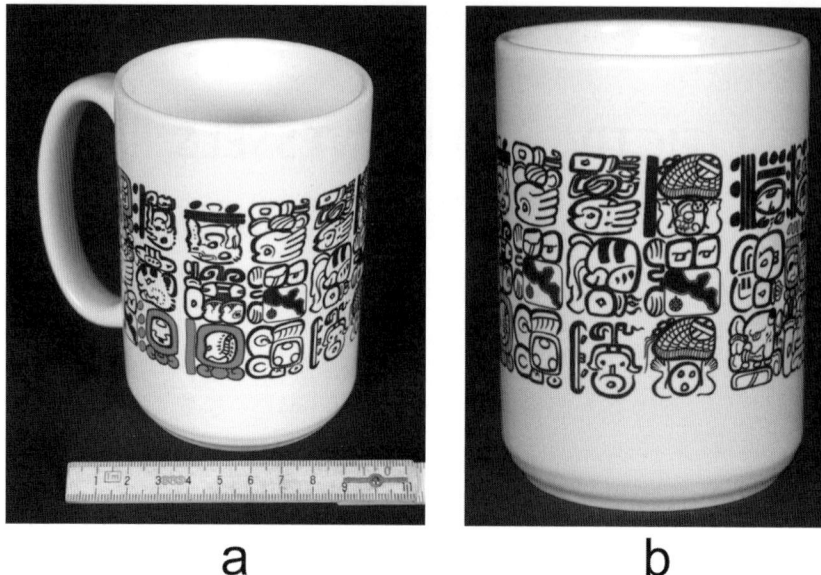

FIGURE 9.1 Photos of the Andrews Coffee Mug: (a) side view showing handle and scale (in centimeters); (b) front view (photos by the author)

Dynastic Vases are ceramic vessels from the northern Maya lowlands with long hieroglyphic texts. They list the divine rulers of the snake dynasty, whose Late Classic capital was at Calakmul (see Figure 1.1). The different Dynastic Vases mention the same kings and coincide in their accession dates (Martin 1997). These kings are rarely attested on carved monuments and other hieroglyphic texts, though, and most of them are historically obscure. Thus, the detailed information on Dynastic Vases is of debatable historical value. Do they provide a king's history or his story?

Codex-style dynastic vases

The Dynastic Vases are a group of about a dozen ceramic vessels with painted hieroglyphic texts (Figure 9.2; Martin 1997; Robicsek and Hales 1981: 97–104). The vessels belong to the Late Classic Zacatel (or Zacatal) Cream tradition and are cylinders, a form that becomes prominent during the eighth century AD (Hansen et al. 1991; Reents and Bishop 1987). None of the known Dynastic Vases comes from controlled excavations. Their forms and styles are, however, consistent with vessels from the central and north-central Maya lowlands.

Red and black bands along the rim and the bottom of the cylinders frame the hieroglyphic texts that cover the entire vessel exterior. Between 24 and 88 hieroglyphs are painted on a cream background in the codex-style tradition (Reents-Budet 1994: 153–5). All hieroglyphs are black except for the Tzolk'iin coefficient and its cartouche, whose interiors are painted red. The red Tzolk'iin dates identify the beginning of each sentence like punctuation marks. The

Real/fictive lords/vessels **225**

FIGURE 9.2 Two vessels of the Dynastic Vase tradition: (a) codex-style vessel K1372; (b) codex-style vessel K2094 (© Justin Kerr; www.mayavase.com)

hieroglyphic texts narrate royal accession (Figure 9.3). Individual phrases begin with a Calendar Round followed by an accession verb and the names and titles of the king. Since Calendar Rounds repeat themselves every 52 years, it is unclear when individuals became rulers. Only the linear reading structure suggests that the accessions line up chronologically. Emblem glyphs at the end of most phrases designate individuals as *k'uhul kaan ajaw*, "divine snake lord." Many of their names include Yuknoom, which is common among snake rulers (Martin and Grube 2008: 100–15; see, for example, glyph blocks H5 [10th king], I2b [12th king], I3b [13th king], J4 [14th king], and K4 [18th king] in Figure 9.3; for naming practices of Maya rulers, see Colas 2003, 2004; Eberl and Graña-Behrens 2004). The *kaloomte'* title attests to the elevated status of some snake lords as supreme rulers (e.g., glyph blocks A4 and N1 on K6751; Figure 9.3). Dynastic Vases contain between five and 19 accessions. They are the painted equivalents of ruler lists on carved monuments. Examples for the latter are the Hieroglyphic Stairway at Copan, the Temple of the Cross Tablet at Palenque, and Lintels 60, 49, 37, and 35 at Yaxchilan.

Vessel K6751 has the lengthiest text, with 88 glyphs, and lists the accession of 19 kings (Figure 9.3). Carved inscriptions attest to some of them, or at least to rulers with the same name (Table 9.1). Yuknoom Yich'aak K'ahk', the 13th king on K6751, was famously defeated at the end of the seventh century AD by Tikal (Martin and Grube 2008: 110–11; Schele and Freidel 1990: 195–212). The 15th king on K6751 bears the same name – Tajoom Uk'ab K'ahk' – as a snake-dynasty king who acceded

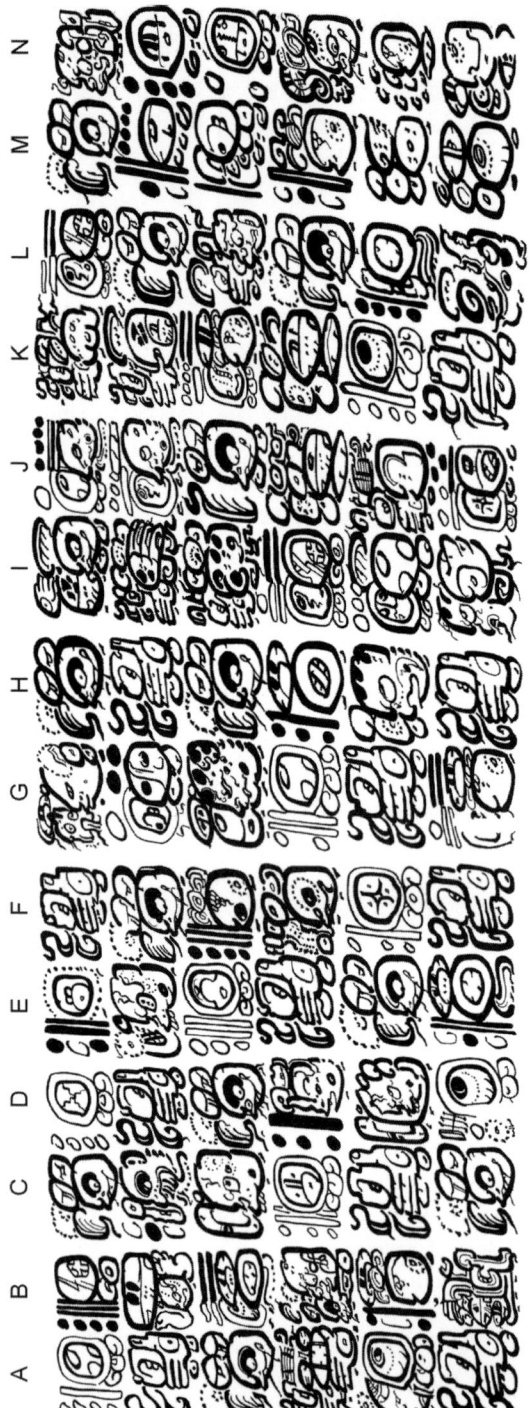

FIGURE 9.3 Hieroglyphic text of codex-style vessel K6751 (rollout drawing by the author)

to office in AD 622 and who died eight years later (Martin and Grube 2008: 106). Sky Witness, whose inscriptions at Caracol and Palenque mention during the second half of the sixth century AD, is listed as the 17th king on K6751 (ibid.: 104). The 18th king on K6751 is Yuknoom Ti' Chan. A snake king with the same name supervises a Caracol king in AD 619 (ibid.: 106). The 19th and last king on K6751 is Scroll Serpent. According to monumental inscriptions he took office in AD 579, and he is attested until AD 611 (ibid.: 105–6).

Five of the 19 kings on vessel K6751 – the 13th, 15th, 17th, 18th, and 19th – are mentioned on monumental inscriptions and correspond to snake kings who ruled during the sixth and seventh centuries. Their internal order on K6751, however, is garbled, and their accession dates never match the ones on monumental inscriptions (Table 9.1). Most puzzling is the absence of prominent snake lords, and in particular of Yuknoom Ch'een the Great, who ruled from AD 636 to 686 (Martin and Grube 2008: 108–9). Since ceramic type, vessel form, and decoration date them to the eighth century, the Dynastic Vases were contemporaneous with the Late Classic carved inscriptions. Different accession dates, names, and order of kings can therefore not be attributed to temporal differences among painted and carved sources.

Snake-dynasty kings appear at Calakmul for the first time during the sixth century AD (Martin 2005). Earlier monuments are rare at the site, and none contain the snake emblem glyph. The occurrence of the snake emblem in Early Classic contexts outside of Calakmul suggests that the snake dynasty moved to Calakmul at the beginning of the Late Classic. Their Preclassic capital was possibly El Mirador (Hansen and Guenther 2005), and Dzibanche may have served as the Early Classic seat (Martin 2005).

The early history of the snake dynasty is fraught with mythological overtones. Skylifter, the first king of the Dynastic Vase tradition (see Figure 9.6b; glyph block B2 in Figure 9.3), appears with his full-figure glyph on codex-style vessel K4117 (Martin 1997: 857). In the accompanying scene, warriors and priests confront each other in a watery environment (Grube 2004; see also Robicsek and Hales 1981: 71–5, 80–82). The warriors are armed, wear animal headdresses, and have faces painted with

TABLE 9.1 Comparison of snake kings on Dynastic Vases (here K6751, the longest king list) and on carved monuments

Snake king[a]	K6751	Accession date	
		K6751	Carved monuments
Sky Witness	17th king	**10 Kaban 10 Pop**	? (before AD 561)
Scroll Serpent	19th king	**9 Imix 9 Yaxk'iin**	9.7.5.14.17 **11 Kaban 10 Ch'en** (AD 579)
Yuknoom Ti' Chan	18th king	**9 Eb 10 Keh**	? (before AD 619)
Tajoom Uk'ab K'ahk'	15th king	**3 Ak'bal 1? Tzek**	9.9.9.0.5 **11 Chikchan 3 Wo** (AD 622)
Yuknoom Yich'aak K'ahk'	13th king	**8 Kaban 5 Xul**	9.12.13.17.7 **6 Manik' 5 Sip** (AD 686)

Sources: Martin 1997 for K6751 and Martin and Grube 2008: 100–115 for carved monuments.
Note: [a] Snake kings in chronological order according to carved monuments.

S-shaped black lines. The priests either gesture towards the warriors or hold a bundle capped by feathers and a *Spondylus* shell. Water symbols or wavy lines indicate that both groups are standing in a watery environment. The accompanying Calendar Rounds include calendrically impossible combinations such as 9 Ajaw 7 Pop that reinforce the mythological character of these scenes. The glyph for *ch'ak* ("to axe") that often follows identifies the scene as a conflict. The dueling warriors and priests represent the primordial tension between chaos and wilderness versus civilized, urban, and community-oriented life (see also Taube 2003: 479–80). Skylifter, the founding father of the snake dynasty, was by Late Classic times a mythological king associated with this primordial conflict (see Grube 2004 [Foliated Ajaw] and Stuart 2007 for comparable cases). While little is known about his successors, Skylifter's case suggests that the early Dynastic Vase rulers straddle myth and history.[2]

Emic concepts of the past

Similar to modern study guides such as CliffsNotes or SparkNotes, the king lists are reduced to a minimum: dates, accessions, and the names and titles of rulers. The Dynastic Vases seem to provide historical facts; yet, a second look exposes many rulers as obscure or even mythological. Should these king lists be dismissed as fictitious?

Epigraphers have debated the reliability of Maya hieroglyphic texts ever since – starting with Tatiana Proskouriakoff (1960), Heinrich Berlin (1958, 1959), and other scholars – they discovered that the texts contain historical information (Coe 1992: 167–84). In *Mesoamerican Writing Systems*, Joyce Marcus (1992a) discusses native texts as history, myth, and propaganda. She defines histories as narratives of the immediate past, myth as narratives of remote events (especially of creation), and propaganda as narratives intended to influence attitudes towards some cause or position (Marcus 1992a: 8–12). In her view, history, myth, and propaganda are not distinguishable in Mesoamerican writing. By further arguing that rulers manipulated events and rewrote history (ibid.: 15–16, 435–45; 1992b: 235–7), she questions the reliability of Maya hieroglyphic texts – a position that many Maya epigraphers reject (e.g., Houston 1994; Stuart 1994; Martin and Grube 2008: 127, 192–3). Together with archaeologists and physical anthropologists, they have, for example, resolved the dilemma surrounding Palenque king K'inich Janaab Pakal I. According to hieroglyphic texts the king died at age 81, but the initial assessment of his skeleton pointed to a much younger man (Marcus 1992b: 235–7). A recent re-examination of Janaab Pakal's physical remains supports the hieroglyphic information (Tiesler and Cucina 2006). Investigations confirmed hieroglyphic texts on the ages of Palenque and Yaxchilan rulers (Hernández and Márquez 2006) and the early history of Copan (Sharer 1999; Sharer *et al.* 1999). Nonetheless, difficulties remain, as in the case of Yax Nuun Ahiin I of Tikal (Wright 2005).

Ancient societies demonstrate awareness of their own pasts by way of social or collective memory (Assmann 1992; Connerton 1989; Halbwachs 1992). So-called primitive societies are often assumed to separate the past clearly from the present and to allow myths to absorb historical events (Errington 1974; McDowell 1985; McKinley 1979; Middleton 1967; Morphy and Morphy 1984; Turner 1988). For example,

Claude Lévi-Strauss (1966: 233–4) distinguishes cold from hot societies. While cold societies annul the possible effects of historical factors on their equilibrium, hot societies internalize the historical process and make it the engine of their development. In his perspective, myth and history constitute a dichotomy and fundamentally different ways of dealing with events. Nonetheless, societies form their own consciousness of past and present (Munn 1992: 112). They divide myth from history not to suppress history but to establish historical awareness (Turner 1988: 235–6).

Instead of classifying Maya hieroglyphic texts *a priori* as history, myth, or propaganda, the decipherment of Maya writing has advanced enough for a contextual analysis (Coe 1992). Several factors need to be taken into account: the inherent plausibility, the position in time and space of the author, the knowledge and cultural status of the author, and the genre of the account (Barber and Berdan 1998: 160–68). In the politically fragmented Classic Maya landscape, parallel, complementary, and competing accounts of the same event exist. For example, Copan Altar Q and Quirigua Zoomorph P provide two perspectives on how K'inich Yax K'uk' Mo' arrived at Copan and founded the royal dynasty there (Stuart 2004). By comparing accounts such as these, the inherent plausibility of a specific text can be judged and a composite history can be written (Houston 1993: 96). At the same time, the decipherment of Maya writing points to the emic understanding of history. "The essential purpose of most monumental texts of Classic times was not simply to record royal life history," observes David Stuart, "but rather to record the activities surrounding the placement, creation, and activation of ritual things and spaces" (Stuart 1998: 375; see also Grube 2006: 148). Yaxchilan Lintels 24 through 26 emphasize ritual at the expense of history in the Western sense:

> Although the Calendar Round dates of Lintels 24–26 place the three events pictured at widely spaced moments in time, they seem to commemorate successive stages of three different instances of the same ritual, since they appear to have a narrative structure, reading from left to right.
> (Josserand 2007: 303)

The king lists on Dynastic Vases fit into the genre of historical texts even though they contain both mythological and historical kings. The Western notion of history as an objective and verifiable study of the past is difficult to apply to them. The king lists encourage, instead, the study of how the ancient Maya perceived history.

The Andrews Coffee Mug

The painted vessel in E. Wyllys Andrews V's private collection is 11.7 centimeters high and has a maximum diameter of 8.4 centimeters. The interior volume of 15 US fluid ounces or 443.6 milliliters is in the normal range of containers used in complex societies to imbibe stimulating liquids. Its cylindrical form is typical for eighth-century or Tepeu 2-period Maya vessels. It has an appliquéd handle that – while attested among jars and bowls – has not been observed on cylinders. The vertical placement of the handle recalls modern coffee mugs, and it is for this reason that the vessel became known as the Andrews Coffee Mug.

The hieroglyphic text is painted in black with red accents on a creamy white background. The excellent preservation of the mug makes it impossible to examine the paste directly. No coarse temper juts out from the smooth surface. The Andrews Coffee Mug shares these feature with Late Classic Zacatel Cream polychrome vessels.

Hieroglyphic text

The hieroglyphic text consists of 30 glyph blocks that are arranged in five double columns of six glyph blocks (Figure 9.4). The hieroglyphs are executed in a calligraphically elaborate style in which heavy outlines counterbalance finely drawn details. Individual hieroglyphs tend to lean to the right. The artist often took liberties in the representation of hieroglyphs. The glyph for "red," for example, is indistinguishable from the glyph for "green-blue" (Figure 9.4, glyph block B2). The syllable **jo** replaces the round interior detail of the hand in glyph block I2, while **K'AN** is infixed into **K'IIN** in glyph block J3. The *tuun* glyph is missing in the distance number in glyph blocks G1 to H1. The text on the Andrews Coffee Mug shares these stylistic characteristics with texts belonging to the codex-style tradition (compare Figures 9.2 and 9.4).

Chronology

Among the 30 glyph blocks are five Calendar Round dates that divide the text into five phrases. The artist highlighted Tzolk'iin glyphs with a red background, similar to the convention found on other Dynastic Vases. Further chronological information is absent for the first two Calendar Rounds, while distance numbers link the last three dates. The reference to the end of the thirteenth Baktun in the last phrase (see discussion below) allows placing the last three Calendar Rounds in absolute time. The linear discourse of the text strongly suggests that the first two Calendar Rounds precede the later ones. They are therefore placed at the nearest corresponding Long Count position (see Table 9.2 for the reconstructed chronology).

Tying the white headband

A careful examination of the glyph that follows the first three Calendar Rounds (glyph blocks A2, D1, and E1) shows that – disregarding the stylistic variation – it is identical. It reads in all three cases **SAK:HUUN:K'AL**. Similar accession statements appear at Palenque, where rulers take the royal headband and tie it to their heads at accession (e.g., on the Palace Tablet; Schele and Miller 1983: 3–21, 36–40). Substitution patterns clarify that the intended reading order was not ★*sak huun(al) k'al* but *k'al sak huun(al)* – "he or she ties the white paper/headband." Accession rituals included several components, such as the taking of the K'awiil scepter, the tying of the crown-like headband, the adoption of a royal name, and the seating on a throne (Eberl and Graña-Behrens 2004: 102–4). Most inscriptions highlight only one

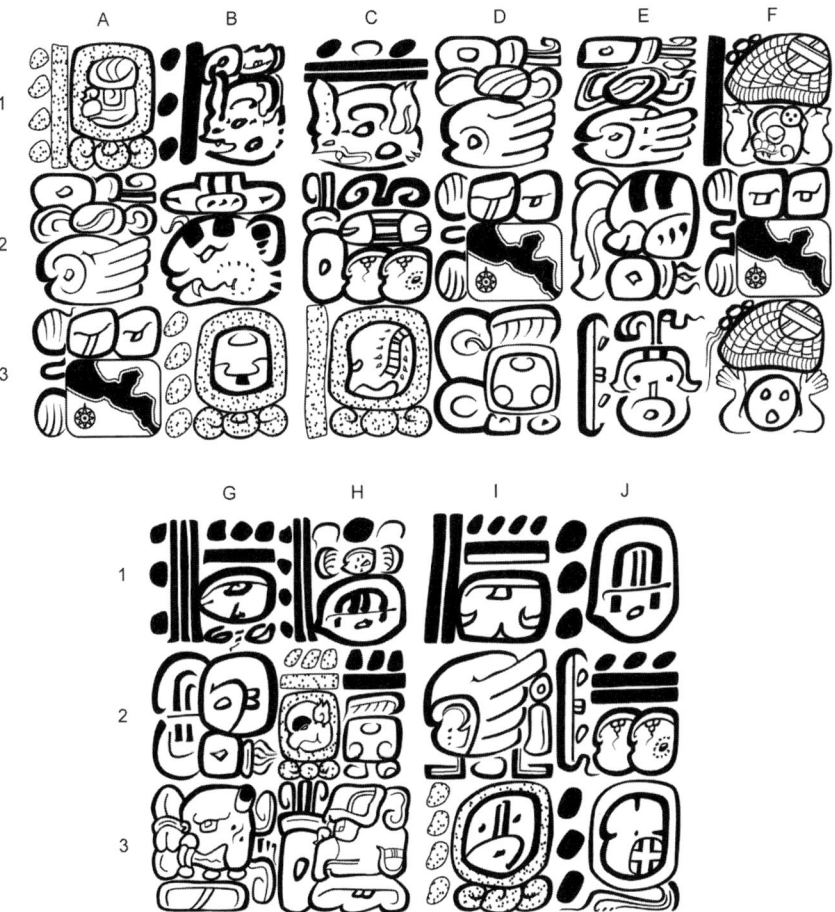

FIGURE 9.4 Rollout drawing of the hieroglyphic text of the Andrews Coffee Mug (stippling indicates areas painted red in the original; drawing by the author)

TABLE 9.2 Chronology of the glyphic text on the Andrews Coffee Mug

	Long Count	Calendar Round	Gregorian date[a]	Comment[b]
1	[12.15.12.4.15]	9 Men 8 Sotz'	July 1, AD 1926	Reconstructed LC
2	[12.16.9.9 4]	4 K'an 12 Sotz'	July 1, AD 1943	Reconstructed LC
3	[12.18.1.17.12] + 1.14.8.18	5 Eb 0 Tzek	July 1, AD 1975	Distance Number
4	[12.19.16.8.10] + 3.9.10	8 Ok 8 Tzek	June 30, AD 2009	Distance Number
5	13.[0.0.0.0]	4 Ajaw 3 K'ank'iin	Dec. 21, AD 2012	End of Baktun 13

Notes: [a] The 584,283 correlation was used to calculate the Gregorian equivalents.
[b] LC stands for Long Count.

component that is specific for a royal dynasty. The "grasping of K'awiil," for example, is typical for Calakmul kings, the "tying of the headband" and the "seating on a throne" for Palenque kings, the "tying into rulership" for Piedras Negras, the "sitting down" for early Yaxchilan kings. Subordinate rulers imitate the accession customs of their superiors. The adoption of "grasping K'awiil" at accession reflects to a certain degree the waxing and waning of the clout of Calakmul in the southern lowlands.

The Dynastic Vases list snake-dynasty rulers, and their texts correspondingly refer to their accession as *ch'am-[a]w k'awiil* – "he is K'awiil-grasping" or, more freely, "he grasps the K'awiil-scepter" (e.g., glyph block A2 in Figure 9.3; Lacadena 2000). The use of *k'al sak huun(al)*, which is common at Palenque, on the Andrews Coffee Mug is therefore surprising. E. Wyllys Andrews V (1974) has long ago revealed, however, that the southwestern lowlands were linked to the northern lowlands. David Stuart (1984) showed that the sajal title occurs in the Usumacinta area and in the northwestern Maya lowlands.

The MARI emblem

Another repetitive glyph can be found in glyph blocks A3, D2, and F2. It consists of three glyphs – **ma.?.AJAW** – that replicate the format of a Classic Maya emblem glyph (see Graña-Behrens 2006: 105–7; Stuart and Houston 1994: 3–7). The superfixed *Ajaw* indicates a high-ranking noble. The variable main element is an as of now undeciphered glyph that resembles the logo of the Middle American Research Institute at Tulane University (Figure 9.5), commonly abbreviated as MARI. The *ma* prefix seems to be a phonetic complement for the initial syllable. It should be noted that the *k'uhul* or "divine" prefix as the third element of an emblem glyph is absent. In the hierarchy of Maya rulers, an *ajaw*, "lord," had a lower standing than a *k'uhul ajaw*, or "divine lord." Yet, some hieroglyphic texts omit the *k'uhul* component for divine kings. Among these are snake kings (e.g., glyph blocks J3 and I1 in Figure 9.3) and the MARI lords.[3]

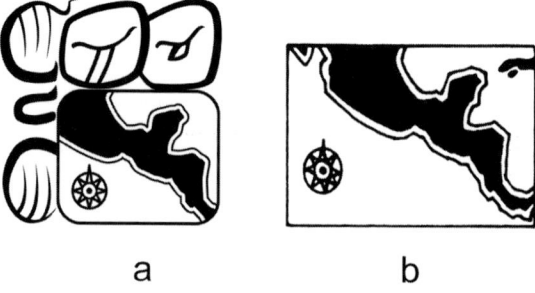

a   b

FIGURE 9.5 (a) emblem (glyph block A3 on the Andrews Coffee Mug) compared to (b) the logo of the Middle American Research Institute at Tulane University (after Bricker 1986: iii)

Phrase 1: Chak Bahlam ties the white headband

The first phrase (glyph blocks A1–A3) begins with the Calendar Round 9 Men 8 Sotz', which presumably corresponds to July 1, AD 1926. The following glyph block A2 is the accession statement *k'al sak huun(al)*, the binding of the white headband. The subject of the phrase is named in glyph block B2 as *chak bahlam*, "red jaguar," followed by the MARI emblem in glyph block A3. The chronological context suggests that this represents a person from the early days of the Middle American Research Institute.

In 1951, Swiss conservationist and photographer Gertrude Duby founded the non-governmental organization Na Bolom together with the Danish archaeologist and MARI director Frans Blom. They bought a house in San Cristobal de Las Casas:

> We wanted to give the house a name and then remembered Frans' first visit with the Lacandones in which they transformed his name to "Balum" which sounds similar to "Jaguar." In Tzotzil, the Maya language of the highlands, "Blom" converts to "Bolom" which practically sounds like Frans' last name. It was from this that we decided to name the house "Na Bolom" which means "the house of the jaguar."
>
> (Duby 2009)

Therefore, it seems prudent to interpret glyph block B2 as Frans Blom's name. **BAHLAM** refers to "Blom," leaving the *chak* ("red") prefix. Since Frans and related names originated as a pejorative term for "Frenchman" (Long 1883: 156), the scribe may have intended to identify Frans Blom as a man from the east or the rising sun, and hence "red." Simon Martin (1997: 853) pointed out that some Dynastic Vases conflate *yax*, "blue/green, first," with *chak*, "red." Alternatively, the intended reading could be *yax bahlam*, "first Blom," and refer to Frans Blom as the founder of the MARI dynasty. The Andrews Coffee Mug bypasses William E. Gates, who led the Department of Middle American Research before Frans Blom replaced him (Lowe 1954). Below, I return to this omission and the origins of the MARI.

Phrase 2: Sak Wokoop accedes

The text continues in glyph block B3 with the Calendar Round 4 K'an 12 Sotz', which likely corresponds to July 1, AD 1943, 17 years after the accession of Chak Bahlam. The "binding of the white headband" in glyph block D1 identifies the following phrase as another accession of a MARI ruler whose emblem is given in glyph block D2. The name of the ruler is found in glyph block C2: **SAK. wo:ko:pi**, for *Sak Wokoop*, "White Wokoop." The second part of the name is easily explained as the phonetic spelling of Bob Wauchope's last name. *Sak* means "white" but also "resplendent." It represents "Robert," a personal name that translates as "fame brilliant" (Attwater 1939: 84).

Phrase 3: accession of E. Wyllys Andrews V

In glyph block C3, the text moves 32 years ahead, to 5 Eb 0 Tzek (the latter is literally written as *chum kasew*, "the seating of Kasew" – the Ch'olan spelling for Haab month Tzek). The distance numbers that link phrases 3, 4, and 5 firmly date the third Calendar Round to 12.18.1.17.12, or July 1, AD 1975. Glyph block E1 repeats the accession statement *k'al sak huun(al)*, or the binding of the white headband. The subject follows in glyph blocks F1 through F3. Glyph block F1 reads **V.KOHAW**°"**Cross**":"**Lifter**"°**e**. Its five glyphs start with the number 5 and continue with a toad that lifts a helmet (*kohaw*) with an infixed cross. The raising of the sky – separating heavens and earth – was an act of creation and not surprisingly attributed to founding fathers such as Skylifter of the snake dynasty (Figure 9.6b). On the Andrews Coffee Mug, though, the *e*-toad lifts a helmet. The cross that is infixed into the helmet resembles the central element found in the sky glyph (T561c in Thompson's glyph catalog) and subtly recalls the "lifting of the sky." At the same time, the diagonal cross in the helmet is the St Andrews cross and invites the interpretion of a logogram for **ANDREWS**. The helmet and the lifting reflect Wyllys, which means "son of will-helmet" (Long 1883: 170–71). Together with the prefixed number 5, glyph block F1 spells "E. Wyllys Andrews V."

The following glyph block E2 is **yo.(P)AAT:ti**, for *yopaat*, "lightning god," a title reserved for high-ranking elites. The penis as main sign of this title has been linked to the power and fertility of its carrier. Yet, the epigraphic debate is still in its infancy, and the alternative interpretation of **(P)AAT:ti** as a female first name remains equally plausible. The MARI emblem follows in glyph block F2. The last glyphs of this phrase provide a parentage statement. Glyph block E3 contains the "son of father" glyph that possibly reads *u mihin*. Glyph block F3 is a stylistic variant of "E. Wyllys Andrews" without a prefixed number and likely refers to a male ancestor.

Phrase 4: untying the headband

The fourth phrase occupies the fourth double column (glyph blocks G1–H3). The distance number 1.14.8.18 links E. Wyllys Andrews V's accession to the Calendar

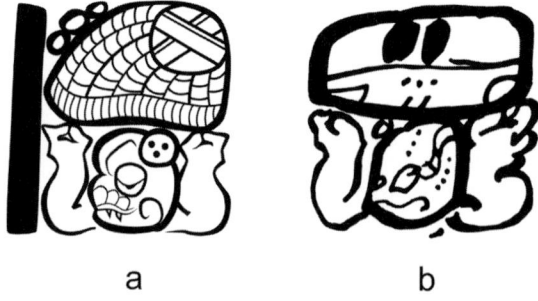

a   b

FIGURE 9.6 (a) E. Wyllys Andrews V's name (glyph block F1 on the Andrews Coffee Mug); (b) Skylifter's name from Dynastic Vase K6751 (glyph block B2; drawings by the author)

Round 8 Ok 8 Tzek (glyph H2), which corresponds to 12.19.16.8.10, or June 30, AD 2009. The glyph for Tuun is missing in the distance number; the 14 Tuun are instead prefixed to the K'atun glyph in glyph block H1. Glyph block G3 records **ja:ma:li.ya**, for *jam(a)l-iiy*, which possibly means "it was opened," followed by **SAK.HUUN:na**, *sak huuna[l]*, "the white headband," in glyph block H3. The opening of the headband refers on the Palace Tablet of Palenque to a ritual in which the ruler surrenders power (Schele et al. 1990). E. Wyllys Andrews V's reign lasted no less than 12,418 days, or 34 vague years, or 47.7615 Tzolk'iin cycles, or 21.2636 Venus cycles. These numbers will upon closer examination turn out to be contrived (Lounsbury 1976) and reveal numerological and astronomical secrets. Andrews's reign compares favorably with approximately seventeen years for Chak Bahlam and 32 years for Sak Wokoop.

Phrase 5: the end is near

The last double column contains the final phrase (glyph blocks I1–J3). It begins with the distance number 3.9.10 that links the preceding Calendar Round 8 Ok 8 Tzek to 4 Ajaw 3 K'ank'iin. Glyph blocks I2 and J2 read: **TZUTZ°jo:ma u.XIII. PIK**, or *tzu[h]tz[a]joom-Ø u[y] uxlajun pik* – "it will be finished the thirteenth bundle (or Baktun)." 4 Ajaw 3 K'ank'iin marks the end of the thirteenth Baktun on December 21, AD 2012. In contrast to the popular excitement about 2012, very few Maya inscriptions actually mention 13.0.0.0.0 4 Ajaw 3 K'ank'iin. The best-known examples are Tortuguero Monument 6 and Block 5 from Hieroglyphic Stairway 2 at La Corona (Eberl and Prager 2005; Gronemeyer and MacLeod 2010: 7–8). The Haab month (glyph block J3) is spelled **K'AN°K'IIN**, or *K'ank'iin*, the Yucatec Maya name for the Classic Ch'olan month *Uniiw* (Xcalumkin Panel 2 [glyph block A14] has a similar spelling). Hieroglyphic inscriptions are written in Classic Ch'olan, and Dynastic Vases are among the rare inscriptions with Yucatec Maya spellings (Houston et al. 2000). On vessel K6751 (glyph block M4), the second Haab month appears both as Classic Ch'olan *Ik'at* (glyph block J6) and as Yucatec Maya **wo-hi** or *Wo* (glyph block M4; Martin 1997: 854). The consistent *ka* prefix added to the snake dynasty's emblem glyph also points to Yucatec Maya *kaan*, "snake," instead of Classic Ch'olan *chan*. The occasional Yucatec Maya words on the Dynastic Vases and the Andrews Coffee Mug distinguish the snake and MARI lords and likely served as identity markers (Wichmann 2006: 288–90).

MARI lords

The Andrews Coffee Mug belongs to the Dynastic Vase tradition. Shared characteristics are the cylindrical form of the vessel, the red backgrounds of Tzolk'iin glyphs, the calligraphic style of the glyphs, and the linguistic affiliation of some glyphs with Yucatec Maya. Its hieroglyphic text provides a king list, yet not of *k'uhul kaan ajaw*, or snake kings, but of *MARI* rulers. The text begins with the accession of Yax or Chak Bahlam, whom I identify as Frans Blom. After mentioning Sak Wokoop, or Bob Wauchope, the text culminates with E. Wyllys Andrews V. It ends with the celebration of the thirteenth Baktun in AD 2012.

Medium and message

The Dynastic Vases formed part of the royal court life. The text on vessel K6751 refers to it literally as a "drinking instrument" (glyph block M5 in Figure 9.3; see also Houston and Taube 1987; Houston *et al.* 1989). In cylinders such as this, cacao was often served. The Andrews Coffee Mug likely served in a similar social context for the consumption of stimulating liquids. The Dynastic Vases were not ordinary tableware but, as the finely executed texts and excellent preservation demonstrate, were equivalent to Meissen porcelain and brought out only for special occasions. Filled with food and drink, painted and inscribed vessels adorned palaces during visits, feasts, and gatherings (Figure 9.7). The vessels and their hieroglyphic texts were too small to be seen by a large audience, but their noble owners and feast participants could fully appreciate them in the intimate setting of a palace room. The painted king lists cannot be separated from their context and usage. The Dynastic Vases objectified the king lists through association with rulers and their ritualized lives.

Creating mythistory

Writing constitutes and legitimizes power (Demarest and Conrad 1992; Freidel 1981; Marcus 1974). Together with art and ritual, it expresses and objectifies political ideologies. Claude Lévi-Strauss observed the impact of writing among the Nambikwara of Brazil:

> No doubt [the Nambikwara chief] was the only one who had grasped the purpose of writing. So he asked me for a writing-pad, and when we both had one, and were working together. If I asked for information on a given

FIGURE 9.7 A court scene involving Dos Pilas king K'awiil Chan K'inich on polychrome vessel K1599; note the four vessels – a jar to the left and a cylinder, a bowl, and a tripod plate – next to the king; the cylinder and the bowl preserve the faint outlines of a glyphic text below their rim (drawing by the author after rollout photo of Justin Kerr)

point, he did not supply it verbally but drew wavy lines on his paper and presented them to me, as if I could read his reply.

(Lévi-Strauss 1992: 296)

Writing can – but does not have to – naturalize a hegemonic discourse (Comaroff and Comaroff 1993; Kertzer 1988). Instead of simply expressing power, writing is a complex system of communication involving writers, messages, media, and readers (Houston 2004). It must be understood in its social and cultural context or in what Keith Basso (1989: 428) called *the situation*: "the status and role of attributes of participants, the form of the message, the code in which it is communicated … and the physical setting in which the message is encoded and decoded." For this reason, scribes had limited control over their writings and audiences interpreted messages differently (for ancient Egypt as case study, see Baines 1983).

The Dynastic Vases exemplify the complex relationship between writing and power. King lists with clearly spelled out accession dates and names demonstrate control over time and legitimation through ancestors as fundamental aspects of royal power (Grube 2004; Stuart 1996: 165–7, 2005: 186–9; Rice 2008). In this chapter, I have shown that the five snake kings who appear on carved inscriptions and on Dynastic Vases are among the last seven kings of the Dynastic Vase king lists and that these kings ruled during the sixth and seventh century AD. The Dynastic Vases themselves were made about a century later. The king lists present a gradient from mythological founding figures to historically attested rulers. Their staccato rhythm of dates, accessions, and names creates a persuasive logic: Z acceded, before him Y, before him X, … before him C, before him B, before him A. If X, Y, and Z are known rulers, then A, B, and C should be, too. The king lists link mythological past with the then-present. By the eighth century, the earliest kings were too far removed in time to be experientially confirmed or disproven. The Dynastic Vases attribute "the quality of unquestionable truthfulness … to unverifiable propositions" (Rappaport 1971: 69). Their discourse creates history.

The Andrews Coffee Mug throws a distinctive light on the origins of the Middle American Research Institute by omitting William E. Gates (1863–1940), an avid collector of manuscripts and books on Mexico and Central America. Tulane University bought half of Gates's collection and made him director of the new Department of Middle American Research to oversee it (Lowe 1954: 32). During his tenure between 1924 and 1926, Gates hired Frans Blom to head the archaeological field operations of the department (ibid.: 33). Other staff included Ralph Roys and Oliver La Farge. In 1925, Blom and La Farge embarked on the now famous expedition to Middle America. They published their observations a year later in *Tribes and Temples*, the first publication of an ongoing series (Blom and La Farge 1926–7). Since Gates overdrew the budget of the department during the same years, Tulane first made Blom directly responsible to the president of the university and then placed the departmental library under the library committee (Lowe 1954: 35). Gates fought in vain against this loss of power and was removed in March 1926. A few months later, Blom officially took over.

FIGURE 9.8 MARI king list from the Andrews Coffee Mug: (a) Chak Bahlam or Frans Blom (glyph block B2); (b) Sak Wokoop or Bob Wauchope (glyph block C2); (c) E. Wyllys Andrews V (glyph block F1; drawings by the author)

After its dysfunctional childhood the MARI grew, as J. Eric S. Thompson (in Lowe 1954: 67) put it, in wisdom and stature. In contrast, the Andrews Coffee Mug presents a streamlined list from Blom to Andrews (Figure 9.8). By conflating *yax*, "blue/green," but also "first," and *chak*, "red," in his name, the text implies Frans Blom as MARI's founder. Blom carries the MARI emblem glyph despite the fact that the Department of Middle American Research became the Middle American Research Institute only in 1938, 12 years after Blom's accession. The Andrews Coffee Mug manifests the Maya concept of history. Its steady beat of accessions creates a convincing discourse by seamlessly linking past and present but skipping the troubled beginnings of the MARI.

Notes

1 The transliteration and transcription of Maya glyphs follow the system used in Thompson's catalogue (1962) and the guidelines for the series *Research Reports on Ancient Maya Writing* (Stuart 1988). Transcribed glyphs are in boldface (with word signs in capital letters) and transliterated glyphs are italicized. Maya kings are spelled according to Martin and Grube (2008).
2 Dynastic Vases are to a certain degree similar to Colonial *títulos primordiales*, or "primordial titles," that "typically claim to date from the sixteenth century, although their vocabulary, orthography, script, and paper indicate a later date of composition" (Horn 2006). The primordial titles emerged during late colonial times when escalating land disputes forced indigenous communities to defend their land claims in Spanish courts. They did this by looking back to their situation during the conquest and by claiming continued possession of their lands since then. Their accounts disagree with other sources. Instead of simply dismissing them as inauthentic, the primordial titles have been scrutinized for native conceptions of history and identity (e.g., Lockhart 1991:39–64).
3 Note from the editor: The less humble title has sometimes been employed by lords of Penn and Harvard, despite the fact that geographic analysis and Thiessen polygons demonstrate that they controlled much smaller territories.

References

Andrews, E. Wyllys, V (1974) Some Architectural Similarities between Dzibilchaltun and Palenque. In *Primera Mesa Redonda de Palenque, 1973, Part I* [*Palenque Round Table Series*, Vol. 1], ed. Merle Greene Robertson, pp. 137–45. Pebble Beach, CA: Robert Louis Stevenson School.

Assmann, Jan (1992) *Das kulturelle Gedächtnis: Schrift, Erinnerung und politische Identität in frühen Hochkulturen*. Munich: C. H. Beck.
Attwater, Donald (1939) *Names and Name-Days*. London: Burns, Oates & Washbourne.
Baines, John (1983) Literacy and Ancient Egyptian Society. *Man* 18: 572–99.
Barber, Russell J., and Frances F. Berdan (1998) *The Emperor's Mirror: Understanding Cultures through Primary Sources*. Tucson: University of Arizona Press.
Basso, Keith H. (1989) The Ethnography of Writing. In *Explorations in the Ethnography of Speaking*, ed. Richard Bauman and Joel Sherzer, pp. 425–32. Cambridge: Cambridge University Press.
Berlin, Heinrich (1958) El glifo "emblem" en las inscripciones mayas. *Journal de la Société des Américanistes* (n.s.) 47: 111-19.
—— (1959) Glifos nominales en el Sarcófago de Palenque. *Humanidades* II(10): 1–8.
Blom, Frans, and Oliver La Farge, II (1926–7) *Tribes and Temples: A record of the Expedition to Middle America Conducted by the Tulane University of Louisiana in 1925*. New Orleans: Tulane University Press.
Bricker, Victoria R. (1986) *A Grammar of Mayan Hieroglyphs*. New Orleans: Tulane University Press.
Coe, Michael D. (1992) *Breaking the Maya Code*. New York: Thames & Hudson.
Colas, Pierre Robert (2003) K'inich and King: Naming Self and Person among Classic Maya Rulers. *Ancient Mesoamerica* 14: 269–83.
—— (2004) *Sinn und Bedeutung klassischer Maya-Personennamen: Typologische Analyse von Anthroponymphrasen in den Hieroglypheninschriften der klassischen Maya-Kultur als Beitrag zur allgemeinen Onomastik*. Markt Schwaben: Anton Saurwein.
Comaroff, Jean, and John L. Comaroff (1993) Introduction. In *Modernity and its Malcontents: Ritual and Power in Postcolonial Africa*, ed. Jean Comaroff and John L. Comaroff, pp. xi–xxxvii. Chicago: University of Chicago Press.
Connerton, Paul (1989) *How Societies Remember*. Cambridge: Cambridge University Press.
Demarest, Arthur A., and Geoffrey W. Conrad (eds) (1992) *Ideology and Pre-Columbian Civilizations*. Santa Fe, NM: School of American Research.
Duby, Gertrude (2009) Homepage of Na Bolom, www.nabolom.org/index_en.html (accessed April 1, 2009).
Eberl, Markus, and Daniel Graña-Behrens (2004) Proper Names and Throne Names: On the Naming Practice of Classic Maya Rulers. In *Continuity and Change: Maya Religious Practices in Temporal Perspective. Fifth European Maya Conference at the University of Bonn, December 2000*, ed. Daniel Graña-Behrens, Nikolai Grube, Christian M. Prager, Frauke Sachse, Stefanie Teufel, and Elisabeth Wagner, pp. 101–20. Markt Schwaben: Anton Saurwein.
Eberl, Markus, and Christian Prager (2005) B'olon Yokte' K'uh: Maya Conceptions of War, Conflict, and the Underworld. In *Wars and Conflicts in Prehispanic Mesoamerica and the Andes*, ed. Peter Eeckhout and Geneviève Le Fort, pp. 28–36. Oxford: British Archaeological Reports.
Errington, Frederick (1974) Indigenous Ideas of Order, Time, and Transition in a New Guinea Cargo Movement. *American Ethnologist* 1(2): 255–67.
Freidel, David A. (1981) Civilization as a State of Mind: The Cultural Evolution of the Lowland Maya. In *The Transition to Statehood in the New World*, ed. Grant D. Jones and Robert R. Kautz, pp. 188–248. Cambridge: Cambridge University Press.
Graña-Behrens, Daniel (2006) Emblem Glyphs and Political Organization in Northwestern Yucatan in the Classic Period (AD 300–1000). *Ancient Mesoamerica* 17: 105–23.
Gronemeyer, Sven, and Barbara MacLeod (2010) *What Could Happen in 2012: A Re-Analysis of the 13-Bak'tun Prophecy on Tortuguero Monument 6*. Wayeb Note 34, www.wayeb.org/notes/wayeb_notes0034.pdf (accessed November 12, 2011).
Grube, Nikolai (2004) El origen de la dinastía Kaan. In *Los cautivos de Dzibanché*, ed. Enrique Nalda, pp. 117–31. Mexico City: Instituto Nacional de Antropología e Historia.

—— (2006) Ancient Maya Royal Biographies in a Comparative Perspective. In *Janaab' Pakal of Palenque: Reconstructing the Life and Death of a Maya Ruler*, ed. Vera Tiesler and Andrea Cucina, pp. 146–66. Tucson: University of Arizona Press.
Halbwachs, Maurice (1992) *On Collective Memory*, trans. Lewis A. Coser. Chicago: University of Chicago Press.
Hansen, Richard D., and Stanley P. Guenther (2005) Early Social Complexity and Kingship in the Mirador Basin. In *Lords of Creation: The Origins of Sacred Maya Kingship*, ed. Virginia M. Fields and Dorie Reents-Budet, pp. 60–61. Los Angeles and London: Los Angeles County Museum of Art and Scala.
Hansen, Richard D., Ronald L. Bishop, and Federico Fahsen (1991) Notes on Maya Codex-Style Ceramics from Nakbe, Peten, Guatemala. *Ancient Mesoamerica* 2: 225–43.
Hernández, Patricia, and Lourdes Márquez (2006) Longevity of Maya Rulers of Yaxchilán: The Reigns of Shield Jaguar and Bird Jaguar. In *Janaab' Pakal of Palenque: Reconstructing the Life and Death of a Maya Ruler*, ed. Vera Tiesler and Andrea Cucina, pp. 126–45. Tucson: University of Arizona Press.
Horn, Rebecca (2006) Primordial Titles. In *The Oxford Encyclopedia of Mesoamerican Cultures*, ed. Davíd Carrasco. Oxford: Oxford University Press. E-reference edition: www.oxford-mesoamerican.com/entry?entry=t221.e518 (accessed 10 December 10, 2009.)
Houston, Stephen D. (1993) *Hieroglyphs and History at Dos Pilas: Dynastic Politics of the Classic Maya*. Austin: University of Texas Press.
—— (1994) Review: Writing in New World Civilizations. *American Anthropologist* (n.s.) 96: 716–18.
—— (2004) The Archaeology of Communication Technologies. *Annual Review of Anthropology* 33: 223–50.
Houston, Stephen D., and Karl A. Taube (1987) "Name-Tagging" in Classic Mayan Script. *Mexicon* 9: 38–41.
Houston, Stephen D., David Stuart, and Karl A. Taube (1989) Folk Classification of Classic Maya Pottery. *American Anthropologist* 91: 720–26.
Houston, Stephen D., John Robertson, and David Stuart (2000) The Language of Classic Maya Inscriptions. *Current Anthropology* 41(3): 321–56.
Josserand, Kathryn J. (2007) The Missing Heir at Yaxchilán: Literary Analysis of a Maya Historical Puzzle. *Latin American Antiquity* 18: 295–312.
Kertzer, David I. (1988) *Ritual, Politics, and Power*. New Haven, CT: Yale University Press.
Lacadena, Alfonso (2000) Antipassive Constructions in Classic Maya Texts. *Written Language and Literacy* 3(1): 155–80.
Lévi-Strauss, Claude (1966 [1962]) *The Savage Mind*, trans. George Weidenfeld. Chicago: University of Chicago Press.
—— (1992 [1955]) *Tristes tropiques*, trans. John Weightman and Doreen Weightman. New York: Penguin.
Lockhart, James (1991) *Nahuas and Spaniards: Postconquest Central Mexican History and Philology*. Stanford, CA: Stanford University Press.
Long, Harry Alfred (1883) *Personal and Family Names: A Popular Monograph on the Origin and History of the Nomenclature of the Present and Former Times*. London: Hamilton, Adams.
Lounsbury, Floyd G. (1976) A Rationale for the Initial Date of the Temple of the Cross at Palenque. In *The Art, Iconography, and Dynastic History of Palenque, Part III: Proceedings of the Segunda Mesa Redonda de Palenque*, ed. Merle Greene Robertson, pp. 211–24. Pebble Beach, CA: Robert Louis Stevenson School.
Lowe, Gareth W. (1954) *William E. Gates: A Biography*. Provo, UT: Brigham Young University Press.
Marcus, Joyce (1974) The Iconography of Power among the Classic Maya. *World Archaeology* 6: 83–94.

—— (1992a) *Mesoamerican Writing Systems: Propaganda, Myth, and History in Four Ancient Civilizations*. Princeton, NJ: Princeton University Press.
—— (1992b) Royal Families, Royal Texts: Examples from the Zapotec and Maya. In *Mesoamerican Elites: An Archaeological Assessment*, ed. Diane Z. Chase and Arlen F. Chase, pp. 221–41. Norman: University of Oklahoma Press.
Martin, Simon (1997) The Painted King List: A Commentary on Codex-Style Dynastic Vessels. In *The Maya Vase Book: A Corpus of Rollout Photographs of Maya Vases*, Vol. 5, ed. Barbara Kerr and Justin Kerr, pp. 847–67. New York: Kerr Associates.
—— (2005) Of Snakes and Bats: Shifting Identities at Calakmul. *PARI Journal* 6(2): 5–15.
Martin, Simon, and Nikolai Grube (2008) *Chronicle of the Maya Kings and Queens: Deciphering the Dynasties of the Ancient Maya*. 2nd ed., London: Thames & Hudson.
McDowell, Nancy (1985) Past and Future: The Nature of Episodic Time in Bun. In *History and Ethnohistory in Papua New Guinea*, ed. Deborah B. Gewertz and Edward Schieffelin, pp. 26–39. Sydney: University of Sydney Press.
McKinley, Robert (1979) Zaman dan Masa, Eras and Periods: Religious Evolution and the Permanence of Epistemological Ages in Malay Culture. In *The Imagination of Reality: Essays in Southeast Asian Coherence Systems*, ed. Alton L. Becker and Aram A. Yengoyan, pp. 303–24. Norwood, NJ: Ablex.
Middleton, John (1967) Some Social Aspects of Lugbara Myth. In *Myth and Cosmos: Readings in Mythology and Symbolism*, ed. John Middleton, pp. 47–62. Garden City, NY: Natural History Press.
Morphy, Howard, and Frances E. C. Morphy (1984) The "Myths" of Ngalakan History: Ideology and Images of the Past in Northern Australia. *Man* 19(3): 459–78.
Munn, Nancy D. (1992) The Cultural Anthropology of Time: A Critical Essay. *Annual Review of Anthropology* 21: 93–123.
Proskouriakoff, Tatiana (1960) Historical Implications of a Pattern of Dates at Piedras Negras, Guatemala. *American Antiquity* 25: 454–75.
Rappaport, Roy A. (1971) Ritual, Sanctity and Cybernetics. *American Anthropologist* 73: 59–76.
Reents, Dorie J., and Ronald L. Bishop (1987) The Late Classic "Codex Style" Pottery. In *Memorias del Primer Coloquio Internacional de Mayanistas*, pp. 775–89. Mexico City: Universidad Nacional Autónoma de México.
Reents-Budet, Dorie J. (1994) *Painting the Maya Universe: Royal Ceramics of the Classic Period*. Durham, NC: Duke University Press.
Rice, Prudence M. (2008) Time, Power, and the Maya. *Latin American Antiquity* 19: 275–98.
Robicsek, Francis, and Donald M. Hales (1981) *The Maya Book of the Dead: The Ceramic Codex*. Norman: University of Oklahoma Press.
Schele, Linda, and Jeffrey H. Miller (1983) *The Mirror, the Rabbit, and the Bundle: "Accession" Expressions from the Classic Maya Inscriptions*. Washington, DC: Dumbarton Oaks.
Schele, Linda, and David Freidel (1990) *A Forest of Kings: The Untold Story of the Ancient Maya*. New York: William Morrow.
Schele, Linda, Peter Mathews, and Floyd Lounsbury (1990) *Untying the Headband*. Austin: University of Texas Press.
Sharer, Robert J. (1999) Archaeology and History in the Royal Acropolis, Copán, Honduras. *Expedition* 41(2): 8–15.
Sharer, Robert J., Loa P. Traxler, David W. Sedat, Ellen E. Bell, Marcello A. Canuto, and Christopher Powell (1999) Early Classic Architecture beneath the Copán Acropolis: A Research Update. *Ancient Mesoamerica* 10: 3–23.
Stuart, David (1984) Epigraphic Evidence of Political Organization in the Usumacinta Drainage. Unpublished manuscript.

—— (1994) Review of *Mesoamerican Writing Systems: Propaganda, Myth, and History in Four Ancient Civilizations* by Joyce Marcus. *Journal of Field Archaeology* 21: 251–53.

—— (1996) Kings of Stone: A Consideration of Stelae in Ancient Maya Ritual and Representation. *Res: Anthropology and Aesthetics* 29/30: 149–71.

—— (1998) "The Fire Enters His House": Architecture and Ritual in Classic Maya Texts. In *Function and Meaning in Maya Architecture*, ed. Stephen D. Houston, pp. 373–425. Washington, DC: Dumbarton Oaks

—— (2004) The Beginnings of the Copan Dynasty: A Review of the Hieroglyphic and Historical Evidence. In *Understanding Early Classic Copan*, ed. Ellen E. Bell, Marcello A. Canuto, and Robert J. Sharer, pp. 215–47. Philadelphia: University of Pennsylvania Museum of Archaeology and Anthropology.

—— (2005) *The Inscriptions from Temple XIX at Palenque: A Commentary*. San Francisco: Pre-Columbian Art Research Institute.

—— (2007) *"White Owl Jaguar": A Tikal Royal Ancestor*, http://decipherment.wordpress.com/2007/11/04/white-owl-jaguar-a-tikal-royal-ancestor/ (accessed January 21, 2010).

Stuart, David, and Stephen D. Houston (1994) *Classic Maya Place Names*. Washington, DC: Dumbarton Oaks.

Stuart, George (1988) A Guide to the Style and Content of the Series Research Report on Ancient Maya Writing. *Special Supplement of the Research Reports on Ancient Maya Writing* no. 15: 7–12. Washington, DC: Center for Maya Research.

Taube, Karl A. (2003) Ancient and Contemporary Maya Conceptions about Field and Forest. In *The Lowland Maya Area: Three Millennia at the Human–Wildland Interface*, ed. Arturo Gómez-Pompa, Michael F. Allen, Scott L. Fedick, and Juan J. Jiménez-Osornio, pp. 461–92. Binghamton, NY: Food Products Press.

Thompson, John Eric Sidney (1962) *A Catalog of Maya Hieroglyphs*. Norman: University of Oklahoma Press.

Tiesler, Vera, and Andrea Cucina (eds) (2006) *Janaab' Pakal of Palenque: Reconstructing the Life and Death of a Maya Ruler*. Tucson: University of Arizona Press.

Turner, Terence S. (1988) Ethno-Ethnohistory: Myth and History in Native South American Representation of Contact with Western Society. In *Rethinking History and Myth: Indigenous South American Perspectives on the Past*, ed. Jonathan D. Hill, pp. 235–81. Urbana: University of Illinois Press.

Wichmann, Søren (2006) Mayan Historical Linguistics and Epigraphy: A New Synthesis. *Annual Review of Anthropology* 35: 279–94.

Wright, Lori E. (2005) In Search of Yax Nuun Ayiin I: Revisiting the Tikal Project's Burial 10. *Ancient Mesoamerica* 16: 89–100.

PART IV
The eastern periphery of Belize

10

THE DYNASTIC HISTORY AND ARCHAEOLOGY OF PUSILHA, BELIZE[1]

Christian M. Prager, Beniamino Volta, and Geoffrey E. Braswell

Pusilha, located in inland southern Belize, was a small Classic Maya city with a population of about 7,000. Despite its modest size, Pusilha is second only to Caracol in the number of known inscriptions in Belize. One of the very first sites in the country subject to professional exploration, Pusilha remained relatively unknown and understudied until 2001. In this chapter, we summarize archaeological fieldwork conducted by the authors at the site between 2001 and 2008, focusing on burials and caches associated with eight excavated structures. Among these is a royal tomb whose occupant has been tentatively identified in the hieroglyphic record. We also describe the inscriptions of Pusilha and present a full dynastic account for the kings and queen who ruled the site between AD 571 and 798.

A key goal of Maya epigraphy is the development of political histories for important regional capitals. Such accounts at their simplest comprise dates and king lists, but ideally these serve as temporal frameworks for organizing more important events in the history of particular kingdoms and for understanding their relations with other polities (e.g., Marcus 1973, 1976). Our comprehension of Maya history began with the decipherment of hieroglyphs describing the birth, accession, and death of the rulers of Piedras Negras (Proskouriakoff 1960) and the identification of emblem glyphs (Berlin 1958). Since then, epigraphers have identified political events such as marriage, alliance formation and betrayal, warfare, ambassadorial visits, the inauguration of minor kings by major players, and ritual performance, as well texts regarding other kinds of behavior, customs, and beliefs (see Martin and Grube 2000). In some cases, it is now possible to study the material culture of Maya cities within a temporal framework defined by the life of particular kings. At Copan, for example, the Early and Late Classic architectural sequence of the acropolis can be discussed in terms of expansions linked to specific rulers, as can changes to the ceramic inventory of the Late Classic period (see Chapter 4).

Most detailed political and dynastic histories constructed by Maya epigraphers describe sites in Peten, Guatemala, or in the adjoining regions of Chiapas and southern Campeche. To date, only one site in Belize – Caracol – has seen extensive epigraphic research (Beetz and Satterthwaite 1981; Grube 1994; Martin and Grube 2000). One reason for this is that most of the Maya sites of Belize exhibit limited signs of literacy. An important exception is the inland Southern Belize Region (*sensu* Leventhal 1992), an area characterized by extensive carved hieroglyphic texts (e.g., Morley 1937–8; Wanyerka 2003, 2009).

Pusilha, the largest site in the region, is particularly rich in texts. Our current knowledge of the political history of the site is sufficient to warrant its inclusion as a chapter in a volume such as *The Chronicle of Maya Kings and Queens* (Martin and Grube 2000). The principal goals of this chapter are (1) to present epigraphic information concerning the political history of Pusilha organized by the life of each ruler; and (2) to contextualize this information by discussing the results of archaeological research conducted between 2001 and 2008.

The Southern Belize Region: definition, characteristics, and settlement history

The Southern Maya Region was one of the first areas in the southern lowlands to see substantial archaeological investigation during the twentieth century. Five major sites – Pusilha, Uxbenka, Lubaantun, Xnaheb, and Nim li Punit – are located in a relatively small inland area circumscribed to the north and west by the foothills of the Maya Mountains, to the east by the infertile soils and thin coniferous forest known locally as "pine ridge," and to the south by the marshy terrain of the Temash and Sarstoon rivers. Within this small region, the five sites are situated on hilltops surrounded by drainable slopes and, with one exception, are more or less evenly spaced in a line spanning less than 50 kilometers. The two largest communities, Lubaantun and Pusilha, are strategically positioned on major rivers connecting them to the Caribbean Sea (see Figures 1.1 and 10.1). A constant water supply and proximity to important coastal trade and salt-producing communities probably accounts for the continued success of Lubaantun well into the Terminal Classic period (McKillop 2005). Uxbenka, although located relatively far from a major river, is positioned along a natural land passage running from the southeastern Peten to the Caribbean. This trade route is still important and parallels the newly paved road from the Guatemalan border at Jalacte to the junction with the Southern Highway (Prufer and Thompson 2013). Lubaantun is just 4 kilometers north of this route and has its own direct access to the Caribbean via the Río Grande. In contrast, Xnaheb and Nim li Punit are situated just above the edge of the coastal plain in locations that strategically control north to south travel. These two sites are just a few hundred meters west of the modern Southern Highway. Thus, the ancient Maya centers of Southern Belize are advantageously positioned in locations that dominate or are connected to important east–west and north–south transportation routes.

Despite the short distances among the major sites of the Southern Belize Region, the rulers of a number of them employed emblem glyphs, implying at least nominal claims of political independence. The emblem glyphs of Nim li Punit and Pusilha are clearly legible, that of Uxbenka is too eroded to read, and the Lubaantun emblem glyph – if that is what it is – employs the head variant of the *k'uhul* glyph

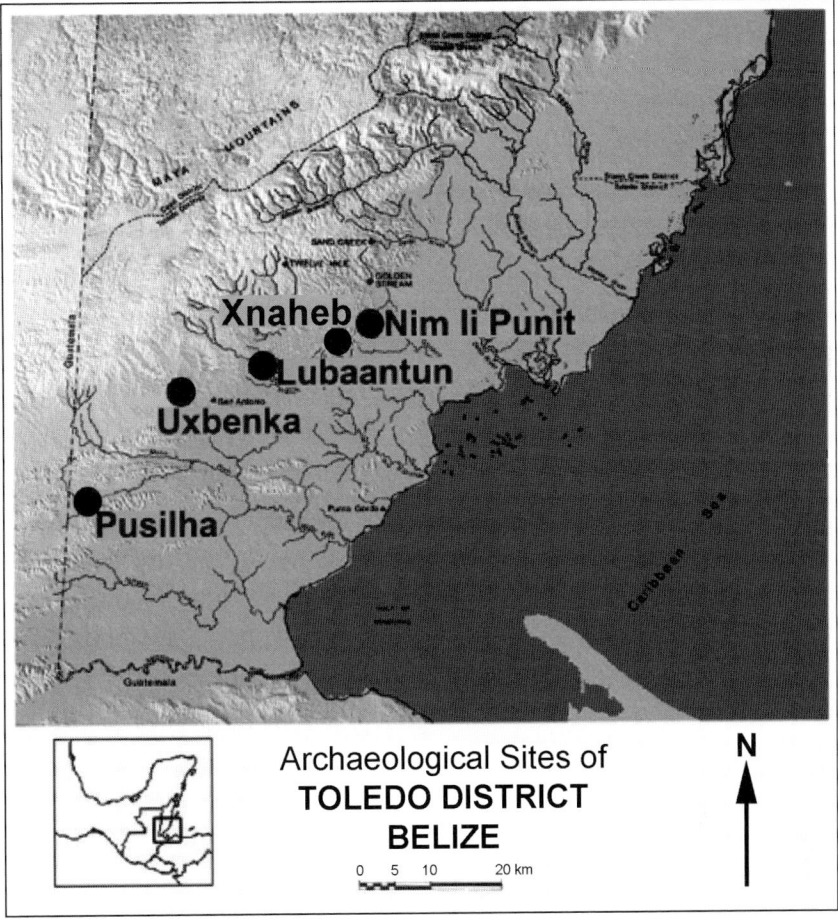

FIGURE 10.1 The Southern Belize Region (after Leventhal 1990: map 1)

as its main sign (Wanyerka 2003: 23; 2009: 415–18). The hieroglyphic texts of Xnaheb are eroded, fragmented, and few in number, but it is possible that an emblem glyph was employed there, as well (Wanyerka 1999). A key question in the archaeology of Toledo District is: Did these closely packed sites form the cores of independent polities, or were some of them united in one way or another?

The greater Southern Belize Region extends well beyond these five sites to encompass all of Toledo District, Belize, and southeastern Peten, Guatemala (Dunham et al. 1989: 263, 269; Leventhal 1992: 145). In total it encompasses more than 4,000 square kilometers. San Luis Peten is the largest modern town in the greater region and – for the Mopan Maya of Toledo – is still a cultural center. The *franja transversal del norte*, a major transportation route for more than a thousand years, runs along the southern boundary of the greater region, joining it to Cancuen and, ultimately, Chiapas and the Gulf Coast (see Chapter 8). To the southwest the area extends well into the upper reaches of the Rio Cancuen (Corzo et al. 2000). The cave site of Naj Tunich (Brady 1989;

Stone 1995) served as a major ceremonial pilgrimage place linking ancient sites on both sides of the modern Belize–Guatemala border. Today, Mopan and Q'eqchi' Maya frequently cross that border, conduct trade and smuggle goods, play soccer in village leagues, worship at sacred caves, and look for spouses in communities located in both nations.

The Southern Belize Region differs from adjacent cultural zones in having distinctive architectural remains, such as terraced platform constructions, ballcourts within walled enclosures, a complete lack of corbelled vaults, and the use of natural terrain to support the façades of "Hollywood"-style pyramid-like structures (Leventhal 1990: 138–9). There also is a complete lack of astronomical groups or "E-groups" (we do not consider the Stela Plaza of Nim li Punit to contain such a complex), in great contrast to the adjoining Valley of Dolores Region (Chocón 2013). "Eastern shrines" are also relatively infrequent, although Structure 5 at Nim li Punit seems to constitute such a platform. Although no single architectural convention is unique, together they help define the region.

The masonry of the Southern Belize Region is also distinctive, but it ranges from very poor in quality to some of the most beautiful in the Maya region. It is fair to say that no site between Copan, Honduras, and the Rio Bec Region, Campeche, exhibits such finely crafted stonework as Lubaantun (Figure 10.2a). Construction techniques in the region all follow the same general pattern. First, a pen or box was built of cut and dressed stones to a height of about 1.5 meters and packed either with earth or with dry fill. At Lubaantun, an inner retaining box of cut but undressed stones often was built first. Platforms could be built higher by constructing a second body set back a few inches from the first, much like adding a layer to a wedding cake. Next, stairblocks were built. Finally, stairside outsets were added. Key here is that these last two features were not dovetailed or integrated into platforms. Instead, they served as separate buttresses supporting platform walls. Almost no platforms supported superstructures with stone walls. The exceptions are miniature shrines with thigh-high walls found at Lubaantun. Limited plaster mortar and thin coats of stucco were employed at Lubaantun and Uxbenka; plaster and limestone mortar are rare or absent at Nim li Punit after the Early Classic period. In great contrast, the poorly finished masonry of Pusilha (Figure 10.2b) was covered with very thick coats of stucco. Unique to Lubaantun are its two major pyramids that lack stairs that climb to the summit.

Other shared cultural practices include collective tombs, the prevalence among elite burials of fully extended individuals on their backs with heads placed to the north and facing east (the opposite of the pattern seen in the Belize Valley), teeth cached as ancestral relics, a regional style of carving, a degree of literacy surprising for sites in Belize, and rather idiosyncratic hieroglyphic inscriptions employing nonstandard Lunar Series data (Braswell *et al.* 2004b, 2005; Fauvelle *et al.* 2013; Grube *et al.* 1999: 3–7; Leventhal 1990: 138–9; Morley 1938: vol. IV; Thompson 1928).

Regional settlement history

The earliest known human occupation of the region dates to the Paleoindian period. A single fishtail point was recovered from a plowed field near Big Falls village,

FIGURE 10.2 Masonry of Southern Belize: (a) Lubaantun Structure 104; (b) Pusilha Operation 8 Structure

downstream from Lubaantun (Lohse *et al.* 2006: 215, fig. 4b; Weintraub 1994). A late Archaic Lowe point from the same general area also has been reported, and in 2013 a possible Archaic context with percussion flakes and cores was located by members of the Uxbenka Archaeological Project (Prufer and Thompson 2013).

Uxbenka is the oldest known Maya center in Toledo District. The earliest construction there has been dated by radiocarbon to the first century AD (Prufer et al. 2011) or, more broadly, to the period 60 BC to AD 220 (Culleton et al. 2012). Nonetheless, the ceramics associated with early construction episodes at Uxbenka date to the Early Classic (Jordan and Prufer 2013). Thus, despite a few earlier carbon dates (derived, perhaps, from old wood), the *archaeological chronology* of Uxbenka – determined from diagnostic artifacts – begins in the third century AD. The pottery of this time belongs to what Juan Pedro Laporte (2007: 539–43) called the Peripheral Chicanel complex, which is a mixture of late waxy slipped monochrome pottery with early polychromes and glossy Peten monochromes typical of the Tzakol sphere (Jordan and Prufer 2013). Few of the carved monuments at Uxbenka contain readable dates (see Wanyerka 2003: 203–31), but some are argued on stylistic grounds to date to the Early Classic and others to the Late Classic. Uxbenka grew during the Late Classic and even has a Terminal Classic occupation (Aquino 2013; Aquino et al. 2013). Nonetheless, the paucity of diagnostic Terminal Classic ceramics – so common at Lubaantun, at Nim li Punit, and in some groups at Pusilha – demonstrate that occupation of Uxbenka at that time was light (Jordan and Prufer 2013; Prufer et al. 2011). In sum, the small Maya center of Uxbenka was occupied around AD 200–800, and perhaps saw limited settlement briefly before and after that time.

Nim li Punit was the next major Maya site to be founded, around AD 400–450 (Daniels and Braswell 2013). Early Classic pottery of this time contains types and groups characteristic of the Tzakol sphere but lacking Chicanel material. Three slab-footed tripods from one of the earliest structures yet excavated at the site imply construction around AD 400 (ibid.; Fauvelle et al. 2013). The rulers of Nim li Punit carved seven stelae during two short periods of monument erection: AD 734–741 and 790–810. An eighth monument contains a rough and peculiarly carved date of Ajaw 7, which probably refers to 10.0.0.0.0 (AD 830). This final date seems to have been carved on an already standing plain monument. There is some ceramic evidence in the form of Thin Orange pottery that supports an occupation of Nim li Punit after that date, but so far such a presence appears to have been light and located mainly in the West Group (Daniels and Braswell 2013; Fauvelle et al. 2012).

Pusilha is by far the largest site in southern Belize and the only one that reasonably can be called a city (Figure 10.3). It was founded at the very end of the Early Classic. Most sherds date to the Late Classic, but we found a handful of pottery characteristic of the Early Classic. This accords well with the historical hieroglyphic dates from Pusilha, which begin at 9.6.17.8.18 (AD 571). Pusilha is fundamentally a Late Classic site, but the Gateway Hill Acropolis and the Moho Plaza contain ample evidence of Terminal Classic occupation or use. So far unique for inland southern Belize, Postclassic ceramics have been found associated with the "Bulldozed Structure" (Bill and Braswell 2005; Braswell et al. 2004b). In many respects, the pottery of Pusilha is the most distinctive in the region (Bill and Braswell 2005; Bill et al. 2005; Daniels and Braswell 2013).

Lubaantun has no firmly dated texts, but three ballcourt markers were dated on stylistic grounds to about AD 780–790 by Sylvanus Morley (1937–8: IV.5–10). Ceramics at Lubaantun imply a short occupation that began sometime in the eighth century

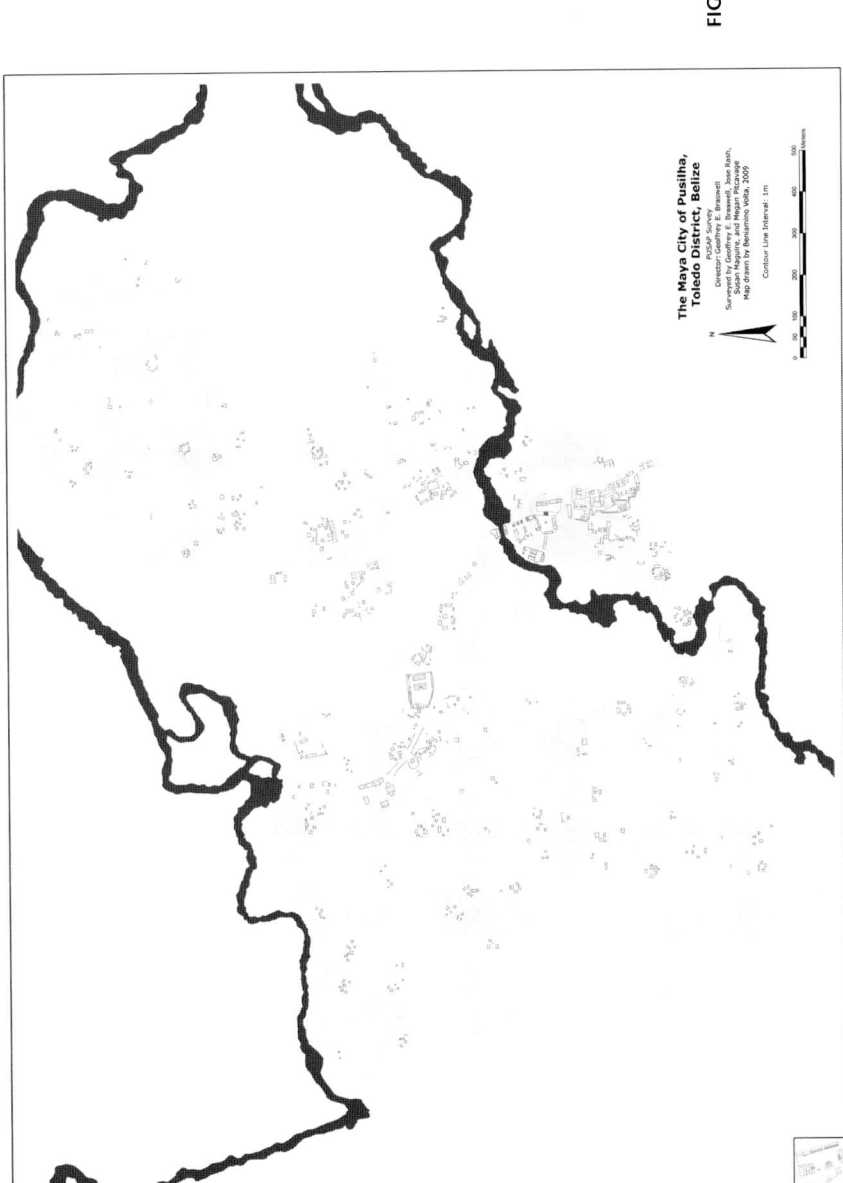

FIGURE 10.3 Partial map of Pusilha, Belize: the Moho Plaza, shown in a box in the lower left corner, is located approximately 150 meters farther to the southwest.

(Hammond 1975). Norman Hammond found Belize Red in deeply buried contexts at the site. Because such pottery is limited elsewhere in the region to contexts dating to the late eighth and early ninth centuries (Daniels and Braswell 2013), we tentatively suggest that Lubaantun was founded after 750 and perhaps as late as 780. The pottery is so similar to materials from Uxbenka that much of what is found at Lubaantun seems to represent a Terminal Classic extension of that site (ibid.; Jillian Jordan, personal communication 2013). Thus, it may be that people from the Uxbenka region moved to Lubaantun shortly before the end of the eighth century. Lubaantun has a rich Terminal Classic occupation but was abandoned around 900 or perhaps somewhat later.

The fifth and final major settlement is Xnaheb. Its location is anomalous because, unlike other centers that are evenly spaced, it is only a few kilometers from Nim li Punit. Xnaheb has seen relatively little archaeological investigation. Peter Dunham's "gravity model" argues that a site built between central places will be located at or near the political boundary that separates them. He calculates that, given the relative sizes of Lubaantun and Nim li Punit, such a site should be found precisely where Xnaheb is situated (Dunham et al. 1989: 275). Key to his argument is that Xnaheb must have been built after both Nim li Punit and Lubaantun, but this remains to be demonstrated. Archaeological data appear to imply that the site was briefly occupied during the second half of the Late Classic (ibid.: 268–9; Jamison 2001: 79). A single stela has an Initial Series date of 9.17.10.0.0 (AD 780), which falls during the hieroglyphic hiatus at Nim li Punit. It might be that Xnaheb already existed or was founded at about that time, and that the royal house of Nim li Punit moved briefly to this center in order to protect its boundary from newly founded Lubaantun. Ceramics from Nim li Punit and Lubaantun dating to the Late Classic are chemically quite distinct (Fauvelle et al. 2013), so it should be rather easy to determine if Xnaheb was tied economically to Nim li Punit or to Lubaantun.

Archaeological investigations at Pusilha

The site of Pusilha was discovered in 1926 and investigated by the British Museum between 1928 and 1930 (Gruning 1930; Joyce 1929; Joyce et al. 1928). The principal focus of this chapter is the dynastic history of Pusilha as recorded on 44 carved limestone monuments and fragments thus far discovered. Although some are still *in situ* (but severely eroded), the best-preserved stelae and monument fragments were moved to the British Museum where they reside today. Between 1930 and 2001, little archaeological work was conducted at Pusilha. During this interval, sporadic excavations were conducted in 1970 by Hammond (1975), in 1979 and 1980 by Richard Leventhal (1990, 1992), and in 1992 by Gary Rex Walters and Lorington Weller (n.d.). The site again saw sustained field investigations by members of the Pusilha Archaeological Project (PUSAP), co-directed by Braswell, Prager, and Cassandra R. Bill, during the years 2001–2, 2004–5, and 2008. Results of the first two seasons of our project and a specialized study have been published in journals (Braswell 2007b; Braswell et al. 2004b, 2005; Pitcavage and Braswell 2009); preliminary results have appeared in numerous symposia volumes (Bill and Braswell 2005; Bill et al. 2005; Braswell 2007a, 2010; Braswell et al.

2004a, 2006, 2007, 2008; Braswell and Gibbs 2006; Braswell and Prager 2003; Braswell and Prufer 2009; Maguire *et al*. 2003; Pitcavage and Braswell 2009, 2010); and data collected by students have formed the basis of five MA theses (Nickels 2008; Pitcavage 2008; Prager 2002; Somerville 2009;Volta 2007). One of the goals of this chapter is to present a brief summary describing more notable finds of the 2004, 2005, and 2008 seasons.

The Stela Plaza of Pusilha (16°06'45" N, 89°11'43 W) is located between the Poite (or Joventud) and Machaca (or Pusilha) rivers along the Guatemalan–Belize border, some 42 kilometers west of Punta Gorda, the capital of Toledo District (see Figure 10.1). To the north and south of Pusilha are an extensive series of karst limestone ridges rising to an altitude of some 200 meters above sea level. Architectural remains and ancient settlements are dispersed over an area of approximately 6 square kilometers (see Figure 10.3). Numerous settlements have been found along the sloping karst foothills north of the Poite River and along the limestone massif to the south of the mapped portion of the site. Cutting through the middle of the site is the Machaca River, which in ancient times was crossed by a triple-span bridge. The abutments of the bridge are still visible today and now support a suspension bridge (Figure 10.4).

The site core runs in a northwest to southeast direction and spans both sides of the Machaca River. From the northwest, the major ceremonial and residential groups include the Stela (or Main) Plaza, the Ballcourt I Group, the Big Tree Group (Figure 10.5), and the Maya Bridge (known locally as "the Pusilha"). The vast majority of carved monuments known from Pusilha are found in the Stela Plaza. Other important groups north of the Machaca River include Leventhal's Blank Stela Group (but there

FIGURE 10.4 The Maya bridge of Pusilha, showing modern suspension bridge (July 2007)

is no stela there) and the Pottery Cave Group (Figure 10.6). Located southeast of the Stela Plaza and on the opposite bank of the Machaca River is a stepped residential complex known as the Gateway Hill Acropolis. This portion of the site begins at the famous bridge and rises roughly 79 meters above the river in a series of terraces that

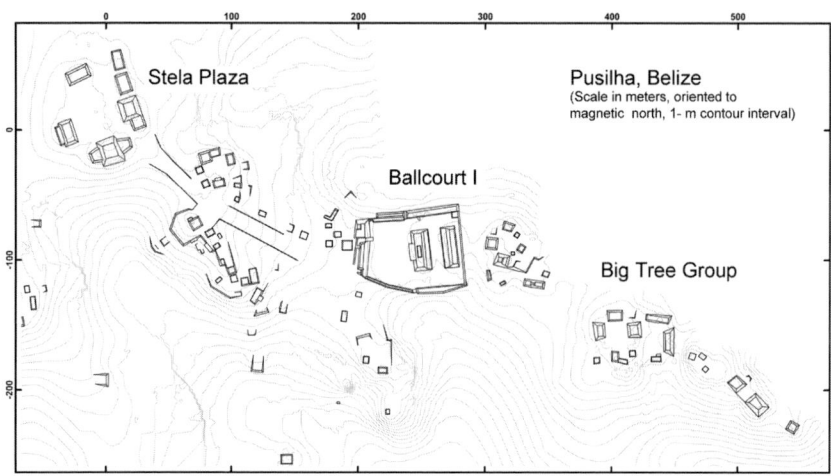

FIGURE 10.5 Major architectural groups north of the Machaca River (grid in meters, as measured from a datum in the Stela Plaza)

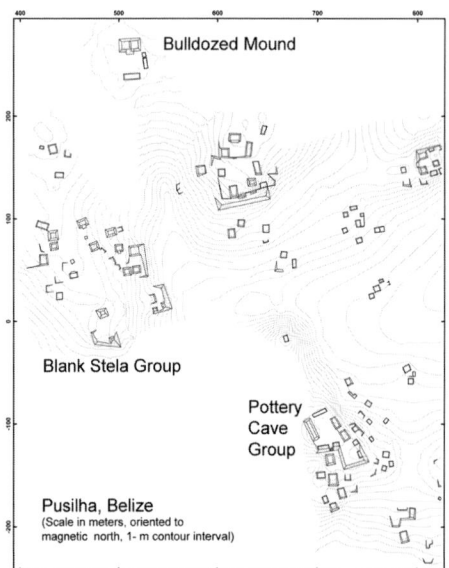

FIGURE 10.6 Major architectural groups north of the Machaca River, showing the location of the Bulldozed Mound (grid in meters, as measured from a datum in the Stela Plaza)

culminate at the tallest pyramids at the site (Figure 10.7). To the west and southwest of the Gateway Hill Acropolis are elite residential groups, among them Lower Group I, Lower Group II, and the Machaca Plaza. This last group was discovered by Leventhal and included in his map of the site (Leventhal 1990: fig. 8.1), but we were unable to gain permission to enter that parcel of land and remap it. Finally, Walters and Weller (n.d.) discovered a major outlying group that they call the Moho Plaza (Figure 10.8).

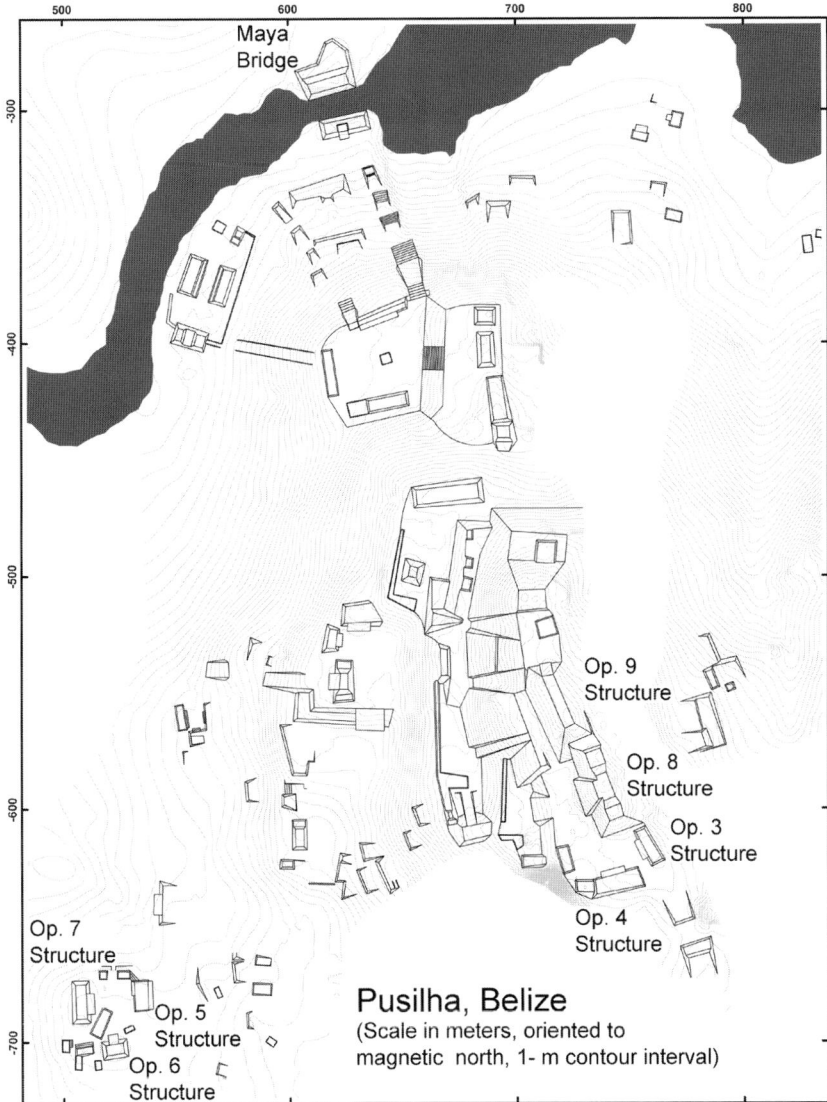

FIGURE 10.7 Gateway Hill Acropolis south of the Machaca River, showing locations of excavated structures: the Operation 5–7 structures are located in Lower Group I.

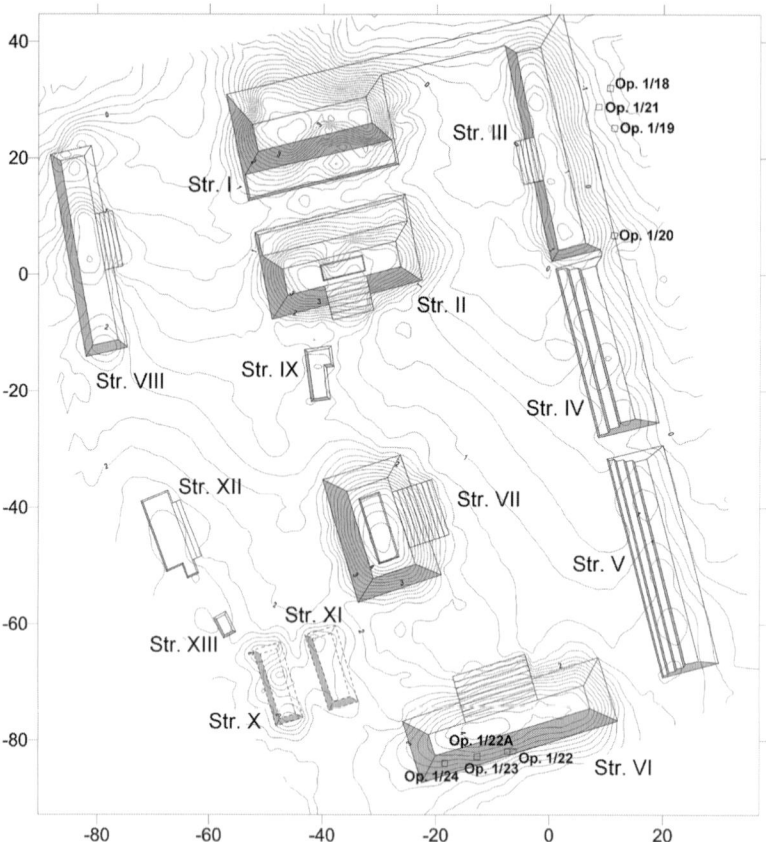

FIGURE 10.8 The Moho Plaza, showing the location of excavated test pits (grid in meters, as measured from a group specific datum; contour interval is 20 centimeters)

This group contains at least one ballcourt (and possibly a second) in which three carved markers were found, as well as the only known hieroglyphic stair in all of Belize (Braswell *et al.* 2004b). Both Leventhal's pace-and-compass and our own total station map are woefully incomplete. More mounds and many groups can be found stretching westward towards the Guatemalan border (and perhaps beyond), on the imposing hills south of the Machaca River, and, especially, north of the Poite River.

Settlement patterns at Pusilha

The mapped portion of Pusilha is just under 2 square kilometers. Within this area, we recorded about 550 structures and platforms. This count does not include non-residential structures found in the Gateway Hill Acropolis, Stela Plaza, and Moho Plaza. Most of the mounds thought to have supported houses are arranged in groups. Depending on how they are defined, between 60 and 70 of these residential groups can be identified in the mapped portion of the site. Assuming that the settlement density is fairly uniform throughout the approximate total area of 6 square kilometers, we estimate that Pusilha was a city with slightly more than 7,000 inhabitants and a settlement density of about 235 structures per square kilometer. This population estimate includes a 25 percent reduction for non-contemporaneous occupation. Thus, although Pusilha was undoubtedly a much smaller city, the density of structures there is equivalent to that of the urban core of Late Classic Tikal and much higher than that of any other major settlement in the Southern Belize Region (Rice and Culbert 1990: table 1.2).

The majority of the residential architecture at Pusilha was built on well-drained, elevated hilltops and ridges. In general, larger and more elaborate platform and terrace arrangements are found at the highest elevations, with smaller clusters of mounds located on terraced areas further downslope. The natural depressions in the karst topography that separate these areas can be inundated for part of the year and probably were used for agriculture in the past, just as they are now. The watercourses provide a secondary focus for residential clustering, with slightly higher settlement densities in a 100-meter-wide strip along the banks of the Poite and Machaca rivers (Braswell *et al.* 2004b: 225).

An analysis of the formal characteristics of residential clusters reveals that higher-status plazuela or patio groups (*sensu* Ashmore 1981: 48), with four or more structures and clearly defined central plazas, are spaced fairly regularly throughout the settlement at an average distance of 300 meters from each other. Fourteen such patio groups have been identified in the mapped portion of the site. There also are seven more elaborate patio groups featuring multiple plazas, more than eight structures, or larger mounds that possibly served ritual functions. These elite groups – which include the Ballcourt I Group, the Blank Stela Group, the Big Tree Group, the Pottery Cave Group, Lower Groups I and II, and an unnamed group directly northeast of the Blank Stela Group – are clustered in an area of 0.5 square kilometers in the vicinity of the northwest–southeast axis that connects Stela Plaza to Gateway Hill (see Figure 10.3). Although this seems to suggest that the site conforms to a "concentric" or centralized settlement pattern (Folan *et al.* 1983, 2009), there are at least two quite large groups with monumental public architecture to the southwest of the Gateway Hill Acropolis – Leventhal's (1990: fig. 8.1) Machaca Plaza and the Moho Plaza. The construction of the latter appears to date to the Terminal Classic, and the occupational history of the former is unknown. Thus, the settlement of Pusilha was organized into a social landscape that at different moments of its history may have been characterized either by a well-defined central area or by multiple nuclei of status and power.

Most of the largest groups at Pusilha share a similar alignment: approximately 16 to 23 degrees west of true north. At the Gateway Hill Acropolis, this alignment follows natural topography. But the NNW alignment of structures in the Stela Plaza, Moho Plaza, Pottery Cave Group, Lunar Group, and Lower Group I do not. The meaning of this alignment is unknown, but it may have replicated that of the royal acropolis.

Studies of the monumental public buildings of Pusilha have identified a unique architectural template that also sets the site apart from other centers in the Southern

Belize Region (Braswell et al. 2005; Volta 2011). This pattern, which consists of a causeway linking an enclosed ballcourt to a large plaza, is found twice at Pusilha. One example is the *sacbe* that heads downhill from the Stela Plaza to Ballcourt I (see Figure 10.5). The other is the short, steep causeway connecting the northernmost terrace of the Gateway Hill Acropolis with Ballcourt II (see Figure 10.7). The first example may display cosmological principles. The Stela Plaza sits at the highest point in the site and is associated with the north, the heavens, and ancestor veneration. Ballcourt I is at a lower elevation and associated with the south, the underworld, and death. The causeway, like the world tree, connects the two (Ashmore 1991). In both examples, the plaza connected to the ballcourt is relatively open to the west and features three low-range structures on its eastern side. At Gateway Hill, these are found on the second terrace, which is connected to the first by means of a stairway (see Figure 10.7). Other examples of this plaza layout – a relatively open west side faced by three structures on the east – are found in at least three other groups: the Moho Plaza, the Pottery Cave Group, and the Lunar Group (about 1,000 meters northeast of the Stela Plaza). It is clear that this template does not duplicate the "E Group" known in other parts of the Maya lowlands, but the arrangement of three structures could be a reference to it (Volta 2007, 2011).

The 2001–2004 field seasons

PUSAP research began in 2001 with a season of mapping (the Gateway Hill Acropolis, the Moho Plaza, the Stela Plaza, and a large area in the northeastern portion of the site cleared by a communal plantation burn) and recording *in situ* monument fragments. During the 2002 field season, we mapped two adjoining transects between the Poite and Machaca rivers. These passed through the Stela Plaza. A test-pitting program was conducted at this time in the Stela Plaza, the Moho Plaza, Weller's Group (located 500 meters south of western end of the Ballcourt I Group), and – most productively – inside and outside of Pottery Cave. During a short break in our work, a platform about 600 meters northeast of the Stela Plaza and 200 meters north of the Blank Stela Plaza was partially bulldozed. Salvage excavations revealed this to be a Terminal Classic structure occupied into the Postclassic period that contained an earlier substructure. The fragmentary remains of an elderly male were recovered from undisturbed fill in the final stage structure (Pitcavage 2008: 20). An offering of three red-slipped cache vessels, a lid, and a jade bead were placed in the stair of the substructure when it was partially dismantled immediately prior to building the final stage Terminal Classic platform. Associated with this cache was abundant charcoal that two distinct assays date to the early portion of the Early Classic, centuries before Pusilha was first occupied. We assume that this represents the burning of an ancient wooden object. The substructure of the "Bulldozed Mound" was partially consolidated and can be found next to the Catholic church in the village of San Benito Poite (Braswell et al. 2004b; see Figure 10.6).

Opportunistic mapping of plantation burns continued in 2004 and five structures were excavated. Two of these (the Operation 3 and Operation 4 structures) are located towards the southern end of the Gateway Hill Acropolis and three (the Operation 5, 6, and 7 structures) are in Lower Group I (see Figure 10.7). The Operation 3 and 5 structures were excavated completely, the entire fill core and front of the Operation 6 structure and the surviving northern end of the Operation 4 structure were excavated (the southern half or more of the latter's platform was destroyed by looting in the weeks before our season began), and test pits were placed in the Operation 7 platform.

Excavations in the Operation 3 structure revealed four burials (Figure 10.9a). Three related interments containing matched polychrome ceramic vessels date to the Late Classic and were located on top of the platform. The central head-cist burial, Burial 3/1, contained an extended supine male (who died in young adulthood) and two companion caches of teeth. Strontium isotope analyses of the teeth of the principal individual in Burial 3/1 and of one of the companions reveal that they were not from Pusilha. Two flexed burials north and south of Burial 3/1 contained one local individual (Burial 3/1B, a female who survived into late adulthood) and one possible foreigner (Burial 3/A, a young adult and probable male) who may have come from a second nonlocal site. A double burial at the base of the Operation 3 structure contained two local individuals – a principal figure and a companion flexed at his feet – who were both local males that survived to an advanced age. Burial 3/2 dates to the Terminal Classic period, based on the presence of Belize Red, Pabellon Modeled-Carved super-system pottery, and a tripod orange bowl in a form diagnostic of that period. A cranium and disarticulated arm bones were found on the surface of the plaza in front of the Operation 4 structure. The head was held in place by a flat stone and a fragmentary vessel was found next to it. These remains could not be dated but are clearly late. Strontium analysis reveals that the adult woman (Burial 4/1) came from a third nonlocal place (Braswell *et al.* 2005; Pitcavage 2008; Pitcavage and Braswell 2010; Somerville 2009).

Excavations in Lower Group I revealed that it was built and occupied entirely during the Late Classic period. The burials of two children were found in the Operation 5 structure (Figure 10.9b). The more interesting of these is Burial 5/1, which contained the remains of a small child accompanied by a shell "pukka"-style necklace. Fifteen deciduous teeth were recovered and permanent teeth were observed within the dental crypts. Together, these allow a precise determination of a dental age of between four and five years. What is most interesting is that the two upper lateral incisors had distal filings and jade inlays. This is the only known example of such modifications made to deciduous teeth in all of Mesoamerica (Braswell and Pitcavage 2009). The Operation 6 structure contained an elaborate crypt with numerous offerings, among them two shell ornaments, four Late Classic vessels (including a polychrome plate with a glyph band and a stuccoed and painted vase), a jade bead, a *Spondylus* shell, slate fragments and pyrite tesserae from a mirror, hematite sequins, a limestone baton and slate paddle, and a tooth cache (Figure 10.10; Braswell *et al.* 2005). The flexed burial of an adult of undetermined sex was found in this platform, south of and behind the offering crypt. The individuals represented by the teeth in the crypt (Burial 6/1) and the flexed interment (Burial 6/2) are both locals (Somerville 2009).

A subsurface remote sensing program also was undertaken in 2004 in the vicinity of Lower Groups I and II but yielded results of limited utility. What was tentatively

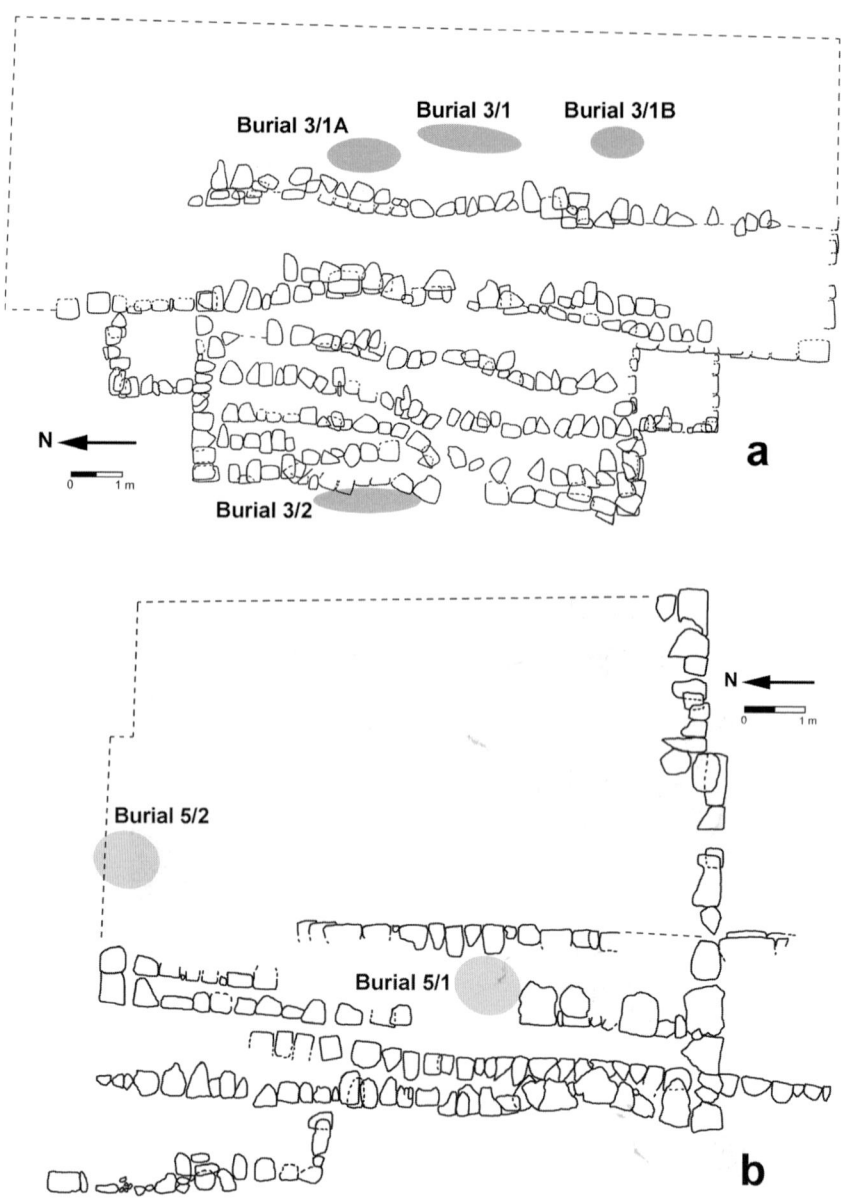

FIGURE 10.9 Plans of the Operation 3 structure (a) and the Operation 5 structure (b) showing the locations of burials (after Braswell et al. 2005: figs 7 and 10)

identified as a midden proved to contain soft soils washed down from a western terrace of the Gateway Hill Acropolis. Within this secondary matrix were found the partial remains of a locally born child of seven to nine years (Burial 1/25/1; Braswell et al. 2004b: 51–4; Pitcavage 2008: 19–20; Somerville 2009).

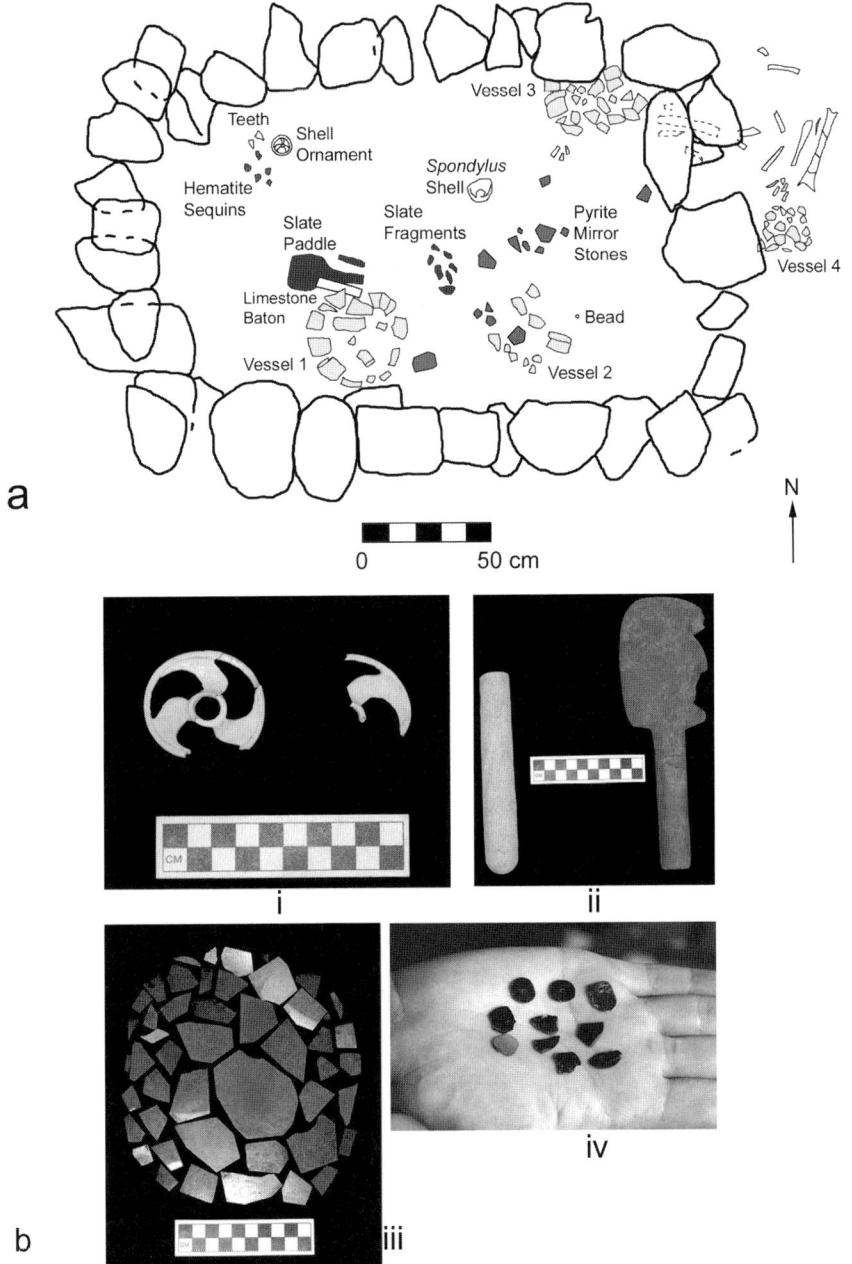

FIGURE 10.10 Offering crypt Burial 6/1: (a) plan; (b) artifacts found within the crypt: (i) shell ornaments, (ii) limestone baton and slate "paddle," (iii) pyrite mirror tesserae, (iv) hematite sequins (after Braswell *et al.* 2005: fig. 8)

The 2005 and 2008 field seasons

During the 2005 season, opportunistic mapping continued in a large burned field stretching north of the Machaca River to the road into Poite village. The Pottery Cave group and a large, unnamed group 300 meters to the north were mapped, as were structures in a burned field on the east side of Gateway Hill. In 2008, we returned for just two weeks of mapping before a long laboratory season. During this time, we cleared and mapped the Big Tree and Blank Stela Group.

Excavations in 2005 concentrated on two of the three tallest pyramidal platforms on the Gateway Hill Acropolis – the Operation 8 and 9 structures (see Figure 10.7). This work consisted of clearing the south and west faces of the Operation 8 structure and of excavating the summit of the Operation 9 structure and a small portion of the horribly looted top of the Operation 8 structure. This last was dug to a depth of about 2.5 meters; the fill was too unstable to go deeper.

We did not originally plan to excavate the Operation 9 structure. For a major platform at Pusilha, it was only slightly looted. Given that virtually every platform at the site has been badly damaged by villagers from San Benito Poite, Dr Jaime Awe of the Belize Institute of Archaeology asked us to conduct preventive salvage work. Excavations revealed that the mass of the platform consists of a large, natural outcrop of rock covered with a cut stone façade lacking a stair. The summit served as an access linking the Operation 8 structure to the northern half of the acropolis.

Excavations on the south side of the Operation 8 structure revealed a small Terminal Classic room constructed at plaza level against the lowermost body of the pyramid. Within this room were found the postcranial remains of a small adult or adolescent of undetermined sex (Burial 8/2). Duplicate arm bones indicate that this is not the same individual represented by Burial 4/1. A cranium and fragmentary postcranial elements were found resting on the lowermost body of the pyramid (Burial 8/1). These belong to an adult male of local origin (Pitcavage 2008: 29–30). In the plaza west of the Operation 8 structure and in front of its stair we excavated a family crypt (Pitcavage and Braswell 2009, 2010). A single pyriform vessel belonging to the Pabellon Modeled-Carved supersystem found in the crypt dates it to the Terminal Classic. The burial appears to have been opened and used in three sequential episodes that cut through the plaster floor. First, a young child was interred. Later, an adult male was added in an extended position. Finally, a woman of advanced age was placed in a flexed position at his head. Both adults are of local origin.

The Burial 8/4 royal tomb

The summit of the Operation 8 structure was found riddled by seven major looters' pits and a tunnel connecting two of them. Scattered and broken cache vessels were found on this disturbed, unstable, and uneven surface. As salvage work, we excavated on top of the Operation 8 structure to see what might still be preserved prior to leveling it with fill. Our excavations quickly revealed an anthropomorphic eccentric (Figure 10.11a), as well as large capstones for a tomb. These stones were found out of place and jumbled, and appear to have been moved in antiquity.

Excavating through collapse, a tomb with a southern antechamber was revealed (Figure 10.12; Braswell 2007a, 2007b; Braswell and Gibbs 2006). A total of 761 obsidian blade fragments, flakes, and debitage were recovered from inside of the tomb, most from collapse and slump contexts above the tomb floor. This suggests that these objects may have been placed as an offering or cache above the tomb proper, perhaps on top of the capstones. With the exception of three pieces that could not be visually sourced, all the obsidian appears to come from the El Chayal sources.

The tomb contained the fragmentary remains of a local male individual who died in advanced adulthood and who shows signs of arthritis, caries, and dental modification (Pitcavage 2008: 33; Somerville 2009). Also found on the floor of the tomb were four eccentrics of chert and obsidian (see Figure 10.11b–e), 13 fragmented serving vessels (Figure 10.13), a crude basin holding jadeite offerings, 197 jadeite and other greenstone artifacts (including three jadeite diadems that were part of a royal headdress), one large drilled pearl, four pyrite mirror stones, two

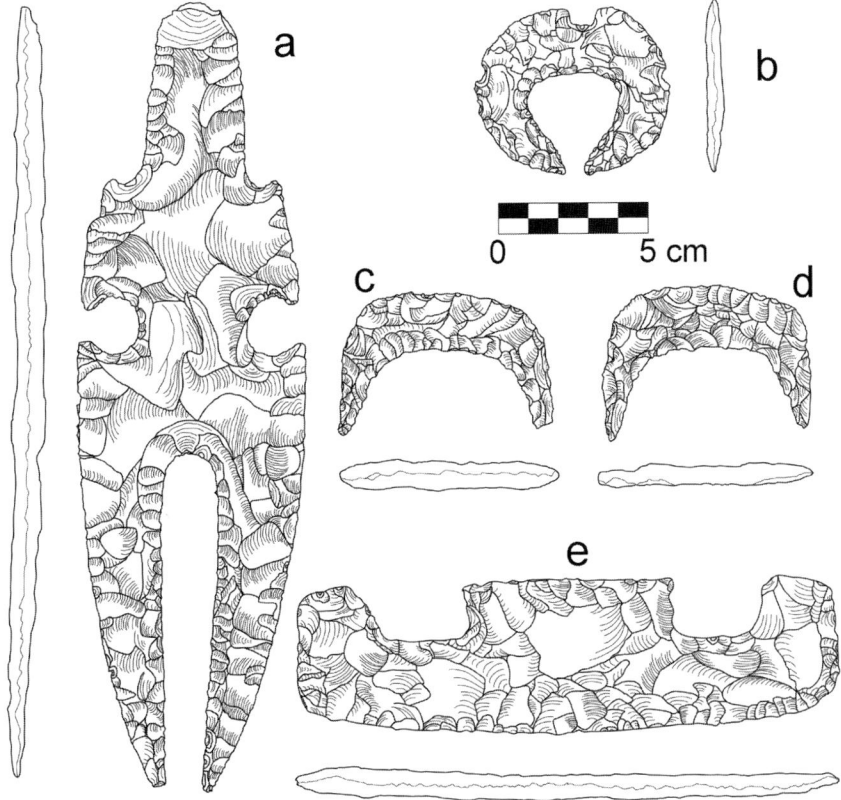

FIGURE 10.11 Eccentric lithic artifacts associated with the Burial 8/4 royal tomb: (a) anthropomorphic chert eccentric, Op. 8/11/5, found outside tomb; (b) lunate chert eccentric Op. 8/10/5; (c–d) lunate obsidian eccentrics, Op. 8/10/5; (e) trilobe obsidian eccentric Op. 8/9/3 (original drawings by Edwin Barnes)

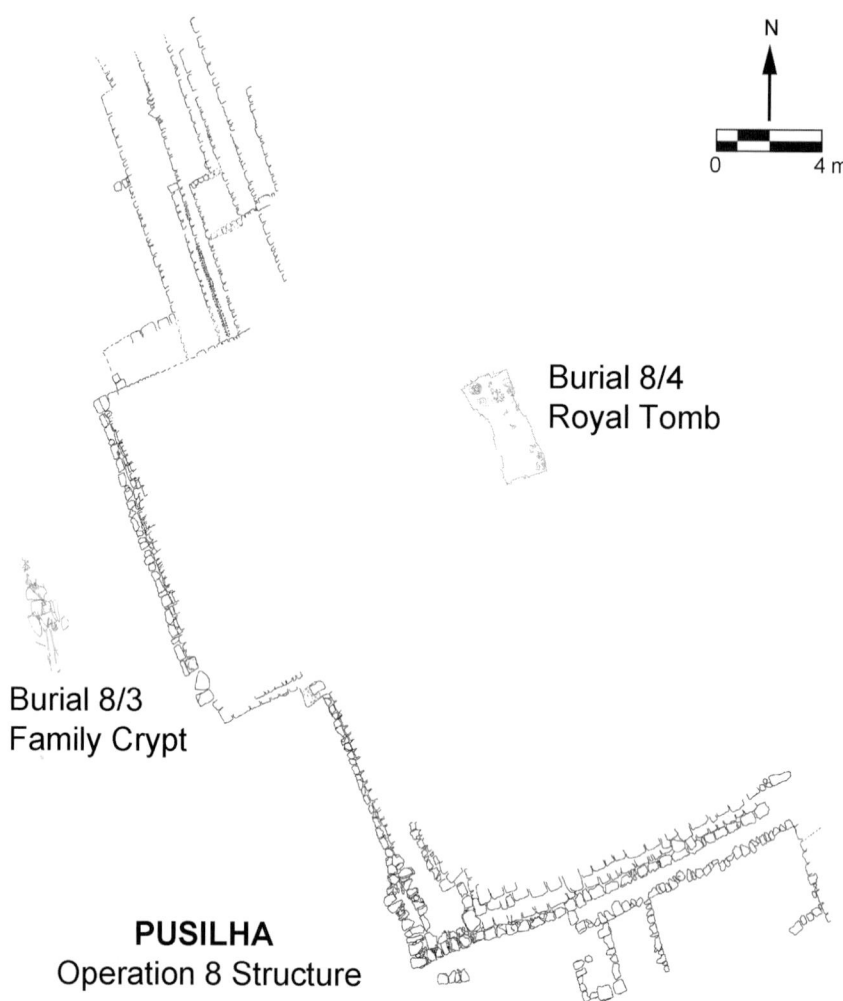

FIGURE 10.12 The Operation 8 structure, showing the location of the Burial 8/3 family crypt and Burial 8/4 royal tomb

complete *Spondylus* shells (one cupping the chin and mouth, another the face of the buried individual), 17 other shells and fragments, and four carved *Spondylus* mosaic pieces. Thirteen broken and disturbed polychrome and monochrome vessels were lined up against the eastern side of the tomb; brightly colored polychromes were present in the north and dark monochromes in the south of this alignment (Cassandra R. Bill, personal communication 2007). Two of the jade diadems were found whole in the cache vessel located north of the head of the individual (Figure 10.14). A small fragment of the third diadem was also present in this vessel, but most of it was found broken in the southeastern corner of the tomb. This supports the observation that the tomb was opened in antiquity.

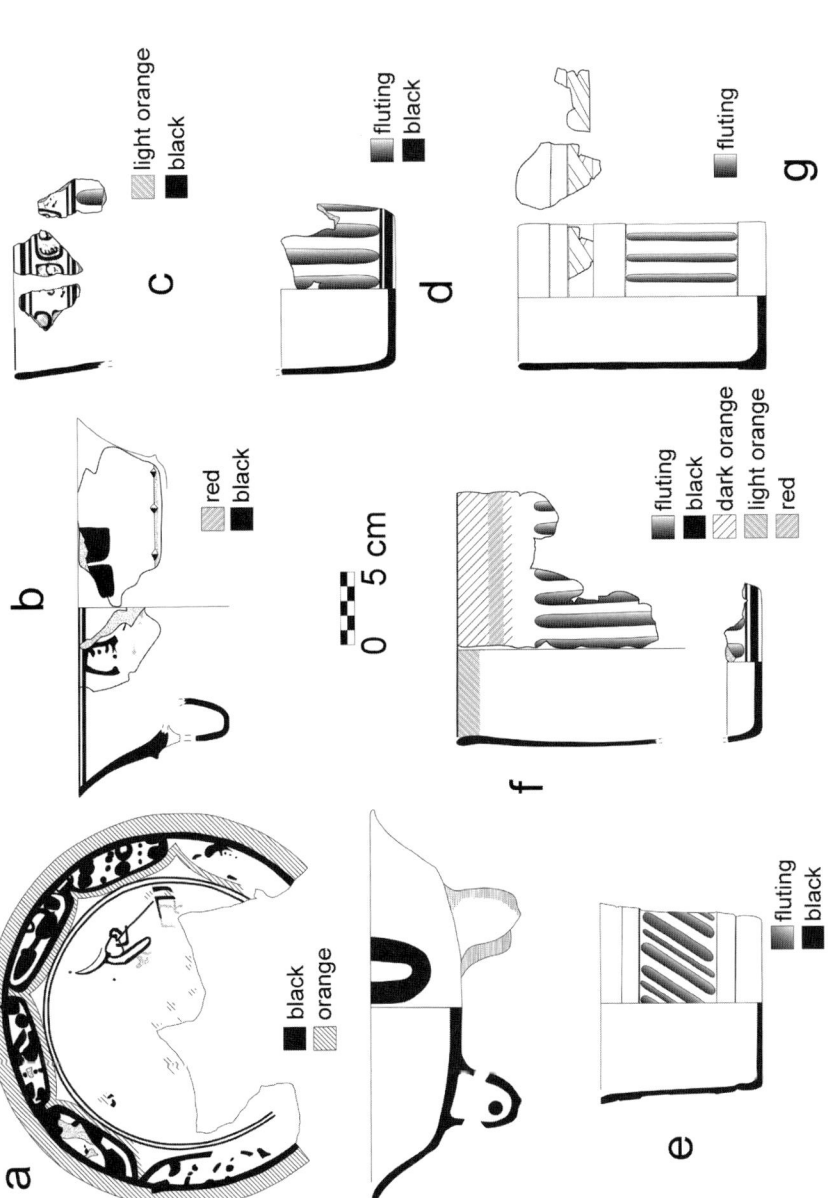

FIGURE 10.13 Late Classic ceramics recovered from the Burial 8/4 royal tomb: (a) Op. 8/10/5, Vessel A; (b) Op. 8/9/3 and Op. 8/10/5, Vessel C; (c) Op. 8/11/5, Vessel E(a); (d) Op. 8/10/5, Vessel F; (f) Op. 8/9/3, Vessel E(b); (e) Op. 8/9/3, Vessel F; (f) Op. 8/10/5, Vessel D; (g) Op. 8/9/3, Vessel G (original drawings by Edwin Barnes)

FIGURE 10.14 Three jade diadems from the Burial 8/4 royal tomb: the third diadem is carved on two sides (bottom row), and most of it was found broken in the southeastern corner of the tomb (Braswell *et al.* 2005: fig. 11).

Who was buried in the royal tomb? Unfortunately, the painted ceramics recovered from Burial 8/4 are too poorly preserved to know if they once contained texts with nominal phrases. Thus, there is no evidence in the tomb that names its occupant. Nonetheless, the location of the tomb, the elaborate nature of the grave furnishings, the presence of the jade diadems, and the sex of the individual suggest it is the burial of a male *k'uhul ajaw*. Furthermore, the age of the ceramics imply that Burial 8/4 dates roughly to the middle of the eighth century. Two rulers who employed the *k'uhul ajaw* title and emblem glyph of Pusilha on carved monuments and a third who did not – Ruler F, Ruler G, and "Ruler" X5 – lived in this period (see below).

The first of these, Ruler F, was a woman, so she is excluded. It is not clear if "Ruler" X5 was a *k'uhul ajaw*. He did not claim that title on his only known monument, Stela F, dedicated in AD 751. In contrast, the diadems in Burial 8/4 certainly indicate *k'uhul ajaw* status. Ruler G – who did employ the *k'uhul ajaw* title and the full emblem glyph of Pusilha – lived until sometime after 731 and presumably died before 751. These make him the strongest candidate for the occupant of Burial 8/4. But it also should be noted that three other rulers – X1, X2, and X4 – whose dynastic positions are unknown, cannot be definitively excluded.

What makes the tentative identification of Burial 8/4 as that of Ruler G (or possibly "Ruler" X5) so exciting is that this is the first and only time in the nation of Belize that the remains of a hieroglyphically known ruler have been identified. Burial 8/4 thus provides a connection between the archaeology and known dynastic history of Pusilha.

The hieroglyphic monuments of Pusilha

Thomas A. Joyce published photographs and several partial sketches of some of the Pusilha stelae (Joyce et al. 1928), as did Sylvanus G. Morley (1937–8) and Berthold Riese (1972). Until recently, the hieroglyphic texts had not been thoroughly illustrated according to standards set forth by the Corpus of Maya Hieroglyphic Inscriptions Project (Graham 1975). Moreover, except for a few brief studies concerning the chronological and astronomical contents of the hieroglyphic inscriptions, the majority of the monuments have never been adequately analyzed. To understand these texts better, Prager conducted field work at the British Museum in London in 1996 and 2000 and at the modern Q'eqchi' village of San Benito Poite in 2001 and 2005 as co-director of the Pusilha Archaeological Project. As part of his research, Prager surveyed, photographed, and drew all of the monuments located in both the British Museum and at the site of Pusilha.[2]

Of particular interest to this study are the hieroglyphic inscriptions from the Stela and Moho Plazas. Most of the carved monuments known from Pusilha were found in the main Stela Plaza, a large area defined by six platforms (Figure 10.15). Structure I was the most important platform in this group, reflected in its large size and the fact that nearly all of the known monuments were concentrated in a row in front of its north side. Each monument found in front of or on Structure I was labeled with an alphabet letter (Stelae A–H, K–T, and Z) by Thomas Gann (Joyce et al. 1928: fig. 2). Stela U was found on the opposite end of the plaza in front of Structure III. This alphabet is still used, with modifications by Morley (1937–8), Riese (1972), and Prager (2002). Following a suggestion by Riese (1972), all of the monument fragments found during the 2001 field season are numbered consecutively (Figure 10.15a). Not one of the newly discovered carved fragments belongs to any of the monuments previously documented.

As first reported by Gann (1928) and Joyce (1929), most of the stelae were found broken and lying on the ground near their respective monument bases except for Stela F, which was found intact. Many fell backwards, preserving their inscribed backs better than their figurative front sides. Shortly after their initial discovery, the best-preserved monuments (Stelae C, D, E, H, M, O, P, Q, R, Z, and Monument Fragments 1–3) were removed from British Honduras and shipped to the British Museum.

In 1992, Gary Rex Walters and Lorington Weller (n.d.) discovered a large residential complex and ceremonial group that they dubbed the Moho Plaza, located about 2 kilometers southwest of the Stela Plaza. It includes a previously unknown ballcourt (see Figure 10.8, Structures I and II). Walters and Weller found three small ballcourt markers and located nine hieroglyphic and iconographic cartouches engraved into the risers of a stair leading up to the top of Structure VI.

During the 2001 season, the PUSAP team found 15 new sculptured monument fragments (and many more blank pieces of known monuments) in the Stela Plaza (Figure 10.15a). A well-preserved fragment of a previously unknown carved stela was brought to our attention in the village. Thus, today the corpus of carved monuments from Pusilha comprises some 46 items: 20 stelae (Stelae A, A1, B–H, K–S, U, Z), three altars (Altars V–X), three ballcourt markers (Ballcourt Markers 1–3), one hieroglyphic

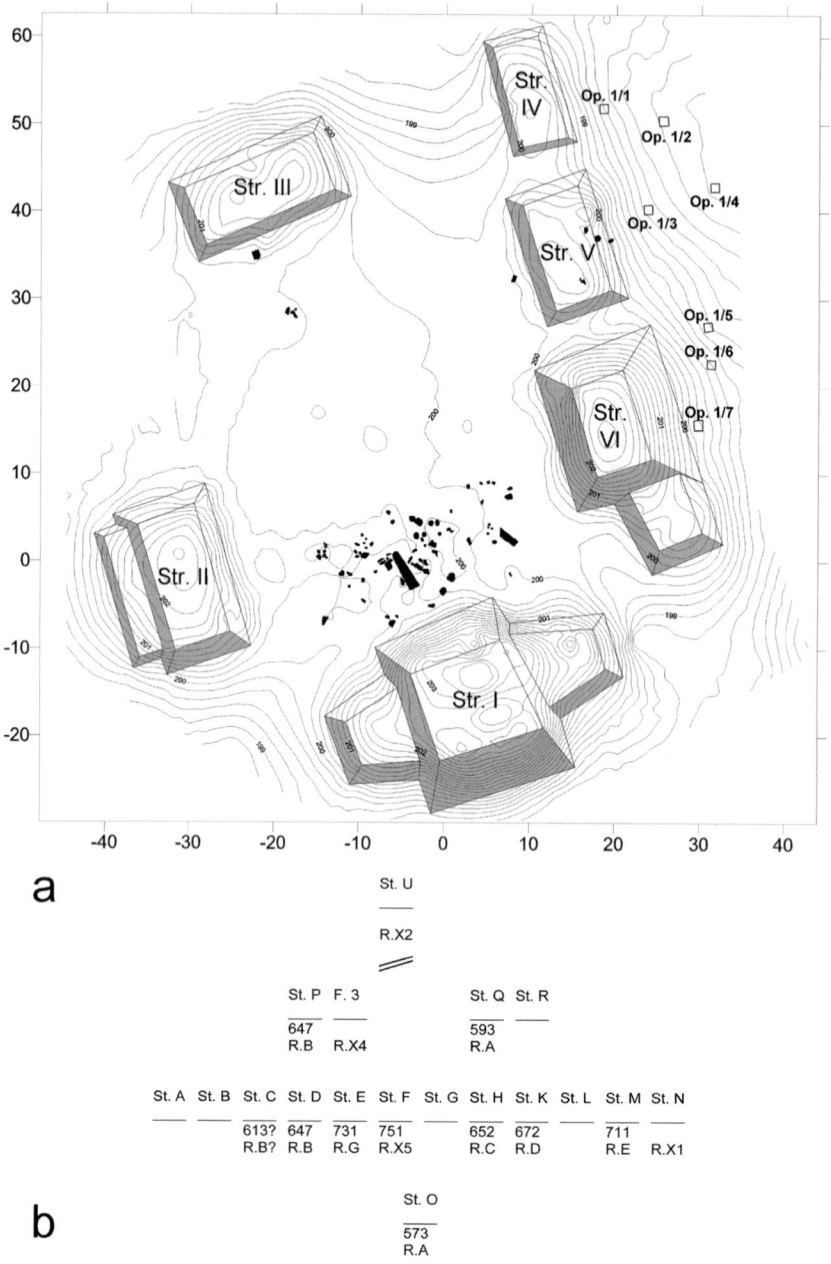

FIGURE 10.15 The Stela Plaza: (a) location of platforms, mapped monument fragments (black), and test pits; (b) ideal schematic of location of stelae, showing dedicating ruler and date (in years AD); Stela F (near center) and Stela N (at eastern end) are still in place (grid is in meters, as measured from a datum in the Stela Plaza; contour interval is 20 centimeters; height of the datum was arbitrarily set at 200 meters but is closer to 153 meters above sea level).

stairway (Hieroglyphic Stairway 1), 17 sculptured monument fragments (Fragments 1–17), and two miscellaneous texts (Miscellaneous Texts 1–2).

Previous epigraphic studies

To date, the hieroglyphic texts of Pusilha have received only moderate attention from epigraphers. Several scholars examined the dates and portions of the Supplementary Series as found on the texts shortly after their discovery (Andrews 1951; Gann 1928; Morley 1937–8; Satterthwaite 1951; Thompson 1928). Riese (1972) compiled a summary and review of the state of epigraphic research on Pusilha during the early 1970s. Table 10.1 presents the hieroglyphic dates in the Pusilha corpus as recorded in ten hieroglyphic inscriptions. The chronological sequence of dates begins in the remote and legendary past with a retrospective date of 8.2.0.0.0 (February 9, 81 BC), and the latest date known at Pusilha, found on the Hieroglyphic Stairway 1, is 9.18.7.10.3 (March 26, 798). Most historical texts date to between 9.6.17.8.18 and 9.16.0.0.0 (June 19, AD 571 and May 9, AD 751), spanning a period of almost two centuries.

One of the few researchers to use and publish data from the Pusilha inscriptions was Heinrich Berlin, who, in his study of Classic Maya emblem glyphs (Berlin 1958: 118), identified the emblem glyph of Pusilha on Stela M. Following Berlin's work, Joyce Marcus (1973, 1976) was the first scholar to consider seriously the hierarchical nature of

TABLE 10.1 Hieroglyphic dates and accompanying Supplementary Series information from Pusilha

Date		Supplementary Series	Monument
[8.2.0.0.0]	5 Ajaw 8 Sak		St. P
[8.6.0.0.0]?	10 Ajaw 13 Ch'en		St. K
[9.6.17.8.18]	[2 Etz'nab 11 Sek]		St. P
9.7.0.0.0	7 Ajaw [3 K'ank'in]	G9, D25, C6, X6, A9	St. O
9.7.0.0.0	7 Ajaw 3 K'ank'in	G9, D3, C3, A10	St. P
[9.7.4.9.12]	[1 Eb 10 Zotz']		St. P
[9.7.10.0.0]	6 Ajaw 13 Sak		St. H
9.7.12.6.7	8 Manik' 10 K'ayab	G9, D2, C5, X5, A10	St. H
[9].8.[0].0.[0]	5 Ajaw [3 Ch'en]		St. Q
9.8★.0.0.0	5 Ajaw 3 Ch'en★	G9, D17, C4, A10	St. D
[9.8.1.12.8]	2 Lamat 1 Zip		St. D
9.10.15.0.0	6 Ajaw 13 Mak	G9, D3, C3, A10	St. P
9.10.15.0.0	6 Ajaw 13 Mak	G9, D23, C3, A10	St. D
9.11.0.0.0	12 Ajaw 8 Keh	G9, D4, C4?, X?, A9	St. H
9.12.0.0.0	10 Ajaw 8 Yaxk'in	G9, D1, C3, X3/4, A10	St. K
[9.12.7.5.0]?	4 Ajaw 13 Yax?		St. U
9.14 0.0.0	[6 Ajaw 13 Muwan]	G9, C16, C?, X3/4, A?	St. M
9.15.0.0.0	4 Ajaw 13 Yax	D11, C1?, X2, A9	St. E
[9].16.[0.0.0]	2 Ajaw 13 Sek		St. F
[9.18.7.10.3]?	4 Ak'bal 2 Sotz'		HS 1

Note: Unattested portions of the dates are shown in brackets, reconstructed texts are indicated by asterisks, and question marks indicate uncertainty about reconstructions.

Maya polities. In so doing, based on her identification of the shared use of the Quirigua emblem glyph by Pusilha, she placed Pusilha within the political realm of Copan and Quirigua. Subsequently, Proskouriakoff (1993: 56) also suggested that Pusilha was subordinate to Copan. Nonetheless, we believe that these identifications of the Pusilha emblem glyph on Quirigua Stela I and Copan Stela 7 are incorrect. Very importantly, Proskouriakoff (1993:96) noted that the name of the eleventh ruler of Copan (nicknamed Butz' Chan) resembles that of the contemporary ruler of Pusilha, known today as Ruler B. Her argument clearly suggests some sort of political interaction or relationship between Pusilha and Copan based on the use of a similar name by both Maya polities. Proskouriakoff's idea was later adopted by Schele and Grube (1994), who deciphered the main sign of the Pusilha emblem glyph as T559 /**TZUK**/, meaning "province" or "partition." In addition, Schele and Grube recognized and accepted the name phrase recorded on Pusilha Stela M as that of the twelfth ruler of Copan, an individual nicknamed Smoke Imix God K. Based on these arguments, they assumed that Pusilha was a province of Copan whose kings reigned temporarily over Pusilha or perhaps subdued the local rulers (ibid.: 118). These interpretations greatly influenced our thinking as we began planning PUSAP in 1998 (Braswell *et al.* 2004b). Braswell and Cassandra Bill's interest in the site, in fact, was stimulated by their previous work at Copan.

In his discussion of the political history of Quirigua, Matthew Looper (in Schele and Looper 1996) casts a critical eye over this regional political model. In regard to the supposed political interactions between Quirigua and Pusilha, Looper emphasizes the formal distinction between the emblem glyphs of Pusilha and Quirigua (T559 and T560). The main sign of the Pusilha glyph (T559) represents an upright avocado tree. In contrast, that of Quirigua is rotated 90 degrees (T560). In addition, Looper suggests that the name on Pusilha Stela M may simply be that of a local lord and not that of the twelfth ruler of Copan. After the seven field and laboratory seasons of PUSAP, we have found virtually no data supporting anything more than the weakest and most tenuous political connection between Pusilha and both Quirigua and Copan (Braswell *et al.* 2004b, 2005). Moreover, economic links are supported only by the presence of three sherds of non-Maya pottery from Honduras (Bill and Braswell 2005; Bill *et al.* 2005). Instead of Copan or Quirigua, the Late Classic occupants of Pusilha most likely came originally from the southwestern Peten.

Before Prager's work, the most substantial study of the dynastic history of Pusilha was an unpublished seminar paper written by Dorie Reents (n.d.), in which she correctly identifies the proper names and epithets of seven Pusilha rulers. She was among the first scholars to identify several parentage statements in the texts of Pusilha. Statements such as *u bah u ch'ab*, meaning "his image [is] her creation," is an explicit "child of parent" expression. Reents also correctly identified the glyphic expression *u bah u juntan*, meaning "he is the cherished one of," as another kind of "child of mother" expression. Both phrases are of help in reconstructing the dynastic sequence of Pusilha and the relationships among rulers of different generations.

Images on the front of the Pusilha monuments emphasize a ruler flanked by bound captives. Both the iconography and hieroglyphic inscriptions suggest that the rulers of Pusilha seem to have participated in numerous wars. Based on the text of Pusilha Stela D, Berthold Riese (1982) was the first scholar to identify the important "flint-and-shield" (*tok' pakal*) warfare expression, while Schele and Grube (1994: 106) identified another war-related expression in the same text, which is paraphrased as the "burning of an object" and linked to a *lakam tun* or "stela." Prager deciphers this as *k'asay lakam tun*, meaning "the stela was broken."

The rulers of Pusilha

Prager (2002) identified 38 individuals in the hieroglyphic inscriptions of Pusilha. Among these are 11 individuals that employ the *k'uhul ajaw* title, meaning "divine ruler." Seven can be placed into a chronological framework. Since most of the personal names cannot be read completely on account of weathering or the lack of proper decipherment, we refer to the lords of Pusilha by the alphabetic designations Ruler A to Ruler G (Table 10.2; Figure 10.16). Three more individuals employ the *k'uhul ajaw* title of Pusilha, but their texts do not include enough information to place them within the chronological framework of the site. Therefore they are labeled Rulers X1, X2, and X4. Ruler X3 is tenuously placed in the chronology, but his name glyph is completely eroded. Hence, it is possible that this individual is one of the other identified rulers. "Ruler" X5 is firmly placed in the chronology at 9.16.0.0.0 in a text consistent with rulership. Nonetheless, Stela F, the only monument on which he is mentioned, does not contain an emblem glyph. Thus it is likely, but not proven, that he was a divine ruler of the site. Four individuals are known from iconographic images and are called Rulers X6 to X9 (Figure 10.17 and Table 10.3). It is entirely possible that some or all of these images correspond to other named rulers identified in the texts. For example, Rulers X3 and X7, both of whom are known only from monuments in the Moho Plaza, could be the same person.

Many of the legible Pusilha texts contain scant biographical information. Moreover, others are severely eroded. Therefore there is limited epigraphic data concerning many of the key individuals in the ruling families of Pusilha. The following reconstruction of the political history of Pusilha comes from the use of indirect epigraphic evidence following the biological and cultural criteria that are generally accepted by most epigraphers today:

1. The age of any person shall not exceed 100 years and the age difference between parents and children must be at least 15 years (Riese 1980).
2. Only one sovereign ruler (the *k'uhul ajaw*) governed the polity at any given time.
3. In order to ensure the continued existence of the dynasty, heirs apparent took power immediately or within one year after the death of their predecessors (exceptions to this rule are known from Caracol; see Grube 1994: 108).
4. Male primogeniture generally governed succession but, in cases where the male line was broken, a brother, a sister, or even a daughter could accede.

Finally, it is important always to remain cautious of the problems associated with the use of historical "truth" and "misrepresentation" associated with the political

TABLE 10.2 The ancient rulers of Pusilha and their biographies

Ruler	Hieroglyphic name	Monument	Birth	Accession/period of rulership	Death
A		St. O, Q	9.4.0.0.1–9.4.19.17.19	9.6.17.8.18?	9.8.14.3.6–9.9.19.17.19
B		St. P, D, C?	9.7.4.9.12?–9.8.15.0.1–9.9.14.17.19	9.8.15.0.1–9.9.14.17.19	9.10.15.0.1–9.11.0.0.0
C		St. H	9.7.12.6.7	9.11.0.0.0	9.11.0.0.1–9.12.0.0.0
D		St. K		9.11.0.0.1–9.12.0.0.0	9.12.0.0.1–9.14.0.0.0
E		St. M		9.12.0.0.1–9.14.0.0.0	9.14.0.0.1–9.15.0.0.0
F				9.14.0.0.1–9.14.19.17.19	
G		St. E		9.14.0.0.01–9.15.0.0.0	
X1		St. N			
X2		St. U			
X3		HS 1 Frag. 3		9.18.7.10.3?	
X4					
X5		St. F			

propaganda on Maya monuments (Marcus 1992, 1995). It is conceivable that the Maya may have distorted the historical record in both contemporary and retrospective texts as well as in posthumous references. Thus, the accuracy of historical statements also must be questioned and examined.

Ruler A

Sources

Ruler A sponsored two known monuments – Stela O (commemorating the 9.7.0.0.0 period ending; Figure 10.18a) and Stela Q (commemorating the 9.8.0.0.0 period ending; Figure 10.18b). Given that only calendar dates survive on these two monuments,

The dynastic history and archaeology of Pusilha **273**

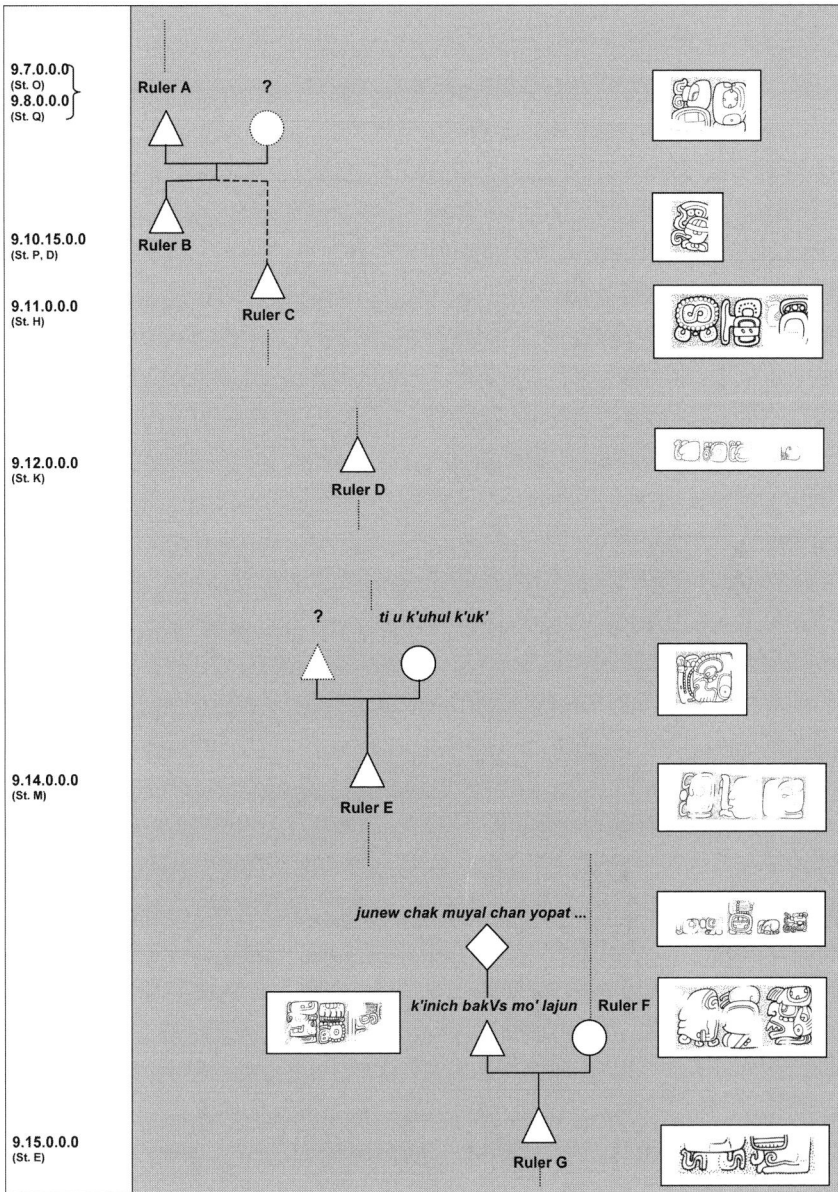

FIGURE 10.16 The royal genealogy of Pusilha (dotted lines show uncertain kinship relationships)

no contemporary historical information can be extracted from them concerning the life of Ruler A. Nonetheless, relevant biographical data were recorded on Stelae D and P (Figure 10.19), two monuments commissioned by Ruler A's son and heir, Ruler B. From these monuments we can conclude that the dates of Ruler A's reign fall between 9.6.17.8.18 (June 17, 571) and 9.10.15.0.0 (November 7, 647).

TABLE 10.3 The chronology of the rulers of Pusilha

Date		Ruler							Problematic rulers									
									with			*no*						
									Emblem glyph			*Iconography*						
K'atun-date	Long Count	A	B	C	D	E	F	G	X1	X2	X3	X4	X5	X6	X7	X8	X9
9.4.0.0.0		♂	♂	♂	♂	♂	♀	♂	St. N	St. U	HS 1	F. 3	St. F	St. C	BM 1	F. 17	St. R
9.5.0.0.0								♂									
9.6.0.0.0	9.6.17.8.18	¤															
9.7.0.0.0	9.7.0.0.0	■? ● St. O															
	9.7.4.9.12		★? ◄	★													
	9.7.10.0.0																
	9.7.12.6.7																
9.8.0.0.0	9.8.0.0.0	● St. Q															
	9.8.1.12.8	□?															
9.9.0.0.0		● St. D, P, C?															
9.10.0.0.0	9.10.15.0.0								No calendar dates from 9.8.1.12.9 to 9.10.14.17.19									

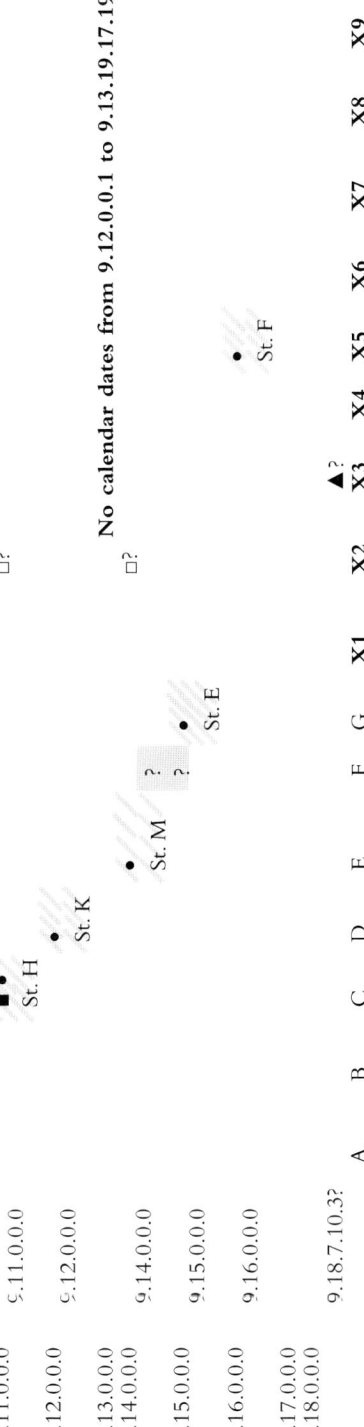

Notes: Rulers A–G and X1–X4 use the Pusilha emblem glyph or are tied to an accession statement; "Ruler" X5's status is deduced from its epigraphic context. Rulers X6–X9 are highly speculative and are known only from iconography; some or all could be duplicated in the hieroglyphically known rulers. The leftmost column displays the dedication dates of the monuments, and the second column displays the Initial Series dates associated with specific events. The rulers are identified by capital letters and their respective lifespans are indicated by bars. Stripes specify a secure lifespan, solid gray indicates an assumed period. Symbols mark specific events: ★ = secure birthdate; ✶ = reconstructed birthdate; ▫ = reconstructed accession date; ■ = secure accession date; ● = period ending and monument dedication; ▲ = unknown event present in texts.

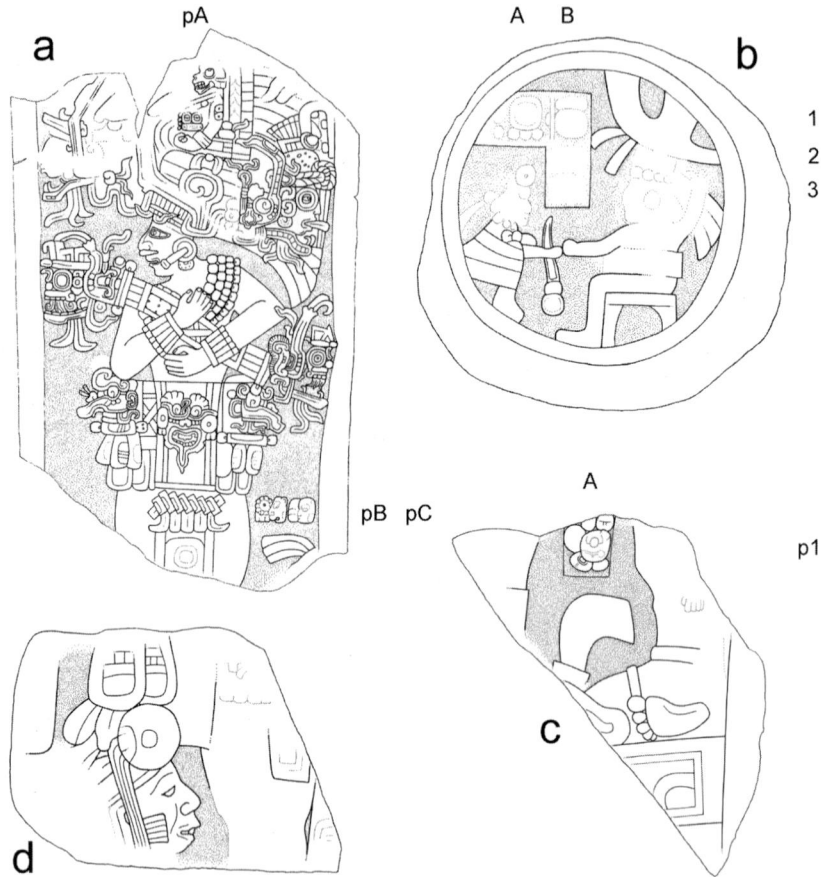

FIGURE 10.17 Monuments showing rulers known only from iconography: (a) Stela C (Ruler X6); (b) Ballcourt Marker 1, Moho Plaza (Ruler X7); (c) Fragment 17 (Ruler X8); (d) Stela R (Ruler X9). The iconographic references to Teotihuacan on Stela C are particularly striking; the inscription at pB names a captive, *Itzamnaaj Balaam*, but his place of origin is too eroded to read (original drawings by Christian Prager).

Names and epithets

The name phrase of Ruler A (dubbed "God K – 1" by Reents n.d.: 2) is recorded on Stelae D and P, both dedicated by Ruler B to commemorate the 9.10.15.0.0 period ending. The complete name phrase of Ruler A, as found on Stela D (C4–D5), reads /**K'AWIL CHAN-na K'IN-ni-chi MUWAN SAK tz'u-nu-na**/ > *K'awil Chan K'inich Muwan Sak Tz'unun*. The second part of his name phrase (*Muwan Sak Tzunun*) may simply be his pre-accession name and means "white hummingbird" (Acuña 1993: 158v). However, Ruler A's proper name is recorded on Stela P (C5–D5, G5–H5) as *K'awil Chan K'inich*. A full title sequence appears on Stela D (D7) and includes the Pusilha emblem glyph: *k'uhul un ajaw*. The main sign of the Pusilha emblem glyph inorporates the T559 logograph /**UN**/, meaning "avocado." This decipherment was derived from its use in the Ch'ol month of *Uniw* and its respective Yukatekan cognate of *K'ank'in* (Grube 1990: 82). Two variants of the Pusilha emblem glyph have been discovered. In most cases, the variable element (the name of the Pusilha polity) is the T559 /**UN**/ (Figure 10.20a), whereas on Stelae D, K, and E the main sign contains an additional element: Tnn+T559 (Stela D: G14–H14; Figure 10.20b). Unfortunately, this additional grapheme has not been deciphered, nor is it featured in any other known hieroglyphic text.

Ruler A's title sequence contains the phrase /**HUK CHAPAT CHAN K'AWIL CHAN-na**/ > *Huk Chapat Chan K'awil Chan*, meaning "the Seventh Celestial Centipede of K'awil" (Stela D: A14–B14). This is the proper name of a supernatural agent related to the god K'awil. Ruler A also bears the epithet /**OCH-K'IN KALOM-TE'**/ > *ochk'in kalomte'*, or the "West *Kalomte*'" (Stela D: C6–D6), which is a directional title of governance. For the most part, only senior members of the most powerful dynasties bore this title, whose precise meaning is still under discussion. Simon Martin and Nikolai Grube (2000: 17) suggest that it "asserts a legitimacy derived from the great Mexican city of Teotihuacan." In many instances – Tikal, Copan, Naranjo, Seibal, and Pusilha – the *ochk'in kalomte'* title refers to the founder of a particular dynastic line. In most cases, such king-makers were themselves *ajawob*, but the first, Siyaj K'ak' of

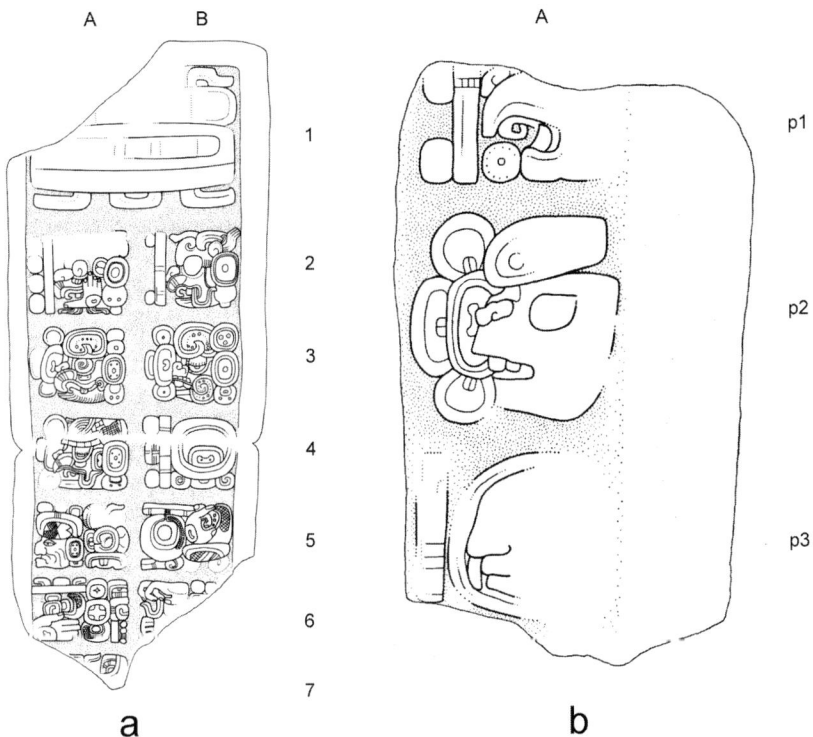

FIGURE 10.18 Stelae dedicated by Ruler A: (a) Stela O, back; (b) Stela Q, back (original drawings by Christian Prager)

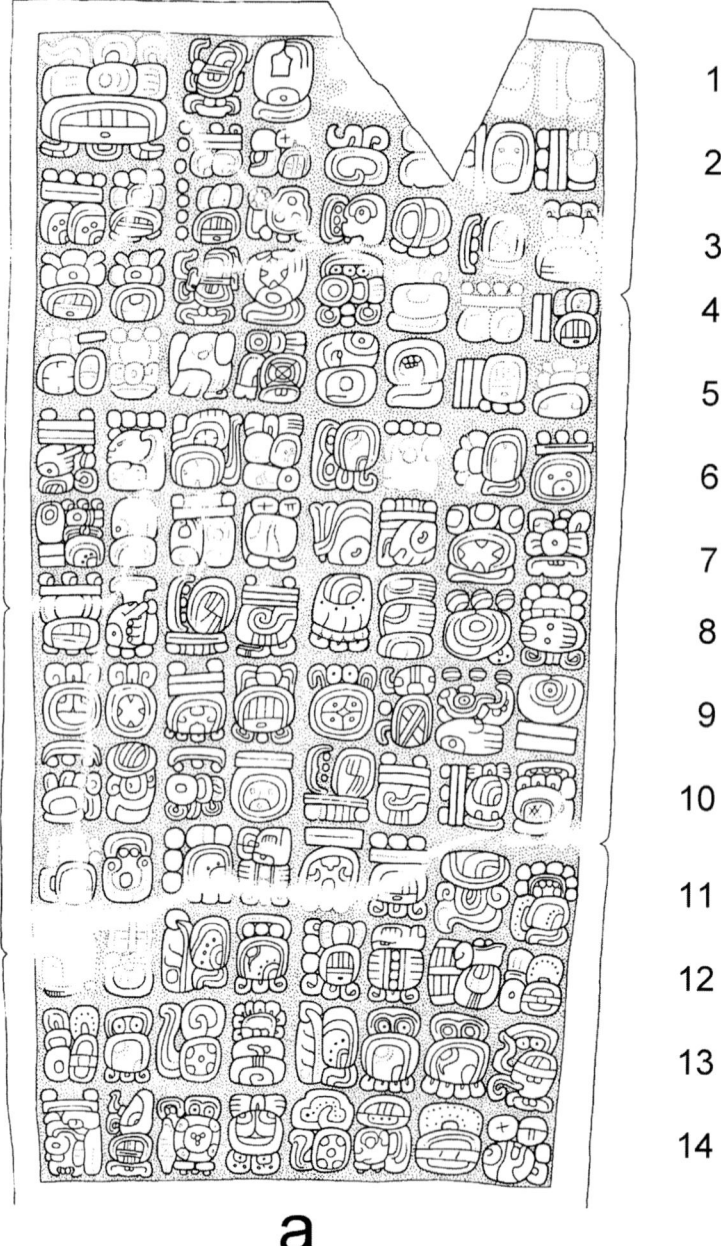

FIGURE 10.19 Stelae dedicated by Ruler B: (a) Stela D, back

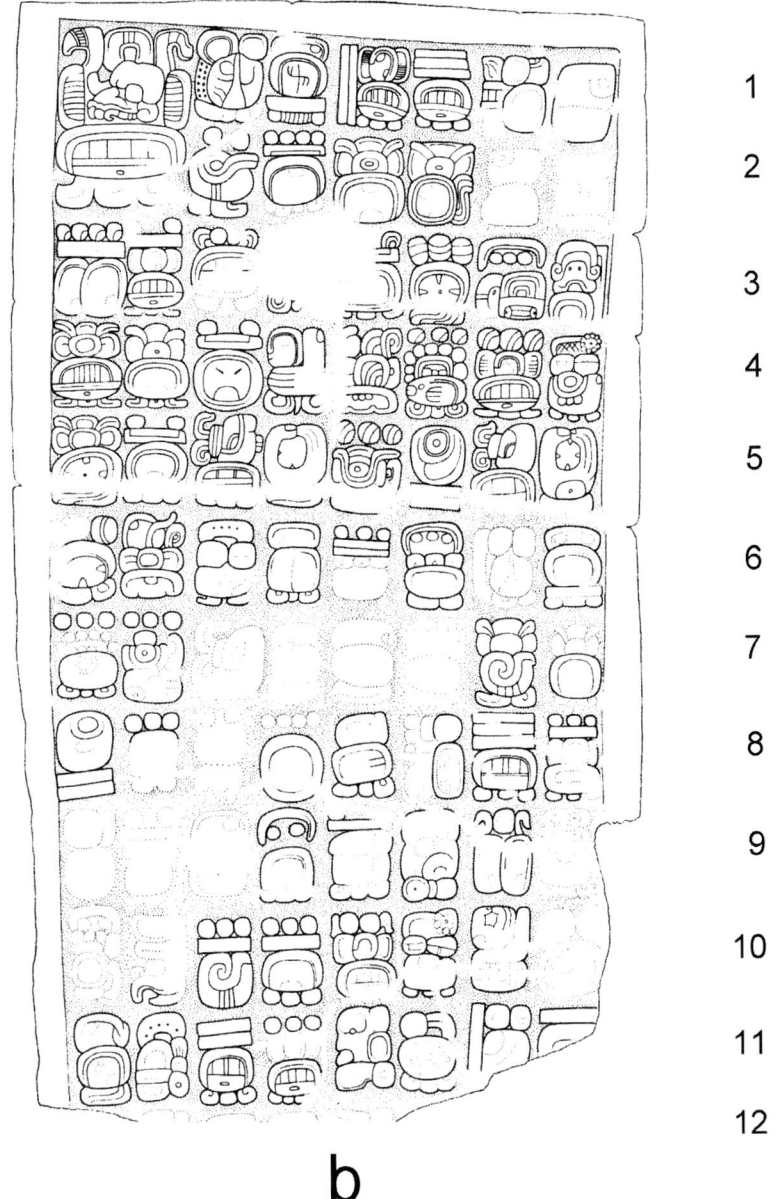

FIGURE 10.19 (b) Stela P, back (original drawings by Christian Prager)

FIGURE 10.20 Variants of the Pusilha emblem glyph: (a) principal variant, Stela M; (b) alternative variant, Stela D (original drawings by Christian Prager)

Tikal, apparently was not. Given that the ceramic sequence of Pusilha begins just before about AD 600, it is reasonable to assume that Ruler A was not only the first member of the Pusilha dynasty but also the actual founder of the city.

Ruler A also carries the title /**CHAN WINIKHAB? Ch'a-jo-ma**/ > *chan winikhab? Ch'ajom*, meaning that he was "four *k'atun* person" (Stela D: C3–D3). This indicates that he was in his fourth *k'atun* of life, or between 60 and eight years of age, when Stela Q (9.8.0.0.0) was dedicated. The sequence of Ruler A's personal titles ends with the expression /**UX BULUK PIK a-AJAW**/ > *ux buluk pik ajaw*, suggesting that he was "3-11 Bak'tun Lord" (Stela D: C2–D2). Together with the 4 *k'atun* expression, this section of the text was previously assumed by epigraphers to be a distance number counting back from the Initial Series date of 9.8.0.0.0 to an implied date of birth (Reents n.d.). Nonetheless, this hieroglyph is simply an epithet that is also recorded in inscriptions elsewhere, such as Tikal, Copan, Naranjo, and Quirigua. According to Marie Gaida (1990), the title expresses the multiplication 3 × 11.0.0.0.0, resulting in the remote Initial Series date 1.13.0.0.0.0 10 Ajaw 8 Zip (February 24, AD 9898). Thus, this numerical title may simply allude to the eternal nature and immortality of the person who uses it.

Biographical data

No text at Pusilha provides direct information about *K'awil Chan K'inich*'s birth. To reconstruct his birthdate, one must use the *k'atun*-age statements recorded on Stela D (C3) and Stela P (G4). The texts on both monuments state that stelae were erected under the aegis of *K'awil Chan K'inich* on 9.7.0.0.0 (Stela P: A10–A11), read as /**u tz'a-pa-wa** T1084 **LAKAM TUN-ni**/ > *u tz'apaw* T1084 *lakam tun*, and 9.8.0.0.0 (Stela D: A10–A11), read as /**u tz'a-pa-wa** T1084 **K'UH-HUL-TUN**/. The text on Stela P (G4) indicates that *K'awil Chan K'inich* was an *ux winikhab ajaw* or "three *k'atun*-lord," implying an age between 40 and 60. Twenty years later, according to the text of Stela D (C3), Ruler A was a "four-*k'atun*-lord," implying an age between 60 and 80. These two "*k'atun*-age" statements imply a time span for the date of his birth of 9.4.0.0.1 to 9.4.19.17.19, also suggested by the first interpretation of the numbered title ("3-11-*pik*") described above. If correct, this interpretation implies a birth on

9.4.7.15.0 12 Ajaw 18 Sek (July 8, 522). There is some epigraphic evidence to suggest that Ruler A probably acceded to kingship on 9.6.17.8.18 (June 19, 571). Recorded on Stela P (D4) in a retrospective text are the remains of a partially effaced verbal expression containing the well-known T670 logograph /**K'AM**/, meaning "to receive." This is a common verbal expression used in formal accession statements. Less than two years later, *K'awil Chan K'inich* celebrated the 9.7.0.0.0 period ending and dedicated a stone monument (Stela P: A10–A11), most likely Stela O, the focal point of the stelae in front of Structure I (see Figure 10.15b). Stela P and Stela D both record the proper name of the specific area of the city of Pusilha where this occurred as /T150-**wi-tzi ti K'UHUL** Tnn/, (T150-*witz k'uhul* ?) or "Platform Mountain at …" (Stela P: B11; Stela D: G12). "Platform Mountain" may have been the ancient name of the Gateway Hill Acropolis where the remains of dozens of pyramidal platforms and terraces were constructed against the natural slope of the hillside. If this is the case, it might be that the oldest stelae at the site were originally placed on the acropolis and moved later to the Stela Plaza. The arrangement of the stelae found there – with the most recent at the center of the monument row – strongly suggests that at least some resetting occurred. Alternatively, "Platform Mountain" could simply be the ancient name of the Stela Plaza.

Interestingly, *Yajaw Te' K'inich II*, the contemporary lord of Caracol, erected Stela 1 at that site in order to commemorate the 9.7.0.0.0 period ending. Both Caracol Stela 1 and Pusilha Stela Q share the same proper name for their respective monuments (T1084 *k'uhul tun*; Figure 10.21). This might provide evidence of contact between the two sites, a relationship that is not evident in the ceramics of Pusilha. 20 years later, the text of Stela D indicates that *K'awil Chan K'inich* was still in power. For the 9.8.0.0.0 period ending he erected a stela, also named T1084 *k'uhul tun*, at the "Platform Mountain" place (Stela D: A10–A13). This stela most likely corresponds to Stela Q, a fragment discovered north of the line of stelae in front of Structure I of the Stela Plaza that carries the Initial Series date 9.8.0.0.0 (see Figure 10.15b).

There are no references to the death of Ruler A on any monument at Pusilha. According to the "*k'atun*-age" statements, Ruler A reached an age of at least 60. The text on Stela D (H10–H14) implies that *K'awil Chan K'inich's* son and heir, *K'ak' U Ti' Chan* (Ruler B), erected a stela on 9.10.15.0.0. This heir carries the title "the divine

a b

FIGURE 10.21 Proper names of stelae at Caracol and Pusilha: (a) Caracol Stela 1 (after Beetz and Satterthwaite 1981: fig. 1); (b) Stela D (original drawing by Christian Prager).

lord of Pusilha." It can be assumed that Ruler A's death was before his son acceded to the throne, which therefore must have happened sometime before 9.10.15.0.0. Moreover, at that time the son is said to be a "2-*k'atun*" lord – that is, under 40 years old. Assuming the age statements for both men are true and that Ruler B really was Ruler A's son, the date of *K'awil Chan K'inich*'s death could not have been before about 9.8.14.3.6, the earliest possible conception date for his heir. Furthermore, if we assume he was no older than 100 years at death (see assumptions above), then he died no later than 9.9.19.17.19. Thus, within a 55-*tun* period that lacks known monuments, we can conclude that Ruler A died within a range of less than 26-*tuns*.

Parentage

No explicit parentage statements are given for Ruler A. A father–son relationship between *K'awil Chan K'inich* and his heir *K'ak' U Ti' Chan* is indicated by the "child of father" parentage statement **U YAX ch'o-ko MIJIN** (*u yax ch'ok mijin*), which can be paraphrased as "his first offspring" (Stela P: G3–H3).

Events during his reign

According to the retrospective texts on both Stela D and Stela P, commissioned by Ruler A's successor, the most notable accomplishment of Ruler A's reign was the erection of two stelae to commemorate the 9.7.0.0.0 and 9.8.0.0.0 period endings. Both stelae were erected at the "Platform Mountain " – again the ancient name of either the Gateway Hill Acropolis or the Stela Plaza (Stela D: A10–A13; Stela P: A10–B11).

A war-related event involving the breaking of stelae is recorded on Stela D (D11–C13), corresponding to the date 9.8.1.12.8 (April 24, AD 595). The subject and object of this attack are ambiguous (i.e., it is not entirely clear if Pusilha instigated or suffered from the battle), but the individual responsible for this action was named ?-*nib*, and appears to be from some unknown polity, perhaps Altun Ha, as suggested by Phillip Wanyerka (personal communication 2003). The inscription itself reads: /**k'a-sa-ya LAKAM TUN-ni U KAB-ji-ya ?-ni-bi**/ > *k'asay lakam tun* ("it got broken the large stone") *u kabjiy* ?-*nib* ("under the supervision of Scroll-*nib*") (Stela D: D11–C12; but see Helmke *et al.* 2010: 104–5 for a different reading). It may be that these actions were against Pusilha and that this portion of the text on Stela D describes the destruction of the stone stelae originally set by Ruler A. Given that there was a 52-year interval between this event and the erection of the next known hieroglyphic monument at Pusilha, it is certainly plausible that the dynasty suffered a serious setback. Following these events the text describes that the flint and the shield of "K'ak'-Scroll" were downed, /**ju-bu-yi U TOK' U PAKAL-la MA' CH'AB MA' AK'AB … K'AK'** T579/ > *jubuy u tok' u pakal ma' ch'ab ma' ak'ab … k'ak'*-? ("was downed the flint and the shield"), followed by a possible metaphor or name of a captive whose proper name remains unclear. All of this was performed under the auspices of *Chan Ek'* (Stela D: F6–E7), a person from *Yok'baj* (Stela D: F7–E8), which is a toponym that has not yet been linked to any known archaeological site. This battle and destruction event occurred at a place whose name has survived only partially, but it includes the well-known expression /**K'O(B?)-TUN**/, nicknamed "Fist-Stone" (Stela D: E5–F5). According to Markus Eberl (2005), this expression refers to a place where corpses were formally laid out. Finally, the extended war-related clause ends with the hieroglyph /**k'i-k'i-yi**/ > *k'ik'-iy*, meaning that "blood exuded" (Stela D: F8).

Ruler B

Sources

Information concerning the life of Ruler B (*K'ak' U Ti' Chan*) comes from two monuments that he commissioned – Stelae D and P (see Figure 10.19). These two companion monuments contain the longest hieroglyphic texts at Pusilha. Both celebrate the 9.10.15.0.0 period ending and were designed to glorify the past deeds of his father, *K'awil Chan K'inich* (Ruler A). Because both monuments are of similar size and style they were probably designed as a pair. Both feature similar images on their fronts (a central figure flanked by seated prisoners), and their obverse faces are completely covered with long hieroglyphic texts. Stela H (Figure 10.22), a monument dedicated by Ruler C (who was probably a brother of Ruler B), is another stela that contains important data concerning Ruler B.

Names and epithets

Ruler B was first identified as a Pusilha lord named "Chan Na God K-West-2" by Reents (n.d.: 2), who places him as the second person in the dynastic sequence. His nominal phrase consists of a full sequence of epithets including his proper name, which probably reads /**K'AK' U TI' CHAN-na**/ > *K'ak' U Ti' Chan*, "Fire is the Mouth of the Heaven" (Stela P: H13).

Schele and Grube (1994: 118) were the first scholars to propose that Ruler 11 of Copan (nicknamed "Butz' Chan") bears the same personal name as Pusilha Ruler B. Copan's "Butz' Chan" acceded to the throne on 9.7.5.0.8 (November 19, AD 578) and enjoyed a 49-year reign, dying at 9.9.14.16.9 (January 23, AD 628). During "Butz' Chan's" reign, the leading elite of Copan oversaw a surge of political power and expanded into the surrounding borderlands. At this time, polities located in the southeastern periphery of the Maya Mountains such as Pusilha – which was established just before the reign of Copan Ruler 11 – might have adopted certain Copan cultural traditions. Among these traditions is the use of proper Copan rulers' name phrases and Copan costumes, eventually including the turban headdress, as seen in a single example at Nim li Punit that dates to the early eighth century (Grube *et al.* 1999). "Butz' Chan's" reign partially overlapped that of Pusilha Ruler B, who took the proper name of his famous counterpart at Copan when he acceded to the throne sometime between 9.8.1.12.8 and 9.10.15.0.0. Based on these similarities, scholars, including Martin and Grube (2000: 201), have suggested the existence of unspecific cultural and political interrelations between Copan and its immediate neighbors to the north in the Southern Belize Region.

Ruler B's extended name phrase appears on Stela P along with several epithets, including a "2-*k'atun*" age statement accompanied by the royal title of *ajaw*, *ch'ajom*,

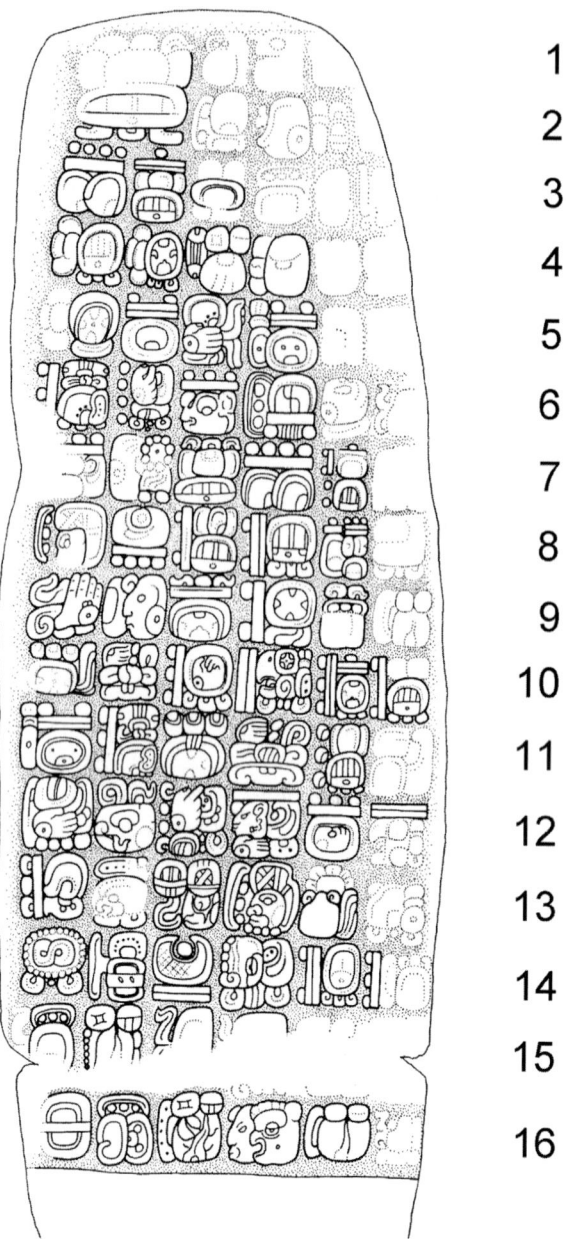

FIGURE 10.22 Stela H (back), dedicated by Ruler C (original drawings by Christian Prager)

"person," *bahte'*, "first tree," and *pitzil*, a ballplayer title (Stela P: F10–F11). The "*k'atun*-age" phrase indicates that *K'ak' U Ti' Chan* was between 20 and 40 years of age when he celebrated the 9.10.15.0.0 period ending. Like his father, Ruler B also carried the *Huk Chapat Chan* […] or "Seventh Celestial Centipede …" title (Stela P: E9). Unfortunately, the rest of Ruler B's name phrase is now eroded.

Biographical data

Ruler B's birthdate is not explicitly recorded on a legible portion of Stela P. It can be reconstructed in two ways. First, as mentioned, Stela P contains a "2-*k'atun*" age statement. Since it was dedicated on 9.10.15.0.0 (November 10, AD 647), the date of Ruler B's birth should lie between 9.8.15.0.1 and 9.9.14.17.19. A second possible birthdate of 9.7.4.9.12 1 Eb 10 Zotz' (May 27, AD 578) may be calculated from an eroded portion of Stela P (D9–D12). This relies on the distance number of 3.10.8.8 leading back from 9.10.15.0.0 to an implied date of birth. Nonetheless, this is more than 30 years earlier than the birthdate implied by the "2-*k'atun*" age statement, suggesting scribal error, the altering of history for some unknown purpose, or imperfect interpretation on our part. Support for this earlier birthdate can be found on Stela H (see Figure 10.22). On that later monument, Ruler B's name is associated with the 9.7.10.0.0 period ending (Stela H: E8), implying that *K'ak' U Ti' Chan* was already alive at that time.

The precise date of Ruler B's inauguration is unknown. We can assume he came to power during a series of wars that began with the 9.8.1.12.8 event and ended by 9.10.15.0.0, when he dedicated Stelae D and P. Stela D (G14–H14) refers to him as a *k'uhul ajaw*, or "divine ruler," of Pusilha during this period. *K'ak' U Ti' Chan* is also said to have rededicated (Stela D: H10) two *k'uhul tun*, or "holy stones" (probably Stela O and Stela Q), that were set by his father in 9.7.0.0.0 and 9.8.0.0.0. The exact date of Ruler B's death is also unknown, but must have occurred after the dedication of Stelae D and P on 9.10.15.0.0 and before the accession of his successor on 9.11.0.0.0.

Parentage

The only parentage reference to *K'ak' U Ti' Chan* is one recorded in a passage on Stela P. There, Ruler B is identified as the firstborn child of *K'awil Chan K'inich* (see above). Ruler B appears to have had a younger brother (Ruler C), who was born on 9.7.12.6.7 (Stela H) and acceded to the Pusilha throne on 9.11.0.0.0.

Events during his reign

As mentioned, Ruler B commissioned Stelae D and P commemorating the 9.10.15.0.0 period ending. Both monuments pay homage to the past deeds of his father. Because of the lack of explicit biographic data, it remains uncertain as to whether the war-related events of 9.8.1.12.8 (the demolition of stone monuments and the downing of the war insignia by the action of "?-*nib*?," or "Scroll-*nib*"; see above) should be associated with Ruler B or with his father. It also is unclear whether the text on Stela D describes a hostile act against Pusilha under the auspices of "Scroll-*nib*," or whether this individual was a local who attacked an unnamed polity. It is interesting to note that the T579 sign in his name occurs with increasing frequency in the hieroglyphic texts of sites north and east of Pusilha, including Altun Ha, Nim li Punit, Naj Tunich, and Tamarindito (see Grube *et al.* 1999: 28; Helmke *et al.* 2010). If "Scroll-*nib*" did not come from Pusilha but instead attacked it, he may have been from one of these other sites. Approximately 47 years after the destruction of his father's monuments, Ruler B rededicated their shattered monuments: /**I' WA'-la-ja** ... T150 **wi-tzi**/ > *I' wa'laj T150-witz*, or "and then was set the ... [at] the Platform Mountain."

K'ak' U Ti' Chan linked the dedication of his two stelae to some unknown past event that occurred in the presence of an ancestral or legendary person at the "*Chi*-Throne Place" on 8.2.0.0.0 5 Ajaw 8 Sak (February 9, AD 81; Stela P: G7–H11). Elsewhere, the "*chi*-throne" glyph is associated with events involving the founding fathers of the most important dynasties of the central Maya lowlands (Grube 1988). It is probably a toponym linked to the major Late Preclassic metropolis of El Mirador (Stanley Guenter, personal communication 2001). Many dynasties throughout the southern Maya lowlands legitimized their claim to power by tracing their origins back to the legendary kings of the "*Chi*-Throne Place." The name glyph of the legendary individual is partially eroded, but it includes the epithet *ho' kab ajaw*, or the "Five Earth Lord" (Stela P: G11), which is the ancient name of the Ixtutz polity of the Dolores Valley. During the Late Classic Period, this toponym appears in various contexts at numerous Maya sites, among them Ixtutz and Naj Tunich, both of which lie about 30 kilometers northwest of Pusilha. Thus, epigraphic evidence implies a heritage shared by Pusilha and several other polities in the southeast Peten. This passage on Stela P suggests that Ruler B considered himself to be the descendant of a legendary ancestor who was a dynastic founder, but who – if real – lived long before any evidence of occupation at Pusilha. It also might be a statement linking the ancestors of the Pusilha rulers to the Ixtutz region.

Ruler C

Sources

Stela H (see Figure 10.22) is the only carved monument dedicated by Ruler C. It commemorates both the 9.11.0.0.0 period ending and the accession of the king on the same day. Unlike the extremely hard, white limestone of Stelae D, P, and C, Stela H was carved on a dark conglomerate. The hieroglyphic inscription that originally faced Structure I is fairly well preserved, but the upper third of the monument is severely eroded and unreadable. Traces of a life-sized human figure occupy the front side.

Names and epithets

Dorie Reents (n.d.: 5) dubs Ruler C "God K-West – 3" and identifies him as the third ruler in the dynastic line of Pusilha. His name appears three times in the text and is read /**MUYAL-la NAH K'UHUL** Tnn **K'AK' U** .../ > *Muyal Nah K'uhul* [unreadable] *K'ak' U* ... (Stela H: A14–A15). The appearance of the Pusilha emblem glyph (B15) identifies him as a supreme Pusilha lord. The use of *K'ak' U ?* in his nominal phrase replicates portions of the name of his predecessor, *K'ak' U Ti' Chan* (Ruler B). Thus we cannot completely rule out the possibility that Ruler B and Ruler C were one and the same person – a suggestion first proposed by Reents (n.d.: 5). Nonetheless, there are several reasons to think they were distinct individuals. First, according to the 2-*k'atun* age statement (Stela P: E10), Ruler B was between 20 and 40 years old at the start of the 9.10.15.0.0 period ending. Because Ruler C's date of birth is known (9.7.12.6.7 8 Manik' 10 K'ayab), he must have been about 66 years of age on 9.11.0.0.0, which would imply a 4-*k'atun* age statement (but see above for contradictory evidence for the birthdate of Ruler B). More importantly, *K'ak' U Ti' Chan* (Ruler B) already was the *k'uhul ajaw* on 9.10.15.0.0. In contrast, the individual on Stela H ascended to the Pusilha throne on 9.11.0.0.0. Because they seem to have had different birthdates and definitively had different accession dates, we conclude that *K'ak' U Ti' Chan* (Ruler B) and *K'ak' U …* (Ruler C) were distinct people.

Biographical data

The life of Ruler C is fairly well documented, as attested by the dates of both his birth and his accession. The text on Stela H states that *K'ak' U …* was born on 9.7.12.6.7.8 8 Manik' 10 K'ayab and that he acceded to the throne on 9.11.0.0.0 at the age of 66 (Stela H: A12 and D14). The respective accession phrase on Stela H (A12–B13) reads /I' **K'AL-la-ja TIL K'AK' WAK** ye-bu tu ba-hi/ > *I' k'a(h)laj k'ak' til wak yeb tu bah*, "tied was the *k'ak' til wak yeb* on his head." Based on comparable accession phrases recorded in texts from the sites of Palenque (the Palace Tablet), Quirigua (Stela J), and Yaxchilan (Hieroglyphic Stair 3, Step III), this expression refers exclusively to the name of the royal headband that was tied to the heir apparent (Schele and Miller 1983: 18; Mathews 1988). Ruler C's precise death date is not known, but it fell before 9.12.0.0.0, the dedication date of Stela K by Ruler D.

Parentage

We have no parentage statements for Ruler C because large portions of Stela H are eroded. Nonetheless, he probably was related to both Ruler A and Ruler B, the "first offspring" of the dynastic founder. Ruler C was born too early to be the son of Ruler B, but his birthdate is consistent with that of a brother (or cousin). The repetition of part of Ruler B's name in Ruler C's nominal phrase also suggests a close family relationship. Thus, although it is not proven, we assume that Ruler C probably was the younger brother of Ruler B and the son of *K'awil Chan K'inich* (Ruler A).

Events during his reign

Two major events occurred during the reign of Ruler C. First, he commissioned Stela H to commemorate the 9.11.0.0.0 period ending and to celebrate his accession to the throne on that same day. Second, Stela H implies that Ruler C engaged in bellicose contact with other sites. A verbal expression that includes the T515 *chuk* sign ("to seize") and the name of a captive are readable (Stela H: D2). The captive appears to carry a *kob-* or *kotz-ajaw* toponym, indicating that he was a "Lord from *Kob/Kotz*" (Stela H: C4). Stela H also recounts the "binding of the stone" (/**K'AL-wi TUN-ni**/ > *k'alaw tun*) rituals that presumably accompanied the 9.11.0.0.0 period ending celebration.

Ruler D

Sources

Little is known of the history of Ruler D. As the fourth ruler of Pusilha dynasty, he was responsible for the dedication of Stela K, which commemorates the 9.12.0.0.0 period ending (Figure 10.23).

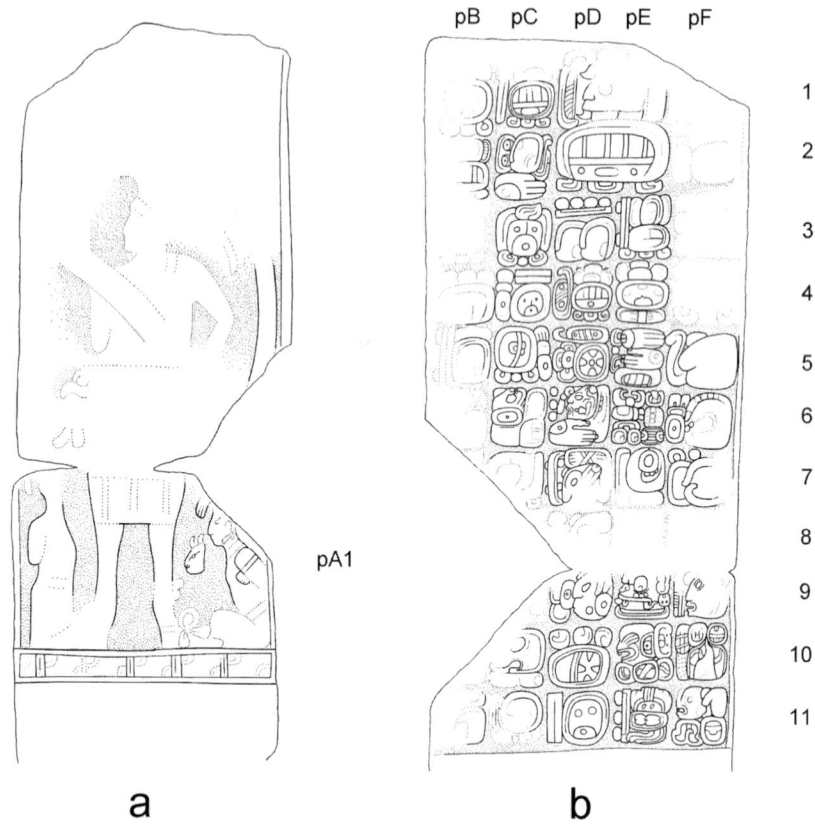

FIGURE 10.23 Stela K, dedicated by Ruler D: (a) front; (b) back (original drawings by Christian Prager)

Names and epithets

Ruler D was first recognized by Reents (n.d.: 5) and dubbed "God K-West – 4." His nominal phrase consists of several elements, including *ne' … sak k'uk' jun … aj …* (Stela K: pF5–pF9), but severe weathering makes most of this unreadable. The first part of the phrase probably contains Ruler D's proper name, and the final part incorporates the Pusilha emblem glyph (Stela K: pF10) along with the epithet /**SUTZ'**-Tnn+T227-**CHAN**/ > *sutz' … chan*, an undeciphered title that may be related to a supernatural location associated with the Rain God *Chak* as depicted in the Dresden Codex (p. 64c).

Biographical data

The lifespan of Ruler D cannot be ascertained because no other monument provides any information concerning him. Although we have no surviving accession statement, that event must have occurred during the interval 9.11.0.0.0 to 9.12.0.0.0 – that is, after the erection of Stela H by Ruler C and before Stela K was dedicated. Ruler D's death date also is unknown, but Ruler E ascended to the office of king sometime before 9.14.0.0.0. Thus we may conclude that Ruler D died between 9.12.0.0.1 and 9.14.0.0.0.

Events during his reign

Pusilha Ruler D celebrated the 9.12.0.0.0 period ending by erecting Stela K. Following a suggestion by Grube and Martin (2001: 11), the inscription on Stela K begins with an unknown distance number leading back in time to 8.6.0.0.0 10 Ajaw 13 Ch'en? (Stela K: pB1–pB5) and linking the 9.12.0.0.0 commemoration to celebrations of that much earlier period ending at the legendary "*Chi*-Throne Place" (Stela K: pC6). Stela K (pC3) names the protagonist for the events surrounding this early date as "Foliated" or "Decorated" Ajaw. He appears to be an important legendary person linked to the origin of Maya kingship and is mentioned in several texts from Tikal, Copan, Calakmul, and other sites (see Martin and Grube 2000: 9ff.). In commemorating and re-enacting the 8.6.0.0.0 *k'atun* celebration, Ruler D legitimized his own power and reign by tying the 9.12.0.0.0 period ending to this legendary event in AD 159 and encapsulated the power and prestige associated with "Foliated" Ajaw.

The iconography on the front face of Stela K (see Figure 10.23a) portrays Ruler D flanked by two kneeling captives. For this reason, it is likely that Ruler D engaged in battle at some point during his reign. Alternatively, such portrayals – which are so common at Pusilha – were propaganda, like the ubiquitous "capture" or "smiting" scenes on the pylons of Egyptian temples.

Ruler E

Sources

Ruler E dedicated Stela M to commemorate the 9.14.0.0.0 period ending (see Figure 10.24). The reference to Ruler E on Stela M provides the only information

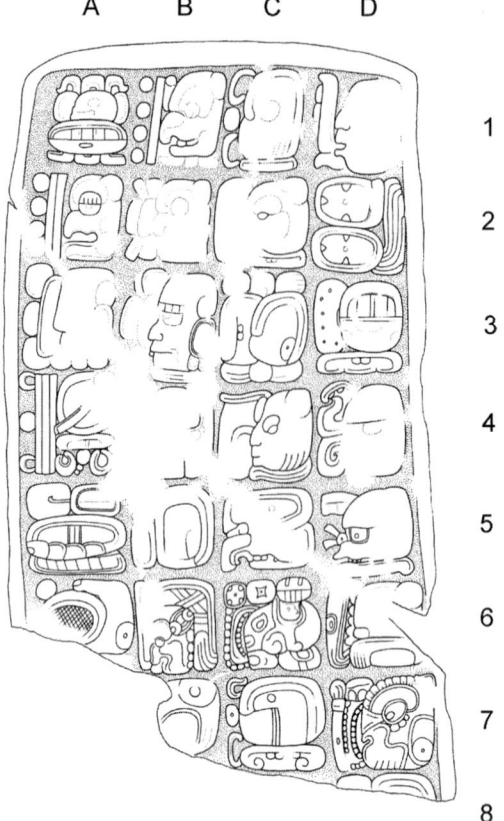

FIGURE 10.24 Stela M (back), dedicated by Ruler E (original drawing by Christian Prager)

we have concerning the life of this ruler. Since no other monument was erected at Pusilha between 9.12.0.0.0 (Stela K) and 9.14.0.0.0 (Stela M), there is a gap of some 40 years in the local dynastic sequence. This hiatus can be explained either as an accident of preservation or as a sign of political turbulence. Reents (n.d.: 6) suggests that the severely eroded Stela U, found in the Stela Plaza in front of Structure III, may be another monument that was erected under the aegis of Ruler E. Her argument is based on the physical features of the monument that are seemingly comparable to those of Stela M. Unfortunately no dates have survived on Stela U, and thus this cannot be confirmed.

Names and epithets

In her unpublished paper, Reents (n.d.) nicknames Ruler E "God K-West – 5" and places him as the fifth ruler in the dynastic sequence. His name phrase consists of his proper name, a title sequence that includes the Pusilha emblem glyph, the *ochk'in kalomte'* title, and a clause that seems to refer to his royal ancestry. The first part of the phrase (Stela M: C1–C2) contains an almost illegible proper name. The second contains the previously discussed *ochk'in kalomte'* title for high-ranking nobles (Stela M: D2–C3) and a long title sequence that reads /**K'UHUL CHAN-na**/ (Stela M: D3), /**yo-ON?-ni**/ (Stela M: C4), /**K'AK' U** .../ (Stela M: D4), /**K'AWIL JOL-**.../ (Stela M: C5–D5), /**K'UHUL UN? AJAW**/ (Stela M: C6) > *k'uhul chan yon? k'ak' u … k'awil jol … k'uhul un? ajaw*, with the final element being the Pusilha emblem glyph. By using the allegedly Teotihuacan-related *ochk'in kalomte'* title, Ruler E refers to his distinguished predecessor in office, *K'awil Chan K'inich*, or Ruler A, the founder of the first Pusilha dynasty and probably also of permanent settlement. This reference to an important royal predecessor is a common feature of the names of most of the rulers of Pusilha and served to legitimize them. The phrase *k'uhul chan yon? k'ak' u … k'awil jol?* comprises three parts: *k'uhul chan*, "godly heaven," *yon*, "his lineage," and *k'ak' u … k'awil jol?*, which probably refers to the name of an earlier ancestral ruler. The first two elements (Stela M: D3–C4) constitute a title also borne by Copan and Quirigua kings. It is most likely associated with the veneration of ancestors, in particular with the concept of divine descent and the eternity of the royal lineage, as outlined by Eberl (2005). Because the third part of the name phrase (Stela M: D4–D5) resembles the proper names of Rulers B and C, it may well be that the last element of this title phrase refers to these kings, a predecessor in office, or a venerated ancestor.

Biographical data

No specific references to the birth, accession, or death of Ruler E survive. Nonetheless, he must have acceded to power before the 9.14.0.0.0 period ending that he commemorated. Similarly, he must have died before the 9.15.0.0.0 period ending celebrated by a successor.

Parentage

Stela M records a parentage statement. The inscription states that Ruler E was the "cared-one" (/**U ba-hi JUN-TAN-na**/ > *u bah u juntan*, "his person is the cared-one of"; Stela M: D6–C7) of a royal woman whose proper name is only partially legible because the text is broken. Her name phrase begins after the "child of mother" expression and reads *ti u k'uhul k'uk'* (Stela M: D7). The classifier (T1000a, **IX**), which usually signifies female names and titles, is omitted in this context. The identity of Ruler E's father remains unknown. Given that Ruler E employed the *ochk'in kalomte'* title, we wonder if he started a new dynastic line at Pusilha whose legitimacy was derived more from his mother's family than from his father's line.

Events during his reign

Stela M was commissioned by Ruler E to commemorate the 9.14.0.0.0 period ending. The depiction of captives on its weathered front hints that Ruler E was involved in warfare during his reign.

Ruler F

Sources

The only woman elevated to the office of king at Pusilha was called *Ix Ich'ak* ... *K'inich*, or Ruler F. Although no monuments survive from her reign, her existence is attested in a parentage statement on Stela E (Figure 10.25), erected by her son Ruler G on 9.15.0.0.0.

Names and epithets

The name of Ruler F appears on Stela E and comprises the female title T1002, her proper name, and the Pusilha emblem glyph. Her personal name is partially eroded, but one can still read /**IX ICH'AK-**...**-ki** ... **K'INICH**/ > *Ix Ich'ak* ... *K'inich*, "Lady Paw ... Sun God" (Stela E: Fp5–Ep7). The initial element is the T1002, a common royal title held by high-ranking female members of a dynasty who gave birth to heirs to the throne (Stela E: Fp5). This title contains the expression *ix k'uh* (*ix* is the female classifier and *k'uh* is glossed as "god") and most likely refers to Goddess O, the aged goddess of birth and housekeeping (Nikolai Grube, personal communication 2000). The last part of her name and title phrase identifies her as a *k'uhul un? Ajaw*, "divine ruler of Pusilha" (Stela E: Fp7).

Biographical data

No biographical data exist for Ruler F. She must have ascended into the office of *ajaw* at some point during the interval between the reign of Ruler E (*ca.* 9.14.0.0.0) and Ruler G, who appears at 9.15.0.0.0 on the front side of Stela E. The accession of a queen at Pusilha suggests that some sort of dynastic upheaval occurred during this 20-year period. There must have been a breakdown in the patriline in order for Lady *Ich'ak* ... *K'inich* to assume the throne – specifically, Ruler F's predecessor probably died without a male heir. She could have been a sister or daughter of Ruler E, who himself might have been the child of a woman of the royal house rather than of a man belonging to it. Whatever her claim to the throne, the queen did not remain in power for long. Her son and successor in office, Ruler G, acceded to power sometime before 9.15.0.0.0. Thus Ruler F's reign can best be characterized as that of an interim lord, comparable with the rulership of Lady *Sak K'uk'* at Palenque (Martin and Grube 2000: 161).

Parentage

There are no statements of parentage for Lady *Ich'ak* ... *K'inich*, but her consort (i.e., the father of Ruler G) was an individual named /**K'INICH ba-ka-si MO' LAJUN k'i-?**/ > *K'inich BakVs Mo' Lajun* ..., a noble of *ajaw* rank (Stela E: Ep9–Fp10). Unfortunately, erosion has rendered much of his name and the emblem glyph he employed unreadable. A parentage statement for *K'inich BakVs Mo' Lajun* ... also names his father (i.e., the paternal grandfather of Ruler G). Finally, Stela E

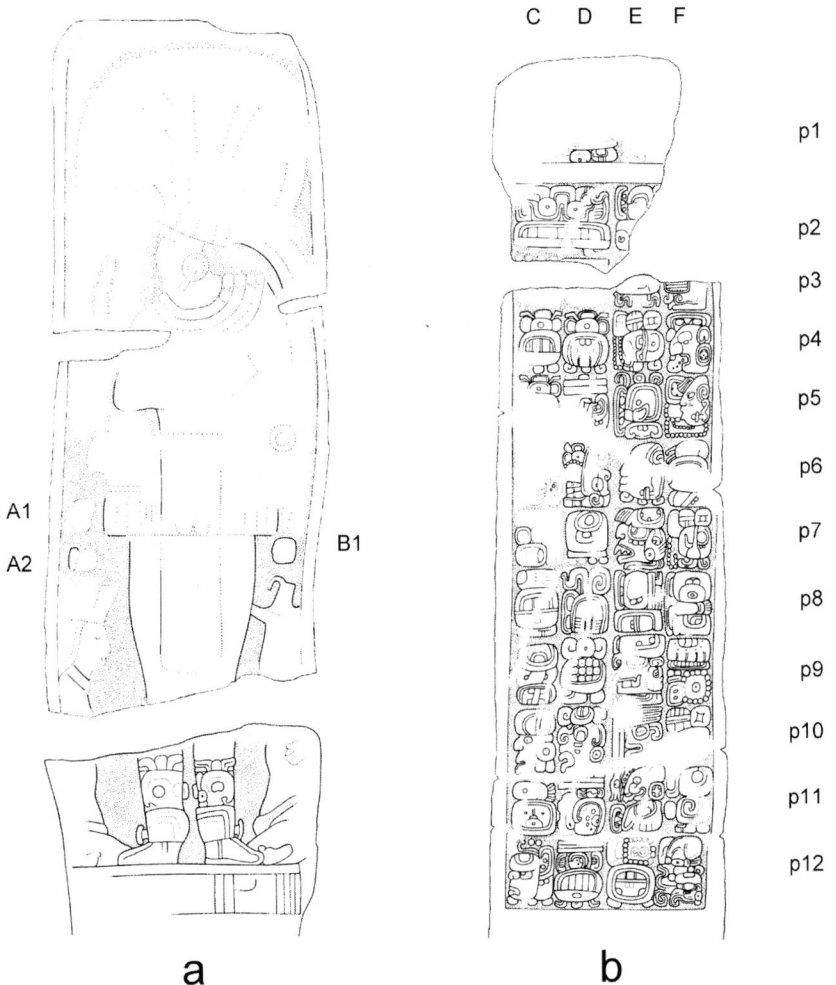

FIGURE 10.25 Stela E, dedicated by Ruler G: (a) front; (b) back (original drawings by Christian Prager)

(Ep3–Fp3) states that the marriage of Ruler F to her consort produced at least one son, ... *k'ak'* ... *chan*, who would later become Ruler G.

Ruler G

Sources

Ruler G presided over the erection of Stela E on 9.15.0.0.0, which is the only monument dedicated during his reign. The front side of the monument portrays the standing ruler flanked by two tied captives (see Figure 10.25a), and the text on the back mainly recounts the ancestry of Ruler G, particularly his parents and his paternal grandfather (Figure 10.25b).

Names and epithets

Dorie Reents (n.d.: 6) identified this ruler by means of the Pusilha emblem glyph that forms the second part of his nominal phrase. His proper name is mostly obliterated, but what remains reads /… **K'AK'** … **CHAN**/; the T561 sign read /**CHAN**/ is infixed with an almost illegible portrait glyph, possibly the T1030 /**K'AWIL**/ glyph. Following his personal name is the Pusilha emblem glyph (Stela E: Ep4).

Biographical data

There are no statements directly dating Ruler G's birth, accession, or death preserved in the hieroglyphic inscriptions of Pusilha. We can place his accession in the 20-year period between the commission of Stela M by Ruler E (9.14.0.0.0) and Ruler G's dedication of Stela E (9.15.0.0.0), shortly after his mother (Ruler F) had either died or stepped down as queen of Pusilha. Stela F (9.16.0.0.0) was dedicated by another individual, "Ruler" X5. If the latter was an *ajaw* of Pusilha, then we can conclude that Ruler G died during the previous *k'atun*.

Parentage

The inscription on Stela E ends with three statements, beginning with the child-of-mother relationship glyph read /**U BAH U JUN-TAN-na**/ > *u bah u juntan*, "his person is the cared-one of." As described above, Ruler G's mother was Lady *Ich'ak* … K'inich, who carried the titles T1002 "… holy woman" and *k'uhul un? Ajaw*, or "divine ruler of Pusilha" (Stela E: Fp5–Fp7). Ruler G's father's name was *K'inich BakVs Mo' Lajun* …, which appears on Stela E just after the "child-of-father" relational metaphor /**U si-hi U CHIT/lo-ti CH'AB**/ > *u sih u chit/lot (u) ch'ab*, meaning "he is the gift and the relative or the creation of." A foreign lord, *K'inich BakVs Mo' Lajun* … married into the ruling family of Pusilha and gave distinction to a dynasty torn by the apparent breakdown of the male line that occurred between 9.14.0.0.0 and 9.15.0.0.0. Although it is pure speculation, the individual found in Burial 3/1 could possibly be Ruler G's father. This Late Classic burial of a foreign male does not appear to be that of a king of Pusilha, yet it occupies the central place on a residential structure next to the tallest platform in the acropolis.

Ruler G gave prominence to his paternal line by adding the names and titles of his grandfather to the inscription on Stela E, which ends with a reference to the father of *K'inich BakVs Mo' Lajun* …. The expression /**U BAH U CH'AB**/ > *u bah u ch'ab*, "his person is the creation of," precedes the proper name of Ruler G's grandfather (Stela E: Ep11–Fp12). He is /**JUN e-wa CHAK MUYAL CHAN YOP-AT-ti K'AK' TI' K'AWIL**/ > *Junew Chak Muyal Chan Yopat K'ak' Ti' K'awil*. His place of origin is not known, but several segments of this personal name, especially *chan yopat*, also were used by lords of Quirigua, Copan, and Naranjo. Thus there is a slight possibility that Ruler G's paternal line might have come from one of these foreign polities. Another personal name phrase is shared by "Ruler" X5 (Stela F; see Figure 10.26a) and a Naranjo king named *K'ak' Ukalaw*

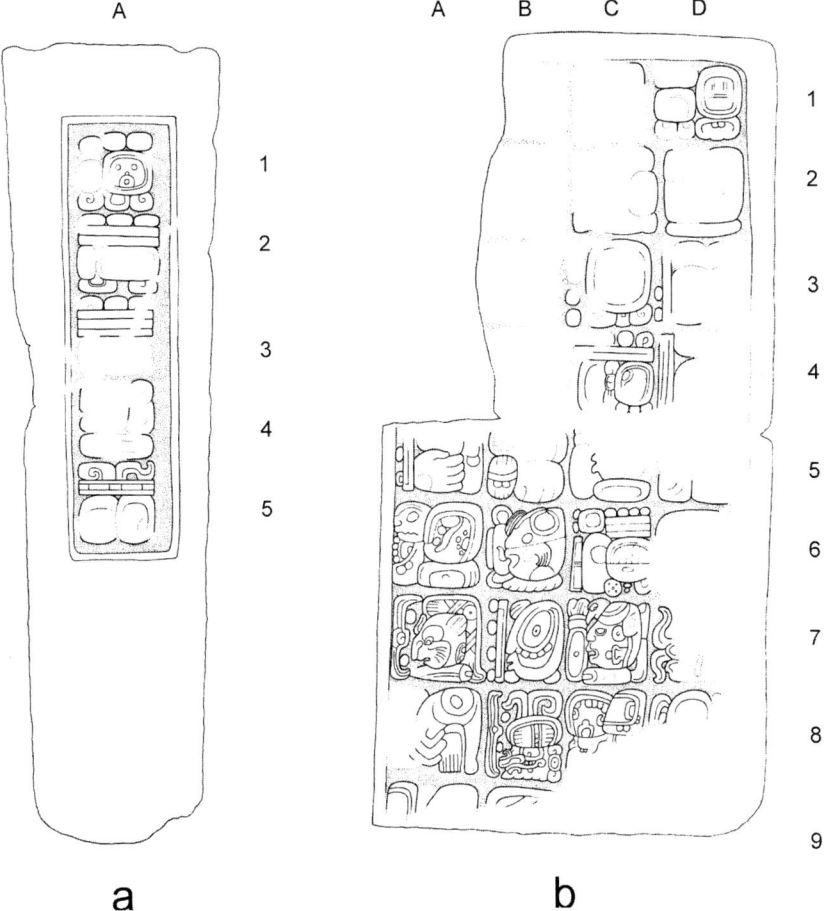

FIGURE 10.26 Late stelae dedicated by "Ruler" X5 and Ruler X2: (a) Stela F, front; (b) Stela U, back (original drawings by Christian Prager)

Chan Chak, who ruled at about the same time as his similarly named counterpart at Pusilha (cf. Martin and Grube 2000: 80–81).

Events during his reign

By 9.15.0.0.0, the dynastic troubles caused by the breakdown of the male line and the accession of a queen were apparently surmounted by the installation of a new king – Ruler G. Ruler G presided over the erection of Stela E that commemorated this important period ending. According to the text, he performed a "stone-binding" ritual, **/U K'AL TUN/** (Stela E: Ep2), ensuring that his name and lineage would live on. Although it is not mentioned in the main text of Stela E, the front face of the monument clearly shows Ruler G taking captives just as his predecessors did before him (see Figure 10.25a). Unfortunately, their name glyphs are now obliterated.

Problematic Pusilha kings

In addition to the seven rulers discussed above, four other individual royal name phrases have been identified in the hieroglyphic inscriptions of Pusilha. These phrases include the Pusilha emblem glyph, or, as on Stela U (Figure 10.26b), the proper name is preceded by an effaced accession statement (… *ti ajawle*). These four rulers, however, cannot be fully integrated into the history of Pusilha because the monuments that mention them lack secure calendar dates; they are therefore nicknamed Ruler X1 (Stela N), Ruler X2 (Stela U), Ruler X3 (Hieroglyphic Stairway 1), and Ruler X4 (Sculptural Fragment 3).

"Ruler" X5

A fifth individual is discussed in the hieroglyphic text of Stela F (Figure 10.26a), which dates to 9.16.0.0.0 and is the tallest monument at the site. The text on the front describes a "hand-scattering" event conducted by a person named *K'ak' Kalaw* (Stela F:A5) to commemorate the 9.16.0.0.0 period ending (Stela F:A3). As mentioned, this personal name is similar to the proper name of a Naranjo king, *K'ak' Ukalaw Chan Chak*, who acceded to the Naranjo throne on 9.16.4.10.18 (Martin and Grube 2000: 80ff.). *K'ak' Kalaw* probably was a ruler of Pusilha (hence nicknamed "Ruler" X5), because he celebrated the all-important *k'atun*-ending ritual usually performed only by the sovereigns of a polity. Nonetheless, his only text neither employs the Pusilha emblem glyph nor contains an accession statement. Thus, although he can be firmly placed within the chronology of the site, it is not entirely clear if he was, in fact, an *ajaw*.

Ruler X3 and the end of Pusilha

The last monarch to accede to the Pusilha throne most likely was Ruler X3. Unfortunately, no aspect of the name of Ruler X3 can be read. Hence, it is possible that he might be the same as some other problematic ruler. Ruler X3 is mentioned in the dedication text of Hieroglyphic Stair 1, found on Structure VI of the Moho Plaza (see Figure 10.8), an outlying group far from the site center. Despite a claim to the contrary (Wanyerka 2003: 174), the glyph blocks in the stair were relocated by PUSAP in 2001 and during later seasons, all are accounted for, and – important for dating the stair – all were found in their original (but slumped) positions (see Braswell *et al.* 2004b: fig. 5). Because of the late architecture of the Moho Plaza – which includes an East–West ballcourt – and the presence of late ceramics, we date its occupation primarily to the Terminal Classic period. Thus, the most likely correlation for the Calendar Round event on Hieroglyphic Stair 1 and overseen by Ruler X3 is the Initial Series date 9.18.7.10.3/4 (March 26/27, AD 798). This is the last known inscription at the site. After this date, the lords of Pusilha fell silent.

A Mexican-inspired date at Pusilha?

The text of Hieroglyphic Stair 1 is remarkable in one respect: it contains the problematical Calendar Round date 4 Ak'bal 2 Sotz' (Braswell *et al.* 2004b: fig. 5, blocks

6–7; Prager 2002; Wanyerka 2003: 174–5). For mathematical reasons, the month coefficient 2 cannot appear in conjunction with the day name Ak'bal in canonical Calendar Round dates.

"Impossible" Calendar Round permutations are known in other Maya inscriptions and have been explained in terms of scribal errors, regional stylistic differences (Proskouriakoff and Thompson 1947), ordinal counting in "current time" (Bricker 2011), extensions of the month Yaxk'in to keep summer solstice events within it (Bricker and Bricker 2011), and night-time events between the clock hours that defined the change of the Tz'olkin and Haab days (Mathews 2001; Stuart 2004; Tokovinine 2010). The last category has two variants – "Haab−1" and "Haab+1" Calendar Round dates, in which the coefficient of the Haab either lags behind an expected value by one (implying that the end/beginning of a Tz'olkin day occurred some clock hours before the changing of the Haab day) or jumps ahead of the expected value by one (implying that the Haab day changed a few clock hours before the Tz'olkin day). Mathews (2001) and Stuart (2004) discuss Haab−1 events (and so, too, do Proskouriakoff and Thompson 1947), which seem to be more common in the northern lowlands. They conclude that, while the Tz'olkin day began before midnight (perhaps at sundown), the Haab day began at sunrise.

In contrast, Tokovinine (2010) discusses Haab+1 events such as that described on Pusilha Hieroglyphic Stair 1. He notes five examples: the Motmot marker and Copan Stela 63 (both containing the date 8 Ajaw 14 Keh), Copan Altar Q (5 K'an 13 Wooh), an inscription at La Sufricaya (11 Eb 16 Mahk), and the Palenque Sarcophagus (11 Chikchan 4 K'ayab). All were carved in the Early Classic or (in the case of Altar Q) describe events during that period. Moreover, Tokovinine ties all five examples to individuals claiming Teotihuacan affiliation. He concludes that Haab+1 dates discuss night-time events from a central Mexican perspective in which the Haab day probably began at sunset.[3] Thus, following Tokovinine, the Pusilha inscription describes the dedication of Moho Plaza Structure VI as taking place after sunset on 9.18.7.10.3 (March 26, AD 798) but before the following sunrise.

Bricker (2011) provides an alternative, elegant, and simpler solution to Haab+1 dates (but which does not explain aberrations of the Haab−1 sort). She suggests that Calendar Round dates of this form reflect notational practices, not ideas about when various days began. Following a discussion by Morley (1915: 46), she maintains that dates such as 4 Ak'bal 2 Sotz' display an ordinal counting of the Haab, and hence should be read as "the second day of Sotz'." Because the seating of the month takes place on a day with the coefficient 0, the cardinal day 1 Sotz' is also the ordinal second day of Sotz'. Bricker ties this way of ordinal numeration or "current time" to central Mexico, echoing Tokovinine (2010).

We cannot be sure which of these interpretations is correct – that is, whether or not the dedication event took place specifically during a night-time transition or more vaguely during a 24-hour period. Fortunately, the difference of only a few hours is not meaningful from an archaeological perspective. What is surprising is that the Pusilha example seems to have been carved many years after all but one of the previous examples – Copan Altar Q. Moreover, the Pusilha example lacks any sort of Teotihuacan referent. Bricker and Bricker (1995) discuss later central Mexican influence in an inscription found at Chichen Itza; perhaps the Pusilha date reflects Terminal Classic rather than earlier contacts with western Mesoamerica. The inscriptions of Pusilha, therefore, end with a minor enigma.

Conclusions

Archaeological survey reveals that Pusilha was a small Maya city with perhaps 7,000 inhabitants and a population density of more than 1,100 individuals per square kilometer (Volta 2007: 39). Nonetheless, it was by far the largest site in the Southern Belize Region and the only one that might accurately be called a true city. Ceramics indicate that permanent settlement began at the very end of the Early Classic and show the strongest ties with southwestern Peten. The city flourished during a relatively short period, roughly AD 600–790. Some groups, including the Gateway Hill Acropolis, also were occupied in the Terminal Classic. Others, such as the Pottery Cave Group and Lower Group I, were abandoned during that period. The large outlying Moho Plaza Group, which resembles the Stela Plaza in some ways but includes at least one ballcourt, was built during the Terminal Classic period. Terminal Classic occupation also was vibrant in the area occupied by the modern village of San Benito Poite. There, the final stage platform of the Bulldozed Mound was built during the Terminal Classic and occupied into the Postclassic period.

Test pits, salvage operations, and excavations in eight structures at Pusilha revealed 17 burial contexts containing the remains of 22 individuals (Pitcavage 2008: 19). These provide detailed information concerning health, diet, origin and migration patterns, interment practices, and ideological beliefs concerning the afterlife (Braswell and Pitcavage 2009; Pitcavage and Braswell 2009, 2010; Somerville 2009). The most elaborate of these is the tomb Burial 8/4. Jade diadems found within the tomb indicate it is the interment of an *ajaw*. The sex of the individual and presence of mid-eighth-century pottery are most consistent with the identification of the individual as Ruler G, but "Ruler" X5 also is a possibility. Either way, this is the only royal burial in Belize that has been linked to a historically known king whose exploits are described in hieroglyphic inscriptions.

Thirty-eight individuals have been documented in the hieroglyphic inscriptions of Pusilha, 21 of whom can be securely placed within the local dynastic and chronological history of the site (Prager 2002: table 1). Reents (n.d.) was able to document seven Pusilha rulers, but the evidence now suggests that the local ruling dynasty comprised at least 11 individuals, including a lone queen (see Figure 10.16 and Table 10.2). The inscriptions reveal a 220-year span of dynastic history dating from 9.7.0.0.0 to 9.18.0.0.0. Earlier historical dates recorded on several monuments (8.2.0.0.0 and 8.6.0.0.0) prove that some Pusilha kings traced their origin back to Late Preclassic times and referred to legendary individuals who, if real, might have been ancestors or even dynastic founders from foreign locations. Similar legends are recorded at Copan, Quirigua, Calakmul, and Tikal and demonstrate that the rulers of Pusilha considered themselves as sharing the same cultural and political legacy. Pusilha itself appears to have been founded by Ruler A in the late sixth century, at the dawn of the Late Classic period. The fact that only a very few number of sherds diagnostic of the Early Classic period have been found at the site supports this conclusion. During Classic times there was a sequence of at least six kings and one queen, spanning a period from 9.6.17.8.18 to 9.15.0.0.0 and beyond.

In general, two major issues hinder the reconstruction of the Pusilha dynasty and its local history. First, the dynastic account is incomplete. It is interrupted by epigraphic gaps around 9.9.0.0.0, 9.13.0.0.0, and 9.17.0.0.0 (see Table 10.3). These could be real hiatuses in the corpus. Alternatively, they could be the results of looting, the erosion and breaking of texts (especially Stelae N and U), and the need to conduct larger-scale excavations in order to find additional inscriptions. The second major issue is the lack of important biographical data for most rulers – including dates of birth, accession, death, and parentage statements. Most personal dates are calculated using indirect evidence, such as *k'atun* age statements, or interpolated between the appearance of one kingly name and that of a successor.

Evidence for inter-site relations between Pusilha and its neighbors are few and one-sided (cf. Wanyerka 2009: 546ff.). The ruling Maya elite of the Late Classic period employed many strategies for seizing, consolidating, and increasing their power, such as warfare, marriage alliances, hierarchical relationships among high kings and subordinate or vassal subject polities, and various forms of diplomatic relations, including royal visits. The hieroglyphic inscriptions of Pusilha and depictions of captives on monuments stress the point that the local elite waged war intensively, but the names of captives generally remain obscure because of weathering. As a result of the present study, new metaphors can be added to the repertoire of war-related clauses, such as *k'asay lakam tun*, "the stela was broken" (Stela D: D11), and *k'ik'iy*, "blood was shed" (Stela D: F8). The child-of-father expression *yax ch'ok mijin*, "first youth, child" for "first offspring," also is unique to Pusilha. Together, such phrases indicate the development of local rhetorics.

Several texts provide indirect evidence that the rulers of Pusilha associated themselves in some way with other important polities. Ruler B refers to a legendary ancestor whose name could be a reference to Ixtutz, a site roughly 30 kilometers northwest of Pusilha. Although the evidence is not strong, a passage on Stela P seems to link the royal houses of these two polities in the distant past. Other hieroglyphic associations suggest some connection with royalty in the Petexbatun–Rio Pasion Region and Copan. Ceramics provide strong suggestive evidence that the inhabitants of Pusilha could have come from southwestern Peten. Ideological or even familial relations between the rulers of Pusilha and Copan seem to be implied by the structural similarity in the proper names of Pusilha Ruler B and the eleventh ruler of Copan, "Butz' Chan." Nonetheless, material evidence for ties with Honduras is virtually non-existent and consists of just three sherds of non-Maya pottery.

Pusilha Stela Q and Caracol Stela 1 (both erected on 9.8.0.0.0) bear the identical proper name. This may indicate that the lords of Pusilha maintained cultural contacts with Caracol around 9.8.0.0.0; later contacts, however, are not reported in the texts. Evidence for ceramic ties with western Belize are lacking at Pusilha until the Terminal Classic period, when Belize Red first appeared at the site. A "water-scroll" toponym is mentioned twice on Pusilha Stela D. This glyph appears quite often in the Petexbatun and Rio Pasion regions (especially at Aguateca and Seibal) and also at Altun Ha. Moreover, the individual credited with demolishing stelae and downing the flint and shield is called "Scroll"-*nib?*. The T579 hieroglyph that is part of his name is found most frequently in the inscriptions of Altun Ha in northern Belize and at Naj Tunich and other sites in southern Peten.

Nonetheless, the inscriptions of Pusilha contain no unambiguous reference to a major Maya polity in the form of a legible foreign emblem glyph or a full royal name. It has been suggested that the Pusilha corpus of inscriptions contains "explicit references to accessions and other important events taking place under the auspices of rulers from foreign polities" (Wanyerka 2003: 6), but we have identified no such unequivocal or clear citations. Tikal, Calakmul, Copan, Caracol, and even the minor site of Quirigua (which displayed a similar emblem glyph) are never explicitly mentioned in the Pusilha corpus. Similarly, these sites do not mention Pusilha on their own monuments. If ambassadorial visits, royal marriages, wars, alliances, or other sorts of interactions between Pusilha and these important sites took place, we do not know of them.[4] With the possible exception of Ruler B, who took the name of a sitting Copan king and who referred to a legendary ancestor associated with Ixtutz, the rulers of Pusilha seem to have studiously ignored their counterparts from other important cities. Despite the use of the prestigious *ochk'in kalomte'* title at Pusilha, the rulers of important polities seem to have returned the favor. As far as we can tell, the lords of Pusilha allied themselves with neither side and took no part in the great struggles between the Tikal and Calakmul dynasties of the sixth and seventh centuries. Instead, they waged war against small, local polities whose names – where legible – have not been linked to archaeologically known polities. Pusilha, therefore, seems to have practiced a "third way" that allowed it to survive in a relatively underpopulated and marginal region situated in a frontier zone at the edge of more powerful kingdoms (Braswell *et al.* 2004b: 232).

What is perhaps most frustrating is that the hieroglyphic inscriptions of Pusilha contain no clear references to Nim li Punit or Lubaantun, two nearby sites in the Southern Belize Region with known emblem glyphs. Uxbenka also had an emblem glyph, but it is too eroded to read. Moreover, Nim li Punit – which has eight inscribed monuments – never mentions either Pusilha or Lubaantun; the limited Lubaantun texts perhaps mention Nim li Punit once but do not reference Pusilha (Wanyerka 2003: 23–4); and readable portions of the Uxbenka inscriptions discuss none of the other three sites. The Southern Belize Region seems positively laconic compared to the Usumacinta zone, where the elite practiced extravagant royal name-dropping in their texts. In fact, pauses and hiatuses in the erection of carved monuments may tell us more about relations among the Southern Belize sites than do the texts themselves.

At Pusilha, Stela F (AD 751) lacks both an emblem glyph and an Initial Series date, Stela U (which contains an accession statement) and Stela N may be later but are undated, and Hieroglyphic Stair 1 contains only a Calendar Round date. Thus, the last monument at Pusilha containing both an emblem glyph and an Initial Series date is Stela E, dedicated by Ruler G to the 9.15.0.0.0 period ending in AD 731. In contrast, the first stela was dedicated at Nim li Punit in AD 734 and two or three more were erected during the following seven years.[5] The lords of Quirigua also began – after a long hiatus – to dedicate stelae in AD 734. Both of these sites had significant Early Classic occupations but did not employ their own emblem glyphs until that year, and some sort of connection between them is demonstrated multiple times in the texts of Nim li Punit. Thus the first appearance of stelae with emblem glyphs at Nim li Punit and Quirigua appears correlated with the end of (or at least a dramatic decrease in) the erection of such monuments at Pusilha. This pattern in the inscriptions could be coincidental and causality is difficult to prove, but there is little doubt that, as the power of Pusilha and more distant Copan waned during the 730s, that of Nim li Punit and Quirigua increased.

The texts and material culture of Pusilha evince idiosyncracies that do not appear elsewhere. Together, these demonstrate the insularity of the Southern Belize Region. One of the most intriguing examples is the pairing of Stelae D and P. The first of these monuments discusses foreign relations, while the second concentrates on local history. This is a unique case in Mayan epigraphy and demonstrates that the rulers of Pusilha considered external and internal history to be distinct. Moreover, this rhetorical device indicates that they wished to keep them separate. As Leventhal (1990, 1992) suggests, Pusilha exhibits local and regional traditions within a broader Classic Maya cultural framework.

Having completed – at least for now – our field and laboratory research at Pusilha, our work continues at two other sites in the Southern Belize Region: Lubaantun and Nim li Punit (Braswell 2010; Braswell et al. 2011a, 2011b; Daniels and Braswell 2013; Fauvelle et al. 2012, 2013). The goal of the new Toledo Regional Interaction Project is to look inwards in order to understand better the economic and political relationships among the major centers of this fascinating region.

Notes

1 Archaeological field and laboratory work at Pusilha was conducted from 2001 until 2008 by the three project co-directors: Geoffrey E. Braswell, Christian M. Prager, and Cassandra R. Bill. The Pusilha Archaeological Project was generously funded by the National Science Foundation Archaeology and International Research Fellowship Programs (SBE-0215068 and INT-02-2581), the Wenner-Gren Post-PhD Program (Gr. 6848), the Foundation for the Advancement of Mesoamerican Studies, Inc. (Gr. 00029), two awards from the School of American Research, and grants from the Faculty Senate of the University of California, San Diego. Among the many colleagues who worked with us over the years were Edwin Barnes (2006), Jennifer B. Braswell (2002), Pierre Robert Colas (2004), Bonnie Dziadaszek (2002), Brittany Frazier (2005), Sherry Gibbs (2005), Susan Maguire (2001, 2002), Karen Nickels (2007), Megan Pitcavage (2007, 2008), Sonja Schwake (2002, 2004), Andrew Somerville (2008), Ben Volta (2005), and Lorington Weller (2001, 2002). We also thank the inhabitants of San Benito Poite village, 105 of whom worked with us in the field. Prager expresses his gratitude to the following people who supported his research: Clara Bezanilla, Pierre Robert Colas (1976–2008), Markus Eberl, Daniel Graña-Behrens, Nikolai Grube, Berthold Riese, Frauke Sachse, and Elisabeth Wagner. He gives special thanks to Phil Wanyerka, who proofread an earlier version of a portion of this text and shared his invaluable epigraphic material from Southern Belize. Finally, we thank Joyce Marcus and Will Andrews for their comments and editing prowess.
2 Early pencil versions of Prager's original Pusilha figures were inked by John Montgomery without our knowledge or consent. Unfortunately, errors in the preliminary drawings

were reproduced in Montgomery's inked copies, which appear throughout Wanyerka's (2003) Southern Belize Epigraphic Project report and his dissertation (2009). These mistakes have since been corrected. For this reason, the final monument illustrations presented here, rather than those inked by Montgomery from Prager's initial sketches, should be considered definitive.

3   The choice of sunset is somewhat arbitrary. The Islamic and *halachic* Hebrew calendars change days at sunset, but *shabbos* and important Jewish holidays end at "nightfall," defined by the appearance of three medium-sized stars. It is possible that such a non-solar astronomical event marked the day transition for the ancient Maya. We probably will never know.

4   Wanyerka (2003: 185–92) discusses a polychrome vase (Kerr 8089) and a slate "wrench" (Kerr 3409) that employ the Pusilha emblem. Both are unprovenienced. The first may come from Pusilha itself, while the second discusses the capture of a Pusilha lord. Unfortunately, this text does not make clear from which polity the captor came.

5   Nim li Punit Stelae 2 and 15 begin with earlier Initial Series dates, but these are retrospective inscriptions. If we date the monuments by their latest calendar reference, it appears that Stela 15 was carved in AD 734 (Wanyerka 2003: 74–5) and Stela 2 in AD 738 (ibid.: 47, 49). Nim li Punit Stela 1 was dedicated in AD 741, and Stela 4 has no date but is roughly contemporary with the other three.

References

Acuña, René (ed.) (1993) *Bocabulario de Maya Than: Codex Vindobonensis N.S. 3833*. Mexico: Instituto de Investigaciones Filológicas, Centro de Estudios Mayas, Universidad Autónoma de México.

Andrews, E. Wyllys IV (1951) The Maya Supplementary Series. In *The Civilizations of Ancient America: Selected Papers of the XXIVth International Congress of Americanists*, ed. Sol Tax, pp. 123–41. New York: Cooper Square.

Aquino, Valorie V. (2013) Chronological Calibration and the Dynamics of Climate and Culture Change at the Lowland Maya Center of Uxbenka, Belize. Paper presented at the 78th annual meeting of the Society for American Archaeology, Honolulu.

Aquino, Valorie V., Keith M. Prufer, Clayton Meredith, Brendan J. Culleton, and Douglas J. Kennett (2013) Constraining the Age of Abandonment of Uxbenká Site Core Using Archaeological Stratigraphy and AMS ^{14}C Dates. *Research Reports in Belizean Archaeology* 10: 269–79.

Ashmore, Wendy (1981) Some Issues of Method and Theory in Lowland Maya Settlement Archaeology. In *Lowland Maya Settlement Patterns*, ed. Wendy Ashmore, pp. 37–69. Albuquerque: University of New Mexico Press.

—— (1991) Site-Planning Principles and Concepts of Directionality among the Ancient Maya. *Latin American Antiquity* 2: 199–226.

Beetz, Carl P., and Linton Satterthwaite (1981) *The Monuments and Inscriptions of Caracol, Belize*. Philadephia: University of Pennsylvania Press.

Berlin, Heinrich (1958) El glifo "emblema" en las inscripciones mayas. *Journal de la Société des Américanistes* (n.s.) 47: 111–19.

Bill, Cassandra R., and Geoffrey E. Braswell (2005) Life at the Crossroads: New Data from Pusilha, Belize. *Research Reports in Belizean Archaeology* 2: 301–12.

Bill, Cassandra R., Geoffrey E. Braswell, and Christian M. Prager (2005) Interacción económica y política en la periferia Maya: Evidencia nueva de Pusilhá, Belice. In *XVIII simposio de investigaciones arqueológicas en Guatemala, 2004*, ed. Juan Pedro Laporte, Bárbara Arroyo, and Héctor Mejía, pp. 467–74. Guatemala City: Museo Nacional de Arqueología y Etnología.

Brady, James E. (1989) *An Investigation of Maya Ritual Cave Use with Special Reference to Naj Tunich, Peten, Guatemala*. PhD dissertation, Department of Anthropology, University of California, Los Angeles. Ann Arbor, MI: University Microfilms.

Braswell, Geoffrey E. (2007a) Late and Terminal Classic Occupation of Pusilha, Toledo District, Belize: Site Planning, Burial Patterns, and Cosmology. *Research Reports in Belizean Archaeology* 4: 67–78.

—— (2007b) Step Mountain and the Kingdom of the Avocado: Engineering Marvels and Forgotten Hieroglyphs at Pusilha, Belize. *Journal of Belizean Studies* 29(2): 1–14.

—— (2010) La organización política y interacción en el sur de Belice: investigaciones recientes en Lubaantún y Pusilhá. *Investigadores de la cultura maya* [Universidad Autónoma de Campeche] 19: 113–24.

Braswell, Geoffrey E., and Sherry A. Gibbs (2006) In the Land of the Avocado: Recent Archaeological Investigations at Pusilhá, Toledo District, Belize. *Research Reports in Belizean Archaeology* 3: 271–86.

Braswell, Geoffrey E., and Megan R. Pitcavage (2009) The Cultural Modification of Teeth by the Ancient Maya: A Unique Example from Pusilhá, Belize. *Mexicon* 31: 24–7.

Braswell, Geoffrey E., and Christian M. Prager (2003) ¿Una unidad politica secundaria en el área Maya? El caso posible de Pusilhá, Belice. *Investigadores de la cultura Maya* [Universidad Autónoma de Campeche] 11: 210–24.

Braswell, Geoffrey E., and Keith M. Prufer (2009) Political Organization and Interaction in Southern Belize. *Research Reports in Belizean Archaeology* 6: 43–54.

Braswell, Geoffrey E., Christian M. Prager, Cassandra R. Bill, and Sonja Schwake (2004a) Recent Archaeological and Epigraphic Research at Pusilha, Belize: Report of the 2001 and 2002 Field Seasons. *Research Reports in Belizean Archaeology* 1: 333–45.

Braswell, Geoffrey E., Christian M. Prager, Cassandra R. Bill, Sonja A. Schwake, and Jennifer B. Braswell (2004b) States in the Southeastern Periphery of the Maya World: A Report of Recent Archaeological and Epigraphic Research at Pusilhá, Belize. *Ancient Mesoamerica* 15: 219–33.

Braswell, Geoffrey E., Christian M. Prager, and Cassandra R. Bill (2005) The Kingdom of the Avocado: Recent Investigations at Pusilhá, a Classic Maya City of Southern Belize. *Anthropological Notebooks* 11(1): 59–86.

Braswell, Geoffrey E., Sherry A. Gibbs, Christian M. Prager, and Cassandra R. Bill (2006) Interaccion, migracion y la emergencia de una ciudad maya: Evidencia nueva de Pusilha, Belice. *Investigadores de la cultura Maya* [Universidad Autónoma de Campeche] 14: 317–28.

Braswell, Geoffrey E., Cassandra R. Bill, and Christian M. Prager (2007) Late and Terminal Classic Occupation of Pusilha, Toledo District, Belize: Site Planning, Burial Patterns, and Cosmology. *Research Reports in Belizean Archaeology* 4: 67–78.

—— (2008) Exchange, Political Relations, and Regional Interaction: The Ancient City of Pusilhá in the Late Classic Maya World. *Research Reports in Belizean Archaeology* 5: 51–63.

Braswell, Geoffrey E., Nancy Peniche May, Megan R. Pitcavage, and Kiri L. Hagerman (2011a) Arqueología en el reino de la calavera de cristal: excavaciones recientes en Lubaantun y otros capitales reales de Belice meridional. In *XXIV Simposio de investigaciones arqueológicas en Guatemala, 2010*, ed. Bárbara Arroyo, Lorena Paiz Aragón, Adriana Linares Palma, and Ana Lucía Arroyave, pp. 1231–43. Guatemala City: Museo Nacional de Arqueología y Etnología.

—— (2011b) Revisiting the Kingdom of the Crystal Skull: New Investigations at Lubaantun. *Research Reports in Belizean Archaeology* 8: 115–26.

Bricker, Harvey M., and Victoria R. Bricker (2011) *Astronomy in the Maya Codices*. Philadelphia: American Philosophical Society.

Bricker, Victoria R. (2011) A Notational Explanation for Maya Calendar Round Dates such as 11 Eb 16 Mac. *PARI Journal* 11(4): 9–10.

Bricker, Victoria R., and Harvey M. Bricker (1995) An Astronomical Text from Chichen Itza, Yucatan, Mexico. *Human Mosaic* 28(2): 91–105.

Chocón, Jorge E. (2013) Los grupos tipo E del sureste de Petén, una vision regional. Paper presented at the XXVII Simposio de investigaciones arqueológicas en Guatemala, Guatemala City.

Corzo, Lilian A., Jorge E. Chocón, Rosa María Flores, Oswaldo Gómez, Nora María López, Héctor E. Mejía, Paulino I. Morales, Erick M. Mejía, Heidy Quezada, Julio A. Roldán, Jorge Mario Samayoa, and Juan Pedro Laporte (2000) San Luis, Petén: exploraciones arqueológicas en el sector montañoso. En *XIII Simposio de investigaciones arqueológicas en Guatemala, 1999*, ed. Juan Pedro Laporte, Héctor Escobedo, Bárbara Arroyo, and Ana Claudia de Suasnávar, pp. 590–612. Guatemala City: Museo Nacional de Arqueología y Etnología.

Culleton, Brendan J., Keith M. Prufer, and Douglas J. Kennett (2012) A Bayesian AMS ^{14}C Chronology of the Classic Maya Center of Uxbenká, Belize. *Journal of Archaeological Science* 39: 1572–86.

Daniels, James T., Jr., and Geoffrey E. Braswell (2013) Procurement, Production, and Distribution of Obsidian in the Southern Belize Region. Paper presented at the 11th Belize Archaeology and Anthropology Symposium, San Ignacio Cayo, Belize.

Dunham, Peter, Thomas R. Jamison, and Richard M. Leventhal (1989) Secondary Development and Settlement Economics: The Classic Maya of Southern Belize. In *Prehistoric Maya Economies of Belize*, ed. Patricia A. McAnany and Barry L. Isaac, pp. 255–92. Greenwich, CT: JAI Press.

Eberl, Markus (2005) *Muerte, entierro y ascensión: ritos funerarios entre los antiguos mayas*. Merida: Universidad Autónoma de Yucatán.

Fauvelle, Mikael, Chelsea R. Fisher, and Geoffrey E. Braswell (2013) Return to the Kingdom of the Eagle: Archaeological Investigations at Nim li Punit, Belize. *Research Reports in Belizean Archaeology* 10: 241–51.

Fauvelle, Mikael, Megan R. Pitcavage, and Geoffrey E. Braswell (2012) Dynastic Capital, Minor Center, or Both? Recent Investigations at Nim li Punit, Toledo District, Belize. *Research Reports in Belizean Archaeology* 9: 51–9.

Folan, William J., Ellen R. Kintz, and Laraine A. Fletcher (1983) *Coba: A Classic Maya Metropolis*. New York: Academic Press.

Folan, William J., Armando Anaya Hernández, Ellen R. Kintz, Laraine A. Fletcher, Raymundo Gonzalez Heredia, Jacinto May Hau, and Nicolas Caamal Canche (2009) Coba, Quintana Roo, Mexico: A Recent Analysis of the Social, Economic, and Political Organization of a Major Maya Urban Center. *Ancient Mesoamerica* 20: 59–70.'

Gaida, Marie (1990) Die Bak'tun-Hieroglyphe mit Doppelkoeffizient in Maya-Inschriften. *Baessler Archiv* (n.s.) 38: 261–9.

Gann, Thomas A. (1928) *Discoveries and Adventures in Central America*. London: Duckworth.

Graham, Ian (1975) *Introduction to the Corpus of Maya Hieroglyphic Inscriptions*. Cambridge, MA: Peabody Museum of Archaeology and Ethnology.

Grube, Nikolai (1988) Städtegründer und "Erste Herrscher" in Hieroglyphentexten der klassischen Mayakultur. *Archiv für Völkerkunde* 42: 69–90.

—— (1990) *Die Entwicklung der Mayaschrift*. Berlin: Von Flemming.

—— (1994) Epigraphic Research at Caracol, Belize. In *Studies in the Archaeology of Caracol, Belize*, ed. Diane Z. Chase and Arlen F. Chase, pp. 83–122. San Francisco: Pre-Columbian Art Research Institute.

Grube, Nikolai, and Simon Martin (2001) *The Coming of Kings: Writing and Dynastic Kingship in the Maya Area between the Late Preclassic and Early Classic: Notebook for the XXVth Maya Hieroglyphic Forum at Texas*. Austin: University of Texas Press.

Grube, Nikolai, Barbara MacLeod, and Phillip J. Wanyerka (1999) *A Commentary on the Hieroglyphic Inscriptions of Nim Li Punit, Belize*. Washington, DC: Center for Maya Research.

Gruning, Edward L. (1930) Report on the British Museum Expedition to British Honduras, 1930. *Journal of the Royal Anthropological Institute* 60: 477–83.

Hammond, Norman (1975) *Lubaantun: A Classic Maya Realm*. Cambridge, MA: Peabody Museum of Archaeology and Ethnology.

Helmke, Christophe, Jaime Awe, and Nikolai Grube (2010) The Carved Monuments and Inscriptions of Xunantunich: Implications for Terminal Classic Sociopolitical Relationships in the Belize Valley. In *Classic Maya Provincial Politics*, ed. Lisa J. LeCount and Jason Yaeger, pp. 97–121. Tucson: University of Arizona Press.

Jamison, Thomas R. (2001) Social Organization and Architectural Context: A Comparison of Nim li Punit and Xnaheb. In *The Past and Present Maya: Essays in Honor of Robert M Carmack*, ed. John Weeks, pp. 73–87. Lancaster, CA: Labyrinthos.

Jordan, Jillian M., and Keith M. Prufer (2013) Contextualizing Uxbenka: Ceramic Analyses from Site Core and Household Contexts. Paper presented at the 11th Belize Archaeology and Anthropology, San Ignacio, Cayo.

Joyce, Thomas A. (1929) Report of the British Museum Expedition to British Honduras, 1929. *Journal of the Royal Anthropological Institute* 59: 439–59.

Joyce, Thomas A., Thomas Gann, Edward L. Gruning, and Richard C. E. Long (1928) Report on the British Expedition to British Honduras, 1928. *Journal of the Royal Anthropological Institute* 58: 323–50.

Laporte, Juan Pedro (2007) *La secuencia cerámica del sureste de Petén: tipos, cifras, localidades, y la historia del asentamiento*. Guatemala: Atlas Arqueológico de Guatemala. Available at www.atlasarqueologico.com/monografias.php?idm=10.

Leventhal, Richard M. (1990) Southern Belize: An Ancient Maya Region. In *Vision and Revision in Maya Studies*, ed. Flora S. Clancy and Peter D. Harrison, pp. 125–41. Albuquerque: University of New Mexico Press.

—— (1992) The Development of a Regional Tradition in Southern Belize. *New Theories on the Ancient Maya*, ed. Elin C. Danien and Robert J. Sharer, pp. 145–53. Philadelphia: University Museum, University of Pennsylvania.

Lohse, Jon C., Jaime Awe, Cameron Griffith, Robert M. Rosenswig, and Fred Valdez, Jr. (2006) Preceramic Occupations in Belize: Updating the Paleoindian and Archaic Record. *Latin American Antiquity* 17: 209–26.

Maguire, Susan, Christian M. Prager, Cassandra R. Bill, Jennifer B. Braswell, and Geoffrey E. Braswell (2003) Investigaciones recientes en Pusilhá, Belice. In *XVI Simposio de investigaciones arqueológicas en Guatemala, 2002*, Vol. 1, ed. Juan Pedro Laporte, Héctor Escobedo, Ana Claudia Monzón de Suasnávar, and Bárbara Arroyo, pp. 97–108. Guatemala City: Museo Nacional de Arqueología y Etnología.

Marcus, Joyce (1973) Territorial Organization of the Lowland Classic Maya. *Science* 180: 911–16.

—— (1976) *Emblem and State in the Classic Maya Lowlands: An Epigraphic Approach to Territorial Organization*. Washington, DC: Dumbarton Oaks.

—— (1992) *Mesoamerican Writing Systems: Propaganda, Myth, and History in Four Ancient Civilizations*. Princeton, NJ: Princeton University Press.

—— (1995) Maya Hieroglyphs: History or Propaganda? In *Research Frontiers in Anthropology*, ed. C. R. Ember, M. Ember, and P. Peregrine, pp. 122–44. Englewood Cliffs, NJ: Prentice Hall.

Martin, Simon, and Nikolai Grube (2000) *The Chronicle of Maya Kings and Queens*. New York: Thames & Hudson.

Mathews, Peter (1988) *The Sculpture of Yaxchilan*. PhD dissertation, Department of Anthropology, Yale University. Ann Arbor, MI: University Microforms.
—— (2001) The Inscription on the Back of Stela 8, Dos Pilas, Guatemala. In *The Decipherment of Maya Hieroglyphic Writing*, ed. Stephen D. Houston, David Stuart, and Oswaldo Chinchilla Mazariegos, pp. 94–115. Norman: University of Oklahoma Press.
McKillop, Heather I. (2005) *In Search of Maya Sea Traders*. College Station: Texas A&M University Press.
Morley, Sylvanus G. (1915) *An Introduction to the Study of the Maya Hieroglyphs*. Washington, DC: Smithsonian Institution, Bureau of American Ethnology.
—— (1937–8) *The Inscriptions of Peten*, 5 vols. Washington, DC: Carnegie Institution.
Nickels, Karen (2008) Food, Function, and Status: Analysis of Faunal Remains from the Maya Site of Pusilha, Belize. MA thesis, Department of Anthropology, University of California, San Diego.
Pitcavage, Megan R. (2008) Companion Burials in the Kingdom of the Avocado: Indirect Evidence of Human Sacrifice in Late and Terminal Classic Maya Society. MA thesis, Department of Anthropology, University of California, San Diego.
Pitcavage, Megan R., and Geoffrey E. Braswell (2009) Entierros múltiples en el reino del aguacate: evidencia indirecta del sacrificio humano durante el período Clásico Tardío y Terminal. In *XXII Simposio de investigaciones arqueológicas en Guatemala, 2008*, ed. Juan Pedro Laporte, Bárbara Arroyo, and Héctor Mejía, pp. 803–9. Guatemala City: Museo Nacional de Arqueología y Etnología.
—— (2010) Diet, Teeth, and Death at Pusilha, Belize. *Research Reports in Belizean Archaeology* 7: 65–72.
Prager, Christian M. (2002) Die Inschriften von Pusilha: Epigraphische Analyse und Rekonstruktion der Geschichte einer klassischen Maya-Stätte. MA thesis, Institut für Altamerikanistik und Ethnologie, Universität Bonn.
Proskouriakoff, Tatiana (1960) Historical Implications of Patterns of Dates at Piedras Negras. *American Antiquity* 25: 454–75.
—— (1993) *Maya History*. Austin: University of Texas Press.
Proskouriakoff, Tatiana, and J. Eric S. Thompson (1947) *Maya Calendar Round Dates Such as 9 Ahau 17 Mol*. Washington, DC: Carnegie Institution.
Prufer, Keith M., and Amy E. Thompson (2013) Settlements as Neighborhoods and Districts at Uxbenka: The Social Landscape of Maya Community. Paper presented at the 11th Belize Archaeology and Anthropology, San Ignacio, Cayo.
Prufer, Keith M., Holly Moyes, Brendon J. Culleton, Andrew Kindon and Douglas J. Kennett (2011) Formation of a Complex Polity on the Eastern Periphery of the Maya Lowlands. *Latin American Antiquity* 22: 199–223.
Reents, Dorie (n.d.) The Hieroglyphic Inscriptions of Pusilha: Preliminary Comments. Unpublished manuscript in possession of the author.
Rice, Don S., and T. Patrick Culbert (1990) Historical Contexts for Population Reconstruction in the Maya Lowlands. In *Precolumbian Population History in the Maya Lowlands*, ed. T. Patrick Culbert and Don S. Rice, pp. 1–36. Albuquerque: University of New Mexico Press.
Riese, Berthold (1972) *Pusilhá: Dokumentation der Inschriften*. Hamburg: privately published by the author.
—— (1980) *Die Inschriften von Tortuguero, Tabasco*. Hamburg: privately published by the author.
—— (1982) Kriegsberichte der klassischen Maya. *Baessler Archiv* (n.s.) 28: 155–80.
Satterthwaite, Linton (1951) Moon Ages of the Maya Inscriptions: The Problems of Their Seven-Day Range of Derivation from Calculated Mean Ages. In *The Civilizations of*

Ancient America: Selected Papers of the XXIVth International Congress of Americanists, ed. Sol Tax, pp. 142–54. New York: Cooper Square.

Schele, Linda, and Nikolai Grube (1994) *Tlaloc-Venus Warfare: The Peten Wars 8.17.0.0.0– 9.15.13.0.0. Notebook for the XVIIIth Maya Hieroglyphic Workshop, March 12–13, 1994.* Austin: University of Texas Press.

Schele, Linda, and Matthew Looper (1996) *The Proceedings of the Maya Hieroglyphic Workshop: Copan and Quirigua, March 9–10, 1996*, ed. Phillip J. Wanyerka. Parma: privately published.

Schele, Linda, and Jeffrey H. Miller (1983) *The Mirror, the Rabbit, and the Bundle: "Accession" Expressions from the Classic Maya Inscriptions.* Washington, DC: Dumbarton Oaks.

Somerville, Andrew (2009) Identifying the Local and the Foreign: Strontium Isotope and Trace Element Analysis of Companion Burials from Pusilha, Toledo District, Belize. MA thesis, Department of Anthropology, University of California, San Diego.

Stone, Andrea (1995) *Images from the Underworld: Naj Tunich and the Tradition of Maya Cave Painting.* Austin: University of Texas Press.

Stuart, David (2004) The Entering of the Day: An Unusual Date from Northern Campeche. Available at www.mesoweb.com/stuart/notes/EnteringDay.pdf.

Thompson, J. Eric S. (1928) Some New Dates from Pusilha. *Man* 28(6): 95–7.

Tokovinine, Alexandre (2010) The Western Sun: An Unusual Tzolk'in–Haab Correlation in Classic Maya Inscriptions. *PARI Journal* 11(2): 17–21.

Volta, Beniamino P. (2007) Archaeological Settlement Patterns in the Kingdom of the Avocado. MA thesis, Department of Anthropology, University of California, San Diego.

—— (2011) Spatial Plans and Community Identity in Ancient Maya Cities: A Case Study from Pusilhá, Toledo District, Belize. In *Ethnicity from Various Angles and through Varied Lenses: Yesterday's Today in Latin America*, ed. Christine Hunefeldt and Leon Zamosc, pp. 58–72. Brighton: Sussex Academic Press.

Walters, Gary R., and Lorington O. Weller (n.d.) Pusilha Project: 1992 Field Report. Manuscript on file at the Institute of Archaeology, Belmopan, Belize.

Wanyerka, Phillip J. (1999) A Brief Description of the Carved Monuments at Xnaheb, Toledo District, Belize. *Mexicon* 21: 18–20.

—— (2003) The Southern Belize Epigraphic Project: The Hieroglyphic Inscriptions of Southern Belize. Report to the Foundation for the Advancement of Mesoamerican Studies, www.famsi.org/reports/00077/index.html.

—— (2009) *Classic Maya Political Organization: Epigraphic Evidence of Hierarchical Organization in the Southern Maya Mountains Region of Belize.* PhD dissertation, Department of Anthropology, Southern Illinois University, Carbondale. Ann Arbor, MI: University Microforms.

Weintraub, Boris (1994) Geographica. *National Geographic* 185(4).

11

FOLLOW THE LEADER

Fine Orange pottery systems in the Maya lowlands[1]

James J. Aimers

While I was a graduate student, unexpected Postclassic-period finds at Baking Pot, Belize, sparked my interest in ceramics, and since then most of my research has been about Maya pottery. In this chapter I discuss some current debates and approaches in Maya pottery analysis with reference to the work of E. Wyllys Andrews V. I conclude with a discussion of the rarely used concept of the ceramic system in reference to the Terminal Classic and Postclassic pottery of Lamanai, Belize.

When I arrived at Tulane, I was obsessed by Maya architecture and planning to write an interdisciplinary dissertation on that topic. By my fifth year, I was also facing a range of serious practical challenges in my field research on monumental architecture at Baking Pot, Belize, but I felt as if I had few other options but to continue. I had already turned down an opportunity to write a dissertation on Maya pottery because, like many others, I considered pottery to be a boring topic. Nonetheless, at about the same time, unexpected Postclassic pottery found at Baking Pot caught my interest and it occurred to me that, because my advisor was a leader in Maya pottery research, I should reconsider the topic. Since then much of my research has been about Maya pottery of the Terminal Classic and Postclassic periods (Aimers 2004a, 2004b, 2004c, 2008, 2009, 2010, 2011, 2012b). In this chapter I discuss some current issues and approaches in Maya pottery studies and, especially, how these relate to the work of E. Wyllys Andrews V.

Style and identity

In his article on early Central Mexican traits at Dzibilchaltun, Andrews addressed the sorts of issues of architectural style and cultural identity that had brought me to Tulane. The article discussed the issue of lowland Maya contact with central Mexico, which Andrews argued may have been part of "a Gulf Coast network of contacts" (Andrews 1979: 247). My dissertation research on the Terminal Classic period in the Belize valley and my subsequent work at Lamanai in northern Belize (see Figure 1.1) also showed provocative stylistic connections to the Gulf Coast, a topic to which I return towards the end of this chapter. In order to investigate this issue and others, I realized that I would need to visit as many ceramic collections as possible. This is another issue that Will has addressed in his work (see Chapter 7).

In "Early Ceramic History of the Lowland Maya," Andrews (1990: 1) notes that the quantity of available data even at that time made it "increasingly difficult for archaeologists to control or even have reasonable access to all of it. This is most true of ceramic collections."[2] He further remarks that that presentation of ceramic data is often inadequate for the assessment of external relationships, and he emphasizes the importance of hands-on comparison of ceramic collections:

> [I]n some cases the final presentation [of ceramic data] is not adequate to allow definitive conclusions about external relationships of a ceramic type of a complex. This problem results partly from the high cost of color illustrations, and partly from the inability of the author to compensate for this by visiting every conceivable comparative collection before drawing his own conclusions. There exists, in addition, no agreed upon set of criteria for judging closeness of relationship – nor should there necessarily be such. The result is that it is often difficult to assess the significance of ceramic collections in a regional or an interregional context without direct study of comparative collections.
>
> (Ibid.)

This may seem obvious but in fact is not said often enough. I have just edited a volume on Maya pottery classification (Aimers 2012a), and one of the most surprising issues evident throughout it is the damage that has been done to Maya archaeology by pottery identifications that are made without firsthand examination of comparative collections. A result of Andrews's examination of a number of collections was his important contribution to the redefinition of the Swasey phase at Cuello (Andrews and Hammond 1990). Visits to type collections left him "with the growing conviction that we have much to learn from examination and reanalysis of excavated collections. We neglect them at our peril" (Andrews 1990: 1). This is probably even truer now, but it is often difficult to find funding for the examination or reanalysis of an excavated collection.

This is not just a research issue but an ethical one for archaeologists, the agencies who fund them, and those writing grant reviews. I tried for years to get funding to examine collections from various sites (as part of what I call the Interregional Pottery Project) and to finish the analysis of excavated collections from Tipu and Lamanai, but I could not sway many reviewers, who associate "real" research with new excavation. I have also seen this attitude on hiring committees. As one well-known Real Mesoamerican Archaeologist explained to me, to get a job or a major grant, I would need a "real" project, and a project that analyzed and compared disparate collections was in no way a "real" project, regardless of the research payoff. I was not successful in attracting US funding, but the British Academy did see the value of it and supported two seasons of work built around visits to collections across the peninsula and analysis at Lamanai. These were two of the most productive seasons I have ever had, and the discussion that follows of Fine Orange stylistic systems and supersystems derives from this comparative research.

A bias towards fieldwork seems to me to have even deeper roots. The highly gendered practice of Maya archaeology leads both men and women to value the stereotypically masculine and highly public activities of exploration and excavation, whereas the less public activities of collections organization and analysis are devalued as the domestic labor of the archaeologist and in that sense are feminized (Aimers 2003). I dislike being called a ceramicist not only because it negates my years of excavation experience (which is what "real" archaeologists do) but also because I believe the word is glossed by some archaeologists as "housewife." As anthropologists and others continue to examine and question and revise the taken-for-granted meanings of machismo in Latin America (Gutmann 2003, 2007), I think that Maya archaeologists should take a closer look at how such structures of meaning infect our own discourses and practices.

Andrews and methodological rigor

When I arrived at Tulane I was in the midst of a familiar love affair for many graduate students; I was infatuated with theory. The hermeneutic spiral had me in a spin and phenomenology was making me feel mighty real. Andrews convinced me to be grounded in the data and to be much more focused on methods. This is probably the most important thing I learned during my time at Tulane – and one of the most important lessons of graduate school anywhere.

In his study of the Xe ceramics, Andrews notes that, because he was interested in issues of contact, he privileged the study of Xe slip characteristics: "It is the slips that most readily allow one to place this complex with its closest relations, although forms, and, especially at the site of Altar de Sacrificios, paste and temper are important indicators" (Andrews 1990: 2). He follows this with more detail about why he emphasizes slips in his discussion and why these were linked directly to his research goals. In my discussions with archaeologists about typological methods, I have been struck by how many seem to believe that there is an ideal form of ceramic classification. As archaeologists since Brew (1946) have pointed out, classifications make sense only in relation to specific research questions. In type-variety classification, disagreements about whether to privilege slip or paste, and whether to treat them separately or together, have been at the root of many of the problems we now have in comparing the ever growing number of pottery complexes which have been developed. Prudence Rice (1976) has written most cogently about this. The problem would be greatly reduced if archaeologists would include the kind of statement Andrews made about what research interests are best met through applying particular classification methods.

This issue has interested me since I began working with type-variety classification in my research. An awareness of the problems of integrating named types into a coherent framework led me to become an advocate of the *ceramic system* concept. I use ceramic systems and supersystems below to discuss the stylistic connections among various named ceramic types that appear to me to be related to types in the various groups of Fine Orange Ware.

Fine Orange Ware

Fine Orange Ware types are among the best known of Maya ceramics, and much of the pottery of the Terminal Classic and the Postclassic periods appears to imitate them. For example, both of the major red-slipped groups of the Postclassic period in Peten and western Belize (the Augustine and Paxcaman groups) resemble Fine Orange Ware types. In the Early Postclassic, types of the Augustine Group (Vitzil Orange-Red Ware) are made with a compact, bright orange paste and have smooth, well-finished red slips. Somewhat later in the Postclassic of Belize and Peten, the trumpet-shaped supports and dish shape of Paxcaman Red (Paxcaman Group, Volador Dull Ware) are very similar to Silho Fine Orange (e.g., Kilikan Composite Type; Smith 1971: 22). I see a parallel to European attempts to re-create Chinese hard paste porcelain in the eighteenth century by making soft paste porcelain. The technology was different and inferior, but Europeans did manage to create stylistic versions of porcelain.

At Lamanai, the Buk phase is currently dated AD 962 to 1200/1250, based on a preliminary assessment of a suite of radiocarbon dates (Graham 2008), although it appears to have had earlier stylistic roots. The designs found on Lamanai pottery in the Buk phase most closely resemble those of Silho (or "X") Fine Orange, which was probably produced near Campeche but possibly at other more distant locations along the Gulf Coast and the Usumacinta River (Bishop 1994). The traditional interpretation of these motifs and styles suggests that they represent either the movement of Mexicanized Maya people from the Gulf Coast during and after the Terminal Classic or some sort of vaguely defined "influence" of Mexicanized groups (i.e., Thompson's Putun Maya) from the Gulf Coast. Silho Fine Orange continues to be closely associated with the Itza (e.g., Bishop 1994; Kepecs et al. 1994; Robles Castellanos 1986).

At Lamanai, imported Fine Orange pottery is very rare. In fact, we have identified only one full vessel of Fine Orange Ware (Figure 11.1) and other isolated sherds. Nevertheless, many motifs from Fine Orange types were absorbed into the existing pottery repertoire of the site. This hybridization suggests that the people of Lamanai consciously chose to adopt these styles and thus their presence was desirable in some way. Because many of the vessels from Lamanai are from grave contexts, there was almost certainly some religious significance to the motifs. I have argued that these motifs were also status markers in the Postclassic (Aimers 2001). My primary goal in this chapter is to trace out the stylistic connections between Fine Orange pottery and the ceramics of Lamanai using the concept of ceramic systems to show its potential for mapping stylistic interaction across large areas. Ultimately, however, I do think that the distribution of these systems can help us hone our interpretations of the cultural and social factors that motivated stylistic behavior at Lamanai.

Systems and supersystems

Ceramic systems are part of the earliest formulations of type-variety, but, for reasons that escape me, in Maya archaeology they have rarely been used outside of Honduras. "A ceramic system … consists of homologous types that are related in terms of aspects

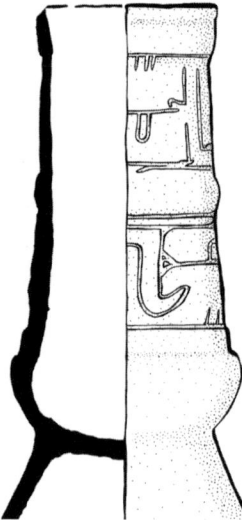

FIGURE 11.1 Lamanai Silho Fine Orange Vessel – Fine Orange Ware: Silho Orange Group: Pocboc Gouged-Incised (drawing by Jenna Anderson, after Pendergast [1985: fig. 7.5a])

of decoration: design elements, element execution, design field layout, and the like" (Henderson and Agurcia 1987: 432). The value of ceramic systems is that they are built around stylistic elements such as surface treatment and decoration and do not consider paste characteristics, as do wares in many type-variety classifications. Systems are superficial; they are all about style over substance. Wares, in contrast, have traditionally been defined through a combination of paste and surface characteristics. Fine Orange is one of the few wares that really seem to make sense based on this definition (Rice 1976). Most other wares show significant variation in paste – especially among sites – even when the surfaces are fairly consistent, and this variation is very difficult to reflect in the hierarchical system of type-variety. I refer to this as the "Curse of the Ware," and it has led to major differences in how people go about the seemingly straightforward process of type-variety classification (Aimers 2007; Rice 1976).

Although systems tell us almost nothing about production, they sidestep the problematic surface-plus-paste definition of ware that has inhibited comparison of types. Systems "facilitate recognition at the conceptual level" (Henderson and Agurcia 1987: 433) and are one of two major ways within type-variety to map the links between stylistically similar ceramics made in a variety of locations (the other integrative concept is the ceramic sphere). Systems tell us about the formal choices made by the producers and consumers of pottery, although they do not (and were not meant to) tell us anything about *how* or *where* the pots were made. That is the realm of materials analysis.

Nevertheless, many of the surface correspondences I see between Fine Orange types and non-Fine Orange types are also reflected in the pastes. The pastes of the analogues are frequently strikingly close in color to the bright orange of the Fine Orange pastes, but, unlike Fine Orange, they are visibly tempered. Thus, the concept of technological style may also be relevant to understanding these types (Lechtman 1977). The fact that later examples of Fine Orange-like types (e.g., Paxcaman Red) often appear in non-orange pastes suggests that after a few centuries the imitation styles had become conceptually disconnected from their Fine Orange antecedents.

I also lump the various Fine Orange systems (based on *types* such as Cumpich Incised) into Fine Orange supersystems (based on *groups* such as Silho Fine Orange). A supersystem is "a category containing two or more systems whose component types exhibit general commonalities of surface treatment and decoration, suggesting a common, if remote, inspiration and which are found over a continuous spatial and temporal span" (Urban and Schortman 1987). Given that supersystems often align with group assignments, one could say group is to supersystem as type is to system.

The ceramics of Lamanai and Fine Orange Ware

Much of the orange-red slipped Buk-phase pottery found in burials and caches at Lamanai can be classified as belonging to the Zakpah Group (Ware Unspecified): Zakpah Orange-Red, Zacbeeb Incised, Zalal Gouged-Incised (Walker 1990), and an as yet undesignated openwork type (or variety). For stylistic similarities to Zakpah Group pottery from sites such as Cerros, Colha, and Marco Gonzalez, one must look north to the ceramics of sites such as Ichpaatun, Chichen Itza, and Mayapan (Sanders 1960; Smith 1971). The discussion that follows is based mostly on my observations of the northern Maya collections stored at the Instituto Nacional de Antropología e Historia (INAH) in Merida and other collections I examined in 2006 and 2007.

Zakpah Group ceramics from Lamanai most closely resemble types in Chichen Red Ware and Mayapan Red Ware in the northern lowlands. In fact, there is a Zalal Gouged-Incised sherd in the Chichen Itza collections that has been classified as Papacal Incised (Mayapan Red Ware, Red Mama Group). This is not surprising given the similarity of Zalal Gouged-Incised to the Red Mama Group types, and the fact that Zakpah Group ceramics are rarer as one moves north.

Smith (1971: 27) also noted the similarity of the Puuc Red Ware types (Red Teabo Group) to the Chichen Red Ware types (Red Dzibiac Group). The differences are in their temper and the more uniform red color of Puuc Red Ware. I also observed their close similarity in the Isla Cerritos collections. I observed also that Red Dzibiac Group sherds can resemble Fine Orange sherds (and, incidentally, the Augustine Group, the major red-slipped group in the Early Postclassic Belize Valley; Figure 11.2). In short, Augustine Group (Vitzil Orange-Red Ware), Teabo Group (Puuc Red Ware), and Dzibiac Group (Chichen Red Ware) ceramics all look like Fine Orange with visible temper. On the surface, however, they can be hard to distinguish. Mayapan Red Ware types, although they rarely have an orange paste, also superficially resemble Fine Orange types.

Inspired by these observations, I am experimenting with aligning the Puuc Red Ware, Chichen Red Ware, and Mayapan Red Ware types with types in Fine Orange. Most of them seem to belong in the Silho Orange and Matillas Fine Orange supersystems, and I put them there in this chapter (see Table 11.1).

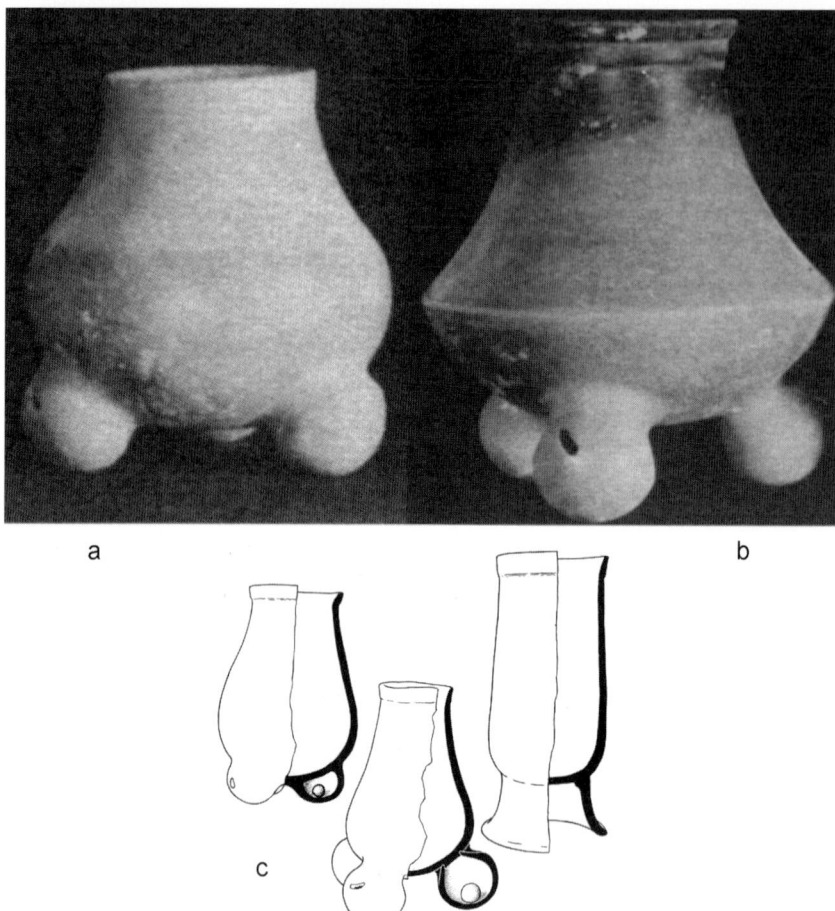

FIGURE 11.2 Comparison of Fine Orange Ware and Chichen Red Ware: (a–b) two vases of Fine Orange Ware: Silho Group; Silho Orange; Silho Variety (Smith 1957: figs 13c, 15a); (c) three vases of Chichen Red Ware: Red Dzibiac Group; Dzibiac Red; Dzibiac Variety (Brainerd 1958: figs 86d–f).

The closest similarities I saw in Merida were between Pocboc Gouged-Incised (a type in the Silho Fine Orange Group) and Holtun Gouged-Incised (a Chichen Red Ware, Red Dzibiac Group type). There are strong similarities in the shape of vessels and especially their decoration (not to mention their bright orange pastes), but I emphasize that the Holtun Gouged-Incised vessels are not *exact* copies of Pocboc Gouged-Incised (Figure 11.3). Brainerd (1958: 282) provides a good description of the differences. At Chichen Itza, as at Lamanai, potters chose to imitate Fine Orange motifs (and, less closely, shapes), but these were absorbed into, or perhaps it is better to say "filtered through," existing conventions. Nevertheless, many of the motifs and the placement on Holtun Gouged-Incised have no precedent at Chichen Itza, and their origin in Fine Orange types seems clear (ibid.: 276). There are also some similarities

TABLE 11.1 Fine Orange systems and supersystems

The Silho Orange supersystem

System	Mayapan	Chichen Itza	Lamanai
Silho Orange system	FO Ware: Silho Grp: Silho Orange: Silho Chichén Red Ware: Red Dzibiac Grp: Dzibiac Red: Dzibiac Variety	FO Ware: Silho Grp: Silho Orange: Silho Chichén Red Ware: Red Dzibiac Grp: Dzibiac Red: Dzibiac Variety	FO Ware: Silho Grp: Silho Orange: Silho (a few sherds?) Ware Unspecified: Zakpah Orange-red Group: Zakpah Orange-red: Variety Unspecified
Calkini Gadrooned system	FO Ware: Silho Grp: Calkini Gadrooned: Calkini Variety	FO Ware: Silho Grp: Calkini Gadrooned: Calkini Variety Chichén Red Ware: Red Dzibiac Grp: Tiholop Gardrooned: Tiholop Variety	
Champan Red-on-orange system	FO Ware: Silho Grp: Champan Red-on-orange: Champan Variety	FO Ware: Silho Grp: Champan Red-on-orange: Champan Variety	
Cumpich Incised system	FO Ware: Silho Grp: Cumpich Incised: Cumpich Variety Puuc Red Ware: Red Teabo Grp. Becal Incised: Becal Variety	FO Ware: Silho Grp: Cumpich Incised: Cumpich Variety	
		Chichén Red Ware: Red Dzibiac Grp: Xuku Incised: Xuku Chichén Red Ware: Red Dzibiac Grp: Xuku Incised: Grooved-Incised Variety Chichén Red Ware: Red Dzibiac Grp: Xuku Incised: Cream-slip Variety	Ware Unspecified: Zakpah Group Zakbeeb Incised: Variety unspecified
	FO Ware: Silho Grp: Cumpich Incised: black-paint Variety	FO Ware: Silho Grp: Cumpich Incised: black-paint Variety	

(Continued)

TABLE 11.1 (Continued)

Kilikan Composite system	FO Ware: Silho Grp: Kilikan Composite: Kilikan Variety	FO Ware: Silho Grp: Kilikan Composite: Kilikan Variety	Motifs on Zakpah Goughed Incised vessels overlap with this system, but painting not present with incising at Lamanai so see Pocboc Gouged-Incised System, below
	FO Ware: Silho Grp: Kilikan Composite: black-slip Variety	FO Ware: Silho Grp: Kilikan Composite: black-slip Variety Chichén Red Ware: Red Dzibiac Grp: Xuku Incised: black slip Variety Chichén Red Ware: Red Dzibiac Grp: Holtun Gouged-Incised: black slip Variety	No correspondence at Lamanai with black-slipped composite?
	FO Ware: Silho Grp: Kilikan Composite: cream-slip Variety	FO Ware: Silho Grp: Kilikan Composite: cream-slip Variety Chichén Red Ware: Red Dzibiac Grp Holtun Gouged-Incised: cream slip Variety	No correspondence at Lamanai with cream-slipped composites?
	FO Ware: Silho Grp: Kilikan Composite: polychrome Variety		No Correspondence at Lamanai with polychrome composites?
Nunkini Modeled system	FO Ware: Silho Grp: Nunkini Modeled: Nunkini Variety	FO Ware: Silho Grp: Nunkini Modeled: Nunkini Variety	Possible correspondences with Buk jars with turkey head appliqués; undesignated
	FO Ware: Silho Grp: Nunkini Modeled: black-paint Variety		
	FO Ware: Silho Grp: Nunkini Modeled: polychrome Variety		
Pocboc Gouged-Incised system	FO Ware: Silho Grp: Pocboc Gouged-Incised: Pocboc Variety	FO Ware: Silho Grp: Pocboc Gouged-Incised: Pocboc Variety Chichén Red Ware: Red Dzibiac Grp: Holtun Gouged-Incised: Holtun	FO Ware: Silho Grp: Pocboc Gouged-Incised: Pocboc Variety (one vessel at Lamanai)

System	Mayapan	Chichen Itza	Lamanai
		Chichén Red Ware: Red Dzibiac Grp: Xuku Incised: Xuku Variety Xuku Incised: Grooved Incised Variety	Ware Unspecified: Zakpah Grp: Zalal Gouged-Incised: ← Zalal Gouge-Incised also resembles these
	FO Ware: Silho Grp: Pocboc Gouged-Incised: black-slip	FO Ware: Silho Grp: Pocboc Gouged-Incised: black-slip Variety	No correspondence at Lamanai?
	FO Ware: Silho Grp: Pocboc Goughed-Incised cream slip	FO Ware: Silho Grp: Pocboc Goughed-Incised cream silp	No correspondence at Lamanai?
Pomuch Polychrome system	FO Ware: Silho Grp: Pomuch Polychrome: Pomuch		
Yalton Black-on-Orange system	FO Ware: Silho Grp: Yalton Black-on-Orange: Yalton Variety	FO Ware: Silho Grp: Yalton Black-on-Orange: Yalton Variety	
		Chichén Red Ware: Red Dzibiac Grp: Chan Kom Black-on-red: Chan Kom Yalton Black-on-Orange: cream-slip Variety	

Matillas Orange supersystem (incomplete)

System	Mayapan	Chichen Itza	Lamanai
Matillas Orange system			
Chilapa Gouged-Incised system	Matillas Fine Orange Chilapa Gouged-Incised: Chilapa Variety Mayapán Red Ware: Red Mama Grp: Mama Red (some have incisions) and Papacal Incised		Mayapán Red Ware: Red Mama Grp: Lamanai Gouged-Incised? ← Close correspondences between Lamanai red types and Mayapán Red Ware vessels
Grijalva Incised-Polychrome system			
Nacajuca Black-on-Orange system			

(Continued)

TABLE 11.1 (Continued)

Salto
Composite
system
Sayula
Polychrome
system
Villahermosa
Incised
system

to Plumbate wares that are beyond the scope of this discussion. Briefly, it seems that the motifs are developed first in Fine Orange and later absorbed into Plumbate. This raises the possibility that some of the Plumbate types could be linked to Fine Orange types through systems, a prospect I have not yet investigated.

The cream-slipped varieties of Pocboc Gouged-Incised, Kilikan Composite (both Silho Fine Orange) and Holtun Gouged-Incised: Cream Slip Variety (Chichen Red Ware) are also similar (Figures 11.4 and 11.5). The few published examples of these types do not convey the similarities – especially in motifs – shared among the types was well as with the sherds in Merida. In the Merida collections there are *identical* gouged-incised motifs in these types, and these are strongly reminiscent of motifs at Lamanai. All of these types are in the same system as Zalal Gouged-Incised (Zakpah Group, Ware Unspecified) at Lamanai, Cerros, Colha, Laguna de On, and other sites in northern Belize (Figure 11.6).

There are also correspondences between Cumpich Incised (Silho Fine Orange) and Xuku Incised (Chichen Red Ware; Red Dzibiac Group) in the Chichen Itza collections (Figure 11.7), and both of these types can be tied to Lamanai through very similar curvilinear motifs on Zakbeeb Incised bowls from Lamanai, Marco Gonzalez, and Cerros (Figure 11.8; Graham and Pendergast 1989: fig. 8j; Walker 1990: 83). Vessels with effigy supports and notched basal flanges are found at Lamanai and in the Matillas Fine Orange Group in Fine Orange Chilapa Gouged-Incised: Chilapa Variety vessels at Mayapan (Figure 11.9). I find it interesting that Matillas Fine Orange is generally dated somewhat later than Silho Fine Orange, because I also suspect that the dishes with large stepped flanges and effigy supports are part of a possible late facet of the Buk phase at Lamanai. Future stratigraphic investigations and radiocarbon dates at Lamanai should allow us to test this hypothesis. Both of these types have parallels in Mayapan Red Ware: Red Mama Group: Mama Red (some have incisions) and Papacal Incised of the same group.

Two Chichen Red Ware types (Xuku Incised: Black Slip Variety and Holtun Gouged-Incised: Black Slip Variety) also close resemble Silho Fine Orange (Kilikan Composite: Black Slip Variety), but at Lamanai the potters and consumers of pottery appear to have had no interest in copying this particular stylistic combination. Orange-red and red slips are overwhelmingly dominant after the Classic period at Lamanai. Another interesting contrast is the apparent lack of black-on-red painting alone or in combination with incising or gouge-incising during the Buk phase at Lamanai. The motifs are shared with Lamanai, but as far as I can tell they are always incised or gouged-incised, never through black or cream slips, and never in combination with black painting.

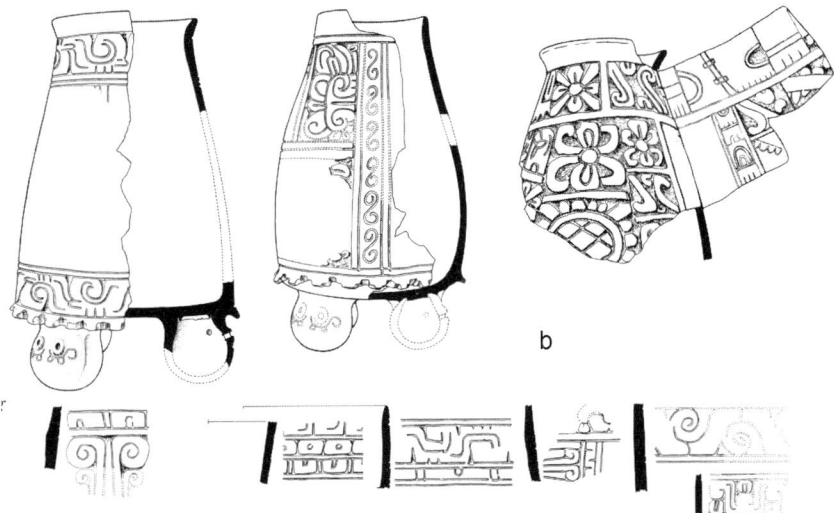

FIGURE 11.3 Comparison of Fine Orange Ware and Chichen Red Ware: (a) Pocboc Gouged-Incised (Fine Orange Ware; Smith 1957: fig. 13e); (b) Holtun Gouged-Incised (Chichen Red Ware; Brainerd 1958: fig. 86a–c, 86g 5, 7–11)

Style and interaction

Table 11.1 is an incomplete and preliminary presentation of some of the system and supersystem relationships I see between Fine Orange Ware types and other non-Fine Orange types across the peninsula. In general, I suspect that many of the Lamanai examples are local adaptations of Fine Orange styles – or at least

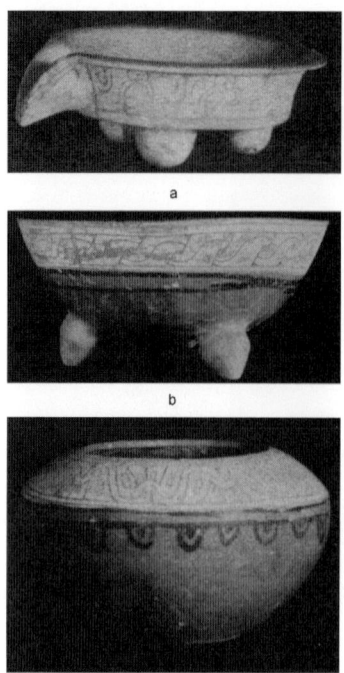

FIGURE 11.4 Comparison of Fine Orange Ware and Chichen Red Ware: (a) Silho Fine Orange Group: Upper: Pocboc Gouged-Incised type: Cream Slip Variety (Smith 1957: fig. 17f); (b–c) Kilikan Composite type: Cream Slip Variety (ibid.: fig. 16d, g)

motifs – especially from types of the Silho Orange Group and (probably later) the Matillas Orange Group. I will continue to assess these ideas, but already there are some interesting implications to the pattern of stylistic sharing that the system assignments suggest. Until now, we have looked to the northern Yucatan peninsula and Mayapan as the inspiration for the vessels of Lamanai, but the stylistic links to Fine Orange require us to take a much closer look at the more distant Gulf Coast.

The connection of these motifs to the Gulf Coast is not a new observation. Spinden (1933) and Kidder *et al.* (1946) noted ties decades ago between ceramics from the Maya area and from the Gulf Coast. In particular, Spinden (1933: fig. 8) showed notable parallels between the hook and scroll motifs of the Classic Veracruz culture (especially El Tajin) to pottery found along the Maya Gulf Coast (Figure 11.10). Later, Brainerd agreed that many of the Fine Orange motifs probably derive from the Veracruz area and were adopted by the makers of Fine Orange and the makers of imitations at Chichen Itza. He wrote: "Whatever may be the historical development of this design, it arrived at Chichén a well-integrated style, underlaid with solid conventions and showing ease and variety in its application" (Brainerd 1958: 276). Some of the parallels in the pottery between the

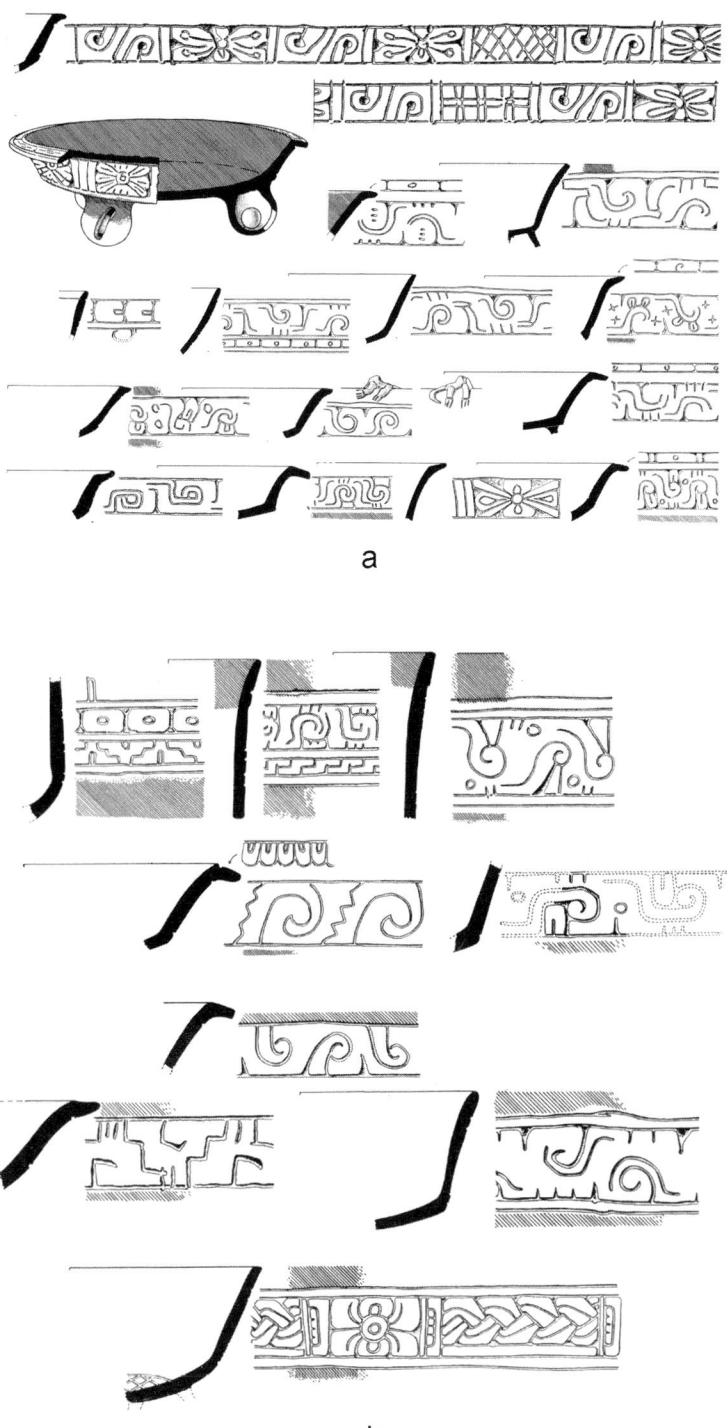

FIGURE 11.5 Chichen Red Ware: (a) Red Dzibiac Group: Holtun Gouged-Incised type: Cream Slip Variety (Brainerd 1958: figs 87a–d, i, k, s, x); (b) Red Dzibiac Group: Holtun Gouged-Incised type: Cream Slip Variety (Brainerd 1958: figs 86g1–3; j1, 3–7).

FIGURE 11.6 Zalal Gouged-Incised from Lamanai (after Pendergast 1981: fig. 15)

ceramic styles of Veracruz and the northern Yucatan peninsula are also reflected in other materials, especially architectural decoration (Figure 11.11). Although Mayapan and Chichen Itza are obviously very important sites for our understanding of the Terminal Classic and Postclassic in the Maya area, I believe that these sites were nodes in a larger interaction sphere that ran along the coasts.

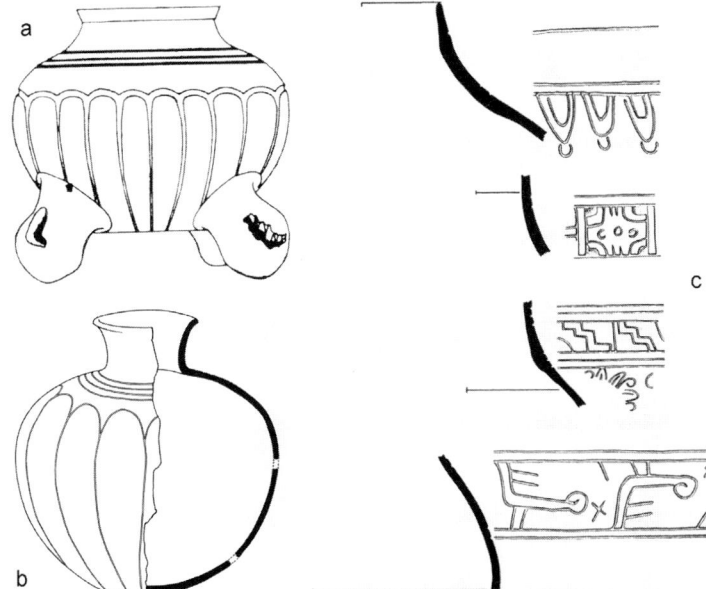

FIGURE 11.7 Comparison of Fine Orange Ware and Chichen Red Ware: (a) Fine Orange Ware: Silho Orange: Cumpich Incised: Cumpich Variety (Smith 1957: fig. 5d); (b) Chichen Red Ware: Red Dzibiac Group: Xuku Incised: Xuku Variety (Brainerd 1958: fig. 85c); (c) Chichen Red Ware: Red Dzibiac Group: Xuku Incised: Xuku Variety (ibid.: fig. 85b1–3, 13)

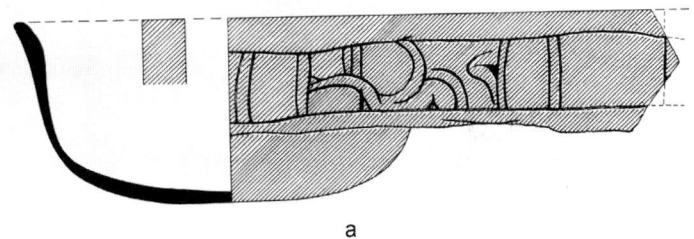

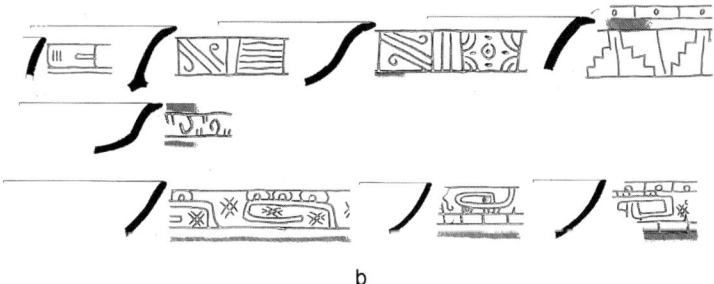

FIGURE 11.8 Comparison of Lamanai pottery with Chichen Red Ware: (a) Ware Unspecified: Zakpah Group: Zacbeeb Incised: Variety Unspecified (Lamanai; Graham and Pendergast 1989: fig. 8j); (b) Chichen Red Ware: Red Dzibiac Group: Xuku Incised: Cream Slip Variety (Brainerd 1958: fig. 87e–h, j, aa–cc)

324 James J. Aimers

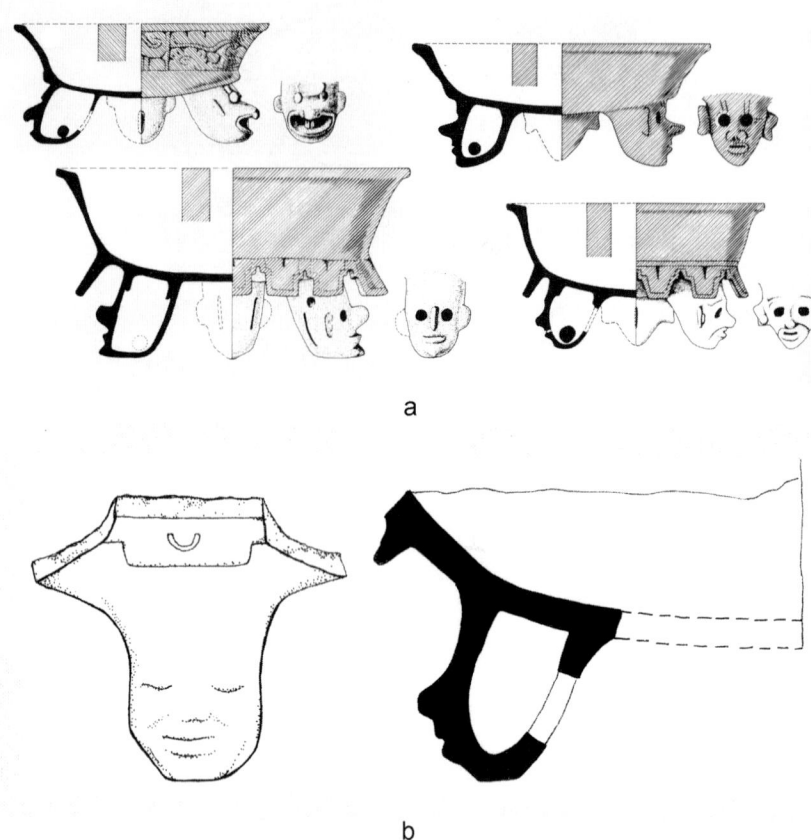

FIGURE 11.9 Vessels with effigy supports and notched basal flanges: (a) Lamanai (undesignated type, Zakpah Group; Pendergast 1981: figs 26h, j, k, m); (b) Mayapan (Fine Orange Ware: Matillas Orange Group: Chilapa Gouged-Incised: Chilapa Variety (drawing by Jenna Anderson, after Smith [1971: fig. 56c, 12])

Coastal interaction

I was interested to see that, in collections from the coastal sites of Xcaret and El Meco (Robles Castellanos 1986), sherds that are virtually identical – in surface color/finish, decoration, and paste – to geometrically incised hemispherical bowls from Lamanai and to other Zalal Gouged-Incised sherds have been placed in the Paxcaman Group, best known from the Peten region (Rice 1987). At El Meco, Robles Castellanos (1986) suggests these sherds could also be Augustine Red, another Peten type. This identification, which has probably been picked up by other archaeologists through the El Meco monograph, has profound implications for interaction models. Instead of being evidence of central Peten influence on the northeast coast of the Yucatan peninsula, these sherds are actually evidence of a coastal interaction sphere and probably have relatively little to do with the central Maya lowlands.

Fine Orange pottery systems in the Maya lowlands

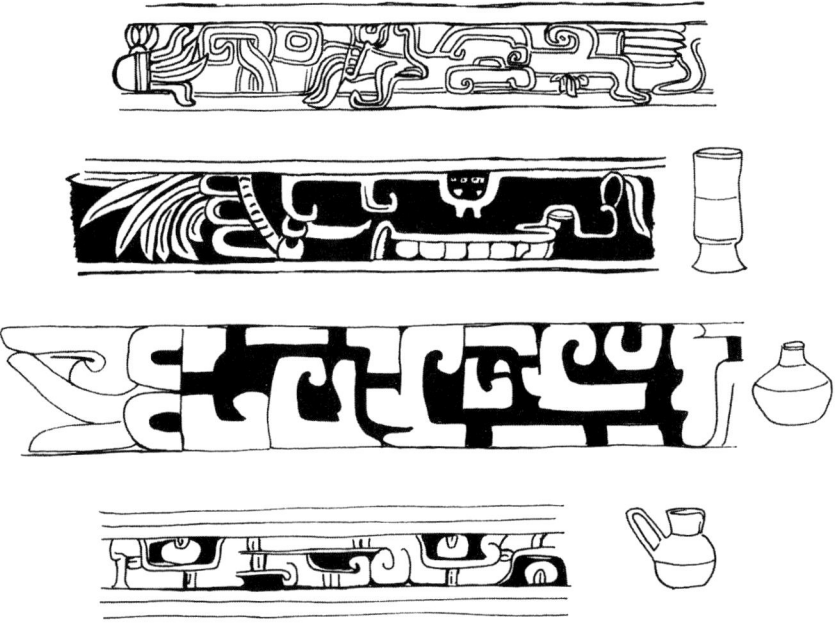

FIGURE 11.10 "Totonac motives" (drawing by Jenna Anderson, after Spinden [1933: fig. 8])

FIGURE 11.11 Architectural elements: (left) El Tajin; (right) Chichen Itza (drawing by Jenna Anderson, after Spinden [1933: fig. 2])

Like many others (e.g., McKillop and Healy 1989), I believe that a great deal of evidence points to the development of a strong coastal interaction sphere in the Terminal Classic and throughout the Postclassic. This interaction sphere (or, more precisely, "interaction arc") probably extended from Veracruz to the coast of Honduras. Since there is not much Fine Orange at Lamanai, but much copying, I suspect that the people of Lamanai were connected to this interaction sphere, possibly through Marco Gonzalez (Graham and Pendergast 1989), just as Chichen Itza was probably connected to it through Isla Cerritos. But what is the significance of this copying of Fine Orange at Lamanai?

Lamanai, Mesoamerica

I placed much of the red-slipped pottery of the Buk phase at Lamanai in the Silho Orange and Matillas Orange supersystems. Nicholson (1981) noted that, "wherever Plumbate or X [Silho] Fine Orange is found throughout Mesoamerica, various Mixteca-Puebloid motifs occasionally occur." More recently, Ringle and his colleagues have reinterpreted the significance of the Mixteca-Puebla style, and they note that the distribution of Silho Fine Orange may correspond rather well with their proposed cult of Quetzalcoatl network (see Chapter 2). In reviewing the evidence for the distribution of Fine Orange, they observe that authentic Silho Orange types are found at sites most closely associated with the Itza (Ringle *et al.* 1998: 217; see also Bishop 1994; Kepecs *et al.* 1994; Robles Castellanos 1986).

Ringle *et al.* (1998: 218) suggest that the imitation of both Plumbate and Fine Orange at sites such as Monte Alban "may reflect the adoption of the cult and its apparatus by local elites, rather than by imposition from without." In reference to Matillas Fine Orange, they note that "virtually the only imported ware of any importance in the Late Postclassic of northern Yucatan was Matillas Fine Orange. This may reflect the continuing importance of the cult network during that period, especially at Mayapán and at such East Coast shrine centers as Cozumel and Tulum" (ibid.).

Given the sharing of many pottery styles between Lamanai and coastal sites such as Marco Gonzalez, Ichpaatun, Tulum, and Cozumel, the Silho and Matillas Orange imitations at Lamanai may link it to the cult of Quetzalcoatl, but this was most likely a purposeful adoption by local people at the site, and there is (at this time) no support for a major population movement – much less invasion – by Itza people into Lamanai as there appears to be at Nohmul (Chase and Chase 1982). Nonetheless, the presence of these Itza-like styles in local elite burials at Lamanai argues for their importance both as a religious and social marker, and this identification, I suspect, was crucial to the survival of the site during the Postclassic period. In the Cib phase that follows Buk, it appears Payil Red and Palmul Incised vessels were imported to the site from elsewhere (possibly the Ichpaatun or Tulum areas) and placed in burials, suggesting that coastal interaction had become stronger and more direct.

Ringle returned to the old idea of the links between Veracruz and the Maya area, but he tied the strong similarities of murals and carvings at El Tajin and Chichen Itza to the cult of Quetzalcoatl, which he more clearly defined as "a set of imagery, beliefs, and practices associated with an ideology of leadership" (Ringle 2004: 167). I cannot summarize the many elements of Ringle's argument here, but I would like to draw attention to a type of figure identified at El Tajin and at Chichen Itza by Spinden (1933) and revisited by Ringle (2004) more than 70 years later (Figure 11.12). These images remind me in many ways of some very distinctive vessels from Lamanai (Figure 11.13). My initial thought was that, like (a probably later) vessel from Marco Gonzalez (Figure 11.14), these vessels depict the diving god known at Tulum. If this is so, the Lamanai vessel could link that site to the coastal interaction sphere. Ringle, instead, follows Spinden (1933) and newer work by Koontz (1994) on the iconography of El Tajin to suggest "that the descending gods at Tajin, both in zoomorphic form, were the local manifestation of Quetzalcoatl" (Ringle 2004: 186). Like Spinden and Koontz, he demonstrates parallels in the sculpture of Chichen Itza (Figure 11.15). Notably, none of the "descending god vessels" at Lamanai or Marco Gonzalez have the characteristic forked tongue shown at El Tajin and Chichen Itza, but Lamanai vessel 1896/4, from a Buk burial (Figure 11.16), does have "fangs" and feathers that resemble another figure from El Tajin and could easily signify a feathered serpent (Figure 11.17).

I have not yet begun to compare these vessels to similar ones found at other sites, and I have no idea at this point what their systems assignments will be. I include them here because it was the systems assignments of the Zakpah Group ceramics at Lamanai that got me looking at coastal interaction, the Gulf Coast, and the cult of Quetzalcoatl in the first place. Ceramic systems and supersystems are not a panacea for the problems we face in type-variety classification, especially problems with the inconsistent definition of ware and its application in the Maya area. Systems do, however, point us in certain directions in assessing interaction among Maya sites and even with other regions of Mesoamerica.

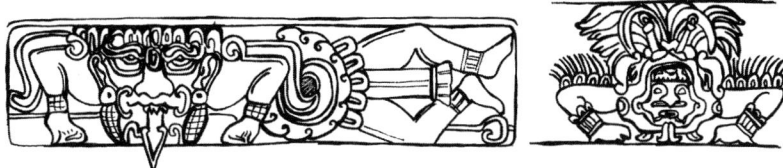

FIGURE 11.12 Descending figures: (left) El Tajin; (right) Chichen Itza (drawing by Jenna Anderson, after Spinden [1933: fig. 5])

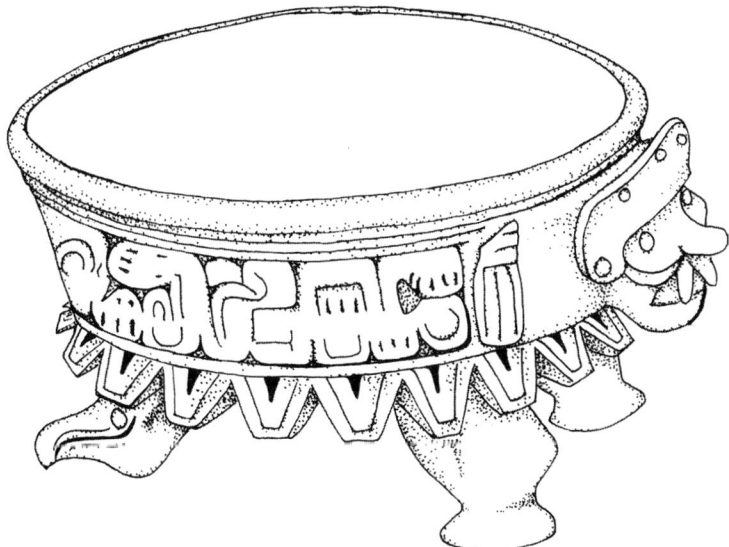

FIGURE 11.13 Vessel from Lamanai Structure N10-48 (drawing by Jenna Anderson, after Pendergast [1982: fig. 19])

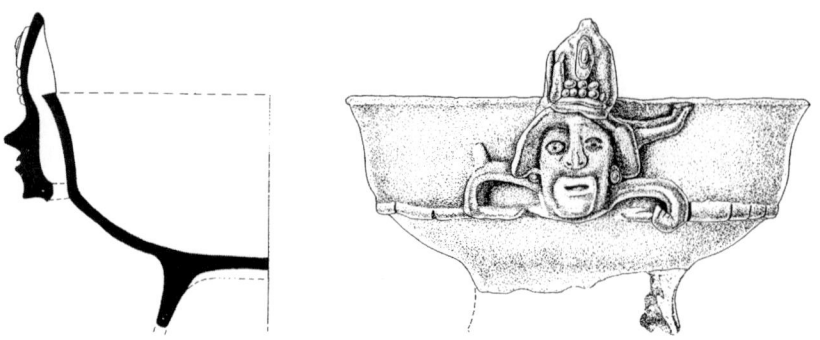

FIGURE 11.14 Diving God dish from Marco Gonzalez (Graham and Pendergast 1989: fig. 11a)

FIGURE 11.15 Column bases at Chichen Itza: (a) South Temple of Great Ballcourt (Ringle 2004: fig. 15d, after Tozzer 1957: 318); (b) Temple of the Warriors (Ringle 2004: fig. 15e, after Tozzer 1957: 317)

FIGURE 11.16 Lamanai vessel 1896/4 (photograph by the author)

FIGURE 11.17 El Tajin relief carving (drawing by Jenna Anderson, after Ringle [2004: fig. 15c])

Ringle suggests that major sites of the Postclassic in Mesoamerica were places of investiture for members of his suggested cult of Quetzalcoatl: "A model holding that certain major sites acted as centers of legitimation for large hinterlands throughout much of Mesoamerican prehistory may be an attractive alternative to explanations based on trade, military conquest, or elite emulation" (Ringle 2004: 213). Could Lamanai be one such investiture site, or, alternatively, did some of the Lamanai elite travel to sites such as Mayapan or Chichen Itza for investiture and return to be buried eventually with vessels signifying their identity and status? I do not presume to have the answers, but there are tantalizing clues suggested by preliminary systems assignments.

Conclusions

In my opinion, the neglect of ceramic systems in Maya type-variety classification is unfortunate and inexplicable. Ceramic systems are very useful for early work with pottery collections when stylistic types have been given different type-variety names in other places and one is unsure either whether to create new type names or which existing type names to choose. Systems also provide a clear-cut way to group pottery types that have been created for different reasons due to different research goals on various projects. In addition, ceramic systems can be used in the construction of ceramic spheres, the other major integrative concept in type-variety classification:

> Ceramic systems permit a much more sensitive assessment of ceramic similarity than either horizon styles, which are defined in terms of widely distributed modes that may be only loosely associated, or ceramic spheres, which are based on aggregate similarities at the type level among entire

ceramic complexes. At the same time, ceramic systems provide a systematic basis for the recognition of ceramic spheres. *Plotting the overlap in distribution of the ceramic systems that include a majority of common types in a series of ceramic complexes would be a simple way of defining spheres.*

(Henderson and Agurcia 1988: 433; emphasis added)

Only systematic comparison of ceramics over broad areas and the alignment of ceramic sequences among sites, zones, and regions of Mesoamerica will allow us to address the "big picture" issues of the meaning of style in the Maya area. The examples from Lamanai above are an attempt to do this.

Because so many ceramics at Maya sites are made locally, stylistic analysis must be used with technological studies to address questions about inter-site and inter-regional interaction. After over a century of research, we have a great deal of the data we need for this endeavor. Thus, I think that style can lead to substance, but only if we take Andrews's advice and visit pottery collections firsthand and foreground our research goals in discussions of our methods. When I met Will Andrews these were not at all the sorts of issues I expected to be excited about two decades later, but I am happy that I decided to follow the leader at Tulane.

Notes

1 The comparative collections research described above is the result of cooperation with many archaeologists in Belize, Guatemala, and Mexico. I am grateful to the British Academy for funding it. I would especially like to thank another of Andrews's former graduate students, Rafael Cobos Palma, for going to great lengths to give me access to the Isla Cerritos pottery and his assistance in my discussions with INAH.
2 These issues are also related to lumping and splitting. Splitters, obviously, create more types, and this can hinder comparison. Andrews is definitely a lumper. He combined Smith's (1971) Navula and Panaba Unslipped into Navula Unslipped and thus moved Chen Mul Modeled from Panaba Unslipped to Navula Unslipped.

References

Aimers, James J. (2001) "Foreign" Elements in the Ceramics of Lamanai, Tipu, and the Belize Valley. Paper presented at the 66th annual meeting of the Society for American Archaeology, New Orleans.

—— (2003) Out in Archaeology: Theories, Methods, Practice. Paper Presented at the 101st annual meeting of the American Anthropological Association, Chicago.

—— (2004a) *Cultural Change on a Temporal and Spatial Frontier: Ceramics of the Terminal Classic to Early Postclassic Transition in the Upper Belize River Valley*. Oxford: British Archaeological Reports.

—— (2004b) The Origins and Significance of the Scroll or Slipper Support in Maya Ceramics. *Mexicon* 26: 36–42.

—— (2004c) The Terminal Classic to Postclassic Transition in the Belize Valley. In *Archaeology of the Upper Belize Valley: Half a Century of Maya Research*, ed. James F. Garber, pp. 147–77. Gainesville: University of Florida Press.

—— (2007) The Curse of the Ware: Using Ceramic Systems in Belize. *Research Reports in Belizean Archaeology* 4: 101–10.

—— (2008) Snakes on Planes: Sinuous Motifs in the Art of Lamanai. *Research Reports in Belizean Archaeology* 5: 115–23.
—— (2009) Bring It On: Using Ceramic Systems at Lamanai. *Research Reports in Belizean Archaeology* 6: 245–52.
—— (2010) You Only Live Twice: The Agency of Ritual Ceramics at Lamanai. *Research Reports in Belizean Archaeology* 7: 119–25.
—— (2011) Results of the 2010 Maya Pottery Workshop. *Research Reports in Belizean Archaeology* 8: 267–73.
—— (2012a) (ed.) *Ancient Maya Pottery: Classification, Analysis, and Interpretation*. Gainesville: University of Florida Press.
—— (2012b) La Belle et la Bête: The Everyday Life of Ceramics at Lamanai, Belize. In *Proceedings of the 13th European Maya Conference, Paris, December 1–8 2008*, ed. P. Nondédéo and A. Breton. Markt Schwaben: Anton Saurwein.
Andrews, E. Wyllys, V (1979) Early Central Mexican Architectural Traits at Dzibilchaltún, Yucatán. *Actes de XLII Congrès International des Américanistes* 8: 237–49.
—— (1990) Early Ceramic History of the Lowland Maya. In *Vision and Revision in Maya Studies*, ed. Peter D. Harrison and Flora S. Clancy, pp. 1–19. Albuquerque: University of New Mexico Press.
Andrews, E. Wyllys, V, and Norman Hammond (1990) Redefinition of the Swasey Phase at Cuello, Belize. *American Antiquity* 55: 570–84.
Bishop, Ronald L. (1994) Pre-Columbian Pottery: Research in the Maya Region. In *Archaeometry of Pre-Columbian Sites and Artifacts*, ed. D. A. Scott and P. Meyers, pp. 15–65. Los Angeles: Getty Conservation Institute.
Brainerd, George W. (1958) *The Archaeological Ceramics of Yucatán*. Berkeley: University of California Press.
Brew, John O. (1946) The Use and Abuse of Taxonomy. In *Archaeology of the Alkali Ridge, Southeastern Utah*, pp. 44–66. Cambridge, MA: Peabody Museum of Archaeology and Ethnology.
Chase, Diane Z., and Arlen F. Chase (1982) Yucatec Influence in Terminal Classic Northern Belize. *American Antiquity* 47: 597–613.
Graham, Elizabeth (2008) Lamanai, Belize, from Collapse to Conquest – Radiocarbon Dates from Lamanai. Paper presented at the 106th meeting of the American Anthropological Association, Washington, DC.
Graham, Elizabeth, and David M. Pendergast (1989) Excavations at the Marco Gonzalez site, Ambergris Caye, Belize, 1986. *Journal of Field Archaeology* 16: 1–16.
Gutmann, Matthew C. (2003) (ed.) *Changing Men and Masculinities in Latin America*. Durham, NC: Duke University Press.
—— (2007) *The Meanings of Macho: Being a Man in Mexico City*. Berkeley: University of California Press.
Henderson, John S., and Ricardo F. Agurcia (1987) Ceramic Systems: Facilitating Comparison in Type-Variety Analysis. In *Maya Ceramics: Papers from the 1985 Maya Ceramic Conference*, ed. Prudence M. Rice and Robert J. Sharer, pp. 431–38. Oxford: British Archaeological Reports.
Kepecs, Susan, Gary Feinman, and Sylviane Boucher (1994) Chichen Itza and its Hinterland: A World-Systems Perspective. *Ancient Mesoamerica* 5: 141–58.
Kidder, Alfred V., Jesse D. Jennings, and Edwin M. Shook (1946) *Excavations at Kaminaljuyú, Guatemala*. Wahington, DC: Carnegie Institution.
Koontz, Rex (1994) *The Iconography of El Tajin, Veracruz, Mexico*. PhD dissertation, Department of Art History, University of Texas. Ann Arbor, MI: University Microfilms.
Lechtman, Heather (1977) Style in Technology: Some Early Thoughts. In *Material Culture: Style, Organization, and Dynamics of Technology*, ed. Heather Lechtman and R. S. Merrill, pp. 3–20. New York: West.

McKillop, Heather, and Paul F. Healy (eds) (1989) *Coastal Maya Trade*. Peterborough, Ontario: Trent University Press.

Nicholson, Henry B. (1981) The Mixteca-Puebla Concept in Mesoamerican Archaeology: A Re-examination. In *Ancient Mesoamerica: Selected Readings*, ed. John A. Graham, pp. 253–8. Palo Alto, CA: Peek.

Pendergast, David M. (1981) Lamanai, Belize: Summary of Excavation Results, 1974–1980. *Journal of Field Archaeology* 8: 29–53.

—— (1982) Lamanai, Belize, durante el Post-Clásico. *Estudios de Cultura Maya* 14: 19–58.

Rice, Prudence M. (1976) Rethinking the Ware Concept. *American Antiquity* 41: 538–43.

—— (1987) *Macanche Island, El Petén, Guatemala: Excavations, Pottery, and Artifacts*. Gainesville: University of Florida Press.

Ringle, William M. (2004) On the Political Organization of Chichen Itza. *Ancient Mesoamerica* 15: 167–218.

Ringle, William M., Tomás Gallareta Negrón, and George J. Bey III (1998) The Return of Quetzalcoatl: Evidence for the Spread of a World Religion during the Epiclassic Period. *Ancient Mesoamerica* 9: 183–232.

Robles Castellanos, Fernando (1986) Cronología ceramica de El Meco. In *Excavaciones arqueológicas en El Meco, Quintana Roo*, ed. Anthony P. Andrews and Fernando Robles Castellanos, pp. 77–130. Mexico City: Instituto Nacional de Antropología e Historia.

Sanders, William T. (1960) *Prehistoric Ceramics and Settlement Patterns in Quintana Roo, Mexico*. Washington, DC: Carnegie Institution.

Smith, Robert E. (1957) *The Marquez Collection of X Fine Orange and Fine Orange Polychrome Vessels*. Washington, DC: Carnegie Institution.

—— (1971) *The Pottery of Mayapán*. Cambridge, MA: Peabody Museum of Archaeology and Ethnology.

Spinden, Ellen S. (1933) The Place of Tajin in Totonac Archaeology. *American Anthropologist* 35: 225–70.

Tozzer, Alfred M. (1957) *Chichén Itzá and its Cenote of Sacrifice: A Comparative Study of Contemporaneous Maya and Toltec*. Cambridge, MA: Peabody Museum of Archaeology and Ethnology.

Urban, Patricia A., and Edward M. Schortman (1987) Copan and its Neighbors: Patterns of Interaction Reflected in Classic Period Western Honduran Pottery. In *Maya Ceramics: Papers from the 1985 Maya Ceramic Conference*, ed. Prudence M. Rice and Robert J. Sharer, pp. 341–95. Oxford: British Archaeological Reports.

Walker, Debra Selsor (1990) *Cerros Revisited: Ceramic Indicators of Terminal Classic and Postclassic Settlement and Pilgrimage in Northern Belize*. PhD dissertation, Department of Anthropology, Southern Methodist University. Ann Arbor, MI: University Microfilms.

PART V
Yucatan

12

THE ROLE AND REALITIES OF *POPOL NAHS* IN NORTHERN MAYA ARCHAEOLOGY[1]

George J. Bey III and Rossana May Ciau

Popol nahs, *or council houses, have been identified for the Late and Terminal Classic periods in the northern Maya lowlands. This chapter focuses on the earliest proposed examples, examining the characteristics and assumptions used to define them and understand their role in the evolution of Classic Maya society. Examples from Ek Balam, Kiuic, and Labna are discussed in detail in order to consider the reality of* popol nahs, *their function in the development of social stratification in the northern Maya lowlands, and how they may also reflect changes in social organization during the Late and Terminal Classic periods (*AD *550–1000). We argue that* popol nahs *are a manifestation in architecture of one of the central organizing principles of northern Maya lowland society from at least the early Late Classic Period onward.*

> Architectural and spatial contrasts among Maya sites ... help us to understand how social, political and religious organization varied from one Maya site to another ... Recording the forms and interpreting the functions of such royal constructions is the first step in understanding the organization and activities of the group that lived in them.
>
> (Andrews *et al.* 2003: 69)

The *popol nah* is one of the best-known building types in Maya archaeology – or at least we think we know it well. The *popol nah*, or council house, was known at the time of the conquest in the Guatemalan highlands and in Yucatan (Carmack 1981; Fox 1987; Ringle and Bey 2001). In Yucatan, it is mentioned in several ethnohistorical documents. In folio 14 of the *Chronicle of Calkini*, it is described as a specific building type where people assembled at the doors in order to participate in public consultation (Barrera Vásquez 1957; Ringle and Bey 2001), and references to the mat house as the "council house" or "community house" are found in the sixteenth-century colonial Motul and San Francisco Yucatec dictionaries (Martinez Hernandez 1929; Pérez 1870). The *popol nah* has been defined archaeologically in the Late Postclassic centers of highland Guatemala (Fox 1987), and in the northern Maya lowlands the colonnaded halls located in the center of Mayapan are commonly considered to have served as council houses (Proskouriakoff 1962; Ringle and Bey 2001). Such buildings are called *popol nah* (literally, "mat house"), *nim ja* ("big house"), or "council house" because of their presumed administrative function (Bey *et al.* 1997; Carmack 1981: 154–60; Cheek 2003; Fox 1987). They served as buildings where various Maya constituencies met to discuss and make decisions on the issues of the polity or lineage. In Postclassic centers they were defined on the basis of lineage and represented the physical manifestations of group identity and decision-making. The ethnohistorical literature also indicates that they served as men's houses and as the location for the storage of important ritual objects (Cheek 2003: 133).

Postclassic *popol nahs* have a set of architectural features that ostensibly permits their identification in the archaeological record. They are long, single-roomed buildings with multiple entrances formed by either doorways or colonnades (Figure 12.1). In highland Postclassic centers, they typically have benches running along the back or side walls and are commonly associated with an additional set of structures that includes a temple pyramid, shrine, and ballcourt (Fox 1987). At Mayapan they lack benches but are typically associated with an oratory or shrine and, in some cases, temples and one or more colonnaded buildings that are smaller than the *popol nah* itself. Over the last two decades there has been interest in identifying Classic-period *popol nahs* in the Maya area (Bey *et al.* 1997; Cheek 2003; Cheek and Spink 1986; Fash *et al.* 1992; Stomper 1996). Based on the archaeology of the northern Maya lowlands, *popol nahs* are recognized from at least the early

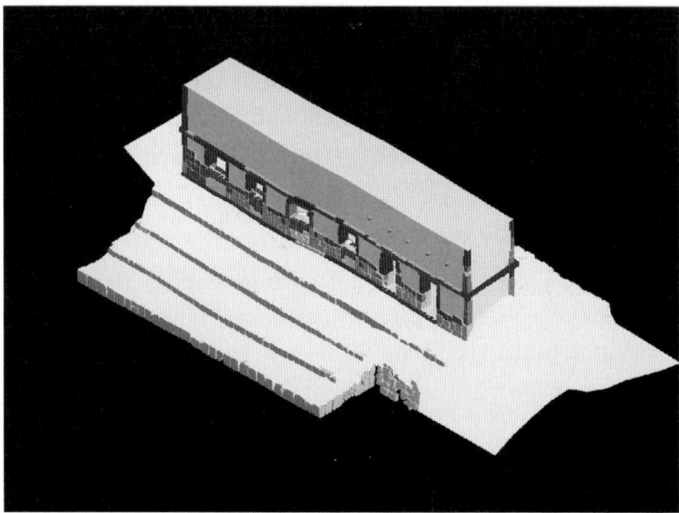

FIGURE 12.1 Reconstruction drawing of Kiuic N1015E1015, a *popol nah* (drawing by David Rivera Arjona)

Late Classic through the Postclassic at a number of sites, suggesting that they represented the architectural manifestation of a highly persistent organizational feature of Maya polities (Bey et al. 1997; Bey and May Ciau 2010).

Here we examine the growing evidence for *popol nahs* in the northern Maya lowlands during the Late and Terminal Classic Periods (AD 550–1000) and what that evidence suggests about both the reality of this structural type and the changing nature of activities that may have been associated with the buildings.

Early Late Classic (AD 550–750) *popol nahs*

No *popol nahs* have been identified dating to the Preclassic or Early Classic in the northern Maya lowlands. Nonetheless, when they appeared in the early Late Classic period they were already well defined, suggesting that the roots of this building type extend into earlier times. Buildings identified as *popol nahs* occurred across the north during the early Late Classic period (Figure 12.2). We have excavated three of these buildings, at Ek Balam (GT-20), at Kiuic (N1015E1015), and at Labna (Structure [Str.] 7; see Figure 1.1) and, on the basis of these excavations, have identified similar structures at five other sites. It is likely that further research will identify many additional examples.

Bey excavated the first of these early *popol nahs* at Ek Balam in 1997 (Figure 12.3). We identified it based on what was known about Str. 10L-22A at Copan, excavated several years earlier (Bey et al. 1997). Str. 10L-22A, a building dated to AD 746 and dedicated to Smoke Monkey, the fourteenth ruler of Copan, was identified as a *popol nah* because of the use of stone mosaic mat (*pop*) motifs on the building and because its upper façade contains sculpted images of men thought to

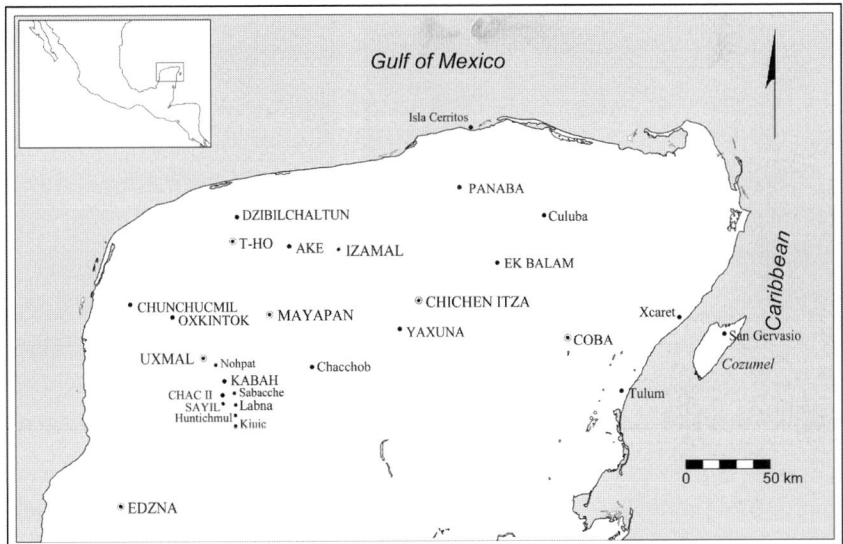

FIGURE 12.2 Map of northern Yucatan with sites mentioned in the text

be lineage leaders sitting on glyphs interpreted as place names (Fash *et al.* 1992). Moreover, it consists of a single room with three doorways. Almost all other rooms in the Copan Acropolis have just one doorway (Cheek 2003). Although it does not look very much like the Postclassic *popol nahs* found in highland Guatemala or the colonnaded halls at Mayapan, these features took precedence over the general form of the structure in identifying it. During the excavation of GT-20 at Ek Balam, a number of stucco glyph medallions were recovered, one of which contained a large *pop* glyph. It was on the basis of this glyph that we initially suggested that, like Copan Str. 10L-22, the building was a *popol nah*. Our excavations also revealed that, like Copan Str. 10L-22A, GT-20 at Ek Balam had multiple entrances.

It now appears that GT-20 has more in common with a second earlier *popol nah* excavated at Copan – Str. 10L-223, located in the northeast corner of the Main Group (Cheek 2003; Cheek and Spink 1986). This building forms the north side of a quadrilateral plaza and is dated to sometime after AD 625 (Cheek 2003). The other major construction in the plaza is 10L-3, a large pyramidal mound that forms the eastern side. The south and west sides of the plaza are defined by long, low mounds and steps. Str. 10L-223 lacks preserved decoration and was identified as a *popol nah* on the basis of its plan, its location, and the use ethnographic analogy (ibid.). It is 80 meters long, larger than any of early Late Classic *popol nahs* in the northern Maya lowlands except for those at Dzibilchaltun. Although part of the interior of the building is subdivided, Str. 10L-223 contains one very long chamber with multiple entrances. At least six entrances of various sizes were identified in the 60 meters of the structure that were excavated. One of the entrances is 10 meters wide, and the overall impression is that Str. 10L-223 is an open-faced building. In fact, it is probable that it consists of one subdivided room with four entrances and a second room composed of piers lacking walls in the section that

a

b

FIGURE 12.3 The interior of Ek Balam GT-20, a *popol nah*: (a) looking north; (b) looking west

was excavated. Another distinctive feature of the structure is that the stairway leading up from the plaza to the building entrance consists of two "landings." These landings provide wide areas for interaction or displays directly in front of the building, connecting the interior and the exterior together in a distinct way. The building is argued to have been the early *popol nah* at Copan, and it likely served a wide variety of functions associated with such structures, including being the main council house for the community as well as a men's house (ibid.: 136).

Although GT-20 and Copan Str. 10L-22A both had stucco decoration, in other respects the Ek Balam *popol nah* looks more like Copan Str. 10L-223. GT-20 consists of a single vaulted room 29 meters long with multiple doorways, a single rear entryway, and a bench at one end. A total of six doorways were revealed in the 19 meters of the building that we excavated. GT-20 also contains a long stair composed of four broad steps placed in front of the building. Each step is approximately 1.5 meters wide, providing a series of landings that give a distinct appearance to the front of the building (Figure 12.4). The walls of GT-20 are not faced with veneer stones, but instead are made of roughly cut stones covered in a thick layer of stucco. The vault is composed of roughly cut slabs. Evidence of a modeled stucco entablature – including the glyph medallions mentioned above – decorating the front of the building was recovered in the collapse. GT-20 is set at a right angle to an unexcavated pyramid (GT-19), and together they form a plaza. This temple/building complex faces onto the large main plaza of Ek Balam.

GT-20 underwent a series of changes during its construction history. One of these is the addition of a large platform on the back that supports a small but

FIGURE 12.4 Exterior view of Ek Balam GT-20, showing its stair

elaborate three-room Chenes-style shrine. At some point in time, three of the six excavated entrances were sealed shut, and it looks as if ultimately the building was "terminated." We excavated ritual deposits at the juncture of the stairway and the building platform, as well as on the floor of the interior of the structure. The last includes a long chert bifacial point and carved conch shell blood-collector or inkpot smashed next to each other on the floor. GT-20 and this part of the site center became peripheral to the main activities associated with the great plaza of Ek Balam by the Terminal Classic period. Not only was GT-20 ritually terminated and several doorways sealed, but also the building was incorporated into the famous wall system that encloses the site center.

Since our work at Ek Balam we have excavated two other similar structures, Str. 7 at Labna (Gallareta Negrón et al. 2003) and N1015E1015 at Kiuic (Figure 12.5). Each of these two buildings contains a long central chamber, multiple open doorways, a stair composed of a series of wide landings, rear entrances, and slab vaulting. They are also both located in conjunction with a pyramid (N1065E1025 at Kiuic and the Mirador at Labna). Nonetheless, recent research suggests that these pyramids were actually constructed later than the *popol nahs* and, in fact, may have been part of a set of events that dramatically changed the meaning and function of the council houses.

These three early Late Classic *popol nahs* are examples of a very standardized building type that we assume was designed to provide open space for groups of people to congregate and interact. The single vaulted room with multiple entrances emphasizes this, but its association with a particular type of stair, composed of wide steps forming landings, indicates the exterior was also an important place of interaction. These stairs with their wide steps could serve as locations for people to socialize, allowing easy access in and out of the building and providing a place to sit and talk.

The single room of the Kiuic *popol nah* is 16.3 meters long, 3 meters wide at the western end, and 2.8 meters wide at the eastern end. The building faces north onto the largest open space in the Yaxche Palace, a presumed civic plaza known as Plaza Dzunun. The Kiuic *popol nah* has six front entrances and two rear ones at each end of the building. The structure has characteristics that are considered typical of Early Puuc-style architecture (Andrews 1986; Gendrop 1983; Pollock 1980), such as walls built with small worked stones, slab vaulting, a load-bearing footing composed of a single rectangular element, and monolithic jambs. The lower molding of the structure is beveled. The simple medial molding has protruding armatures, suggesting that it once supported modeled stucco decoration. Nonetheless, no modeled stucco was discovered during excavation. Stair C (the first built of three) is located on the north side of the building and is 13.4 meters long. It is composed of six steps with slightly inclined faces placed approximately 80 centimeters apart. The final stair (Stair A) is composed of just four steps placed 1.8 meters apart.

Str. 7 at Labna is a *popol nah* consisting of three rooms. Although it appears that the building contained a single vaulted chamber split into three rooms, it is possible there were three separate vaults. The building is 19.5 meters long and 3 meters

a

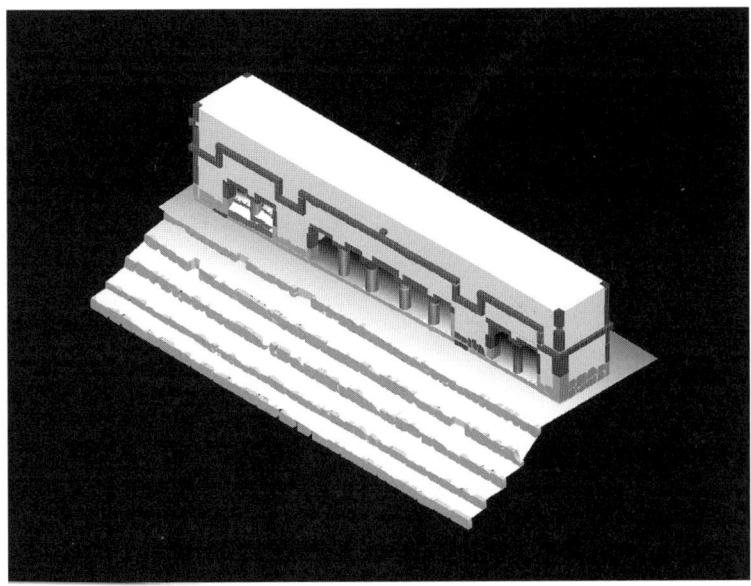

b

FIGURE 12.5 Kiuic N1015E1015 and Labna Str. 7, two *popol nahs*: (a) exterior view of N1015E1015; (b) reconstruction drawing of Str. 7 (drawing by David Rivera Arjona)

wide. The two lateral rooms (Rooms 1 and 3) both have two entrances formed by two jambs and a column in the center. The central room (Room 2) has five entrances formed by two jambs and four columns. The stair, 21 meters long, is composed of five steps forming landings 2 meters wide.

Doorways in both the Kiuic and Labna *popol nahs* were sealed. Just two doorways at the west end of the Kiuic *popol nah* were left open. The other four front entrances as well as the two rear doorways were sealed. The principal entrance of the northernmost room (Room 1) of Str. 7 at Labna was closed. All the other entrances were left open.

Our investigations of the structures at Labna and Kiuic also provide information about the evolution of these building types and their relationship to their associated architectural groups. Each of the buildings is part of an enclosed architectural group that we argue represent early "palaces" at their respective sites (Figure 12.6). They seem to form a core building in the early civic-ceremonial area of these palaces, which makes sense if they served as *popol nahs*. Other features associated with these complexes include ramps leading into the plaza and, as mentioned, pyramids. Using these criteria, we have identified *popol nahs* and associated plaza groups at other sites, particularly in the Puuc region of Yucatan. Among these sites are Nohpat, Xcanacruz, Sabbache, Chac II, and Huntichmul (see Figure 12.2). As discussed previously, a *popol nah*, together with a "temple" and often a small altar in the shared plaza between them, formed the core of many northern Maya civic centers (Bey and Ringle 1989; Ringle and Bey 1992).

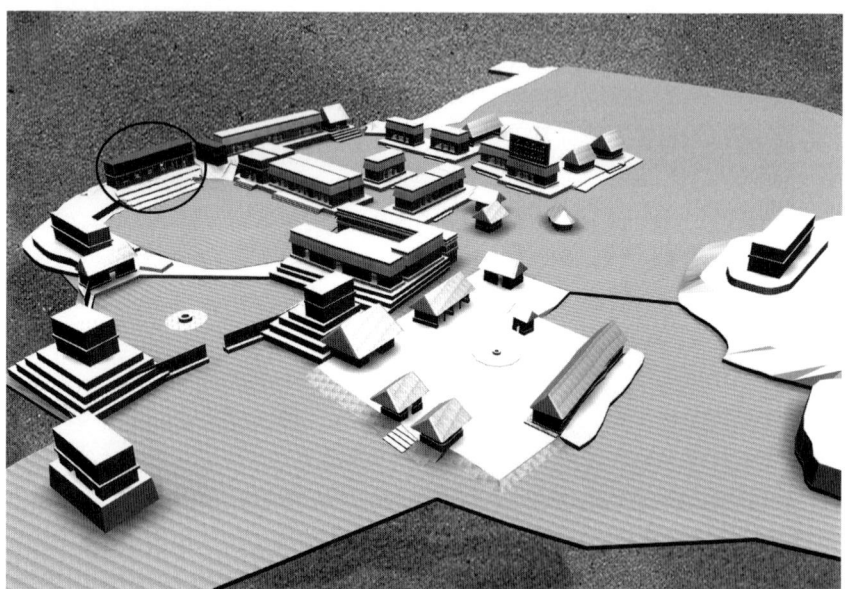

FIGURE 12.6 Reconstruction drawing of the Late Classic Yaxche Group at Kiuic, highlighting the location of N1015E1015 (drawing by David Rivera Arjona)

Because we have identified these architectural groups in the Puuc region, we have called them "Early Puuc Ceremonial Complexes" (Ringle et al. 2006). Nonetheless, the presence of an early *popol nah* at Ek Balam also demonstrates that such structures were built at emerging centers across the northern Maya lowlands. In addition to GT-20 at Ek Balam, we identify Str. 42 at Dzibilchaltun as a large and early variant of the *popol nah*. This building originally consisted of a single extended hall with 21 entrances, a single rear entrance, and a slab vault (Maldonado Cárdenas et al. 2002: 82; Ringle and Bey 2008). It further appears that one of the substructures of Str. 44 at Dzibilchaltun was a *popol nah* (Maldonado Cárdenas 1997: 67). The *popol nahs* at Dzibilchaltun are larger than the other northern Maya examples discussed here and are similar in length to Str. 10L-223, the early and large *popol nah* at Copan.

Detailed excavations of the Yaxche palace at Kiuic have provided fine-tuned diachronic control of the development of this complex, adding further insight into the evolutionary history of early Late Classic *popol nahs*. N1015E1015 is located on the south side of the civic-ceremonial plaza of the Yaxche palace, opposite the largest pyramid at the site. There were six major construction phases in the plaza based on its floor sequence: three associated with the Preclassic (and perhaps Early Classic) and three associated with the early Late through Late/Terminal Classic periods. N1015E1015 was built directly over the Preclassic/Early Classic construction and is associated with the fourth renovation of the plaza. A piece of carbon recovered from inside the construction fill of the building beneath the floor (Beta-266393) has a calibrated one-sigma date of AD 450–580 with an intercept of radiocarbon age with the calibration curve at AD 550. The fifth renovation of the plaza floor is associated with changes to the stair of N1015E1015. A carbon sample associated with this event (Beta-213545) has a calibrated one-sigma date of AD 690–780 with an intercept of radiocarbon age with the calibration curve at AD 690. It was one of the first major buildings associated with the transformation of the Yaxche Group from an open platform into a palace composed of three interconnected plazas and over 25 structures. It is the only slab-vaulted building in the Yaxche Group and, according to William Ringle (personal communication 2009), may be the first vaulted structure constructed at Kiuic.

Although we lack a radiocarbon date for GT-20 at Ek Balam, we found Early Classic sherds along the exterior base of the west wall of the building and a complete Early Classic basal flange polychrome vessel buried as an offering beneath its floor. These support the idea that GT-20 was also built in the late Early Classic to early Late Classic period (Ringle et al. 2006). The fact that all three of the early Late Classic *popol nahs* we studied are so similar and contain slab vaulting suggests that their construction took place more or less at the same time and indicates a response to similar sociopolitical needs. Their role in the lives of these emerging Late Classic polities must have been of great importance, probably representing one of the central organizing principles in their regulation and decision-making structure. If the buildings truly were *popol nahs* – that is, if they were used in ways similar to Postclassic and historical examples – they indicate an emphasis on lineage or group decision-making as these centers developed into complex polities and states. If the early vaulted structures at these centers were designed to promote lineage-based decision-making, it suggests that the leaders of the northern lowlands were less powerful than the kings of the southern lowlands at the dawn of the Late Classic period. The lack of dynastic history in writing and art that typifies the north at this time reinforces this idea (Bey 2006; Ringle and Bey 2008). It is worth noting that it is the earliest building phase of Str. 10L-223 at Copan (dated to AD 625) that shows the greatest similarity to the northern lowland *popol nahs*. Charles Cheek argues that Str. 10L-223 "may have served as the *popol nah* for the entire community in the earlier part of the Late Classic" and, if so, "then consultation among lineage heads took place here in the seventh century, as did several of the other activities ascribed to these kinds of buildings" (Cheek 2003: 136).

The building of *popol nahs* at Kiuic, Labna, and other Puuc centers such as Huntichmul took place before the construction of the first major palaces of these centers – that is, around AD 550 to 700. These community houses likely served as the early centers of administrative life at such Puuc sites and were designed to be accessible to a large number of community members, particularly the various lineage leaders who met to address the increasingly complex decisions faced by emerging polities. Open-faced structures sitting on largely open platforms, they would have been the centers for the daily buzz of activity at these early Late Classic cities, with people gathering in the buildings, spilling out of them onto the landings, and sitting on the steps. At smaller centers such as Kiuic and Labna, there was likely just one *popol nah*, suggesting that these communities were managed by a single lineage-group. At larger centers such as Huntichmul, the remains of several early Late Classic *popol nahs* raise the possibility that multiple lineages were involved in the administration of the city.

Following AD 700, the *popol nahs* were the focus for a major expansion at these centers. Council houses formed core elements associated with the development of large palaces characterized by enclosed multiple plaza groups (see Figure 12.6). The construction of these early palaces resulted in changes to the *popol nahs*. At first, they were open structures with largely unimpeded community access, but later they became structures located inside the palace. As parts of enclosed plazas within a warren of vaulted architecture, after about AD 700 *popol nahs* had highly restricted and private access.

Although it would have been recognized as the original community building, by the early eighth century the *popol nah* was co-opted by the royal family that lived in and controlled the palace. In the case of N1015E1015 at Kiuic, it was during this time that benches were added at either end of the building and a third placed directly in the middle, looking out the front entrance. The mat house at Kiuic now had a throne in its center.

Late/Terminal Classic (AD 750–900) changes to *popol nahs*

The power of elite families within these centers increased throughout the eighth century. By the beginning of the ninth century, the type of *popol nah* represented by GT-20, N1015E1015, and Str. 7 was obsolete. Dramatic sociopolitical and demographic changes took place across the peninsula at the beginning of the Terminal Classic, and architectural changes associated with this period indicate that the function and central role of the *popol nah* altered as well. In the case of the three excavated early Late Classic *popol nahs* discussed above, the plaza or palace group associated with them changed function, making the *popol nahs* significantly less central – if not peripheral – to the life of the court. In the case of GT-20 at Ek Balam, many of the doorways were sealed and the building itself eventually became part of the wall system. Left in the shadow of two huge structures, GT-2 and the massive GT-1 acropolis, GT-20 was terminated and transformed into a minor feature in the sociopolitical structure of the Ek Balam court. Doorways were also sealed in the *popol nahs* at Kiuic, Huntichmul, and Labna.

As Ringle and Bey (2008) note, the tendency in the Puuc region was to replace Early Puuc Ceremonial Complexes or the first palaces (as at Labna, Kiuic, and Huntichmul) with huge, new palaces composed of much larger buildings. These much larger and later palaces are often connected to the earlier ones by *sacbes*. We argue that the early palaces were transformed in function from the primary seats of power into ceremonial/ritual compounds that served to legitimize the authority of a more centralized rulership headquartered in the new grand palaces. In the cases of Ek Balam and Dzibilchaltun, we associate this transformation with the arrival of a *kalomte'*, or divine king and dynastic founder (ibid.). As part of the changing location and redefinition of power and sociopolitical activity, the residential quarters of the ruler in the early palaces at Kiuic and Labna were transformed into pyramids that buried the earlier vaulted buildings. The original *popol nahs* no longer served as council houses. It was at this time that a number of their entrances were closed, turning them into long dark chambers with only one or two doorways. As discussed above, at Kiuic all but two of the entrances were sealed up.

Ringle and Bey (2008) argue that, as a result of transformations in the sociopolitical life of rulers, some of the smaller *popol nahs* at sites in the northern plains of Yucatan were replaced by much larger "super-*nahs*." Examples of these are seen at Dzibilchaltun and Edzna (Figure 12.7). At Dzibilchaltun, the large and early *popol nah* Str. 42 was replaced by Str. 44, an enormous building measuring 130 meters in length. Str. 42 continued to be used, but like early *popol nahs* elsewhere it was modified. The central hall of Str. 42 of Dzibilchaltun was subdivided and a superstructure was eventually constructed over the central section of the building, basically obliterating its original configuration and altering its function. Several of its original entrances were walled up, as well. Its replacement, Str. 44, had 35 entrances with an interior hall divided into three sections. Maldonado Cárdenas (2003) has also drawn attention to the Nohochna of Edzna (Str. 424) as a parallel to Str. 44. This building was partially excavated by Luis Millet Camera and then later by Antonio Benavides C. (personal communication, 2008), who notes that the base of the building has rounded corners and general Peten affinities. Nevertheless, because he encountered heavy deposits of Terminal Classic ceramics while clearing its rooms, the superstructure of Edzna Str. 424 may have been built after the Late Classic period.

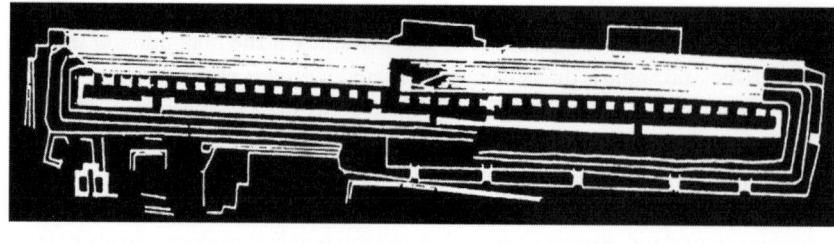

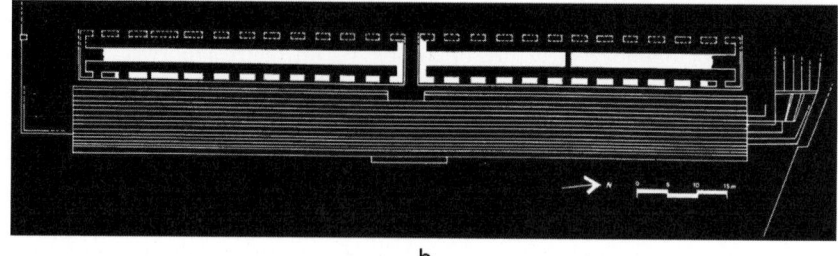

FIGURE 12.7 Terminal Classic "super-*nahs*": (a) Dzibilchaltun Str. 44; and (b) the Nohoch Nah structure at Edzna

Elsewhere, the direct architectural parallels between the early *popol nahs* and the super- *nahs* are less clear. At Ek Balam, Ringle and Bey (2008) identify GT-2 as the corresponding replacement of GT-20. This range structure, 54 meters long, was built on a platform 10 meters high; divided into two halves, it sits along the western edge of an expansive summit consisting of a large open area suitable for public gatherings. The Puuc-style architecture of this building is clearly later than that of GT-20 and dates to the wave of major construction associated with the arrival of the *kalomte'* title at Ek Balam. Another as yet unexcavated super-*nah* is located at Kumal, a site 17 kilometers southeast of Ek Balam. This structure, 160 meters long, is the largest of any of the super-*nahs*, but unfortunately it is so badly collapsed that we were unable to determine anything about its superstructure (Ringle and Bey 2000).

In the Puuc region, other buildings identified as possible super-*nahs* include the Nunnery Quadrangle and the Governor's Palace at Uxmal. In fact, at Uxmal there appears to be evidence of the transition between the slab-vaulted early *popol nahs* and the full-blown super-*nahs* of the late Late/Terminal Classic. There are several long, single vaulted structures with open fronts composed of a number of columns that also are likely candidates for *popol nahs*. One is Str. 6, located just southwest of the Temple of the Magician and on the south side of the Pajaros Group. This group of buildings is constructed on the smaller scale associated with Early Puuc architecture and has been interpreted by us as originally serving as an early palace, probably pre-dating the Nunnery, similar to the early palaces at Kiuic and Labna. The east building, or Temple of the Magician, like N1065E1025 at Kiuic, was originally a set of buildings. These were later buried within the massive pyramid temple. It therefore appears that Str. 6 was constructed before the pyramid and, based on its features, is a very likely candidate for a *popol nah*. The use of columns on *popol nahs* versus masonry walls seems to be a feature of sites in the Puuc region; the early *popol nahs* of Labna and Xcanacruz also have columns instead of walls. Nonetheless, Str. 6 at Uxmal lacks the broad risers that we have identified as a consistent feature of the early *popol nahs*. Moreover, it has a boot-stone vault instead of a vault built of slab stones, as found at earlier *popol nahs*. Uxmal Str. 6 also contains a set of interior rooms behind the long, open chamber. There is another almost duplicate building (Str. 9) located approximately 20 meters south of the Pajaros Group and facing the ballcourt. The construction of two such *popol nahs* virtually right next to each other reflects the greater sociopolitical complexity of Uxmal even before its dramatic expansion during the Late/Terminal Classic period.

Here a *nah*, there a *nah*...

Despite the elegance of this evolution of *popol nahs* into super-*nahs* (and even some evidence of a transitional stage in this process), and the way such a development fits with our thinking about shifts in power and sociopolitical organization from the early Late Classic to the Terminal Classic period, there are some inherent problems with this interpretation. Most important for this chapter is the fact that identifying the super-*nahs* as buildings that were derived from the early *popol nahs* is problematic. Although super-*nahs* have multiple entrances, they are associated with multiple rooms rather than long, single chambers. There is little consistency in how these buildings look beyond the fact that they tend to be very long. They have a wide variety of room configurations, stairs, and contextual arrangements. The end result is that, with the dramatic and ubiquitous construction of range structures after AD 800, we face the danger of seeing super-*nahs* everywhere, even though they do not form a category that is as precisely defined or as distinctive as the early Late Classic *popol nah* building form.

At Yaxuna, Str. 6F-68 has been identified as a Terminal Classic *popol nah* based on the mat iconography found along its basal molding and the presence of a long platform extending from the structure. This is interpreted as a dance platform (Ambrosino 2003). The building, 26 meters long, is composed of three rooms – not a single room – and has veneer-stone rather than slab vaulting. It also lacks the distinctive wide steps associated with the early Late Classic *popol nahs*. Thus, the iconography of Str. 6F-68 and the dance platform suggests it is a *popol nah*, but it incorporates features of the super-*nah*, such as multiple rooms. Is this evidence that supports our interpretation that at least some of the long, multi-chambered range structures are actually super-*nahs*? It does seem to indicate that a *popol nah* can have multiple rooms. Or perhaps Str. 6F-68 is not a *popol nah* at all.

Further evidence of the association or development of multiple rooms with *popol nahs* may be seen in Str. 7 at Labna. Although containing many of the characteristics of the early Late Classic *popol nah* (slab vaulting, wide steps in front of an open-columned long structure, rear doorway, and its position as part of the early palace at Labna), Str. 7 clearly has three rooms. It appears, however, that the building may have consisted of a single long vault and that the interior dividing walls were not supporting structures; it was likely conceived as a single, long slab-vaulted structure in which walls dividing it into three chambers were added during or after its initial period of construction. If so, this may provide evidence of an early Late Classic *popol nah* being reconfigured as a multi-room structure.

Three rooms seem to be quite common (e.g., Str. 44 at Dzibilchaltun and the three sections of the Governor's Palace at Uxmal) and may represent the development of a specific set of sociopolitical structures (offices or estates) that were discrete enough that they required separate spaces within what had once been common and public space in the early *popol nahs*. Along these same lines, perhaps the addition of three benches inside N1015E1015 at Kiuic (one at either end and one directly in the middle of the room) represents some sort of tripartite division. These benches were not part of the original construction of the *popol nah* but were added later and probably are associated with a set of additional changes to the Yaxche Group. These other changes include the partial dismantling of the stair in front of N1015E1015 and its movement a couple of meters to the east of its original orientation on the platform.

We are suggesting that buildings previously called range structures might represent the development of large-scale *popol nahs* associated with the breakdown of segmentary-based rulership and its replacement by more powerful and centralized kingship. Ringle and Bey (2008) have argued that the major architectural changes at Ek Balam and Dzibilchaltun are associated with the arrival of a *kalomte'* at each site and the establishment of a royal dynasty. Nonetheless, the changes we see at many Rank 2 and 3 sites in the Puuc also suggest that a focus on the *popol nah* and its associated political functions broke down or changed at roughly the same time. The early *popol nahs* imply that authority was significantly less developed and centralized than during the Late/Terminal Classic period.

Thus, the first appearance of *popol nahs* – as at Kiuic, where N1015E1015 may be the first vaulted building at the site – would seem to reflect a transition in power from a more egalitarian form of sociopolitical organization in the Puuc region during the Early Classic to the rise of powerful local councils by the early Late Classic period. This was followed by the fairly rapid rise of centralized leadership in the Late Classic period, which by the later part of the Late/Terminal Classic found no need for the once important longhouses.

It may be that our super-*nahs* are not really *popol nahs* at all, but a new form of building designed to meet the needs of centralized kingship and a greatly expanded bureaucratic system of social, political, military, and religious positions. Super-*nahs* may have so little in common with the *popol nahs* of the early Late Classic that it may not be useful to discuss them as such. They are, however, often found in plaza contexts that seem to reflect the contexts of earlier *popol nahs*. They also echo the longhouse idea in that they are in fact very large – up to 160 meters long at Kumal. Nonetheless, there are many long, multi-chambered, vaulted structures throughout the northern Maya lowlands, so we must consider whether such long buildings with multiple rooms and doorways really provide us evidence that they are *popol nahs* or are instead a whole new form of building, which may represent any number of different functions in more complex and centralized Late/Terminal Classic political systems. Nonetheless, the Yaxuna and Labna examples suggest that the idea of the *popol nah* may still have been recognized during the Late/Terminal Classic period.

There is an additional problem regarding the identification of Terminal Classic buildings in the northern Maya lowlands as *popol nahs* beyond those related to size and form. This is the use of the mat (*pop*) sign as an iconographic identifier for *popol nahs* (Schele 1998). Schele and others have identified buildings as *popol nahs* based on the appearance of mat designs on their façades. In some cases, such as Copan Str. 10L-22, Ek Balam GT-20, and Yaxuna Str. 6F-68, mat signs are associated with other characteristics, such as building form or additional iconography to establish a building as a *popol nah*. In other cases, such as with Linda Schele's identification of the Codz Pop at Kabah and the northern wing of the central patio of Structure 1 at Labna as *popol nahs*, the identification hinges almost exclusively on the identification of mat signs on them. Gallareta Negrón's recent research (2012) argues that Labna Structure 1 was not a *popol nah* but that the rooms with mat signs on them served as a throne room with the images framing the doorway. His identification of this room as a throne room is based on extensive analysis with other similar structures at Labna. Gallareta Negrón's work makes a strong case that mat signs are also found at throne rooms during the Terminal Classic and not just at council houses. Stone and Zender (2011) further caution us in considering the mat sign (the *jal* glyph) as marking a building as a *popol nah*. They note that it is likely that in some cases it refers to textiles and their economic value to elite households. Mat signs were no doubt used in multiple ways to define the function of Late/Terminal Classic buildings and cannot be assumed on their own to mark a building as a *popol nah*.

The Terminal Classic transition (AD 900–1000): post-monumental architecture and C-shaped structures

At the end of the Terminal Classic period, monumental construction ceased at every one of the Maya centers discussed in this chapter. Nonetheless, many of these centers saw later post-monumental construction. This late period of construction was first noted at Uxmal in the late 1950s and elsewhere after the 1980s (Barrera Rubio and Huchím Herrera 1990; Bey *et al.* 1997; Gallareta Negrón 1989; Ruppert and Smith 1957; Ruz Lhuiller 1952). The ceramics associated with this post-monumental occupation are not Postclassic (i.e., they are *not* classified as belonging to the Tases ceramic complex) but are Terminal Classic in character (Bey *et al.* 1997). Late inhabitants of these sites continued to make and use pottery that can be assigned to the greater Cehpech ceramic sphere. Researchers such as Christopher Gunn of the Bolonchen Regional Archaeological Project are now beginning to differentiate the qualitative changes in paste, surface finish, and form that took place at the very end of the Terminal Classic period, but in general what we find is the continuation of Cehpech-sphere ceramic production and distribution systems. We have already described much of our initial thinking about post-monumental occupation in the northern Maya lowlands (ibid.).

A hallmark of post-monumental construction at many sites is the C-shaped building. Such structures are also known from Late and Terminal Classic sites, as at Kiuic, where they appear to be kitchen and staff buildings built on patios behind, outside, or near palaces. During the post-monumental phase, however, such buildings became the major form of construction. The structure type is defined by its C- or sometimes L-shape. Most frequently, such buildings have three walls that supported a thatch or perishable roof, an open front, and a configuration of benches that often extends the length of the back wall. Similar types of constructions appear at Terminal Classic sites in the southern Maya lowlands, such as Finca Michoacan and Ixlu in the Peten lake district, and they are the most common architectural form at Bayal-phase Seibal (AD 830–930; Bey et al. 1997). In the northern Maya lowlands, post-monumental C-shaped structures have been identified at Sayil, Uxmal, Huntichmul, and Ek Balam (Barrera Rubio and Huchím Herrera 1990; Bey et al. 1997; Gallareta Negrón 1989; Gallareta Negrón et al. 2007).

At Ek Balam, GS-12 (one of three C-shaped structures identified in the urban survey) is part of the Sacrificios Group. The Sacrificios Group includes a 10 meter pyramidal mound, four vaulted structures, a ballcourt, elite residences, small platforms, and a central altar and thus is reminiscent of the Postclassic "temple-long structure/altar complexes" described by Fox (1987) for sites in the Maya highlands and by Proskouriakoff (1962) for Mayapan (Bey and Ringle 1989; Ringle and Bey 1992). GS-12 and the other Terminal Classic C-shaped structures are almost identical to the Postclassic longhouses that have been identified as kinship-based administrative buildings called *popol nahs* in the northern lowlands and *nim ja* in the southern highlands. As with the super-*nahs*, there is the danger of identifying every C-shaped structure as a *popol nah*, which is highly unlikely. And, unlike the range structures, we have the additional complication of identifying some of the C-shaped structures as post-monumental when some, such as those at Kiuic, are clearly not. Nonetheless, unlike the Late and Terminal Classic range structures, the C-shaped structures are not as varied in size or configuration. A common subtype is defined by a long, continuous, and low bench built against the back wall. Of these, several examples – including GS-12 and some structures from Uxmal, Sayil, and Huntichmul – are clearly located in post-monumental contexts on top or to the side of monumental constructions and often are built with reused stones from surrounding structures. The most impressive of these is the unnamed structure uncovered during the restoration of the north side of the Great Platform of Uxmal (Barrera Rubio and Huchím Herrera 1990: 31). "The building itself has been interpreted as a single chamber with an open front and a thatch roof. A built-in benchlike construction, about .20 m high, was in the three walls of the structure" (Gallareta Negrón 1989: 6). We are therefore confident that these C-shaped structures at Ek Balam, Uxmal, and Sayil, and at least some of those in the Chan Chich group of Huntichmul (Gallareta Negrón et al. 2007), are Terminal Classic and post-monumental versions of the Postclassic *popol nahs* found at Mayapan and in the Guatemalan highlands.

With the appearance of C-shaped *popol nahs*, we see the return of the single long room, this time with benches, as the defining characteristic of the structure. Although they lack stairs with wide steps, the emphasis was once again – as it was during the early Late Classic – on open public space. The scale of these late *popol nahs* is also similar to that of early Late Classic examples. In the case of GS-12 at Ek Balam, we see the construction of an associated set of buildings similar not only to the Postclassic model found in the highlands and at Mayapan but also to early Late Classic configurations. That is, the *popol nah* is central to a particular set of residential and ceremonial structures, probably reflecting the post-monumental court at Ek Balam. In contrast, the late *popol nahs* of Uxmal are embedded in the collapsing splendor of the Late Classic ceremonial center adjacent to the ballcourt, Nunnery Quadrangle, Temple of the Magician, and Palace of the Governor.

Final comments: the council house as an organizing principle

The council house emerged early on as the central administrative structure of northern Maya centers. It reflected the close relationship of the leadership with a set of high-ranking members of the community, which was likely at first to have been kin-based and to have downplayed the distance between individuals. The council house was an open and public building designed to allow decision-makers to meet face to face and to rub shoulders. The space was meant to be available and visible to the larger community, and it allowed commoners to socialize publicly with the highest-ranking members of the sociopolitical hierarchy. One room and one community might have been the motto of the council house. With the intensification of centralized leadership in the northern Maya lowlands after the late eighth century, such spaces were lost. They were replaced by awe-inspiring super-*nahs*, which reflected the increased complexity of the sociopolitical system, the importance of kingship, and the breakdown of the relationship between community leadership and political hierarchy. What was public became private, what was singular became differentiated, and what was controlled by the community became controlled by the king and his court.

With the breakdown of the Late/Terminal Classic sociopolitical system, particularly the system of divine kingship and its attendant control structures, we see the re-emergence of the community-centered *popol nah*. Once more the center of power was open and space was undifferentiated. Such structures had long benches in single long chambers and fronts open to public viewing. These post-monumental *popol nahs* became the standard for the Postclassic communities that emerged with the final abandonment of the major Classic polities. In major centers such as Ek Balam and Uxmal, where there are a number of these longhouses, we are probably seeing the reappearance of lineage or segmentary-based sociopolitical organization after the collapse of divine kingship.

This process of development, breakdown, and re-emergence suggests that the council house and the activities, roles, and sense of community that were associated with such buildings were central features of Maya sociopolitical organization from at least the early Late Classic through the Postclassic period. The fact that they reappeared after the collapse in a relatively intact form – although undoubtedly changed by the breakdown of the rule of the *kalomte'* or divine king – provides us with evidence that the principles of community-based decision-making were never completely lost. Such principles probably were maintained in a number of ways, both within the complex centralized government of kings and in community- and kin-based organizations that lacked the high-profile spaces and power associated with traditional *popol nahs*.

Our survey of the history of *popol nahs* over five centuries also highlights the fact that it may seem too easy to identify these buildings in the archaeological record. We must use caution in equating a set of architectural characteristics with the function of a building. In particular we need to recognize that some Late/Terminal Classic buildings may represent direct descent from the early Late Classic council houses, but that their functions may have changed so dramatically that they should not be considered *nahs* (super or not). Many of the long range structures we see during this period may owe nothing to the idea of a community house, and trying to fit them into the model could be wrong. The same may also be true for many of the C-shaped post-monumental structures commonly considered to be *popol nahs*. Although we argue that some of these C-shaped buildings clearly served as community houses, others were elite residences or other building types that had nothing to do with the activities we associate with council houses. In addition we need to be careful not to assume that all C-shaped structures date to the post-monumental period of occupation at these sites, because we find the building type in use during the Late/Terminal Classic period in wider contexts that suggest domestic activities.

We believe that the idea of the *popol nah* as an organizing feature in the evolution of northern Maya polities is useful and should be further investigated, but we need to examine carefully the greater context, associated artifacts, and chronology of each structure in order to identify its function. We should not simply stamp a building as a community house based on its architectural features. We also recognize that the best way to study the structure and function of a *popol nah* is through careful excavations that allow for the building to be understood dynamically by identifying the changes it underwent during its history. Building functions change over time. Thus, although N1015E1015 began its life as the community house of Kiuic, it apparently served a very different role in its final years when all but two of its many doors were sealed.

Note

1   This chapter has benefited from discussion with Tomás Gallareta Negrón and William Ringle. Their ideas have been invaluable and are so interwoven into the text that we

might as well include them as co-authors. We would also like to thank Tomás and Bill for access to their data from Labna and Huntichmul. The research at Ek Balam and Kiuic was supported by the National Science Foundation, INAH, Millsaps College, the National Geographic Society, and several private foundations. We would also like to note our appreciation to the citizens from Yaxhachen, Ek Balam, and Hunuku who assisted in the excavation of GT-20 and N1015E1015.

References

Ambrosino, James (2003) The Function of a Maya Palace at Yaxuna: A Contextual Approach. In *Maya Palaces and Elite Residences: An Interdisciplinary Approach*, ed. Jessica Joyce Christie, pp. 253–73. Austin: University of Texas Press.

Andrews, E. Wyllys, V, Jodi L. Johnson, William F. Doonan, Gloria E. Everson, Kathryn E. Sampeck, and Harold E. Starratt (2003) A Multipurpose Structure in the Late Classic Palace at Copan. In *Maya Palaces and Elite Residences: An Interdisciplinary Approach*, ed. Jessica Joyce Christie, pp. 69–97. Austin: University of Texas Press.

Andrews, George F. (1986) *Los estilos arquitectónicos del Puuc: una nueva apreciación*. Mexico City: Instituto Nacional de Antropología e Historia.

Barrera Rubio, Alfredo, and José Huchím Herrera (1990) *Architectural Restoration at Uxmal, 1986–1987*, trans. C. A. Uribe. Pittsburgh: University of Pittsburgh Press.

Barrera Vásquez, Alfredo (ed.) (1957) *Códice de Calkiní*. Campeche: Talleres Gráficos del Estado.

Bey, George J., III (2006) Changing Archeological Perspectives on the Northern Maya Lowlands. In *Lifeways in the Northern Maya Lowlands: New Approaches to Archaeology in the Yucatán Peninsula*, ed. Jennifer Mathews and Bethany Morrison, pp. 13–40. Tucson: University of Arizona Press.

Bey, George J., III, and Rossana B. May Ciau (2010) The Role and Reality of *Popol Nas* in Northern Maya Archaeology. Paper presented at the 75th annual meeting of the Society for American Archaeology, St Louis.

Bey, George J., III, and William M. Ringle (1989) The Myth of the Center: Political Integration at Ek Balam, Yucatan, Mexico. Paper presented at the 54th annual meeting of the Society for American Archaeology, Atlanta.

Bey, George J., III, Craig A. Hanson, and William M. Ringle (1997) Classic to Postclassic at Ek Balam, Yucatan: Architectural and Ceramic Evidence for Defining the Transition. *Latin American Antiquity* 8: 237–54.

Carmack, Robert M. (1981) *The Quiché Mayas of Utatlan: The Evolution of a Highland Guatemala Kingdom*. Norman: University of Oklahoma Press.

Cheek, Charles D. (2003) Maya Community Buildings: Two Late Classic Popol Nahs at Copan, Honduras. *Ancient Mesoamerica* 14: 131–8.

Cheek, Charles D., and Mary L. Spink (1986) Excavaciónes en el Grupo 3, Estructura 223 (Operación VI). In *Excavaciónes en el área urbana de Copán*, vol. 1, pp. 27–154. Tegucigalpa: Instituto Hondureño de Antropología e Historia.

Fash, Barbara, William Fash, Sheree Lane, Rudy Larios, Linda Schele, Jeffrey Stomper, and David Stuart (1992) Investigations of a Classic Maya Council House at Copan, Honduras. *Journal of Field Archaeology* 19: 419–42.

Fox, John W. (1987) *Maya Postclassic State Formation*. Cambridge: Cambridge University Press.

Gallareta Negrón, Tomás (1989) The Postclassic Period in the Northern Maya Lowlands: Some Preliminary Observations. Manuscript on file, Middle American Research Institute, Tulane University, New Orleans.

—— (2012) *The Social Organization of Labna, a Classic Maya Community in the Puuc Region of Yucatan*. PhD dissertation, Department of Anthropology, Tulane University. Ann Arbor, MI: University Microfilms.

Gallareta Negrón, Tomás, Rossana May Ciau, Ramón Carrillo Sánchez, Julieta Ramos Pacheco, and Maribel Gamboa Angulo (2003) Investigaciones arqueológicas y restauración arquitectónica en Labná, Yucatán, México: la temporada de campo de 2002, capitulo 5:5.1–5.13. Report submitted to the Instituto Nacional de Antropología e Historia, Merida, Mexico.

Gallareta Negrón, Tomás, George J. Bey III, and William M. Ringle (2007) Investigaciones arqueológicas en las ruinas de Kiuic, Huntichmul, y la zona Labná-Kiuic, Distrito de Bolonchén, Yucatán, México: temporada de campo 2006. Report submitted to the Instituto Nacional de Antropología e Historia, Merida, Mexico.

Gendrop, Paul (1983) *Los estilos Río Bec, Chenes y Puuc en la arquitectura maya*. Mexico City: Universidad Nacional Autónoma de México.

Maldonado Cárdenas, Rubén (1997) La exploración y restauración de la Subestructura 44 de Dzibilchaltún. In *Yucatán a través de los siglos*, ed. Ruth Gubler and Patricia Martel, pp. 67–76. Merida, Mexico: Ediciones de la Universidad Autónoma de Yucatán.

—— (2003) Dzibilchaltún, desarrollo e interrelaciones en la planicie norte de Yucatán. In *Escondido en la selva: arqueología en el norte de Yucatán*, ed. Hanns J. Prem, pp. 39–52. Mexico City: Instituto Nacional de Antropología e Historia; and Bonn: Bonn University.

Maldonado Cárdenas, Rubén, Alexander Voss, and Ángel Góngora (2002) Kalom Uk'uw, señor de Dzibilchaltún. In *La organización social entre los Mayas prehispánicos, coloniales y modernos: memoria de la Tercera Mesa Redonda de Palenque I*, ed. Vera Tiesler Blos, Rafael Cobos, and Merle Greene Robertson, pp. 79–100. Mexico City: Instituto Nacional de Antropología e Historia.

Martinez Hernandez, Juan (ed.) (1929) *Diccionario de Motul maya-español, atribuído a Fray Antonio de Ciudad Real y Arte de lengua maya por Fray Juan Coronel*. Merida, Mexico: Compañía Tipográfica Yucateca.

Pérez, Juan Pío (1870) Apuntes para un diccionario de la lengua maya: compuestos con vista de varios catálogos antiguos de sus voces y aumento con gran suma de los de uso común y otras que se han extractado de manuscritos antiguos. Manuscript, University of Pennsylvania Museum Library, Philadelphia.

Pollock, Harry E. D. (1980) *The Puuc: An Architectural Survey of the Hill Country of Yucatan and Northern Campeche, Mexico*. Cambridge, MA: Peabody Museum of Archaeology and Ethnology.

Proskouriakoff, Tatiana (1962) Civic and Religious Structures of Mayapan. In *Mayapan, Yucatan, Mexico*, ed. Harry E. D. Pollock et al., pp. 87–164. Washington, DC: Carnegie Institution.

Ringle, William M., and George J. Bey III (1992) The Center and Segmentary State Dynamics. Paper presented at the Wenner-Gren Conference on the Segmentary State and Classic Maya Lowlands, Cleveland State University.

—— (2000) Proyecto Ek Balam: Preliminary Report on the 1999 Field Season. Report submitted to the Ahau Foundation and to the Instituto Nacional de Antropología e Historia, Mexico City and Merida, Mexico.

—— (2001) Post-Classic and Terminal Classic Courts of the Northern Maya Lowlands. In *Royal Courts of the Ancient Maya*, Vol. 2: *Data and Case Studies*, ed. Takeshi Inomata and Stephen D. Houston, pp. 266–307. Boulder, CO: Westview Press.

—— (2008) Preparing for Visitors: Classic-Period Political Dynamics on the Northern Plains of Yucatan. Paper presented at the VI Mesa Redonda de Palenque, Chiapas.

Ringle, William M., George J. Bey III, and Tomás Gallareta N. (2006) The Urban Process in Northern Yucatan: Puuc to Plains. Paper presented at the 71st meeting of the Society for American Archaelogy, San Juan, Puerto Rico.

Ruppert, Karl, and Augustus L. Smith (1957) *House Types in the Environs of Mayapan and at Uxmal, Kabah, Sayil, Chichen Itza, and Chacchob*. Cambridge, MA: Carnegie Institution.

Ruz Lhuillier, Alberto (1952) Uxmal: temporado de trabajos 1951–1952. Manuscript on file at the Archivo Tecnico de Monumentos Prehispanicos del Instituto Nacional de Antropología e Historia, Merida, Mexico.

Schele, Linda (1998) The Iconography of Maya Architectural Façades during the Late Classic Period. In *Function and Meaning in Classic Maya Architecture*, ed. Stephen D. Houston, pp. 479–517. Washington, DC: Dumbarton Oaks.

Stomper, Jeffrey Alan (1996) *The Popol Na: A Model for Ancient Maya Community Structure at Copan, Honduras*. PhD dissertation, Department of Anthropology, Yale University. Ann Arbor, MI: University Microfilms.

Stone, Andrea, and Marc Zender (2011) *Reading Maya Art: A Hieroglyphic Guide to Ancient Maya Painting and Sculpture*. New York: Thames & Hudson.

13

ALTERNATIVE NARRATIVES AND MISSING DATA

Refining the chronology of Chichen Itza[1]

Beniamino Volta and Geoffrey E. Braswell

The history of the ancient Maya city of Chichen Itza, Yucatan, Mexico, has been a subject of debate in archaeology, epigraphy, and art history for more than a century. Despite abundant scholarly attention, little agreement has been reached on a coherent chronological framework for the site. Contradicting chronologies based on hieroglyphic inscriptions, ethnohistorical sources, ceramic typologies, architectural styles, and absolute dates have been proposed. Such alternative chronologies reflect past and current interpretations of ancient Maya history. Nonetheless, they often limit new understanding. In this chapter we review existing chronologies of Chichen Itza and attempt to resolve some of the inconsistencies among them. We combine different lines of evidence with data from recent stratigraphic excavations of the Great Terrace, employing Bayesian calibration of radiocarbon determinations to generate a more precise chronology for the site. The results of our analysis refine our understanding of the dynamics of occupation at Chichen Itza during the ninth, tenth, and early eleventh centuries AD. Future research should be aimed at elucidating initial settlement of the site during the Preclassic and Early Classic periods, exploring a possible temporary decline during the first half of the tenth century, and understanding the collapse of Chichen Itza during the eleventh century.

The nature and timing of the transition between the Terminal Classic and Early Postclassic periods are important and controversial issues in the archaeology of the northern Maya lowlands (Andrews *et al.* 2003; Andrews and Sabloff 1986; Bey *et al.* 1997; Chase and Chase 2004; Demarest *et al.* 2004; Sabloff 2007). As one of the primary political and economic centers in northern Yucatan for at least part – if not all – of the time span between AD 800 and 1200, Chichen Itza plays a major role in any attempt to identify and explain the social processes underlying this significant change (see Figures 1.1 and 13.1; Aimers 2007; Anderson 1998; A. P. Andrews 1990; E. W. Andrews 1979; Ball 1979; Cobos 2004, 2011; Cobos

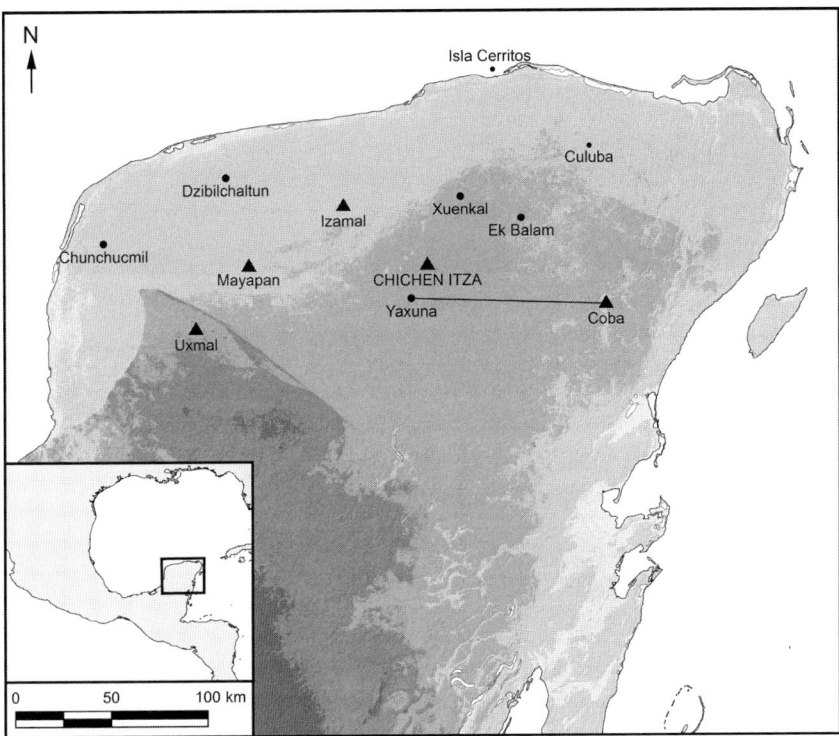

FIGURE 13.1 The northern Maya lowlands, showing the location of Chichen Itza and other sites; gray scale indicates meters above sea level: light gray = 0–2 m; light-medium gray = 2–20 m; medium gray = 20–65 m; medium-dark gray = 65–160 m; dark gray = 160–320 m

and Winemiller 2001; Lincoln 1986; Sabloff 2007; Suhler *et al.* 2004). Nonetheless, and despite more than a century of archaeological research at the site, our understanding of the occupational history of Chichen Itza remains uncertain and controversial. Progress on the question is hampered in part by the persistence of entrenched chronological assumptions that limit our understanding of both old and newly acquired data.

Recent stratigraphic excavations on the Great Terrace (Braswell and Peniche May 2012) and two studies of the ceramics of Chichen Itza (Chung 2009; Pérez de Heredia Puente 2010, 2012) have generated valuable new information whose chronological implications are discussed here. In an effort to generate more precise interpretations from what is still a sparse and problematic data set, we employ Bayesian calibration of radiocarbon determinations to generate more precise anchor-points for the archaeological chronology of Chichen Itza.

Excavations conducted by staff from the University of California, San Diego (UCSD), in the Great Terrace, constituting the northern half of the site center, are described in two publications and an internal report (Braswell and Peniche

May 2012; Hahn and Braswell 2012; Peniche May *et al.* 2009). This work consisted of two distinct operations within a broader project directed by Rafael Cobos of the Universidad Autónoma de Yucatán. One set of excavations was placed east of the Castillo pyramid, connecting it to the Group of the Thousand Columns (Figures 13.2 and 13.3). The horizontal extent of our excavations was just under 600 square meters in area, and most test pits were dug to bedrock. Our long and deep stratigraphic cuts were designed not only to link these important structures directly but also to connect to previous excavations (Schmidt and Pérez de Heredia Puente 2006). This is fortunate, because we do not have access to the pottery collected from our excavations. Instead, we rely on the analysis by Pérez de Heredia Puente (hereafter Pérez) of materials from the same stratigraphic levels revealed through earlier excavations, which are either next to or actually intersect with our own.

During UCSD excavations conducted in 2009, we revealed two or three Late Classic platforms (AC16, AC3, and – possibly – AC21), important north- and eastward Terminal Classic expansions of these platforms (AC10, AC4, and AC7), and two Terminal Classic superstructures (AC18 and patio-gallery AC8). The construction of the Castillo-sub saw the Great Terrace floor (AC2) expand to the western entrance of what is now the Group of the Thousand Columns. After two more reflooring events (AC1 and "piso sin nombre"), the Castillo (Str. 2D5) and final floor (AC6) east of that pyramid were built during the Early Postclassic period. Stratigraphic analysis reveals that all this was before the construction of most of the structures now visible on the Great Terrace, including the Temple of the Warriors and its substructure, the Great Ballcourt, the Lower Temple of the Jaguars, the

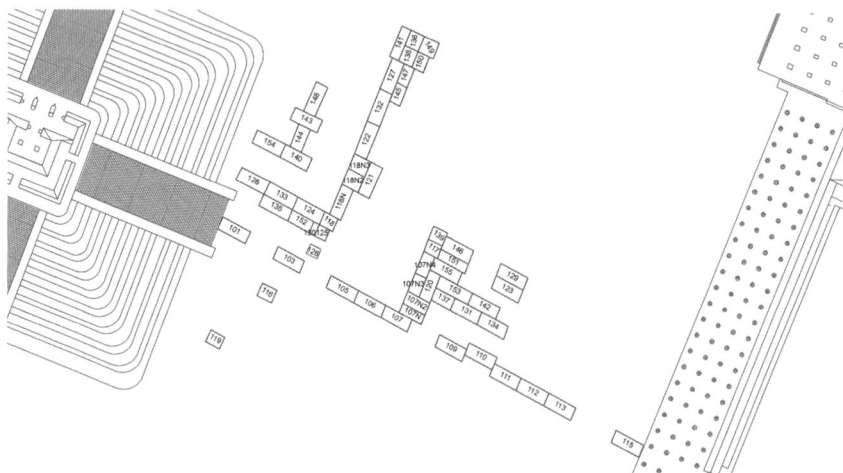

FIGURE 13.2 Excavations conducted by UCSD staff in 2009, between the Castillo and the Western Colonnade of the Group of the Thousand Columns (Braswell and Peniche May 2012: fig. 9.5)

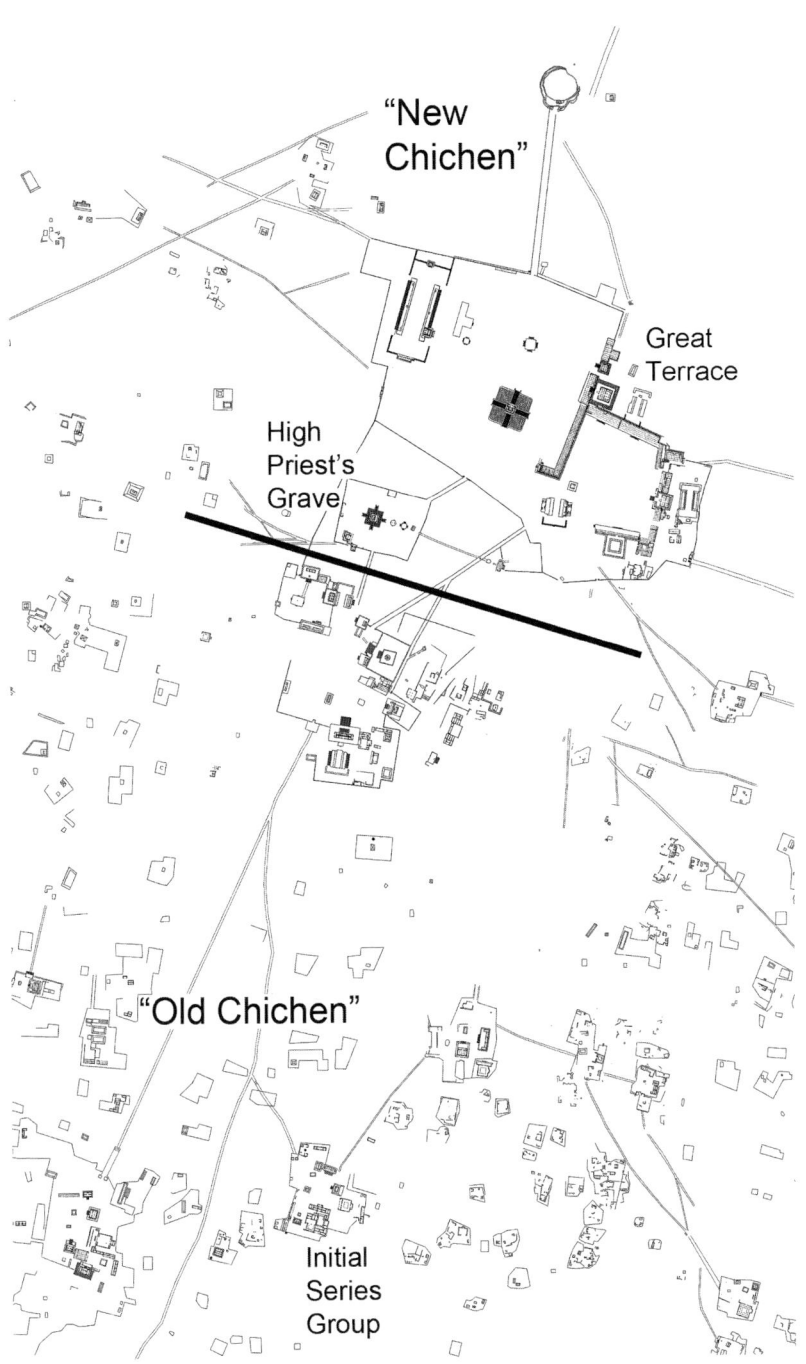

FIGURE 13.3 Chichen Itza, showing the location of Maya-style architecture in "Old Chichen" and International-style architecture in "New Chichen" (Braswell and Peniche May 2012: fig. 9.3)

Upper Temple of the Jaguars, the Venus Platform, and the Temple of the Big Tables and its substructure, also built during the Early Postclassic (Braswell and Peniche May 2012: 238–52, figs 9.8–9.19).

Early chronological models: Chichen Itza and the Toltecs

The most influential chronological models for Chichen Itza have their origins in the late nineteenth and early twentieth centuries and the work of Désiré Charnay (1887), Eduard Seler (1909), and George Vaillant (1961). These ideas were most completely developed and elaborated by Sylvanus G. Morley (1946), Alfred M. Tozzer (1957), and J. Eric S. Thompson (1970). These scholars – as well as many others – sought to understand similarities recognized in the architecture, art, and even ceramics of Tula and Chichen Itza. Their interpretations share similar general outlines.[2] According to the "traditional model," local Maya people first established Chichen Itza. Somewhat later, invaders or immigrants with central Mexican connections – often said to come directly from Tula – arrived at the site and imposed foreign ideas upon an already existing city.

Put another way, Chichen Itza was considered to have had at least two distinct occupations. The first occupation, called the "Maya period," was thought to date to before about AD 900 or 1000. It was during this period that the southern half of the site center, containing structures such as Monjas, the Akab Dzib, and the Caracol, was built (see Figure 13.3). In contrast, the "Toltec-Maya" period was thought to date somewhat later, to about AD 900/1000–1250. The chronology of this later period was derived in part through comparison with legendary Tula, known to predate the historical Aztecs yet postdate Classic-period Teotihuacan (Jiménez Moreno 1941; Kirchhoff 1955). For this reason, the Toltec-Maya period, to which most of the monumental architecture on the Great Terrace was assigned (including the Castillo, the Great Ballcourt, and the Group of the Thousand Columns), was placed in the Early Postclassic period, making it contemporary with Tula. Chichen Itza and Tula therefore came to define Early Postclassic Mesoamerica. A key aspect of the traditional model that is now widely rejected is that long-distance migration played an important role in the history of the site. Almost all scholars who now work in the northern lowlands consider Chichen Itza to have been a Maya site throughout its history, although the exact origin of the Itza remains a topic of discussion (e.g., Boot 2010; Schele and Mathews 1998).

The books of Chilam Balam

Aztec legends about Tula are not the only indigenous sources that provide chronological information used to understand the culture history of Chichen Itza. More directly, the great city and the Itza play prominent roles in the books of Chilam Balam, especially the Chumayel (Medíz Bolio 1930) and Tizimin (Makemson 1951). Ralph Roys (1933), Ermilio Solís Alcalá (1949), Alfredo Barrera Vásquez (Barrera Vásquez and Rendón 1948), Munro Edmonson (1982, 1986), and Susan

Milbrath and Carlos Peraza Lope (2003) all have tried to extract chronological information from these documents that could be correlated with Western calendar years. With few exceptions, all dates in the books of Chilam Balam are given in the *k'atun-ajaw* format, which lends itself to multiple interpretations based on what 13-*k'atun* (or *may*) cycle, correlation factor, and calendrical seat one believes should be used in converting a chronological expression into Gregorian years (see Edmonson 1976, 1982: 195–9, for a summary discussion).

The historical framework for early ideas about Chichen Itza is based in part on Roys's interpretation of *k'atun* chronicles and prophecies from the Chilam Balam of Chumayel. He lists the relevant events as follows:

> K'atun 6 Ajaw (AD 452): Chichen Itza founded.
>
> K'atun 8 Ajaw (AD 689): Chichen Itza abandoned. Chakanputun settled.
>
> K'atun 4 Ajaw (AD 985): Occupation of Chichen Itza by Kukulcan and the Itza.
>
> K'atun 8 Ajaw (AD 1201): Conquest of Chichen Itza by Hunac Ceel.
>
> (Roys 1933: 204)[3]

Two events were interpreted as indicating an invasion of Chichen Itza: its occupation by Kukulcan and the Itza in K'atun 4 Ajaw and its conquest by Hunac Ceel during K'atun 8 Ajaw. Following Roys's publication of the Chumayel, the first of these periods, ending in the Long Count date 10.8.0.0.0 and corresponding to the years AD 968–987 in the GMT correlation, became the most commonly accepted date for the so-called Mexican *entrada* at Chichen Itza (Morley 1946: 87; Thompson 1937: 190, 1970: 10). Other correlations for a supposed conquest event include placing the Hunac Ceel episode one *may* cycle earlier, at 10.6.0.0.0 (AD 948; Tozzer 1957: 25–32), as well postulating an earlier invasion at 10.4.9.7.3 (AD 918) as part of Thompson's (1970: 10–25) two-stage "Putun hypothesis" (cf. Kremer 1994). Edmonson's (1986: 37–47) more recent reading of the Chumayel contains conquest or destruction events at Chichen Itza in AD 674, 948, 1059, 1244, and 1382.

Tozzer, Thompson, and their colleagues expended considerable effort constructing historical chronologies from native accounts that were written down in the early colonial period. But, as several scholars have pointed out, it is unlikely that texts such as the books of Chilam Balam contain reliable historical information about legendary events that occurred three to six centuries before they were composed (Bricker 1981: 6–8; Edmonson 1986: 2; Smith 2011: 586–91). Moreover, the books of Chilam Balam do not present events in strict chronological order, nor are they linear in structure. Instead, they reflect Maya concepts of the organization of time – not Western ideas. To this end, events are grouped according to dramatic categories and ascribed to corresponding *k'atuns*, each of which has certain characteristics (Bricker 1981: 154). Great cities, for example, are said to have been abandoned during K'atun 8 Ajaw, a period of destruction and rebirth. We should understand this not as the literal truth, but as a deliberate organizational, thematic, and explanatory device employed by the authors of the books. Moreover, cities that we know were not contemporary – such as Uxmal and Mayapan – are said to have been occupied at the same time (cf. Milbrath and Peraza Lope 2003). Although some scholars have tried to assign the final destruction of Chichen Itza and Mayapan to different *may* cycles, it appears that the authors of the books of Chilam Balam saw them as linked events occurring in precisely the same K'atun 8 Ajaw. The unlikely alternative is that some individuals mentioned in the chronicles lived longer than one 256-year *may* cycle. Victoria Bricker (1981: 149–54) has referred to this compression and expansion of historical events that are transformed into legend as "telescoping."

Thus, although the books of Chilam Balam tell us a lot about how the post-Conquest Maya structured their own cyclical history and legends, the events described in them are often difficult to organize into a linear time line from oldest to most recent. Furthermore, it is naïve to consider these texts as objective historical records. As Matthew Restall (1998; see also Marcus 1992) and others have shown, the histories contained in colonial-period documents are inextricable from their expedient political purposes. Thus, we should neither compel the books of Chilam Balam to conform to Western notions of history nor force archaeological data to fit our understanding of those books.

Ceramic studies

The pottery of Chichen Itza, first analyzed by George Vaillant (1961) in the 1920s, was described extensively by George Brainerd (1958) and later classified by Robert Smith (1971) as part of his regional study of the northern lowlands. Brainerd defines three stages of pottery found at Chichen Itza: the Regional Stage, corresponding roughly to the Late Preclassic and Early Classic periods; the Florescent Stage, dated to the second half of the Late Classic; and the Mexican Stage, divided into Early, Middle, and Late sub-stages. Smith calls these respectively the Cochuah and Motul phases (although he does not report any Motul ceramics from Chichen Itza itself), the Cehpech phase, and the Sotuta, Hocaba, and Tases phases – names that we still use today even though we question some of the dates Smith assigned to these phases (Figure 13.4). Brainerd reports that Regional-Stage pottery is rare at Chichen Itza and that Mexican-Stage (i.e., Sotuta and later) sherds constituted the largest portion of the collection that he studied. Similarly, Smith's (1971: table 1b) sample contained only 12 Cochuah and 404 Cehpech sherds, compared to more than 18,000 fragments of Sotuta pottery.[4]

There has been some confusion as to whether Brainerd studied pottery from any unmixed Florescent (i.e., Cehpech) contexts. Brainerd (1958: 94), in fact, states that "there are several seemingly pure [Early Mexican] deposits, many deposits showing varying degrees of Middle Mexican and Florescent mixture, but no pure Florescent deposits." Nevertheless, in the very next sentence he writes that caches found within the substructure of the Caracol (Str. 3C15) date it to the Florescent Stage.[5] Furthermore, he states one reason why just "several" pure Sotuta deposits

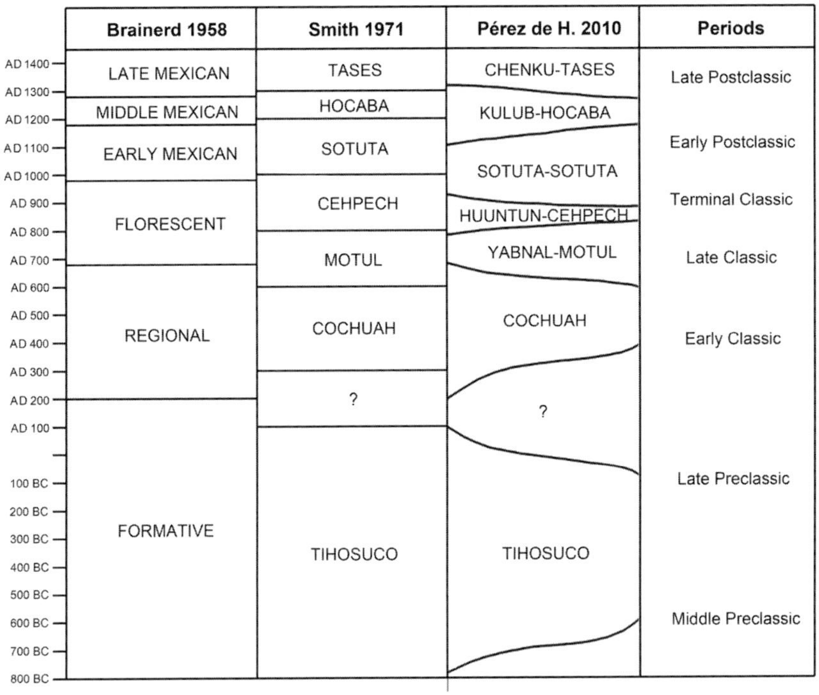

	Brainerd 1958	Smith 1971	Pérez de H. 2010	Periods
AD 1400 / AD 1300	LATE MEXICAN	TASES	CHENKU-TASES	Late Postclassic
AD 1200	MIDDLE MEXICAN	HOCABA	KULUB-HOCABA	
AD 1100 / AD 1000	EARLY MEXICAN	SOTUTA	SOTUTA-SOTUTA	Early Postclassic
AD 900 / AD 800	FLORESCENT	CEHPECH	HUUNTUN-CEHPECH	Terminal Classic
AD 700		MOTUL	YABNAL-MOTUL	Late Classic
AD 600 / AD 500 / AD 400 / AD 300	REGIONAL	COCHUAH	COCHUAH	Early Classic
AD 200 / AD 100		?	?	
100 BC / 200 BC / 300 BC / 400 BC / 500 BC	FORMATIVE	TIHOSUCO	TIHOSUCO	Late Preclassic
600 BC / 700 BC / 800 BC				Middle Preclassic

FIGURE 13.4 Ceramic chronologies for Chichen Itza (Brainerd 1958: chart 22; Pérez 2010: fig. 2; Smith 1971: chart 1)

were encountered at Chichen Itza: mixture was created by a heavy Toltec-Maya occupation. He goes on to argue that the excavation strategy, which focused on the consolidation of late architecture, "did not often pierce earlier deposits." Similarly, the five trenches that provided Smith's ceramic sample for Chichen Itza were designed "for determining the component parts of the Sotuta Ceramic Complex" (Smith 1971: 162), not for elaborating a full ceramic sequence for the site.

We stress Brainerd's and Smith's actual words in order to make four points: (1) there were at least some caches from the Caracol substructure that lacked Sotuta material and therefore predate that phase; (2) Brainerd had relatively few pure deposits of any kind, including those dating to the Sotuta phase; (3) there are cultural and archaeological reasons why his and Smith's samples would not have come from pure Cehpech or other early contexts; and (4) the question of whether there exists a pure Cehpech phase at Chichen Itza is open to discussion.

Some of the pottery recovered by early excavations in the major structures of Chichen Itza is still available for study in the Instituto Nacional de Antropología e Historia (INAH) *ceramoteca* in Merida. Smith's extensive type collections from Chichen Itza, Mayapan, and other sites are still important tools for researchers. Although no one wishes to criticize the work of pioneers, it is widely if quietly acknowledged that some of the original identifications are incorrect. More to the point, the ever growing literature concerning the slate wares of the northern Maya lowlands indicates that there are still many questions regarding how to identify them (Bey *et al.* 1997, 1998; Chung 2009; Chung and Lee 2005; Espinosa *et al.* 2000; Jiménez Álvarez *et al.* 2006; Johnson 2012; Robles Castellanos 1988; Suhler *et al.* 1998; Varela Torrecilla 1998). It is often difficult to distinguish at the group – let alone the type – level whether a particular sherd with black trickle decoration should be classified as Say (or Sat or Early) Slate, Muna (or Puuc) Slate, Dzitas (or Chichen) Slate, or even Kukula Cream (or Peto Cream Ware or Coarse Slate). Rather than being always distinct groups, the slate wares are more accurately considered as clouds that overlap to such a degree that both conflation and false discrimination are common, and only extremes of each particular group or type can be identified with confidence without employing petrographic analysis. Classification decisions, for example, concerning the difference between Sat and Muna Slate might be made solely on differential firing, with better fired examples of Sat being assigned to the second – and supposedly later – group (Joseph W. Ball, personal communication 2013). Given the difficulties that even the most experienced analysts have in distinguishing among these frequently overlapping pottery types and groups – which, in turn, are used to determine chronology and inter-site affiliations – it is reasonable, cautious, and legitimate to point out how easily such misidentifications can occur.

It is also important to ask to what degree various ceramic complexes should be viewed as representing the complete pottery assemblage of a given phase and if they constitute a true sphere. This is particularly true of the Late Classic Motul complex, but it also is true to some degree of the widely accepted Cehpech complex and phase:

> Cehpech is an unusual and somewhat tricky-to-work with construct in that its diagnostic content-package, as first crystallized in the Cehpech complex at Uxmal, more closely resembles an elite class or fine wares subcomplex appended to an already established Copo sphere complex than it does a full and independent complex in its own right. In all probability it does so because, in fact, that is what it really is.
>
> *Cehpech diagnostic elements tend to appear in already existing complexes in clusters* and subsequently to become integral parts of them, generally in conjunction with other stylistic, formal, and/or typological modifications to their preintroduction composition.
>
> (Ball 1976: 328; emphasis added)

Among the many import aspects of this observation is that we should be cautious when employing the Cehpech construct at sites such as Chichen Itza. The spread of Cehpech pottery, like the expansion of Early Classic Tzakol Peten Gloss Ware into pre-existing Peripheral Chicanel complexes in the southern Maya lowlands, might best be thought of as indicating participation in a widespread elite interaction network. It is a "mode of integration" (ibid.: 329). Hence, we should expect to find some Cehpech pottery embedded within other complexes at Chichen Itza, and that this pottery would both create change in the underlying complex and be transformed by it. From another perspective, much of what is called "Sotuta" at Chichen Itza and "Cehpech" at Uxmal are just regional and temporal variants of the same kinds of pottery.

Recent ceramic studies

Since the 1990s, Eduardo Pérez (2010, 2012) has analyzed nearly 2 million sherds excavated by the Proyecto Arqueológico Chichen Itza, directed by Peter Schmidt. In this extremely important and well-documented work, Pérez identifies a significant number of what he calls Yabnal-Motul deposits and even some pure (if small and few) Huuntun-Cehpech deposits at the site. The first of these ceramic complexes is distinguished from Smith's (1971: 142) original definition of the Motul complex by the recognition of early Slate Ware belonging to the Say Slate Group (Pérez 2007, 2012: 383–4).[6] Such pure Late Classic deposits, which Pérez sees as dating to before about AD 800/830, are found not only in the construction fill of what we call "Early Chichen"-style structures and platforms but also in primary-context burials. At the moment, these Late Classic contexts are best known from the Group of the Initial Series, from the Group of the Three Lintels (Pérez 2012), and from within the Great Terrace.

Pérez also identifies some pure Huuntun-Cehpech contexts at Chichen Itza, but they are much fewer in number and contain many fewer sherds. Most importantly, Pérez (2010: 128) writes: "construction fill of 'Maya' or 'Puuc' buildings is not associated with Sotuta ceramics, but rather with very Early or Early Facets of the Cehpech complex." In other words, he found no Sotuta pottery in or beneath such structures. Surprisingly, the fill of the platforms supporting the House of the Phalli (Str. 5C14) and the Temple of Three Lintels (Str. 7B3), as well as the fill of the roof comb of the Casa Colorada (Str. 3C9), contained no Cehpech pottery either, but only earlier materials (ibid.: 138–42). The fill of the roof and supporting platform of the Akab Dzib (Str. 4D1) contained Late Classic Yabnal-Motul ceramics and some Terminal Classic Huuntun-Cehpech pottery (ibid.: 143–5). Together, this suggests that either these structures were built just before the Huuntun-Cehpech phase or very early in it (if such a phase, in fact, exists). Pérez prefers the second explanation, and argues that the Huuntun-Cehpech phase – associated by him with all the "Maya" or "Puuc" structures built during K'ak'upakal's reign – was quite short, lasting from AD 800/830 to AD 920/950 – that is, just 90 to 150 years. But the phase might be significantly shorter. Pérez explains the dearth of Cehpech pottery in the fill of Puuc-style structures as indicating that construction of these buildings took place at a time when Cehpech pottery was already in use but before it had sufficient time to enter the waste stream. He also has identified "pure deposits of … Huuntun-Cehpech complex [ceramics] in a vast majority of the collections" (ibid.: 159) recovered in excavations supervised by Peter Schmidt in the Great Terrace surrounding the Castillo pyramid. These critical data have not yet been published.

For reasons described above, we still question whether Cehpech materials constitute a full complex or merely a ceramic subcomplex – that is, whether or not there really was a Huuntun-Cehpech phase after Yabnal-Motul, before Sotuta-Sotuta, and distinct from both (see also Bey and Ringle 2011: 307–9). We also wonder if *some* of what is called Muna Slate at Chichen Itza might be at one extreme of the firing continuum of Say Slate, as Joseph W. Ball (personal communication 2013) warns. Pérez's (2010) thorough dissertation highlights that very little Cehpech pottery was actually found associated with the structures that he says were built during that phase. What is clear from his work is that the construction of the Maya-style structures is not associated with "early" Sotuta pottery (cf. Cobos 2004). In fact, based on his analysis, the division of Sotuta into early and late facets, the first associated with Maya-style architecture and the second with "Toltec"-style structures, is unsupported.

The beginning of the following Sotuta-Sotuta phase – the time when most, if not all, of the visible structures on the Great Terrace were built – is dated by Pérez (2010: 182) to AD 920/950. This potentially allows for a short overlap of the Cehpech and Sotuta complexes at Chichen Itza, but he does not favor a robust and lengthy overlap of the two, as Charles Lincoln (1986) and others have proposed (e.g., Andrews *et al.* 2003; Ball 1979; Cobos 2004, 2011). Pérez dates the end of the Sotuta phase at Chichen Itza to about AD 1150/1200 but admits that it could be earlier. How much earlier is unknown.

Finally, Pérez (2010: 333) places the end of monumental construction at Chichen Itza during the Kulub-Hocaba complex, dated by him to AD 1150/1200–AD 1250/1300. Kulub-Hocaba ceramics are not found in the fill of any "Toltec"-style structure, but only in minor additions and in the occupational debris of buildings. Pérez does not allow for any overlap of the Sotuta and Hocaba complexes. Similarly, the later Chenku–Tases complex is represented by minor constructive episodes and light occupation continuing until the arrival of the Spaniards.

Absolute dates for Chichen Itza ceramics and an alternative ceramic chronology

As Michael Smith (2011: 471) points out, the ceramic sequence of Chichen Itza needs to be tied to radiocarbon determinations from stratigraphic contexts. That is, it is a relative sequence that remains to be directly anchored in absolute time. A recent attempt to do so through thermoluminescence (TL) dating of the volcanic glass temper in ceramic sherds has yielded mixed results (Chung 2008, 2009; Chung *et al.* 2010). Heajoo Chung and her colleagues (2010) report TL dates for eight Slate Ware sherds "from different cultural layers" of 13 test pits excavated at Chichen Itza. More detailed contextual data are presented in Chung's (2009) published dissertation.

The earliest TL date (AD 875 ± 88) comes from sample CH18, derived from a type defined by Chung and called "Tintin Slate" (Chung et al. 2010: table 4). The error range of this TL date is reasonable for all three widely recognized slate groups: Say/Sat (to which Tintin probably should be assigned), Muna, and Dzitas. A "Puuc Slate" sherd (sample CH19), from the Muna Slate Group in Pérez's Huuntun-Cehpech complex, is dated to AD 1154 ± 76. A second Puuc Slate sherd – sample CH11, which was actually excavated at Mayapan (Chung 2009: table 14) – is dated to AD 1063 ± 47. These dates are much too late for Pérez's chronology and are inconsistent with hieroglyphic dates found on structures at Chichen Itza that contain Muna Slate in their fill (e.g., the Akab Dzib). A sample of "Early Chichen Slate" (CH16), another type defined by Chung that she argues is coeval with the Muna Slate group (ibid.: 94), produced a TL date of AD 1055 ± 85. This also seems unduly late to us for pottery thought to predate the full Sotuta complex. Finally, four "Chichen Slate" samples (CH13, CH14, CH15, CH17), all from the Dzitas Slate Group of the Sotuta complex, have TL dates of AD 1532 ± 26, AD 1110 ± 53, AD 1132 ± 69, and AD 1221 ± 30, respectively. The first date is certainly far too late, and the last one also seems late to us but certainly consistent with the traditional chronology of Chichen Itza (Chung et al. 2010: 119). Thus, roughly half of the TL dates reported by Chung and her colleagues seem to be consistent with the pottery from which they are derived, while four or five of the eight are not and appear to be quite late.[7]

Using these TL dates and stratigraphic data from her test pits, Chung also establishes a chronological sequence for the ceramics of Chichen Itza that differs in several respects from that proposed by Pérez. We stress two points. First and most importantly, Chung (2009: 225) does not recognize the existence of the full Cehpech complex at Chichen Itza and therefore rejects Smith's (1971) single linear framework proposed for the entire northern lowlands. Thus, it is not necessary to imagine that the Dzitas Slate Group of the Sotuta complex was derived from the Muna Slate Group of the Cehpech complex, but instead followed *directly* from Say Slate (in Chung 2009, "Early Dzitas" is a local stepping stone between "Tintin" and Dzitas Slate). In this model, Cehpech and Sotuta can be viewed as parallel "sister" complexes – fundamentally regional variants of the same ceramic ideas found in different geographic areas within the northern Maya lowlands – that represent a trend towards regional ceramic divergence rather than sequential stages in a uniform and unbranching sequence. We favor this perspective (see Andrews et al. 2003; Ball 1979) and suspect that, at Chichen Itza, the locally produced types of the Sotuta complex – especially the slates, red wares, and unslipped pottery – followed more or less directly from local Late Classic antecedents.[8] We argue that this transition probably took place during the late ninth and early tenth centuries. We strongly suspect that the earliest appearance of Peto Cream Ware – ascribed by Pérez, following Smith (1971), to the Kulub-Hocaba complex – also dates to the early tenth century (see Ochoa Rodriguez 1999: 77–8; Ringle et al. 1998: 189–90).

Second, based on her TL dates, Chung places the heart of the Chichen Itza ceramic sequence quite late in time. She sees the appearance of Sotuta pottery – and therefore the bulk of International-style structures associated with such pottery – as dating to the period AD 1070 to AD 1350. We do not accept this late chronology.

A final point also is concerned with the absolute dates of pottery. Scholars frequently have dated the ceramics of Chichen Itza by establishing cross-ties with other sites in the area (e.g., Anderson 1998; Andrews and Sabloff 1986; Ball 1979; Bey et al. 1997: 115–16; Robles Castellanos and Andrews 1986: 66–7). While recognizing the importance of this, we follow Smith (2011) and stress that such endeavors do not obviate the need for more chronometric data from Chichen Itza itself, especially from stratigraphic contexts containing ceramics.

Architecture

Since the beginning of research at Chichen Itza, scholars have noted the presence of at least two – and we argue for four – architectural styles at the city. As with ceramics, there is disagreement as to the degree to which these may overlap in time. The earliest is what we call the "Early Chichen" style. Rather presciently, Morley (1946) hypothesized that such a style or period should exist and called it "Initial Series." Such Early Chichen-style architecture was recently described by José Osorio León (2004) in his excavations of the House of the Stuccoes (Str. 5C4-I) underneath the Temple of the Initial Series (see Figure 13.3). Since then, Braswell and Peniche May (2012: 241–3) have identified at least two more platforms (AC16 and AC3) built in this early style east of the Castillo and within the Great Terrace. Characteristic of the Early Chichen style is the use of roughly faced stones covered with a thick layer of stucco for supporting platforms (Figure 13.5). To date, the only superstructure of the Early Chichen style that has been excavated is the House of the Stuccoes. The walls of this three-room building were built of very crude stones and mud and covered with thick plaster. The upper façade appears to have been richly decorated with modeled stucco, but it is not clear if the roof was stone or made of perishable materials (Osorio León 2004). Many pieces of painted stucco found just off platform AC3 on the Great Terrace suggest that other structures were painted at this time (Figure 13.5, painted stucco found just above the exposed human remains). The fill of the House of the Stuccoes contains Late Classic Yabnal-Motul but no Cehpech or Sotuta pottery (Osorio León 2006; Pérez 2012: 390–91). We assume that Platforms AC3 and AC16 of the Great Terrace also date to the very end of the Late Classic, perhaps to about AD 800. This assumption is supported by Pérez's unpublished analysis of ceramics recovered from INAH excavations in the Great Terrace east of the Castillo during the 1980s and early 2000s, which found Yabnal-Motul ceramics in stratigraphic levels that correspond to the construction of these platforms (Figure 13.6; Schmidt and Pérez 2006). Finally, it seems likely that the earliest subplatform of the Monjas Complex (Str. 4C1) was also built in the Early Chichen style (Bolles 1977: 86).

Refining the chronology of Chichen Itza   369

FIGURE 13.5   Platform AC3 of the Great Terrace, an Early Chichen-style construction dating to *ca.* AD 800 (Braswell and Peniche May 2012: fig. 9.9)

The second architectural style at Chichen Itza has been called "Pure Florescent," "Maya," or "Puuc," although perhaps the Temple of the Three Lintels (Str. 7B3) is the only pure Classic Puuc-style structure (Figure 13.7). We use the phrase "Maya style" but stress that we consider all the buildings of Chichen Itza to have been constructed by the Maya using local techniques. Many of the most impressive Maya-style structures, such as the Casa Colorada, Monjas, the Akab Dzib, and the Temples of the Three and Four Lintels, contain texts with hieroglyphic dates that

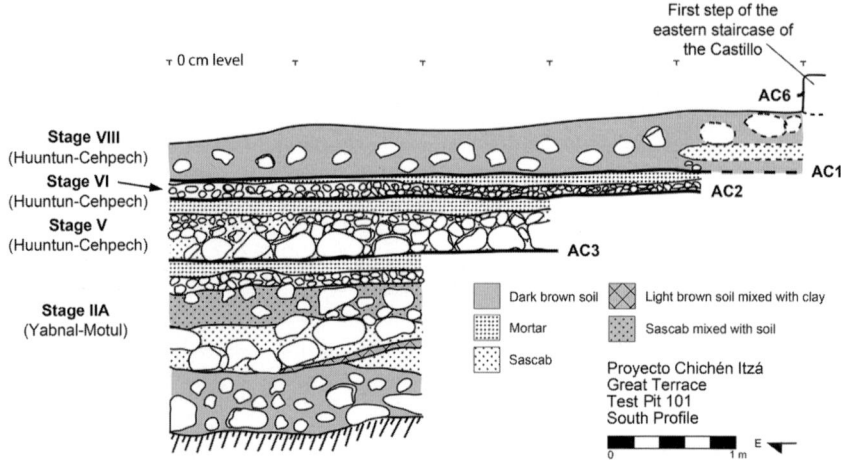

FIGURE 13.6 Test pit 101, south profile (after Peniche May and Braswell 2009: fig. 3.22), showing ceramic phases identified by Pérez in corresponding stratigraphic levels from INAH excavations in the Great Terrace (Schmidt and Pérez 2006); the Castillo was built in Stage VIII and the Castillo-sub in Stage V

place them in a rather narrow period in the late ninth century. There are currently no known Maya-style structures on the Great Terrace, but it is possible that a posited first version of the Castillo, buried beneath and within the substructure of the Castillo itself, was built in the Maya style (Schmidt and Pérez 2006; see also Braswell and Peniche May 2012).

A third style is dubbed "Transitional" and was first described by Ignacio Marquina (1951: 852) in his discussion of the Castillo-sub. An alternative name could be "Early International style," because Transitional-style architecture demonstrates familiarity with certain elements of the full International style but incorporation of only some of those elements. For example, the Castillo-sub has a *chacmool* sculpture and is decorated with marching felines and intertwined snakes, but it lacks warrior columns and is not a radial pyramid (Figure 13.8). Other Transitional-style structures include an early gallery-patio structure excavated within the Great Terrace (Str. AC8; Braswell and Peniche May 2012: 248–50), the Castillo Viejo (Str. 5B18) of Old Chichen, and perhaps intermediate construction stages of the Caracol. Nonetheless, there are few known Transitional-style structures at Chichen Itza, suggesting either that the period during which the International style was adopted was short or that the Transitional style dates to a time when relatively few buildings were constructed. According to William Ringle (personal communication 2012), certain aspects of the substructure of the Temple of the Big Tables and the Lower Temple of the Jaguars also are "Maya" in style, even though the artwork is purely International. This fusion might allow them to be called Transitional, as well, even though they were built at a later time.

FIGURE 13.7 Temple of the Three Lintels, a Maya-style structure dating to AD 878/879

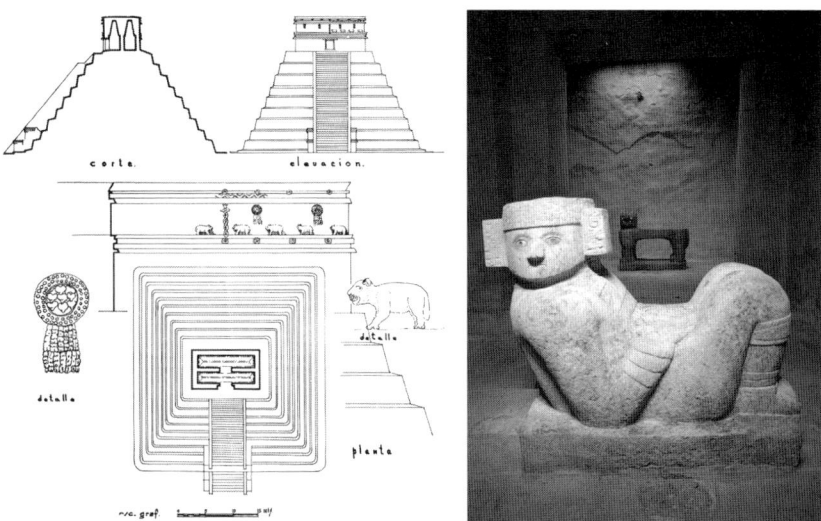

FIGURE 13.8 Section and elevation of the Castillo-sub (left; Marquina 1951: plate 263) and photo of sculpture located within the two rooms of the superstructure (right); the Castillo-sub is a Transitional-style structure dating to about AD 900–950

The fourth style has been called "Mexican," "Toltec," "Maya-Toltec," "Modified Florescent," and "International." We employ the last term, but again stress that there is nothing foreign about the construction techniques of any of the styles at Chichen Itza and that core-veneer masonry has a long history in the northern Maya lowlands. The oldest International-style structure currently visible on the Great Terrace is probably the Castillo itself (Figure 13.9). We say this because all other excavated visible structures there were built above the floor that lips up on the base of the Castillo (Floor AC6; see Figure 13.6) or are associated with horizontal expansions of that floor to the north and west. Later International-style buildings include the High Priest's Grave (Str. 3C1), the Temple of the Warriors (Str. 2D8), the Group of the Thousand Columns, and the Great Ballcourt (Str. 2D1). It should be noted that Thompson (1970) placed the beginning of "Toltec" architecture at Chichen Itza to about AD 987, or 10.8.0.0.0 in the Maya calendar, a date in relatively close accord with our own understanding of the temporal placement of the style.

For more than a century, archaeologists have argued about the relative temporal positions of Maya-style structures in "Old Chichen" and International-style architecture on the Great Terrace. Most scholars have recognized that Maya-style structures are somewhat older than International-style buildings. In contrast, Charles Lincoln (1986), Marvin Cohodas (1978), Linda Schele, and

FIGURE 13.9 The Castillo, an early International-style structure dating to about AD 950–998, as seen from the Temple of the Warriors, a later International-style structure; in the background at the right is the Great Ballcourt, which, like the Temple of the Warriors, dates to sometime around or after AD 1000

David Freidel (Schele and Freidel 1990) embrace total overlap models. Although several Maya-style structures have dated inscriptions, only three International-style buildings – the Temple of the Hieroglyphic Jambs (Str. 6E3), the High Priest's Grave, and the Temple of the Initial Series – are unambiguously associated with hieroglyphic dates. In two cases, these seem to have been reset from earlier structures.

Hieroglyphic dates

The history of the study of Maya hieroglyphic inscriptions at Chichen Itza is long and rich. José Miguel García Campillo (2000), Daniel Graña-Behrens (2002), Erik Boot (2005), and Nikolai Grube and Ruth Krochock (2011) have recently discussed the texts of the site. A key factor hampering our understanding of the chronology of these texts is that many contain only Calendar Round or *tun-ajaw* dates, as recognized by Thompson (1937). The dates of the earliest and latest texts of the site, therefore, often have been reassessed or questioned (Table 13.1).

TABLE 13.1 Hieroglyphic dates associated with buildings from Chichen Itza and its hinterland

Location	Calendar Round or tun-ajaw	Long Count	AD
T. of the Hieroglyphic Jambs, east jamb	9 Ben 1 Sak	10.0.2.7.13	832
T. of the Hieroglyphic Jambs, west jamb	9 Ben 1 Sak	10.0.2.7.13	832
Great Ballcourt stone	11 Kimi 14 Pax	10.1.15.3.6	864
Water Trough lintel	11 Ben 11 Kumk'u	10.1.17.5.13	867
Casa Colorada band, blocks 2–4	6 Muluk 12 Mak	10.2.0.1.9	869
Casa Colorada band, blocks 27–9	7 Ak'bal 1 Ch'en	10.2.0.15.3	870
Halakal lintel	**Tun 1 in 1 Ajaw**	**10.2.1.0.0**	**869–870**
Akab Dzib lintel	Tun 1 in 1 Ajaw	10.2.1.0.0	869–870
Casa Colorada band, blocks 10–12	Tun 1 in 1 Ajaw	10.2.1.0.0	869–870
Casa Colorada band, blocks 17–19	Tun 1 in 1 Ajaw	10.2.1.0.0	869–870
Casa Colorada band, blocks 33–4	Tun 1 in 1 Ajaw	10.2.1.0.0	869–870
Casa Colorada band, blocks 47–8	Tun 1 in 1 Ajaw	10.2.1.0.0	869–870
Casa Colorada band, block 51	Tun 2 in 1 Ajaw	10.2.2.0.0	870–871
Casa Colorada band, block 54	**Tun 3 in 1 Ajaw**	**10.2.3.0.0**	**871–872**
Yula, Lintel 2	2 Imix 4 Mak	10.2.4.2.1	873
Yula, Lintel 1	8 K'an 2 Pop	10.2.4.8.4	874
Yula, Lintel 2	**3 Eb 10 Pop**	**10.2.4.8.12**	**874**
Caracol hieroglyphic band, fragment 9	Tun 8 in 1 Ajaw	10.2.8.0.0	876–877
Temple of the Initial Series lintel	**9 Muluk 7 Sak**	**10.2.9.1.9**	**878**
Temple of the Initial Series lintel, side	Tun 10 in 1 Ajaw	10.2.10.0.0	878–879
Temple of the Three Lintels, Lintel 1	**Tun 10 in 1 Ajaw**	**10.2.10.0.0**	**878–879**
Temple of the Three Lintels, Lintel 2	Tun 10 in 1 Ajaw	10.2.10.0.0	878–879
Temple of the Three Lintels, Lintel 3	Tun 10 in 1 Ajaw	10.2.10.0.0	878–879
Monjas, Lintel 1	**8 Manik 15 Wo**	**10.2.10.11.7**	**880**

(Continued)

TABLE 13.1 (Continued)

Location	Calendar Round or tun-ajaw	Long Count	AD
Monjas, Lintel 2	8 Manik 15 Wo	10.2.10.11.7	880
Monjas, Lintel 3	8 Manik 15 Wo	10.2.10.11.7	880
Monjas, Lintel 4	8 Manik 15 Wo	10.2.10.11.7	880
Monjas, Lintel 5	8 Manik 15 Wo	10.2.10.11.7	880
Monjas, Lintel 6	8 Manik 15 Wo	10.2.10.11.7	880
Monjas, Lintel 7	8 Manik 15 Wo	10.2.10.11.7	880
Akab Dzib lintel	**Tun 11 in 1 Ajaw**	**10.2.11.0.0**	**879–880**
Temple of the Four Lintels, Lintel 1	9 Lamat 11 Yax	10.2.12.1.8	881
Temple of the Four Lintels, Lintel 3	9 Lamat 11 Yax	10.2.12.1.8	881
Temple of the Four Lintels, Lintel 4	9 Lamat 11 Yax	10.2.12.1.8	881
Temple of the Four Lintels, Lintel 2	**12 K'an 7 Sak**	**10.2.12.2.4**	**881**
Temple of the Owls capstone	**4 Imix 14 Sip**	**10.2.13.13.1**	**883**
Monjas East Annex capstone	**4 Imix 14 Sip**	**10.2.13.13.1**	**883**
T. of the Wall Panels "reset monument"	Tun 15 in 1 Ajaw	10.2.15.0.0	884
Caracol hieroglyphic band, Fragment 17	Tun 16 in 1 Ajaw	10.2.16.0.0	884–885
Caracol, Panel 1 ("Stela" 1)	Tun 16 in 1 Ajaw	10.2.16.0.0	884–885
Caracol hieroglyphic band, Fragment 16	5 K'an 7 Muwan	10.2.16.7.4	885
Caracol, Panel 1 ("Stela" 1)	Tun 17 in 1 Ajaw	10.2.17.0.0	885–886
Caracol, Panel 1 ("Stela" 1), side	Tun 17 in 1 Ajaw	10.2.17.0.0	885–886
Caracol hieroglyphic band, Fragment 18	3 Imix 4 Ch'en	10.3.0.2.1	889
Caracol, Panel 1 ("Stela" 1)	**Tun 1 in 12 Ajaw**	**10.3.1.0.0**	**889–890**
Stela 2, near Casa Colorada	12 Manik 5 Sak	10.3.1.0.0	890
Unknown Tomb capstone	6 K'an 1 Pop	10.3.8.14.4	897
Caracol, circular stone	Tun 2/3 in 8 Ajaw	10.5.2.0.0	930–931
High Priest's Grave, Column 4	10 K'an 2 Sots'	10.8.10.6.4	998
High Priest's Grave, Column 4	**2 Ajaw 18 Mol**	**10.8.10.11.0**	**998**
High Priest's Grave, sculptural fragment	?	10.9.0.0.0	1007

Source: Compiled from Bey and Ringle 2011; García Campillo 2000; Graña-Behrens 2002; Grube 1994, 2003; Grube and Krochock 2011.

Note: Dates assumed to mark the construction of a building are in **bold** type.

We accept Krochock's (1997) early reading for the inscriptions at the Temple of the Hieroglyphic Jambs. She dates the texts to 10.0.2.7.13, or AD 832, making them the oldest inscriptions at Chichen Itza. It is important to note that the Temple of the Hieroglyphic Jambs is a gallery-patio structure built in the full International style (Ruppert 1950). If the jambs were carved specifically for incorporation in this structure, this could be taken as evidence for a significant overlap of the Maya and International styles. Alternatively, it could be that the jambs were salvaged from an earlier structure and reset in a building constructed 100 to 200 years after the inscription was carved (cf. Proskouriakoff 1970). Chung (2009: 66–7, 130–32) excavated within the group and concludes that it was built in a single construction stage associated with Sotuta pottery. The hieroglyphic date of AD 832 is far too early for the appearance of Sotuta pottery at the site. Instead, Yabnal-Motul material would be expected at that early time. An alternative date of AD 884, according to a previous reading by David Kelley (1982), is still too early for Sotuta pottery. Therefore, given that both the architectural style of the Temple of the Hieroglyphic Jambs Group and the ceramics recovered from its fill are consistent with a construction date of the late tenth or early eleventh century, it is almost certain that the earliest known inscription at Chichen Itza was reset. The lintel dating to AD 878 found on the final stage of the Temple of the Initial Series – another International-style structure with Sotuta pottery – also was reset from an earlier building (Peter Schmidt suggests the House of the Phalli; see Grube and Krochock 2011: 182).

After the early text of the Temple of the Hieroglyphic Jambs there was a hiatus in monument carving of 37 years. The vast majority of securely dated texts at Chichen Itza discuss events during a roughly 20-year period from AD 869 to 890. Texts dating to this interval are all associated with Maya-style structures, providing a very tight chronology for the construction of many of the most important buildings in this style. Within this short epigraphic florescence, Grube and Krochock (2011: 183–4) identify three bursts of activity. The first was the construction of the Casa Colorada around AD 871. This corresponds to a period before K'ak'upakal became the ruler of the polity. The second burst of activity was at Monjas, whose texts describe K'ak'upakal's descent and divine patronage. The Akab Dzib, another Maya-style structure, was also built in AD 880 (García Campillo 2000: 89–92). Its texts name it as the residence of a Kokom lord who does not appear to be related to K'ak'upakal. The third set of construction was further south, in the Group of the Initial Series and at the Temples of the Three and Four Lintels. Texts there date to AD 878–882 and tend to focus on dedicatory events by K'inil Kopol, the brother of the ruler (Grube 1994: 344; Grube and Krochock 2011: 169–72). Stela 2, from the Casa Colorada Group, is the last monument to mention K'ak'upakal and dates to AD 890 (Graña-Behrens 2002: 457). Thus, almost all of the texts from Chichen Itza pertain to the life of a single ruler. Finally, a few dates associated with the Caracol and its substructure may correspond to AD 876–890, or possibly even AD 930, but these dates are insecurely ascribed (García Campillo 2000: 34).

Grube and Krochock (2011: 176) state, citing Cobos (2004), that "[t]he short epigraphic florescence at Chichen Itza very much coincides with early Sotuta ceramics identified with the first important occupation of Chichen Itza." Braswell (in Braswell and Peniche May 2012: 230), also following Cobos, has written the same thing, but this needs to be corrected. As we have seen, the Proyecto Arqueológico Chichen Itza has demonstrated that the fill of Maya-style structures – including the Casa Colorada, the Akab Dzib, and the Temple of the Three Lintels – contains no Sotuta pottery. In fact, with the exception of the Akab Dzib, not even Cehpech pottery has been found in these structures (Pérez 2010: 138–45).

After the short epigraphic florescence and flurry in building activity associated with K'ak'upakal, a second hiatus in inscriptions lasted from AD 897 until AD 998 – that is, roughly a century. Three final texts, associated with an International-style temple, date to this period. Two dates of AD 998 are found on a column within the High Priest's Grave. There has been some disagreement concerning this attribution (see Graña-Behrens *et al.* 1999), but we see no reason to question it. This reading of the date, the artistic style of the column on which it is found, and the International style of the structure supported by that column are all consistent with the end of the tenth century. A final date of AD 1007 has been tentatively identified from a block of uncertain context excavated at the High Priest's Grave (Graña-Behrens 2002: 458).

In summary, hieroglyphic inscriptions demonstrate at least three periods of construction (Figure 13.10). The first, in the early 800s, is associated with a gallery-patio structure. We consider the date at the Temple of the Hieroglyphic Jambs to be correct, but also that it is almost certain – based on both architectural style and the ceramics recovered from the fill of the platform – that this inscription was reset from an earlier structure. The second construction period demonstrated by hieroglyphic texts is AD 870–897 and is associated with Maya-style structures built during the life of K'ak'upakal. No Sotuta pottery has been shown to be associated with these structures. It is possible that later stages of the Caracol date to the early 900s. Finally,

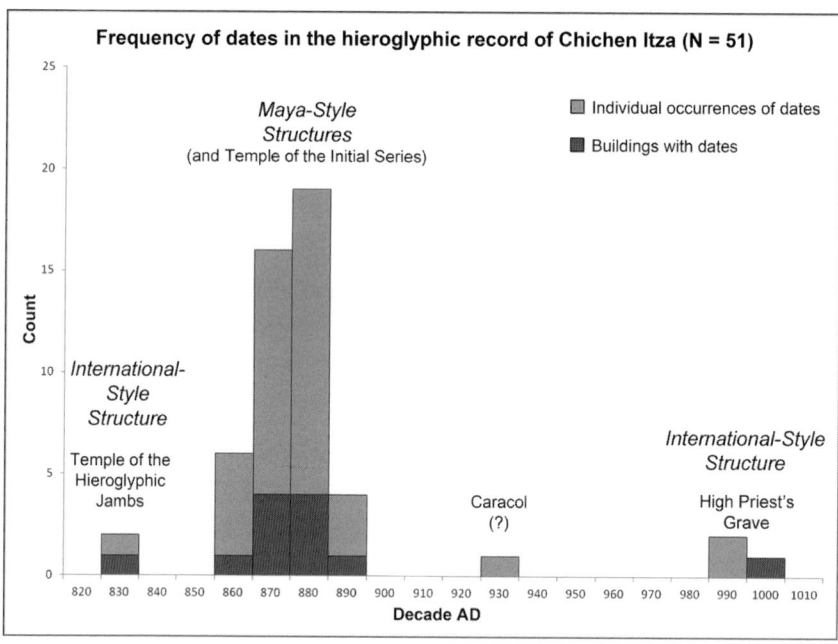

FIGURE 13.10 Histogram of individual hieroglyphic dates from Chichen Itza and its peripheral settlements of Yula and Halakal, showing a trimodal distribution: construction events for individual buildings, as inferred from the hieroglyphic record, are shown in dark gray. The date of the Caracol round stone is uncertain. We consider the texts in the Temples of the Hieroglyphic Jambs and the Initial Series, both International-style structures with Sotuta ceramics, to be reset

there appears to be a major burst of construction activity at the very end of the tenth or beginning of the eleventh century, focused on the Great Terrace and its vicinity, but only one structure from that time has hieroglyphic inscriptions that date the building.

Radiocarbon dates

The final chronological data set that we examine are the radiocarbon dates for Chichen Itza. Given both the importance of the site and lingering questions about its chronology, we find it surprising that so few carbon samples have been processed. To date, just ten samples from Chichen Itza and two from Balankanche Cave have been assayed (see Andrews 1979: table 1). One of the samples from the Castillo was rerun, as were both samples from Balankanche, yielding a total of 15 dates (Table 13.2). In the case of Chichen Itza itself, samples come from wooden beams, a lintel, and structural fill, so must predate the structures with which they are associated. Moreover, we expect that some beams and lintels were reused during the occupation of the site.

TABLE 13.2 Radiocarbon dates from Chichen Itza and Balankanche, ordered by radiocarbon age

Sample provenience	Laboratory code	Material	Year collected	Conventional radiocarbon age BP
Great Terrace				
East – Stage V	Beta-295908★	Charcoal from fill	2009	1700 ± 40
Iglesia	TBN-313-2	Wood from beam	1962	1350 ± 70
Casa Colorada	TBN-313-3	Wood from beam	1962	1340 ± 60
Iglesia	TBN-313-1	Wood from beam	1962	1170 ± 70
Castillo	Y-626	Wood from lintel	1958	1160 ± 70
	Y-626-bis	(Rerun of Y-626)		1140 ± 100
Great Terrace				
East – Stage IV	Beta-295907★	Charcoal from fill	2009	1160 ± 40
Monjas East Annex	LJ-87	Wood from beam	< 1959	1140 ± 200
Great Terrace				
East – Stage IV	Beta-295911★	Charcoal from fill	2009	1140 ± 30
Great Terrace				
East – Stage IV	Beta-295910★	Charcoal from fill	2009	1110 ± 40
Great Terrace				
East – Stage VI	Beta-295909★	Charcoal from fill	2009	60 ± 30
Balankanche Cave	LJ-272	Charcoal inside urns	1959	1090 ± 200
	P-1132	(Rerun of LJ-272)		1072 ± 51
Balankanche Cave	LJ-273	Charcoal from hearth	1959	1090 ± 200
	P-1133	(Rerun of LJ-273)		1028 ± 42

Note: ★ indicates accelerator mass spectrometry date.

Four radiocarbon dates were determined for three Maya-style buildings in the 1950s and early 1960s, the early days of radiocarbon dating. It is therefore reasonable to question the accuracy of these dates. They were determined from samples taken from beams in the Casa Colorada, the Iglesia (Str. 4C1; two dates), and the Monjas East Annex (Chandler et al. 1963; Hubbs et al. 1960). The midpoint of the two-sigma calibrated range for the Casa Colorada date falls at cal AD 700, roughly 170 years before the hieroglyphic text that dates its construction (Figure 13.11).[9] It seems likely, then, that either the sample came from old wood or the assay is in error. The same can be said for one of the two dates from the Iglesia (TBN-313-2), which falls around cal AD 690. Nonetheless, a second date from the Iglesia (TBN-313-1; midpoint cal AD 840) and the date from the Monjas East Annex (LJ-87; midpoint cal AD 905) are in better accord with hieroglyphic evidence for the construction of these buildings in the late ninth century. Of course, their error ranges are extremely large, especially in the case of LJ-87 (see Figure 13.11).

Four radiocarbon assays come from fill contexts in the Great Terrace predating the Castillo-sub. Beta-295908 comes from a Stage V context in the construction of the Great Terrace, between floors AC2 and AC7 (Figure 13.12).[10] Its midpoint of cal

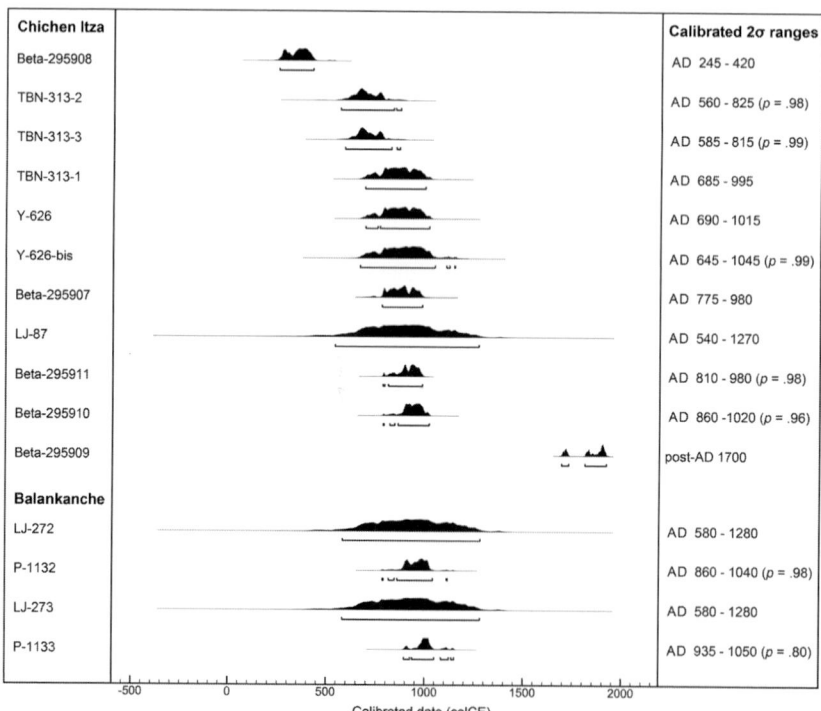

FIGURE 13.11 Individual calibration of radiocarbon dates from Chichen Itza and Balankanche: probability distribution plots were generated in OxCal 4.2 (Bronk Ramsey 2009)

AD 330 places it firmly in the Early Classic period. It probably comes from old charcoal incorporated into fill. Beta-295907 and Beta-295911 fall into a fairly narrow two-sigma range of less than 200 years, with midpoints of cal AD 875 and 895. Beta-295910 is slightly later, with a midpoint of cal AD 940 (see Figure 13.11). All date Stage IV construction, which corresponds to a major expansion to the east and the building of gallery-patio Structure AC8 (built with floor AC7; see Figure 13.12). Taken together, these dates suggest that both Structure AC8 and the Castillo-sub that followed it in Stage V were built sometime after AD 900. A final determination from Stage VI of the Great Terrace construction sequence (a reflooring event), Beta-295909, dates to after cal AD 1700 and is clearly a result of modern sample contamination.

Two additional dates, Y-626 and Y-626-bis, were derived from two runs of a sample collected from a wooden lintel of the Castillo in 1958 (Deevey et al. 1959; Stuiver et al. 1960). Their two-sigma midpoints fall at cal AD 850 and 845, respectively (see Figure 13.11). The lintel must come from a tree that predates the construction of the Castillo. Finally, two charcoal samples from inside (LJ-272 and P-1132) and below (LJ-273 and P-1133) an incense burner in Balankanche Cave were both run twice (Hubbs et al. 1962; Stuckenrath 1967). The second assays yielded very similar dates to the first attempts but with much narrower calibration ranges. Overall, the four dates have midpoints that range from cal AD 930 to 990 and correspond chronologically to Sotuta ceramics in the cave and in the construction fill of International-style buildings at Chichen Itza.

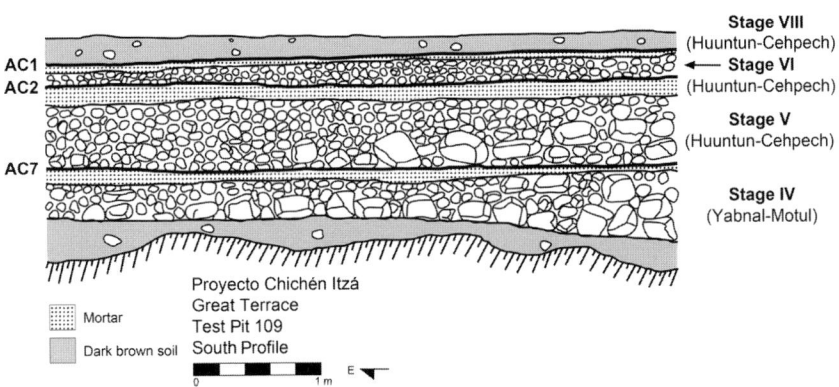

FIGURE 13.12 Test pit 109, south profile (after Peniche May and Braswell 2009: fig. 3.11), showing constructive stages IV–VI of the Great Terrace, along with ceramic phases identified by Pérez in corresponding stratigraphic levels from INAH excavations in the Great Terrace (Schmidt and Pérez 2006). Gallery-patio Structure AC8 was built directly on top of floor AC7 during Stage IV. The Castillo-sub and floor AC2, which abuts its base, were built in Stage V

Bayesian analysis of radiocarbon determinations

The radiocarbon dates reviewed above are in general agreement with the broad outlines of the chronology of Chichen Itza derived from hieroglyphic sources, ceramic analysis, and architectural sequences. Nonetheless, because of their wide standard deviations, taken as a whole they do not add much temporal resolution to our understanding of the history of the site. This uncertainty can be reduced by using available absolute and relative chronological data from other sources to inform the calibration process. In non-statistical terms, Bayesian modeling allows us to consider radiometric dates not merely as isolated facts but as probability statements subject to other known information (such as stratigraphic superposition), other absolute data (including hieroglyphic dates), and even relative ceramic chronologies. Bayesian statistical inference works by incorporating known or inferred information about the samples – called "prior probabilities" – into the analysis (Bronk Ramsey 2009; Buck 2004; Buck *et al.* 1999; Michczyński and Pazdur 2003). This incorporation results in a more precise "posterior probability" distribution, thus improving chronological resolution of the calibrated dates. In addition, Bayesian modeling allows the identification of outliers in groups of samples (Christen 1994). Applications of these statistical techniques are becoming more common in archaeology (e.g., Beramendi-Orosco *et al.* 2009; Culleton *et al.* 2012; Higham *et al.* 2005) with the development of specialized software packages such as OxCal (Bronk Ramsey 2009) and BCal (Buck *et al.* 1999, 2001).

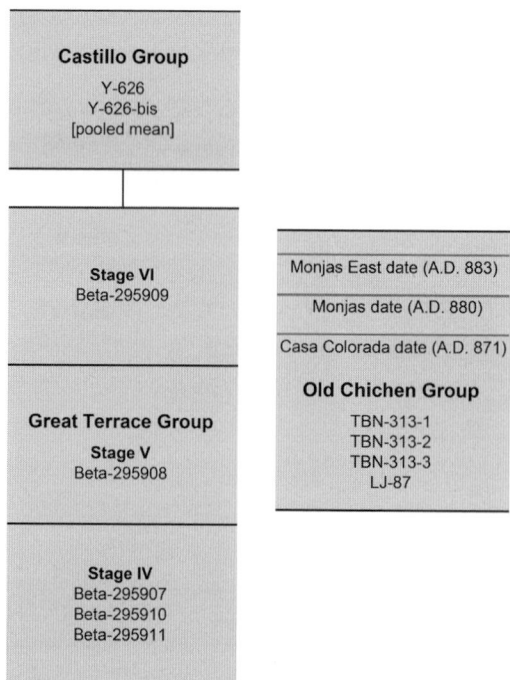

FIGURE 13.13 Structure of Bayesian calibration model in BCal (Buck *et al.* 1999, 2001)

We carried out calibration with Bayesian analysis of the 15 dates from Chichen Itza using BCal (Buck *et al.* 1999, 2001). The dates were arranged into three groups based on stratigraphic and architectural association (Figure 13.13). The "Old Chichen" group contained the four dates from the Casa Colorada (TBN-313-3), the Iglesia (TBN-313-1 and TBN-313-2), and the Monjas East Annex (LJ-87). It also contained three "floating parameters" – events for which the prior probability is an absolute chronological determination. These parameters were the construction dates for the Casa Colorada (AD 871), Monjas (AD 880), and the Monjas East Annex (AD 883) derived from hieroglyphic texts. Radiocarbon dates were associated with these floating parameters following the assumption that each sample from one of the Maya-style buildings must be earlier than the date of its construction (or, in the case of the Iglesia sample, earlier than the construction date of Monjas). Put another way, we assume that the beams were cut before the dedication events recorded in hieroglyphic texts in the structures.

The Great Terrace Group (Figure 13.13) contains five dates separated into three stratigraphically ordered abutting levels, corresponding to the construction stages of the Great Terrace: Stage IV (Beta-295907, Beta-295910, Beta-295911), Stage V (Beta-295908), and Stage VI (Beta-295909). The Castillo Group contains only one radiocarbon determination, a pooled mean of Y-626 and Y-626-bis (Figure 13.14). Pooled means in themselves are not part of the Bayesian analytical method and are used simply to combine statistically the different measurements taken from the same sample (Bowman 1990: 58). We set the Castillo group of dates to be later than the Great Terrace group based on stratigraphy (the Castillo dates to construction Stage VIII of the Great Terrace; Braswell and Peniche May 2012). No relative placement was specified either within the Old Chichen Group or between it and the other two groups.

We ran this initial Bayesian calibration model assigning to each sample a 5 percent prior probability of being an outlier. Once we confirmed in various runs that both the Early Classic (Beta-295908) and the modern (Beta-295909) samples returned a "one-hundred percent" posterior probability of being outliers, we removed them from the model. We ran this second model a few times in order to ensure the validity of the results and also performed a sensitivity analysis by running independent calibrations for each group. The results, reported in Figure 13.15, represent the average of three runs, rounded to the nearest five-year interval.

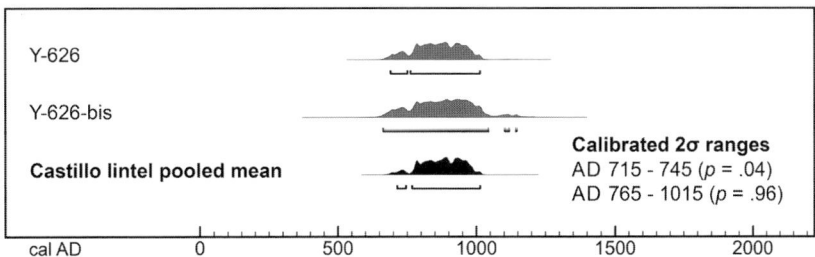

FIGURE 13.14 Pooled mean of the Castillo radiocarbon dates (Y-626 and Y-626-bis); probability distribution plots were generated in OxCal 4.2 (Bronk Ramscy 2009)

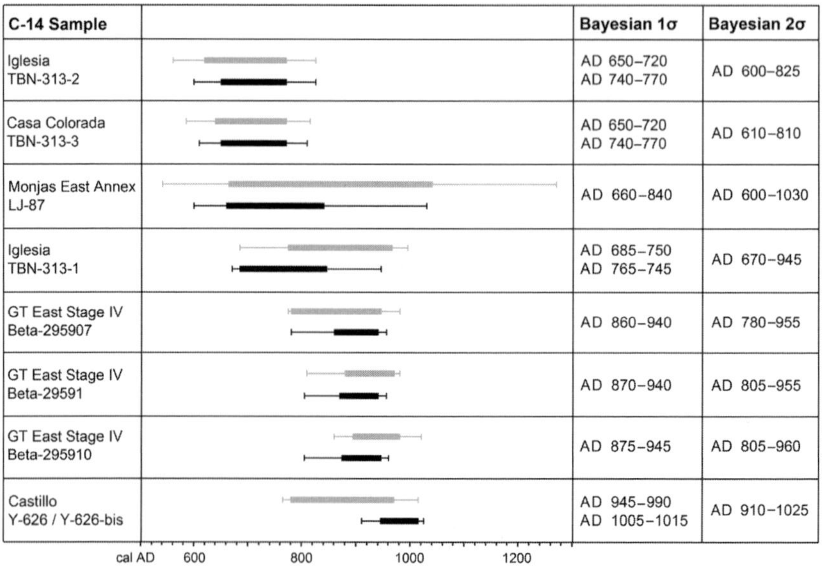

C-14 Sample		Bayesian 1σ	Bayesian 2σ
Iglesia TBN-313-2		AD 650–720 AD 740–770	AD 600–825
Casa Colorada TBN-313-3		AD 650–720 AD 740–770	AD 610–810
Monjas East Annex LJ-87		AD 660–840	AD 600–1030
Iglesia TBN-313-1		AD 685–750 AD 765–745	AD 670–945
GT East Stage IV Beta-295907		AD 860–940	AD 780–955
GT East Stage IV Beta-29591		AD 870–940	AD 805–955
GT East Stage IV Beta-295910		AD 875–945	AD 805–960
Castillo Y-626 / Y-626-bis		AD 945–990 AD 1005–1015	AD 910–1025

FIGURE 13.15 Results of Bayesian calibration (shown in black) compared to individual calibration (shown in gray): thin lines indicate two-sigma ranges; thick bars represent one-sigma ranges. Discontinuous ranges have been simplified for ease of visualization but are reported numerically

The Bayesian calibration results in a slight tightening of the standard deviation ranges for the two early dates from the Iglesia (TBN-313-2) and the Casa Colorada (TBN-313-3), as well as a small shift forward in time. Their two-sigma midpoints cluster around cal AD 710. Although the date from the Monjas East Annex still has a fairly wide two-sigma range, it has been reduced by about 40 percent, from 730 to 430 years, with a midpoint of cal AD 815. Similarly, the range for the second Iglesia date (TBN-313-1) now has a midpoint of cal AD 805. Thus, it appears likely that the beams for these three Maya-style structures date to a time 70 to 150 years before their hieroglyphic texts were carved. We suspect that these Terminal Classic structures were constructed using wood scavenged from earlier Late Classic buildings, but it is also conceivable that the beams were cut from the hearts of very old trees. A final and significant possibility is that these radiocarbon determinations, processed more than 50 years ago, are flawed.

More significantly, the Bayesian analysis aligns and tightens the three Stage IV dates from the Great Terrace. Their two-sigma midpoints fall in the decade between cal AD 870 and 880, and their ranges have been reduced to 150 years. Along with the dramatically improved date from the Castillo lintel, with a midpoint of cal AD 965, these dates essentially bracket the construction of the Str. AC8 gallery-patio and the Castillo-sub to the late ninth and mid-tenth centuries.

Specific attention should be given to the Great Terrace dates for Stage IV. One of these – Beta-295907 – comes from a primary burning episode conducted on bedrock below the surface (floor AC7) that supports the AC8 gallery-patio structure (see Figure 13.12). In this case, a significant fire was lit in a discrete area and both wood and other materials were burned. We lack sufficient evidence to assert that this was a ritual or dedicatory event, but the preservation and lack of dispersal of charcoal imply that the floor above it was built shortly after the fire was extinguished. Allowing a few years for the wood to mature, a date of roughly AD 900 for this event seems quite likely. This is consistent with the other two radiocarbon dates for Stage IV. Put another way, Stage IV construction of one of the first Transitional-style buildings at Chichen Itza seems to date to the very beginning of the tenth century. The Castillo-sub, a Transitional-style building constructed during Stage V, is somewhat later based on stratigraphy, and our best guess for the Castillo itself is the second half of the tenth century. For stylistic reasons, we think it likely that the Castillo was constructed before the High Priest's Grave, built in AD 998 according to a hieroglyphic text.

The two reruns of samples from Balankanche Cave, with midpoints at cal AD 950 and 990, date the ritual use of Sotuta ceramics there to the tenth or eleventh century. For this reason, we date the first appearance of Sotuta ceramics at Chichen Itza to roughly AD 900–950. Thompson's dating for the initial appearance of "Toltec"-style architecture and Sotuta ceramics at 10.8.0.0.0 therefore does not seem too far off, but perhaps a few decades later than what the data currently support for the pottery.

In sum, the newly calibrated radiocarbon dates for Chichen Itza and the reruns from Balankanche Cave – along with the pottery found associated with these contexts – imply that the Sotuta phase could not have begun much before AD 900. Sotuta pottery certainly is found in construction fill and ritual contexts dating to the late tenth century. Both of these conclusions are supported by hieroglyphic dates. Radiocarbon dates are also consistent with both architectural stratigraphy and hieroglyphic dates and suggest that much of the International-style architecture visible at Chichen Itza was built after AD 950 and especially around AD 1000.

Radiocarbon dates also agree with the placement of Maya-style architecture in the middle to late ninth century. The beams, dating from the early eighth to the early ninth centuries, provide only *termini post quem* dates because of the likeliness of reuse or the more remote possibility that they were cut from the center of old trees. The Transitional-style Castillo-sub does not date to before about AD 900. Finally, we currently lack clear chronometric data concerning construction after AD 1000 and the waning of the site at an even later time.

Ceramic overlap and radiocarbon dates from other sites

Still looming over Chichen Itza archaeology is the burdensome question of "overlap." Such overlap has been described not only for architectural styles but also especially for the Cehpech and Sotuta ceramic complexes. We are fairly confident now that, despite prior claims, there is little reason to posit an overlap in the construction of Maya- and International-style structures (cf. Cohodas 1978; Schele and Freidel 1990; Schele and Mathews 1998). Stratigraphic superposition indicates that structures such as the Great Ballcourt, thought by some to be early, really date to AD 1000 or so – more than a century after the period when Maya-style buildings with hieroglyphic texts were constructed (cf. Wren and Schmidt 1991). But the question of a temporal overlap between the Cehpech and Sotuta ceramic complexes remains. It is important to stress that we do not seek to answer this question for the entire peninsula – overlap is related as much to spatial as to temporal placement – but limit our thoughts here to Sotuta at Chichen Itza itself and two related sites that have radiocarbon dates. We remind readers that the Cehpech–Sotuta problem originally arose because Smith (1971) attempted to form a single sequence for the entire northern lowlands rather than proceeding site by site and considering the differential regional distribution of ceramic complexes.

It is our contention that we still lack clear and convincing evidence for a stand-alone Cehpech complex at Chichen Itza. The vast majority of the pottery found in the fill of Maya-style structures analyzed by Pérez (2010, 2012) is assigned by him to the Yabnal-Motul complex, and only a very small number of Cehpech sherds were recovered from limited fill contexts in such structures. We find it simpler, more elegant, and more likely that the period AD 870–890 was typified largely by Yabnal-Motul pottery, which includes a relatively small number of sherds belonging to an *incomplete* Cehpech subcomplex overlapping Yabnal-Motul. Moreover, because of the difficulty inherent in distinguishing pottery on both sides of the seamless transition from Say/Sat to later slate wares, it might even be that some sherds identified as belonging to the Cehpech subcomplex are particularly well-fired examples of Yabnal-Motul slates. We are unsure whether later Dzitas Slate was derived directly from Late Classic to early Terminal Classic Say Slate (Chung 2009), from locally produced Terminal Classic Muna Slate (Johnson 2012), or from both. Either way, Dzitas Slate of the tenth century is a late but close relative of all the other slates produced in Yucatan in the Late and Terminal Classic periods.

Pérez's work shows that there is no good reason to date Sotuta pottery at Chichen Itza to any time before the very end of the ninth century. The most likely interval during which it began to be manufactured and consumed at Chichen Itza is AD 900–950 – that is, during the period for which we have little ceramic data. Stated differently, Pérez's Sotuta-Sotuta phase – limited to Chichen Itza proper – does not overlap strongly with Cehpech in the Puuc (see Braswell et al. 2011). Any such overlap could have occurred during the final, rapid, and glorious period of construction at Uxmal, and especially during its aftermath. But *most* of the temporal range of the Puuc phenomenon and the Cehpech phase there precedes the first appearance of Sotuta pottery at Chichen Itza. The overlap – judging from the perspective of Sotuta-phase Chichen Itza – seems to be limited (potentially) to the early tenth-century zenith and (certainly) epigonal, post-collapse activities in the Puuc after about AD 920/950. Seen from the perspective of the Puuc, however, the overlap is limited largely to this later period because most Sotuta ceramics found there come from contexts subsequent to monumental construction (Braswell *et al.* 2011; Ringle 2012: 198).

Radiocarbon dates from Isla Cerritos

Of course, it may be that Sotuta pottery was first produced somewhere other than Chichen Itza before about AD 900. If that is the case, then there is – from a peninsular perspective – a broader overlap. To date, however, radiocarbon assays of samples associated with Sotuta ceramics have yet to support this supposition. Two sites other than Chichen Itza with large quantities of Sotuta ceramics have radiocarbon dates. Five dates are reported from Isla Cerritos, a port of the great city (Ringle *et al.* 1998: table 1). Four of these are associated with Sotuta or "Hocaba-Sotuta" ceramics. For one of these (Beta-14085), "Project members thought the sample was contaminated and the resultant date too late" (ibid.: table 1, fn. e). This date has a one-sigma range of cal AD 1056–1253, which we consider consistent with a Hocaba-Sotuta context at a coastal site beyond Chichen Itza. Such coastal sites could have survived the collapse of the great city itself. The other assays relevant to the date of Sotuta and Hocaba-Sotuta ceramics have midpoints of cal AD 960–1039 (Teledyne I-14244, Beta-14082, Beta-14083), which also are consistent with the first appearance of Sotuta at that site sometime after AD 900. In contrast, a single date for a Cehpech context has a one-sigma range of cal AD 663–782, which makes it contemporary with the Yabnal-Motul phase at Chichen Itza. Thus, the radiocarbon dates from Isla Cerritos do not *on their own* support a significant Cehpech–Sotuta overlap at that site.

Radiocarbon dates from Xuenkal

Six carbon dates have recently been determined for contexts with Sotuta pottery at Xuenkal, a site with distinct Cehpech and Sotuta contexts (Manahan *et al.* 2012: table 1). Two of the carbon dates for Sotuta are far too late and must be discounted (AA86755 and AA86760). A lone date (AA86759) – with a two-sigma range covering the late seventh to mid-tenth centuries – might suggest an overlap but seems a bit early for Sotuta pottery. Three assays, however, firmly date Sotuta ceramics at Xuenkal to the late tenth and eleventh centuries (AA86756, AA86757, and AA86759). Five additional dates for Cehpech contexts also were processed. Unfortunately, four of these are far too late to pertain to any prehistoric period (AA86762–AA86765). One assay (AA86761), derived from burned maize found at the base of a wall, is dated with a 99 percent probability to cal AD 685–895. This overlaps with only one of the Sotuta dates (AA86759) from Xuenkal and none from Isla Cerritos, and it also seems to fall before the posited range for the Sotuta-Sotuta phase at Chichen Itza. Thus, given the few relevant radiocarbon dates from other sites in the northern Maya lowlands, the supposition that Sotuta ceramics first appear at Chichen Itza during the period AD 900–950 seems supported. Moreover, any potential overlap between Cehpech and Sotuta seems likely to be limited to the tenth century.[11]

The chronology of Chichen Itza: a current assessment

Any attempt to derive a coherent temporal framework for the development of Chichen Itza from the current tangle of chronologies is hampered by large uncertainties associated with the data. Architectural stratigraphy, hieroglyphic texts, ethnohistorical documents, artistic styles, ceramic classifications, and radiocarbon dates all constitute partial narratives with missing data. Nonetheless, we can draw some useful conclusions and questions from this synthetic overview.

Occupation Phase I (before AD 600)

Chichen Itza was first occupied – as demonstrated through ceramics – in the Preclassic period (González de la Mata 2006). There also was an Early Classic occupation (Pérez 2007). Neither of these is well understood, and we still lack evidence of any architecture that survives from this very early period of occupation. The shallow soils and high bedrock of the northern Maya lowlands provide a palimpsest that was scraped clean of prior structures before the city as we know it began to take shape sometime after AD 600. In contrast, nearby Yaxuna was a thriving city during this period (Ambrosino 2006; Ardren 1997; Johnstone 2001; Suhler *et al.* 1998).

Occupation Phase II (AD 600/750 to AD 800/870)

The Early Chichen style in architecture corresponds to the occupation of the site during the Yabnal-Motul ceramic phase. We have little evidence for the beginning of this ceramic complex, but, as Pérez (2010, 2012) suggests, it could not have been before about AD 600 and perhaps began no earlier than the eighth century. Thus, we consider the beginning of the Early Chichen architectural style as dating to the Late Classic period. Braswell has analyzed obsidian recovered from Osorio León's (2004) excavations of the House of the Stuccoes (Str. 5C4-I) underneath the Temple of the Initial Series. This is the only Early Chichen style structure so far excavated that contained obsidian in its fill. Even at this early time, obsidian came from a mix of Guatemalan and Mexican sources, implying that this structure, at least, cannot date too long before AD 800 and possibly dates to the early ninth century. Thus, the Early Chichen architectural style and Yabnal-Motul ceramic complex began in the Late Classic but might be said to continue into the early Terminal Classic period.

Occupation Phase III (AD 800/870 to AD 900)

The next stage of occupation is typified by Maya-style structures and represents the first great period in the history of Chichen Itza. It is firmly dated to the Terminal Classic period, especially the decades immediately before the great building program of Lord Chaak at Uxmal (Kowalski 1987; Ringle 2012). At Chichen Itza, we think it is reasonable to extend Pérez's end date for the Yabnal-Motul phase from AD 800/830 to AD 870/900. This is because very few Maya-style buildings have been shown to contain any ceramics that are later than the Yabnal-Motul complex. Continuity in construction – for example, in the Initial Series Group – suggests that there was no hiatus in occupation between the Early Chichen and Maya styles.

What is clear now is that Sotuta ceramics – "early" or "late" – are *not* associated with the construction of Maya-style structures. In fact, the existence of "early" and "late" Sotuta facets (Cobos 2004, 2011) does not seem supported, unless one hypothesizes that "early" Sotuta pottery is associated with Transitional-style structures dating to the early tenth century – something that still needs to be demonstrated. Moreover, an argument can be made that an "early" Sotuta lacking both Tohil Plumbate and Silho Fine Orange is not a meaningful construct (Johnson 2012). Instead, Maya-style structures are associated overwhelmingly with Yabnal-Motul pottery, which – given their hieroglyphic dates of *ca.* AD 870–890 – seems to suggest that this ceramic complex continued at Chichen Itza throughout much of the ninth century and could also be said to be Terminal Classic in date. There is still some question as to whether there was a stand-alone Huuntun-Cehpech phase between the Yabnal-Motul and Sotuta-Sotuta phases (Chung 2009; cf. Pérez 2010, 2012). Securely dated contexts in which just a handful of Cehpech sherds have been found are Maya-style structures built from about AD 870 to AD 890, corresponding to the reign of K'ak'upakal. Nonetheless, the vast majority of the pottery recovered from such contexts is assigned to the Yabnal-Motul complex. Schmidt and Pérez (2006) also place construction Stages V to VII (corresponding to Transitional-style architecture) of the Great Terrace (Braswell and Peniche May 2012) within the Huuntun-Cehpech phase. We *did* observe some Cehpech sherds during our excavations there and date these construction stages to sometime after about AD 900, but stress that these are fill contexts. Thus there are two possibilities: either the Huuntun-Cehpech phase lasted a very short time, and we have yet to identify many pure contexts dating to that phase, or Cehpech material constitutes an incomplete ceramic subcomplex at Chichen Itza and overlaps with the Yabnal-Motul phase of the late ninth century and possibly also with the Sotuta-Sotuta phase during the poorly understood early tenth century. We view the slates, red wares, and Fine Oranges of Cehpech and Sotuta as regional variants on a common theme rather than as evolutionarily sequential pottery, so favor this second hypothesis.

Occupation Phase IV (AD 900 to AD 950/980)

Except for evidence from the Great Terrace for the emergence of the Transitional style (the building of gallery-patio structure AC8 at roughly AD 900 and the Castillo-sub sometime later), the early tenth century remains poorly documented. Ceramics studied by Pérez that come from the same archaeological strata as these structures – revealed in the 2009 Great Terrace excavations – are assigned by him to the Yabnal-Motul and the Huuntun-Cehpech complexes (see Figures 13.6 and 13.12, Stages V–VI). Nonetheless, these are fill contexts, and it is possible that the ceramics are redeposited older material. We cannot yet describe the pottery of the period AD 900–950/980 with any certainty. Perhaps it should be assigned to the Yabnal-Motul complex (although this seems unlikely to us), perhaps it should be called Huuntun-Cehpech (if such a stand-alone complex exists at Chichen Itza), perhaps it belongs to the Sotuta-Sotuta complex (and most of the ceramics are older sherds incorporated into fill), or perhaps we have some sort of ceramic overlap or transition. We currently favor a gradual transition from the Late Classic Yabnal-Motul complex to the Sotuta complex in a manner parallel to, but centuries later than, the transition to Cehpech in the Puuc. Specifically, at Chichen Itza we think it likely that pottery belonging to the Say Slate or Muna Slate groups – or both – was gradually replaced by Dzitas Slate types during this period and that types belonging to the Dzibiac Red group also appeared at this time.

The picture that is emerging now is that the early tenth century represents a significant decline or slowdown in construction activity after the Maya style of the late ninth century and before the full International style of the late tenth century. Thus, Transitional-style architecture is dated to this period of reduced construction, and the greatest building in this style – the Castillo-sub – probably was constructed towards its end. Moreover, except for a possible date of AD 930 from the Caracol round stone, there is no evidence for writing during the interval AD 897–998. If both the seeming architectural lull and the hieroglyphic pause are real – and if it can be shown that there is little pottery dating to this period – then a strong argument could be made that Chichen Itza suffered a decline or even a hiatus during the early tenth century.

The period AD 900–950 corresponds not only with the great construction boom of Mosaic-style architecture in the Puuc but also with the collapse and near abandonment of that region sometime after about AD 920 (Dunning and Kowalski 1994). A reasonable hypothesis for further testing is that Chichen Itza, too, suffered a significant decline during the early tenth century. Its temporary eclipse could have begun during the reign of Lord Chaak of Uxmal, but more importantly would have been contemporary with the collapse of much of the northern Maya lowlands. What should be stressed is that, if Chichen Itza also waned during the early tenth century, we should no longer consider that the decline of other sites – such as Uxmal, Coba, Ek Balam, and Dzibilchaltun – was the result of the militaristic expansion of the Itza state (cf. Andrews and Robles Castellanos 1985; Andrews and Sabloff 1986: 450–51; Carmean et al. 2004: 445; Kelley 1984; Robles Castellanos and Andrews 1986: 84; Schele and Mathews 1998: 234; Suhler et al. 2004: 454–8). Conquest often implies subjugation rather than steep demographic decline or abandonment, and the latter is a closer match to what happened in the Puuc and many other inland sites during the second half of the tenth century.

Unlike Uxmal and most other cities across the northern Maya lowlands, Chichen Itza re-emerged from decline during the late tenth century. The reasons why it rebounded are not certain but may be related to its specialized function as a pilgrimage site (see Ringle et al. 1998). But, given how much more we need to learn about the early tenth century at Chichen Itza, we are not sure whether it is more proper to describe Occupation Phase IV as Terminal Classic, Early Postclassic, or transitional in character.

Occupation Phase V (AD 950/980 to AD 1050/1100)

Pérez defines the Sotuta-Sotuta phase as starting at about AD 920/950. But he also reports Sotuta ceramics from the fill of the platform extension in the Initial Series Group upon which the Temple of the Owls is built. If we accept Graña-Behrens's (2002: 370) tentative reading of the hieroglyphic date from the Temple of the Owls (Str. 5C7) capstone of sometime between AD 870 and AD 889 and assume that the monument was not reset, we could push back the earliest Dzitas Slate to about AD 880/890. Thus, production of Sotuta pottery at Chichen Itza began sometime between the end of the ninth century and the late tenth century. The problem again is identifying primary (rather than fill) contexts dating to the early tenth century.

The earliest International-style structure visible on the Great Terrace – identified as such by tracing stratigraphically superimposed floors – is the Castillo. Following Schmidt (2011), we argue that it was built during the interval AD 950–998 – that is, before the stylistically more complex High Priest's Grave. The construction of International-style architecture is associated with Sotuta ceramics. We know that there was a flurry of building on and around the Great Terrace during the late tenth and possibly early eleventh centuries. Most of the structures visible there today date to this second construction boom. Although the relative chronologies of these structures are well understood (see Braswell and Peniche May 2012), what is not clear is for how long and until when such construction continued: AD 1000 seems a little early to us but is possible, AD 1050 is a reasonable conjecture, and AD 1100 cannot yet be ruled out with certainty; in contrast, AD 1200 now seems too late on ceramic grounds. Just as we lack adequate data on the ceramics of the early tenth century at Chichen Itza, we also need more chronometric dates relevant to the end of significant construction at the site.

Given the apparent decline in construction activity and the lack of hieroglyphic texts dating to Occupation Phase IV, we suggest that a significant lull or even interruption existed between the two greatest periods at Chichen Itza. While the first occurred during the late ninth century, the second is separated from it by 50 to 80 years. Thus, we assign the period of construction of Maya-style architecture to the Terminal Classic period and consider the final glorious period in the history of Chichen Itza – roughly AD 950/980 to AD 1050 or so – as dating to the Early Postclassic period. For us, the internationalism seen in the architecture, artwork, and trade of materials, as well as the presence of a significant corpus of hieroglyphs written in a new and foreign style (Love and Schmidt 2011), argue more for participation in the broader Postclassic Mesoamerican world than in the narrower Classic Maya world of the northern lowlands. Nonetheless, there are great continuities linking the ceramics, architectural techniques, and other aspects of material culture of the Late Classic and Early Postclassic periods. Occupation Phase V represented neither a non-Maya invasion nor a total break from the past.

Occupation Phases VI and VII (AD 1050/1100 to AD 1500+)

The last occupation phases at Chichen Itza date to a period after major monumental construction ceased. Minor changes, such as modifications to the wall surrounding the Great Terrace (Hahn and Braswell 2012; Pérez Ruiz 2005), were made during this time. Some of the last major buildings to be constructed during Occupation Phase V, such as the Temple of the Warriors, were restuccoed many times (Morris *et al.* 1931), suggesting that they remained in use for a long time after they were built. But we cannot quantify the time span indicated by these restuccoing events. Brainerd's (1958: 37) work with materials from the Caracol implies that floors in that building were resurfaced well into the Late Postclassic, so it is possible that restuccoing of the Temple of the Warriors continued into this very late period. Population levels and the state-level government centered at Chichen Itza could have collapsed as early as AD 1050 or perhaps not until AD 1100. Nonetheless, the city was never completely abandoned.

Pérez (2010: 333) places the end of monumental construction at Chichen Itza during his Kulub-Hocaba ceramic phase, which he dates to between AD 1150/1200 and AD 1250/1300). Kulub-Hocaba ceramics are not found in significant quantities in the fill of any International-style structure but only in small platforms and minor additions, such as a dais and two fireboxes (Brainerd 1958: 38; Pérez 2010: 298, 319, 323). A tomb located on the Monjas terrace also contained Hocaba pottery (Bolles 1977: 237; Pérez 2010: fig. 242), but most has been recovered from the post-construction occupational debris of buildings. Pérez does not allow for any overlap of the Sotuta and Hocaba complexes, as argued by Ringle *et al.* (1998: 189–90), who prefer to consider Hocaba as an incomplete complex overlapping Sotuta at Chichen Itza during the period AD 1000–1150 and Tases at Mayapan during the thirteenth century. Peto Cream Ware – an important component of Hocaba – has been found in an architectural context at Uxmal dating to the early tenth century and at Balankanche Cave and Isla Cerritos during the later tenth century (ibid.). Ochoa Rodriguez (1999) has studied the distribution of Peto Cream at more than 50 sites – mostly on the east coast – and concludes that it dates to the period AD 900/1050 to AD 1250/1300. The temporal silhouette of Peto Cream seems to have formed a long battleship curve. It seems likely to us that Coarse Slate (another name for Peto or Kukula Cream) – what might be considered a poor man's imitation slate ware – appeared alongside the other "nicer" slates for a long time, and that the coarser pottery continued to be made after production of the finer slates ceased. Thus, while early Coarse Slate represents an attempt to copy well-made pottery, later Coarse Slate represents the continuation of an older aesthetic during a time of waning technological ability. This pattern is consistent not only with a decline in elite consumption and the sponsorship of production (two signs of collapse) but also with a continuation of demand for a product whose surface treatment was part of a long tradition.

Hocaba pottery – whether considered as forming a full complex or an incomplete one overlapping with Sotuta and Tases – is relatively uncommon at inland sites in the northern lowlands and dates mostly to a time when population levels were low and concentrated on the coasts. Whether one wishes to consider Hocaba and the later centuries during which it appears as Early Postclassic or Middle Postclassic in character is not very important. What is apparent is that, despite an early tenth-century origin, much of it dates to a "dark age" spanning the decline of Chichen Itza and the rise of Mayapan as powerful polities.

Even later post-monumental-construction pottery assigned to the Late Postclassic Chenku–Tases complex has been identified at Chichen Itza, perhaps most notably and dramatically manifested by the presence of effigy censers at the High Priest's Grave (Schmidt 2011). Extremely minor construction episodes and light occupation characterized by Tases pottery continued at Chichen Itza until the arrival of the Spaniards.

Conclusions, questions, and continuing problems of interpretation

It is trite to end a chapter with a call for further research. Nonetheless, there are several periods in the history of Chichen Itza that warrant much more investigation if we are to understand developmental processes at the site. We particularly need more information concerning Preclassic to Early Classic occupation, the period AD 900–950/980, and the end of monumental construction.

Beginnings and a possible Terminal Classic decline

Peter Schmidt's Proyecto Arqueológico Chichen Itza contained an important subproject conducted by Rocío González de la Mata (2006) that was designed to study early occupation, especially around the Temple of Three Lintels and nearby sinkholes. Some early pottery was found, but no structures dating to this early time have been identified. It may be that none exist now, but it is important to keep on looking for them. Moreover, it may be possible to identify the loci and extent of early settlement through the distribution of Preclassic and Early Classic pottery.

For us, a clear interpretative problem is created by the relative lack of information concerning the critical early tenth century – that is, the period between the construction of Maya-(or "Puuc"-) and International-(or "Toltec"-)style architecture. Only a few Transitional-style structures built at this time have been identified, but two are fairly well dated by multiple radiocarbon assays bracketing their construction. We cannot yet securely categorize the pottery of this period but hypothesize that it represents the transition from Late Classic to Sotuta pottery without an intervening, stand-alone Cehpech phase. Moreover, there was a prolonged hiatus in the carving of dated hieroglyphic monuments.

It is critically important to understand developmental processes during the early tenth century, one that was characterized by the rapid decay of Terminal Classic civilization in much of the northern Maya lowlands. We suspect that Chichen Itza, too, declined – but how much? – during this period. This implies that the Itza did not dramatically expand their state by conquest but instead were subject to the same forces of decay seen elsewhere. Thus, a contemporary decline (but not abandonment or even complete hiatus of construction) at Chichen Itza might have been caused by the same factors – such as a prolonged drought coupled with political and economic competition – seen across the region. Braswell and Peniche May (2012) have argued for a gradual transition to the full International style, but, if this transition took place during a period of relative hiatus and population loss, it may be more proper to link the appearance of the full International style with a dramatic resurgence.

The return of the Early Postclassic?

In some respects, our current understanding of the chronology of Chichen Itza resembles the much older "traditional model." During the Terminal Classic period – especially AD 870–890 or so – the ruling families of Chichen Itza built structures in the Maya style and carved Mayan hieroglyphic texts. They also used Yabnal-Motul pottery, closely related to – but somewhat different from – the Cehpech pottery of their neighbors in the Puuc region. At least some ceramics assigned to this second complex were consumed at Chichen Itza at this time. The early to mid-tenth century is not well understood, but the building frenzy of the late ninth century seems to have ended. This apparent decline might suggest a temporary loss of population, political breakdown, or both. By the late tenth century, however, Chichen Itza entered a second golden age. The pottery of this period belonged to the Sotuta complex, many massive structures were built in the new International style, dated Mayan hieroglyphic texts reappeared (but were very few in number), and even a new International writing style – mostly in the form of names tagged to individuals shown on warrior columns – was adopted.

The differences in the material culture of the late ninth and late tenth centuries – and the apparent lull, pause, or decline at Chichen Itza between these two periods – allow us to argue that the first should be called Terminal Classic while the second is more properly considered Early Postclassic in character. We view late tenth-century Chichen Itza as sharing more social, political, and architectural affinities with Mayapan than with the many cities of the Classic period. The general collapse seen throughout much of the northern Maya lowlands during the early tenth century and the later emergence of a new internationalism also fortify our resolve to resurrect the phrase "Early Postclassic."

Nonetheless, we acknowledge that many scholars stress continuity going back to the Late Classic. The architecture of the late tenth century employs the core-veneer technique developed in the northern Maya lowlands. Locally produced Early Postclassic Sotuta pottery (excluding the imports) is, essentially, a relatively late regional variant of Terminal Classic Cehpech and does not represent a complete technological or aesthetic break from the Late to Terminal Classic Yabnal-Motul complex. In fact, a difference of scale – whether one looks at individual ceramic types versus complexes or architectural techniques versus overall form – tends to force one to see either continuity or disruption. Such scholars who emphasize continuity over change will, no doubt, continue to refer to the late tenth and early eleventh centuries as the Terminal Classic.

Despite our preference for the phrase "Early Postclassic" to describe the second great period of construction at Chichen Itza, we differ strongly from the traditional model in that we do not see evidence for positing a foreign invasion of either "Toltecs" from Tula or "Putun Maya" from the Gulf Coast. Instead, we believe that most of the Early Postclassic occupants of Chichen Itza were the descendants of the Terminal Classic Maya who lived in the great city and other parts of the northern Maya lowlands. The emulation of foreign styles, wide-ranging trade relations, and a shared world religion are all plausible explanations for the participation of Chichen Itza in the Early Postclassic Mesoamerican world. Moreover, given that the second great period of Chichen Itza took place several decades after the collapse of powerful cities elsewhere on the peninsula, it seems more proper to explain the growth of the Early Postclassic Itza state in terms of opportunistic expansion into a political vacuum and demographic void rather than as a militaristic conquest. The Early Postclassic at Chichen Itza was a period of great reorganization and experimentation in the aftermath of a general Terminal Classic collapse felt throughout much of the north. But there is no need to resort to foreign migration, invasion, or even regional conquest models as explanations.

The end of Early Postclassic Chichen Itza

A final problem is dating the conclusion of the last great period at Chichen Itza – that is, the cessation of monumental construction at the site, political collapse, and demographic decline. Wooden lintels and beams in the Upper Temple of the Jaguars and the Temple of the Warriors – two relatively late structures probably constructed around or after AD 1000 – have never been subject to radiocarbon dating. Numerous carbon samples collected by the Proyecto Arqueológico Chichen Itza remain to be assayed. We may never know when the last major building was raised at Chichen Itza, but it seems likely to have taken place no more than a century or so after the final great building phase began. Most importantly, we need data that will help us understand why Chichen Itza seems to have rebounded so strongly from the general collapse felt across the northern Maya lowlands during the tenth century, only to fail a century or two later.

Notes

1 We thank Rafael Cobos Palma, Director of Chichén Itzá: estudio de la comunidad del Clásico Tardío, for his invitation to form a team of UCSD archaeologists and excavate on the Great Terrace in 2009. Our two subprojects (Operations AB and AC) were conducted alongside Universidad Autónoma de Yucatán (UADY) subprojects in other portions of the site. UCSD staff included the authors, Nancy Peniche May, Lauren D. Hahn, Kiri L. Hagerman, Misha Miller-Sisson, and Megan R. Pitcavage. We also acknowledge the

UADY scholars Lilia Fernández Souza, Mauricio Germón Roche, and Rodolfo Canto Carrillo for their daily colleagueship, as well as Dylan Clark (Harvard University) and Kate Jarvis and Oliver Boles (University College London). We further thank Elisabeth Flores Torruco, Director of the Archaeological Zone of Chichen Itza, and her staff for their constant help and sincere welcome. We gratefully acknowledge our longtime friends from the Proyecto Chichén Itzá, particularly Peter J. Schmidt, Rocío González de la Mata, José F. Osorio León, Francisco Pérez Ruiz, Eduardo Pérez de Heredia Puente, and Heajoo Chung for their many years of collaboration and colleagueship. Funding for UCSD research was generously provided to Braswell by UC MEXUS-CONACYT and UCSD. The greater project was funded by awards to Cobos from the UADY and INAH. We also thank Bill Ringle, George Bey, Will Andrews, Heajoo Chung, Eduardo Pérez de Heredia Puente, and Chris Gunn for sharing ideas and hard-to-find manuscripts with us. We are especially grateful to Will Andrews, Joyce Marcus, and George Cowgill for their comments and corrections to this chapter. Finally, Joe Ball was exceptionally generous in sharing his great experience with ceramics from the northern lowlands and provided indispensable help in crafting our understanding and discussion of slate wares.

2   For more detailed historical reviews of the chronology of Chichen Itza, see Anderson (1998), Kristan-Graham and Kowalski (2011), and Lincoln (1986). Gillespie (2011) provides a thorough and illuminating discussion of the origins of the Toltec invasion hypothesis.

3   Roys's Gregorian date equivalents are based on the Morley–Spinden (12.9.0.0.0) correlation.

4   Given Pérez's (2010, 2012) recent identification of Say Slate at Chichen Itza, an abundant group that he assigns not to Cehpech but to the earlier Motul complex, we wonder if most of Smith's "Cehpech" sherds were Say Slate that was misidentified and erroneously assigned to the Cehpech complex.

5   For example, he reports a cache "25 cm. below the lower platform floor on north side of the upper platform" of the Caracol, consisting of an "Early Florescent Medium Slate-ware" slab-legged basal break bowl covering an unslipped jar (Brainerd 1958: 36, figs 67a and 68a).

6   Say Slate and Sat Slate are different names for the same group in the Chichen Itza and Puuc regions. We prefer the complex and phase name "Yabnal" by itself to any phrase containing the word "Motul." This is because we are uncertain of the existence of a "Motul sphere" and because the Yabnal-Motul complex is recognized principally by the presence of the Say Slate group rather than by Motul types established by Smith (1971). Smith did not himself identify any Motul ceramics at Chichen Itza and, as stated in note 4 above, may have misclassified the most important markers of the Yabnal-Motul complex as belonging to the Cehpech complex.

7   There are some slight differences in the TL dates as reported by Chung (2008) and in her more recent publication. In the earlier work, samples CH16 (AD 1006 ± 85) and CH19 (AD 1107 ± 83) are assigned dates that are roughly 50 years earlier than reported by Chung et al. (2010), sample CH14 (AD 1114 ± 34) has a smaller error, and there is an additional sample (CH4) labeled "Gray Slate" that is given a TL date of AD 384–398. Such an early date for any Slate Ware suggests that TL is not yet a particularly reliable chronometric method, as does the colonial period date determined for sample CH13.

8   The problems in understanding the history of Chichen or Dzitas Slate are related more to issues of taxonomy than to real differences in what is observed by ceramicists. It is a case where nomenclature creates distinct interpretations. Confusions lie in the use of terms with specific local and regional referents rather than neutral and potentially transregional phrases such as "Early," "Medium," "Thin," and "Coarse" Slate Ware. Early Slates (i.e., "Sat" in the Puuc region and "Say" or "Tintin" at Chichen Itza) are relatively poorly fired, and the small differences between them were created by local or regional soil geology. Early Slates were followed by better-fired Medium Slates but are often otherwise difficult to distinguish from their local antecedents. In the Puuc region, these

are assigned to the Muna group. Johnson (2012) and Pérez (2010) also call the first Medium Slates at Chichen Itza – which probably appeared in the decades before AD 900 – Muna Slate. The implication of this term is that the first Medium Slates of Chichen Itza were derived from or converge with those of the Puuc region. Pérez (ibid.) in particular emphasizes an inherited relationship with the Puuc by switching from a local name (Say Slate) to foreign terms (both Muna Slate and the Cehpech complex). This creates the impression that a local complex was *replaced* by a foreign one. In contrast, Chung (2009) calls the first Medium Slate at Chichen Itza "Early Dzitas," which gives more emphasis to its relationship with a later *local* slate than with contemporary pottery from the Puuc region. During the first half of the tenth century, a second local Medium Slate derived from the first (Muna or Early Dzitas) began to be produced at Chichen Itza. There is a general consensus that this should be called "Dzitas" or "Chichen" Slate, but Johnson (2012) convincingly argues that this, too, could be considered a category within Muna Slate. Nevertheless, the fact that Puuc rather than Chichen Itza terminology is employed on the peninsular level is an artifact of the history of ceramic studies, not of the pottery itself.

In sum, the locally made pottery of Chichen Itza and the Puuc region exhibit close similarities during the Late and Terminal Classic periods. There is much agreement that a single, broad surface-finishing tradition was shared across much of the northern Maya lowlands. Despite this consensus, the taxonomy employed by Pérez (2010) emphasizes changes in affiliation from a local complex (Yabnal) to a foreign one (Cehpech) and back again to a local one (Sotuta). Johnson (2012) is certainly technically correct in classifying slates using terms from the Puuc region, but this inadvertently creates the impression that those from Chichen Itza should be understood principally in terms of external influence. Chung (2009) avoids the use of complex names (and formal taxonomy in general) and emphasizes the local development of Slate Wares at Chichen Itza within a broad tradition spanning much of the northern Maya lowlands. We think that Chung's interpretation (but not her TL chronology) best represents the historical trajectory of Slate Wares at Chichen Itza.

9 All radiocarbon assays were calibrated using OxCal 4.2 (Bronk Ramsey 2009) with the IntCal04 atmospheric calibration curve (Reimer *et al.* 2009). Probability distributions and two-sigma ranges for each date are reported in Figure 13.11. For convenience, we discuss the dates in terms of the midpoints of their calibrated two-sigma ranges. All calibrated dates are rounded to the nearest five-year interval.
10 For a detailed description of the construction stages of the Great Terrace, see Braswell and Peniche May (2012).
11 Braswell *et al.* (2011) discuss 30 radiocarbon and 13 TL dates from the Puuc site of Xkipche. Only two dates – both TL – pertain to the Cehpech–Sotuta overlap. These are AD 645 (870) 1095 (HdTL33 B19-1; 1127 BP, one-sigma range) and AD 861 (969) 1077 (HdTL33 B23-1; 1028 BP, one-sigma range). Both come from contexts dating to a time after monumental construction ceased and are consistent with the supposition that Sotuta pottery appears in the Puuc region during the tenth century. Nonetheless, their error ranges are large. Ringle (2012: 199, table 8.1) discusses radiocarbon dates from the Nunnery Quadrangle at Uxmal and does not find them useful.

References

Aimers, James J. (2007) What Maya Collapse? Terminal Classic Variation in the Maya Lowlands. *Journal of Archaeological Research* 15: 329–77.
Ambrosino, James N. (2006) Warfare and Destruction in the Maya Lowlands: Pattern and Process in the Archaeological Record of Yaxuna, Yucatan, Mexico. PhD dissertation, Department of Anthropology, Southern Methodist University, Dallas.

Anderson, Patricia K. (1998) Yula, Yucatan, Mexico: Terminal Classic Ceramic Chronology for the Chichen Itza Area. *Ancient Mesoamerica* 9: 151–65.

Andrews, Anthony P. (1990) The Fall of Chichen Itza: A Preliminary Hypothesis. *Latin American Antiquity* 1: 257–67.

Andrews, Anthony P., and Fernando Robles Castellanos (1985) Chichen Itza and Coba: An Itza–Maya Standoff in Early Postclassic Yucatan. In *The Lowland Maya Postclassic*, ed. Arlen F. Chase and Prudence M. Rice, pp. 62–72. Austin: University of Texas Press.

Andrews, Anthony P., E. Wyllys Andrews V, and Fernando Robles Castellanos (2003) The Northern Maya Collapse and its Aftermath. *Ancient Mesoamerica* 14: 151–6.

Andrews, E. Wyllys, V (1979) Some Comments on Puuc Architecture of the Northern Yucatan Peninsula. In *The Puuc: New Perspectives*, ed. Lawrence Mills, pp. 1–17. Pella, IA: Central College.

Andrews, E. Wyllys, V, and Jeremy A. Sabloff (1986) Classic to Postclassic: A Summary Discussion. In *Late Lowland Maya Civilization: Classic to Postclassic*, ed. Jeremy A. Sabloff and E. Wyllys Andrews V, pp. 433–56. Albuquerque: School of American Research and University of New Mexico Press.

Ardren, Traci (1997) The Politics of Place: Architecture and Cultural Change at the Xkanha Group, Yaxuná, Yucatán, Mexico. PhD dissertation, Department of Anthropology, Yale University. Ann Arbor, MI: University Microfilms.

Ball, Joseph W. (1976) Ceramic Sphere Affiliations of the Barton Ramie Ceramic Complexes. In *Prehistoric Pottery Analysis and the Ceramics of Barton Ramie in the Belize Valley*, ed. James C. Gifford, pp. 323–30. Cambridge, MA: Peabody Museum of Archaeology and Ethnology.

—— (1979) Ceramics, Culture History, and the Puuc Tradition: Some Alternative Possibilities. In *The Puuc: New Perspectives*, ed. Lawrence Mills, pp. 18–35. Pella, IA: Central College.

Barrera Vásquez, Alfredo, and Silvia Rendón (1948) *El libro de los libros de Chilam Balam*. Mexico City: Fondo de Cultura Económica.

Beramendi-Orosco, Laura E., Galia González-Hernández, Jaime Urrutia-Fucugauchi, Linda R. Manzanilla, Ana M. Soler-Arechalde, Avto Goguitchaishvili, and Nick Jarboe (2009) High-Resolution Chronology for the Mesoamerican Urban Center of Teotihuacan derived from Bayesian Statistics of Radiocarbon and Archaeological Data. *Quaternary Research* 71: 99–107.

Bey, George J., III, Tara M. Bond, William M. Ringle, Craig A. Hanson, Charles W. Houk, and Carlos Peraza Lope (1998) The Ceramic Chronology of Ek Balam, Yucatan, Mexico. *Ancient Mesoamerica* 9: 101–20.

Bey, George J., III, Craig A. Hanson, and William M. Ringle (1997) Classic to Postclassic at Ek Balam, Yucatan: Architectural and Ceramic Evidence for Defining the Transition. *Latin American Antiquity* 8: 237–54.

Bey, George J., III, and William M. Ringle (2011) From the Bottom Up: The Timing and Nature of the Tula–Chichén Itzá Exchange. In *Twin Tollans: Chichén Itzá, Tula, and the Epiclassic to Early Postclassic Mesoamerican World*, rev. ed., ed. Jeff K. Kowalski and Cynthia Kristan-Graham, pp. 299–340. Washington, DC: Dumbarton Oaks.

Bolles, John S. (1977) *Las Monjas: A Major Pre-Mexican Architectural Complex at Chichen Itza*. Norman: University of Oklahoma Press.

Boot, Erik (2005) *Continuity and Change in Text and Image at Chichén Itzá, Yucatán, Mexico: A Study of the Inscriptions, Iconography, and Architecture at a Late Classic to Early Postclassic Maya Site*. Leiden: Research School CNWS, Leiden University.

—— (2010) Chichen Itza in the Mesoamerican World: Some Old and New Perspectives. In *The Maya and Their Neighbors: Internal and External Contacts through Time*, ed. Laura van

Broekhoven, Rogelio Valencia Rivera, Benjamin Vis, and Frauke Sahse, pp. 73–88. Markt Schwaben: Anton Saurwein.

Bowman, Sheridan (1990) *Radiocarbon Dating*. Berkeley and Los Angeles: University of California Press.

Brainerd, George W. (1958) *The Archaeological Ceramics of Yucatan*. Berkeley and Los Angeles: University of California Press.

Braswell, Geoffrey E., and Nancy Peniche May (2012) In the Shadow of the Pyramid: Excavations in the Great Platform of Chichen Itza. In *The Ancient Maya of Mexico: Reinterpreting the Past of the Northern Maya Lowlands*, ed. Geoffrey E. Braswell, pp. 229–63. Sheffield: Equinox.

Braswell, Geoffrey E., Iken Paap, and Michael D. Glascock (2011) The Obsidian and Ceramics of the Puuc Region: Chronology, Lithic Procurement, and Production at Xkipche, Yucatan, Mexico. *Ancient Mesoamerica* 21: 135–54.

Bricker, Victoria R. (1981) *The Indian Christ, the Indian King: The Historical Substrate of Maya Myth and Ritual*. Austin: University of Texas Press.

Bronk Ramsey, Christopher (2009) Bayesian Analysis of Radiocarbon Dates. *Radiocarbon* 51(1): 337–60.

Buck, Caitlin E. (2004) Bayesian Chronological Data Interpretation: Where Now? In *Tools for Constructing Chronologies: Crossing Disciplinary Boundaries*, ed. Caitlin E. Buck and Andrew R. Millard, pp. 1–24. London: Springer.

Buck, Caitlin E., J. Andrés Christen, and Gary N. James (1999) BCal: An On-line Bayesian Radiocarbon Calibration Tool. *Internet Archaeology* 7.

—— (2001) BCal software, http://bcal.shef.ac.uk/.

Carmean, Kelli, Nicholas Dunning, and Jeff Karl Kowalski (2004) High Times in the Hill Country: A Perspective from the Terminal Classic Puuc Region. In *The Terminal Classic in the Maya Lowlands: Collapse, Transition, and Transformation*, ed. Arthur A. Demarest, Prudence M. Rice, and Don S. Rice, pp. 424–49. Boulder: University Press of Colorado.

Chandler, John B., Russell Kinningham, and Don S. Massey (1963) Texas Bio-Nuclear Radiocarbon Measurements I. *Radiocarbon* 5: 56–61.

Charnay, Désiré (1887) *The Ancient Cities of the New World, being Voyages and Explorations in Mexico and Central America from 1857–1882*, trans. J. Gonino and Helen S. Conant. New York: Harper & Brothers.

Chase, Diane Z., and Arlen F. Chase (2004) Hermeneutics, Transitions, and Transformations in Classic to Postclassic Maya Society. In *The Terminal Classic in the Maya Lowlands: Collapse, Transition, and Transformation*, ed. Arthur A. Demarest, Prudence M. Rice, and Don S. Rice, pp. 12–27. Boulder: University Press of Colorado.

Christen, J. Andrés (1994) Summarizing a Set of Radiocarbon Determinations: A Robust Approach. *Applied Statistics* 43:489–503.

Chung, Heajoo (2008) Analysis and Interpretation of Chichen Itza Chronology Problem. *Asian Journal of Latin American Studies* 21(4):113–37.

—— (2009) *La cronología de Chichén Itzá*. Paju: Korea Studies Information.

Chung, Heajoo, and Insung Lee (2005) Search for the Origin of Volcanic Glass in Chichen Slate Ware. Paper presented at the 35th Annual Symposium on Archaeometry, Beijing.

Chung, Heajoo, Pedro González, Angel Ramírez, Peter Schaaf, and Insung Lee (2010) Rethinking about Chronology of Chichen Itza by Thermoluminescence Dating of Volcanic Glass. *Mediterranean Archaeology and Archaeometry* 10(4): 115–20.

Cobos, Rafael (2004) Chichén Itzá: Settlement and Hegemony during the Terminal Classic Period. In *The Terminal Classic in the Maya Lowlands: Collapse, Transition, and Transformation*, ed. Arthur A. Demarest, Prudence M. Rice, and Don S. Rice, pp. 517–44. Boulder: University Press of Colorado.

—— (2011) Multepal or Centralized Kingship? New Evidence on Governmental Organization at Chichén Itzá. In *Twin Tollans: Chichén Itzá, Tula, and the Epiclassic to Early Postclassic Mesoamerican World*, rev. ed., ed. Jeff K. Kowalski and Cynthia Kristan-Graham, pp. 249–71. Washington, DC: Dumbarton Oaks.

Cobos, Rafael, and Terance L. Winemiller (2001) The Late and Terminal Classic-Period Causeway Systems of Chichén Itzá, Yucatán, Mexico. *Ancient Mesoamerica* 12: 283–91.

Cohodas, Marvin (1978) *The Great Ball Court of Chichen Itza, Yucatan, Mexico*. New York: Garland.

Culleton, Brendan J., Keith M. Prufer, and Douglas J. Kennett (2012) A Bayesian AMS 14C Chronology of the Classic Maya Center of Uxbenká, Belize. *Journal of Archaeological Science* 39: 1572–86.

Deevey, Edward S., L. J. Gralenski, and Väinö Hoffren (1959) Yale Natural Radiocarbon Measurements IV. *Radiocarbon (American Journal of Science Radiocarbon Supplement)* 1: 144–72.

Demarest, Arthur A., Prudence M. Rice, and Don S. Rice (2004) The Terminal Classic in the Maya Lowlands: Assessing Collapses, Terminations, and Transformations. In *The Terminal Classic in the Maya Lowlands: Collapse, Transition, and Transformation*, ed. Arthur A. Demarest, Prudence M. Rice, and Don S. Rice, pp. 545–72. Boulder: University Press of Colorado.

Dunning, Nicholas P., and Jeff Karl Kowalski (1994) Lords of the Hills: Classic Maya Settlement Patterns and Political Iconography in the Puuc Region, Mexico. *Ancient Mesoamerica* 5: 63–95.

Edmonson, Munro S. (1976) The Mayan Calendar Reform of 11.16.0.0.0. *Current Anthropology* 17: 713–17.

—— (1982) *The Ancient Future of the Itza: The Book of Chilam Balam of Tizimin*. Austin: University of Texas Press.

—— (1986) *Heaven Born Merida and its Destiny: The Book of Chilam Balam of Chumayel*. Austin: University of Texas Press.

Espinosa, Manuel, Heajoo Chung, Alfredo Victoria Moralez, D. Mendoza, Rosario Domínguez, and V. Rodríguez (2000) A Study of Mayan Slate Ware Slip. Paper presented at the 32nd Annual Symposium on Archaeometry, Mexico City.

García Campillo, José Miguel (2000) *Estudio introductorio del léxico de las inscripciones de Chichén Itzá, Yucatán, México*. Oxford: Archaeopress.

Gillespie, Susan D. (2011) Toltecs, Tula, and Chichén Itzá: The Development of an Archaeological Myth. In *Twin Tollans: Chichén Itzá, Tula, and the Epiclassic to Early Postclassic Mesoamerican World*, rev. ed., ed. Jeff K. Kowalski and Cynthia Kristan-Graham, pp. 61–92. Washington, DC: Dumbarton Oaks.

González de la Mata, Rocío (2006) Agua, agricultura y mitos: el caso de tres rejolladas de Chichen Itza. In *XIX simposio de investigaciones arqueológicas en Guatemala, 2005*, ed. Juan Pedro Laporte, Bárbara Arroyo, and Héctor Mejía, pp. 305–18. Guatemala City: Museo Nacional de Arqueología y Etnología.

Graña-Behrens, Daniel (2002) Die Maya-Inschriften aus Nordwestyukatan, Mexiko. PhD dissertation, University of Bonn.

Graña-Behrens, Daniel, Christian Prager, and Elizabeth Wagner (1999) The Hieroglyphic Inscription of the "High Priest's Grave" at Chichén Itzá, Yucatán, Mexico. *Mexicon* 21(3): 61–6.

Grube, Nikolai (1994) Hieroglyphic Sources for the History of Northwest Yucatan. In *Hidden among the Hills: Maya Archaeology of the Northwest Yucatan Peninsula*, ed. Hanns J. Prem, pp. 316–58. Möckmühl: Von Flemming.

—— (2003) Hieroglyphic Inscriptions from Northwest Yucatán: An Update of Recent Research. In *Escondido en la selva: arqueología en el norte de Yucatán*, ed. Hanns J. Prem, pp. 339–70. Bonn: University of Bonn/Anton Saurwein; and Mexico City: Instituto Nacional de Antropología e Historia.

Grube, Nikolai, and Ruth J. Krochock (2011) Reading between the Lines: Hieroglyphic Texts from Chichén Itzá and its Neighbors. In *Twin Tollans: Chichén Itzá, Tula, and the Epiclassic to Early Postclassic Mesoamerican World*, rev. ed., ed. Jeff K. Kowalski and Cynthia Kristan-Graham, pp. 157–93. Washington, DC: Dumbarton Oaks.

Hahn, Lauren D., and Geoffrey E. Braswell (2012) Divide and Rule: Interpreting Site Perimeter Walls in the Northern Maya Lowlands and Beyond. In *The Ancient Maya of Mexico: Reinterpreting the Past of the Northern Maya Lowlands*, ed. Geoffrey E. Braswell, pp. 264–81. Sheffield: Equinox.

Higham, Thomas, Johannes van der Plicht, Christopher Bronk Ramsey, Hendrik J. Bruins, Mark Robinson, and Thomas E. Levy (2005) Radiocarbon Dating of the Khirbat-en-Nahas Site (Jordan) and Bayesian Modeling of the Results. In *The Bible and Radiocarbon Dating: Archaeology, Text, and Science*, ed. Thomas E. Levy and Thomas Higham, pp. 164–78. Sheffield: Equinox.

Hubbs, Carl L., George S. Bien, and Hans E. Suess (1960) La Jolla Natural Radiocarbon Measurements. *Radiocarbon (American Journal of Science Radiocarbon Supplement)* 2: 197–223.

—— (1962) La Jolla Natural Radiocarbon Measurements II. *Radiocarbon (American Journal of Science Radiocarbon Supplement)* 4: 204–38.

Jiménez Álvarez, Socorro, Rafael Cobos, Heajoo Chung, and Roberto Belmar Casso (2006) El despertar de la complejidad sociocultural visto desde el estudio tecnológico de la cerámica: explicando las transformaciones sociopolíticas en el occidente de Yucatán. In *XIX simposio de investigaciones arqueológicas en Guatemala, 2005*, ed. Juan Pedro Laporte, Bárbara Arroyo, and Héctor Mejía, pp. 532–42. Guatemala City: Museo Nacional de Arqueología y Etnología.

Jiménez Moreno, Wigberto (1941) Tula y los Toltecas según las fuentes históricas. *Revista Mexicana de Estudios Antropológicos* 5: 79–85.

Johnson, Scott A. J. (2012) Late and Terminal Classic Power Shifts in Yucatan: The View from Popola. PhD dissertation, Department of Anthropology, Tulane University. Ann Arbor, MI: University Microfilms.

Johnstone, David (2001) The Ceramics of Yaxuná, Yucatan. PhD dissertation, Department of Anthropology, Southern Methodist University, Dallas.

Kelley, David H. (1982) Notes on Puuc Inscriptions and History. Supplement to *The Puuc: New Perspectives*, ed. Lawrence Mills. Pella, IA: Central College.

—— (1984) The Toltec Empire in Yucatan. *Quarterly Review of Archaeology* 5: 12–13.

Kirchhoff, Paul (1955) Quetzalcoatl, Huemac y el fin de Tula. *Cuadernos Americanos* 84: 163–96.

Kowalski, Jeff Karl (1987) *The House of the Governor, a Maya Palace at Uxmal, Yucatan, Mexico*. Norman: University of Oklahoma Press.

Kremer, Jürgen (1994) The Putun Hypothesis Reconsidered. In *Hidden among the Hills: Maya Archaeology of the Northwest Yucatan Peninsula*, ed. Hanns J. Prem, pp. 289–307. Möckmühl: Von Flemming.

Kristan-Graham, Cynthia, and Jeff K. Kowalski (2011) Chichén Itzá, Tula, and Tollan: Changing Perspectives on a Recurring Problem in Mesoamerican Archaeology and Art History. In *Twin Tollans: Chichén Itzá, Tula, and the Epiclassic to Early Postclassic Mesoamerican World*, rev. ed., ed. Jeff K. Kowalski and Cynthia Kristan-Graham, pp. 1–58. Washington, DC: Dumbarton Oaks.

Krochock, Ruth J. (1997) A New Interpretation of the Inscriptions on the Temple of the Hieroglyphic Jambs, Chichén Itzá. Manuscript on file, Department of Art and Art History, University of Texas, Austin.

Lincoln, Charles E. (1986) The Chronology of Chichen Itza: A Review of the Literature. In *Late Lowland Maya Civilization: Classic to Postclassic*, ed. Jeremy A. Sabloff and E. Wyllys Andrews V, pp. 141–96. Albuquerque: School of American Research and University of New Mexico Press.

Love, Bruce, and Peter Schmidt (2011) Catálogo preliminar de glifos ajenos de la tradición maya en Chichén Itzá. Unpublished manuscript in possession of the authors. Proyecto Arqueológico Chichén Itzá, Merida.

Makemson, Maud W. (1951) *The Book of the Jaguar Priest: A Translation of the Book of Chilam Balam of Tizimin with Commentary*. New York: Henry Schuman.

Manahan, T. Kam, Traci Ardren, and Alejandra Alonso Olvera (2012) Household Organization and the Dynamics of State Expansion: The Late Classic–Terminal Classic Transformation at Xuenkal, Yucatan, Mexico. *Ancient Mesoamerica* 23: 345–64.

Marcus, Joyce (1992) *Mesoamerican Writing Systems: Propaganda, Myth, and History in Four Ancient Civilizations*. Princeton, NJ: Princeton University Press.

Marquina, Ignacio (1951) *Arquitectura Prehispánica*. Mexico City: Instituto Nacional de Antropología e Historia and Secretaría de Educación Pública.

Medíz Bolio, Antonio (1930) *Libro de Chilam Balam de Chumayel: traducción del idioma maya al castellano*. San José: Lehmann.

Michczyński, Adam, and Anna Pazdur (2003) The Method of Combining Radiocarbon Dates and Other Information in Application to Study the Chronologies of Archaeological Sites. *Geochronometria* 22: 41–6.

Milbrath, Susan, and Carlos Peraza Lope (2003) Revisiting Mayapan: Mexico's Last Maya Capital. *Ancient Mesoamerica* 14: 1–46.

Morley, Sylvanus G. (1946) *The Ancient Maya*. Stanford, CA: Stanford University Press.

Morris, Early H., Jean Charlot, and Ann Axtell Morris (1931) *The Temple of the Warriors at Chichen Itza, Yucatan*, 2 vols. Washington, DC: Carnegie Institution.

Ochoa Rodriguez, Virginia Josefina (1999) Spatial Distribution of Peto Cream Ware in the Yucatan Peninsula. MA thesis, Department of Geography and Anthropology, Lousiana State University.

Osorio León, José F. J. (2004) La estructura 5C4 (Templo de la Serie Inicial): un edificio clave para la cronología en Chichen Itza. Licenciatura thesis, Universidad Autónoma de Yucatán, Merida.

—— (2006) La presencia del Clásico Tardío en Chichen Itza (600–800/830 DC). In *XIX simposio de investigaciones arqueológicas en Guatemala, 2005*, ed. Juan Pedro Laporte, Bárbara Arroyo, and Héctor Mejía, pp. 455–62. Guatemala City: Museo Nacional de Arqueología y Etnología.

Peniche May, Nancy, and Geoffrey E. Braswell (2009) Operación AC: exploración de la sección este de la Gran Nivelación durante el lapso del 21 de abril al 24 de julio. In *Excavaciones de la UCSD en Chichén Itzá: Informe de la temporada de campo 2009 al Proyecto Chichén Itzá*, ed. Nancy Peniche May, Lauren D. Hahn, and Geoffrey E. Braswell, pp. 109–96. Unpublished report on file at the Universidad Autónoma de Yucatán, Merida, and at the University of California, San Diego. Available at http://dss.ucsd.edu/~gbraswel/docs/InformeChichen-Itza2009UCSD_opt.pdf.

Peniche May, Nancy, Lauren D. Hahn, and Geoffrey E. Braswell (2009) *Excavaciones de la UCSD en Chichén Itzá: Informe de la temporada de campo 2009 al Proyecto Chichén Itzá*, unpublished report on file at the Universidad Autónoma de Yucatán, Merida, and at the

University of California, San Diego. Available at http://dss.ucsd.edu/~gbraswel/docs/InformeChichenItza2009UCSD_opt.pdf.

Pérez de Heredia Puente, Eduardo J. (2007) *Chen K'u: la cerámica del Cenote Sagrado de Chichén Itzá: estudio de los fragmentos cerámicos de las exploraciones de los años sesentas*. Report submitted to the Foundation for the Advancement of Mesoamerican Studies, www.famsi.org/reports/97061es/97061esPerezdeHeredia01.pdf (accessed September 18, 2012).

—— (2010) Ceramic Contexts and Chronology at Chichen Itza, Yucatan, Mexico. PhD dissertation, La Trobe University.

—— (2012) The Yabnal-Motul Complex of the Late Classic Period at Chichen Itza. *Ancient Mesoamerica* 23: 379–402.

Pérez Ruiz, Francisco (2005) Recintos amurallados: Una interpretación sobre el sistema defensivo de Chichen Itza, Yucatán. In *XVIII simposio de investigaciones arqueológicas en Guatemala, 2004*, ed. Juan Pedro Laporte, Bárbara Arroyo, and Héctor E. Mejía, pp. 881–90. Guatemala City: Museo Nacional de Arqueología y Etnología.

Proskouriakoff, Tatiana (1970) On Two Inscriptions at Chichén Itzá. In *Monographs and Papers in Maya Archaeology*, ed. William R. Bullard, Jr., pp. 459–67. Cambridge, MA: Peabody Museum of Archaeology and Ethnology.

Reimer, Paula J., Mike G. L. Baillie, Edouard Bard, Alex Bayliss, J. Warren Beck, Paul G. Blackwell, Christopher Bronk Ramsey, Caitlin E. Buck, George S. Burr, R. Lawrence Edwards, Michael Friedrich, P. M. Grootes, Thomas P. Guilderson, Irka Hajdas, T. J. Heaton, Alan G. Hogg, Konrad A. Hughen, K. F. Kaiser, Bernd Kromer, F. G. McCormac, S. W. Manning, Ron W. Reimer, D. A. Richards, John R. Southon, Sahra Talamo, C. S. M. Turney, Johannes van der Plicht, and Constanze E. Weyhenmeyer (2009) IntCal09 and Marine09 Radiocarbon Age Calibration Curves, 0–50,000 Years Cal BP. *Radiocarbon* 51(4): 1111–50.

Restall, Matthew (1998) *Maya Conquistador*. Boston: Beacon Press.

Ringle, William M. (2012) The Nunnery Quadrangle of Uxmal. In *The Ancient Maya of Mexico: Reinterpreting the Past of the Northern Maya Lowlands*, ed. Geoffrey E. Braswell, pp. 191–228. Sheffield: Equinox.

Ringle, William M., Tomás Gallareta Negrón, and George J. Bey III (1998) The Return of Quetzalcoatl: Evidence for the Spread of a World Religion during the Epiclassic Period. *Ancient Mesoamerica* 9: 183–232.

Robles Castellanos, Fernando (1988) Ceramic Units from Isla Cerritos, North Coast of Yucatán (Preliminary Results). *Ceramica de Cultura Maya* 15: 65–71.

Robles Castellanos, Fernando, and Anthony P. Andrews (1986) A Review and Synthesis of Recent Postclassic Archaeology in Northern Yucatan. In *Late Lowland Maya Civilization: Classic to Postclassic*, ed. Jeremy A. Sabloff and E. Wyllys Andrews V, pp. 53–98. Albuquerque: School of American Research and University of New Mexico Press.

Roys, Ralph L. (1933) *The Book of Chilam Balam of Chumayel*. Norman: University of Oklahoma Press.

Ruppert, Karl (1950) Gallery-Patio Type Structures at Chichén Itzá. In *For the Dean: Essays in Anthropology in Honor of Byron Cummings on His Eighty-Ninth Birthday, September 20, 1950*, ed. Erik K. Reed and Dale S. King, pp. 249–58. Tucson: Hohokam Museums Association; and Santa Fe: Southwestern Monuments Association.

Sabloff, Jeremy A. (2007) It Depends on How We Look at Things: New Perspectives on the Postclassic Period in the Northern Maya Lowlands. *Proceedings of the American Philosophical Society* 151(1): 11–26.

Schele, Linda, and David Freidel (1990) *A Forest of Kings: The Untold Story of the Ancient Maya*. New York: William Morrow.

Schele, Linda, and Peter Mathews (1998) *The Code of Kings: The Language of Seven Sacred Maya Temples and Tombs.* New York: Simon & Schuster.

Schmidt, Peter J. (2011) Birds, Ceramics, and Cacao: New Excavations at Chichén Itzá, Yucatan. In *Twin Tollans: Chichén Itzá, Tula, and the Epiclassic to Early Postclassic Mesoamerican World*, rev. ed., ed. Jeff K. Kowalski and Cynthia Kristan-Graham, pp. 113–55. Washington, DC: Dumbarton Oaks.

Schmidt, Peter J., and Eduardo J. Pérez de Heredia Puente (2006) Fases de construcción de la Gran Nivelación de Chichén Itzá. Paper presented at the XVI Encuentro Internacional "Los Investigadores de la Cultura Maya," Campeche, November.

Seler, Eduard (1909) *Die Ruinen von Chich'en Itzá in Yucatan.* Vienna: A. Hartleben.

Smith, Michael E. (2011) Tula and Chichén Itzá: Are We Asking the Right Questions? In *Twin Tollans: Chichén Itzá, Tula, and the Epiclassic to Early Postclassic Mesoamerican World*, rev. ed., ed. Jeff K. Kowalski and Cynthia Kristan-Graham, pp. 579–617. Washington, DC: Dumbarton Oaks.

Smith, Robert E. (1971) *The Pottery of Mayapan, including Studies of Ceramic Material from Uxmal, Kabah, and Chichen Itza*, 2 vols. Cambridge, MA: Peabody Museum of Archaeology and Ethnology.

Solís Alcalá, Ermilio (1949) *Códice Pérez: traducción libre del maya al castellano.* Merida: Liga de Acción Social.

Stuckenrath, Robert, Jr. (1967) University of Pennsylvania Radiocarbon Dates X. *Radiocarbon* 9: 333–45.

Stuiver, Minze, Edward S. Deevey, and L. J. Gralenski (1960) Yale Natural Radiocarbon Measurements V. *Radiocarbon (American Journal of Science Radiocarbon Supplement)* 2: 49–61.

Suhler, Charles, Traci Ardren and David Johnstone (1998) The Chronology of Yaxuná: Evidence from Excavations and Ceramics. *Ancient Mesoamerica* 9: 167–82.

Suhler, Charles, Traci Ardren, David Freidel, and Dave Johnstone (2004) The Rise and Fall of Terminal Classic Yaxuna, Yucatán, Mexico. In *The Terminal Classic in the Maya Lowlands: Collapse, Transition, and Transformation*, ed. Arthur A. Demarest, Prudence M. Rice, and Don S. Rice, pp. 450–84. Boulder: University Press of Colorado.

Thompson, J. Eric S. (1937) *A New Method of Deciphering Yucatecan Dates, with Special Reference to Chichen Itza.* Washington, DC: Carnegie Institution.

—— (1970) *Maya History and Religion.* Norman: University of Oklahoma Press.

Tozzer, Alfred M. (1957) Chichen Itza and its Cenote of Sacrifice: A Comparative Study of Contemporaneous Maya and Toltec. Cambridge, MA: Peabody Museum of Archaeology and Ethnology.

Vaillant, George C. (1961) *The Chronological Significance of Maya Ceramics.* Washington, DC: Society for American Archaeology; and Madison: University of Wisconsin Press.

Varela Torrecilla, Carmen (1998) El Clásico Medio en el noroccidente de Yucatán: la fase Oxkintok Regional en Oxkintok (Yucatán) como paradigma. Oxford: British Archaeological Reports.

Wren, Linnea H., and Peter Schmidt (1991) Elite Interaction during the Terminal Classic Period: New Evidence from Chichen Itza. In *Classic Maya Political History: Hieroglyphic and Archaeological Evidence*, ed. T. Patrick Culbert, pp. 199–225. Cambridge: Cambridge University Press.

PART VI
Before and beyond
A comparative perspective

14

PEER-POLITY INTERACTION IN THE NORTE CHICO, PERU, 3000–1800 BC[1]

Winifred Creamer, Jonathan Haas, and Allen Rutherford

Thirty major ceremonial and residential centers dating to the Late Archaic period (3000 to 1800 BC) have been identified in the four valleys of the Norte Chico region of Peru. In terms of area, the number of monumental structures, and size, there is no sign of a hierarchical relationship among the sites. Radiocarbon evidence suggests most were occupied contemporaneously during the period 2400–2000 BC. We explore the idea that these centers represented relatively independent polities engaged in peer-to-peer competition for religious participants and labor.

> When a significant organizational change, and in particular an increase in complexity, is recognized within one polity, it is generally the case that some of the other polities within the region will undergo the same transformation at about the same time.
>
> (Renfrew 1986: 7)

The coast of Peru is a single environmental zone: north to south a narrow strip of desert bisected by short rivers carries melt water from the Andes to the Pacific Ocean. In four closely spaced river valleys and their desert surroundings called the Norte Chico region (Figure 14.1), huge mounds and sunken circular courts flanked by upright monoliths were built in at least 30 localities during the period 3000–1800 BC. In general terms, this surge of monumental construction is viewed as the development of civilization. Nonetheless, our example from the Norte Chico region presents some specific questions:

> What was it? Was occupation as dense as it appears from archaeological survey and radiocarbon dating? What kind of cultural expression was this region full of large mound complexes and sunken circular courts?

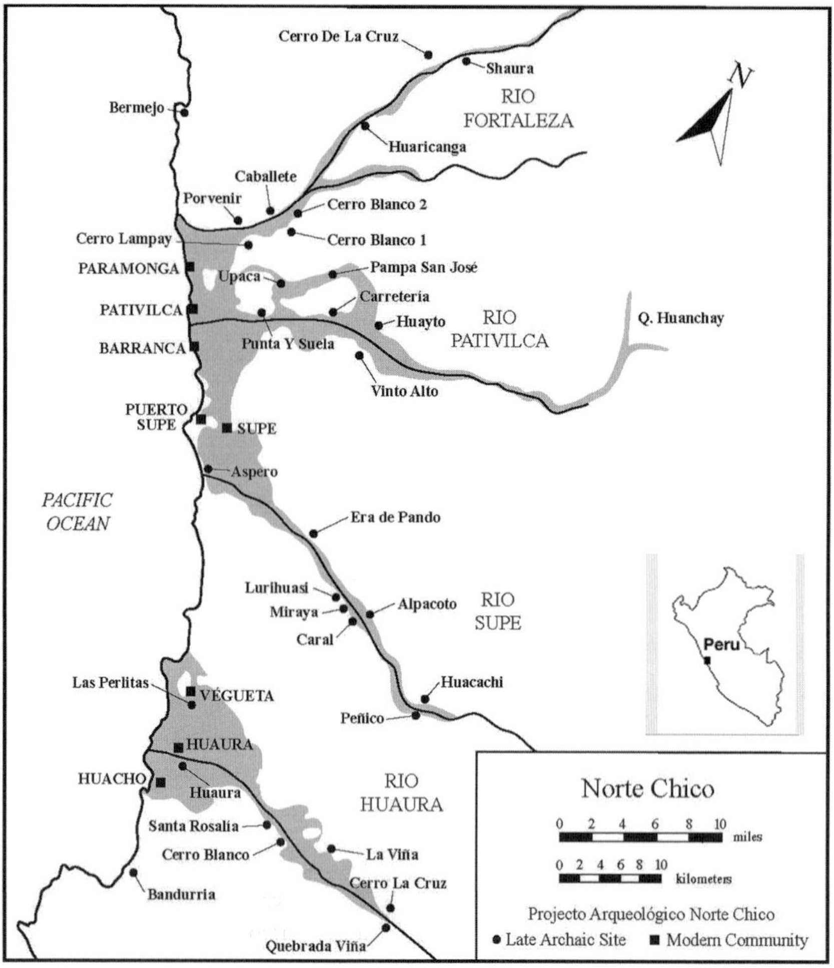

FIGURE 14.1 Map of the Norte Chico region

Why here? Why did monumental construction begin in this particular segment of the coastal zone, earlier than anywhere else?

How? What sustained this cultural expression for more than a thousand years of cultural development?

This chapter examines the first of these questions. As archaeologists who have applied a neo-evolutionary perspective to a number of archaeological data sets over the past 20 years or more, we confess that the Late Archaic florescence in the Norte Chico stoutly resists classification as band, tribe, chiefdom, *or* state (Service 1975). Among the alternatives to consider is peer-polity interaction, first outlined by Renfrew (1986).

Defining peer-polity interaction

Renfrew's model of peer-polities suggests there were regions in which a number of settlements grew in size and existed in a single cultural and economic milieu, sharing some, but not all, characteristics. He describes these settlements or units as polities, implying that they do not have to be of any specific size, although they are "the highest order socio-political unit[s] in the region" (Renfrew 1986: 2). At an initial point, these polities are autonomous but aware of neighboring groups. Renfrew proposes similarities and differences among the settlements that are connected in a peer-polity network of communication and competition, yet he focuses on the institutionalization of political organization and ritual as a key step in the transformation of a network of polities to a civilization. He indicates (ibid.: 7) that communication among participants in the network leads to a sharing of symbolic systems and technology and the development of similar political and symbolic structures.

Interaction among peer-polities may have taken the form of competition through (1) conflict or competitive emulation; (2) the transmission of innovative, shared symbols; or (3) the increased exchange of goods (Renfrew 1986: 8). We examine each of these for the Norte Chico.

Late Archaic sites in the Norte Chico

The Norte Chico region of Peru consists of four closely spaced river valleys: the Fortaleza, Pativilca, Supe, and Huaura. The rivers in each valley are similar in that they descend from the foothills of the Andes, crossing a narrow coastal plain for 20 to 30 kilometers before emptying into the Pacific. Outside the confines of the valley bottom the landscape is a sere desert that supports a few cactus and *Tillandsia* sp., a variety of air plant. The three northerly valleys – Fortaleza, Pativilca and Supe – empty into the Pacific Ocean so close together that they have been considered a single conjoined parcel of land watered in common, or rather by the Pativilca, as "it can completely irrigate the joint coastal plain of these three rivers throughout most of the year" (Kosok 1965: 218). Kosok and Schaedel identified three segments of canal they believed to be ancient in the Pativilca area (ibid.).

There are differences among the valleys, as well. The annual volume of water in each river varies greatly, as does the seasonal variation in water flow (Creamer *et al.* 2007: fig. 1). Access to the highlands differs from valley to valley. The Fortaleza Valley is a major transportation route from the coast to the highlands. The Huaura Valley has an equally long history of use as a transportation route, although the contemporary infrastructure is not as highly developed. The other valleys descend from smaller highland watersheds.

Although irrigation has probably been used for most of the past 5,000 years to convert valley bottomlands into agricultural fields, no particular valley displays evidence of unusually early occupation. Little is known about human occupation of the Norte Chico region before the Late Archaic period (3000–1800 BC). Sites in the Norte Chico with large mounds were recorded by Uhle in 1906, by Kosok and Schaedel (1965) in the late 1940s, by Engel (1987) in the 1970s, and by Vega-Centeno *et al.* (1998) in the 1990s. Large sites located away from the coast were thought to be agricultural centers dating to the Initial period (ibid.), similar to, though smaller than, sites such as Sechin Alto and El Paraiso (Engel 1966; Kosok 1965; Quilter 1985). Testing by Zechenter (1988) established for the first time that some of large inland sites were occupied during the third millennium BC. Shady's work at the Supe Valley site of Caral in the 1990s demonstrated the pre-ceramic characteristics of the inland mound and sunken court pattern, and radiocarbon dates from Caral placed it firmly in the Late Archaic period, 3000–1800 BC (Shady *et al.* 2001; Shady and Leyva 2003).

Mound sites of the Late Archaic are not the first occupation of the Norte Chico, but they are the first large-scale constructions in the region (Perales Munguía 2006, 2007). Further, there appear to be far fewer, if any, sites with the features characteristic of the Late Archaic in either the Río Seco/Chancay Valley to the south (Wendt 1964) or the Huarmey Valley to the north (Bonavia 1982). Comprehensive survey has not yet been carried out in either area, so this could change. At the same time, years of research in the Casma Valley, north of Huarmey, reveal nothing comparable during the Late Archaic (Pozorski and Pozorski 1990), despite recent finds of circular courts dating to the middle fourth millennium BC (Fuchs *et al.* 2010). What distinguishes the phenomenon of mound and sunken court centers in the Norte Chico is the limited region in which this rapid and large-scale construction occurred, its early date, and the density of sites, especially considering the massive size of the works erected. Enormous labor investment is visible in each construction and in the near constant remodeling that can be seen in the gigantic looters' pits that have been dug into some of these sites (Figure 14.2).

Again and again, archaeological research has shown that simple explanations of the so-called spread of civilization – by diffusion and migration – are inadequate for anything beyond recognition that change has occurred across space, with larger structures and larger settlements replacing smaller ones (Carneiro 1970; Haas 1982). Examining how change actually takes place has become a more compelling approach, from Binford's (1982) examination of site structure to contemporary landscape archaeology (Ashmore and Knapp 1999).

In the Norte Chico case, the concept of peer-polity interaction may explain this otherwise puzzling density of sites. Large multi-mound complexes, each up to 100 hectares in area, set close to one another is a pattern not found in other sections of the Peruvian coast. Many of these sites are located in such close proximity that one can be seen from another. Why do these appear only in the Norte Chico during the Late Archaic?

Elements of a peer-polity model

To consider the applicability of the peer-polity model for the Norte Chico region, we must establish the parameters that identify the highest order sociopolitical unit, with the expectation that there will be several of these and that there will be evidence

FIGURE 14.2 Clearing a looter's pit at Pampa San Jose

of interaction among the identified polities. A polity in this region during the Late Archaic consisted of a central place distinguished by the construction of one or more large step-sided mounds built with stone-filled *shicra* bags and one or more circular courts, along with the placement of monoliths, or *huancas*. Around this center, residential areas can be identified. Some of these include stone structures with carefully prepared floors, but other residential areas consist of temporary structures built of canes and woven mats, with floors of tamped earth or clay. Together, the range of structures present and the range of materials incorporated into each of these suggests the mobilization of labor to construct monumental works, a system divided socially into two or more strata and production of goods sufficient to support a resident population as well as a temporary or periodic population of individuals involved in the construction of public works.

The sites identified in the region that fit these parameters display Late Archaic characteristics in different combinations. Late Archaic polities in the Norte Chico were centered on sites having a single mound and circular court, or as many as six mounds and three circular courts. Occasionally, a circular court is found in an isolated location associated with only a small ancillary structure. Fifteen monoliths form a circle around a court area at Caballete, but individual monoliths placed at the top of a mound or by the steps into a circular court are a more common configuration (Figure 14.3). There is variability in the range of elements included in each center and in their arrangement on the landscape, although there is a defining set of features. All are built on a monumental scale.

Renfrew (1986: 7) noted: "when one polity is recognized, other neighbouring polities of comparable scale and organization will be found in the same region." Since starting research in the region, Shady and her colleagues have identified sites in the Supe Valley in addition to Caral that have monumental architecture and date to the Late Archaic (Shady et al. 2003). Testing since 2002 by the Proyecto Arqueologico Norte Chico (PANC) in the valleys to the north of Supe confirmed the presence of 13 pre-ceramic centers in the Fortaleza and Pativilca valleys that date to the Late Archaic period (see Figure 14.1; Creamer et al. 2007, 2013; Haas and Creamer 2006; Haas et al. 2004). Survey by Nelson and Ruiz (2005) in the Huaura Valley recorded eight additional sites with all the hallmarks of the Late Archaic, including step-sided mounds, sunken circular courts, and upright *huanca* monoliths. These and others that have been identified (Vega-Centeno 2005, 2007; Vega-Centeno et al. 1998) show more than 30 Late Archaic centers with monumental architecture in the Norte Chico region as a whole. To date, circular courts have not been identified at Cerro Blanco 1 in the Fortaleza Valley, at Huayto, Potao, and Vinto Alto in the Pativilca Valley, at Lurihuasi in the Supe Valley, or at Cerro Blanco in the Huaura Valley. In half of these cases, circular courts were probably present and have been destroyed by recent agricultural and construction activities (Haas and Creamer 2010). Excavation at four of these sites demonstrates associated habitation areas (Béarez and Miranda 2003: 123–4; Creamer et al. 2007; Flores 2006; Haas and Creamer 2006; Vega-Centeno 2005, 2007; Winker 2011; Wulffen 2009). Thus, in the area we would consider as a zone of peer-polity interaction, which extends from the Huaura Valley in the south to the Fortaleza Valley in the north, there are numerous sites having a range of components that include the defining elements of the Late Archaic.

Identifying peer polities

Among archaeological indicators of interaction are the degree of contemporaneity among sites, a shift in site layout towards a common pattern, and regular site spacing across the landscape. The peer-polity model suggests there will be multiple neighboring polities of comparable size and complexity. By this definition, peer-polities must be contemporaneous or have overlapping occupations. In the case of the Norte Chico, more than 100 radiocarbon dates from Late Archaic mound sites show that the vast majority were built and occupied at roughly the same time (Figure 14.4; Haas et al. 2004), or close enough in time that radiocarbon dating cannot easily distinguish a sequence or direction of construction. Based on these data, we suggest the bulk of the large Late Archaic mound sites in the Norte Chico were occupied during the period from 2400 to 2000 BC and would have constituted peer-polities in temporal terms. Not

FIGURE 14.3 Examples of Norte Chico circular court and mound sites: (a) circular court surrounded by upright monoliths, *huancas*, at Caballete, Fortaleza Valley; (b) mound at Pampa San Jose, Pativilca Valley; (c) mound at Vinto Alto, Pativilca Valley. In (b), the washed-out central slope indicates the main staircase; trees and bushes in the foreground mark the circular court

only have 30 or more large centers been identified, but comparison of their area and architectural components yields a range of sizes with equivocal indications of site hierarchy. There are differences from site to site that are cumulative but that may also be modular. At Caballete, for example, a mound and circular court were constructed in Sector E (Figure 14.5). Another mound and circular court were constructed adjacent to those in Sector E, and later construction was aligned with that in Sector A. At a later date, a third mound and circular court complex was constructed in Sector C. Caballete covers a larger area than sites with a single mound and circular court complex, but, if each complex was built and occupied sequentially, site hierarchy suggested by size is deceptive.

Although as many as 11 mound and circular court sites in the Norte Chico may have been contemporaneous, there is an increase in the total number of mound sites over time. Early on, 3700–2800 cal BC, a maximum of three sites with monumental architecture were occupied at any given time (Table 14.1). By 2700 cal BC there were six, by 2600 cal BC there were seven, and by 2200 cal BC there were 11 contemporaneous sites with monumental architecture in the region. This number continued for at least a century, followed by a decline; three to six sites yielded contemporaneous dates between 2000 and 1700 BC, and after 1600 cal BC there were never again more than three contemporaneous mound and circular court sites.

Site layout provides an example of the variability among centers that is inherent in the peer-polity concept as well as suggesting the development of a basic architectural convention. Some Late Archaic sites have an irregular layout, but in many there is a symmetrical arrangement of structures. A change from individual, overlapping, or irregularly spaced mounds towards a U-shaped layout can be identified at several but not all the centers in the Norte Chico. Huaricanga, for example, consists of overlapping and adjacent mounds. Carreteria and Shaura consist of single

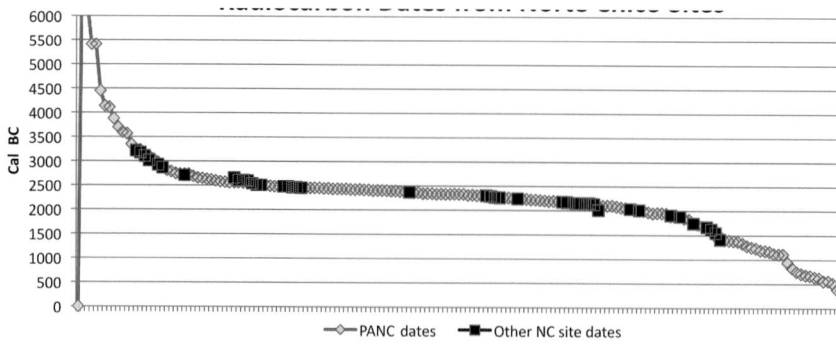

FIGURE 14.4 Radiocarbon dates from Norte Chico sites, showing the concentration of occupation 2500–2000 cal BC PANC sites, N = 67; other radiocarbon dates from Norte Chico region sites, N = 25

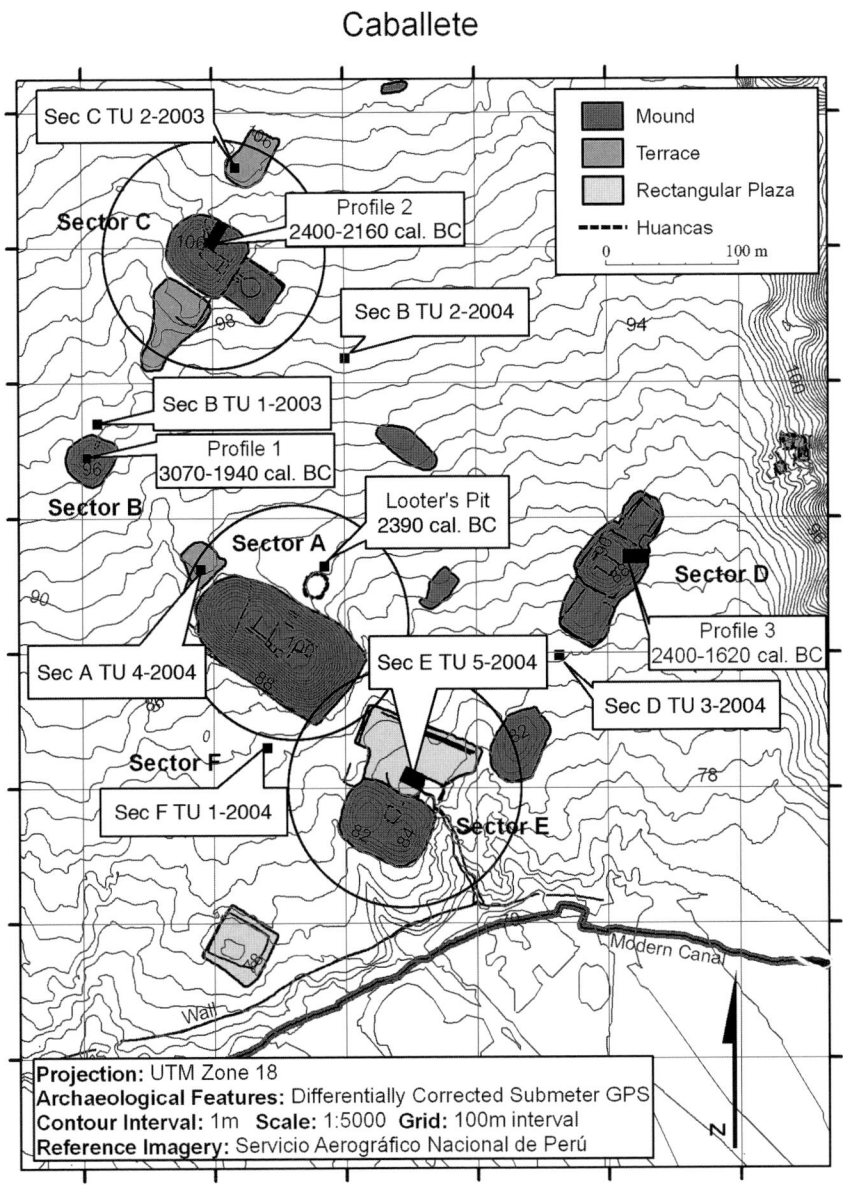

FIGURE 14.5 Caballete, showing "modular" construction; each similarly constructed pyramid and circular court group is circled

TABLE 14.1 Contemporaneity of sites in the Fortaleza and Pativilca valleys based on radiocarbon dates (N = 132)

Sites occupied:	1	1	1	4	4	6	6	8	9	5	3	5	3	3	0	1	2	2	2	2	2	Dated samples
Millennium BC	4th					3rd							2nd									
Cerro Blanco 1																	(3)	(1)★		(2)	(2)	8
Shaura												(1)			(1)	(1)	(1)★					3
Cerro Blanco 2								(1)				(1)	(1)			(1)						3
Carreteria								(1)				(1)										1
Huayto								(2)														2
Pampa San Jose								(1)	(2)		(2)	(2)	(1)									6
Punta y Suela								(1)	(1)						(1)							3
Cerro Lampay						(1)		(8)	(12)	(1)	(4)		(1)									26
Vinto Alto				(2)		(5)	(1)	(1)	(1)			(1)										9
Upaca		(1)		(1)	(1)★	(1)(3)★	(3)	(2)	(1)											(3)		12
Huaricanga		(1)		(1)★	(1)(1)★	(1)(3)★	(2)(1)★	(1)★	(1)★													13
Porvenir		(1)		(1)	(1)	(1)	(2)	(1)	(1)		(1)	(1)	(1)						(1)			12
Caballete	(1)	(1)★	(1)	(1)	(2)(1)★	(3)(1)★	(3)(4)★	(2)	(6)	(4)	(1)	(1)	(1)			(1)						34
Cal BC:	3100	3000	2900	2800	2700	2600	2500	2400	2300	2200	2100	2000	1900	1800	1700	1600	1500	1400	1300	1200	1100	132

Sources: Dates from Cerro Lampay are from Vega Centeno (2005); all others are from PANC research (Haas *et al.* 2004, Creamer *et al.* 2007, 2013).

Notes: Eight samples dated earlier than 3200 cal BC and eight samples dated later than 1000 cal BC were omitted.

★ Dates from charcoal; all others are on annual plant materials.

mound/circular court units. Porvenir, Caballete, and Huayto each have a symmetrical U-shaped arrangement of structures. In some cases the U-shape is a horseshoe of distinct mounds encircling a dry wash (e.g., Lurihuasi), while in others it resembles an open rectangle (e.g., Caballete). A transition from the most irregular arrangements to the U-shaped layout (*templo en U*) becomes the norm for large sites by the beginning of the Initial period, a new institutional feature that accompanied the development of interacting polities (Renfrew 1986: 7).

In addition to considering mound and circular court sites as the centers of polities – determined by the presence of monumental architecture and different types of habitation areas – we can examine the regularity of spacing at a sample of sites. Renfrew (1986: figs 1.1, 1.2) suggests that polities will be regularly spaced on the landscape, an indicator of competition (Hodder and Orton 1976: 46–55). Thiessen polygon analysis shows that the spacing of Late Archaic sites in the Norte Chico is relatively even (Figure 14.6). Although this analysis may not provide a true gauge of land ownership, it shows a spatial relationship consistent with Renfrew's (1986) original model. There also may be a correlation between multi-mound and

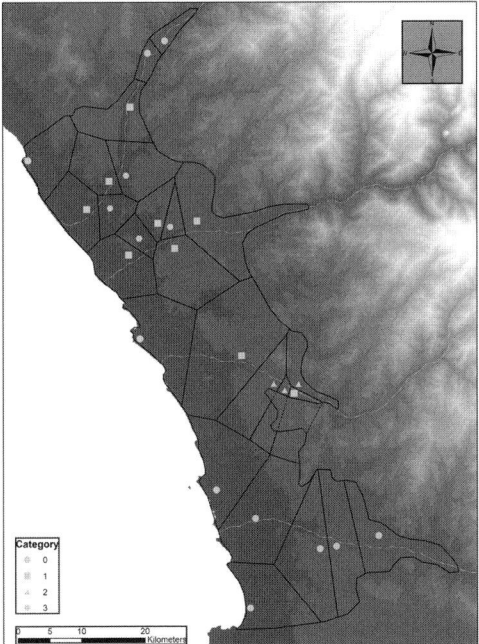

FIGURE 14.6   Thiessen polygon analysis of all identified Late Archaic sites in the Norte Chico: the eastern extent of the boundary is the *chala* zone, at 500 meters above sea level, and the north and south boundaries are the arbitrary extent of the Norte Chico region. The categories correspond to Rutherford's (2008) architectural analysis of Late Archaic sites with cal BC dates. The sites categorized as zero were not measured in Rutherford's analysis. Note the relatively even distribution of site location

single-mound sites and their spatial locations. Rutherford (2008: 70) established three categories of site based on area, the number of structures, and architectural accessibility. He identified nine large (Category 1) sites in three of the four valleys of the Norte Chico, as well as Category 2 and 3 sites, which are smaller and provide easier access to major architectural features (such as sunken circular courts and mound summits). Category 1 and 3 sites show evidence of regular spacing in the Fortaleza and Pativilca valleys (ibid.; Figure 14.6).

The presence of both site hierarchy and regular spacing suggests there was competition among the Category 1 sites and that trade was among the factors involved in the development of the overall system. Rutherford's Category 3 sites are small, generally having a single mound and sunken circular court. Many of these sites are located at approximately the mid-point between pairs of Category 1 sites. Following Christaller, this pattern may occur when, "due to the importance of lines of communication, centres are placed at the midpoints of the roads linking larger centres" (Hodder and Orton 1976: 60). Thus, the distribution of sites suggests regular communication and trade among polities of varying sizes that shared common architectural elements – the mound and sunken circular court – to mark central places.

The spatial relationship between Category 1 and Category 3 sites may also be an indication of a developing and intensifying social hierarchy associated with competition over land and trade routes between 2400 and 2200 cal BC. According to Renfrew (1986: 2), "subordinate units, which may themselves have been independent polities at an earlier time, are often simply administrative or territorial subdivisions." Category 1, 2, and 3 sites are relatively evenly distributed in the region, yet Category 1 sites are distinct in size and organization. This likely reflects the development of polity centralization at sites that eventually contained multiple mounds (e.g., Caballete, Caral, and Pampa San Jose) and the subordination of others where construction ceased before additional mounds were built (e.g., Cerro Lampay, Carreteria, Cerro Blanco 2, and Shaura). The process of hierarchical intensification may have been the result of competition over in-valley trade routes or polity alliances. It may also have been a part of a strategy to increase arable landholdings. Each site was part of a religious complex, a political center for a given territory, and a center for exchange. The system grew rapidly from an initial few sites having these characteristics at 3000 cal BC, peaking at a minimum of 12 contemporaneous interacting polities in 2200 cal BC, and declining to none by 1500 cal BC.

Identifying interaction

The mere presence of similar-sized sites dating to a particular millennium does not demonstrate peer-polity interaction. The distinctive aspect of the peer-polity model is the emphasis on interaction: "the process of transformation is frequently brought about not simply as a result of internal processes … but as a result of interaction between the peer polities" (Renfrew 1986: 8). That is, interaction among sites must be shown along with organizational change. Such interaction may take the form of competition, warfare, competitive emulation, symbolic entrainment, transmission of innovation, and increased flow in the exchange of goods (ibid.: 7–8).

Competition

We must first consider the resources underlying competitive action. Variation in natural resources across the region and variability in subsistence activities are two ways in which competition may arise as individuals diverge from family-based foraging subsistence towards specific productive niches. In the Norte Chico, two resource areas dominated: the shore (the source of marine foods) and the valley bottom (the location of land that could be cultivated). By 3000 BC both zones were occupied, as indicated by the presence of a few mound sites and by the fact that people at shoreline sites used cotton nets for fishing and ate a variety of plant foods. Similarly, middens at inland sites yield cotton fiber, string, and seeds along with fruits, vegetables, and fish bone. These people rarely ate meat from terrestrial animals but regularly ate small fish and shellfish (Haas and Creamer 2006; Shady 2003: 103).

Marine resources available to people living near the shore varied in abundance according to the type of nearby coastal environment (headland or beach), by the weather that affected the waves and the tides, and, occasionally, by El Niño events that changed the range of species available, killed off shellfish species, and caused rain and flooding. The inland resource base depended upon the availability of water. There is evidence for construction of irrigation canals in northern Peru by 3400 BC and perhaps much earlier (Dillehay *et al.* 2005). The size of sites and the volume of plant remains recovered from middens suggest that irrigation technology is likely to have been in use in the Norte Chico region by 3000 BC. The geographic location of sites in the region also indicates an even distribution of arable land. The proximity of agriculturalists who could farm year round to fishing communities who could fish year round creates a situation where both exchange and competition were likely.

Conflict

We have discussed spatial indicators of competition such as settlement pattern and regular spacing. Competition over farmland, fishing areas, or trade routes could lead to the construction of boundary walls or defensive features, such as hilltop sites, fortifications, palisades, ditches, and moats. There is no evidence of these types of defenses among the large Late Archaic polities of the Norte Chico. Sites are located in dry washes or *quebradas* that are often ringed by hills –almost the exact opposite of a defensive location. Other sites are situated at the edge of the valley backing onto natural hills, also a position lacking defensive properties. The absence of defensive features suggests there was no regular inter-site skirmishing and throws cold water on Carneiro's (1970) elegant model for the origins of the state based on warfare in the coastal valleys of Peru. Conflict is not a necessary outcome of competition; it occurs when resources become scarce due to population growth, climate change, or unanticipated changes in local circumstances (Haas and Creamer 1993).

Competitive emulation

Competitive emulation is another possible explanation for the millennium of construction in the Norte Chico. "Neighboring polities may be spurred to ever greater displays of wealth or power in an effort to achieve higher inter-polity status" (Renfrew 1986: 8). The contemporaneous dates, the size of the structures, and the similarity of site layouts resemble Renfrew's description of competitive emulation, as does the close proximity of sites to one another. For example, sites in the Norte Chico were subject to continual remodeling that changed the configuration of space while maintaining the overall layout at both the structure level (Figure 14.7) and the site level, as was shown by the modular composition of Caballete.

Competitive emulation also suggests there was a comparable level of surplus among sites in the Norte Chico and open channels of communication among valleys. Carlson and Craig's (2005) analysis of least-cost pathways across the region suggests that routes of communication appear to have crossed from one valley through the hills rather than following the bed of the river, as paved roads do. Based on their example, Bermejo may have been the source of marine foods consumed at Huaricanga (see Figure 14.1). Why mounds were not constructed in coastal valleys beyond the Norte Chico is problematical if we assume valley margins did not constrain travel. Perhaps natural barriers slowed the spread of the trade network that connected coast and inland sites beyond the region. There is a broad stretch of desert between the mouth of the Fortaleza and Huarmey rivers that may have acted as a barrier to regular contacts. On the southern margin of the Norte Chico,

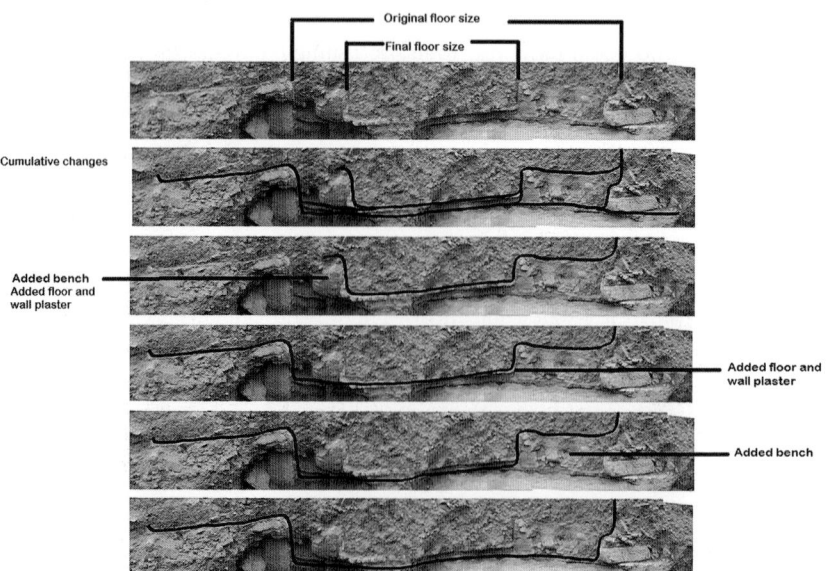

FIGURE 14.7 Sequential remodeling of a temple at Huaricanga

the mouth of the Huaura River is much farther from the mouth of the Río Seco in Chancay than from the other rivers of the Norte Chico, possibly impeding communication and exchange and forming a regional boundary.

Symbolic entrainment

The peer-polity model also suggests mechanisms of interaction that are not based on competition. "Symbolic entrainment" is the "tendency for a developed symbolic system to be adopted when it comes into contact with a less-developed one with which it does not strikingly conflict" (Renfrew 1986: 8). Although we know little of symbolic systems that predate the Late Archaic, there are some indications of continuity of Late Archaic iconography that endured over time. This may represent a first step in the process of symbolic entrainment. Gourd fragments in the Norte Chico engraved with a simple standing figure have been radiocarbon dated to the third millennium BC (Haas *et al.* 2003), and this form is repeated over and over during the following millennia (Figure 14.8). The process of symbolic entrainment may have been a technique used to incorporate groups into regional and pan-regional networks by offering symbols, rituals, and prestige to smaller groups.

FIGURE 14.8 (a) Upright figure with fangs and claws holding a staff, engraved on a gourd fragment from Cerro Pacay in the Norte Chico region; (b) the Raimondi Stela from Chavin de Huantar, showing a fanged deity holding a staff

Transmission of innovation

In addition to the transmission of symbols and prestige, the transmission of innovation among interacting peer-polities may be a key factor in the development of complexity. Irrigation was not "invented" in the Norte Chico, as the recent identification of short irrigation canals in the Zaña Valley suggests (Dillehay et al. 2005). The Zaña find actually strengthens the possible importance of irrigation in the transformation of the Norte Chico. "Either irrigation preceded supravillage aggregation or it did not, and if it followed state formation, then it cannot have been its cause" (Carneiro 1970: 222). Clearly, irrigation preceded state formation on the coast of Peru. It is not the specific invention that is important. Rather, it is the acceptance and spread of the innovation in society (Renfrew 1986: 10). The Norte Chico may not be the place where the first irrigation canal was dug, but it may well be the first region widely to use and rely on the fruits of canal irrigation, with lasting structural effects on society.

We can consider the impact canal irrigation may have had upon this region in expanding the capacity to grow cotton and other agricultural products. As many others have noted, cotton is of particular importance on the coast. When it was spun into string, cotton was used to make nets that are needed to catch the innumerable but tiny fish that were the staff of life. The remains of these species are found in every midden and coprolite that has been tested in the Norte Chico (Haas et al. 2013). To increase the catch would require increasing quantities of cotton string, providing a stimulus for the intensification of canal irrigation to expand fields. Canal irrigation also provided domesticated plant resources that were critical to a balanced diet on the coast. The relationship between irrigated agricultural production and fishing shows economic interaction between parts of the cultural system and provides another key characteristic of peer-polity interaction – the increased exchange of goods. Regional-scale movement of cotton, agricultural products, and fish yielded food for the residents with a surplus that could be converted into durable items, such as large mounds and sunken courts. The need for construction might have been reinforced by leaders invoking civic pride, by entrepreneurs seeking to increase the benefits of exchange, or by priests validating work through ritual. As sites became more numerous while the range of exchange goods stayed the same, a basis for increased competition developed that resulted in more sites, ever more closely spaced, with more mounds, courts, and *huancas*.

Increased flow of exchange

It is difficult to track economic interaction between specific sites in the Norte Chico. The products involved in exchange are well known and consist primarily of cotton, fish, and plant products. The details of how these goods circulated remain to be identified and require sourcing techniques that are still being developed (cf. Benson et al. 2008; Cordell et al. 2001). The presence of fish and shellfish remains confirms that marine foods arrived at inland sites. Moreover, the distance of these

FIGURE 14.9 Stela at Huaricanga (photo by J. Haas) and the Lanzon, Chavin de Huantar (after Tello 1923)

sites from the shore suggests exchange as the most likely mechanism (Creamer *et al.* 2011). At the same time, surplus generated in the Norte Chico – in the form of fish, shellfish, cotton, and plant foods – appears to have been employed in exchange and to support individuals involved in the numerous regional construction projects. There is little evidence of surplus converted to craft production or the development of craft specialists. There is a notable absence of ceramic production, loom-weaving, painting, bead-making, shell-working, and other crafts. Workshops for weaving cane bags, mats, and rope are the only specialized work areas yet identified (Creamer *et al.* 2013). Stone carving produced masonry blocks and roughly shaped monoliths, with none of the elaboration found at later sites such as Cerro Sechin, Caballo Muerto, or Chavin (Figure 14.9).

Conclusion: peer-polity interaction in the Norte Chico

The Norte Chico consisted of a number of interacting units that, based on their architectural components, the distribution of sites across the region, and evidence of ongoing exchange, may be described as peer-polities. In addition to exchange contacts, competitive efforts to attract participants to a site may have included planning ever larger monumental complexes, organizing ritual activities, and producing a sufficient volume of goods to keep the process going. One way to enhance the volume of production would have been to expand irrigated areas.

In the Norte Chico, the impetus for expansion and change may well have been technological as irrigation agriculture spread, perhaps accompanied by ritual and symbols associated with new knowledge and prestige. The scale of monument construction compared to the areas of habitation at most sites suggests a periodic influx of people from a large sustaining area (Wulffen 2009). As shown here, by 2400 cal BC, monumental structures were relatively closely spaced in the Norte Chico, suggesting that there was active competition among centers for labor. At the same time, there is no evidence at present for the development of a class of laborers who worked in construction full-time like the pyramid-builders of ancient Egypt.

After achieving the level of complexity indicated by monumental structures, sunken courts, and *huancas*, the number of contemporary and competing polities in the regional system increased over time to a maximum around 2100 cal BC. Further changes in complexity may have been taking place among the peer-polities of the region that led to expansion beyond the Norte Chico and the end of the Late Archaic period. Changes in complexity are accompanied by novel institutional features (Renfrew 1986: 7–8), and, at three of the centers occupied the longest, sunken square temples, or "Mito temples," have been identified (Haas *et al.* 2010; Shady and Macachuay 2003). These may mark the next level of institutional complexity in the region.

The model of peer-polity interaction is reflected in the Norte Chico region during the Late Archaic period but ceases to describe the region effectively after about 2000 cal BC. By this time, several of the factors that contributed to the formation of peer-polities had changed. Irrigation technology seems to have been adopted in other valleys, such as the Chillon and Casma. If there had been a substantially larger population in the Norte Chico region than elsewhere, those differences diminished as irrigation technology made it possible to support increasing populations in other coastal valleys. The effective exchange network contributed to the development of increasingly hierarchical society. In later times, this was marked by non-local status markers, such as *Spondylus spp.* shell beads, found in much greater numbers than during the Late Archaic. Further, there is evidence for craft specialization within the Norte Chico as pottery production was introduced, along with loom-weaving, figurine-crafting, bead-making, and metallurgy. Perhaps the conclusive end of the Norte Chico as a region of peer-polities came with the expansion of interregional relationships and the development of ever more complex political units beyond the boundaries of the region.

Note

1 The authors gratefully acknowledge support from the National Science Foundation (Collaborative Research Grants 0211010 and 0542088 to Creamer and Haas), the Center for Latino and Latin American Studies at Northern Illinois University (grants to Creamer and to Rutherford), the Field Museum, and wonderful friends of the Proyecto Arqueológico Norte Chico.

References

Ashmore, Wendy, and A. Bernard Knapp (1999) *Archaeologies of Landscape: Contemporary Perspectives*. Malden, MA: Blackwell.

Béarez, Philippe, and Luis Miranda (2003) Analisis arqueo-ictiologico del sector residencial del sitio arqueologico de Caral-Supe, Costa Central del Peru. In *La ciudad sagrada del Caral-Supe: los orígenes de la civilización andina y la formación del estado prístino en el antiguo Perú*, ed. Ruth Shady and C. Leyva, pp. 123–32. Lima: Instituto Nacional de Cultura.

Benson, Larry, Howard Taylor, K. A. Peterson, B. D. Shattuck, Cindy Ramotnik, and John Stein (2008) Development and Evaluation of Geochemical Methods for the Sourcing of Archaeological Maize. *Journal of Archaeological Science* 35: 912–21.

Binford, Lewis (1982) The Archaeology of Place. *Journal of Anthropological Archaeology* 1: 5–31.

Bonavia, Duccio (1982) *Los Gavilanes: mar, desierto y oásis en la historia del hombre: precerámico peruano*. Lima: Ausonia.

Carlson, Keith, and Nathan Craig (2005) Late Preceramic Mound Site Locational Patterning in the Norte Chico of Coastal Peru: A GIS Approach. Paper presented at the 70th annual meeting of the Society of American Archaeology, Salt Lake City.

Carneiro, Robert L. (1970) A Theory of the Origin of the State. *Science* 189: 733–8.

Cordell, Linda, Steven Durand, Ronald Antweiler, and Howard Taylor (2001) Toward Linking Maize Chemistry to Archaeological Agricultural Sites in the North American Southwest. *Journal of Archaeological Science* 28: 501–13.

Creamer, Winifred, Alvaro Ruiz and Jonathan Haas (2007) *Archaeological Investigation of Late Archaic Sites (3000–1800 BC) in the Pativilca Valley, Peru*. Fieldiana: Anthropology (n.s.) no. 40.

Creamer, Winifred, Jonathan Haas, Edward Jakaitis III, and Jesus Holguin (2011) Far from the Shore: Comparison of Marine Invertebrates in Midden Deposits from Two Sites in the Norte Chico, Peru. *Journal of Island and Coastal Archaeology* 6(2): 176–95.

Creamer, Winifred, Alvaro Ruiz, Manuel Perales Munguía, and Jonathan Haas (2013) *The Fortaleza Valley, Peru: Archaeological Investigation of Late Archaic Sites (3000–1800 BC)* Fieldiana: Anthropology (n.s.), no. 44.

Dillehay, Tom D., Herbert H. Elling, Jr., and Jack Rossen (2005) Preceramic Irrigation Canals in the Peruvian Andes. *Proceedings of the National Academy of Sciences* 102(47): 17241–4.

Engel, Frederic (1966) Le complexe précéramique d'el Paraiso (Pérou). *Journal de la Société des Américanistes* 55(1): 43–95.

—— (1987) *De las begonias al maíz: vida y producción en le Perú antiguo*. Lima: Universidad Agraria La Molina.

Flores, Luis (2006) Estudio de Unidades Residenciales en el subsector 12 de Caral, Valle de Supe, Peru. Licenciatura thesis in Archaeology, UNMSM, Lima.

Fuchs, Peter R., Renate Patzschke, Germán Yenque y Jesús Briceño (2010) Del Arcaico Tardío al Formativo Temprano: las investigaciones en Sechín Bajo. In *El Period Formativo: enfoques y evidencias recientes: cincuenta años de la misión arqueológica japonesa y su vigencia*, Part 2, ed. Peter Kaulicke and Yoshio Onuki, pp. 55–86. Lima: Fondo Editorial de la Pontificia Universidad Católica del Perú.

Haas, Jonathan (1982) *The Evolution of the Prehistoric State*. New York: Columbia University Press.

Haas, Jonathan, and Winifred Creamer (1993) *Stress and Warfare among the Kayenta Anasazi of the Thirteenth Century AD*. Fieldiana: Anthropology (n.s.) no. 21.

—— (2006) The Crucible of Andean Civilization. *Current Anthropology* 47: 745–75.

—— (2010) Reuse of Late Archaic (3000–1800 BC) Monument Sites in the Norte Chico Region of Peru. Paper presented at the 75th annual meeting of the Society for American Archaeology, St Louis.

Haas, Jonathan, Winifred Creamer, and Alvaro Ruiz (2003) Gourd Lord. *Archaeology* 56(3): 19.

—— (2004) Dating the Late Archaic Occupation of the Norte Chico Region in Peru. *Nature* 32: 1020–23.

—— (2010) Late Archaic Temples in the Norte Chico Region of Peru. Paper presented at the 38th annual meeting of the Midwest Conference on Andean and Amazonian Archaeology and Ethnohistory, Indiana University–Purdue University, Fort Wayne.

Haas, Jonathan, Winifred Creamer, Luis Huaman, David Goldstein, Karl Reinhard, Cindy Vergel, and Alvaro Ruiz (2013) Evidence for Maize (*Zea mays*) in the Late Archaic (3000–1800 BC) in the Norte Chico Region of Peru. Proceedings of the National Academy of Science, www.pnas.org/cgi/doi/10.1073/

Hodder, Ian, and Clive Orton (1976) *Spatial Analysis in Archaeology*. Cambridge: Cambridge University Press.

Kosok, Paul (1965) *Land, Life and Water in Ancient Peru*. New York: Long Island University Press.

Nelson, Kit, and Alvaro Ruiz (2005) Proyecto de investigación arqueológica: Valle de Huaura, Perú. Report deposited in the Instituto Nacional de Cultura, Lima.

Perales Munguía, Manuel F. (2006) Proyecto de investigación: reconocimiento arqueológico en el Valle Bajo de Pativilca, Lima, Perú. Report filed at the Instituto Nacional de Cultura, Lima.

—— (2007) Proyecto de investigación: reconocimiento arqueológico en el Valle de Fortaleza, Lima-Ancash, Perú. Report filed at the Instituto Nacional de Cultura, Lima.

Pozorski, Shelia, and Thomas Pozorski (1990) Reexamining the Critical Preceramic/Ceramic Period Transition: New Data from Coastal Peru. *American Anthropologist* 92: 481–91.

Quilter, Jeffrey (1985) Architecture and Chronology at El Paraiso, Peru. *Journal of Field Archaeology* 12: 179–97.

Renfrew, Colin (1986) Introduction: Peer-Polity Interaction And Sociopolitical Change. In *Peer Polity Interaction and Sociopolitical Change*, ed. Colin Renfrew and John Cherry, pp. 1–18. Cambridge: Cambridge University Press.

Rutherford, Allen (2008) Space and Landscape in the Norte Chico Region, Peru: An Analysis of Socio-Political Organization through Monumental Architecture. MA thesis, Department of Anthropology, Northern Illinois University.

Service, Elman (1975) *Origins of the State and Civilization*. New York: W. W. Norton.

Shady, Ruth (2003) El sustento económico del surgimiento de la civilización en el Perú. In *La ciudad sagrada del Caral-Supe: los orígenes de la civilización andina y la formación del estado prístino en el antiquo Perú*, ed. Ruth Shady and Carlos Leyva, pp. 101–5. Lima: Instituto Nacional de Cultura.

Shady, Ruth, and Carlos Levya (eds) (2003) *La ciudad sagrada del Caral-Supe: los orígenes de la civilización andina y la formación del estado prístino en el antiquo Perú*. Lima: Instituto Nacional de Cultura.

Shady, Ruth, and Marcos Macachuay (2003) El Altar del Fuego Sagrado del Templo Mayor de la Ciudad Sagrada de Caral-Supe. In *La ciudad sagrada del Caral-Supe: los orígenes de la civilización andina y la formación del estado prístino en el antiquo Perú*, ed. Ruth Shady and Carlos Leyva, pp. 169–85. Lima: Instituto Nacional de Cultura.

Shady, Ruth, Jonathan Haas, and Winifred Creamer (2001) Dating Caral, a Preceramic Urban Center in the Supe Valley on the Central Coast of Peru. *Science* 292: 723–6.

Shady, Ruth, Camilo Dolorier, Fanny Montesinos, and Lyda Casas (2003) Los orígenes de la civilización en el Perú: el área norcentral y el valle de Supe durante el Arcaico Tardío. In *La ciudad sagrada del Caral-Supe: los orígenes de la civilización andina y la formación del estado prístino en el antiquo Perú*, ed. Ruth Shady and Carlos Leyva, pp. 51–91. Lima: Instituto Nacional de Cultura.

Tello, Julio C. (1923) Wira Kocha. *Inca* [Universidad Nacional Mayor de San Marcos, Lima] 1: 93–320.

Vega-Centeno, Rafael (2005) *Ritual and Architecture in a Context of Emergent Complexity: A Perspective from Cerro Lampay, a Late Archaic Site in the Central Andes*. PhD dissertation, Department of Anthropology, University of Arizona. Ann Arbor, MI: University Microfilms.

—— (2007) Construction, Labor Organization, and Feasting during the Late Archaic Period in the Central Andes. *Journal of Anthropological Archaeology* 26: 150–71.

Vega-Centeno, Rafael, Luis F. Villacorta, Luis E. Cáceres, and Giancarlo Marcone (1998) Arquitectura monumental temprana en el valle medio de Fortaleza. *Boletín Arqueológico* 2: 219–38.

Wendt, W. (1964) Die präkeramische Siedlung am Rio Seco, Peru. *Baessler Archiv* (n.s.) 11(2): 225–75.

Winker, Rebecca (2011) Searching for Function and Social Hierarchy at Operación VI, Caballete, Norte Chico Region, Peru. MA thesis, Department of Anthropology, Northern Illinois University, DeKalb.

Wulffen, Jennifer (2009) Two Test Excavations at Caballete, Norte Chico, Peru. MA thesis, Department of Anthropology, Northern Illinois University, Dekalb.

Zechenter, Elzbieta (1988) *Subsistence Strategies in the Supe Valley of the Peruvian Central Coast during the Complex Preceramic and Initial Periods*. PhD dissertation, Department of Anthropology, University of California, Los Angeles. Ann Arbor, MI: University Microfilms.

INDEX

2012 (December 21, 2012), end of 13th Baktun 231, 235

Aguateca, Guatemala 207, 300
Aimers, James A. xvii, 15
Akhetatan, Egypt 30
Algaze, Guillermo 115–16, 141
Alotenango, Guatemala 117, 119, 130, 142
   ceramics 136
   settlement 123, 131–4, 144
   Volcano 5
Alta Verapaz, Guatemala 4, 105, 179, 184, 187, 206–7
Altar de Sacrificios, Guatemala 4–5, 104, 177–80, 183, 187, 189–90, 193, 207, 310
Alvarado, Pedro and Jorge de 69
Andrews V., E. Wyllys 2–5, 7–8, 10, 12–14, 17, 25–8, 30–3, 36–41, 43–4, 46–7, 49, 56–7, 59–60, 63, 65, 68, 150, 171, 177–9, 195–7, 201, 223, 234–5, 238, 301, 308–10, 330, 335, 394
   coffee mug 223–4, 229–38
Antigua, Guatemala 6–7, 107, 119–21, 123–4, 142, 150–1, 159–62, 169–71
   ceramic chronology 127–8, 136, 143, 152–3, 162–3, 165–6
   environment 134–6, 152, 167
   radiocarbon dates 121, 167
   sculpture 7, 121, 158, 164, 167–9
   settlement 123, 131, 133, 140, 143–4, 153, 167
   site typology 123, 154–8
Aquino, Valorie 143

Archaic Period 4–5, 8–9, 115, 121, 138, 405–22
   corn pollen 138
   Lowe point, Belize 249
   in Peru 405–22
architecture 2, 4, 6, 9, 11, 26, 27, 29, 31, 194, 308, 335, 340, 344, 346, 349, 410, 412, 415
   in Archaic Peru 9
   at Cancuen 207, 209–10, 214–15
   construction techniques 31, 40
   of Kaqchikel region 6, 132, 138, 151, 153, 167, 170
   popol nahs or council houses 335–52
   at Quelepa 7, 27, 29, 40–5, 59–62, 65
   in southern Belize 248–9, 257, 296
   styles at Chichen Itza 359, 360, 363, 366, 368–73, 383, 386–9, 391–2
arenas, public 43, 49
Armillas, Pedro 27, 37–8, 56
Ashmore, Wendy xvii, 7, 17
audience chamber, Cancuen 212, 214
Avocado, Kingdom of (*see also* Pusilha) 10, 270, 277
Awe, Jaime 196, 262
Aztecs 1, 47, 360

Bagaces Period 67
Baking Pot, Belize 308
Balankanche Cave, Mexico 377–9, 383, 390

ballcourt, ballgame 12, 47–8, 57, 61–2, 65, 168–9, 181, 336, 347, 350–1
  at Cancuen 212–17
  at Chichen Itza 328, 358, 360, 364, 372–3, 378
  in Kaqchikel region 153, 155, 157, 160–3, 170
  at Pusilha and southern Belize 248, 250, 253, 256–8, 267, 276, 285, 296, 298
  at Quelepa 30–1, 34, 37, 39–40, 42–3, 45, 61–2
Barnes, Edwin 263, 265, 301
basin monoliths 32–4
"Bayesianized" dates 16, 117, 356–7, 380–2
Benavides C., Antonio 345
Berlin, Heinrich 269
Bermejo, Peru 418
Bey, George J., III xvii, 11, 47, 337, 394
Bezanilla, Clara 301
Bilbao, Guatemala 601, 166–7
Bill, Cassandra R. xvii, 12–14, 252, 270, 301
Blackman Eddy, Belize 4–5,
Blom, Frans 233, 235, 237–8
bloodletting 39
boatmen at Cancuen 210
border, definition 58–9
botija 73
Braswell, Geoffrey E. i, xvii–xvii, 166, 171, 301
Braswell, Jennifer B. 301
British Museum (*see also* Pusilha) 252, 267

C-shaped structures 11, 349–52
Caballete, Peru 410–16, 418
Caballo Muerto, Peru 421
cacao 30, 72–3, 151, 236
Cahal Pech, Belize 4–5, 177–80, 183–5, 187–9, 191–6
Cahokia, USA 130
Calakmul, Mexico 10, 12, 204, 207, 227, 232, 289, 298, 300
  rulers 224, 227, 232
  Snake Dynasty 10, 224, 227
calendar round dates 10, 225, 228–31, 233–5, 296, 300
  earliest at Chichen Itza 373
  impossible date at Pusilha 296–8
  latest at Chichen Itza 374
calibration, Bayesian method (*see* "Bayesianized" dates)
camino real 75
Campeche, Mexico xix, 62, 246, 248, 311
Cancuen, Guatemala xviii, 11–12, 102, 105, 201–18, 247
  monuments 204, 214–16

Cara Sucia, El Salvador 32, 60
Caracol, Belize 227, 245–6, 271, 281, 299–300
Caral, Peru 408, 410, 416
Caribbean Sea 15, 66, 201, 217–18, 246,
Carniero, Robert L. 9, 417
Carreteria, Peru 412, 414, 416
Casma Valley, Peru 408, 422
caves 32–3, 135, 159, 169, 204, 247–8, 254, 257, 258, 262 298, 377, 379, 383, 390
celts, stone 37–8
censers 38, 40, 46, 48, 96, 99, 101–4, 106, 126, 165, 391
ceramic chronology, revised
  Chichen Itza 16, 363, 365–8, 394–5
  Preclassic Kaminaljuyu 117–18, 136–7, 143
ceramics *see* pottery
Cerezeda, Andrés de 69
Cerritos de Izapa, Guatemala 123–4
Cerro Blanco (Huaura Valley), Peru 410
  Cerro Blanco 1 410, 414
  Cerro Blanco 2 414, 416
Cerro Palenque, Honduras 30, 66
Cerro Sechin, Peru 421
Chac II, Mexico 342
Chalchuapa, El Salvador 27, 30–1, 43, 66, 142
Chancay Valley, Peru 408, 419
Chavin, Peru 419, 421
Cheek, Charles 344
Chiapas, Mexico 4, 12, 62, 106, 129, 133, 150, 178, 180, 207–8, 210, 215, 245, 247
Chichen Itza, Mexico xix, 12–13, 15–17, 30, 298, 313–15, 317–18, 320, 322, 325–9, 356–395
  Akab Dzib 360, 365, 367, 369, 373–5
  Caracol 360, 362–3, 370, 373–6, 388, 390, 394
  Castillo 16, 358, 360, 366, 368, 370–2, 377–9, 381–3, 387–9
  ceramic phases 362–8, 370, 379, 384–91, 394–5
  collapse of 361, 390–3
  Early Chichen style 365, 367–9, 386–7
  early occupation 368, 386, 390–1
  Great Ballcourt 358, 360, 372–3, 384
  Great Terrace 17, 356–8, 360, 365–6, 368–70, 372, 377–9, 381–3, 387, 389–90, 393, 395
  Group of the Initial Series 365, 368, 373, 375–6, 386–7, 389

Chichen Itza, Mexico *cont.*
    Group of the Thousand Columns 358, 360, 372
    Group of the Three Lintels 365, 369, 371, 373, 375, 391
    hieroglyphic texts 356, 367, 369, 373–8, 380–4, 386–9, 391–2
    High Priest's Grave 372–4, 376, 383, 389, 391
    House of the Phalli 365, 375
    House of the Stuccoes 368, 386,
    Huuntun-Cehpech phase 365–7, 387–8
    Iglesia 377–8, 381–2
    International style 17, 359, 368, 370, 372–6, 379, 383–4, 388–90, 392
    Lower Temple of the Jaguars 358, 370
    Maya period 360
    Maya style 16, 359, 366, 369–73, 375–6, 378, 381–4, 386–9, 392
    Monjas Complex 360, 368–9, 373–5, 377, 381, 390
    Monjas East Annex 377–8, 381–2
    obsidian 386
    occupation phases 386–91
    Slate Ware *see* ceramics
    Sotuta phase 15–17, 362–3, 365–8, 374–6, 379, 383–5, 387–92, 395
    Stela 2 374–5
    Temple of the Big Tables 360, 370
    Temple of the Four Lintels 369, 374–5
    Temple of the Hieroglyphic Jambs 373–6
    Temple of the Initial Series 368, 373, 375–6, 386
    Temple of the Owls 374, 389
    Temple of the Three Lintels 365, 369, 371, 373, 375, 391
    tenth-century hiatus 16, 356, 388, 391–2
    Toltec-Maya period 360, 363
    traditional chronology 360
    Transitional-style architecture 370–1, 383, 387–8, 391
    and Tula 360, 393
    Yabnal-Motul phase 16, 365–6, 368, 375, 384–8, 392, 394–5
Chilam Balam, Books of 360–2
Chilibrillo Cave, Panama 135
Chillon Valley, Peru 422
Chimaltenango, Guatemala 5, 115, 117, 119–20, 123, 128, 143, 159, 169
Chitak Tzak, Guatemala 120, 142
Choatalum, Guatemala 120
Chocola, Guatemala 116, 141–3
Ch'olan Mayan 131, 234–5
Chuisac, Guatemala 120–1

circular court 405, 408–13, 415–16
cistern, Cancuen 214–15
Ciudad Vieja, El Slavador 66, 70
Cival, Guatemala 181, 183
Colas, Pierre Robert 301
Colha, Belize 4, 313, 318
collapse *see* Maya Collapse; Preclassic Period
collective memory 228–9
Comayagua Valley, Honduras 59, 66–7, 103
competitive emulation 9, 407, 417–19
compositional tracing 203
conflict 9, 11, 61, 64, 70, 158–60, 170, 204, 228, 407, 417, 419
Copan, Honduras 2, 8, 10, 12–15, 17, 30–1, 39–40, 42–4, 46, 48, 63–7, 83–106, 137, 225, 228–9, 245, 248, 270, 277, 280, 283, 289, 291, 294, 297–301, 337–9, 343–4, 349
    Acbi phase 89, 92, 101
    collapse of 12–15, 83–4, 87, 94, 96–8, 104–6
    Early Coner phase 84–7, 89, 95
    Ejar phase 13, 17, 98–105
    Late Coner phase 12–13, 86–96, 106
    relations with southern Belize 270, 283, 291, 294, 298–301
    Str. 10L–22A 337–9
    Str. 10L–223 338–9, 343–4
    Terminal Coner phase 12, 88–98
corbelled vault 212, 248
Córdoba, Francisco Hernández de 70
corn pollen 121, 138
Cortés y Larraz, Archbishop 76–7
cosmos 32, 36–7
Cotzumalguapa 152–3, 169
    Region 7, 152–3, 170
    sculpture 7, 151, 164, 167–9
council house (*see also popol nah*) 11, 335–6, 339–40, 344–5, 349, 351–2
crafting 210, 394, 422
Creamer, Winifred xviii, 2, 8–9, 49
creation narratives, Maya 37
Cuello, Belize 4, 178–9, 187–9, 309
Cueva, Cristóbal de 69

Dávila, Gil González 70
Dávila, Pedrarías 69
defensive features 6, 150, 159, 212, 417
    in Huista-Acatec region 150, 154, 159
    in Kaqchikel region 151, 159–60, 169–70
Demarest, Arthur A. xviii, 11–12
dendritic economy 66–7, 169

Department of Middle American Research 233, 237–8
deposition contexts 31, 34–40, 44–5
derrotero 71
discs 37–9
Dos Pilas, Guatemala 12, 14, 204, 207, 214, 236
Duby, Gertrude 233
Dunham, Peter 252
dynastic vases 10, 223–5, 227–30, 232–8
Dziadaszek, Bonnie 301
Dzibanche, Mexico 227
Dzibilchaltun, Mexico 308, 338, 345–6, 348, 388
   Str. 42 343
   Str. 44 343, 346, 348

Early Classic 7–8, 13, 29, 60, 62, 65, 90, 101, 117–18, 120, 125, 131, 133–4, 136, 152, 165, 167–8, 181, 183, 227, 248, 250, 258, 297–9, 301, 343, 348, 356, 362, 364, 379, 381, 386, 391
   at Calakmul 227
   at Chichen Itza 362, 364, 379, 381, 386, 391
   at Copan 13, 90, 101
   in Maya highlands 117–18, 120, 125, 131, 133–4, 136, 152, 165, 167–8
   origin of *popol nahs* 337, 348
   at Quelepa 29, 60, 62, 65
   in southern Belize 248, 250, 258, 298–9, 301
Early Postclassic Period 12–13, 15–17, 68, 83, 98–106, 134, 152, 311, 313, 356, 358, 360, 388–9, 391–3
   at Chichen Itza 16–17, 356, 358, 360, 388–9, 391–3
   at Copan 12–13, 83, 98–105
   definition of 104–5, 389, 392
   at Lamanai 15, 17
Early Preclassic Period 4, 6, 9, 115, 117–18, 121–3, 126, 138, 196
Early Puuc Ceremonial Complexes 343, 345
Early Puuc-style architecture 340, 346
Eberl, Markus xviii, 10, 283, 291, 301
Edzna, Mexico 345–6
Ek Balam, Mexico xvii, 335, 337–40, 343, 345–6, 348–51, 353, 388
   GS-12 350–1
   GT-19 339
   GT-20 337–40, 343, 345–6, 349
   Sacrificios Group 350
El Baul, Guatemala 164–5, 167–8
El Boquerón eruption 62
El Castillo, Guatemala 164, 167–8
El Chayal obsidian source 129–30, 137–9, 142, 166, 206, 263
El Hato, Guatemala 160–2
El Mirador, Guatemala 13, 207, 227, 286
El Paraiso, Peru 408
El Perén, Guatemala 120
El Peru/Waka, Guatemala 204, 207
El Portal, Guatemala 153, 156, 159, 161–2, 169
El Raudal, Guatemala 207
El Ujuxte, Guatemala 142
emblem glyph (*see also* Maya rulers) 10, 225, 227, 232, 235, 238, 245–7, 266, 269–71, 274–7, 280, 289–92, 294, 296, 300–1
   of Pusilha 266, 269–71, 274–7, 280, 289–92, 294, 296, 300
enclaves, ethnic 46
Encuesta Arqueológica del Área Kaqchikel (EAK) 119–20, 154
epigraphy xviii, 202, 345, 301, 356

feasting 62, 165, 216–17
feathered serpent *see* Quetzalcoatl/Kukulkan
fire 44, 168, 283, 383, 390
flutes, ceramic 47
Fortaleza Valley, Peru 407, 410–11, 414, 416, 418
four-sided (four-part) figures 32–3, 35, 37
Frazier, Brittany 301
frontiers and boundaries i, xix, 7–8, 11, 56–63, 65, 67, 69, 77, 83, 150–1, 169–70, 300
   definition 58, 170
   in eastern El Salvador 7–8, 56–63, 65, 67, 69, 77
   in Kaqchikel region 7, 150–1, 169–70

gallery-patio structures 370, 374, 376, 379, 382–3, 387
Gann, Thomas 267
García García, Edgar Vinicio 119, 143
Garníca, Marlen 142, 171
Gates, William E. 223, 233, 237
Gateway Hill Acropolis, Pusilha 250, 254–8, 260, 262, 281–2, 298
Gibbs, Sherry 301
Golondrinas Rockshelter, Guatemala 118, 123, 142, 168–9
Graña Behrens, Daniel 301
Greenstone *see* jade/jadeite
Grube, Nikolai 301
Guatemala, Santiago de 69–70

Gulf Coast, Mexico 15, 40, 43–4, 47, 62, 65, 67–8, 103, 178, 195, 207, 210–11, 247, 308–9, 311, 320, 327, 393
Gunn, Christopher 349

Haas, Jonathan xviii
hachas 47, 62, 65
Hack, William 71
  Atlas 8, 56, 71–6
Hammond, Norman 252
head of navigation 11, 207, 209–12, 217
hematite 5, 39, 184, 187, 189, 259, 261
hieroglyphic writing 1, 7, 10, 16–17, 57, 83, 86–7, 133, 214, 223–6, 228–32, 235–6, 245–8, 250, 252, 256, 267–300, 356, 373, 376–8, 380–4, 386, 389, 392
  content debate 228–9, 236
highlands
  of Guatemala i, xix, 1, 3, 5–7, 9, 11, 39, 62–3, 66, 88, 92, 103, 105, 115–71, 177, 201, 203–4, 207–10, 215–16, 233, 335, 350–1
  of Mexico 178
Holmul, Guatemala xviii, 4–5, 177–9, 181–5, 187–90, 192–6
  K'awil ceramic complex 5, 177, 183–4, 187, 190, 192, 194–5
Huanca (monolith), Peru 409–11, 420, 422
Huaricanga, Peru 412, 414, 418, 421
Huarmey Valley, Peru 408, 418
Huaura Valley, Peru xix, 407, 410, 419
Huayto, Peru 410, 414–15
Hughbanks, Paul 143
Hunac Ceel 361
Huntichmul, Mexico 342, 344–5, 350–1

iconography 31, 60, 167, 194, 202, 270, 274–6, 289, 326, 347, 349, 419
  jaguar, serpent, water 32
iconological style 180–1, 194–5
Ilopango eruption 31, 62
impossible calendar round dates 296–8
indigo 70–3, 75–6
inhabitation 7, 26, 45
Initial Period (Peru) 408, 415
Inomata, Takeshi 117, 143
interaction sphere 12, 62, 66, 94, 104, 322, 324–6
internationalism 213, 389, 392
Isla Cerritos, Mexico 313, 325, 330, 385, 390
isochrestic style 180, 195
isotopic analysis 46, 259
Itza Maya 15, 311, 326, 360–1, 388, 391, 393
Izapa, Mexico 27, 32, 60, 142

jade/jadeite 12, 36–8, 65, 204, 209–10, 217, 258–9, 263–4, 266, 298
Jaguar Altar *see* Quelepa
Janaab Pakal (Palenque ruler) 228
Jiquilisco, Bay of 70, 75
Joyce, Thomas A. 267

K'ak' U Ti' Chan (Pusilha ruler) 281–7
K'ak'upakal (Chichen Itza ruler) 365, 375–6, 387
Kalomte'/Kaloomte' (*see also* Maya rulers) 225, 277, 290–1, 300, 345–6, 348, 352
Kaminaljuyu 4, 6, 14, 27, 32, 46, 60, 115–19, 121, 125–31, 133–43, 150, 152–3, 166, 170, 189
  Arenal complex 130, 133, 136–8
  Arevalo complex 6, 130
  La Culebra mounds 126
  Majadas phase, status 117
  monuments 116, 120, 125–6, 143
  obsidian artifacts of 128, 130, 137–9, 141–2
  Providencia complex 117–18, 126, 128, 139
  Verbena complex 118, 136
Kaqchikel region xviii–xix, 3, 5–7, 115–44, 150–71, 189
k'atun 235, 274, 289, 294, 296, 361–2
k'atun-age 280–3, 285, 287, 299
K'awiil (Maya god) 230
  "grasping the … scepter" (Maya accession statement) 230, 232
K'awiil Chan K'inich (Dos Pilas ruler) 214, 236
K'awil Chan K'inich (Pusilha ruler) 276–83, 285, 287, 291
king lists 10, 223, 227–9, 235–8
K'inich BakVs 292, 294
K'inich Yax K'uk' Mo' (Copan ruler) 31, 229
K'inil Kopol (Chichen Itza noble) 375
Kiuic, Mexico xvii–xviii, 4, 178, 186, 188, 193, 335–7, 340–6, 348, 350, 352–3
  N1015E1015 336–7, 340–4, 348, 352
  N1065E1025 340, 346
  Plaza Dzunun 340
  Yaxche Palace 340, 343
K'iche'an peoples 7, 117, 131, 133, 140, 170
  interaction with neighbors 7, 131, 170
  migrations 117, 133, 140
Kokom 375
Komchen, Mexico 2, 4, 177–8, 186–8, 193
K'uhul ajaw (*see also* Maya rulers) 204, 214–15, 225, 232, 266, 271, 285, 287
k'uhul tun 281, 285

Kukulcan *see* Quetzalcoatl/Kukulkan
Kumal, Mexico 346, 348

La Corona 204, 235,
La Laguneta, El Salvador 42–3
La Sufricaya, Guatemala 181, 297
La Venta, Mexico 35, 46, 139
Labna, Mexico xviii, 335, 337, 340–2, 344–9, 353
   Str. 7 337, 340–2, 347–9
   Mirador xviii, 340
labor investment 40–1, 62, 408–9, 422
Lake Amatitlan, Guatemala 134
Lake Miraflores, Guatemala 133
Lake Quilisimate, Guatemala 121, 134
Lamanai, Belize 13, 15–17, 106, 308–9, 311–20, 322–30
   Buk phase 15, 17, 311, 318
   Cib phase 326
   surviving the collapse 13, 15
land routes 204, 207–8, 210, 215
landscape xix, 5, 7–8, 26–7, 29–33, 35, 40–2, 45–6, 48–9, 58, 60, 64, 73, 77, 126, 142, 159–61, 194, 229, 257, 407–8, 410, 415
   of opportunity 30, 42, 48–9, 77
Laporte, Juan Pedro 250
Late Archaic (Peru) 8, 405–22
Late Classic Period 6–7, 10–11, 13, 16, 84, 87–8, 90, 92, 94, 101, 150–3, 159–60, 168–70, 181, 201, 215, 245, 259, 287, 298–9, 335, 337, 343–5, 348, 386
   popol nahs 11, 335–49, 351–2
lateral displacement 25, 30–1, 45–6, 48–9
Lenca, Lenkan 13, 28, 57, 59, 63
Leventhal, Richard 252–3, 255–7
lip-to-lip vessel pairs 35–8, 49
long-distance exchange 67, 201, 210, 217–18
Looper, Matthew 270
Lord Chaak (Uxmal ruler) 386, 388
Los Llanitos, El Salvador 42–3
Los Naranjos, Honduras 27, 30, 60, 103
Los Terrenos, Guatemala 123, 152–3, 156–7, 160–1
Lubaantun, Belize 246, 248–250, 252, 300–1
Lunar Series data 248
Lurihuasi, Peru 410

Machaca River 253–8, 262
Machaquila, Guatemala 204, 207, 215–16
Maguire, Susan 301
mail routes, nineteenth-century 76
maize 37, 121, 138, 385
Maldonado Cárdenas, Rubén 345
Manahan, Kam 14, 98–9

Manchon Swamp, Guatemala 134–5
Marcus, Joyce 143, 228, 269, 301, 394
marriage alliance 204, 245, 299
Martin, Simon 233, 277
masonry 30, 61, 204, 208–9, 212, 214–15, 248–9, 347, 372, 421
   of Southern Belize Region 248–9
mat house *see popol nah*
mat (*pop*) motif 337
materiality 7, 26, 35, 38–9, 45, 47–9
May Ciau, Rossana xviii, 11
Maya Collapse i, 2, 7, 11–7, 83–4, 87, 94–8, 104–6, 167, 202, 351–2, 356, 384–5, 388, 390, 392–3
   at Cancuen 12, 202
   at Copan and revisionist narrative 12–15, 83–4, 87, 94–8, 104–6
   in Maya highlands 7, 167
   in northern Maya lowlands 11, 16–17, 351–2, 356, 384–5, 388, 390, 392–3
Maya rulers 9–12, 84, 90, 92, 94, 97, 143, 204, 214–15, 223–5, 228, 230, 232–3, 235–7, 245–6, 250, 266, 268, 270–96, 298–301, 337, 375
   accession statements 10, 224–5, 227–8, 230, 232–5, 237–8, 245, 272, 275, 281, 285–7, 289, 291–2, 294–6, 299–300,
   titles (*ajaw*, emblem glyph, *Kaloomte'*, *pitzil*, sajal, *yopaat*, etc.) 10, 204, 214–15, 225, 228, 232, 234–5, 266, 271, 276–7, 280–1, 283, 285–92, 294, 296, 300, 346
Maya kingship 9–11, 13, 130, 143, 289, 348, 351
Mayan languages 4–5, 11, 13, 63, 131, 150, 234–5, 277
   Ch'olan 131, 234–5, 277
   Jakaltek 150
   Kaqchikel 11, 151
   K'iche'an 63, 151
   Mopan 247–8
   Q'eqchi' 248, 267
Mayapan, Mexico 11, 15, 106, 313, 315, 317–18, 320, 322, 324, 326, 329, 336, 338, 350–1, 362–3, 367, 390–2
mercenaries 47
merchants 12, 47, 57, 210
mestizo 71
Middle American Research Institute xvii, 143, 150, 171, 177, 196, 223, 232–5, 237–8
Middle Preclassic Period 4–6, 9, 60, 63, 115–18, 123, 125–30, 134, 137–40, 143, 152, 177–97

432 Index

military (conflict, conquest, expansion, invasion, positions) 11, 30, 44, 48, 142, 212, 215, 329, 388, 393
Miraya, Peru 410, 415
Mito temples 422
Mixteca-Puebla style 326
mobilization of labor 409
Moho Plaza, Pusilha 250–1, 255–8, 267, 271, 276, 296–9
monument breakage 33, 271, 282, 285–6, 299
monumental architecture and construction xviii, 29, 30, 42, 45, 126, 167, 257, 308, 349–50, 360, 366, 385, 390–1, 393, 395, 405–6, 409–10, 412, 415, 421–2
Morley, Sylvanus G. 250, 267, 297
Moscoso, Luís 69
Moundville, USA 130
mythistory 236–7

Naco Valley, Honduras 61, 64, 67, 106
Naj Tunich Cave, Belize 247, 286, 300
Nambikwara of Brazil 236
Naranjo, Guatemala 6, 118, 125–8, 277, 280, 294, 296
   Las Charcas complex at 6, 118, 125, 127–8
Neivens, Niña xviii, 4–5
Nickels, Karen 301
Nim li Punit, Belize 246, 248, 250, 252, 283, 286, 300–2
Nimajuyu, Guatemala 140
Nohpat, Mexico 342
Norte Chico zone, Peru 405–22

obsidian 12, 14, 115, 120, 124, 137, 142–3, 166, 171, 217, 386
   of Copan 103
   exchange 12, 67–8, 118, 129–30, 138–9, 143, 206, 210, 217
   hydration dating at Copan 13–14
   of Kaminaljuyu 130, 137–41
   lithic industries 129, 166
   of Middle Preclassic Kaqchikel region 118, 120, 122, 125, 128–30, 139
   of Pusilha 263
   of Quelepa 7, 39, 67–8
   sources 39, 68, 103, 120, 122, 124, 129–30, 132, 137–8, 141, 152, 166, 171, 206, 211, 263, 386
ocarinas 47
Olmecs 1, 5, 35, 46, 60, 62, 64–5, 128, 139, 177–8, 180
onyx 36
origin of the state, models 8–9, 115–16, 141, 407, 408, 410, 415–17, 419, 422

Pachay, Guatemala 119–21, 125
Pacific coast and Piedmont, Guatemala 4–5, 7, 48, 62, 103, 117, 119, 125–9, 133, 138–40, 151, 184, 187, 189, 192, 195, 207
Palenque, Mexico 12, 189, 225, 227–8, 230, 232, 235, 287, 292, 297
Paleoindian Period 248
   fishtail point, Belize 248
palmas 47, 62, 65
Pampa San Jose, Peru 409, 411, 414, 416
Pativilca Valley, Peru 407, 410, 411, 414, 416
patronage 47, 204, 375
peer–polity interaction 8–9, 406–7, 416, 419–20
   in Archaic Peru 9, 405–22
   in Maya region 8–9
Peñol of Chilanga 70
performance 31–2, 34, 37, 43, 245, 282, 295–6
period ending 272, 275–6, 281–3, 285–9, 291, 295–6, 300
Peten, Guatemala 1, 5, 11, 47, 103, 133, 139, 178–80, 191, 194, 201–8, 215, 217, 245–7, 250, 270, 286, 298–300, 311, 324, 345, 350, 364
Petexbatun kingdom 102, 204, 299–300
Piedra Parada, Guatemala 125–6
Piedras Negras, Guatemala 36, 207, 232, 245
pilgrimage 47, 248, 388
Pitcavage, Megan 301, 393
Platform Mountain, Pusilha 281–2, 286
plumage 11, 204, 228, 327
Poite river, Belize 253, 256–8
Pompeya, Guatemala 123, 151–3, 156–7, 159–61, 165–7, 170, 171
Ponce, Fray Alonso de 71
pop 227–8, 338, 349, 373–4
Popenoe de Hatch, Marion 130, 143
popol nah 11, 335–52
ports 11–12, 71–6, 116, 201–18, 385
Porvenir, Peru 414–5
Postclassic Period 6, 11–13, 15–17, 68, 102–5, 106, 118–21, 134, 138, 140, 152, 158–9, 168, 171, 217–18, 250, 308, 311, 313, 322, 325–6, 329, 336–8, 343, 349–52, 356, 360
   Early Postclassic at Chichen Itza 15–17, 356, 358, 360, 388–93
   Early Postclassic at Copan 12–13, 17, 83, 94, 98–9, 100, 102–5
   Early Postclassic at Lamanai 15, 17, 311–30
   at Pusilha 250, 258, 298
Pot Belly sculptures 121
Potao, Peru 410

pottery
  Acbi complex 89, 92, 101
  Agua complex 122, 127–9, 136, 152
  Amatle ware 152–3, 162–3, 165–6
  Arevalo complex 6, 130
  Augustine Ceramic Group 311, 313, 324
  Bah complex 178
  Bolo Orange 64
  Buk complex 15, 17, 311, 313, 316, 318, 326–7
  Cehpech complex/sphere 16, 349–50, 362–8, 385, 387, 388, 391–2, 394–5
    association with Maya-style architecture 365–6, 368, 375, 387
    overlap with Sotuta complex 365–7, 383–5, 391, 395
    pure deposits at Chichen Itza 362–3, 387, 394
  ceramic supersystems 15–16, 89, 259, 262, 310–11, 313, 315, 319, 326–7
  ceramic systems 15, 310–13, 315–16, 318–20, 327, 329–30
  Chicanel complex/sphere 117, 133, 183, 250, 364
  Chichen Red Ware 313–14, 318–21, 323–4, 367, 387
  Chuya Red-on-White 136
  Cochuah complex 362
  Coner complex 12–13, 84–101, 104–5, 106
  Cream Paste tradition 84–5, 90–1, 96
  Cunil/Kanocha complex 5, 177, 179, 183–4
  Delirio Red-on-White 38, 48, 66, 94
  Eb complex 5, 177, 179, 183–4
  Ek complex 177
  Fine Orange ware 15–16, 66, 103, 210, 308–30
    at Chichen Itza 387
    at Lamanai 15, 311–30
  Fine paste 65, 210
  Hocaba ceramic complex 362, 366–7, 385, 390–1
  Huuntun-Cehpech complex 365–7, 387–8
  Izote ware 136
  Jobal Red 5, 183–7, 189
  K'awil complex 5, 177, 183–95
  Las Charcas complex 6, 117–18, 125–8, 130, 138
  Majadas complex 117
  Mamom complex/sphere 117, 179–80, 182–4, 187, 192, 197
  Matillas Fine Orange 313, 317–18, 320, 324, 326

pottery *cont.*
  Mayapan Red Ware 313, 318
  "Miraflores sphere" 64, 116, 128, 130–1, 133, 136–8
  Motul complex *see* pottery, Yabnal-Motul complex
  Navarro ware 136
  paste composition analysis 64
  Pastores Simple ware 162, 165–6
  Paxcaman Ceramic Group 311, 313, 324
  Peto Cream ware 364, 367, 390
  Plumbate ware 99, 318, 326
    San Juan Plumbate 153, 165–6
    Tohil Plumbate 66, 98–9, 103, 105, 387
  Polished Black/Brown tradition 84, 86–92, 105
  Preclassic (Formative) 117–18, 120, 123, 125, 127–8, 136–7, 140–1, 143, 177–96
  "Pre-Mamom" 5, 6, 178–84, 187–9, 192–4, 196–7
  production and distribution 12, 15, 64, 84, 87, 91, 96, 102, 104–6, 128, 170, 195, 312, 350, 389–90, 421–2
  Providencia complex 117–18, 125–6, 128, 130, 133, 136–7, 139
  Sacatepequez complex 117–8, 122, 126, 128–9, 131, 134, 139, 143, 152, 189
  Santa Rosa Anaranjado 162–3
  Silho Fine Orange Group 15, 311–8, 320, 323, 326, 387
  Slate Ware 16, 364, 366–7, 384, 387, 394
    Dzitas 364, 367, 384, 388–90, 394
    Early/Say/Sat/Tintin 16, 364–7, 384, 388, 394
    Muna/Puuc 16, 364, 366–7, 384, 388, 394
  Solano tradition 64, 118, 133
  Sotuta complex 15, 17, 362–3, 365, 367, 379, 384–5, 388, 391, 395
    absence from Maya-style architecture 16, 365, 375–6, 387
    association with International-style architecture 17, 374–5, 383, 387, 389, 392
    beginning of 366–8, 374–5, 383–5, 389
    end of 366, 385, 389
    overlap with Cehpech 362–3, 366–7, 383–5, 387, 395
    overlap with Hocaba 366, 385, 390
  Swasey complex 4, 179, 197, 309
  Tases complex 349, 362, 366, 390–1
  technological diversity 96
  technological style 312

pottery *cont.*
   technological traditions 96, 99, 105
   Tepeu complex/sphere 97, 209–10, 229
   Tenampua Polychrome 66
   Tiquisate ware 165–6
   type-variety classification 15, 196, 310–12, 327, 329
   Tzakol complex/sphere 204, 250, 364
   Uapala sphere 4, 7, 27–8, 31, 33, 35, 40–1, 43–5, 60, 62–5, 94
   Ulua/Yojoa Polychromes 64, 66, 91–5
   Usulutan 63–5, 90, 136
   wares, problems of definition 312, 327
   Xe/Real Xe complexes 5, 177–9, 183, 190, 310
   Xuc ware 128, 136, 139, 189
   Yabnal-Motul complex 362, 364, 365–6, 368, 375, 384–8, 392, 394
      association with Early Chichen-style architecture 365, 386
      beginning of 386
      end of 365, 386
   Zakpah Ceramic Group 313, 315–17, 318, 323–4, 327
Pottery Cave Group, Pusilha 254, 257–8, 262, 298
practice theory 26, 49
Prager, Christian M. xviii, 10, 267, 270–1, 301
Preclassic Period 2–7, 9, 16, 27, 29, 33, 59–60, 63–5, 88, 94, 101, 115–44, 152, 158–9, 162, 166, 168, 171, 177–97, 203, 227, 286, 298, 337, 343, 362, 391
   abandonment and population loss 6, 131–4, 137
   climate 6, 135, 143
   drought 133–5, 140
Proskouriakoff, Tatiana 270
proxy war 215
Proyecto Arqueológico Chichén Itzá 365, 375, 391, 393–4
Proyecto Arqueológico del Área Kaqchikel (PAAK) 120–1, 142, 154, 158, 171
Puc Raxon, Castulo 119
Punta de Chimino, Guatemala 204
Punta Gorda, Belize 253
Pusilha, Belize 10–12, 102, 106, 245–302
   architectural alignment 257
   architectural templates 257–8
   Ballcourt I Group 253, 257–8
   Big Tree Group 253, 257, 262
   Blank Stela Group 253, 257–8, 262

Pusilha, Belize *cont.*
   British Museum research at 252, 267
   "Bulldozed Mound" 250, 254, 258, 298
   burials 248, 259, 260–5, 266, 294, 298
   caches 258–9, 262–4
   dental modification 263
   Gateway Hill 250, 254–8, 260, 262, 281, 282, 298
   jade artifacts 258–9, 263–4, 266, 298
   Lower Groups I and II 255, 257, 259, 298
   Machaca Plaza 255, 257
   Maya Bridge 253–4
   Moho Plaza 250–1, 255–8, 267, 271, 276, 296–8
   monuments 252–3, 257–8, 266, 267–76, 280–1, 283, 285–6, 289–90, 292–3, 296, 298–302
   Operation 3 255, 258–9, 260
   Operation 4 255, 258–9
   Operation 5 255, 258–9, 260
   Operation 6 255, 259
   Operation 7 255, 259
   Operation 8 255, 249, 262, 264
   Operation 9 255, 262
   Platform Mountain *see* Platform Mountain, Pusilha
   Pottery Cave Group *see* Pottery Cave Group, Pusilha
   royal tomb 262–6, 298
   Ruler A 271–7, 280–3, 287, 291, 298
   Ruler B 270, 271–7, 278, 281–7, 294, 299–300
   Ruler C 272–5, 283–9
   Ruler D 272–5, 287–9
   Ruler E 272–5, 284, 289–92, 294
   Ruler F 266, 272–5, 292–4
   Ruler G 266, 271–5, 292–5, 298, 300
   Ruler X1 266, 271–2, 274–5, 296
   Ruler X2 271–2, 274–5, 295, 296
   Ruler X3 271–2, 274–5, 296
   Ruler X4 271–2, 274–5, 296
   "Ruler" X5 266, 271–2, 274–5, 294–6, 298
   Ruler X6 271, 274–6
   Ruler X7 271, 274–6
   Ruler X8 271, 274–6
   Ruler X9 271, 274–6
   settlement patterns at 256–8
   Stairway 1 269, 296
   Stela Plaza 253–4, 256–8, 267–8, 281–2, 290, 298
   stelae *see* Pusilha monuments
   strontium isotope analysis of teeth 259
   Weller's Group 258

Pusilha Archaeological Project (PUSAP) 252, 258, 267, 270, 296
Putun Maya 311, 361, 393
Puuc region, Mexico 11, 16, 340, 342–8, 384, 388, 392, 394–5
  abandonment of 16, 384, 388
Pye, Mary 120, 171
pyrite 204, 259, 261, 263

Quelepa, El Salvador 2, 7–8, 17, 25–50, 56–77, 94, 150
  caches at 31, 34–40, 43–5, 47–50, 62
  ceramics of 7, 27, 33, 36–40, 42, 44–9, 62–6, 94
  Jaguar Altar 27, 32–4, 48, 60
  Lepa phase 7, 106, 29–31, 33, 36, 38–46, 48, 61–2, 65, 68
  monuments of 27, 31–4, 38, 40–1, 60, 65
  Shila phase 7, 29–31, 33, 35–6, 38, 41–5, 60–1, 65
  structures of 7, 27, 29–31, 34–46, 50, 59–62
  test pits at 33, 35, 38, 40, 44
  Uapala phase 7, 27–8, 31, 33, 35, 40–1, 43, 45, 60, 62, 64–5
quetzal 11, 204
Quetzalcoatl/Kukulkan, cult of 16, 47–8, 326–7, 329
quincunx 33–4, 36
Quirigua, Guatemala 84, 105, 229, 270, 280, 287, 291, 294, 298, 300–1

radiocarbon dates 14, 16, 106, 117–18, 121, 125, 138, 153, 179, 182, 194, 196, 250, 311, 318, 343, 366, 377–86, 391, 393, 395, 405, 408, 410, 412, 414, 419
  calibration of 357, 377–83, 395
  from Chichen Itza 366, 377–83, 386, 391
rain making 32–3, 38, 48
ramps 29, 36–8, 43, 45, 60–1, 156, 162, 170, 212, 342
range structures 42, 208–9, 212, 258, 346–8, 350, 352
Raxruja Viejo, Guatemala 215
Reents, Dorie 270
Ri Rusamäj Jilotepeque 120, 142
Riese, Berthold 301
Ringle, William 2, 47, 49, 326, 352, 394
Rio Bec region, Mexico 248
Rio Lempa, El Salvador 27, 60, 69, 73
Rio Motagua, Guatemala 5, 106, 203
Rio Pasion, Guatemala 11, 66, 105, 203–7, 215–16, 299–300
Rio San Esteban, El Salvador 27, 33, 41–2, 45, 70

Rio Sebol, Guatemala 207
Rio Seco, Peru 408, 419
Rio Usumacinta, Guatemala and Mexico 203, 207, 232, 300, 311
ritual 12, 26–7, 31–48, 50, 60, 62–3, 90, 92, 121, 123–4, 126–7, 139, 168, 204, 207, 212–13, 215, 217, 229–30, 235–6, 245, 257, 288, 295–6, 336, 340, 345, 383, 407, 419– 22
  "cleansing" 41
  engineering 35
road system, colonial 72–3
Robinson, Eugenia J. xviii, 5–7, 119–20, 142, 154
royal courts of the Maya 2, 9, 31, 86, 206, 236
royal tomb, Pusilha *see* Pusilha
Rucal, Guatemala 117, 119–21, 123–4, 126–8, 138–9, 142, 151, 153–4, 156–7, 160–1, 166, 171
rulers of Pusilha *see* Pusilha
Rutherford, Allen xix, 8, 416, 422

Sabbache, Mexico 342
Sac Witz 215
sacbe 212, 258, 345
Sachse, Frauke 301
Salama Valley, Guatemala 4, 187, 189
Salinas de Nueve Cerros, Guatemala 206–7
Salitron Viejo, Honduras 60
salt 206, 246
Sampeck, Kathryn xix, 7–8, 30, 49
San Bartolome Milpas Altas obsidian source 129, 166, 171
San Benito Poite, Belize 258, 262, 267, 298, 301
San Cristobal de Las Casas 233
  Na Bolom 233
San Juan del Obispo, Guatemala 157, 161
San Lorenzo El Tejar, Guatemala 123–4
San Luis, Guatemala 157, 160–2
San Martin Jilotepeque, Guatemala 117–21, 125–6, 128–30, 136–9, 141, 144, 167
  obsidian source 120, 129–30, 137–9, 152, 166
  settlement 120–1, 125, 131, 133–4, 136
San Miguel, El Salvador 8, 27, 30, 59, 69–77
Santa Rosa, Guatemala 120, 140, 142, 151, 155, 158, 160–2, 164, 168–71
  architectural features 125, 155, 161–3, 170
  ceramics 140, 153, 162–3, 165, 170
  obsidian 166
Sayil, Mexico 31, 350
Schaedel, Richard 407

Schele, Linda 349
Schwake, Sonja 301
Scroll Serpent (Calakmul ruler) 227
Sechin Alto, Peru 408
Seibal, Guatemala 2, 4–5, 9, 31, 66, 104, 177–80, 183–4, 186–90, 193–4, 207, 277, 300, 350
settlement patterns
  in Antigua valley 6–7, 120–4, 131, 133–4, 140, 143
  in Kaqchikel region 6–7, 118–26, 130–6, 154–62, 169–70
  at Pusilha 256–8
  at Quelepa 2, 7, 27–9
  in San Martin Jilotepeque 120–1, 125, 131, 133
Sharpe, Captain Bartholomew 71
Shaura, Peru 412, 414, 416
shell ornaments 36, 259, 261, 264, 422
shicra bags 409
Shila phase, Quelepa *see* Quelepa, El Salvador
Shook, Edwin 124, 128, 143, 153, 155–8, 161
shrines 47–8, 169, 204, 248, 326, 336, 340
Sierra de Chinaja, Guatemala 207, 215
Sky Witness (Calakmul ruler) 227
Skylifter (Calakmul ruler) 227–8, 234
slate artifacts 259, 261, 302
Smoke Monkey (Copan ruler) 337
Snake Dynasty (Calakmul and elsewhere) 10, 224–5, 227–8, 232, 234–5, 237
social memory 7, 34
Somerville, Andrew 301
Sonsonate, El Salvador 72–3, 76
Southern Belize Region 11–12, 135, 246, 257, 283, 298, 300–1
  characteristic features 248
  definition 246–8
  masonry 248–9
speleothems 135
Spondylus shell 228, 259, 263, 422
Squier, Ephraim G. 76
status 6, 63, 84, 116, 124, 139, 170, 217, 225, 229, 237, 257, 266, 275, 311, 329, 418, 422
stone balls 37, 65
storage pits 34, 49
strontium isotope analysis 259
Stuart, David 229
stucco 86, 182, 214–15, 248, 259, 338–40, 368, 386, 390
subsistence 123, 206, 217, 417
Sumpango, Guatemala 117, 119–20, 123–4, 128, 130–1, 136, 140, 142–3
  settlement 123, 131, 133–4

Supe Valley, Peru 407–8, 410
"super-*nahs*" 345–8, 350–1
Swezey, William R. 119–20, 154
symbolic entrainment 9, 417, 419
symbolism 36, 38, 215

Tabasco, Mexico 62, 207–8, 210, 215
Taj Chan Ahk, Cancuen ruler 212, 214–15
Tajoom Uk'ab K'ahk' (Calakmul ruler) 225, 227
Tak'alik Ab'aj, Guatemala 14, 60, 116, 142–3
Tamarindito, Guatemala 207, 286
Tapexco, Guatemala 153, 162, 165
Tecomate form 64, 184–5, 187, 193
temporary structures 409
Teotihuacan, Mexico 1, 46, 48, 88, 116, 130, 141–2, 151, 181, 276–7, 291, 297, 360
Terminal Classic Period 2, 12, 61, 66, 68, 76, 118, 151, 181, 246, 250, 252, 308, 311, 322, 325, 340, 349–52, 356, 391–3, 395
  at Cancuen 211, 218
  at Chichen Itza 16–17, 358, 365, 382, 384, 386–9, 391–3, 395
  at Copan 12, 15, 84, 94–9, 103–4
  popol nahs 337, 343–52
  at Pusilha 257–9, 262, 296, 298–9
Terminal Preclassic Period 29, 130–3, 137–8, 140, 142–3, 162, 181
termination rituals 26, 33, 34, 40, 44, 46
terraces 27, 29, 34–8, 41–3, 45, 60–1, 95, 157–61, 208, 212, 248, 254, 257–8, 281, 390
Terrenos, Guatemala 123, 152–3, 156–7, 160–1
thermoluminescence (TL) dating 366–7, 394–5
Thiessen polygon analysis 142, 238, 415
Thompson, J. Eric S. 238, 361, 383
Tikal, Guatemala 4–5, 10, 31, 43, 46, 177–8, 180–1, 183–4, 187–90, 192–6, 204, 207, 213, 225, 228, 257, 277, 280, 289, 298, 300
Tipu, Belize 309
Toledo District, Belize *see* Southern Belize Region
Toltecs 1, 360, 393
  occupation of Chichen Itza 360–1, 363, 393, 394
  timing of *entrada* 361
Topoxte 201
total overlap model 373
trade routes 12, 15, 66, 203, 207, 215, 246, 416–17

transformation 33, 38, 44–6, 343, 345, 407, 416, 420
transmission of innovation 407, 417, 420
transversal 205, 207, 210–11, 213, 215, 247
Tres Islas, Guatemala 204, 207
Trinidad de Nosotros, Guatemala 201
Tula, Mexico 103, 360, 393
tun-ajaw date 373–4
type-variety classification (*see* pottery)

U-shaped layout 412, 415
Ulua Valley, Honduras 64, 66–7
Urías, Guatemala 117, 119–20, 121, 123–8, 139, 142
   architecture 124–6, 139
   ceramics 121, 124–8
   obsidian 129–30
Uxbenka, Belize 246, 248–50, 252, 300
Uxmal, Mexico 346, 349–51, 362, 364–5, 384, 386, 388, 390
   Nunnery Quadrangle 346–7, 351, 395
   Palace of the Governor 346, 348, 351
   radiocarbon dates 395
   Str. 6 346–7

Valdés, Juan Antonio 130, 143
Valley of Guatemala 6, 116–17, 119, 126–7, 130–1, 134, 137–42, 152, 170, 189
Veracruz, Mexico 4, 7, 15, 46–8, 62, 65, 207–8, 210–11, 320, 322, 325–6
Verapaz, Guatemala 4, 105, 179, 184, 187, 204–7, 209–10, 216
Vinto Alto, Peru 410–11, 414
Volta, Beniamino xix, 10, 16, 301

Wagner, Elisabeth 301
Walters, Gary Rex 252, 255, 267
Wanyerka, Phillip J. 282, 301–2
warfare 9, 44, 46, 158, 245, 271, 291, 299, 417
water 14, 15, 27, 32–3, 38, 41–2, 50, 75, 106, 123, 133–5, 152, 157, 159, 161–2, 168, 209, 212, 215, 227–8, 246, 257, 299, 373, 405, 407, 417
   management system 134
Wauchope, Robert 233, 235, 238
Weller, Lorington 252, 255, 258, 267, 301

Xcanacruz, Mexico 342, 347
Xnaheb, Belize 246–7, 252
Xuenkal, Mexico 385

Yarumela, Honduras 59, 63
Yax Nun Ahiin I (Tikal ruler) 228
Yaxchilan, Mexico 207, 225, 228, 229, 232, 287
Yaxha, Guatemala 201
Yaxuna, Mexico 349, 386
   Str. 6F–68 347, 349
yokes 47, 62
Yuknoom Ch'een the Great (Calakmul ruler) 227
Yuknoom Ti' Chan (Calakmul ruler) 227
Yuknoom Yich'aak K'ahk' (Calakmul ruler) 225, 227

Zaragoza, Puebla, obsidian source 211

Taylor & Francis
eBooks
FOR LIBRARIES

ORDER YOUR FREE 30 DAY INSTITUTIONAL TRIAL TODAY!

Over 22,000 eBook titles in the Humanities, Social Sciences, STM and Law from some of the world's leading imprints.

Choose from a range of subject packages or create your own!

Benefits for you
- Free MARC records
- COUNTER-compliant usage statistics
- Flexible purchase and pricing options

Benefits for your user
- Off-site, anytime access via Athens or referring URL
- Print or copy pages or chapters
- Full content search
- Bookmark, highlight and annotate text
- Access to thousands of pages of quality research at the click of a button

For more information, pricing enquiries or to order a free trial, contact your local online sales team.

UK and Rest of World: **online.sales@tandf.co.uk**
US, Canada and Latin America: **e-reference@taylorandfrancis.com**

www.ebooksubscriptions.com

ALPSP Award for BEST eBOOK PUBLISHER 2009 Finalist

Taylor & Francis eBooks
Taylor & Francis Group

A flexible and dynamic resource for teaching, learning and research.